MAGILL'S SURVEY OF AMERICAN LITERATURE

Revised Edition

MAGILL'S SURVEY OF AMERICAN LITERATURE

Revised Edition

Volume 1

Abbey—Chopin

Edited by

Steven G. Kellman

University of Texas, San Antonio

SALEM PRESS, INC.

Pasadena, California   Hackensack, New Jersey

Editor in Chief: Dawn P. Dawson

Editorial Director: Christina J. Moose *Production Editor:* Joyce I. Buchea
Project Editor: Tracy Irons-Georges *Acquisitions Editor:* Mark Rehn
Copy Editors: Sarah M. Hilbert *Research Supervisor:* Jeffry Jensen
Elizabeth Ferry Slocum *Research Assistant:* Rebecca Kuzins
Editorial Assistant: Dana Garey *Graphics and Design:* James Hutson
Photo Editor: Cynthia Breslin Beres *Layout:* William Zimmerman

Cover photo: Truman Capote (Hulton Archive/Getty Images)

Library of Congress Cataloging-in-Publication Data

Magill's survey of American literature / edited by Steven G. Kellman. — [Rev. ed.].
    p. cm.
Includes bibliographical references and index.
ISBN-10: 1-58765-285-4 (set : alk. paper)
ISBN-13: 978-1-58765-285-1 (set : alk. paper)
ISBN-10: 1-58765-286-2 (vol. 1 : alk. paper)
ISBN-13: 978-1-58765-286-8 (vol. 1 : alk. paper)
  1. American literature—Dictionaries. 2. American literature—Bio-bibliography. 3. Authors, American—Biography—Dictionaries. I. Kellman, Steven G., 1947- II. Magill, Frank Northen, 1907-1997. III. Title: Survey of American literature.
  PS21.M34 2006
  810.9′0003—dc22
                                                                        2006016503

First Printing

CONTENTS

Contents

PUBLISHER'S NOTE

Magill's Survey of American Literature offers profiles of major U.S. and Canadian writers from all time periods, accompanied by analyses of their significant titles of fiction, drama, poetry, and nonfiction. This six-volume set covers 339 writers at the heart of literary studies for middle and high school students and at the center of book discussions among library patrons. It is currently the only set from Salem Press that brings together information on the lives and works of American writers from all genres.

REVISION DETAILS

The original set, published in 1991 with a 1994 supplement with Marshall Cavendish Corporation, profiled 266 writers. For this *Revised Edition,* 73 new authors were added. For the first time, Canadians are included, such as Margaret Atwood, Robertson Davies, Mavis Gallant, Anne Hébert, Farley Mowat, Alice Munro, and Michael Ondaatje. In addition, an effort was made to cover even more minority and women writers. Also featured are authors of young adult literature, such as Judy Blume, M. E. Kerr, Madeleine L'Engle, Walter Dean Myers, Gary Paulsen, and Laura Ingalls Wilder.

All the original essays were evaluated for their currency, and more than 100 were given substantial revision, in many cases by the original contributor. Material was added to cover recent developments: new titles or awards, changes in residence or employment, and alterations in critical and popular reception. In addition, one or more sections on specific titles—novels, poems, short stories, plays, essays—were added. For every entry, the bibliography was updated to provide readers with the latest information.

An exciting new feature for this edition is a sidebar in each essay called "Discussion Topics." They address such topics as the writer's body of work, specific works, or life as it relates to his or her literature. Intended for students, teachers, and members of reading groups, they can be used as paper topics or conversation points.

FORMAT AND CONTENT

Magill's Survey of American Literature is arranged in an A-Z format, beginning with nature essayist Edward Abbey and ending with young adult novelist and playwright Paul Zindel. The essays vary from approximately six to thirteen pages in length. Each one begins with a block of reference information in a standard order:

- Name by which the author is best known
- **Born:** place and date
- **Died:** place and date
- A statement explaining the writer's literary importance

The main text is divided into the following sections:

- **Biography**—a chronological overview of the author's life
- **Analysis**—a discussion about the author's style, dominant themes, and literary characteristics
- **Works**—profiles of one or more individual titles (novels, novellas, plays, poems, short stories, essays)
- **Summary**—one or two brief paragraphs summarizing the author's legacy

Each title section lists the year in which the work was first published. For short stories, poems, essays, or other short pieces, a collection of the author's works in which the reader can find the title is also indicated.

Every essay ends with a bibliography listing both the author's works in all genres (**By the Author**) and sources for further study (**About the Author**) and contains the thought-provoking "Discussion Topics" sidebar. All essays include the byline of the expert who wrote the entry. In addition, more than 800 author portraits and thumbnail photographs of book covers illustrate the text.

REFERENCE FEATURES

At the beginning of each volume are the Table of Contents for that volume, including the works featured in the title sections, and a Complete List of Contents for the entire set.

Four reference features can be found at the end of volume 6. A Glossary defines crucial literary terms for the reader. A Category List groups authors by genre, country, gender, and ethnic identity:

- African American/African Descent
- American Indian
- Asian American/Asian Descent
- Canadian
- Gay or Bisexual
- Jewish
- Latino
- Nonfiction Writers
- Novelists
- Playwrights
- Poets
- Short-Story Writers
- Women
- Young Adult Authors

The Author Index lists all authors profiled in the set, along with their profiled works, while the Title Index lists all featured works.

ACKNOWLEDGMENTS

We would like to thank our Editor, Steven G. Kellman, professor of literature at the University of Texas at San Antonio, for his invaluable expertise. We also owe our gratitude to all the outstanding writers who contributed material for this *Revised Edition* of *Magill's Survey of American Literature* and for the original set and its supplement. A list of their names and affiliations can be found in the front of volume 1.

CONTRIBUTORS

Michael Adams
*City University of New York
    Graduate Center*

Patrick Adcock
Henderson State University

Thomas P. Adler
Purdue University

Claudia Emerson Andrews
*University of North Carolina,
    Greensboro*

Terry L. Andrews
Rutgers University

Andrew J. Angyal
Elon University

Karen Antell
University of Oklahoma

Karen L. Arnold
Independent Scholar

Bryan Aubrey
Maharishi International University

Philip Auslander
Georgia Institute of Technology

James Baird
University of North Texas

Jane L. Ball
Independent Scholar

Janet M. Ball
The Mogollon Gazette

Mary H. Barnes
Monmouth College

Dan Barnett
California State University, Los Angeles

Melissa E. Barth
Appalachian State University

Milton Berman
University of Rochester

Anthony Bernardo, Jr.
Delaware College of Art and Design

Alan Blackstock
University of New Mexico

Pegge Bochynski
Salem State College

Jo-Ellen Lipman Boon
Independent Scholar

William Boyle
State University of New York, New Paltz

Harold Branam
Temple University

Gerhard Brand
California State University, Los Angeles

John Brehm
Independent Scholar

J. R. Broadus
University of North Carolina

Keith H. Brower
Dickinson College

Alan Brown
Livingston University

James S. Brown
Bloomsburg University of Pennsylvania

Molly Brown
Stanford University

Mary Hanford Bruce
Monmouth College

Carl Brucker
Arkansas Tech University

Jeffrey L. Buller
Georgia Southern University

Joseph P. Byrne
Belmont University

Edmund J. Campion
University of Tennessee

Pamela Canal
Independent Scholar

Thomas Carmichael
University of Toronto

Warren J. Carson
*University of South Carolina,
    Spartanburg*

Linda M. Carter
Morgan State University

Leonard Casper
Boston College

Thomas Cassidy
University of Wisconsin, Stevens Point

Hal Charles
Eastern Kentucky University

Balance Chow
San Jose State University

C. L. Chua
California State University, Fresno

John J. Conlon
University of Massachusetts, Boston

Holly Dworken Cooley
Independent Scholar

Rebecca Curtiss-Floyd
University of South Florida

Mary Virginia Davis
University of California, Davis

Frank Day
Clemson University

Donald L. Deardorff II
Cedarville University

Bill Delaney
Independent Scholar

James E. Devlin
State University of New York, Oneonta

Joseph Dewey
University of Pittsburgh, Johnstown

Ted William Dreier
Portland State University

Gweneth A. Dunleavy
University of Louisville

Bruce L. Edwards
Bowling Green State University

Clifford Edwards
Fort Hays State University

Robert P. Ellis
Independent Scholar

Thomas L. Erskine
Salisbury University

James Feast
New York University

John W. Fiero
University of Southwestern Louisiana

Edward Fiorelli
St. John's University, New York

Rebecca Hendrick Flannagan
Francis Marion University

Bruce E. Fleming
United States Naval Academy

Robert J. Forman
St. John's University, New York

Joseph Francavilla
Columbus State University

Carol Franks
Portland State University

Robert L. Gale
University of Pittsburgh

Ann D. Garbett
Averett University

Jill B. Gidmark
University of Minnesota

Sheldon Goldfarb
University of British Columbia

Marc Goldstein
Independent Scholar

John L. Grigsby
*Appalachian Research & Defense Fund
of Kentucky, Inc.*

Daniel L. Guillory
Millikin University

James Gunn
University of Kansas

Charles Hackenberry
Pennsylvania State University, Altoona

Jay L. Halio
University of Delaware

Natalie Harper
Simon's Rock of Bard College

Susan Tetlow Harrington
*University of South Florida,
Sarasota/Manatee*

Sharon M. Harris
Temple University

Melanie Hawthorne
Texas A&M University

Terry Heller
Coe College

Diane Andrews Henningfeld
Adrian College

Joyce E. Henry
Ursinus College

Allen Hibbard
Middle Tennessee State University

Joseph W. Hinton
Independent Scholar

Rebecca Stingley Hinton
Miami University

James L. Hodge
Bowdoin College

W. Kenneth Holditch
University of New Orleans

John R. Holmes
Franciscan University of Steubenville

David R. Howell
*University of North Carolina,
Wilmington*

Edward W. Huffstetler
Bridgewater College

David Huntley
Appalachian State University

Chandice M. Johnson, Jr.
North Dakota State University

Sheila Golburgh Johnson
Independent Scholar

Leela Kapai
Prince George's Community College

Richard S. Keating
United States Air Force Academy

Steven G. Kellman
University of Texas, San Antonio

Richard Kelly
University of Tennessee, Knoxville

Howard A. Kerner
*Polk Community College
Nova Southeastern University*

Marilyn Kongslie
Independent Scholar

Paula D. Kopacz
Eastern Kentucky University

Selina Lai
University of Heidelberg

Eugene Larson
Los Angeles Pierce College

William T. Lawlor
University of Wisconsin, Stevens Point

Linda Ledford-Miller
University of Scranton

Josephine M. Lee
South Dakota School of Mines and Technology

Leon Lewis
Appalachian State University

Paul R. Lilly, Jr.
State University of New York, Oneonta

Emily Lindner
Appalachian State University

Victor Lindsey
East Central University

James Livingston
Northern Michigan University

Janet Lorenz
Independent Scholar

R. C. Lutz
CII Group

Janet McCann
Texas A&M University

Joanne McCarthy
Independent Scholar

Philip McDermott
Independent Scholar

Andrew Macdonald
Loyola University, New Orleans

Gina Macdonald
Nicholls State University

Roxanne McDonald
Independent Scholar

Edythe M. McGovern
West Los Angeles College

S. Thomas Mack
University of South Carolina, Aiken

John L. McLean
Missouri Valley College

A. L. McLeod
Rider University

Marian B. McLeod
Trenton State College

David W. Madden
California State University, Sacramento

Barry Mann
Independent Scholar

Kristin L. Matthews
Brigham Young University

Charles E. May
California State University, Long Beach

Laurence W. Mazzeno
Alvernia College

Patrick Meanor
State University of New York, Oneonta

Ray Mescallado
Independent Scholar

Philip Metcalfe
Independent Scholar

Kathleen Mills
Independent Scholar

Christian H. Moe
Southern Illinois University, Carbondale

Robert A. Morace
Daemen College

Robert E. Morsberger
California State Polytechnic University, Pomona

Charmaine Allmon Mosby
Western Kentucky University

Edwin Moses
Bloomsburg University

John M. Muste
Ohio State University

William Nelles
University of Massachusetts, Dartmouth

Matthew Nickel
State University of New York, New Paltz

Terry Nienhuis
Western Carolina University

Holly L. Norton
University of Northwestern Ohio

Lisa Paddock
Independent Scholar

John G. Parks
Miami University

David B. Parsell
Lurwau University

Leslie Pearl
Independent Scholar

David Peck
Independent Scholar

Robert W. Peckham
Sacred Heart Major Seminary

William E. Pemberton
University of Wisconsin, La Crosse

Tom Petitjean
Louisiana State University, Eunice

John R. Pfeiffer
Central Michigan University

Adrienne Pilon
North Carolina School of the Arts

Bonnie C. Plummer
Eastern Kentucky University

Marjorie J. Podolsky
Pennsylvania State University at Erie, The Behrend College

Charles H. Pullen
Queen's University, Ontario

Catherine Rambo
Independent Scholar

John D. Raymer
Holy Cross College

Jere Real
Lynchburg College

Peter J. Reed
University of Minnesota

Rosemary M. Canfield Reisman
Charleston Southern University

H. William Rice
Shorter College

Rodney P. Rice
South Dakota School of Mines and Technology

Dorothy Dodge Robbins
Louisiana Tech University

Kenneth Robbins
Louisiana Tech University

James W. Robinson, Jr.
Chaminade University

Carl Rollyson
Baruch College, City University of New York

Paul Rosefeldt
University of New Orleans

Diane M. Ross
Independent Scholar

Gabrielle Rowe
McKendree College

Susan Rusinko
Bloomsburg University

Richard Sax
Fort Lewis College

William J. Scheick
University of Texas, Austin

Judith Schnee
University of Massachusetts, Boston Bentley College

Steven P. Schultz
Independent Scholar

Thomas C. Schunk
University of Wisconsin, Oshkosh

Kenneth Seib
University of Illinois

Barbara Kitt Seidman
Linfield College

R. Baird Shuman
University of Illinois, Urbana-Champaign

Jamie Sondra Sindell
Onondaga Community College

Amy Sisson
University of Houston, Clear Lake

Marjorie Smelstor
University of Wisconsin, Eau Claire

Ira Smolensky
Monmouth College

Katherine Snipes
Eastern Washington University

Katherine Socha
St. Mary's College of Maryland

Joseph Michael Sommers
University of Kansas

Michael Sprinker
State University of New York, Stony Brook

August W. Staub
University of Georgia

Louise M. Stone
Bloomsburg University

Gerald H. Strauss
Bloomsburg University

James Sullivan
California State University, Los Angeles

David Sundstrand
Association of Literary Scholars & Critics

Roy Arthur Swanson
University of Wisconsin, Milwaukee

Peter Swirski
Hong Kong University

Thomas J. Taylor
Independent Scholar

Terry Theodore
University of North Carolina, Wilmington

Michele D. Theriot
Nicholls State University

Linda Jordan Tucker
Kennesaw State University

Eileen Tess Tyler
United States Naval Academy

George W. Van Devender
Hardin-Simmons University

Steven Weisenburger
University of Kentucky

James M. Welsh
Salisbury University

Barbara Wiedemann
Auburn University, Montgomery

Albert E. Wilhelm
Tennessee Technological University

John Wilson
Independent Scholar

Michael Witkoski
Independent Scholar

Amanda B. Wray
Eastern Kentucky University

Karin A. Wurst
Michigan State University

Robert E. Yahnke
University of Minnesota

Vincent Yang
Pennsylvania State University

Joanna Yin
University of Hawaii

COMPLETE LIST OF CONTENTS

Volume 1

Volume 2

Volume 3

Volume 4

Volume 5

Volume 6

Complete List of Contents

MAGILL'S SURVEY OF AMERICAN LITERATURE

Revised Edition

EDWARD ABBEY

Michael Hendrickson

Born: Indiana, near Home, Pennsylvania
January 29, 1927
Died: Tucson, Arizona
March 14, 1989

Abbey is best known for his iconoclastic attacks on the forces of modern society that have encroached on the wilderness areas in the United States, particularly the mountains and deserts of the Southwest.

BIOGRAPHY

Edward Abbey was at once intensely private and self-revelatory. The facts of his intellectual and professional life are accessible; those of his private life remain mostly unknown. He was born and educated in the Allegheny Mountains of Pennsylvania. In the summer of 1944, registration for the World War II draft loomed large on the horizon for American males about to turn eighteen, so the seventeen-year-old Abbey opted for a trip by thumb across the United States before graduating from high school and being swallowed up by the draft. He hitchhiked from Pennsylvania to Seattle, passing through Chicago and Yellowstone National Park. From Seattle, he traveled south through California as far as Bakersfield, then journeyed home by way of Barstow, California; Flagstaff, Arizona; and Albuquerque, New Mexico.

He recounts this rite of passage into adulthood in "Hallelujah on the Bum" (1977), an essay filled with the warmth, wonder, and enthusiasm of youthful adventure. The vision of this Western land and its people marked Abbey in an inescapable way. Of his first sight of the Rocky Mountains, he wrote:

On to Wyoming, where near Greybull I saw for the first time something I had dreamed of seeing for

ten years. There on the western horizon, under a hot clear sky, sixty miles away, crowned with snow (in July), was a magical vision, a legend come true: the front range of the Rocky Mountains. An impossible beauty, like a boy's first sight of an undressed girl, the image of those mountains struck a fundamental chord in my imagination that has sounded ever since.

Perhaps nothing that Abbey has written so perfectly captures the intensity and passion of his love for the landscapes of the West. Thus, it is not surprising that the focus of his life and work has been on the preservation of this vision.

Soon after completing high school, Abbey was drafted into the Army. The years following his discharge found him yearning to return to the open spaces of the West. During this period he began to write, publishing his first novel, *Jonathan Troy*, in 1954. Like Abbey, the title character is caught between two worlds, the confining one of the East which he inhabits and the vision of the West, where personal freedom is only attainable in the open spaces of an untrammeled landscape.

Troy's escape to the West reflects Abbey's own break with his roots upon moving to New Mexico, where he attended the state university, completing his B.A. in 1951. Abbey then won a Fulbright Scholarship to the University of Edinburgh to study philosophy. Upon returning to the United States, he made an unsuccessful attempt to undertake graduate studies at Yale University. Abbey, feeling that he was not meant to live and work in the East, re-

1

turned to the University of New Mexico to pursue his M.A.

In 1956, he published his master's thesis, titled "Anarchism and the Morality of Violence," and his second novel, *The Brave Cowboy: An Old Tale in a New Time.* Both works examine the nature and effects of violence. In his thesis, Abbey wrestles with the sticky question of when and to what degree violence is justified. In *The Brave Cowboy,* the anachronistic hero, Jack Burns, must cope with the forces of a bureaucratic brutality that employs violence to impose its will as a matter of course. These thematic concerns remain central to Abbey's work.

With the publication of *The Brave Cowboy,* Abbey gained critical and public recognition. The novel was well reviewed and made into a successful motion picture in 1962 under the title *Lonely Are the Brave,* starring Kirk Douglas as Jack Burns. Unfortunately, Abbey sold his story outright for ten thousand dollars, so his financial gain was small indeed. Money problems continued to be a part of Abbey's life. He worked as a United States National Parks ranger and as a fire lookout for the forest service, and he did occasional stints as a college teacher. Although he could be considered a prolific writer, he was not to be widely read until the publication of *Desert Solitaire: A Season in the Wilderness* (1968), a collection of personal reflections that remains popular among students of nature, environmentalists, and lovers of the Western landscape.

As Abbey witnessed the encroachment of strip mining, development, and the beginning of what he termed "industrial tourism," his work took on a sense of desperation. In *Fire on the Mountain* (1962), the central character struggles against the forces of a faceless bureaucracy seeking to turn his ranch into a weapons test site. In the 1975 novel *The Monkey Wrench Gang,* the socially disenfranchised characters go on quixotic raids against the forces of development, burning billboards and plotting the destruction of the Glen Canyon Dam. Its sequel, *Hayduke Lives!* was published posthumously in 1990 and continues relating the gang's works in defense of the earth. In *Good News* (1980), set in the near future, ignorance and folly have prevailed; the landscape is blighted, and the government has become an expression of a darkly totalitarian state fueled by greed.

The increasing rage and despair of the latter work is reflective of Abbey's own perception of the human condition. Despite his efforts to maintain a glimmer of hope, he reveals a misanthropic disgust with the "featherless biped" so intent on destroying his beloved West and the planet itself. As early as 1967, in the introduction to *Desert Solitaire,* he wrote that his work was an elegy to a lost land; he told the reader, "You're holding a tombstone in your hands."

Despite Abbey's pronouncements that the battle was already lost, he continued to write, to exhort his readers to action, and to be hopeful in the face of hopelessness. In *The Fool's Progress* (1988), Abbey chronicles the adventures of a man suffering from a mortal ailment desperately trying to go home before dying. The main character, Henry Lightcap, reflects on the misadventures of his life. Retrospectively, one can see that the novel is thinly disguised autobiography written by a dying author trying to sum up his own efforts, to settle accounts before being overtaken by death. Abbey is nothing if not contradictory, for the book is both outrageously funny and painfully honest. It honors the love of life and makes one glad that Abbey was here to make his readers think, to make them angry, and above all to be passionate in the defense of beauty.

As was *Hayduke Lives!,* three other works were published after Abbey's death. *Vox Clamantis in Deserto: Some Notes from a Secret Journal* (1989) was republished in 1990 as *A Voice Crying in the Wilderness (Vox Clemantis in Deserto): Notes from a Secret Journal,* with an introduction Abbey dated less than two weeks before his death. In 1994, selections from Abbey's multivolume journal were published together as *Confessions of a Barbarian: Selections from the Journals of Edward Abbey.* The same year saw the appearance of a slim volume of verse titled *Earth Apples = (Pommes des terre): The Poetry of Edward Abbey.*

Abbey has become a cult hero to radical environmental groups. It was a mantle that he himself never put on. He insisted on being an individual; above all, he despised "group-think." Yet his voice remains.

ANALYSIS

It is tempting to see Abbey as an itinerant preacher, with "love" tattooed on one hand and "hate" on the other. The dichotomy of his preferences appears to be crystal clear. Wilderness is good. Civilization, manifesting itself in the form of urban sprawl and industrialization, is bad. Stop the latter and preserve the former. Indeed, he has been dismissed as an "eco-crank," a leftover Luddite, and an anarchist, but Abbey's voice challenges the common assumptions that modern society has come to accept complacently about the nature of progress and the idea of the "good life."

Abbey's first novel, *Jonathan Troy*, reveals the unhappy contrast between the decadent civilization of the East and the promising wilderness of the West. The title character encounters conflict and disappointment in his native Pennsylvania—squalor and hopelessness in the mining towns and barbarism in the backwoods. It is a place that suffers from rot, a rot he must escape by flight to the liberating landscape of the West, where there is room for the individual to be free.

The Brave Cowboy, Abbey's second novel, further develops the contrast between the landscape of the wilderness and the contamination of urban life established in *Jonathan Troy*. Jack Burns, the cowboy of the title, is one of Abbey's most memorable characters. He loves the freedom of his life as an itinerant herder, a life characterized by physical labor, personal freedom, and respect for the land, but he is a man out of step with his time. Abbey sends his hero riding into Duke City on horseback. Burns is a happy-go-lucky sort who hates fences, highways, and urban sprawl. When he comes to a fence, he cheerfully cuts it. When he comes to a highway, he and his horse have difficulty, but they manage to cross it. Burns lives by a personal code that has nothing to do with the constraints of modern civilization.

When Burns comes into conflict with the law and is asked to produce his identification cards, he replies, "Don't have none. Don't need none. I already know who I am." To know Burns is to like him, but he is doomed by his refusal to knuckle under to the forces of change. When he and his beloved little mare are run down on the highway by a truck carrying a load of bathroom fixtures, it is tragic but not unexpected. The message is clear. There is no room for a Burns and the way of life he represents in urban, industrial society. The future belongs to the developers and bureaucrats who are the faceless representatives of modern repression.

The notion of government as an expression of the violent repression of the individual is more explicit in *Fire on the Mountain*. The United States government wants John Vogelin's ranch for a weapons testing site. Vogelin refuses to sell. He sees himself as a part of the land upon which he has lived his life. The conflict is intrinsically unequal, for it pits the collective power of government against the individual. Like Burns, Vogelin is doomed to perish in the defense of a lost cause, and like Burns, he must resist the inevitable or lose his essential nature, the very core of his individuality.

The publication of *Desert Solitaire*, a series of reflective essays centered on Abbey's experiences as a park ranger at Arches National Monument, propelled Abbey into public attention and the center of controversy. Unconfined by the strictures of fiction, Abbey speaks in his own voice, and it is a voice that soars in lyrical praise of the land he loves and drips with contempt for the destructive forces of industrial and commercial development. For Abbey, the bringing of roads and automobiles into the wilderness means the beginning of its end and the onset of what he calls "industrial tourism."

The Monkey Wrench Gang might be considered a prescription for sedition, insurrection, and sabotage. It contains detailed descriptions of procedures for destroying earth-moving equipment and using explosives to destroy bridges. It counsels the destruction of private property in defense of the wilderness and the burning of billboards in the name of preserving beauty. His characters are fueled by rage against a society that would trade profit in the present against the future of the remaining wilderness; they believe their actions to be not only justified but also essential. Doc, Hayduke. Seldom Seen Smith, and Bonnie are fragments of Abbey that take action against an industrial society bent on destruction of the land. In *Desert Solitaire*, Abbey insisted that "wilderness is not a luxury but a necessity of the human spirit, and as vital to our lives as water and good bread."

In both his later fiction and nonfiction, Abbey's voice frequently becomes strident. The essays collected in *The Journey Home: Some Words in Defense of the American West* (1977) and *Abbey's Road* (1979) repeatedly lash out in furious anger or drop into despair. In *Good News*, set in a dark and grim future, both the land and the individual have fallen victim to the pervasive power of greed, the inevitable outcome when government becomes the tool of industrialism.

Abbey's last major work, *The Fool's Progress*, is transparently autobiographical, a darkly comic tale of a dying man wandering across the damaged landscape of America and the damaged landscape of his own life. The voice of Henry Holyoak Lightcap is one of comic despair. He is an irascible antihero who has an opinion about everything from French cuisine to feminism. Like his creator, for whom he speaks, Lightcap raises offensiveness to an art form. Nobody's cows are sacred. Nothing escapes his scathing observations, including himself. Lightcap's journey is filled with flashes of brilliance and a clarity of vision that is at once comical and deeply disturbing, for behind Lightcap's lament is a sense of loss, not so much for himself as for a United States that has lost its way—its land destroyed by rapacious development, its language debased by jargon, and its character dominated by loveless materialism. Yet despite the disquieting presence of impending death, Lightcap's life has been a joyous one, for he has fought the good fight, loved immoderately, and been loved in return.

DESERT SOLITAIRE

First published: 1968
Type of work: Essays

Abbey's iconoclastic reflections on his experiences as a park ranger at Arches National Monument touch on everything from rattlesnakes to philosophy.

Desert Solitaire: A Season in the Wilderness is the work for which Abbey is best known and by which he is most frequently defined. It contains his views on a variety of subjects, from the problems of the United States Park Service to an angry indictment of the evils of technology masquerading under the guise of progress. No voice is more eloquent in the praise of America's remaining wilderness nor more vitriolic in attacking those who would exploit and destroy it for profit.

In the introduction to *Desert Solitaire*, Abbey informs his readers that he has combined the experiences of three summers spent as a park ranger at Arches National Monument into one for the sake of narrative consistency. He writes that the first two summers were good but that the last summer was marred by the introduction of industrial tourism.

For Abbey, the tourist in the automobile (worse yet, in the huge recreational vehicle) spells the end of the wilderness spirit. Abbey's ambivalent stance toward the tourists, ostensibly fellow lovers of the outback, reflects the work's central dichotomy. Abbey's eloquent voice describes the beauty of the desert landscape, only to pause on the intrusion of industry and commerce into one of the last remaining wilderness areas in the United States.

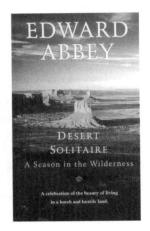

The first sentence of *Desert Solitaire* declares, "This is the most beautiful place on earth." Although Abbey believes that the wilderness is as close as one can come to something sacred, his view is not simplistic. He sees wilderness as essential to the quality of human life. His quarrel is not with civilization itself but with civilization made manifest as industrial technology thrust on the physical and spiritual landscape of the human condition: "A civilization which destroys what little remains of the wild, the spare, the original, is cutting itself off from its origins and betraying the principle of civilization itself."

Although Abbey is not a naturalist, *Desert Solitaire* is filled with the observations of the trained eye. He makes scientific observation serve the eloquence of his prose. The sureness of the scientific landscape lends validity to the thrust of his ideas. Nowhere in the book is the power of his prose or the sureness of his eye more apparent than in the chapter titled "Down the River."

For Abbey, the construction of the Glen Canyon Dam was one of the great sins of American society. In a discussion of human failings, he suggests that "original sin, the true original sin, is the blind destruction for the sake of greed of this natural paradise which lies all around us—if only we were worthy of it." The rafting trip he and his friend Ralph Newcomb take down the Colorado River through Glen Canyon just before it is flooded under the waters of Lake Powell becomes a song of lamentation for a lost Eden.

Abbey intersperses the tale of their journey with

excerpts from the journals of Major John Wesley Powell, who was the first white man to explore the Colorado River through Glen Canyon and the Grand Canyon. Despite the deprivation and hardships he experienced, Powell filled his journals with wonder. Abbey's voice joins Powell's, as he, too, pauses on the untouched beauty of the place: the shimmering waterfalls, whose mists create rainbows across the red sandstone sides of the canyon, the changing sounds of the river on its journey to the Sea of Cortez, the shifting patterns of the sky, and the voices of the wildlife soon to be displaced by rising waters. The landscape of the canyon becomes a part of the landscape of the mind. As Abbey and Newcomb are swept past side canyons beckoning for exploration, they are aware that the canyons will remain unexplored—at least by them, their children, or their children's children.

Abbey and Newcomb camp at the mouth of the Escalante River, where it joins the Colorado. Newcomb remains behind to fish for catfish while the adventurous Abbey explores upstream. He wanders up the labyrinthine canyon past untouched cliff dwellings of the Anasazi, the ancient people who inhabited the land before the Navajo. He realizes that these, too, will be submerged under the flooding water of the Colorado. Moreover, Abbey points out that the waters of Lake Powell will irrigate no land, will grow no crops. Instead, the trapped water will produce power—power to make possible the continued urban sprawl of Phoenix and Albuquerque—and provide an aquatic playground for well-to-do suburbanites, whose noisy powerboats will drown out the cry of the red-tailed hawk, the calls of the killdeer and sandpiper.

When Abbey returns down the canyon at nightfall to rejoin his fellow adventurer Newcomb, he is greeted by the smell of cooking catfish and the night sounds of the river. He reflects that this is all the paradise that is needed. The beauty of the place is heartbreaking, as is the tragedy of its imminent disappearance under mud and water. As Abbey and Newcomb approach the construction zone of the dam, a large sign that Abbey derisively dubs "first billboard erected in Glen Canyon" reminds them that government, in the service of greed, is willing to prosecute those who would trespass on the march of progress. The lyricism of Abbey's prose captures the mind and imagination; the

force of his passion invites the reader to share his outrage. The temple has been profaned by the money changers, and one is invited to help drive them out.

Abbey's journey is spiritual as well as physical. He probes the boundaries of his beliefs. He searches for divinity among the rocks and canyons and finds it lacking. He muses that he suspects that the surface of reality is also its essence. Yet he resists the temptation to remake nature into a more comforting pattern. He refuses to succumb to the idea that human nature is special and separate from the natural environment, from the earth itself. Thus the desert, the wilderness, becomes a part of the temple of existence—an Edenic landscape and a part of that primeval source from which humans spring and to which they return. Abbey discovers the nature of his belief in his love of the land. He proclaims, "I am not an atheist, but an earthiest. Be true to the earth."

Near the confluence of the Green and Colorado Rivers there is a labyrinthine landscape called the Maze. It held a particular place of affection in Abbey's heart, for he considered it one of the last places that was truly terra incognita—a place unmapped, untrodden by the foot of the casual tourist. Much like Abbey, it resists the domestication of being fully known, preserving its integrity and the mystery of its spirit; it is part of the voice that cries in the wilderness.

SUMMARY

The most frequent criticisms of *Desert Solitaire* are that it is contradictory, inconsistent, excessive, and angry—charges that are largely true. Such criticism, however, misses the point on two scores. Abbey's work reflects the complexities of the human condition, which is filled with contradiction, inconsistency, folly, and anger more often than not. Moreover, such criticism fails to see that Abbey's work is deliberately provocative. If he resorts to invective, he provokes response. When he reviles human behavior, it is to save humanity from itself. In the posthumously published volume *A Voice Crying in the Wilderness*, Abbey writes that "love implies anger. The man who is angered by nothing cares about nothing."

David Sundstrand

BIBLIOGRAPHY

By the Author

FICTION:

The Brave Cowboy: An Old Tale in a New Time, 1956
Fire on the Mountain, 1962
Black Sun, 1971
The Monkey Wrench Gang, 1975
Good News, 1980
The Fool's Progress, 1988
Hayduke Lives!, 1990

NONFICTION:

Desert Solitaire: A Season in the Wilderness, 1968
Appalachian Wilderness: The Great Smoky Mountains, 1970
Slickrock: Endangered Canyons of the Southwest, 1971
Cactus Country, 1973
The Journey Home: Some Words in Defense of the American West, 1977
Abbey's Road, 1979
Down the River, 1982
Beyond the Wall: Essays from the Outside, 1984
Slumgullion Stew: An Edward Abbey Reader, 1984
One Life at a Time, Please, 1988 (working title: "Rock Salt and Cherry Pie")
A Voice Crying in the Wilderness: Vox Clamantis in Deserto: Notes from a Secret Journal, 1990
Confessions of a Barbarian: Selections from the Journals of Edward Abbey, 1951-1989, 1994

POETRY:

Earth Apples = (Pommes des terre): The Poetry of Edward Abbey, 1994

About the Author

Bishop, James, Jr. *Epitaph for a Desert Anarchist: The Life and Legacy of Edward Abbey*. New York: Atheneum, 1994.

Cahalan, James M. *Edward Abbey: A Life*. Tucson: University of Arizona Press, 2001.

Hepworth, James, and Gregory McNamee, eds. *Resist Much, Obey Little: Remembering Edward Abbey*. San Francisco: Sierra Club Books, 1996.

Loeffler, Jack. *Adventures with Ed: A Portrait of Abbey*. Albuquerque: University of New Mexico Press, 2002.

McCann, Garth. *Edward Abbey*. Boise, Idaho: Boise State University Press, 1977.

Quigley, Peter, ed. *Coyote in the Maze: Tracking Edward Abbey in a World of Words*. Salt Lake City: University of Utah Press, 1998.

Ronald, Ann. "Edward Abbey." In *A Literary History of the American West*. Fort Worth: Texas Christian University Press, 1987.

_____. *The New West of Edward Abbey*. 2d ed. Reno: University of Nevada Press, 2000.

DISCUSSION TOPICS

- What is the explanation of Edward Abbey's failure to find "divinity" in natural landscape in the West?

- At what is Abbey's anger directed in *Desert Solitaire*? Is it under control and therefore effective?

- Judging from this essay or your familiarity with Abbey's later writings, how do you account for the decline in his work after *Desert Solitaire*?

- Some people consider puns and word play a low and weak form of humor. Is this true of Abbey's assertion "I am not an atheist, but an earthiest"?

- *Desert Solitaire* is not found among the many books for sale in the shop at Arches National Park. What could account for this apparently purposeful exclusion? Is it justifiable?

- To what extent is Abbey a kindred spirit of Henry David Thoreau?

HENRY ADAMS

Born: Boston, Massachusetts
February 16, 1838
Died: Washington, D.C.
March 27, 1918

Adams's literary work, which is crowned by his internationally acclaimed autobiography, examines the multiple challenges of the early twentieth century against the backdrop of earlier ages.

Library of Congress

BIOGRAPHY

Henry Brooks Adams, who dropped his middle name at age thirty-two, was born in Boston on February 16, 1838, the child of the writer and politician Charles Francis Adams and the homemaker Abigail Brooks Adams. The fourth of seven children, Henry came from an impressive New England family: He was grandson to John Quincy Adams, who was still alive during his childhood, and great grandson to John Adams; both men had been American presidents. This legacy of achievement bestowed a lifelong, influential sense of familial obligation on Adams at a very early age.

While young, Henry Adams, like his siblings, profited immensely from the liberal and intellectual atmosphere at home. By opening his huge library to him, his father gave Henry early access to works of literature and history. Soon, the quiet and observant boy watched his father work and converse with his political friends. Adams entered Harvard College in 1854 and graduated with a bachelor of arts degree in 1858. Looking back later, Adams did not think Harvard worthwhile; however, it gave him the intellectual background com-

mon to the elite of his time. The new *Harvard Magazine* also offered him an outlet for his first writing and awarded him with its editorship.

Following graduation, Adams went to Europe, where, while writing for the *Boston Daily Courier* in 1860, he scored a minor coup with an interview of Italian rebel leader Giuseppe Garibaldi. After his move to Washington, D.C., in the fall of 1860, Adams matched his writing powers with his interest in politics. As private secretary to his father, a congressman, he combined access to information and journalistic skill in his work for the Bostonian *Daily Advertiser.* "The Great Secession Winter, 1860-1861," was his dramatic summary of the secession of the South.

The appointment of his father as minister to the English court in 1861 gave Adams an inside view of global politics and a larger share of responsibility. Working for a while as an anonymous correspondent for *The New York Times*, Adams soon began to broaden the scope of his pen to move beyond politics to science, history, and economics. Combining a journalist's eye for the topical with a scholar's emphasis on knowledge and intellectual vigor, his articles soon attracted notice within the transatlantic intellectual community.

Adams's return to the United States in 1868 saw him becoming an important political journalist in Washington, where he wrote for reform and lambasted corruption. A few years later, however, he followed familial advice by accepting the professorship of medieval history at Harvard. From then on, his involvement in politics would remain indirect: Even though he continued to comment on current

7

issues as an outspoken writer and as editor of the *North American Review* from 1870 to 1876, he would never hold political office.

Adams married Miriam "Clover" Hooper in 1872. He resigned from Harvard in 1877 to go back to Washington to write *The Life of Albert Gallatin* (1879), the biography of President Thomas Jefferson's secretary of the treasury, whom Adams celebrated for his moral uprightness. Moving directly across from the White House in 1879, then relocating a few yards down the street in 1885, Adams made his home the social center for an exclusive group of influential friends. Based there, he became an incessant traveler and would see the Far East, the South Seas, and the Caribbean region; further, he undertook regular visits to Europe that, from 1899 to 1911, included annual summer stays in Paris.

His intimate knowledge of power politics made Adams's first (anonymously published) satire, *Democracy: An American Novel*, an instant success in 1880. A second work, *Esther: A Novel*, followed in 1884, but Adams's prohibition of all advertisement made it virtually unknown to the public. The suicide of his wife, with whom he had enjoyed a loving marriage, on December 6, 1885, visibly shook Adams. The young Elizabeth Cameron, wife of an elderly senator, already had been a friend of the family; now, she and Adams grew closer. Throughout their ensuing years as friends, they, according to all sources, never took their intense relationship beyond a platonic level.

The final publication of Adams's great historical masterwork in nine volumes, the *History of the United States During the Administrations of Thomas Jefferson and James Madison*, occurred in 1889 and 1891. It was greeted with great critical acclaim and was widely popular. With the completion of this gigantic work, Adams embarked on a two-year journey to the South Seas and Europe, during which he must have finally decided to remain only friends with Cameron. Back in Washington in 1892, he completed a promised biography. In a manner that would become typical, he privately printed *Memoirs of Marau Taaroa, Last Queen of Tahiti* for his friends in 1893 (revised in 1901 and published in 1947).

A first visit to the cathedrals of Normandy in 1895 sparked the privately printed *Mont-Saint-Michel and Chartres* of 1904 (revised in 1912 and published in 1913). In it, Adams presents an imagi-

nary "niece" with a grand tour of the architectural masterpieces of Norman France.

In 1907, Adams printed for his friends *The Education of Henry Adams* (published in revised form in 1918). In this, his most famous work, the author struggles with the implied promise of his life and his apparent "failure" to live up to it; his autobiography has become one of the classic texts of American literature. His final work, *The Life of George Cabot Lodge* (1911), is a biography of a close friend. After a stroke in 1912, Adams recovered sufficiently to travel again in 1913. The outbreak of World War I found him in Paris, where he took leave of Cameron. Shortly after his eightieth birthday, he died in his sleep in his home in Washington on March 26, 1918.

ANALYSIS

His familial heritage seemed to destine Adams for a life in politics; however, he discovered that the ideals of the past were no longer applicable to the realities of a modern mass democracy in which alliance and obligation to a political party seemed to eclipse independent statesmanship. Unwilling to adapt, Adams turned from active participation in politics to a literary and scholarly career and became a brilliant, highly moral, and idealistic observer of the public life of the United States on the verge of entering the twentieth century.

Adams's great interest in politics is never far from the forefront of his writing, and it comes as no surprise that his first piece of fiction, *Democracy: An American Novel*, tests the inner strength of his heroine, Madeleine Lee, to run the maze of power-obsessed Washington while trying to keep her morals intact and her ideals uncompromised. Adams amply studied his subject; his later autobiography, *The Education of Henry Adams*, is full of instances in which he received a practical "education" in the corrupt means of contemporary power politics.

The crucial point that emerges in both his fiction and autobiography is Adams's firm conviction (validated in principle by modern research) that the then-current system of partisan appointments led to an undignified run on offices with the onset of every new federal administration. With a keen eye on the abuses of the system, which Adams had observed with a wide-awake intelligence and well-trained moral sensitivity, and which he had lambasted directly in his earlier political writing, he succeeded in making *Democracy: An American Novel* a powerful mirror of the ills of a system that had lost its earlier ideals in the quagmire of party politics.

Thus, the central question expressed directly in his first novel, and strongly implied in his autobiography, is whether a qualified person should compromise in order to achieve a position of power from which he or she may do some common good, or whether the risk of contaminating one's ideals is too high a price to pay. The fictional Lee flees the arms of a corrupt senator who tempts her with power; the Henry Adams of his autobiography decides that "failure" to achieve political office is the only thing for which his idealistic and moral education has fitted him to suffer. The topic is again taken up in his 1895 reflection "Buddha and Brahma" (published in 1915), in which Adams's reworking of an Eastern legend privileges neither the active nor the contemplative life.

Critics have charged that much of Adams's disaffection with the American style of politicking was rooted in his unwillingness to compromise and his somewhat elitist tendency to remain aloof. His friend Justice Oliver Wendell Holmes once put it thus: "If the country had put him on a pedestal, I think Henry Adams with his gifts could have rendered distinguished public service. . . . He wanted it handed to him on a silver platter." Yet there is something of the power of the idealist in Adams's writing, and it is the finely honed ironic style and superb wit that accompany his observer point of view that give his works their unique voice. By keeping himself free to watch and analyze, Adams allowed his art to develop a sureness of touch, successfully conveying his critical opinions in a graceful and exciting manner—a style that would work equally well when he examined, for example, the topic of religion, as he did in his second novel, *Esther.*

Further, Adams's disgust at political corruption is not only the thematic concern of his literary work; it also looms large—indeed, it is the trademark—of his rich political and historical writing. Endowed with a brilliant analytical mind, and traveling widely from his dearly cultivated home base across from the White House, Adams was in a privileged position to see and analyze the dramatic shifts in power and culture that technology and industrialization brought following the Civil War, both in the United States and all over the globe.

Increasingly concerned with the breathtaking tempo with which these changes were happening wherever he placed his foot, be it the then-popular industrial "World" exhibitions, the Westernized islands of the South Seas, or the rapidly technologized Western Europe lying cheek by jowl with the inert giant of czarist Russia, Adams began looking for a means of understanding and rationalizing what was happening. Toward the end of the century, he became convinced that the future would hold no more fixed truths or unifying ideas that could make sense of the increasingly fragmented "multiverse" he saw developing. For Adams, twentieth century multiplicity extended to all fields of human endeavor, ranging from science to economics to religion, and the centrifugal forces of unfettered progress threatened to tear apart what was left of historic systems.

Against this backdrop, a first visit to Norman France in 1895 offered Adams a vision of a time in history when spiritual unity was perfect and humanity lived in harmony with God and the cosmos. From his repeated travels to the abbeys and cathedrals of northern France, Adams created his *Mont-Saint-Michel and Chartres,* intended as a travel guide for his friends but developed into an artistic statement offering an answer to the troubling present. Adams planned this work, which he subtitled "A Study in Thirteenth Century Unity," to stand alongside *The Education of Henry Adams,* which he gave the subtitle "A Study in Twentieth Century Multiplicity" to make obvious their close thematic relationship.

In these late works, Adams attached the different forces governing the thirteenth and twentieth centuries to the central symbols of the Virgin Mary and the technological wonder of the dynamo; he also put the conflict into poetic form with his splendid "Prayer to the Virgin of Chartres" (published posthumously in 1920). In his autobiography, the dynamo epitomizes the accelerating dynamic of change in the Western world and finely dramatizes the author's frustrated apprehension of a process which threatens to sweep away history itself. The Virgin, in *Mont-Saint-Michel and Chartres,* becomes synonymous with Adams's lifelong longing for a center that will hold:

She [the Virgin] never calls for sympathy by hysterical appeals to our feelings; she does not even altogether command, but rather accepts the voluntary, unquestioning, unhesitating, instinctive faith, love and devotion of mankind. She will accept ours, and we have not the heart to refuse it; we have not even the right, for we are her guests.

DEMOCRACY: AN AMERICAN NOVEL

First published: 1880
Type of work: Novel

Tempted to gain immense political power by marrying a ruthless and corrupt senator, the heroine decides for morality and rejects him.

Because of the sarcastic critique of his contemporary Washington which his first novel offered, Adams decided to publish *Democracy: An American Novel* anonymously; he succeeded in keeping his secret to his death and continued to move in the society whose moral flaws and rampant corruption he had exposed with such incisiveness.

As the novel opens, the thirty-year-old Madeleine (Mrs. Lightfoot) Lee decides to go to Washington, D.C., to observe the play of power politics in an effort to overcome the sense of hollowness with which the death of her husband, the Southerner Lightfoot Lee, and her infant baby have filled her. Clearly modeled after both the author and his wife, Miriam "Clover" Adams, Lee has independent means and great social charm, and she is inevitably drawn to "the action of primary forces," "the machinery of society, at work," thus echoing one of Adams's personal longings.

Further, the fact that Lee's arrival comes after a disappointing series of attempts to make herself and her inherited fortune useful to society is a fine play on the author's own most burning obsessions. Her frustrations with the products of higher education parallel the author's recent resignation from Harvard University in 1877, and she moves to a "newly hired house on Lafayette Square" opposite the White House, effectively next door to Adams's own. Most important, her sarcastic wit and ironic self-detachment from the political jungle she observes are the voice of Adams himself.

In her endeavor to see "POWER" at work, Lee is aided by her distant relation, the forty-one-year-old southern veteran-turned-lawyer John Carrington, who introduces her to the political powerhouse Senator Silas P. Ratcliffe, the "Prairie Giant of Peonia." While her younger sister Sybil Ross helps to make her salon a success, a variety of minor characters are introduced, all typical of people wrapped up in the machinations at the Capitol.

The inauguration of a new president, a masterful composite caricature of Ulysses S. Grant and the young Abraham Lincoln, sets in motion the game, as everybody begins hustling for appointments and political power. After their initial sizzling meeting at a political dinner, Adams lets Ratcliffe, a fiftyish widower of considerable attraction, charm himself into Lee's confidence, while she dreams of using power to reform this appallingly corrupt system. Asking her for political advice, Ratcliffe offers Lee a first draught of power; she still shies away from the responsibility that comes with it.

Carefully worming his way into the confidence of the bumbling new president, Ratcliffe is equally adept at enticing Lee, whom society begins to see as a potential occupant of the White House if she chooses the ambitious senator for a husband. In the southerner Carrington, however, Adams has created a central conscience who is aided in his destruction of Ratcliffe's pretensions of morality by the accident of privileged knowledge of the latter's evil deeds.

During a carefully set excursion to the tomb of George Washington, who rather obviously stands for a better, moral America now betrayed by politicians, Carrington brings Ratcliffe to a first admission of having instrumented political fraud. The latter fires back, however, and sends Carrington on a distracting mission to Mexico. Yet Carrington's alliance with Sybil Ross thwarts Ratcliffe, whose proposal of marriage is delayed until the two sisters have a private heart-to-heart talk.

What began as a political satire now becomes a romantic drama as, critics have insisted, the characters develop lives of their own and draw the reader into their conflicts. Presented with final evidence of Ratcliffe's corruption, Lee confronts him the morning after his proposal and is given the opportunity to reject soundly his Machiavellian belief that the end—the welfare of himself and his party, in which he subsumes that of the nation—justifies the dirty means he has employed. Rejected (and physically assaulted by a minor character), Ratcliffe receives a thorough dose of poetic justice and is left abandoned by the time of the epilogue, a letter of Ross's to Carrington, in which she hints at possible success for his proposal to the purified heroine.

While the romantic plot of the novel is somewhat conventional and the rejection of Ratcliffe comes as no surprise, Adams nevertheless delivers an interesting social satire. His well-drawn characters indeed come alive once their problems take center stage, and the political conflict moves toward a more universal clash between morals and ambition. Adams's contemporary critics rather liked the novel, which they compared to the fiction of Henry James and Anthony Trollope. It is still regarded as a minor achievement that can capture a modern reader interested in its central conflict.

MONT-SAINT-MICHEL AND CHARTRES

First published: 1913 (privately printed, 1904)
Type of work: Essay

Presenting the architectural masterpieces of medieval northern France, the author combines his description with reflections on the history of the period.

Initially written only for a small circle of friends, *Mont-Saint-Michel and Chartres* became so popular that Adams finally consented to have the American Institute of Architects publish a trade edition in 1913. The work's thought-provoking mixture of presentation of the religious monuments of medieval Normandy and the author's intelligent (and often idiosyncratic) reflections on the history and philosophy of a bygone era (and their potential applications to his own time, the early twentieth century) have lost nothing of their power to fascinate a reader.

Mont-Saint-Michel and Chartres opens with a powerful portrait of the abbey of Saint Michael on the northern coast of France. As is the case throughout the text, the physical description of the abbey and its features is embedded in Adams's narration of the history of the place. In a move perhaps typical for the American view of Europe of the time, Adams tries to entice his readers into the narrative further by telling of the Norman migration across the English Channel into England after the battle of Hastings and then of the eventual immigration of the descendants of the builders of Mont Saint Michel to the New World, where they would become Adams's ancestors.

The oldest surviving parts of the abbey church serve as the starting point for Adams's reflections on the history, culture, and spiritual mind-set of the eleventh century. In what is clearly his own reading, Adams sees the century united in its "masculine" Christian belief in power, heroic battle, and a philosophic materialism exemplified by the Romanesque style of architecture. Contemporary and later historians often have disagreed with this, and other of Adams's views, stressing disunity and civic strife where he saw harmony and community.

Although later critics stressed individual ambition as central to the age, Adams's personalized account of one of the abbots is still in general accordance with the modern picture: "One might linger over Abbot Robert of Torigny, who was a very great man in his day, and an especially great architect, but too ambitious. All his work, including the two towers [for Mont Saint Michel], crumbled and fell for want of proper support." Thus, Adams's fascinating travel guide may still serve as one possible approach to the era; his own disclaimers that he writes for an intelligent and interested tourist, rather than crusty scholars, is the best antidote when his vision collides with treatments that stress abstract historic fact over feeling.

From the abbey church on the mount, the narrative moves to the great cathedral of Chartres near Paris. There, a fascinatingly detailed and extremely loving account of the outstanding features of the building captures the imagination of the reader, who is introduced to art still in existence in France. Again, the material objects are brought to life as Adams begins to render his interpretation of the meaning of this great architectural masterpiece: "The Church at Chartres belonged not to the people, not to the priesthood, and not even to Rome; it belonged to the Virgin [Mary]."

The cult of the Virgin Mary, whose "fetish power" has overcome the masculine obsession with

God and his fiery Archangel Michael that is celebrated at Mount Saint Michael, is for Adams central for the period of the Transition Gothic of the twelfth century in France. A deep "feminine" mysticism has replaced rationalism, he says, and the veneration of the Virgin bestows a deep sense of unity on its culture—a unity, Adams is quick to point out, that his own early twentieth century has lost forever.

From the deeply sympathetic discussion of Chartres, Adams moves to show the depth of the cult of the Virgin in the medieval world. In the chapter "Les Miracles de Notre Dame" (the miracles of Our Lady), Adams guides the reader through a compilation of anecdotes and historical material enriched by his quotation and translation of medieval French texts related to his topic.

To conclude his spiritual and geographical tour of medieval northern France, Adams adds three chapters dealing with the philosophy of the age. "Abelard" deals with the famous abbot and schoolmaster of that name, whose central debate with another scholar is playfully rendered by Adams much in the style of a senatorial debate in the Capitol. A chapter on the mystics of the twelfth century, among whom Francis of Assisi stands out, precedes Adams's discussion of Thomas Aquinas. For Adams, Aquinas presents the terminal point of scholastic philosophy; from his religious premises, nothing more than his attempted synthesis of faith and reason could be achieved. Adams directs his reader to then-current problems in theoretical physics, in which people struggled again with the issues of unity versus multiplicity in the order of the cosmos.

What started out as a travel guide, then, has become a philosophical meditation on the state of the universe by the time Adams finishes *Mont-Saint-Michel and Chartres*. Even though his reading of French medieval history and culture has been criticized, Adams's vision of an age so different from an increasingly fragmented twentieth century remains a fascinating journey into a foreign country and a past mind-set. In Adams's celebration of a gentle, unifying Virgin, the reader can see a deep longing for a world different from that encountered at home in Washington, across the street from the White House.

THE EDUCATION OF HENRY ADAMS

First published: 1918 (privately printed, 1907)
Type of work: Autobiography

Obsessed with an apparent "failure" to be as successful as his ancestors, Henry Adams insists that his education did not prepare him for the rough reality of a new century.

The Education of Henry Adams, the most famous work of its author, was originally intended only for a small audience; after its posthumous publication in 1918, it promptly won the prestigious Pulitzer Prize in 1919, and it is still regarded as a masterpiece of American literature.

At the core of Adams's autobiography lies his concern that his education was rooted in the eighteenth century and thus was of little value in preparing the boy to become a success in what Adams calls the "twentieth" century (actually the second half of the nineteenth). Further emphasis is placed on the fact that in the newly emerging, rapidly changing world, all education will have to be continuous and can no longer guarantee success. Despite its author's focus on "failure," however, and its self-deprecating irony and gentle wit, *The Education of Henry Adams* chronicles a remarkably successful, productive, rich, and influential life.

The Education of Henry Adams opens with a skillfully drawn account of the author's youth in the family home of Boston and the summer residence of Quincy, Massachusetts, where the historic legacy of his great New England family was always in strong evidence. Adams personifies the early factors of his development through a warm portrayal of his admired father; it was through him that the boy received an education which, the author half-mockingly insists, "condemned [him] to failure" because he was not educated to stoop to the low ways of a corrupt present.

Adams vigorously dismisses his formal schooling as dull memorizing and perceives personal experience as the true educator. Thus, a boyhood trip to Washington across the morally repulsive, slave-holding South is given more weight than the whole of his time at Harvard College. At Harvard,

Adams insists, was bred "an inferior social type, quite as ill-fitted as the Oxford type for success in the next generation." Similarly, on his first trip to Europe, Adams ends his plan to study German law with his listening to the music of composer Richard Wagner; throughout his travels, his "accidental education" is worth more than carefully laid-out schemes.

Following his young self back to Washington, Adams interprets the insights gained during practical work for his congressman father as an education in the corrupt and devious ways of contemporary politics. There, the narrative implies, morality and idealism are dangerously out of fashion. The author continues his account of his practical education—contrasting starkly to familial values—as the young man follows his father to England. There, his "education" acquaints him with the price of political scandal and compromise, alienating social customs, and the experience of the United States' sudden coming of age with the assassination of President Lincoln in 1865.

As a turning point in his career, Adams depicts his decision in 1870 to accept a professorship at Harvard, after about only two years back in the cauldron of Washington, where he was further educated in the corruption of the present day. His narrative—in a chapter significantly titled "Failure"—reads like an apology for this act, which seemingly forever rejected any possibility that he would live up to his birthright of a shining political career. Accordingly, the narrator informs the reader that with this act, "Henry Adams' education, at his entry into life, stopped, and his life began." Characteristically, his self-assessment of the following seven years is carried by the familiarly self-mocking tone as he insists that as "a professor, he regarded himself as a failure."

Against the dark vision of the failed eighteenth century man Adams, the narrative presents the fate of Clarence King, close friend of the author who, as an enterprising geologist and self-made man, "had given himself education all of a piece, yet broad." Yet King's ensuing bankruptcy in 1893 and a confrontation with the gigantic dynamos of the Chicago Exhibition in that year seem to render hopeless all trust in education: What use can come of the cultivation of a mind in a world where the brute forces of capitalism and electricity threaten the very existence of a self hoping to live in harmony with a unified cosmos?

From this pessimistic vantage point, Adams develops the final third of his autobiography, which becomes increasingly theoretical and philosophical. The author connects the perceived failure of his life with a broader sense of chaos and vulnerability; he sees the "multiplicity" of the emerging twentieth century—symbolized by the dynamo—as opposed to the unity of medieval spiritualism and veneration of the Virgin Mary.

Adams's important observation of dramatically accelerating technological progress and its accompanying cultural change leaves his narrative struggling to produce a formula that could describe these processes with the same mathematical accuracy with which his contemporary scientists began to discover the rules governing the behavior of ideal gases. Mixing history and thermodynamics, Adams articulates a "dynamic theory of history" and a "law of acceleration"; both theories convince in their analysis of the past but fall far short from being natural laws.

Adams's autobiography ends on a note that is both resigned to the inevitability of the new and guardedly optimistic about the vistas the new powers serving humanity may open. Taking the death of a beloved friend as an occasion to conclude his autobiography, Adams ends with a vision of a future world which may be regarded "without a shudder."

Despite its obvious laments and occasionally massive self-deprecation, *The Education of Henry Adams* fascinates in its profound examination of a powerful mind growing up at a crucial period in American and human history. If his autobiography excludes important aspects of his life—his wife, Miriam, is not mentioned once—it is nevertheless a powerful meditation on how to prepare the mind to succeed in a rapidly changing, uncaring world. Taken as such, Adams's work is of a strikingly modern quality and has not lost its relevance for the reader of today.

SUMMARY

The work of Adams offers his readers a powerful view of a United States in transition and artistically examines the struggles of idealistic people who, aware of their cultural legacy, are trying to come to terms with the immense challenge of a new century and era. His fiction succeeds in combining entertaining stories with greater moral and philosophical concerns that are still relevant. His two late masterpieces blend discussion of architectural wonders and a presentation of the author's own life with fascinating reflections on the place of humanity in an ever-changing cosmos. Adams's gentle, ironic voice never lets a reader's interest lapse; it is full of wit and devoid of doctrine.

R. C. Lutz

BIBLIOGRAPHY

By the Author

NONFICTION:
The Life of Albert Gallatin, 1879
John Randolph, 1882 (biography)
The History of the United States of America, 1889-1891
  (9 volumes)
Historical Essays, 1891
Mont-Saint-Michel and Chartres, privately printed, 1904, repb., 1913
The Education of Henry Adams, privately printed, 1907, repb., 1918 (autobiography)
The Degradation of the Democratic Dogma, 1919
A Cycle of Adams Letters, 1861-1865, 1920 (W. C. Ford, editor)
Letters of Henry Adams, 1892-1918, 1938 (Ford, editor)
Henry Adams and His Friends: A Collection of Unpublished Letters, 1947 (H. D. Cater, editor)
The Correspondence of Henry James and Henry Adams, 1877-1914, 1992 (George Monteiro, editor)

LONG FICTION:
Democracy: An American Novel, 1880
Esther, 1884

EDITED TEXTS:
Documents Relating to New-England Federalism, 1801-1815, 1877
The Writings of Albert Gallatin, 1879 (2 volumes)

About the Author
Brookhiser, Richard. *America's First Dynasty: The Adamses, 1735-1918.* New York: Free Press, 2002.
Bush, Clive. *Halfway to Revolution: Investigation and Crisis in the Work of Henry Adams, William James, and Gertrude Stein.* New Haven, Conn.: Yale University Press, 1991.
Chalfant, Edward. *Better in Darkness: A Biography of Henry Adams, His Second Life.* Hamden, Conn.: Archon Books, 1994.
_____. *Both Sides of the Ocean: A Biography of Henry Adams, His First Life, 1838-1862.* Hamden, Conn.: Archon Books, 1982.

DISCUSSION TOPICS

- In what significant ways does Henry Adams differ from his father and grandfather?

- Are Adams's political and religious ideas more effectively presented in his fiction or in nonfiction works such as his autobiography?

- Does Adams offer a convincing interpretation of Roman Catholic devotion to the Virgin Mary in *Mont-Saint-Michel and Chartres*?

- Why is Adams so critical of his formal education? Does it seem to have benefited him more than he realized?

- Characterize Adams's attitude toward the time in which he was living.

- How convincing do you find Adams's assertion of his own "failure"?

Contosta, David R., and Robert Muccigrosso, eds. *Henry Adams and His World.* Philadelphia: American Philosophical Society, 1993.

Decker, William. *The Literary Vocation of Henry Adams.* Chapel Hill: University of North Carolina Press, 1990.

Harbert, Earl. *Henry Adams: A Reference Guide.* Boston: G. K. Hall, 1992.

————, ed. *Critical Essays on Henry Adams.* Boston: G. K. Hall, 1981.

O'Brien, Michael. *Henry Adams and the Southern Question.* Athens: University of Georgia Press, 2005.

Rowe, John Carlos, ed. *New Essays on "The Education of Henry Adams."* New York: Cambridge University Press, 1996.

Samuels, Ernest. *Henry Adams.* Cambridge, Mass.: Belknap Press of Harvard University Press, 1989.

Wasserstrom, William. *The Ironies of Progress: Henry Adams and the American Dream.* Carbondale: Southern Illinois University Press, 1984.

JAMES AGEE

Born: Knoxville, Tennessee
November 27, 1909
Died: New York, New York
May 16, 1955

Agee brought subtlety of thought and intensity of emotion to his portrayal of the people, issues, and sensibilities of the American South.

Library of Congress

BIOGRAPHY

James Rufus Agee was born in Knoxville, Tennessee, on November 27, 1909. His father, Hugh James Agee, a warm and simple man, had worked for the U.S. Postal Service in Panama and later for the railroad in Tennessee. His mother, the former Laura Whitman Tyler, was from a wealthier family and kept a religious household. A turning point came early in Agee's life when, on May 18, 1916, his father died in an automobile crash.

Left alone to raise James and his sister Emma, Laura Agee's religiosity grew; it brought feelings of guilt and anger to James and led the family to a Catholic mountain retreat, where he found substitute parents in Father Harold and Grace Flye. A serious, lonely boy who loved reading, Agee experienced a spiritual crisis at the age of fourteen that further alienated him from his background and surroundings.

With his mother's remarriage in 1924 to a conservative churchman, Agee was ready to leave home. In 1925 he entered Phillips Exeter Academy in rural New Hampshire, where he wrote poetry and contributed stories to the school's monthly publication. Though his grades were poor, upon graduation in June of 1928 he was accepted to Harvard College. There he wrote for the newspaper and literary review and cultivated friendships with rising literary figures such as I. A. Richards, Ber-

nard Schoenfeld, and Dwight Macdonald. Agee's college years, like much of his life to follow, were characterized by heavy drinking and severe depressions. Though he had felt occasional homosexual leanings, involvements with a series of women culminated in his courtship of Olivia Saunders, whose family had effectively adopted Agee, and the couple was married early in 1933.

A *Harvard Advocate* parody of *Time* magazine brought Agee to the attention of publisher Henry Luce, and upon graduation in 1932 Agee moved to New York to write for *Fortune*. Meanwhile, he worked sporadically on several autobiographical novels. In 1934, some of his poetry was anthologized in *Modern American Poetry* and was selected for publication by Yale University under the title *Permit Me Voyage*. A *Fortune* assignment in 1936 to report on tenant farmers in Alabama led to a piece which was rejected by the magazine but developed into the book *Let Us Now Praise Famous Men* (1941).

In 1937, Agee met and fell in love with Alma Mailman. After years of discontent, he and Olivia divorced, and Alma became his second wife in 1938. This marriage lasted three years and resulted in the birth of a son, Joel. By 1940, Agee had met and fallen in love with Mia Fritsch, his third wife, to whom he remained married until his death and by whom he fathered three children, Julia, Andrea, and John.

Having become a book reviewer at *Time* in 1938, Agee capitalized on his fascination with the cinema to become the magazine's film reviewer in 1941 and to accept the same post at *The Nation* in 1942. He also served as a steady consultant in the expansion of the Library of Congress Film Archives. He had always loved film, and his work as a reviewer and consultant led naturally to filmmaking itself. His first venture was "In the Street," made with photographer Helen Levitt in 1945. In 1948, Agee left his positions with *Time* and *The Nation* and turned his efforts to film and fiction. Agee established friendships with directors Charlie Chaplin and John Huston and was hired by Huston in 1950 to write a screenplay for C. S. Forester's 1935 novel *The African Queen*; the film was released in 1951. A coronary thrombosis in early 1951 interrupted Agee's work and precipitated his physical decline.

Agee's first novel, *The Morning Watch*, based on his years at St. Andrew's retreat, appeared in 1951. The following year, he penned a series on U.S. president Abraham Lincoln for television, and in 1953 a film he wrote based on Stephen Crane's story "The Bride Comes to Yellow Sky" was released. With his constant smoking and drinking and frequent angina attacks, Agee took on numerous projects, only to abandon them, and tried to complete others on which he had been working for years. On May 16, 1955, in New York City, a final heart attack took his life at the age of forty-five.

A Death in the Family, a novel published in 1957, received the Pulitzer Prize. Other posthumous publications include *Agee on Film: Reviews and Comments* (1958), *Agee on Film: Five Film Scripts* (1960), and *Letters of James Agee to Father Flye* (1962).

ANALYSIS

During the course of his career, James Agee wrote in a wide variety of genres. It is difficult to place a single label on him, and even within a given genre his work often frustrates conventional expectations. Through the broad range of his poems, stories, essays, articles, novels, reviews, and screenplays, his voice expresses the clarity of thought and depth of passion that characterized his life.

Agee first considered himself a poet and as a young man admired the poetry of John Keats, William Blake, the seventeenth century "metaphysical poets"—John Donne, George Herbert, and Andrew Marvell—and, among his contemporaries, W. H. Auden. From these poets Agee took formal and stylistic influences—a devotion to metrical formulae, a meditative tone, complex thought and imagery, romantic lyricism—that give his poetry intellectual and spiritual elevation and sometimes

an archaic or stilted quality. His volume of verse, *Permit Me Voyage*, includes portrayals of urban and rural scenes, a tragic narrative about an infertile farmwife, sonnets of marital discontent, versified prayers, and an impassioned dedication to an exhaustive list of the poet's personal heroes, friends, and inspirations.

The ability to combine given forms with intense personal passion is seen beyond Agee's poetry. All of his works draw on his personal life or attitudes: His style is inherently subjective. This tendency to interpret his subjects in a personal and intimate manner is reflected even when he is on assignment to cover a luxury cruise, roadside America, the new Tennessee Valley Authority, or the Borough of Brooklyn, New York. By the same token, Agee's fiction is always partially or wholly autobiographical. He had little interest in making up or disguising stories; rather, he sought to observe and experience real life and then to render and evoke it through the written word.

On the other hand, Agee's years as a staff and freelance journalist inculcated in him the ability to tell a story simply and directly when necessary and to render detail with detached and even scientific precision. While his poetry betrays occasional emotional indulgence, his novels and essays exhibit steady control. Mere suggestions serve to add brief but vivid color, after which the narrative or thrust of the argument is duly resumed. In some cases, Agee's concern with maintaining the movement or structural integrity of a piece may seem to deny the emotional or evocative power inherent in the subject matter; however, the emotional power is enhanced through the subtle treatment, and realism is not sacrificed to artistic license. In this way, Agee's writing is often deceptive in its simplicity; character transformation and the depiction of mood are achieved not explicitly but gradually, almost imperceptibly.

Agee's family and educational background inform his unique style. Raised in a religious home, he spent his life defining his relationship to Christian institutions and beliefs. This background steeped him in the Bible, the catechism, the confession, and the sermon; his writing therefore often exhibits biblical simplicity and rhythm, an attention to detail, a relentless examination of moral condition, and a passionate rhetorical power. Similarly, Agee's wide knowledge of philosophy and music (above all, the music of nineteenth century composer Ludwig van Beethoven), along with the traditional canon of English and American literature, gave him a grounding in cultural history and a rich pool from which to draw intellectual or allusive power.

This cultured and literate background enhanced Agee's natural abilities with language, and his writing is masterfully crafted, with a subtlety of gesture and careful attention to detail. While capable of extremely economical usage in turning a striking phrase or image, Agee is not a particularly economical writer. His attention to detail and desire to replicate real people or situations with unflawed accuracy, in both external attributes and internal implications, result in long sentences, complex constructions, expansive catalogs, meticulously qualified arguments, and use of some of the finer technical devices of logic and rhetoric. While brevity was not a central concern of Agee, however, his writing is not verbose or diffuse, for the full and often dense prose reflects the precision and breadth of Agee's powers of observation and discernment.

Nowhere are these powers more evident than in his writings for and about film. On one hand, his love of the quickly developing medium infused his journalistic and novelistic endeavors with the power to evoke images and entire scenes with cinematic fullness. On the other hand, it led him to devote his intellect and labor to elevating film as an art form, and Agee's reviews helped revolutionize attitudes toward film. He approached film with lucidity and treated it with as much respect and severe scrutiny as have been devoted to poetry and painting through the centuries. In writing about film, Agee found an eloquence that few others had—and that he himself often lacked elsewhere. Rather than simply report on a film's entertainment value or intellectual content, Agee brought to his reviews an inside, craftsmanlike approach. Even before he had begun making films himself, he saw and reviewed them with an eye to the specific cinematographic techniques involved in creating the series of images. Thus his reviews are often as informative and provocative as the works on which they focus.

LET US NOW PRAISE FAMOUS MEN

First published: 1941
Type of work: Essay

The lives of tenant farmers in Alabama, and their relationship to two journalists who come to report on them, are complex, difficult, and inspiring.

Let Us Now Praise Famous Men is a unique work of literature. It was first conceived as a feature article for *Fortune* magazine: In the summer of 1936, Agee was sent to Alabama along with photographer Walker Evans to document the lives of tenant farmers. The article they produced, however, was much too passionate and impressionistic for the editors of *Fortune,* so Agee worked on the project privately and eventually published the "article" as a four-hundred-page book. When it first appeared, only two years after John Steinbeck's novel *The Grapes of Wrath,* with which it shares certain similarities, the book received bad reviews and sold a mere six hundred copies. It was only after Agee's death, and especially in the political turbulence and social awareness of the 1960's, that the book achieved popularity and literary standing.

Let Us Now Praise Famous Men is as much about Agee's personal experiences among three poor sharecropping families as it is about their lives per se. For Agee, the two could not be considered separately, and the moral and emotional implications of his and Evans's presence among their subjects—seeing themselves as spies—are central to any meaningful contemplation of tenant farming during the Depression. Thus, the piece moves back and forth, sometimes overtly in large sections, sometimes momentarily in parentheses, between precisely objective reportage and relentless self-examination.

The structure of the book reflects the care that

Agee obviously invested in it. The composition is divided into various sections, and movements at times seem nearly spontaneous or improvised. Agee uses a series of prefatory pieces to create a sense of false beginnings that nullifies any expectations the reader may have and establishes the book's painstaking pace. Then, sections are introduced with titles, labels, and enumerations that reflect no overall pattern but rather mirror the complexity of the material they cover. They are not placed in chronological order, order of composition, or any order sequence of logical development. Each new section may be a new beginning, marked by an epigram, a poem, a list, or a dramatic shift in tone. Transitions are often sudden and connections unclear. Such an unorthodox structure, far from being a gratuitous game devised to baffle, derives from the earnest effort to make sense of the experience of observing, interacting with, and living among sharecroppers.

In spite of this complexity, Agee is rigorously direct with the reader as to his purposes in the book and his awareness of the limitations its form places on him. He asks for no suspension of disbelief—the book is admittedly only paper—and makes no claims to extraordinary powers of insight or expression. He simply trusts in words. This trust and the earnest effort to be truthful, like so many attributes of the work, are relentless, and therein lies their emotional and philosophical power.

Within this context of moral and literary anxiety, Agee documents, with the help of Evans's photographs (which precede and are to be considered coequal with sections of the text), the poverty, aspirations, and pathos of the people he encounters. The Gudger, Ricketts, and Woods families live in poverty: Agee exhaustively details their surroundings, their clothing, their daily activities, their conversations, their work, their educations, their diets, their health, and any other aspect of their lives he can attempt to portray. He also depicts his own interactions with them and the relationships that result. He contemplates the social and political implications of their lives for society as a whole and, through the intense and relentless examination of their existence, poses practical and philosophical questions of universal relevance.

A DEATH IN THE FAMILY

First published: 1957
Type of work: Novel

A man's sudden death in an automobile crash leaves his wife and small children to try to continue without him.

A Death in the Family is a novel of delightful and deceptive simplicity. As the title implies, it is the story of a man's death and its effects on the family he leaves behind. Jay Follet is happily married to his devout wife, Mary, and they have two children, Rufus and Catherine, ages six and four. Early one morning, Jay is summoned by his drunken brother Ralph to drive from Knoxville to their father's deathbed in rural LaFollette. As Jay suspects, the journey turns out to be unnecessary—Ralph exaggerated the severity of the old man's condition—so he sets out to return home, hoping to arrive before the children go to bed. Formerly an alcoholic, Jay may have had something to drink; apparently, high speeds and a loose pin in the steering mechanism cause his car to go off the road. Jay, with only two tiny bruises on his face, experiences a fatal concussion. His family is first alerted that he was in an accident, and then that he died. His body is returned to Knoxville, and the funeral is held. That, with several interpolated flashbacks (sections in italics which the editors, after Agee's death, placed where they thought best) is the entire action of the novel.

Within this bare plot, Agee uses careful and subtle detail to create character and emotional movement. The narrative voice is nearly absent; it either describes the external attributes of a particular moment or records the impressions and inner thoughts of any of a number of characters. From chapter to chapter, the point of view often shifts among Mary, Rufus, Catherine, Ralph, Mary's brother Andrew, and her Aunt Hannah. Each character brings to the narrative a particular sensibil-

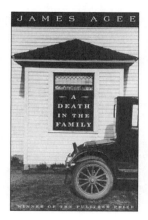

ity through which events are viewed, and Agee often provides parallel, simultaneous perspectives on a given scene or moment. Contrasting with Mary's emotional spirituality are Hannah's even-headed wisdom and Andrew's often bitter skepticism. Moreover, against the seeming clarity of the adults, Agee offers the perceptions of the children, who attempt to understand their elders, their own roles in the world, and their father's disappearance with a balanced mixture of innocence, selfishness, and confusion.

Within the larger story of Jay's death and burial, most of which is recounted directly but from the distance of the Follet home, smaller events establish the novel's dramatic life and texture. Agee provides a wealth of otherwise ordinary incidents or encounters—Jay and Rufus seeing a Chaplin film, Jay's early morning departure, Hannah buying Rufus a hat, Rufus and Catherine bickering, Mary being comforted by the priest from Chattanooga—that take on special power or significance on this particular day in the life of the family. Agee portrays moments vividly but without pretension or fanfare; the moments both stand alone and accumulate to create a textured portrait of a group of people and a meaningful event in their lives.

BIBLIOGRAPHY

By the Author

SHORT FICTION:
"A Mother's Tale," 1952
Four Early Stories by James Agee, 1964
The Collected Short Prose of James Agee, 1968

LONG FICTION:
The Morning Watch, 1951
A Death in the Family, 1957

SCREENPLAYS:
The Red Badge of Courage, 1951 (based on Stephen Crane's novel)
The African Queen, 1952 (based on C. S. Forester's novel)
The Bride Comes to Yellow Sky, 1952 (based on Crane's short story)
Noa Noa, 1953
White Mane, 1953
Green Magic, 1955

A Death in the Family is a deeply autobiographical novel. Not only does Jay Follet's death mirror that of Agee's father, but other details—the name Rufus and the taunting it occasions, the mother's extreme religiosity, and the priest's refusal to administer full rites—are also drawn directly from the author's past as well. No effort is made to fictionalize the story; rather, Agee has given imaginative, artistic, and unsentimental expression to his vivid memories of a crucial period in his life.

SUMMARY

As a man who lived somewhat recklessly and died much too young, Agee left behind a small body of work by no means commensurate with his extraordinary talents. His life was a tragedy of promise only partially fulfilled, and his writings offer, through careful examination of specific subjects, a universal vision of human suffering, longing, and hope.

Barry Mann

DISCUSSION TOPICS

- The title *Let Us Now Praise Famous Men* is a quotation from a sacred book in which the "famous men" are prophets and patriarchs. What are the effects of his applying it to poor sharecroppers?

- How does James Agee make the reader feel the impact of Jay Follet's death in *A Death in the Family*? Does the author's restraint play a part?

- Since Jay Follet's fatal accident parallels that of Agee's own father so closely, why did he not write directly about his father's death? What does he gain by fictionalizing it?

- *A Death in the Family* is called "a novel of delightful and deceptive simplicity." How can one be "delighted" by such a story?

- Locate the "deceptive" elements in Agee's novel. What motives might account for an attempt to "deceive" the reader?

The Night of the Hunter, 1955
Agee on Film: Five Film Scripts, 1960

POETRY:
Permit Me Voyage, 1934
The Collected Poems of James Agee, 1968

NONFICTION:
Let Us Now Praise Famous Men, 1941
Agee on Film: Reviews and Comments, 1958
Letters of James Agee to Father Flye, 1962
James Agee: Selected Journalism, 1985

About the Author

Barson, Alfred. *A Way of Seeing: A Critical Study of James Agee.* Amherst: University of Massachusetts Press, 1972.

Bergreen, Laurence. *James Agee: A Life.* New York: E. P. Dutton, 1984.

Hersey, John. Introduction to *Let Us Now Praise Famous Men,* by James Agee. Boston: Houghton Mifflin, 1988.

Hughes, William. *James Agee, Omnibus, and Mr. Lincoln: The Culture of Liberalism and the Challenge of Television, 1952-1953.* Lanham, Md.: Scarecrow Press, 2004.

Kramer, Victor A. *Agee and Actuality: Artistic Vision in His Work.* Troy, N.Y.: Whitston, 1991.

_____. *A Consciousness of Technique in "Let Us Now Praise Famous Men": With Thirty-one Newly Selected Photographs.* Albany, N.Y.: Whitston, 2001.

Lofaro, Michael, ed. *James Agee: Reconsiderations.* Knoxville: University of Tennessee Press, 1992.

Madden, David, ed. *Remembering James Agee.* 2d ed. Baton Rouge: Louisiana State University Press, 1997.

Spiegel, Alan. *James Agee and the Legend of Himself.* Columbia: University of Missouri Press, 1998.

AI

Born: Albany, Texas
October 21, 1947

Ai uses disturbing, often violent imagery to explore the darker aspects of human nature.

BIOGRAPHY

The poet now known as Ai was born Florence Anthony in Albany, Texas, on October 21, 1947. Her mother was sixteen at the time, and married, but Ai was born out of wedlock. She did not know who her father was until she was twenty-six.

Ai's ancestry was a mixture of Choctaw, Caucasian, Japanese, and Filipino. Although Anthony clearly looked black, as did her mother, she found it difficult in early life to identify with any particular ethnic group. She was born at her grandparents' house after her mother's husband had found out about his wife's affair and had beaten his wife in retribution.

Anthony was sent to an "integrated" Catholic school in Albany that was, in fact, largely black; there, she was taunted by her schoolmates (she has remembered being called a "nigger-jap," among other things). She therefore rejected her obvious ethnic background and adopted the name of Ai, the Japanese word for love. Her first academic degree, a bachelor's degree from the University of Arizona awarded in 1969, was in Oriental Studies.

In 1971, Ai earned a master's degree in creative writing from the University of California; about that time, she began writing poetry under her adopted name. Along the way, she worked at a variety of jobs, including modeling and teaching.

Ai's unconventional beginnings and her rage at having no ethnic "home" are clearly reflected in her poetry. As part of no particular ethnic group, she shunned established ways of viewing the world, and her anger and her sense of homelessness permeated her work.

When her first collection of poetry, *Cruelty*, was published in 1973, Ai met with a variety of critical responses. She received Guggenheim and Radcliffe Fellowships in 1975 and a Massachusetts Arts and Humanities Fellowship in 1976. These honors proved that she was a poet to be taken seriously, but there were negative reactions as well.

Ai's poetry was far from gentle. She wrote of graphic violence, rape, child molestation, and murder, and her work was condemned by many critics as pornographic. When *Killing Floor* (1979) was named the 1978 Lamont Poetry Selection by the Academy of American Poets, Ai had to be taken more seriously, even by those who had disparaged her in the past. Still, there was continued objection to her graphic depictions of sex and violence.

Ai has been lauded by many but has also been criticized for her forthright manners. She has been loudly attacked by feminists for her graphic descriptions of rape and violence against women. She has been applauded as a speaker for minority groups, but she has also been attacked for her refusal to identify herself with any particular group. In response, Ai has declared, "I was forced to be loyal to myself as a multiracial person or be immersed in the black struggle for identity with which I had little in common. Except a desire to be accepted as I was."

Ai's poetry, her life, even her chosen name have made it quite clear which road she has taken. She has chosen the Japanese culture as her own, but she has clearly shown through her works that she can identify with the human race in general and especially the darker aspects of the human soul.

The publication of *Sin* (1986), *Fate* (1991), and *Greed* (1993) added to Ai's reputation. Her 1999 collection of new and selected poems, *Vice*, won the National Book Award and established her as a major poet despite the controversy surrounding her work.

Ai held the Mitte Chair in Creative Writing for 2002-2003 at Southwest Texas State University. She became a professor of English at Oklahoma State University and moved to Stillwater, Oklahoma. She continued to write poetry and to comment on her life and work in interviews and prose articles. Far from being a voice of black or feminist literature, Ai remained her own person, not tied to any ethnic or racial group but, rather, identifying with the most intense aspects of humanity in general.

ANALYSIS

The first observation one cannot help making about Ai's poetry is that she uses a straightforward narrative style to describe the most horrible people and events. Almost all of her works are first-person narratives in which she assumes the voices of a variety of people—men and women, adults and children, murderers and victims. Her characters come from many times and places, but they all have one thing in common: They are experiencing, in various ways, the darkest parts of human nature.

Ai's first published collection, *Cruelty* (1973), is essentially a series of one-page monologues told from the points of view of a variety of anonymous people. A short poem called "Abortion," told from a father's point of view, expresses his anger that his wife or lover (it is not clear whether this is a married couple) has killed "his son." "The Hitchhiker" is the story of a man who hitches a ride and then kills the woman who has picked him up. There is even a monologue told from the point of view of a child beater. What all these people share is violence. Ai's world is not a pretty one. People kill and die, rape and murder. They do not pick flowers or look at sunsets.

In *Killing Floor* (1979), Ai continued in this direction. These poems are generally much longer and are more varied in style. There are dialogues between characters and even a few prose poems, written in the same narrative style but in paragraph form, rather than broken into lines as poetry usually is. Moreover, in *Killing Floor,* the characters do not exist in isolation as they did in the first collection. They are placed within their environments and in some cases within historical settings. Some of the narrators are historical figures, including actress Marilyn Monroe and Ira Hayes, an American Indian World War II hero who died broke and drunk after the war. Other poems are written from the point of view of people who are not named but who are archetypes of the most horrid sorts.

The poem "Jericho" is told from the point of view of a fifteen-year-old girl in bed with an older man who feeds her candy and who has already gotten her pregnant. "The Mortician's Twelve-Year-Old Son" is the story of a boy who makes love to a corpse. "Almost Grown" is a prose poem about a boy visiting a prostitute for the first time. In this collection, sixteen of the twenty-four narrators are men. The poet here is clearly identifying with all humanity, or at least with the darker side of all human souls.

These first two collections of poetry have much in common. Death, violence, and sex are of paramount importance. Children appear often in both collections, but they are never happy boys and girls. The unifying factor in both books is misery, but there is also something else, something astounding, at work here. Readers identify with these characters. Horror, including horror poetry, has long been a popular genre of writing. Ai's poetry is completely different, however, with respect to the points of view taken.

Readers are drawn inside the minds of rapists, child molesters, murderers, and victims of violent death, perspectives that are rarely seen in literature. This is not to say that Ai's readers are sympathetic to these monsters; her readers do not feel compassion for the rapist, do not come to think that it is a good idea to have sex with a corpse. Her readers do, however, understand how these people feel, and this is Ai's greatest strength.

In *Sin*, Ai goes one step further in her attempt to encompass all humanity. The book makes strong political and religious statements in addition to the sorts of statements the poet had previously been making about human nature in general. Many of the figures here are well known; as usual, though, they are seen from a new perspective.

"Two Brothers," the poem that opens the book, is told from the points of view of American politicians John and Robert Kennedy. The poem is about death, not surprisingly, but it is also about immortality. These two personages are already dead, after all, and they are not speaking as if they were alive. Indeed, they discuss their deaths. Yet the poem ends with a suggestion that death is not final: "Give 'em a miracle. Give 'em Hollywood. Give 'em Saint Jack." There is a suggestion that, ultimately, God is responsible for all that has occurred, that the human players involved are secondary.

"The Prisoner" takes a similar tone. This poem is told from the point of view of an anonymous prisoner who is regularly tortured; his jailer refers to himself as "Our Father." "The Testimony of J. Robert Oppenheimer: A Fiction" is an imagined confession by the man generally considered the "father of the atomic bomb" after he has seen the bomb's effects. He is horrified at what has happened, horrified that people now have a godlike control over the very fabric of the universe.

Perhaps Ai's poetic point of view is best summed up in her note to *Fate*: "Fate is about eroticism, politics, religion, and show business as tragicomedy, performed by men and women banished to the bare stage of their obsessions." This can be said to be true of all of her works. Ai's poems are indeed about people laid bare, and her poetic style attests this. There is no embellishment, no flowery speech, no use of complex metaphors. She is simply telling people about the deepest and darkest parts of themselves.

In *Greed*, poems about events and figures in popular culture show the consequences of selfishness not only for the individuals who commit acts of greed but also for their victims, whether they are members of a community that has been imploded by riots ("Riot Act, April 29, 1992"), citizens of a country that has been deprived of a leader who gives them hope in a time of turmoil ("Jack Ruby on Ice"), or economically deprived as a result of the greed of others ("Miracle in Manila," a meditation on the dysfunctional marriage and political regime of Ferdinand and Imelda Marcos).

The collection of poems in previous books and new poems in *Vice* shows the trajectory of Ai's career. Her unswerving commitment to exposing corruption in politics and private lives gives new meaning to the statement that the political is personal. The title of Ai's 2003 book of poems, *Dread*, signals the hesitation to confront the most difficult experiences but courage and determination to meet them head-on nevertheless, as she does in "Delusion," written from the standpoint of a woman whose sister was killed in the 2001 attack on the World Trade Center. In "Greetings Friend" Ai describes her experience growing up as a child of mixed race and feeling marginalized, or "with a slight sense of dislocation." In stating, "I guess that means I'm not real either," Ai makes those feelings of not fitting in real.

Ai has changed the face of American poetry by her forthright, often horrific renderings of some of the grimmer aspects of reality. She has been extolled as a great poet and reviled as a writer of pornography. Ai can identify with so many types of people because she has such a strange and varied history herself and has never really identified with any one ethnic or racial group. She can deal with pain and anger so well because she has been hurt and she is angry.

"THE KID"

First published: 1976 (collected in *Vice*, 1999)
Type of work: Poem

A young boy describes his murderous acts and his state of mind.

"The Kid" is perhaps the most disturbing of Ai's poems. Told in the first-person voice, this is the story of a boy of fourteen who is far from ordinary. The poem begins in a fairly straightforward way. The boy clearly lives on a farm; he is busy whacking the tires on the family's truck with an iron rod. His father calls to him "to help hitch the team," and then his mother calls him. He tosses a rock at the kitchen window, but he is unsuccessful in making his point in such a tame manner.

In the second stanza, this boy has given up whacking tires, and he splits his father's skull open with the iron rod; when his mother comes running, he bludgeons her as well. He then proceeds to abandon the rod for a gun and starts shooting, first killing horses and then his little sister. The short poem is, however, more than a mere picture of bloody violence. It is the boy's attitude that gives this poem its power: "Yeah. I'm Jack, Hogarth's son. / I'm nimble, I'm quick. // I'm fourteen. I'm a wind from nowhere. / I can break your heart."

There is no attempt by some outsider to justify the boy's acts. The reader is not told about overly stern parents, about a "disturbed" child, or any such situation. Yet, obviously, something is wrong.

After the boy has killed his family, he puts on his father's best clothes, packs his sister's doll and his mother's nightgown in a suitcase, and heads for the highway. It is as if, by taking his family's belongings and symbolically identifying with his father, he has somehow justified his actions.

The most terrifying aspect of the poem is that the reader is compelled to identify with the boy and, in some strange way, to feel sorry for him. Modern culture tends to assume that a boy of fourteen who murders has somehow been mistreated by society. The point is that even a child can be a monster, and perhaps the way in which children are viewed is a large part of the problem. As the poem opens, there is a tendency to picture a cute, innocent-looking boy who is merely being hassled by his parents and annoyed by his sister while he is trying to play. The fact that this play turns to grisly murder hardly changes that opinion. Readers can hardly excuse the boy's acts, but they wish they could, somehow.

"THE GOOD SHEPHERD: ATLANTA, 1981"

First published: 1986 (collected in *Vice*, 1999)
Type of work: Poem

"The Good Shepherd: Atlanta, 1981" is a dramatic monologue by a mass murderer of children.

"The Good Shepherd: Atlanta, 1981" was inspired by the case of Wayne Williams, who made headlines by committing a series of murders of black children in and around Atlanta from 1979 to 1981. The poem begins with a graphic description of the murderer pushing a child's body over an embankment. He identifies with the boy and imagines himself within the dead body: "I watch it roll/ and feel I'm rolling with it." He speaks of "the little lamb/ I killed tonight," and then he goes and has some hot cocoa. The murderer then describes washing out the blood that stains his bathroom. He cleans and cleans, then finishes his hot chocolate.

Once again, the reader can understand how this man is thinking. He is clearly pleased by his actions: He is "a good shepherd," seducing little boys to their deaths. Yet there is more involved here; the killer opens a book on mythology and remarks,

> Saturn, it says, devours his children.
> Yes, it's true, I know it.
> An ordinary man, though, a man like me
> eats and is full.
> Only God is never satisfied.

This is a rather strange religious statement. Saturn, a god of Roman mythology, killed and ate all of his children except for Jupiter, who escaped and later killed his father, thus becoming king of the gods. It is clear that the murderer is identifying himself with divinity. As a god, he has the right to dispose of his subjects and feels no particular guilt in doing so. The poet's basic idea is that, ultimately, God is responsible for everything and that humans are merely pawns in a great game. These sometimes destroy other pawns, but it really does not matter, because God is never quite satisfied.

Sin is full of such ideas, but this is an unusually powerful presentation. It is difficult to feel sympathy for a mass murderer, but it is also difficult not to see his way of looking at the situation. Even a man who kills young children has a point of view worth considering. Lastly, there is a sense of satisfaction once the children are murdered and the mess is cleaned up: "Only God is never satisfied," the killer says. Does this mean that the murderer is somehow more merciful, or more just, than God? This is a question left open by the poem.

"THE TESTIMONY OF J. ROBERT OPPENHEIMER"

First published: 1986 (collected in *Vice*, 1999)
Type of work: Poem

Written from the perspective of J. Robert Oppenheimer, this poem describes the scientific process that led to his development of the atomic bomb.

"The Testimony of J. Robert Oppenheimer," subtitled "A Fiction," presents the story of a theoretical physicist who, in the early 1940's with the threat of Japanese attack looming, was selected to head a team of scientists to work on atom bomb development, despite his contributions to left-wing organizations. Written in Oppenheimer's voice, the poem describes the evolution of his passion for science as well as his justifications for the role that he played in developing the uranium bomb that destroyed Hiroshima and the plutonium bomb that decimated Nagasaki.

The speaker describes his shedding of consciousness at Los Alamos, where the bombs were created, as attaining "enlightenment," where he "threw off the night like an old skin," and his eyes "filled with light." The moment that he "fell to the ground" is presented as a spiritual experience. He compares himself to the bomb, describing how "some say" that when *he* hit, "there was an explosion." In this identification with the bomb, Oppenheimer shows how much of his life had been consumed by this project, almost as if he had become one with the bomb. However, he also describes how "there was only silence" rocking him "in its cradle of cumulus cloud," creating a false image of peacefulness after the destruction.

To further justify his participation in this event, the persona of Oppenheimer suggests, "It is better to leap into the void./ Isn't that what we all want anyway?—" When "we accept the worst in ourselves," he proposes, we are "set free," as if to absolve himself of involvement in the project.

The scientist then relates the origin of his passion for science, describing a "ferocious need to know," as signified by the hypothesis "what if" that all scientists are trained to ask. He asks if readers, addressed as "gentlemen," have that insatiable curiosity, too—the desire to be "born again and again/ from that dark, metal womb."

Still, even science is not absolute, the speaker argues, comparing it to a "bed we make and unmake at whim." "The truth is always changing," he states, "always shaped by the latest/ collective urge to destroy." Despite these rationalizations, he is "gnawed down by the teeth" of his nightmares, a guilty conscience that "will not heal." He takes a cynical approach to nationalistic pride, as typified by "our military in readiness,/ our private citizens/ in a constant frenzy of patriotism/ and jingoistic pride." "Good soldiers," he says, "we do not regret or mourn,/ but pick up the guns of our fallen." In the process, the scientist states, we destroy ourselves "atom by atom," leading to our ironic "transcendent annihilation."

"THE PRIEST'S CONFESSION"

First published: 1986 (collected in *Vice*, 1999)
Type of work: Poem

A priest describes the guilt he feels for sexual involvement with a young girl.

In "The Priest's Confession," Ai presents the thought process of a priest who believes he has sinned and battles his own temptations, fearing the wrath of God. He confesses, "I didn't say mass this morning" and then goes on to describe "Rosamund, the orphan," who tempts him with her laughter and "the almond scent of her body" that wraps around his neck "like a noose." This image of a noose is repeated in part 3 of the poem, where he contemplates hanging a rope from the rafter of the church and kicking away "the needlepoint footstool" so that he can "swing out over the churchyard."

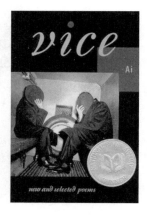

Images of Rosamund and her developing body haunt him. Despite his attempts at self-control, he gives in to temptation, breaks his rosary, and then rolls "on the floor/ in a kind of ecstasy" for his transgression. He describes to God how he craves parts of Rosamund's body, such as the "bird's nest of hair/ barely covered by her drawers" and her breasts that "grew in secret/ like two evil thoughts," but he still wants to know that God loves him.

The priest confesses that, in a moment of sadistic violence, he pressed his face between Rosamund's legs and "bit down" so hard that his mouth bled, but that he did not stop. Although the priest describes Rosamund as "so quiet" and then suddenly crying out, the reader is doubtful that she "moved closer and closer" to the priest's lips, as he describes. Since Rosamund is not given a voice or a choice in this poem, perhaps the priest is having delusions of transcendence. After this encounter, he is haunted by both her laughter and her screams, and he resigns himself to being a sinner, entreating, "Lord, come walk with me" because he knows it is his only hope for redemption.

"EVE'S STORY"

First published: 1990 (collected in *Fate*, 1991)
Type of work: Poem

A sixteen-year-old girl recounts her experiences with a fraudulent evangelist.

"Eve's Story" is a clear statement about established religion and its most evangelistic proponents. The poem is told from the viewpoint of a sixteen-year-old girl who leaves home after her father strangles a deformed kitten; she winds up in an evangelist's tent.

The girl is quickly seduced by the evangelist. She becomes his servant, even helping him to procure prostitutes. When he becomes increasingly successful, the girl is edged out of his inner circle by more photogenic women: "We had gone video,/ but I wasn't in them./ I did not fit his image anymore./ Cheryl did, with her blue contacts, blonde hair,/ and silicone implants." The girl avenges herself by filming the evangelist engaged in a lurid sex act and exposing him as a hypocrite. His followers desert him, and blond, blue-eyed Cheryl becomes a talk-show celebrity. Yet the speaker stays with the fallen preacher, explaining, "So now we live like any other/ retired couple in Sarasota."

Ai is commenting not merely upon the preacher himself but also upon the religious system that has produced him and people like him: "Of a sudden, I realize/ this is how Eve must have done it./ The snake and God were only props/ she discarded when she left Adam/ writhing on the ground." Unlike most of Ai's narrators, this girl inspires real compassion and real pity. She is clearly a victim of other people's actions. The actual blame is still hard to place. Is it the preacher himself who is to blame? Is it the religion he espouses? Or, in the final analysis, is it God who is to blame? If sex is original sin, and also one of the most pleasant actions a human being can experience, does this mean that it is sinful to have fun?

As always in Ai's work, the reader is not told very much about the girl in question, whether, for example, she is black or white, Christian, another religion, or atheist. She is simply presented as having been victimized by a religious system and a man who embodies it. The reader is also confused about how much blame to lay on the evangelist; perhaps he, too, should be considered a victim.

"SLEEPING BEAUTY: A FICTION"

First published: 1999 (collected in *Vice*, 1999)
Type of work: Poem

A comatose patient describes being raped by a hospital aide.

From the beginning of "Sleeping Beauty: A Fiction," dedicated to an actual comatose patient raped by an aide, it is clear that a violation has occurred when the speaker addresses the aide who raped her, saying, "You steal into my room/ between darkness and noon/ to doff the disguise as nurse's aide." She describes him as "furtive" and his violation as violent, as he spreads her legs apart and breaks through "the red door" to her "chamber."

The speaker reminds the rapist of how he wipes away the evidence of how he mingled his life with "what is left" of hers, despite the evidence that is still inside her. This leads to thoughts of how any baby that would grow inside her would only know her "as its host" and never as Mother, nor the rapist as Father. The speaker then remembers the image of her mother praying to Saint Jude for a miracle so that her daughter would no longer be in a coma. Yet the speaker is still someone "for whom language is silence,/ language is thirst/ that is not slaked." Despite this powerlessness, the victim asserts to the rapist, "My eyes were open,/ while you violated me" and " I could see/ beyond the veil of your deceit."

The poem ends with the speaker recalling the image of Sleeping Beauty and how, instead of being woken with a kiss, she is "pricked" with the "thorn of violence." She realizes that there is no happy ending for her story, that unlike the fairy tale that her mother once read to her, it will not end with "forever" but eternity.

SUMMARY

Ai's poetry is forthright and pulls no punches. Her characters are murderers, child molesters, rapists, and prostitutes, types of people most readers do not like to think about and most writers do not address. Life is not necessarily pretty, and Ai shows the ugliest parts of it. While readers might not like to admit that the people Ai talks about exist, her work makes them impossible to ignore.

Marc Goldstein; updated by Holly L. Norton

BIBLIOGRAPHY

By the Author

POETRY:
Cruelty, 1973
Killing Floor, 1979
Sin, 1986
Cruelty/Killing Floor, 1987
Fate: New Poems, 1991
Greed, 1993
Vice: New and Selected Poems, 1999
Dread, 2003

NONFICTION:
"On Being 1/2 Japanese, 1/8 Choctaw, 1/4 Black, and 1/16 Irish," 1974 (*Ms.* 6, June)

About the Author
Cramer, Steven. Review of *Fate*, by Ai. *Poetry* 159 (November, 1991): 108-111.
Kilcup, Karen. "Dialogues of the Self: Toward a Theory of (Re)reading Ai." *Journal of Gender Studies* 7, no. 1 (March, 1998): 5-20.
Monaghan, Pat. Review of *Fate*, by Ai. *Booklist* 87 (January 1, 1991): 902.
Ostriker, Alicia. Review of *Sin*, by Ai. *Poetry* 144 (January, 1987): 231-237.
Seidman, Hugh. Review of *Killing Floor*, by Ai. *The New York Times Book Review*, July 8, 1979, 14.
Seshadri, Vijay. Review of *Dread*, by Ai. *The New York Times Book Review*, May 4, 2003.

DISCUSSION TOPICS

- Violent imagery and taboo subjects are prevalent in Ai's poems. What function could they serve other than to shock readers?

- Despite the cruelty, anger, and sadness of the people portrayed in Ai's poems, in what ways could they be inspiring?

- What do the titles of Ai's books (*Cruelty*, *Killing Floor*, *Sin*, *Fate*, *Greed*, *Vice*, and *Dread*) and the subjects of her poems suggest about her view of humanity and her role as a poet?

- Most of Ai's poems are written from the first-person point of view. What effect does this have on the poem and reader?

- How does Ai use language to capture the personae, or personalities, of the speakers in her poems?

EDWARD ALBEE

Born: Virginia
March 12, 1928

A prolific but controversial playwright, Albee has earned acclaim for his work in the modern theater and its vigorous pursuit of the truth and the dramatic expression of the human condition.

Library of Congress

BIOGRAPHY

Mystery surrounds the origins of Edward Franklin Albee III. He was born to Louise Harvey (father unknown) somewhere in Virginia on March 12, 1928 (not in Washington, D.C., as is frequently listed). Almost three weeks later on March 30, Albee was given up for adoption to Reed A. and Frances Albee (twenty-three years younger than her husband). He was taken to Larchmont, New York, where he was raised in luxury. The name Edward was taken from Reed's father, wealthy theater magnate Edward Franklin Albee, who owned part of the Keith-Albee Theater Circuit until businessman Joseph P. Kennedy forced him out in 1929. Despite several efforts, the playwright has never been able to trace his natural parents. He did discover, after his adoptive mother's death, that his birth name was Edward Harvey.

Albee grew up in a large, luxurious stucco Tudor house. He was surrounded by servants, horses, toys, tutors, and chauffeured limousines. His winters were spent in Palm Beach, Florida, or Arizona and summers sailing in Long Island Sound. Albee developed a love for horses and riding from his adoptive mother, whom he adored as a child; she was a tall, beautiful woman who once modeled for Bergdorf Goodman. He was quite close to his grandmother. It was her trust fund that later enabled Albee to leave home and sustain his efforts as a writer.

Albee's love for the theater developed very early, fueled by his frequent trips to Broadway matinees (in a Rolls-Royce) and by the visits of famous theatrical guests to the Albees' sprawling estate. Excited by meeting such show business personalities as Ed Wynn, Jimmy Durante, and Walter Pidgeon, Albee began writing plays at an early age. He penned his first play at the precocious age of twelve—a full-length sex farce titled *Aliqueen*, about passengers on an English ocean liner.

Albee suffered from a troubled childhood despite his apparent social, economic, and cultural advantages. Keenly aware that he was adopted, the future dramatist harbored a deep-seated resentment against his biological parents for abandoning him. That resentment resonated throughout his plays. Albee's hostility, however, was not reflected toward his adoptive parents. Still, he gave them enough concern about his disruptive behavior that his mother enrolled the eleven-year-old boy in a strict boarding school in Lawrenceville. It would be the first stop of many schools, including Valley Forge Military Academy (termed by Albee the "Valley Forge Concentration Camp") and Choate School. An indifferent student at best, Albee received tremendous encouragement as a writer from his instructors at Choate. During his one-year stay there he wrote numerous pieces, including poems, short stories, a novel entitled *The Flesh of the Unbelievers*, and a play titled *Schism*. Much of his work appeared in the *Choate Literary Magazine*, and one poem was published in *Kaleidoscope*, a Texas literary magazine.

Following graduation from Choate, Albee attended Trinity College beginning in 1946, but he did not apply himself to his studies. He became involved in dramatics, however, and played the role of Emperor Franz Joseph in Maxwell Anderson's 1936 play *The Masque of Kings*. Midway into his second year, Albee left Trinity (actually, he was ordered to leave because he would not attend math lectures or chapel); he never completed his college education. His first job was at radio WNYC, performing a variety of assignments. In 1950, he moved out of his adoptive parents' home despite their entreaties to stay, and moved to Greenwich Village. He was determined to become a writer.

For the next ten years Albee moved around frequently and took numerous positions, including office boy, bartender, book salesman, record clerk at Bloomingdale's, and Western Union messenger. All these jobs gave him ample opportunity to communicate with people. Albee also met and corresponded with playwright Thornton Wilder, who encouraged him to write for the stage. Saddled with job instability, Albee was able to survive because of the $100,000 trust fund established by his grandmother. Its provisions spelled out that Albee should receive fifty dollars a week until his thirtieth birthday, then the remaining sum. During the decade, Albee would write a number of poems and plays that he repudiated in later years.

Albee's coming-of-age as a playwright occurred in 1958, on his thirtieth birthday, when he quit his Western Union job, cashed in his grandmother's inheritance, and sat down and wrote *The Zoo Story* (1959) in three weeks. No Broadway producer was interested in it. Fortunately, William Flanagan (Albee dedicated the play to him), who had roomed with Albee for about nine years, sent the script to a friend in Italy, and it eventually ended up on the desk of German producer Boleslaw Barlog. Barlog presented it at the Schiller Theatre in Berlin on September 28, 1959. Albee attended the Berlin production, despite the fact that he could not understand German. Almost four months later, on January 14, 1960, the play received its successful New York premiere, in conjunction with Samuel Beckett's *Krapp's Last Tape* (1958). Albee's playwriting career was launched; he would soon be known as the "King of Off-Broadway."

In that same year, 1960, Albee would produce three more plays—*The Sandbox*, *The Death of Bessie Smith*, and *Fam and Yam*. Every year thereafter he wrote or adapted one or more plays for the New York stage, and each new Albee work would be eagerly awaited. His biggest success and first Broadway production occurred in 1962 with *Who's Afraid of Virginia Woolf?*, which won numerous awards. He later won Pulitzer Prizes for *A Delicate Balance* (1966), *Seascape* (1975), and *Three Tall Women* (1991) and a Tony Award for *The Goat: Or, Who Is Sylvia?* (2002).

Albee continues to turn out new plays each year, conducts workshops for aspiring dramatists, lectures extensively in the United States and abroad, serves as artistic director for various theater companies, and often reads or directs revivals of his plays. He serves as president of the Edward F. Albee Foundation, Inc., an organization that funds the William Flanagan Creative Persons Center, which actively supports the writers and artists colony in Montauk, New York.

ANALYSIS

Albee is one of the most discussed and analyzed playwrights of American theater. Many books, countless reviews, and hundreds of articles have been published examining the artist and his plays. Most critics agree that Albee is an important writer whose recurring themes include the condemnation of cruelty, emasculation, social complacency, and vacuity. His characters appear to wallow in their own fantasies; the plays exhibit a pervading and overwhelming sense of loss, probably triggered by his own disturbed childhood. Albee is concerned with the illusions that keep people from seeing reality. He believes that he lives in a time when religious, moral, political, and social structures have collapsed. The dramatist is also preoccupied with the fear of death—a continuing motif since his first play. Albee's plays do not end happily, but he never strains to make them tragic.

Albee has a love-hate relationship with his critics, submitting to numerous interviews in which he proceeds to give cryptic answers. He is alternately praised for his consummate craftsmanship, intelligence, and sensitivity and criticized for his clumsiness, dim-witted mentality, or crassness. Albee looks with scorn at attempts to analyze him or his work. He consistently reads all material written about him but derisively views it as well-meaning fiction. Probed about his own artistic credo, Albee is usually coy, but he has written that "the health of a nation, a society, can be determined by the art it demands." The statement may be a key to understanding Albee's own work, because he is openly critical at what passes for entertainment today on Broadway, in films, and on television. Albee praises the technological achievements in all three media and the high level of competence in acting and directing, but he decries the stereotyped, superficial, and sentimental literary material.

Albee's work is unusual for his attempts to fuse comedy and terror. He has said that he wants simultaneously to entertain and offend his audiences. In fact, audience indifference to his plays is one thing Albee abhors. He firmly believes that the theater must be "possessed" by the playwright rather than by the actor, director, producer, or audience. Throughout his career, he has steadfastly refused to condescend to changing theatrical fashions and resolutely follows his own inner visions.

Albee remains one of the great innovators of the theater, having experimented with various genres and techniques over the years, and he has been labeled at one time or another an absurdist, surrealist, existentialist, and satirist. He avoids easy labels or descriptions; about his own work, Albee has said that he does not concern himself with thinking about his style or direction: "I'm interested in the fact that I write plays in such different styles from time to time. . . . I'm not doing it to avoid, or to revenge, or to confuse, or to be fresh in my own mind, even. I just do it because that is the way each one wants to be."

Whatever Albee's approach may be, he has not slowed his output of plays, creating at least one a year. Critics and audiences alike think that *Who's Afraid of Virginia Woolf?* remains his masterpiece, and *The Zoo Story* remains his most popular one-act work. Albee himself is noncommittal about naming a favorite play, but he has expressed a fondness for *The Sandbox*, which he feels is his most perfectly written play (it is also his shortest).

Albee's weakest literary efforts have not been his own creations but his championing of other writers through his role as stage adapter. He has adapted six works into plays, including Carson McCullers's 1951 novella *The Ballad of the Sad Café* (1963); *Malcolm* (1966), the 1959 novel by James Purdy; *Everything in the Garden* (1967), by playwright Giles Cooper; and Vladimir Nabokov's 1955 novel *Lolita* (1981), and only the first one received mixed reviews. The other three were rigorously criticized and have rarely been performed. Albee remained particularly incensed about the failure of the Broadway production of *Lolita*. In the introduction to his *Selected Plays of Edward Albee*, published in 1987, Albee assailed the production for its "combination of disrespect for Nabokov's and my text, directorial vulgarity . . . and a lax and insensitive turn by a leading performer." *Bartleby* (1961), an operatic adaptation of Herman Melville's short story "Bartleby the Scrivener," also failed. An Albee adaptation of Truman Capote's 1958 work *Breakfast at Tiffany's* never opened.

Albee's work has rarely been adapted to the screen; it is generally viewed by filmmakers as too difficult, talky, uninteresting, and static. The one major exception was *Who's Afraid of Virginia Woolf?*, in 1966. The film adaptation starred Elizabeth Taylor and Richard Burton and was well received by the public. The playwright had nothing to do with the film version, but he has stated that he enjoyed it overall despite certain liberties taken with the text. Albee remains prolific, and no one can say in which direction his career will continue to develop. Time and again, he has been dismissed as washed up, and yet some of his best, award-winning work, such as *Three Tall Women* and *The Goat: Or, Who Is Sylvia?*, has come during the latter part of his career.

Albee refuses to be categorized, and each new work is different from the last. He says of his writing simply that "my mind fills with plays, and I write them down from time to time to unclutter my mind." It is interesting to note that Albee is computer illiterate and writes out all his plays in longhand. When directing his own work, he admits to holding heated "conversations" with the playwright about the use of certain passages, and usually the director wins out. It may be too soon to tell if the death of his life partner, sculptor Jonathan Thomas, on May 2, 2005, will have a significant impact on his future work.

THE ZOO STORY

First produced: 1959 (first published, 1959)
Type of work: Play

A vagrant's death wish finds fulfillment after he meets a stranger in New York's Central Park.

The Zoo Story, Albee's first important play, was partially written on his thirtieth birthday, in 1958, as a present to himself. Albee composed the play in three weeks but then could not find an American producer who would stage it. Albee had created a highly unusual and original work in his first venture that bears comparison with Samuel Beckett's first play, *En attendant Godot* (pb. 1952; *Waiting for Godot*, 1954). Eventually, a German production of *The Zoo Story* was arranged on September 28, 1959, at the Schiller Theatre *Werkstatt* in Berlin. Four months later, the American premiere took place—on a double bill with Beckett's *Krapp's Last Tape*—on January 14, 1960, at the Provincetown Playhouse in New York City and ran for 582 performances. Albee won the Vernon Rice Memorial Award for *The Zoo Story*.

The Zoo Story is a stunning tour de force by a new playwright. It is theatrically simple yet thematically complex. The long one-act play has only two characters, strangers to each other, who meet in Central Park on a summer Sunday afternoon. When the curtain rises, Peter is sitting on a park bench reading a book. Albee describes him as "a man in his early forties, neither fat nor gaunt, neither handsome nor homely." The other character, Jerry, walks in and sees Peter. Albee's brief description is as follows: "a man in his late thirties, not poorly dressed, but carelessly." He exhibits "a great weariness."

The Zoo Story is classically structured into three main segments that develop in a climactic order. The introductory section introduces Peter and Jerry and the many differences between them: their clothing, economic and social backgrounds, literary tastes, philosophies of life, and ways of communicating. In the middle section, Jerry narrates a long story about himself and an old, mangy dog that lives at his rooming house. The final section builds to a violent conclusion after Jerry tells Peter what happened to him at the zoo.

Peter and Jerry are oppositional characters in *The Zoo Story*. The only thing they have in common is their age. Albee's description of Peter is a man "moving into middle age," although "his dress and his manner would suggest a man younger." Peter is in no way remarkable or distinctive. He represents a kind of bourgeois Everyman who is comfortable with his sedentary life and avoids taking risks. Jerry, on the other hand, lives on the outer edge of society. He is a rootless person whose "fall from physical grace should not suggest debauchery." Jerry immediately goads Peter into conversation, a maneuver that the overly polite Peter finds disturbing, because he does not want anyone to penetrate his carefully polished facade. Peter tries to steer the conversation to duller topics, but Jerry will have none of it. Jerry eventually strips away all of Peter's protective layers and reveals the raging animal within him.

The separation of humans from their true animal nature is an important theme in *The Zoo Story*. Peter remains blissfully ignorant of the animal within himself until Jerry, who always knew that he was an animal and that meaningful communication with others is difficult because of the individual's isolation, makes him face it. Hence the importance of the "Jerry and the dog" story, which reaffirms humankind's animal heritage and hatred of anything that invades personal security. Jerry finally goads the once-passive Peter into a fight in defense of his honor. The terrified Peter, responding like a savage beast, picks up Jerry's knife and is tricked into killing him.

Another important theme in *The Zoo Story* is the salvation of the individual through sacrifice. Jerry sacrifices himself, removing his isolation by reaching out to Peter, changing Peter for the better. The play ends with Jerry giving a Christlike exhortation to Peter, his disciple. *The Zoo Story* unfolds like a Greek tragedy that builds relentlessly to a horrifying and preordained conclusion. Peter's final howl, "OH MY GOD," amplifies Jerry's onstage whimper as the curtain falls.

THE AMERICAN DREAM

First produced: 1961 (first published, 1961)
Type of work: Play

In this savage satire, Albee portrays the American family as substituting artificial values for real ones.

The American Dream was the fourth play written by Albee. It received its American premiere at the York Playhouse on January 24, 1961, and ran for 370 performances. Four of the five characters in the play—Mommy, Daddy, Grandma, and Young Man—also appeared in an earlier Albee work, *The Sandbox.* Unlike *The Zoo Story, The American Dream* is an absurdist play.

The long one-act is structured into three major sections and eleven groupings of the five characters. The first part deals with the family unit itself—Mommy, Daddy, and Grandma—and the decision of whether Grandma should be put into a nursing home. The second section involves the introduction of Mrs. Barker, a social chum of Mommy, who once worked for the Bye-Bye Adoption Service. The final part begins with the arrival of the Young Man and Grandma's attempt to keep from being institutionalized.

In *The American Dream,* Albee attempts to show that the much-vaunted American Way of Life is absurd. The playwright seeks to show how deprived of meaning Americans' normal human feelings and relationships have become. He points out that people go through the ritualistic motions of loving and caring for one another, and respond to sexual attractiveness or neighborly concerns, but no feelings are engaged. All five characters may speak to each other, but they live in their own worlds, isolated from one another. Their repetitive language of endearments to each other is deflated and hollow.

The play opens with Mommy and Daddy waiting for someone to come and fix the toilet. Mommy tells a story about buying a beige-colored hat, but she exchanges it when her club chairwoman, Mrs. Barker, tells her that it is wheat-colored. Grandma enters carrying many neatly wrapped boxes; it appears that she spends her time wrapping these mysterious boxes. Soon, Mommy reveals her plan to send Grandma to a nursing home and convinces

Daddy to agree. Grandma will not go quietly, however, and proves to be a stubborn match for her daughter. She tells Daddy that Mommy stated at age eight that she would marry a rich old man and even implies that their marriage is a disaster.

Albee pokes merciless fun at what he perceives to be a matriarchal society and at the impotence of the American family head. Sterility is an important theme: Mommy and Daddy cannot conceive a child. Daddy's character is vague, ineffectual, and without determination compared to the nightmarishly efficient Mommy. Mommy is the driving force in the family unit. Only Grandma can stand up to her daughter's wiles and match her. Into this feminine beehive of activity comes Mrs. Barker, the club chairwoman. She makes herself very comfortable and even removes her dress when asked. Through Mrs. Barker's arrival, it is revealed that Mommy and Daddy adopted a little child from her years ago. They systematically dismembered their "bumble of joy," however, because it behaved in a normal and natural manner instead of adapting to their artificial values.

Following that revelation, the Young Man enters and converses with Grandma. He is a handsome, vital, and completely empty-headed dolt whom Grandma calls "The American Dream." He wants to be a film actor and will do anything for money. He tells of an identical twin and of their separation at childhood; he feels as though he lost part of himself. In short order, Mommy and Daddy adopt him, with Mrs. Barker's blessing. The new adoptee will move into Grandma's old room, and Mommy will use him as a lover. Grandma closes the play with a short address: "So, let's leave things as they are right now . . . while everybody's happy . . . while everybody's got what he wants . . . or everybody's got what he thinks he wants. Good night, dears."

The American Dream is a less successfully realized and integrated work than *The Zoo Story.* Unlike the concise structure of *The Sandbox,* which it superficially resembles, the play is overly long, and some of the speeches appear padded. Yet Albee has neatly skewered the American way of life, taking the false images promulgated by television, films, advertising, and political exploitation and revealing them to be totally empty and devoid of any meaning.

Who's Afraid of Virginia Woolf?

First produced: 1962 (first published, 1962)
Type of work: Play

Two married couples pass the night together, hurling verbal abuse at each other until they come to a better understanding of themselves and their spouses.

Who's Afraid of Virginia Woolf? is regarded as Albee's most successfully realized play. It premiered on October 13, 1962, and ran for 664 performances. The original cast starred Uta Hagen, Arthur Hill, George Grizzard, and Melinda Dillon and was directed by Alan Schneider, who has been closely associated with staging Albee's work on the New York stage. Audiences and critics alike enthusiastically received the play. The play won the New York Drama Critics Circle Award, the Antoinette Perry Award (Tony), and the Foreign Press Award. *Who's Afraid of Virginia Woolf?* caused a sensational controversy when it did not win the Pulitzer Prize as well. Two distinguished members of the Pulitzer committee resigned in protest. Albee subsequently won two Pulitzer Prizes, for *A Delicate Balance* and *Seascape.*

Who's Afraid of Virginia Woolf? was Albee's first full-length original play. It represents a departure for him, not only in form but also in focus. In his earlier work, Albee stood outside society and vented his anger as an outraged social commentator whose passionate concern for justice and equality made him side with society's victims. He had been a champion of the lonely and oppressed. In *Who's Afraid of Virginia Woolf?*, Albee shifts his concern from the have-nots to the haves—in this case, college professors. They represent the core of civilized society (they educate their country's future leaders), and what he discovers there is perverse, cruel, hypocritical, immoral, and sterile.

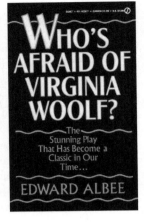

Albee's play has little or no plot, but it moves forward rapidly. It has four characters: two married couples, with husbands teaching at the same small college. Martha is middle-aged, the daughter of the college president, and unhappily married to younger husband George. He has somehow disappointed her by not living up to her high expectations. Nick and Honey, the other (much younger) couple, are also locked into an unhappy marriage. Nick married her for money and what turned out to be "hysterical pregnancy."

Throughout the long evening George and Martha (Albee names them after the childless George and Martha Washington) argue violently and trade insults with furious savagery. Albee has fashioned a highly fascinating battle of the sexes. The intense love-hate relationship of the couple is evident from the first moment, when they enter their house from a party slightly drunk and weary at 2:00 on a Sunday morning. Eager to go to bed, George is amazed that Martha has invited a new biology instructor and his wife over for drinks. It becomes clear that George and Martha enjoy verbally abusing each other, and the arrival of Nick and Honey only exacerbates the situation.

Albee has given subtitles to each of the three acts in *Who's Afraid of Virginia Woolf?* The first one is titled "Fun and Games," the second, "Walpurgisnacht," and the third, "The Exorcism." Throughout the first act, George and Martha relentlessly bait and exasperate the other couple until Nick and Honey reluctantly enter into the spirit of it. Martha reveals to them that she and George have a grown, secretive son. In act 2, Albee draws a clear parallel between the two couples and shows that frustration is what fuels them—particularly sexual frustration, as exemplified by Nick's failure to satisfy Martha.

During the first two acts, George has suffered the most abuse, but in act 3 he breaks free of his personal devils and attempts to exorcise the same from Martha; he tries to make her realize that there is not, and never was, a son. Martha's howling realization and acceptance of the truth brings the embattled pair closer together by the final curtain. Again, Albee reintroduces the recurring themes of the destruction of children by their parents and of men and women by each other.

Unlike other playwrights who allow their characters to keep some of their lies and illusions—most notably Eugene O'Neill and Tennessee Williams—Albee strips all of them away from his characters. He makes it clear in *Who's Afraid of Virginia Woolf?* that he believes self-deception is evil and that no fraud should be entertained, no matter how comforting. Only the passionate search for the truth can nurture and fulfill human beings. Albee says that people must live without illusion and accept the inevitable consequences.

TINY ALICE

First produced: 1964 (first published, 1965)
Type of work: Play

A naïve lay brother of the Catholic Church is seduced by the world's wealthiest woman.

Tiny Alice was first staged at the Billy Rose Theater on December 29, 1964, and it ran for 167 performances. It starred Sir John Gielgud, Irene Worth, William Hutt, Eric Berry, and John Heffernan; Alan Schneider directed. *Tiny Alice* provoked a fury of critical responses at its premiere, ranging from "brilliant" to "sophomoric." Most critics, as well as the performers involved, confessed to not understanding the play and called it a metaphysical muddle. One reviewer dismissed it as a Faustian drama written by a highly endowed college student. Subsequent revivals of the work have aroused the same acrimonious response.

Albee, in introductory remarks to the published text in 1965, kept the controversy alive by writing:

> It has been the expressed hope of many that I would write a preface to the published text of *Tiny Alice*, clarifying obscure points in the play—explaining my intention, in other words. I have decided against creating such a guide because I find—after reading the play over—that I share the view of even more people: that the play is quite clear.

What is clear is that Albee did not include *Tiny Alice* as an important or representative work when he published *Selected Plays of Edward Albee* in 1987.

Despite its confusing allegorical structure, *Tiny Alice* has more of a plot coherence than most of Albee's other plays. Miss Alice is the world's richest woman; she will donate two billion dollars to the Catholic Church if the cardinal's secretary, lay Brother Julian, will be sent to her for further instructions. Brother Julian is a strange individual, dedicated to service in the Church; however, he spent six years of his life in a mental institution. In time, Miss Alice seduces him into marriage, and that sacrament, blessed by the Church, proves to be his undoing. He discovers that Miss Alice is a sham and is the personification of Tiny Alice, who lives inside a model house that is an exact replica of the real mansion. The play ends with Julian dying, alone and abandoned by everyone as he faces death.

The play is written in three acts; unlike *The Zoo Story*, which opens weakly and then builds in dramatic intensity, *Tiny Alice* has a strong first scene. It begins with the cardinal and the lawyer (church and state) crisply discussing the monetary gift to be bestowed on the Church by Miss Alice. Unfortunately, the high level of tension introduced cannot be maintained in later scenes, as they are minor characters in the play. Later the audience is introduced to Brother Julian and Miss Alice, and it is their star-crossed union that forms the centerpiece of the action.

Albee again brings in his familiar themes of aloneness, isolation, and the illusions to which people desperately cling. He also is concerned with the abandonment of one's faith and the relationship between sexual and religious ecstasies. Brother Julian, for example, spent six years in a mental institution because his faith left him. While there, he may or may not have had a hallucinatory sexual experience with a demented woman who believed she was the Virgin Mary. Miss Alice seduces Julian through her deeds rather than with words. Near the end of the play, having rejected him, she cradles the dying Julian in a pietà embrace.

Albee doubtless meant the model with Tiny Alice inside to represent a Platonic symbol of the bright world of ideals that people carry inside their minds. For Albee, Julian's confusion and penance at the end of the play give him absolution and a state of grace. Julian has examined his conscience, abandoned his delusions, and will make the necessary sacrifice to God and Tiny Alice. His acceptance of death finally releases Julian from a lifetime of doubt and gives him insight into himself. Albee makes it clear that Julian's illusory faith has finally been stripped away.

THREE TALL WOMEN

First produced: 1994 (first published, 1995)
Type of work: Play

Three women of widely varying ages come together to discuss the human condition of life, love, loss, and death.

The Pulitzer Prize award-winning *Three Tall Women* premiered in New York City on March 18, 1994. The play proved a popular success and ran for two years, first opening at the Vineyard Theatre and later continuing its run at the Promenade Theatre. It was widely hailed by the theater critics and won not only the Pulitzer, but also the Drama Critics Circle Award, the Lucille Loritel Award, and the Outer Critics Circle Award for best play. The drama's critical success rejuvenated Albee's fading playwriting career, which had been in a slump for more than a decade.

The play is structured in two acts populated by three women generically named A, B, and C. The setting of act 1 is a "wealthy bedroom, French in feeling," the residence of A, a dying matriarchal figure in her nineties who is attended by her companion B, who is fifty-two. The play opens with C, twenty-six years old and A's young lawyer, arguing with A about her true age. The old woman fiercely rails on about her life, her health, her approaching death, and the many painful memories that she still carries. A is especially embittered because she believes that her estranged homosexual son does not come to visit, although B tells the audience that he does. Despite B's attempts at conciliation between the two women, C's character reacts negatively to the old woman. A lively, sometimes hostile, funny, and often profane discussion erupts among all

three women. The act concludes when A's majestic, Lear-like character suffers a stroke.

Act 2 opens full of dramatic surprises. At first A appears to be propped up in bed and wearing a breathing mask, while B and C discuss A's legal situation and the importance of a will. Suddenly a very lively A enters from offstage and jumps into the legal fray. It quickly becomes apparent that all three characters embody the same woman at different stages of her life. The ensuing exchange of opinions about who they really are takes on a deeper resonance, with C loudly protesting that she will never become like either of them. The audience knows, of course, that she will in time. In fact, B tells her with a "(Sour smile.) Well . . . you just *wait.*" The son now appears (remaining mute throughout) and is berated by B and defended by A, while C looks at him in amazement.

The latter part of the act focuses on all three women beginning to merge their memories, thoughts, and recriminations into a continuing collective consciousness, simultaneously becoming a larger-than-life Everywoman. Following A's denunciation of the other two, the playwright suddenly reverses the dramatic tension by having all three women give life-affirming speeches. He ends the play with them holding hands and looking at the audience, facing life and death unafraid. It is Albee's most upbeat ending.

Three Tall Women is Albee's most autobiographical work. The playwright has acknowledged as much, and the central character of A (as well as B and C) is inspired by his own adoptive mother, a tall, "thin, aristocratic, proud" woman who was also racist, homophobic, and anti-Semitic. Albee is willing to look critically as his mother and their dysfunctional relationship with widely divergent emotional views, which led to his fleeing home at an early age. In the preface to his published play, Albee writes, "I knew I did not want to write a revenge piece—could not honestly do so, for I felt no need for revenge."

Three Tall Women is Albee's older self attempting to understand his own formidable, unloving mother. In real life, Albee never reconciled with his mother, but here he largely succeeds in coming to terms with his conflicting feelings toward her and creates a believable, sympathetic, and largely moving figure.

PETER AND JERRY

First produced: 2004
Type of work: Play

A husband and wife reveal some unpleasant truths about their supposedly happy marriage.

Forty-six years after *The Zoo Story*, Albee's playwriting career appeared to have come full circle. His play *Peter and Jerry*, a prequel to *The Zoo Story*, opened on May 28, 2004, to celebrate the fortieth season of the Hartford Stage Company, a theater long associated with Albee's work. Critical reaction to the new work was mixed, with most reviewers praising it but others decrying his attempt to rework and update a classic.

Actually, the full title of the work is *Peter and Jerry. Act I: Homelife. Act II: The Zoo Story.* Albee says he was quite happy with the original *The Zoo Story* but wanted to flesh out and offer more insight into the character of Peter. In *Homelife*, Peter is now seen in his Upper West Side home, where he lives with his wife, two daughters, cats, and a parakeet. He is absorbed in a book (by Stephen King this time) that he will later bring to the park. Ann, his wife, wishes to have a frank talk with him about their married life together and joins him.

Peter attempts to continue reading his book; however, Ann will have none of it. She says that she loves him but is unhappy with their present life despite the obvious creature comforts. Ann wants her husband to let go emotionally and allow his passionate animal instincts to emerge more fully. Peter attempts to explain and justify his behavior, but Ann is disgusted with his explanations. She is far more interested in dissecting what she perceives as a failed marriage. Their brutally frank exchange of dialogue is Albee at his best: sharp, revealing, sexually explicit, and absurdly funny. By act's end, mild-mannered Peter's character is fully revealed as a far more interesting individual as he proceeds to the park where Jerry will accost him.

With the creation of *Homelife*, *The Zoo Story* now no longer needs to be paired with other one-act plays to make a full evening of theater. While the newer work is less striking than its predecessor, the plays have a synergistic effect on each other, with the characters of both Peter and Jerry revealed in a fuller light. Albee always felt that the character of Peter was more of a sketch and revealed primarily through Jerry's eyes. The prequel *Homelife* corrects that imbalance, gives Peter greater emotional depth, updates both plays to the present day, and makes the tragic ending dramatically more confrontational and gripping.

SUMMARY

Albee has for almost fifty years remained one of America's most important playwrights. A prolific dramatist, he produces work that is original, significant, controversial, contradictory, and full of absurdist humor. What remains unique about Albee is his stunning integrity: He will not compromise his artistic ideals, and he resists efforts to become commercially successful. Albee continues following his own inner visions, and each new effort is different from its predecessor. Regardless of his popularity, however, Albee's place in theatrical history is secure. On June 5, 2005, Albee was awarded the prestigious Special Tony Award for Lifetime Achievement, a well-deserved capstone to a distinguished literary career in the American theater.

Terry Theodore

BIBLIOGRAPHY

By the Author

DRAMA:
The Zoo Story, pr., pb. 1959
The Death of Bessie Smith, pr., pb. 1960
The Sandbox, pr., pb. 1960
Fam and Yam, pr., pb. 1960
The American Dream, pr., pb. 1961
Bartleby, pr. 1961 (libretto, with James Hinton, Jr.; music by William Flanagan; adaptation of Herman Melville's "Bartleby the Scrivener")

Who's Afraid of Virginia Woolf?, pr., pb. 1962
The Ballad of the Sad Café, pr., pb. 1963 (adaptation of Carson McCullers' novel)
Tiny Alice, pr. 1964, pb. 1965
A Delicate Balance, pr., pb. 1966
Malcolm, pr., pb. 1966 (adaptation of James Purdy's novel)
Everything in the Garden, pr. 1967, pb. 1968 (adaptation of Giles Cooper's play)
Box and Quotations from Chairman Mao Tse-tung, pr. 1968, pb. 1969 (2 one-acts)
All Over, pr., pb. 1971
Seascape, pr., pb. 1975
Counting the Ways, pr. 1976, pb. 1977
Listening, pr., pb. 1977
The Lady from Dubuque, pr., pb. 1980
Lolita, pr. 1981, pb. 1984 (adaptation of Vladimir Nabokov's novel)
Another Part of the Zoo, pr. 1981.
The Man Who Had Three Arms, pr., pb. 1982
Finding the Sun, pr. 1983, pb. 1994
Marriage Play, pr. 1987, pb. 1995
Three Tall Women, pr. 1991, pb. 1994
The Lorca Play, pr. 1992
Fragments: A Sit Around, pr. 1993, pb. 1995
The Play About the Baby, pr. 1998, pb. 2002
The Goat: Or, Who Is Sylvia?, pr., pb. 2002
Occupant, pr. 2002
Peter and Jerry. Act I: *Homelife*. Act II: *The Zoo Story*, pr. 2004.

DISCUSSION TOPICS

- What does Edward Albee mean when he writes in *The Zoo Story*, "sometimes it's necessary to go a long distance out of the way in order to come back a short distance correctly"?

- How has Albee's concept of civility in marriage evolved from *Who's Afraid of Virginia Woolf?* to *Homelife*?

- Is physical violence, either expressed or inferred, a necessary component of Albee's work?

- Albee's assessment is that his plays are usually stylistically different from one another. What do you think?

- Critics have seen homosexual echoes/images in all of Albee's plays. Do you agree?

- The statement has been made that Albee is obsessed with death and that it is a running character in his plays. What is your opinion?

About the Author

Bloom, Harold, ed. *Edward Albee*. Philadelphia: Chelsea House, 2001.
Bottoms, Stephen J. *The Cambridge Companion to Edward Albee*. Cambridge, England: Cambridge University Press, 2005.
Gussow, Mel. *Edward Albee: A Singular Journey*. New York: Simon & Schuster, 1999.
Kolin, Philip C., ed. *Critical Essays on Edward Albee*. Boston: G. K. Hall, 1986.
Mann, Bruce J. *Edward Albee: A Casebook*. New York: Routledge, 2003.
Nayar, Rana. *Edward Albee: Towards a Typology of Relationships*. New Delhi, India: Prestige Books, 2003.
Roudane, Matthew C. *Understanding Edward Albee*. Columbia: University of South Carolina Press, 1987.

LOUISA MAY ALCOTT

Born: Germantown, Pennsylvania
   November 29, 1832
Died: Boston, Massachusetts
   March 6, 1888

Although she wrote for both adult and juvenile audiences, Alcott is most admired for her children's books, which were popular in her day and which continue as favorites with young adults.

BIOGRAPHY

While Louisa May Alcott is associated with the New England setting where she lived most of her life, she was born in Germantown, Pennsylvania, on November 29, 1832, the second of four daughters born to Amos Bronson and Abba May Alcott. Louisa's father, friend and admirer of Ralph Waldo Emerson and Henry David Thoreau, was a man of great vision and idealism but few practical skills. His inability to provide for his family of six became increasingly apparent as time went on. Soon after Louisa's birth, Bronson moved his family to Boston, where he organized the Temple School. While the school had much to recommend it, it was much more liberal than many Bostonians could accept, and six years later Bronson was forced to close its doors and personally shoulder many of the financial obligations incurred. This was the last time the Alcott family was to have a regular income. The financial instability under which Louisa lived provided material for many of her later writings.

After a trip to England, Bronson Alcott initiated a utopian communal experiment, Fruitlands, in Harvard, Massachusetts. This, too, ended in failure, only eight months after it was begun. Fruitlands was a pivotal experience for the whole Alcott family, for it taught them that Bronson simply would not be able to support them. Following her husband's nervous breakdown, Abba became the head of the household, and the women took on odd jobs. Louisa Alcott's abiding interest in women's work stems from this period.

Alcott's familiarity with poverty provided not only the content and substance of much of her later writing but also a serious incentive to write. Because her father was neither financially nor emotionally dependable, Alcott found herself increasingly at the center of the family. She assumed responsibility, living and working to support the family, a role she never relinquished throughout her life. After Fruitlands, the family lived in various Massachusetts towns—Still River, Concord, and Boston—and in Walpole, New Hampshire. When the family lived away from the business and intellectual center that was Boston, Alcott adopted the pattern of living for a few months in Boston, writing and picking up odd jobs to earn money, and then returning to be with her family. Family loyalty became tied to self-denial—a theme that was to run through some of her most successful writings.

Alcott had written since childhood, but publication came somewhat later. In 1851, her poem "Sunlight" was published in *Peterson's Magazine* under the pseudonym of Flora Fairfield. In the following year, her first story, "The Rival Painters: A Tale of Rome," appeared in *Olive Branch*. Other stories appeared in the *Saturday Evening Gazette* and in *The Atlantic Monthly*. As teacher for Emerson's daughter, Alcott had written several fairy stories, and in 1854 these were collected and published under the title *Flower Fables*. From an early age, Alcott had written and acted in family theatricals, and on May 4, 1860, her farce, *Nat Bachelor's Pleasure Trip*, was presented at the Howard Atheneum. During the decade of the 1850's, Alcott became the "spinster scribbler" about which she sometimes wrote in her later fiction. It was also during this period that she wrote the many sentimental stories that appealed to the audience at that time.

Nearing thirty years of age at the onset of the Civil War, Alcott went to Washington in 1862 as a hospital nurse. Conditions were appalling. In six weeks she became ill with typhoid fever, and, when strong enough to make the trip, she was sent home to recuperate. This was a turning point in her life; she was never again in the exuberant good health of her youth. During her convalescence, she turned again to her writing, and she published the letters she had written home to her family from Washington (*Hospital Sketches* was published in 1863). During this period, too, she wrote the gothic thrillers that Victorians clamored for; these sold well, but because she published them under a pseudonym, they did not acquire a reputation for their author. *Hospital Sketches*, however, did earn for Alcott the reputation of a serious writer, which encouraged her work on a serious novel, *Moods*, published in 1864.

After completing a European tour as companion to a disabled girl, Alcott once again turned to writing to support her family. She became editor of and contributor to *Merry's Museum*, a magazine for children. In 1867, Thomas Niles, a publisher with Roberts Brothers, urged her to write a novel for girls. Although Alcott balked, she turned out the first half of *Little Women*, drawn largely from family experiences. The novel became a great success when it was published in 1868. Encouraged, she moved to Boston and wrote a chapter a day until the second half of the book was finished early in 1869. *Little Women* established Alcott's reputation as a writer of children's books.

Little Women was followed by *An Old-Fashioned Girl* (1870), *Little Men* (1871), *Work* (1873), *Eight Cousins* (1875), and *Rose in Bloom* (1876). By this time, Alcott had become interested in women's issues, including suffrage, and she expressed her opinions in *Woman's Journal*, founded by Lucy Stone and Henry Blackwell in 1870. In 1879, Alcott was the first woman to register to vote in Concord. After the death of her mother in 1879, the family circle widened again with the arrival of her sister's daughter from Europe, May Alcott Nieriker having

died shortly after childbirth. With another person to care for, Alcott continued to write, but *Jo's Boys* (1886) was clearly intended to be her last novel. Both Louisa and her father suffered from ill health as they aged. On March 4, 1888, Bronson died during the night. Early on the morning of March 6, Louisa died in her sleep. Father and daughter had a joint funeral and were buried in Sleepy Hollow Cemetery in Concord.

ANALYSIS

Because Alcott is so well known for *Little Women*, much of her other work is generally overlooked. Yet she was a highly prolific writer who wrote throughout her life, virtually from childhood to the grave. The many stories and home theatricals that she wrote as a child constituted an apprentice period for her craft; much of her mature writing summons up this early period.

The mid-1850's found Alcott writing the sentimental stories popular in the Victorian era. She was always attuned to her audience, writing what would sell to a publisher and be enjoyed by a real audience. While this shows a certain kind of sensitivity, it also restricted her writing. Victorian sentimentality was something she could always fall back upon, and in some of her later novels, when the modern reader hopes for a more mature engagement of ideas and testing of hypotheses, Alcott seems to take the easy way out into the old sentimentality that had worked so well in the past.

Although she was a hospital nurse for only six weeks during the Civil War, the experience was a turning point for Alcott. It had both good and bad outcomes. On the negative side, she never fully recovered her health from the typhoid fever she contracted or from the medication given to cure her. On the positive side, she had the time and the inclination to rewrite the letters she had written home, which were published in 1863 as *Hospital Sketches*. This work, published under her own name, established Alcott's reputation as a serious writer. Of particular note were her frankness and graphic detail, qualities that would continue to serve her well as her career developed.

At the same time, she was writing the gothic stories that were published anonymously or under a pseudonym (frequently A. M. Barnard). In *Little Women*, when Jo March, generally considered to be Alcott's self-portrait, writes thrillers, she does so with a sense of shame and hides her identity from her publishers, her family, and friends. She soon abandons this form of writing, even though she is good at it and needs the money that can result from these stories, agreeing with Professor Bhaer that money earned in this way is not worth the moral degradation it necessitates.

Jo no doubt betrays some of Alcott's own misgivings about the genre. Her gothic thrillers and sensation stories were and are good reading material, however; they are fast-paced and full of suspense. Characterization is lively, although plots are sometimes unbelievable. With that willing suspension of disbelief demanded by all writers of the gothic, Alcott created some memorable characters who play roles in dramatic and compelling plots. No doubt Louisa's own experiences as a hospital nurse, as traveling companion for a disabled woman in Europe, and as a woman attempting to earn money in and around Concord and Boston introduced her to a number of colorful personalities with rich stories, who provided inspiration for the heroes and heroines of her thrillers. The gothic thrillers must have provided not only a rich outlet for her imagination but also a safe way of living vicariously experiences that conventions and responsibilities prohibited in real life.

Many of the gothic thrillers feature strong, courageous, and independent heroines who are bent on carrying out some plot of revenge or ambition. Passionate and dramatic, these women manage to control and manipulate others to accomplish their dire ends. Generally, they succeed in their plans, although the outcome may entail more than originally intended. In Alcott's 1866 story "Behind a Mask," for example, the bold heroine manages to entice several brothers to love her in order to humble them and teach them a lesson about their pride. Although her plot almost fails, she entices the uncle to marry her. She thus secures for herself a devoted husband as well as the security of becoming a legitimate member of a highly reputable, wealthy, and good family despite her own unsavory past. Although it is quite clear that the heroine is an evil woman, Alcott makes the reader appreciate her daring, her shrewdness, and her power to carry it all off. The reader ends up celebrating the villain's triumph. No doubt it is for this reason that Alcott chose to write these gothic thrillers under a pseudonym and had moral qualms about them.

Not all the gothic thrillers flaunt quite so blatantly a different set of values from those conventionally upheld, but many deal with the bringing down of proud families by individuals with the boldness to use less than praiseworthy means to accomplish their ends. While sometimes these means are necessitated by personal desperation and social injustice, the thrillers are intended to entertain rather than to invoke moral debate.

When she began writing for children, Alcott necessarily had to tone down the murders and ghosts, the passions and dramatic actions that marked the gothic and sensation stories. Morality in Alcott's writings took a decided turn toward the conventional expectations of nineteenth century, middle-class America. The existence of the wealthy was no longer a call to arms, a challenge to use one's initiative to find the chink in the wall that would provide access for oneself; it became an opportunity to exercise virtues of patience, humility, and submission to one's own humble station in life. Poverty no longer was a condition to be overcome but a reminder to appreciate other gifts— talent, family, loyalty and devotion, love, charity, and others.

Some critics have remarked that the stories written for children are saccharine, and undoubtedly this is so for the modern reader. It must be remembered, however, that Alcott was aware of her need to write what her publishers and audience desired. She did not have the luxury of a secure economic foundation, an independent income that would sustain her no matter whether she pleased an audience or not. Having tried her hand at other occupations (as teacher, governess, and companion), she turned to writing as one of a very few acceptable ways for a woman to earn a living. To write what would sell, she turned to novels that inculcated the "right" values and celebrated the virtues and delights of family life. The successes and accomplishments of individuals are measured against the backdrop of family and community responsibility and well-being.

Another difference between the gothic thrillers and the writings for children is the increased realism of plot and setting. One reason for the enormous success of *Little Women*, for example, is the fact that the personality types depicted and the situations in which they find themselves are detailed in such a way as to be credible. In writing such novels,

Alcott relied upon incidents of her own childhood, and the authenticity of these experiences is verified by the tone and style of the novels.

Under different circumstances, Alcott may have been a different kind of writer, one who would have ranked among the great artists of the nineteenth century. Nevertheless, most readers acknowledge the considerable talent evident in her work—her vivid characterization, her shrewdness in accommodating the fluctuating needs of various audiences, her expert management of plot events for interest, suspense, and dramatic effect, her lively description of setting, and the remarkable range of her subject matter and tone.

LITTLE WOMEN

First published: Part 1, 1868; part 2, 1869
Type of work: Novel

In the nineteenth century United States, a tightly knit family experiences the joys and disappointments of four young girls growing to adulthood.

Little Women was, and remains, Alcott's best-known and most widely read work. It was her first novel for young girls and was so popular that her audience demanded sequels, a request that Alcott fulfilled, although most readers believe that *Little Women* is the most compelling of Alcott's novels about the March family.

As the novel opens, the four girls—the oldest, Meg (sixteen), tomboyish Jo (fifteen), sweet Beth (thirteen), and the youngest, Amy (twelve)—are sitting around the hearth contemplating a Christmas without presents, for their father is away serving as chaplain for a unit of men fighting in the Civil War, and the family has very limited funds.

From this opening dialogue, a reader gets insights into the basic personality types of the various characters. Meg feels most strongly the family's limited resources. It is she who struggles hardest with envy of the wealthier girls in town. Jo is the most spirited of the lot, physically the most active and psychologically the most independent; she nevertheless is most comfortable when she is safely ensconced within the family circle of Marmee (the

girls' nickname for their mother) and the four girls. Beth is the sweetest and most generous of the girls, the one who complains least and tries hardest to ease the difficulties of the others. She is the character whom some readers think is really too good to be true. As might be expected, she dies an early death, as if she is too good for this world. The youngest, Amy, has rather grand visions of herself but these are tempered as she tests her artistic skills abroad and eventually marries the boy next door.

Several themes emerge in the book as the girls develop into adults. One is the difficulty that women of the period had in finding suitable work. Marriage was the most obvious hope for economic stability, but for the woman who did not choose marriage, options were extremely limited and the pay not sufficient. The girls try a number of ways to earn money—as companion, governess, and writer, for example—but nothing that they can do succeeds very well. Another theme is the importance of maintaining the family circle. Even marriage is not greeted unhesitatingly, because it threatens to remove one sister from the family. Disruptions to the family circle are inevitable as children grow up, but in *Little Women* they are always greeted with only begrudging kindness.

Materialism is decried, as are the frivolities of the dances and entertainments in which girls with only a little more money than the Marches indulge. The virtues of patience, submission, and devotion are lauded instead. Finally, no discussion of the novel is complete without mention of the spirited individualism of Jo. She is the most independent of the four girls, although she probably shocks everyone by turning down a very attractive marriage proposal from the wealthy young man next door. Her later acceptance of the older Professor Bhaer (in part 2) has been a source of some criticism for Alcott, because it seems a fictional denial of the feminism that grew ever stronger in Alcott's own life.

Perhaps the most important feature of *Little*

Women is its depiction of domestic harmony in convincingly realistic detail. In the trivial daily activities and the modest goals and setbacks of family members, Alcott depicts a supportive family environment that anyone committed to the ideal of the family can approve. Further, although *Little Women* eschews the single-minded goals of revenge or passion that characterize the gripping gothic tales, each of the four sisters' separate stories nevertheless determinedly marches along, with the various threads intertwining in a delightfully twisting, sometimes knotted, sometimes surprising, yarn of family life. For its adept juggling of subplots, the conversational dialogue of characters, the realism of setting and situation, and the idealism of personal morality and family harmony, *Little Women* will continue to be read for pleasure, for escape, and for education.

SUMMARY

Alcott was a productive and astute writer, assessing the needs of her audience and writing what would sell. Whether writing in the sentimental or gothic vein, realistic novels for children or for adults, Alcott expressed her respect for individualistic women, her scorn for women's limited economic opportunities, and her esteem for the family unit. Her characters are memorable, her dialogues demonstrate an ear for conversation, her descriptions are strong and picturesque, and her narratives are unfailingly vivid and fast-paced.

Paula D. Kopacz

BIBLIOGRAPHY

By the Author

LONG FICTION:
Moods, 1864, revised 1881
Little Women, 1868
Little Women, Part 2, 1869 (also known as *Good Wives*, 1953)
An Old-Fashioned Girl, 1870
Little Men, 1871
Work: A Study of Experience, 1873
Eight Cousins, 1875
Rose in Bloom, 1876
A Modern Mephistopheles, 1877
Under the Lilacs, 1878
Jack and Jill, 1880
Jo's Boys, and How They Turned Out, 1886

SHORT FICTION:
Flower Fables, 1854
On Picket Duty, and Other Tales, 1864
Morning-Glories, and Other Stories, 1867
Aunt Jo's Scrap-Bag, 1872-1882 (6 volumes)
Silver Pichers: And Independence, a Centennial Love Story, 1876
Spinning-Wheel Stories, 1884
A Garland for Girls, 1887
Lulu's Library, 1895
The Early Stories of Louisa May Alcott, 1852-1860, 2000

DISCUSSION TOPICS

- How is Louisa May Alcott's experience of having a brilliant but impractical father who was a poor provider reflected in *Little Women*?

- Does reading this summary of Alcott's career make you want to explore her "generally overlooked" works, or is she best regarded as a children's writer?

- Does Alcott's dedication to write popular domestic fiction to order to support her family cause her to compromise her feminist convictions?

- Would Alcott be better appreciated today if she had written more in the manner of today's often very candid and realistic writers of fiction for children and young adults?

- In her diary, an eleven-year-old Alcott wrote, "I wish I could be gentle always." Could she have retained this attitude and written all of the books described here?

Louisa May Alcott

POETRY:
The Poems of Louisa May Alcott, 2000

DRAMA:
Comic Tragedies Written by "Jo" and "Meg"; and Acted by the "Little Women," 1893

NONFICTION:
Hospital Sketches, 1863 (essays)
Life, Letters, and Journals, 1889 (Ednah D. Cheney, editor)
The Journals of Louisa May Alcott, 1989 (Joel Myerson and Daniel Shealy, editors)
The Sketches of Louisa May Alcott, 2001

About the Author

Boyd, Anne E. *Writing for Immortality: Women and the Emergence of High Literary Culture in America.* Baltimore, Md.: The Johns Hopkins University Press, 2004.

Brooks, Geraldine. "Orpheus at the Plough: The Father of 'Little Women'." *The New Yorker* (January 10, 2005): 58.

Delamar, Gloria T. *Louisa May Alcott and "Little Women."* London: McFarland, 1990.

Eiselein, Gregory, and Anne K. Phillips, eds. *The Louisa May Alcott Encyclopedia.* Westport, Conn.: Greenwood Press, 2001.

Elbert, Sarah. *A Hunger for Home.* Philadelphia: Temple University Press, 1984.

Lyon Clark, Beverly, ed. *Louisa May Alcott: The Contemporary Reviews.* New York: Cambridge University Press, 2004.

Showalter, Elaine. *Sister's Choice: Traditions and Change in American Women's Writing.* Oxford, England: Clarendon Press, 1991.

Stern, Madeleine B. *Louisa May Alcott.* Norman: University of Oklahoma Press, 1950.

_____. *Louisa May Alcott: From Blood and Thunder to Hearth and Home.* Boston: Northeastern University Press, 1998.

_____, ed. *L. M. Alcott: Signature of Reform.* Boston: Northeastern University Press, 2002.

SHERMAN ALEXIE

Born: Spokane Indian Reservation,
Wellpinit, Washington
October 7, 1966

In novels, short stories, poetry, and screenplays, Alexie has exhibited his literary skills as he examines the plight of the Indian both on the reservation and in the cities of the Pacific Northwest.

© Marion Ettlinger

BIOGRAPHY

Sherman Alexie was born in Spokane, Washington, on October 7, 1966, the son of Sherman Joseph Alexie and Lillian Agnes (née Cox) Alexie. Alexie was hydrocephalic, necessitating brain surgery at the age of six months. The surgery was successful, but he had seizures throughout his youth which were likely related to the birth condition. The seizures, a long history of bed-wetting, and a voracious appetite for reading all conspired to separate him from his childhood peers.

Alexie frequently acknowledges both his Spokane and Coeur d'Alene tribal heritage, even as he notes that he is a "breed," not a "blood," being 13/16 (as the poem of the same name from *The Business of Fancydancing* describes) Indian. Alexie's alcoholic father was absent most of Alexie's youth, while his mother worked in the Wellpinit Trading Post and sold her handmade quilts. It may or may not be true that he had read all of the books in the Wellpinit school library by the end of the eighth grade. He attended Rearden High School, where he excelled academically and on the basketball court, earning a scholarship to Gonzaga University. After two years at Gonzaga, a drinking problem and a girlfriend at Washington State University caused him to transfer there, and he received his

B.A. in English in 1991, benefiting there from the mentorship of one of his teachers, Alex Kuo.

Within a year of graduating from college, Alexie received the Washington State Arts Commission Poetry Fellowship and the National Endowment for the Arts Poetry Fellowship. Alexie has said that receiving the two fellowships, followed by a book contract with Hanging Loose Press to publish *The Business of Fancydancing*, motivated him to quit drinking and that he has remained "sober" ever since. The following decade revealed his talent and determination to excel in a number of different literary genres, and he was named on multiple lists as one of the most promising writers under the age of forty.

Following strong critical praise for *The Business of Fancydancing* (1992), Alexie published a number of poetry chapbooks in addition to four full-length collections of poetry: *First Indian on the Moon* (1993), *Old Shirts and New Skins* (1993), *The Summer of Black Widows* (1996), and *One Stick Song* (2000). He has published three collections of short stories, all to critical acclaim: *The Lone Ranger and Tonto Fistfight in Heaven* (1993), *The Toughest Indian in the World* (2000), and *Ten Little Indians* (2003). He has published two novels: *Reservation Blues* (1994) and *Indian Killer* (1996).

Alexie moved on his own into the area of screenwriting, adapting the short story "This Is What It Means to Say Phoenix, Arizona" into the screenplay of *Smoke Signals* and persuading Cheyenne/Arapaho Chris Eyre to direct the film. The unheralded film won both the Audience Award and the Filmmakers Trophy at the 1998 Sundance

Film Festival, causing Miramax Films to agree to distribute the film. Alexie wrote, as well as directed and produced, his second feature film, *The Business of Fancydancing* (2003), which won awards throughout North America, most notably the Best Narrative Feature Film at the 2002 Durango Film Festival and Audience Awards at the San Francisco and Philadelphia Gay & Lesbian Film Festivals.

Alexie is a funny and engaging interviewee on television and in front of a variety of audiences. He continues to perform as a stand-up comedian and as a garage-band musician (with other notable writers in a band called The Remainders), even as he continues to produce works of fiction, poetry, and film. Alexie repeatedly refuses to be considered a spokesman; he claims simply to be providing his own personal vision. However, it is difficult for readers and critics not to look toward Alexie as one of the most promising writers in the world at the beginning of the twenty-first century and certainly a writer who, if he does not speak for Indian people, certainly provides insight and worthy reflection on what it means to be an American Indian in the modern world.

ANALYSIS

Alexie, from his earliest poems and short stories, has created a particular style that distinguishes his poetry, prose, and screenplays. His writing flashes repeatedly with insights, often stated via outrageously creative and subject-specific figurative language. Alexie essentially teaches about the cultures that he knows without being didactic. His reading audiences often learn about Indian traditions and expectations through what his characters have lost, through what they miss by its absence. Alexie's characters are vulnerable and compelling; they are fraught with personal and systemic shortcomings, but their human fallibility underscores their ability to illustrate poignant moments of the common human condition.

Alexie's work is suffused with irony. He generally creates characters who care deeply about others yet who often act with insensitivity and anger, rendering them dangerous. His characters, especially the young Indian men, seek to forge a noble

and heroic adult identity, yet Alexie complains on multiple occasions that most of them keep their birth names through their entire lives rather than having a vision and defining experience which would lead them to achieve and receive their adult names.

At the same time, however, Alexie understands that modern-day ceremonies can be as simple and poignant as a loving father who repeatedly opens his wallet at Christmastime for his children, only to find each time that it is empty of money. The recurrent themes of loss, identity, poverty as cause and poverty as result of substance abuse continue to be treated in Alexie's work, even as the characters of Thomas Builds-the-Fire, Victor and Aristotle and Junior Polatkin, among others, continue to appear in his fiction and poetry.

Alexie's first novel, *Reservation Blues* (1994), deserves greater attention as well as a film adaptation. The plot of the novel is based on the unlikely premise that blues legend Robert Johnson did not, in fact, die in Mississippi in 1938 but survived into 1991, when he was hitchhiking on the Spokane Indian Reservation, was picked up by Thomas, and purposefully left the guitar on the floor of the van. Johnson's Faustean deal with the devil, "The Gentleman," is thereafter transferred to Thomas, Victor, and the others as the all-Indian blues band Coyote Springs rises quickly to regional stardom, then plummets just as quickly.

Although Alexie has gained international attention and a significant place in North American college literature syllabi through his poetry and fiction, his two screenplays, *Smoke Signals* and *The Business of Fancydancing*, may ultimately be of greater significance to his reputation and to positioning Indian concerns and Indian subcultures on the national arts and visual media agenda. *Smoke Signals* was the first nationally distributed film with an all-Indian cast. It continues to enjoy popularity on college campuses and at conferences. *The Business of Fancydancing*, perhaps hampered by a more limited release, filled art house and college venues and was the darling of film festivals through 2002-2003.

THE BUSINESS OF FANCYDANCING

First published: 1992
Type of work: Poetry and short stories

Alexie's first collection of poetry and short stories introduces his unorthodox style, his quirky humor, and the characters of Thomas, Junior, and Crazy Horse.

"THE APPROXIMATE SIZE OF MY FAVORITE TUMOR"

First published: 1993 (collected in *The Lone Ranger and Tonto Fistfight in Heaven,* 1993)
Type of work: Short story

This story, told in first-person voice by Jimmy Many Horses, details his relationship with his wife and his defense mechanisms—principally, humor—to cope with a sentence of terminal cancer.

The Business of Fancydancing refers to Alexie's first collection, a compendium of five short stories and forty poems; a single, seven-stanza poem within that collection; a screenplay published by Hanging Loose Press in 2003; and a film produced from the screenplay in 2003.

The seven-stanza poem, though without meter or rhyme scheme, contains powerful figurative language which supports the narrative of the poem, describing fancydance aspirants driving all night to compete and hoping to cover their expenses with prize money in order to be able to drive to the next fancydance contest. Alexie uses traditional folk traditions and objects yet renders them in a modern setting as he moves toward metaphorical flourishes of language.

The fancydancers in the poem are characteristic Alexie characters in that they are familiar with their traditional past but live quite clearly and com-

pletely in a contemporary American world which is unforgiving and rife with irony and disappointment. Traditional belief systems have been replaced with ersatz mainstream values which are empty in comparison to the coherent worldview that has been disdained. Vernon WildShoe, the only identified fancydancer in the poem, rep-

resents the hope and promise of prize money in the future; he is indeed "a credit card we/ Indians get to use." Ultimately, the fancydance is reduced to a simple means of sustenance, and an unreliable one at that.

"The Approximate Size of My Favorite Tumor" reprises some of Alexie's recurrent concerns: relationships, traditional values versus modern society, alcoholism, and ironically doomed lives. Jimmy Many Horses retells the history of his relationship with his wife, Norma, from the initial meeting at the Powwow Tavern through their problematic relationship, including grappling with alcohol addiction and Jimmy's death sentence of terminal cancer. Jimmy's recollection of their relationship includes a classic Indian Country pickup line, "Listen . . . if I stole 1,000 horses, I'd give you 501 of them." Although their wedding took place at the Spokane Tribal Longhouse and although Norma is known as the world champion fry bread maker, traditional belief and custom do not especially inform their lives.

Jimmy's cavalier humor about his terminal condition enrages Norma to the point that she leaves him temporarily to go on the powwow circuit. She ends up in Arlee, Montana, with a "second kind of cousin" before returning to be with Jimmy in his last days because, as she explains, "making fry bread and helping people die are two things Indians are good at." The title of the story comes from Jimmy's description of an X ray of one of his tumors which was the approximate size and shape of a baseball—with faint stitch marks on it. Norma finds distasteful Jimmy's attempt to make a joke out of his medical diagnosis; however, she has returned by the end of the story to be with Jimmy in his last days, and their joking together and their domestic dialogue prove the metaphorical point that Jimmy makes in narration in the middle of the story: "Humor was an antiseptic that cleaned the deepest of personal wounds."

"THIS IS WHAT IT MEANS TO SAY PHOENIX, ARIZONA"

First published: 1993 (collected in *The Lone Ranger and Tonto Fistfight in Heaven*, 1993)
Type of work: Short story

Victor Polatkin and Thomas Builds-the-Fire travel to pick up the ashes of Victor's father near Phoenix, then return to the Res in Washington State.

"This Is What It Means to Say Phoenix, Arizona," which several years after it was written provided most of the plot underpinnings of Alexie's first movie, *Smoke Signals*, presages some of the later concerns of Alexie's novel *Reservation Blues* (1995), in which Victor and Thomas and several other "skins" create an all-Indian blues band known as Coyote Springs, and they go on the road. This story, however, is neatly structured around news of Victor's father's death in Arizona and the task of retrieving his ashes, old pickup truck, and modest savings and returning north.

Thomas is perhaps Alexie's most compelling character in terms of being deeply esconced within his tribal traditions yet still willing and able to critique those traditions and articulate various ironies. As Thomas greets Victor at the tribal trading post and expresses condolences for his loss, Victor asks how Thomas learned of Victor's father's passing. Thomas, the tribal storyteller, says: "I heard it on the wind. I heard it from the birds. I felt it in the sunlight. Also, your mother was just in here crying." Thomas continues throughout the story as both an avatar of traditional practice and an ironic commentator on it.

Although Victor had a problematic relationship with his father, as well as with Thomas, part of their trip to Arizona involves Thomas recounting experiences with Victor's father. This creates a sort of modern storehouse of new tales, set in cities and at national-chain restaurants. Thomas recalls having a vision at age thirteen, causing him to travel more than fifty miles to get to Spokane Falls. Although Thomas expects to have a vision at the falls, it is Victor's father who finds Thomas on the bridge overpass, feeds him at Denny's restaurant, and drives him back to the reservation, allowing Thomas to

infer that his vision consisted of the understanding that people are here to take care of one another.

This insight and vision provide the essential meaning of the story. Even though Thomas's mother died in childbirth, and he was raised by his grandmother, he knows the loss that Victor feels in losing even an absent father. Thomas's money and companionship are freely given to Victor in order to care for him in this literal, physical passage toward adulthood. The story concludes with the two young men back in Washington State. As they part after their long journey, Victor gives one-half of his father's ashes to Thomas, and both men plan to return the ashes to the river at Spokane Falls, continuing to add chapters to the stories which Thomas has already been telling and retelling.

"CRAZY HORSE SPEAKS"

First published: 1993 (collected in *Old Shirts and New Skins*, 1993)
Type of work: Poem

This work provides a first-person perspective from the point of view of Oglala Lakota mystic Crazy Horse, concerning General Custer, Little Big Horn, Sitting Bull, and issues of race, identity, and mortality.

"Crazy Horse Speaks," which can be understood as a companion piece or response piece to "Custer Speaks" (also a seven-part poem collected in *Old Shirts and New Skins*), is the first of a number of instances in Alexie's literary corpus in which he invokes the character of Crazy Horse, Tashunka Uitko of the Oglala, both for the nobility of his character and for the irony of his destiny. Crazy Horse (c. 1842-1877) seems to appeal to Alexie's literary consciousness for a number of reasons: his mystical visions as a child and throughout his short life; his success as a warrior at the Battle of the Rosebud and at Little Big Horn; his mostly unrequited love and tribally tragic affair with Black Buffalo Woman; the suspicious circumstances of his bayoneting and death at Fort Robinson. Crazy Horse provides a shorthand representation of tragic vulnerability to which Alexie continued to return in prose and poetry over a decade.

From the perspective of Crazy Horse, the poem considers in seven numbered stanzas the responsibilities and burdens of tribal leadership, whether practiced by Sitting Bull (Hunkpapa Lakota leader) or the adversary George A. Custer or by Crazy Horse himself. In the fourth stanza, Crazy Horse recalls sitting across the fire from Sitting Bull: "We both saw the same thing/ our futures tight and small/ an 8 × 10 dream/ called the reservation./ We had no alternatives/ but to fight again and again/ live our lives on horseback."

Alexie's speculation raises a fascinating question: Did Crazy Horse, and perhaps Sitting Bull as well, perceive the inevitability of Indian military defeat yet continue to wage war with the U.S. cavalry to forestall the ultimate retreat to demarcated reservation land? The closing two-line stanza, however, shows Crazy Horse's indefatigable spirit, even as it implies that the battle is indeed not over.

"CAPITAL PUNISHMENT"

First published: 1996 (collected in *The Summer of Black Widows*, 1996)
Type of work: Poem

This poem is narrated by a prison cook who is preparing the last meal for an "Indian killer."

"Capital Punishment" consists of fifty-eight mostly two-line stanzas, punctuated six times with the same parenthetical, single-line comment by the cook: "(I am not a witness)." The cook thus periodically refuses the status of witness yet is clearly a sympathetic observer. As the cook prepares a simple dinner of a baked potato, salad, and glass of water, he wants desperately to make the last meal memorable and appetizing to the unnamed Indian on death row. The ethnic identity of the cook is unknown, but he is sympathetic to the inordinate percentage of minorities on death row. Such political commentary and inference from crime statistics imply a critique of capital punishment, the title of the poem, which becomes clearer as the poem continues.

The cook admits to tasting the food of the condemned prisoner before serving it, as a means to humanize and essentially to share the last meal of

this condemned human. As the cook proceeds to imagine the "wispy flames decorating" the prisoner in the process of electrocution, the justification of a society that legally kills people is called into question. The cook glumly admits: "I turn off the kitchen lights/ and sit alone in the dark/ because the whole damn prison dims/ when the chair is switched on." By turning off the lights and not noticing the power surge during the moments of electrocution, he is able only temporarily to forget the lethal justice that is being meted out elsewhere in the building.

Finally, without considering at all the crime or the circumstances of the crime, the cook reduces his quandary to simple mathematics: "1 death + 1 death = 2 deaths," and seems to say that state-sanctioned death, whatever seeming justice may be sought, ultimately results in a second death, a second ending of life, a new and more horrible set of disappointments and endings without continuation.

"DEFENDING WALT WHITMAN"

First published: 1996 (collected in *The Summer of Black Widows*, 1996)
Type of work: Poem

The nineteenth century American poet is brought into a pickup basketball game on a twentieth century Indian reservation.

"Defending Walt Whitman" provides Alexie with an opportunity to write about reservation basketball, one of his favorite topics, even as he responds to a nineteenth century icon of American poetry who was singularly responsible for breaking away from standard meter, rhyme, and subject matter. Alexie imagines that the bisexual Whitman would be quite charmed with the vision of sweaty, brown young men who are gallant in their own way yet who are initially defined as "twentieth-century warriors who will never kill."

Alexie is aware of the primacy of basketball among Indian youth throughout the United States, and he is only one of a number of Indian writers who have noticed the phenomenon. Alexie seems unaware that Whitman died in the same year that basketball was invented by James Naismith (1892). Alexie is certainly aware of the powerful dynamic of combining the inclusive, poetic Whitman with the energies and angles of a game of basketball.

"HOW TO WRITE THE GREAT AMERICAN INDIAN NOVEL"

First published: 1996 (collected in *The Summer of Black Widows*, 1996)
Type of work: Poem

This work articulates many of the recurrent stereotypes about American Indians in serious fiction.

"How to Write the Great American Indian Novel" is one of Alexie's most notable and fully realized poems. It has enjoyed a second life as the poem that Seymour Polatkin reads in its entirety at a Seattle book store early in the screenplay and film of *The Business of Fancydancing* (2003). In two-line stanzas that build toward an inevitable but depressing conclusion, Alexie lists a series of supposed assumptions implicit in the title that are requisite in such a work: "The hero must be a half-breed, half white and half Indian, preferably/ from a horse culture. He should often weep alone. That is mandatory." There is a connected cluster of cultural assumptions even in those two lines, but in the poem Alexie does not examine deeply each cultural presupposition. Instead, he heaps additional cultural presuppositions onto the ones just uttered: "If the hero is an Indian woman, she is beautiful. She must be slender/ and in love with a white man. But if she loves an Indian man/ then he must be a half-breed, preferably from a horse culture."

Such absolute statements demand response and argument, but Alexie purposefully continues to state new stereotypes that are increasingly disturbing. Such large-swath stereotyping isolates images of Indians as artifacts from a past America, even as it allows Anglo-Americans to develop themselves as Indian wannabes with little real understanding of the patronized culture. Alexie's conclusion reveals that if all of these stereotypes are perpetuated in such a novel, "all of the white people will be Indians and all of the Indians will be ghosts."

SUMMARY

Alexie has made significant and original contributions in a number of related literary and visual genres, and his prolific output has given him well-earned status as a significant literary figure. Although his characters are generally Indians from the Pacific Northwest, his themes of loss, substance abuse, identity, and poverty are readily understood and appreciated by a wide cross section of writers and critics. Alexie shows every indication of continuing to produce significant work in poetry, short fiction, and screenwriting, meriting the attention which he handles so well.

Richard Sax

DISCUSSION TOPICS

- In what sense is the title, *Reservation Blues*, an apt title for the events of that novel?

- What is the significance of the band that forms within the novel, Coyote Springs?

- Given the fact that Sherman Alexie is an Indian with two tribal traditions from the Pacific Northwest (Coeur d'Alene, Spokane), why does he repeatedly invoke Crazy Horse, an Oglala Lakota (northern Plains) Indian? Does it have anything to do with the refrain from the poem "How to Write the Great American Indian Novel": "the hero must be . . . from a horse culture"?

- Determine the effectiveness of the gallows humor that Alexie uses in his poetry and short fiction.

- Alexie frequently describes young Indian men as warriors without a war to fight. What sorts of modern-day replacements do Alexie's young men use instead of horses and weapons? What sorts of rites of passage and experiences do they need to undergo in order to forge coherent adult identities?

- What sorts of racial prejudice do Alexie's fictional characters suffer, and how do they mediate such prejudice?

BIBLIOGRAPHY

By the Author

SHORT FICTION:
The Lone Ranger and Tonto Fistfight in Heaven, 1993
The Toughest Indian in the World, 2000
Ten Little Indians, 2003

LONG FICTION:
Reservation Blues, 1995
Indian Killer, 1996

POETRY:
I Would Steal Horses, 1992
Old Shirts and New Skins, 1993
The Man Who Loves Salmon, 1998
One Stick Song, 2000

SCREENPLAYS:
Smoke Signals, 1998
The Business of Fancydancing, 2002

MISCELLANEOUS:
The Business of Fancydancing: Stories and Poems, 1992
First Indian on the Moon, 1993
The Summer of Black Widows, 1996 (poems and short prose)

About the Author

Brill, Susan Berry. *Contemporary American Indian Literatures and the Oral Tradition*. Tucson: University of Arizona Press, 1999.

Caldwell, E. K. *Dreaming the Dawn: Conversations with Native Artists and Activists*. Lincoln: University of Nebraska Press, 1999.

Fast, Robin Riley. *The Heart as a Drum: Continuance and Resistance in American Indian Poetry*. Ann Arbor: University of Michigan Press, 2000.

Grassian, Daniel. *Understanding Sherman Alexie*. Columbia: University of South Carolina Press, 2005.

Kilpatrick, Jacquelyn. *Celluloid Indians: Native Americans and Film*. Lincoln: University of Nebraska Press, 1999.

Lincoln, Kenneth. *Sing with the Heart of a Bear: Fusions of Native and American Poetry, 1890-1999*. Berkeley: University of California Press, 2000.

Vickers, Scott B. *Native American Identities: From Stereotype to Archetype in Art and Literature*. Albuquerque: University of New Mexico Press, 1998.

NELSON ALGREN

Born: Detroit, Michigan
   March 28, 1909
Died: Sag Harbor, New York
   May 9, 1981

*A lifelong critic of American society, Algren championed
its victims in fiction renowned for an idiosyncratic style
that is both realistic and lyrical.*

Library of Congress

BIOGRAPHY

Born Nelson Ahlgren Abraham in Detroit, Michigan, on March 28, 1909, Nelson Algren is usually identified with Chicago, where his family moved in 1913. His mother, Goldie, was an ill-tempered, violent woman, and his uncouth father, Gerson, a mechanic, was an often remote presence. The emotionally insecure Algren preferred to identify with the wandering grandfather he never met, Nels Ahlgren, a Swedish convert to Judaism. A normal middle-class boy in most respects, Algren began frequenting pool halls, speakeasies, and gambling dens as a teenager.

Algren's strongest family bond was with Bernice, the younger of two older sisters. It was she who encouraged his literary interests and insisted he attend college, and her death in 1940 left a space no one ever filled. Socially aloof, Algren discovered his love of books at the University of Illinois, Urbana, and led an ascetic and "spiritual" life of study, with the occasional lapse. In college, he wrote stories which demonstrate his identification with the oppressed—an identification that his experiences on the road would deepen. In 1931, with a degree in journalism, he went in search of a job that was

not to be had during the Great Depression. Taking up the hobo's life, he traveled to New Orleans, which, together with Chicago, was one of the two major cities of his fiction. There he was a door-to-door salesman before accompanying two drifters to Texas, where he became involved in an ill-fated scheme to run a gas station and later worked at a carnival.

After further travels, gathering experiences that he would turn into fiction, Algren returned home, joined a writers' group, and started submitting stories using Nelson Algren as his pen name (only changing it legally during World War II). Politically radical, he frequented the John Reed Club, a Communist Party organization, and met writers such as Richard Wright, the future author of *Native Son* (1940). Over the years, he would have close ties with the Communist Party, but it is not certain that he was ever a member.

After several rejections, he was published by *Story* and *A Year* in 1933. When Vanguard Press paid him an advance for a novel, Algren, who always wrote best from immediate experience, went back on the road. In Alpine, Texas, he spent almost a month in jail for stealing a typewriter from the local community college. Though his stories and reporting enhanced his reputation, Algren was devastated when *Somebody in Boots* (1935) was not a success. Despite favorable reviews, the novel did not sell, and he attempted suicide during an extended period of depression. Tough but compassionate in his interviews, Algren was actually deeply insecure and very self-destructive; he did not spare those around him, either, about which he felt guilty even as he denied it. This is clearest in his three ambivalent, tortured marriages, two of them to Amanda Kontowicz, whom he met following the "failure" of his first novel.

In 1936, Algren took a job with the Works Progress Administration, or WPA, a federal program then providing writers and artists with jobs. In 1939, to write his second novel, he moved to the Polish "triangle," the setting of his Chicago novels, a world of taverns, pool halls, gambling dens, police lineups, and brothels, where he recorded dialogue and anecdotes. With the success of *Never Come Morning* (1942), his confidence and spirits rose, though he made so little money that he was soon back on the public payroll with the Venereal Disease Control Project. During World War II, he served in the medical corps, seeing little action but enjoying wartime Marseilles, where he gambled away his black-market profits. Returning to Chicago, he settled down to a more austere life to complete a collection of stories, *The Neon Wilderness* (1947).

Algren's reputation growing in literary circles, he met Simone de Beauvoir, the French novelist and feminist author of *Le Deuxième Sexe* (1949; *The Second Sex*, 1953). His affair with her, the most fulfilling and passionate of his life, ended because of de Beauvoir's commitment to Jean-Paul Sartre, the existentialist writer and philosopher.

The controversial *The Man with the Golden Arm* (1949) brought Algren to the height of his fame and success. Unfortunately, it did not solve his financial problems. He suffered gambling losses; in addition, he was so confident of his own shrewdness that he made several unfortunate financial deals, especially in Hollywood. Fame also isolated him from his subject, the dispossessed. Though he championed the downtrodden in his book-length essay *Chicago: City on the Make* (1951), he found it impossible to complete the novel with which he was struggling, *Entrapment*. Finally, he transformed *Somebody in Boots* into *A Walk on the Wild Side* (1956). Though its reputation continues to grow, it was not a success at the time, and Algren was almost as depressed by its failure the second time as the first, possibly going so far as a second suicide attempt.

Worse, he used popular rejection as an excuse to stop serious writing. Cashing in on his reputation, he lectured and taught. Aside from a few stories, he restricted his writing to journalism, magazine articles, and travel books, such as *Who Lost an American?* (1963) and *Notes from a Sea Diary: Hemingway All the Way* (1965). In 1968, he went to Vietnam, where, instead of covering the war, he had a disastrous experience with the black market.

As Algren became older, his writing turned bitter and satirical. Though he was often amusing and stimulating company, his physical condition deteriorated, which alarmed old friends, many of whom he snubbed without reason. Increasingly obsessed with money, he began a racetrack novel, but he seemed more interested in receiving advances than in actually finishing it; several segments came out in the collection *The Last Carousel* (1973). He was still politically committed enough to move to Paterson, New Jersey, in 1975 to write a nonfiction book on the black boxer Rubin "Hurricane" Carter, whom many considered unjustly convicted of murder. Failing to sell the manuscript, he turned it into the posthumous and poorly received *The Devil's Stocking* (1983).

With considerable help from friends, Algren moved to Sag Harbor, New York, in 1980. He relished this congenial town, but he had already suffered one heart attack which, characteristically, he refused to acknowledge. A second killed him the night before a party to celebrate his election to the American Academy of Arts and Letters.

ANALYSIS

The work of Algren is best understood within the context of naturalism, a literary tradition deriving from realism's truthful representation of life darkened by "Darwinian" notions of survival of the fittest and determinism. Though naturalism began in nineteenth century France with authors such as Émile Zola, a strong American tradition runs from Stephen Crane through Frank Norris, Theodore Dreiser, Upton Sinclair, and James T. Farrell to Algren. Their novels tend to foreground the marginal elements in industrial society, where factors of heredity, chance, and social conditions determine an individual's fate regardless of his or her will. Though characters are depicted as insignificant, their plight is often presented in a romanticized and melodramatic manner, as in some of Algren's writing.

During the Great Depression of the 1930's, with the apparent collapse of capitalism and the rise of

Fascism, naturalism adapted easily to the left-wing dissent that blossomed at the time. Believing that "the role of the writer is always to stand against the culture he is in . . . with the accused," Algren, like many others, sympathized with the Communist Party. Despising capitalism's hypocritical rejection of addicts and criminals whose condition mirrored capitalism's materialist addiction and vicious competition, Algren put his pen at the service of the underdog, whom he saw as victim and scapegoat. This resulted in an often heavy-handed preachiness, though this element was less pervasive in his stories, usually, than the novels.

Algren claimed never to have been a Communist Party member; his compassion for the underclass was more personal—as was that of Studs Terkel, his lifelong friend. At home with a segment of society that most people refuse to see—con artists, drug addicts, prostitutes, and petty criminals—Algren regarded these people as victims of an economic system under which the rich are simply the successful hustlers. The only crime of the dispossessed is that they are losers, their guilt "the great, secret, and special American guilt of owning nothing, nothing at all, in the one land where ownership and virtue are one."

Doing what he called "emotionalized reportage," Algren wrote from life, speaking for those spiritually starved and trapped in the bleak struggle with their social surroundings. Always valuing the human over the theoretical, he lived in the urban settings he described—alley, bar, brothel, jail, tenements, and flophouses—just as he traveled the countryside of his novels, the poverty-stricken United States of the Depression.

In the world of Algren's fiction, there seems no way out except through the always-imminent violence, and the only fatal weakness is the expression of doubt and compassion. For his main characters, never brutal enough, there is no hope for salvation except by trusting other people. Unfortunately, they are the products of a society in which trust, even self-trust, is impossible; the promise of love is counterfeit—or seems so until it is too late. Throughout Algren's work, characters destroy love; then, guilt-haunted, they are unable to escape their fates. Indeed, they seek their doom as expiation of their betrayal of love, while the policemen who hound them are burdened by their sense of shared guilt.

Though these themes remained constant, over time the tone of Algren's writing changed, irony giving way first to the comical before turning bitter and satirical, subsiding at times into slapstick and the bizarre. This reflected not only Algren's belief in the underlying absurdity of the human condition but also his growing despair that writing would ever change anything: Parody was ultimately his only response to society's callousness.

Though this cynicism suits naturalism, Algren was influenced stylistically by the poetry of Walt Whitman and Carl Sandburg, as well as the splenetic, free-form novels of the Frenchman Louis-Ferdinand Céline. Algren's prose catches what he called the poetry of human speech, its rhythms and repetitions, while repeated catch-phrases and song lyrics give it both a dreamlike quality and structural cohesiveness. A mix of specific details, low-life jargon, and well-observed idiosyncrasies of thought and behavior make this style both realistically exact and lyrically grim, though occasionally overwritten. Characteristic is the heavily symbolic and colorful imagery that conveys a nearly pervasive foreboding, as in *The Man with the Golden Arm.*

> Goggling upward at it, shivering a bit in the shabby coat, he felt for a moment as if he, too, were something impaled on city wires for only tenement winds to touch.

Leaving out the spare parts, as he put it, Algren created an unorthodox grammar of fragments and short run-ons arranged to suggest the movement of thought and able to convey a wide range of moods, from the contemplative to the urgent. In these ways, he communicated mental states that his uneducated characters could not articulate for themselves.

From 1935 to 1981, Algren wrote only five novels. Though able to churn out stories and articles for money, he was never able to write his novels easily. Never planned, each developed by a process of aggregation as he expanded it from the inside. To complete this difficult process, Algren needed firsthand experience, but he became increasingly isolated. This partly explains why he completed so few long works; he was also hindered by increasing bitterness about his place in American letters.

Identifying with the writers of the 1930's, who were poor but committed, Algren was critical of the literary scene after World War II. Not only was he ambivalent about the prosperity of other artists (which his gambling habit denied him anyway), but he also considered himself to be the victim of an anti-Communist backlash that he believed extended into literature through the auspices of the New Criticism. This movement removed writing from its social context, dismissing special pleading for a social cause in the belief that true art is self-contained. Attacking this as falsely limiting, Algren believed that "literature is made upon any occasion when a challenge is put to the legal apparatus by conscience in touch with humanity."

Unfortunately, in the turbulent political climate of the 1950's, when to be liberal was to be suspect, many critics turned their backs on the social issues, dismissing Algren's work as sentimental and romantic. Yet the responsibility for his meager output was Algren's also, as he abdicated control of his own artistic life, choosing to see himself as a victim.

NEVER COME MORNING

First published: 1942
Type of work: Novel

A young boxer from Chicago's slums destroys himself in his struggle for identity and independence.

Never Come Morning, like all of Algren's novels, is a study of doom working itself out. Bruno "Lefty" Bicek is a young Polish American imprisoned in the Polish slums of Chicago, so oppressively isolated that the outside filters through only in films and tabloids. These promise a glorified version of success, but the American Dream is closer to nightmare in this world of police lineups, gangs, petty crime, and brothels. Here everyone is either the hunter or the hunted, who have nothing to lose but are too worried about being cheated of what they are owed to trust anyone else.

Like the rest, Bruno, hungering for boxing glory, scorns the Old World values of hard work and religious faith, but he is not strong enough to live by the New World's capitalistic code of violence and deception. Bruno thinks of himself as a wolf,

but he is a dreamer instead of a schemer; though sensitive and humane, he is too crippled by conscience to protect himself and too insecure to protect others. Despite his boxing prowess, he cannot stand up to his more brutal inferiors, either the knife-wielding Fireball Kodadek or the blackmailing Bonifacy "the barber" Konstantine, who wants to control his boxing career.

In a world where everything is a cheat, love seems as false as every other promise, but to destroy love in Algren's novels is to destroy oneself. This is what happens when Bruno, asserting himself as a gang leader, seduces and betrays Steffi Rostenkowski. Steffi, born with similarly limited choices, gives in to Bruno because he seems the best she can expect. Then Bruno, unsure of himself and afraid of Kodadek's knife, lets the rest of the gang have their way with Steffi. After this, Bruno's fate is sealed. Stubbornly proud, he channels his shame into rage, murdering a Greek outsider trying to join in the rape.

Knowing that there can be no forgiveness for killing Steffi "in his heart," he is ready to accept any punishment and goes to jail for a crime he did not commit. Still in search of forgiveness, he returns and gets a job at Mama Tomek's brothel where Steffi, now Bonifacy's mistress, works. Hoping to free Steffi and himself, Bruno establishes his independence by arranging his own boxing match and proves his manhood by beating up Bonifacy's henchmen. All escape is illusory, however; Bruno wins in the boxing ring, but only for Bonifacy to denounce him to the police for the Greek's murder.

Never Come Morning is a stylistic improvement over *Somebody in Boots*, with complex shifts in tone and pacing, subtler characters, and well-developed scenes. The brothel scenes, in particular, are praised for their authenticity and compassionate understanding, conveying simultaneously the comic and the threatening. Critics differ about this and other digressions in the novel, however, which weaken the story's tension to dwell on capitalism's oppressive exploitation. To heighten the sense of futility and hopelessness, Algren uses images of imprisonment and rain. Equally bitter are the song lyrics whose cheerfulness is merely ironic in a dark world where people are compared to mutilated flies and decapitated dolls. In many parts, the story often pushed to the side, *Never Come Morning* reads like a mood poem on the imminence of violence and death.

THE MAN WITH THE GOLDEN ARM

First published: 1949
Type of work: Novel

Doomed from the beginning, card dealer Frankie Machine struggles hopelessly against drug addiction and guilt.

The Man with the Golden Arm, Algren's one great popular success, caught public attention because of the then-shocking drug addiction of its protagonist. For Algren, this aspect—a late addition to the novel—merely contributed to the story of the self-destructive relationship of Francis Majcinek, known as Frankie Machine because of his skill as a dealer, and his possessive, hypochondriacal wife, Sophie (or Zosh).

Like all Algren protagonists, Frankie is not as tough as he pretends; he talks big, but he is a coward who dreams of becoming a drummer. His fixer, Nifty Louis Fomorowsky, sees immediately that Frankie is among the world's sheep, not the shearers, and that like so many, he chooses his addiction and his doom. As always in Algren's work, when strength is used, it leads to violence and self-destruction; in an unthinking moment, Frankie kills Louie.

The wheelchair-bound Sophie is the most complicated female character in any of Algren's novels. Her pride stung by Frankie's indifference to her love, she had trapped him into marriage with a false pregnancy. Now, though there is nothing wrong with her legs, she insists that Frankie crippled her in a driving accident, binding him all the tighter to her through guilt. Throughout the book, she becomes more demanding and destructively compulsive, driving Frankie away while descend-

ing into insanity. Instead of abandoning her, Frankie makes halfhearted attempts to please her, because "a guy got to draw the line somewhere on how bad he can treat somebody who can't help herself no more just account of him." Unfortunately, Frankie does not know where to draw the line and so relies on morphine.

In another characteristic Algren touch, it does not matter that Frankie became addicted by chance in an Army hospital. He is doomed anyway, because he cannot rid himself of this "monkey on his back" (a phrase introduced into general use with this novel). For Algren there are no fresh starts, even though trust and love always hold out hope. Molly Novotny offers love to Frankie, but he cannot accept it because his tortured guilt over Sophie alienates him more and more from himself.

In the novel's world, self-destruction is pursued in the hope of penance, and Frankie gets his one chance for redemption when he is caught shoplifting. In prison, he breaks his addiction, only to return to Division Street and find that Molly is gone, Sophie is crazy, and the one person he trusted, Sparrow "Solly" Saltskin, has betrayed his trust. When he loses his touch with cards, Frankie goes back on drugs, while the tenacious police captain Record Head Bednar uses Sparrow, as well as Frankie's own addiction, to nail him for Louie's killing. On the run, wounded and exhausted, Frankie hangs himself in a flophouse.

In no other novel did Algren mix serious, lyrical, and comic elements to such effect. Writing it, he still thought that books could change society because "every man was secretly against the law in his heart . . . and it was the heart that mattered." Believing that there are no absolute moral values— only people—Algren rated compassion over justice, especially that based on property laws, and he tried in this novel to move the reader to believe that as well.

This is particularly clear in the example of the tortured police captain, Record Head Bednar, who has an answer for every pathetic excuse except when an arrested man says, "We are all members of one another." As the one responsible for arresting criminals, Bednar finally admits, but cannot embrace, his identification with the "guilty" who are closer to redemption than he is because he denies his connection with them. Instead, he continues his spiritual con game, apportioning society's justice when he is "more lost, more fallen and more alone than any man at all."

Though Algren was the grandson of a convert to Judaism and the son of a Jewish mother, it is Christian imagery that predominates in this book, though in an inverted manner. Everyone is guilty. Christ is the accuser, not the savior, as no one can be saved. All the characters feel crucified or impaled, but there is no afterlife, no point to the suffering, only death: "When you come to the end it's the end, that's all." There was some criticism of the book's loose two-part structure, and Algren regretted its chase ending, but the novel excels in its focus on mood. The author cared more for changes of consciousness as the characters suffer the consequences of destroyed love than for plot. In depicting this, Algren's style is at its finest. Algren used jargon accurately and drew his lively images from the characters' lives: "He still looked like the business end of a fugitive warrant to Frankie."

At its best, the writing is both realistic in matter of detail and grim in tone, and it manages a lyrical quality with its freewheeling grammar. "Caught between the dealer's slot and the cat-gray stroke of the years, Frankie saw a line of endless girders wet with the rain of those years to be. Where all night long, in that far time, the same all-night salamanders burned. Burned just as they had so long ago. Before the world went wrong. And any gray cat had purred at all."

At the same time, humor is used more and to more effect than in his earlier novels, in keeping with Algren's sense of the absurd in all human matters, even the tragic. Consequently, the comic elements provide more than laughs: They resonate with foreboding and the horror of life's meaninglessness. For example, the alcoholic dog Rumdum is redeemed, though Frankie is doomed, along with the whole colorful cast of grotesques at the Tug & Maul who drink their lives away. The near-slapstick affair between Sparrow and Vi, whose old husband, Stash Koskoska, is a slow-witted old man with a taste for day-old bread and cut-rate Polish sausage, affords more than comic relief. This travesty of marriage heightens, by contrast, the oppressiveness of Frankie and Zosh's mutual hell.

A WALK ON THE WILD SIDE

First published: 1956
Type of work: Novel

The wise fool Dove Linkhorn sets out to conquer women and the world, only to be thoroughly vanquished.

A Walk on the Wild Side started as a revision of *Somebody in Boots*, but as it progressed, Algren transformed his serious first novel into a parody of the American Dream. Algren justified this on the grounds that, times having changed, he had to entertain readers. Moreover, disgusted by the triumph of materialism, he no longer believed that writing could change attitudes, only mock them. This apparently defensive response betrays a lack of confidence in what some critics considered to be a great idiosyncratic masterpiece of the absurd that prepared the way for such writers as Thomas Pynchon, Ken Kesey, Joseph Heller, and Hunter S. Thompson.

Dove Linkhorn is the last of a line of poor Texas rebels against authority. Illiterate but canny, Dove is a loser who is too innocent to feel like a loser. Incapable of recognizing society's moral code, and so amoral, he does know when he has betrayed those who helped him. Deprived of any meaningful childhood, as Algren may have believed he himself was, Dove at sixteen wants two things, education and love, which he finds in Terasina Vidavarri. While trying to teach Dove the alphabet, she awakens his indefatigable virility, convincing him that he is a born world shaker. When she resists his later advances, he rapes her and flees, only to find he can escape neither his love nor his guilt for violating the reverence he feels for her.

In his subsequent adventures, he meets a cast of strange, but human, characters. He is as odd as the others, certainly, a wise fool, practically a cartoon figure. He learns the ways of the road from

Kitty Twist; however, as so often happens in Algren's works, the man lets the woman down. She gets caught during a robbery while he manages to escape, going on to sell door-to-door and work in a condom factory before having his great success as the Big Stingaree, "deflowerer" of "virgins" in a sex show. This rise to the top of the bottom is central to Algren's parody. In one scene, Dove watches a headless turtle crawl to the top of a pile of decapitated turtles before toppling to the bottom, where there is always room for one more. Dove himself slides to the bottom when he runs off with a teacher turned prostitute, whose lover, the legless Achilles Schmidt, will eventually blind Dove during a savage beating just after he learns to read.

Despite the many amusing and colorful scenes set in brothels and condom factories, the book's core is its examination of love and guilt. Love is resisted because it can kill, as it does the little girl who goes after her doll under the wheels of a train, or threaten one's self-sufficiency, as it does Schmidt's. Dove rebels against Terasina's power, only to learn that violence renders him permanently dependent through guilt. Initially, domination may seem the only basis for emotional relationships in a society that rewards deceit and force, but violence puts a man beyond salvation by destroying his contact with others.

Though less preachy than *Somebody in Boots*, *A Walk on the Wild Side* indicts a society where there is "self-reliance for the penniless and government help to the rich" and where the men who profit from vice are the very ones who inveigh against it and where the losers are jailed, having been given their "chance." During the Depression, the ladder of success was inverted; everyone was on the street hustling for a living and selling something. Dove is warned to watch out for trust and friends, but he comes to wonder if he wants success when it is always at the expense of "them who have already been whipped."

At the end, as Schmidt beats Dove's face into a bloody pulp, others stand around and exult "as though each fresh blow redeemed that blow that his life had been to him." Algren believed that this is what capitalism reduces people to: the violence of despair. When the same crowd rushes Schmidt to his death, he goes as "a saint of the amputees," knowing that he has done their work for them. This Christ-like acceptance of guilt and connection with others is the only salvation the world offers: Dove returns home, ready for love at last and hoping Terasina will take him in.

THE NEON WILDERNESS

First published: 1947
Type of work: Short stories

In realistically grim and lyrically idiosyncratic portraits, Algren depicts America's down-and-out.

With *The Neon Wilderness*, Algren emerged as a mature and original spokesman for a whole class of people usually excluded from literature except as marginal and stereotyped caricatures. In place of the condescending tone of most writing about the poor, Algren demonstrates the compassion of a man determined to live up to the people he is writing about. The stories bristle with many of Algren's characteristic thematic and stylistic concerns. The more focused short-story form undermines his didactic, Communist streak, and though there are times when Algren sentimentalizes his characters, this does not diminish the overall power of these stories.

"So Help Me," his first published story, is a dramatic monologue using a favorite Algren device, the interrogation of a criminal. His use here of only the criminal's voice lessens the effect, but the solidity of detail and attention to human voice create a convincing account of human isolation and the inevitability of violence, those constants of Algren's work. Another characteristic touch is the repeated use of the title phrase, prompting both sympathy and doubt.

In "Design for Departure," one of his attempts to write an important story, Algren carefully creates the urban jungle motif and brings out the religious parallels in this story of Mary and Christiano, victims of psychological and economic deprivation. Born into a world of despair, Mary wants only to die, and her whole life is directed toward that departure as she succumbs to the pervasive sense of doom. Unable to connect with the world, she suffers through an unloving upbringing, drug addiction, and prostitution before finally committing suicide. Deaf Christy, who helps her die when he cannot save her, is one of a whole line of cripples in Algren's writing who are brutal yet not vicious so much as callous and spiritually starved.

The ending teeters between the moving and the sentimental, and some critics prefer Algren's more spontaneous stories. With "How the Devil Came Down Division Street," Algren dashed off one of his first comic masterpieces. Outrageous and bizarre, this supernatural story is told with a casual air that belies its grim moral, that the salvation of one character often necessitates the perdition of another. Irony is equally pronounced in "Depend on Aunt Elly," a bitter love story about a prizefighter and a prostitute. Despite their devotion to each other and their recognition that they are each other's only salvation, their lives are so determined that neither talent nor courage is proof against the simple bad luck of being who they are and being at the mercy of a greed more powerful than love.

Algren worked several of these stories into his novels. "A Bottle of Milk for Mother," for example, tells of the accidental shooting for which Bruno "Lefty" Bicek takes the rap in the middle segment of *Never Come Morning*. Another interrogation story, this is an improvement over "So Help Me" because of the use of character interaction and an ironic narrator to depict Bruno's self-incrimination under Captain Kozak's masterful questioning. Kozak is one of Algren's weary, guilt-haunted but clever cops, such as the captain in "The Captain Has Bad Dreams," used in *The Man with the Golden Arm*.

In "The Face on the Barroom Floor," later refashioned as the end of *A Walk on the Wild Side*, a thoughtless comment sparks a murderous brawl between Railroad Shorty, a powerful fighter cut in half by a train, and a callow young bartender. The story is a graphic tale of the inevitability of violence, given the desperate need for identity and self-respect in a world that denies them.

Throughout the book, characters are not seen as warped or degenerate but as ordinary humans with their lives twisted by circumstances. Their aberrant behavior is, for them, the active expression of their individuality, their defense in a world where violence and deceit are necessary because the highest value is survival and morality is useless. In "A Lot You Got to Holler," for example, the protagonist says, "I was always in the clear so long as I was truly guilty. But the minute my motives were honest someone would finger me."

SUMMARY

Termed "bard of the stumblebum" and "poet of the Chicago slums," Algren combined an idiosyncratic style and a keen eye for detail in his compelling depictions of the dispossessed. Convinced that "lost people sometimes develop into greater human beings than those who have never been lost in their whole lives," Algren created characters dignified even in defeat.

Philip McDermott

BIBLIOGRAPHY

By the Author

LONG FICTION:
Somebody in Boots, 1935
Never Come Morning, 1942
The Man with the Golden Arm, 1949
A Walk on the Wild Side, 1956
The Devil's Stocking, 1983

SHORT FICTION:
The Neon Wilderness, 1947
The Last Carousel, 1973 (also includes sketches and poems)

NONFICTION:
Chicago: City on the Make, 1951
Who Lost an American?, 1963

Conversations with Nelson Algren, 1964 (with H. E. F. Donohue)
Notes from a Sea Diary: Hemingway All the Way, 1965

EDITED TEXT:
Nelson Algren's Own Book of Lonesome Monsters, 1962

About the Author

Cappetti, Carla. *Writing Chicago: Modernism, Ethnography, and the Novel.* New York: Columbia University Press, 1993.

Cox, Martha Heasley, and Wayne Chatterton. *Nelson Algren.* Boston: Twayne, 1975.

Donohue, H. E. F. *Conversations with Nelson Algren.* New York: Hill and Wang, 1964.

Drew, Bettina. *Nelson Algren: A Life on the Wild Side.* New York: G. P. Putnam's Sons, 1989.

Giles, James R. *Confronting the Horror: The Novels of Nelson Algren.* Kent, Ohio: Kent State University Press, 1989.

Pitts, Mary Ellen. "Algren's El: Internalized Machine and Displaced Nature." *South Atlantic Review* 52 (November, 1987): 61-74.

Ray, David. "Housesitting the Wild Side." *Chicago Review* 41 (1995): 107-116.

DISCUSSION TOPICS

- Does Nelson Algren's success at portraying the undesirable elements of society owe more to his literary technique or his personal experiences?

- Can a writer who believes that "there are no absolute moral values" write a morally satisfying novel?

- What suggestions does Algren convey to you by referring to Frankie Machine's arm as "golden"?

- Algren is said to regard compassion as a "fatal weakness." Does his writing ever reveal himself as partaking of this weakness?

- Discuss the claim that Algren "used popular rejection as an excuse to stop serious writing." Algren was in many ways a man of his time. What aspects of his social criticism seem most relevant today?

PAULA GUNN ALLEN

Born: Cubero, New Mexico
October 24, 1939

A storyteller, poet, and essayist, Allen advocates awareness of tribal cultures as integral to a balanced, harmonious understanding of American Indian literatures.

© Tama Rothschild

BIOGRAPHY

Paula Gunn Allen was born in Cubero, New Mexico, in 1939, to Elias Lee Francis, a Lebanese American who had once been lieutenant governor of New Mexico, and Ethel Gunn Francis, a Laguna Sioux-Scottish woman of the Keres Indians, an intensely gynecocratic-centered culture. Allen's multiethnic (or "breed") origins are not unusual in the Laguna Pueblo, which consists of a multitude of cultural worlds uniting through mutual desire into a reciprocal tribal whole.

Allen was born in the seventh year of a thirty-year drought and in the first year of the area's uranium mining. She remembers blocking windows and doors to keep out dust, which at times was so thick that it was difficult to see across a room. Equally vivid are her memories of her stone-walled home, surrounded by white flowers and safely nestled in a hollow, where she would read and listen to her sister play classical music on the family's upright piano. Both her parents were also musicians, and Allen learned early in life to recognize and value the distinctive rhythms of both music and language in the cultures that nurtured her.

The road by their house fascinated Allen. In one direction, it ran to a city; in another, it ran to a mountain. Yet it also remained there, in her homeland. This road is dominant in Allen's life and in her writing. Allen sees herself as standing at a cross-roads, valuing the mountain (sacred wilderness) more highly than the city (civilization) and measuring civilization in terms of the mountain.

The bicultural alienation that haunts Allen appears to have begun when she was sent to an Albuquerque convent school, where she was taught that all humans are innately hopeless, guilt-ridden sinners and that Indians are worthless savages. In "Easter Sunday: Recollection," Allen describes herself on Good Friday "waiting for the earth to tear itself apart and swallow me,/ to reveal my murderous intent" and believing "cold wind and dust and snow sure signs of my guilt,/ the murderous compulsion of those I loved/ god-killers condemned to grief." These teachings are in direct contradiction to the nonpunitive, life-affirming teachings of her mother and her tribal culture, yet they were pronounced as truth by purportedly holy women, convent nuns, and reinforced with punishments. Consequently, Allen as a young girl was unable to reconcile the dichotomies, hated school, and withdrew as quickly as possible into reading, with a strong preference for popular literature rather than the classics.

Nevertheless, her Laguna culture values learning, and Allen persevered. After attending Colorado Women's College, she received her B.A. in English in 1966 and her M.F.A. in creative writing in 1968 from the University of Oregon. While working on her master's degree, Allen felt so fragmented, dissociated, and alone that she experienced a suicidal despair. Her Laguna mother's teachings to nurture all the living and to avoid self-indulgent negativity because it sickens the earth did not alleviate her depression. Allen's poems in *The Blind Lion: Poems* (1974) come from this dark journey.

Allen credits the arrival of a Santee Sioux friend and the publication of N. Scott Momaday's *House Made of Dawn* (1968) with restoring her sense of tribal community. "Land sickness" is a state of grief over not being with the land where one's heart is. To the American Indian, experiences are related to and defined by the places in which they occur. *House Made of Dawn* helped Allen to restore her groundedness in the earth as well as her sense of humor. As she explains, any kind of humor, even gallows humor, is integral to life. Momaday's book demonstrated to her that she was not crazy but, even if she were, at least she was no longer alone.

Although Allen wanted to continue her doctorate in English, no program was available for her to concentrate in Native American literature; therefore, she specialized in Native American literature under the University of New Mexico's American Studies program and received her Ph.D. in 1975. Allen's postdoctoral awards include a 1978 National Endowment of the Arts Creative Writing Fellowship, a 1980-1981 University of California at Berkeley fellowship in Native American Studies, and a 1984-1985 Ford Foundation research grant. *Spider Woman's Granddaughters: Traditional Tales and Contemporary Writing by Native American Women* (1989), edited by Allen under the Ford Foundation grant, won a 1990 American Book Award.

ANALYSIS

American Indians honor all existence as sacred. They do not set up arbitrary barriers between spirit and matter, human and other-than-human. Instead, they perceive the universe as living, dynamic, and fluid, with each being (such as trees, rocks, animals, water, and humans) contributing its own awareness to the integrated and constantly reforming continuance of the whole. In all of her writings, Allen is an "environmental advocate" who reveals the consequences of harmonious and disharmonious relations with the universe. In "Los Angeles, 1980," Allen describes the "vitamin-drenched consciousness" of the city-dwellers: "The death people do not know/ what they create, or how they hide/ from the consequences of their dreams."

To Allen, the female force is "about balance and mutual respect and reciprocal obligation." Reality involves a vigilant awareness of, and caring for, self, others, and place, because all realities coexist in the cycle of life. Time itself is fluid, and spirit is the

creative force. The journeymaker who walks in balance recognizes the essential beauty of the universe and explores each experience for its fundamental, communal truth. In *Grandmothers of the Light: A Medicine Woman's Sourcebook* (1991), Allen teaches a spiritual discipline through twenty-one stories of tribal tradition and sacred power.

Allen was taught that her mind is irrevocably hers, an aspect of her reality that no one else can ever possess. To a people who have survived a genocidal colonization and who are still hostages facing nonexistence on their own land, this is a crucial message. Allen sees American Indian literature as a means of "taking control of the image making again," of choosing ritual right action to reestablish an earth-connectedness and to abandon the illusory path of powerlessness. "Hoop Dancer," in *Shadow Country* (1982), is an unforgettable, synesthetic experience in poetry of these principles.

American Indian literature and Western literature are fundamentally different. Approaching Indian literature metaphysically, psychically open to all of its levels of reality, rather than didactically superimposing an external critical or cultural context, is essential. As a teacher, an essayist, and an editor, Allen has contributed with distinction to integrating American Indian literature into Western awareness as well as to providing the appropriate contexts through which the literature can best be understood. She is the editor of, and contributor to, *Studies in American Indian Literature: Critical Essays and Course Designs* (1983), a definitive text published by the Modern Language Association.

Rather than emphasizing an individual in crisis, American Indian literature focuses upon tribal continuity and the nature of the individual's connection to it, with the purpose of enhancing the fulfillment of both. Self-expression for its own sake would be considered invasive, self-indulgent negativity. Therefore, if an individual is isolated, the isolation is examined in terms of how the individual and the cosmos can be reconnected.

The American Indian universe is integrated, rather than divisive: Great Mystery (God) does not sit apart in judgment from the elements of the universe but lives within all in reciprocity. Place is never incidental; instead, place is crucial to the significance of an action. All planes of existence are recognized as "real." Time is cyclical and coexistent. The treatment of time provides important contextual clues as to the consciousness with which the work can most appropriately be approached. Finally, American Indian literature is life-affirming rather than death-preoccupied.

As a professor of English at the University of California, Los Angeles, until her retirement in 1999, Allen lived in both the Native American and the Western worlds. Her writing, however, is profoundly Native American. In describing her life, she does not speak of a straight-line journey from one event to another but of an energy flow along a path that resembles a Mobius strip.

Many of Allen's books of poetry attest the reality that her journey has not been without turbulence: *The Blind Lion, Coyote's Daylight Trip* (1978), *A Cannon Between My Knees* (1981), *Star Child* (1981), *Shadow Country,* and *Skins and Bones: Poems 1979-87* (1988). Each shares her search for balance and groundedness: from the mountains to the cities, through idealism and despair, to survival, affirmation, and healing transformation.

Self-alienation, often a consequence of bicultural or multicultural experience, is a recurrent theme in Allen's work. An individual displaced by ancestry is highly susceptible to psychic deterioration from the absence of both internal and communal grounding. In addition, Allen focuses upon the scarring effects of a patriarchal colonialism forced upon gynecocratic tribal cultures. The debilitation of land sickness, the powerlessness of nonexistence for tribal women, and the imposition of an alien dualistic, materialistic culture brought searing disharmony and imbalance to the American Indian world.

Myth, ritual action, and oral tradition are the healing foundations of the Native American universe. All three are visionary and real. Allen reinforces their curative, sacred powers with rhythm and sound repetition to create shifts in consciousness that open awareness. The Western use of symbolism is unrecognized in American Indian literature; if all existence is sacred, then a river can be a river and stand for itself in its sacredness.

As a desert dweller, Allen has a special affinity for the mountains, water, and dawn. Her use of shadows is strikingly intense: "shadow too stricken to flow/ dream in your silent shadow/ celebrate." Shadows are places of interdimensional exploration. They are opportunities for earth-connectedness and mutual creation. Allen's only novel, *The*

Woman Who Owned the Shadows (1983), exemplifies these characteristics as it follows the walking path of a half-breed woman to intrapsychic centeredness.

Allen's style has become less obscure over the years; the author attributes this transformation to her long-held belief that after the age of forty, a woman has the power of enhanced clarity. That she no longer holds as deep an emotional investment in avoiding being misunderstood, a condition she had once equated with death, has also contributed to the evolution of her style.

"MAY IT BE BEAUTIFUL ALL AROUND"

First published: 1991 (collected in *Grandmothers of the Light*, 1991)
Type of work: Short story

Two Navajo sisters are taught healing ceremonies by a group of supernatural beings.

"May It Be Beautiful All Around," in *Grandmothers of the Light*, is one of eight stories in which Allen demonstrates the role of ritual magic in the interplay between humans and supernaturals. Allen has stated that "the essential nature of the cosmos is female intelligences," and she has created the word "cosmogyny" to represent this enduring and transformative gynocentric cosmos.

Navajo chantways are intricate healing ceremonies based upon the knowledge that reintegration with the inviolate inner forces of the land and the natural elements restores a diseased individual into balance with the sacred order. The chantways can last from two to nine days and can involve fifteen or more trained practitioners. Although many chantway rituals are shared, each chantway belongs to a specific healing group and contains its own songs, stories, herbal medicines, prayers, and curative processes.

In "May It Be Beautiful All Around," Older Sister and Younger Sister have been pledged to two strong but old warriors whom they do not love. During a raid, the two sisters are separated from their family. Although they are afraid, they ignore tribal knowledge to consider the possibility that they might not have to fulfill their uncle's pledge to marry the old warriors, Bear Man and Snake Man.

As the women search the mountains for their family, two handsome young men appear and offer their help. Because the hour is late, the four decide to take shelter until daybreak in nearby ruins, where Older Sister and Younger Sister are each joined by a virile warrior for the night. In the morning, despite omens that all may not be as it seems, Younger Sister follows her young warrior to a rock that opens at his four knocks (four being the most sacred of numbers) onto another land.

The warrior leaves her at his home to help his mother with her tasks. For the next four days, she is given a different chore each day. Although the tasks are simple ones, she fails every time through inattention, impatience, and undisciplined behavior. Each time, her mother-in-law responds with serene patience. On the fifth day, her warrior-husband offers to teach her a ceremony that she can take to her people.

This time, Younger Sister works diligently to learn every movement and every sound of the ceremony. After four days of right action, she is successful. Her husband, now old and bent, leads her home. As she and her family talk, Younger Sister learns that she has been gone for months, not days. She is rejoined by Older Sister, who has been with Bear Man's mother all these months, and the two women return with their knowledge to their people. After the sisters have taught their ceremonies to their brothers, they rejoin their supernatural husbands, and "because of their continuing thought the ceremonies continue to have the power to heal."

"DEAR WORLD"

First published: 1984 (collected in *Skins and Bones*, 1988)
Type of work: Poem

Bicultural self-alienation is represented by the poet's half-breed mother, who has contracted lupus.

"Dear World" is an agonizing eulogy for the living and the dead who have experienced the internal isolation of nonbelonging. Undercurrents of rage and grief score the poem's essence. In her foreword to Jane Caputi's *Gossips, Gorgons, and Crones: The Fates of the Earth* (1993), Allen explains the context of the poem, which concerns illnesses and death.

Allen once worked for the New Mexico Cancer Control Project, which dismissed discussion of such issues as radiation poisoning and toxic waste in favor of a more publicly acceptable antismoking campaign. Yet in 1976, Allen claimed, her home was using water in which "the level of lethal radiation-associated toxins" was life-threatening. Allen's mother contracted not only lupus and diverticulitis but also lung and heart diseases. Furthermore, Allen questioned whether her mother died of the diseases or the treatments of radiation and chemical therapy. Experiencing the poem with this knowledge adds an ironic dimension to the title "Dear World."

In the poem's first stanza, Allen presents her mother's point of view. Her mother sees lupus as a "self-attack"; she says that the disease is like calling the police when a mugger breaks into her home and then seeing the police attack the victim instead of the mugger. In the second and the third stanzas, Allen acknowledges the truth of her mother's perception before continuing in an ironic tone. Historical precedents, she writes, prove that Indians and Westerners cannot coexist harmoniously. Therefore, she sees it as logical that the different genetic compositions in her mother's blood—"its conflicting stains"—would obliterate each other.

The concluding fourteen lines of "Dear World" employ graphic sensory images to detail the disease's progression until "the crucible and its contents vaporize." The sadness, the devastating powerlessness, of watching a mother dying in incurable pain is exacerbated for the poet by her mother's inability to breathe. Breath to breath is how sacred energy flows in the poet's universe, and even that, in the end, is denied.

Self-alienation, the poet concludes, is an internalized battle between seemingly irreconcilable facets of a single sacred existence. Often, self-alienation is accompanied by other-alienation and isolation. The process, Allen says, is progressive and all-devouring unless a healing connection is reestablished and the imbalance is corrected.

THE SACRED HOOP

First published: 1986
Type of work: Essays

Seventeen literary and feminist essays provide contexts from which to evaluate tribal traditions and the tribal roles of American Indian women.

The Sacred Hoop: Recovering the Feminine in American Indian Traditions is a distinguished scholarly exposition of American Indian traditions with an emphasis upon women-centered tribal life. In Native American tradition, the Sacred Hoop, or Medicine Wheel, is the all-encompassing circle of universal life. The Spider Woman is the central figure who thought the universe into being and who continues to weave her web of existence. The first section, "The Ways of Our Grandmothers," deals with her many aspects in tribal myth, tradition, and ritual. The genocidal impact through the centuries of patriarchal colonization upon the gynocracies is detailed. Allen also dispels several popular misinterpretations of Native American behavior toward women. The last essay in the section is a personal account of the author's experiences as a Keres Laguna woman.

Oral tradition has been an integral factor in tribal survival, and the second section of *The Sacred Hoop* is titled "The Word Warriors." Both traditional and modern tribal literature is studied in terms of Native American culture; thought, structure, symbolism, style, ceremony, and authenticity are among the analytic considerations. Allen not only explicates the tribal perspective but also clarifies the problems inherent in approaching tribal literature from a Western bias.

The final section of *The Sacred Hoop*, "Pushing Up the Sky," concentrates upon modern American Indian women and the social issues (such as feminism, personal power, the female spiritual way, politics, lesbianism, and reformation of a gynocentric tribal structure) that affect them. "Pushing Up the Sky" is pro-female advocacy at its best. For women who lack a sense of continuity, community, self-esteem, or belonging, the essays in this section are healing words. For the self-alienated, *The Sacred Hoop* in its entirety offers the tools for survival.

SUMMARY

Allen is a powerful Native American author who writes with wisdom and passion. Her work has significantly increased both awareness of and understanding of American Indian literature. Two of Allen's key strengths are her mastery of her subject matter and the care with which she expresses her ideas, whether in fiction, poetry, or criticism. Although her earlier writings are at times uneven and obscure, her later writings have an undeniable sharpness of vision. Her body of work is evocative, potent, and life-affirming.

Kathleen Mills

BIBLIOGRAPHY

By the Author

POETRY:
The Blind Lion, 1974
Coyote's Daylight Trip, 1978
A Cannon Between My Knees, 1981
Star Child: Poems, 1981
Shadow Country, 1982
Wyrds, 1987
Skins and Bones, 1988
Life Is a Fatal Disease: Collected Poems, 1962-1995, 1997

LONG FICTION:
The Woman Who Owned the Shadows, 1983

NONFICTION:

The Sacred Hoop: Recovering the Feminine in American Indian Traditions, 1986

Grandmothers of the Light: A Medicine Woman's Source Book, 1991

As Long as the Rivers Flow: The Stories of Nine Native Americans, 1996 (with Patricia Clark Smith)

Off the Reservation: Reflections on Boundary-Busting, Border-Crossing Loose Canons, 1998

Pocahontas: Medicine Woman, Spy, Entrepreneur, Diplomat, 2003

EDITED TEXTS:

Spider Woman's Granddaughters: Traditional Tales and Contemporary Writing by Native American Women, 1989

Voice of the Turtle: American Indian Literature, 1900-1970, 1994

Hozho: Walking in Beauty, 2001 (with Carolyn Dunn Anderson)

About the Author

Ballinger, Franchot, and Brian Swann. "A MELUS Interview: Paula Gunn Allen." *MELUS* 10 (Summer, 1983): 3-25.

Bruchac, Joseph. *Survival This Way: Interviews with Native American Poets.* Tucson: University of Arizona Press, 1987.

Cook, Barbara. "The Feminist Journey in Paula Gunn Allen's *The Woman Who Owned the Shadows.*" *Southwestern American Literature* 22 (Spring, 1997): 69-74.

Cotelli, Laura, ed. *Winged Words: Native American Writers Speak.* Lincoln: University of Nebraska Press, 1990.

Ferrell, Tracy J. Prince. "Transformation, Myth, and Ritual in Paula Gunn Allen's *Grandmothers of the Light.*" *North Dakota Quarterly* 63 (Winter, 1996): 77-88.

Hanson, Elizabeth I. *Forever There: Race and Gender in Contemporary Native American Fiction.* New York: Peter Lang, 1989.

Jahner, Elaine. "A Laddered Rain-Bearing Rug: The Poetry of Paula Gunn Allen." In *Women and Western American Literature*, edited by Helen Winter Stauffer and Susan J. Rosowski. Troy, N.Y.: Whitson Press, 1982.

_____. "The Style of the Times in Paula Allen Gunn's Poetry." In *Speak to Me Words: Essays on Contemporary American Indian Poetry*, edited by Dean Rader and Janice Gould. Tucson: University of Arizona Press, 2003.

McDaniel, Cynthia. "Paula Gunn Allen: An Annotated Bibliography of Secondary Sources." *Studies in American Indian Literatures* 11 (Summer, 1999): 29-49.

Perry, Donna. "Paula Gunn Allen." In *Backtalk: Women Writers Speak Out*, edited by Donna Perry. New Brunswick, N.J.: Rutgers University Press, 1993.

Purdy, John. "'And Then, Twenty Years Later . . .': A Conversation with Paula Gunn Allen." *Studies in American Indian Literatures* 9 (Fall, 1997): 5-16.

Swann, Brian, and Arnold Krupat, eds. *I Tell You Now: Autobiographical Essays by Native American Writers.* Lincoln: University of Nebraska Press, 1987.

Toohey, Michelle Campbell. "Paula Allen Gunn's *Grandmothers of the Light*: Falling Through the Void." *Studies in American Indian Literatures* 12 (Fall, 2000): 35-51.

DISCUSSION TOPICS

- What role does Paula Gunn Allen's multi-ethnic background play in the subjects and themes of her works?

- Discuss how the theme of alienation plays a part in Allen's works.

- Discuss how a sense of American Indian tribal community is expressed in Allen's works.

- Allen has said that humor is essential to life. Show how she uses humor to convey her themes.

- How is environmentalism central to Allen's works?

- Explain how a poem or story by Allen is indicative of the American Indian perception of levels of reality.

- How does Allen show that ceremony is central to American Indian culture in *The Sacred Hoop*?

JULIA ALVAREZ

Born: New York, New York
March 27, 1950

Alvarez has earned an eminent position among contemporary minority writers for her depiction of the immigrant experience.

BIOGRAPHY

Julia Alvarez was born on March 27, 1950, in New York. Her family returned to the Dominican Republic, where Alvarez spent the first ten years of her life in comfort, surrounded by an extended family. Alvarez's grandfather, a cultural attaché to the United Nations, and her uncles, educated at Ivy League colleges, maintained their ties with the United States. Along with her sisters, Alvarez attended the American schools; in her words, she had an "American childhood" on the island.

From 1930 to 1961, the Dominican Republic was under the ruthless dictatorship of Rafael Leonidas Trujillo Molina, a tyrant who had maintained his hold on power by unprecedented repression. As Trujillo's thirst for absolute control bred further corruption, Alvarez's father became involved in anti-Trujillo activities. Alvarez's idyllic childhood came to an abrupt end when a plot to remove the dictator from power was unearthed. With the looming possibility of Dr. Alvarez's arrest, the family left for the United States.

Life in Queens, New York, offered a stark contrast to the family's earlier lifestyle. Her "American childhood" had not prepared the ten-year-old Julia for the realities of American life. She missed her friends and cousins and yearned to be accepted in school, but her accented English set her apart from others. In desperation, Alvarez turned to books

and eventually writing, which became a substitute for her island home and initiated her future career.

Alvarez and her sisters were educated in Catholic boarding schools. Alvarez attended Connecticut College initially. To keep the girls in touch with their culture, the parents sent them to spend their summers in the Dominican Republic. These stays made Alvarez aware of the double standard applied to the sexes and of the treatment of the poor, uneducated underclass. It was difficult for Alvarez to reconcile her American feminism with Dominican patriarchy, but it reinforced her decision to continue her college education. Winning the Benjamin T. Marshall Poetry Prize in 1968-1969 further encouraged her to pursue a literary career. She transferred to Middlebury College, Vermont, and in 1971 earned her B.A. summa cum laude. She earned her M.F.A. in 1975 from Syracuse University.

After serving as a poet-in-schools, teaching in schools, colleges, and universities, in 1988, Alvarez accepted a position at her alma mater, Middlebury College. Though she had published two collections of poetry in the 1980's, it was her first novel, *How the García Girls Lost Their Accents* (1991), that brought her critical acclaim. The book received the 1991 Josephine Miles Award from PEN Oakland for excellence in multicultural literature and was named a Notable Book by the American Library Association in 1992.

Alvarez had always been fascinated by the courage of the Marabel sisters, who were murdered for opposing the regime in Dominican Republic. Her second novel, *In the Time of the Butterflies* (1994), chronicles the lives of these four sisters. The book was a finalist for the National Book Critics Circle Award in 1995. Two more novels, *¡Yo!* (1997) and *In the Name of Salomé* (2000), followed. Three collections of poetry—*The Other Side/El otro lado* (1995), *Seven Trees* (1998), and *The Woman I Kept to Myself* (2004)—and a collection of essays, *Something to Declare* (1998), also came out during this period. Alvarez has also authored three books for children: *The Secret Footprints* (2000), *How Tía Lola Came to Stay* (2001), and *Before We Were Free* (2002).

To devote more time to her writing and pursuing her other interests, Alvarez gave up her tenured professorship in 1998 but maintains her connection with Middlebury College. She and her husband, Bill Eichner, an eye surgeon, are involved in many humanitarian activities.

ANALYSIS

Alienation and disorientation in a new country, complexities of family relationships, the place of women in Latino culture, and the politics of class and power in the Dominican Republic are dominant themes in Alvarez's works. Her personal experiences form the core of her creative endeavors in her poetry as well as fiction.

In her first novel, *How the García Girls Lost Their Accents*, Alvarez draws upon her own experiences to capture the turbulent lives of the García sisters as they navigate the years of adolescence in the new land. In the process, Alvarez touches upon several of her dominant themes. Speaking with an accent, the four girls—Carla, Sandi, Yolanda, and Sofia—are considered outsiders by their peers. Sometimes rejection comes in the garb of stereotyping, as Yolanda realizes in "The Rudy Elmenhurst Story."

To complicate matters, the parents impose the island code on their daughters. They hold firm that training the girls to be subservient to men and guarding their chastity is the right way of preparing them for life. All around, the mainstream American culture tempts the girls with the vision of freedom and romance. Disorientation, resulting from conflicting expectations, no doubt, accounts for the anorexia of Sandi, nervous breakdown of Yolanda, and the outright rebellion of Sofia.

The tyranny of parental authoritarianism can be seen in "Daughter of Invention." When Yolanda is assigned to give a speech on the Teacher's Day, she writes in her authentic voice, only to be told by her infuriated father that the speech was boastful and showed disrespect to teachers. He tears the pages to shreds. The incident remains a painful reminder to Yolanda of her powerlessness as a daughter.

Disorientation, however, is not the province of the young alone. The older generation is lost, too, in the new land. In the absence of the old familiar environment, common language, and clearly defined roles for men and women, the parents also falter in coping with unpredictable situations. In "Floor Show," at the family dinner with Dr. Fanning, the man responsible for helping the family emigrate, the father betrays his uncertainty and awkwardness in dealing with the inebriated Mrs. Fanning.

The macho culture in Dominican society encourages men to overlook one another's transgressions yet guard their women's purity zealously. This attitude is revealed in "A Regular Revolution." When Sofia is sent to live on the island with her relatives, she is transformed into a "Spanish-American Princess." She dresses like her fashion-conscious cousins and behaves like them in her relationship with a "nice" young man. Appalled by Sophie's subservience and her suitor's dictatorial manner, the sisters decide to rescue her by conspiring to get the lovers caught without a chaperone.

Alienation and complexity of family relationships lie at the heart of *¡Yo!*, a sequel to the first novel. The work has been a called "the portrait of an artist," for it focuses on Yolanda after the publication of her first novel. In addition to humorous episodes reflecting the family's reaction to becoming characters in her work, her preoccupation with class and power in Dominican Republic gets a fuller treatment here. Her denunciation of the continuing exploitation of the underclass in Dominican society scandalizes her family and friends. Interspersed among the chapters are the issues of cultural differences, the risks involved in pursuing a life of creative imagination, and the lure of the old world that stands in the way of true assimilation.

With *In the Time of the Butterflies* and *In the Name of Salomé*, Alvarez experiments with historical fiction. Both novels are set in the Dominican Republic. *In the Time of the Butterflies* memorializes the lives of the Marabel sisters, popularly known as *Las Mariposas* (the Butterflies). *In the Name of Salomé* celebrates the life of Salomé Urena, a well-known political poet in the Dominican Republic. She employs the technique of using Camila, the daughter and editor of her mother's papers, to present a panoramic view of political and moral issues of the period from the mid-1990's to the late twentieth century. The book allows Alvarez to explore political and social issues affecting the lives of women in the Caribbean region.

Alvarez's experimentation with plot and point of view in fiction often poses a problem for readers. *How the García Girls Lost Their Accents* seems more like a collage of interconnected episodes than a novel with a traditional plot. Alvarez's handling of chronology of events in *How the García Girls Lost Their Accents* and *In the Name of the Butterflies* is also challenging. However, Alvarez's later fictional works reveal more effective structures. She excels in the use of multiple points of view, an effective means of developing a complex character, though excessive shifts can sometimes overwhelm the readers.

The strength of Alvarez lies in her exploration of the themes of displacement and the painful process of cultural assimilation common to all immigrants. A widening of her sphere is discernible in the shift from personal to larger historical issues. She succeeds in engaging readers in the lives of her characters. Her historical novels, in particular, serve as excellent introductions to the cultural history of the Dominican Republic.

HOW THE GARCÍA GIRLS LOST THEIR ACCENTS

First published: 1991
Type of work: Novel

Conflict between cultures of homeland and the new country leaves its mark on each García girl.

How the García Girls Lost Their Accents, Alvarez's first novel, has an episodic plot covering a time span of thirty-three years, from 1956 to 1989, revolving around the García family—the parents and their four daughters, Carla, Sandi, Yolanda, and Sofia. Set against a backdrop of the political upheavals in the Dominican Republic and in the turbulent years of the 1960's in the United States, the narrative focuses on the struggles of the García family to make sense of the practices and expectations in the New World and reconcile them with the traditions they brought with them.

Arranged in three sections, the events are arranged in reverse chronological order. Beginning with the present, section 1 covers the present, 1989-1972; section 2 focuses on the events of ten years (1970-1960) following the family's arrival in the United States; and 3 on the period 1960-1956, prior to the family's escape. The narrative point of view shifts between objective third person and first person. Collectively, these stories chronicle the life of the García family just before and a decade after their move to America.

The book begins and ends with Yolanda, the compiler of these memories. Also, her experiences reflect typical difficulties faced in the process of assimilation. In "Joe," Yolanda is in a mental hospital recovering from a nervous breakdown after ending her latest relationship. As she reminisces, it becomes clear that her and her boyfriend's difference in temperament had caused their problems: John was a pragmatist, while she was a romantic idealist. He dealt with dry facts; she wanted to savor words. However, John attributed their differences to her ethnic background.

Similarly, Rudy ("The Rudy Elmenhurst Story"), the first love of Yolanda's life, expected her to be a passionate Latina. Circumscribed by her ethnicity in the States, she returns to the Dominican Republic to reclaim her heritage ("Antojos"). She observes at the outset that her mode of dressing, loving, and thinking is very different from that of the islanders. Finally, Yolanda's encounter with two farmworkers brings her to the realization that she is now more of an American than a Dominican and that the island has no easy solution to her identity crisis.

Yolanda has always desired to be a writer. "Daughter of Invention" describes the preparation of her first formal speech. In an effort to find her own voice, she emulates Walt Whitman's proud and distinctive tone. The resulting work is a remarkable accomplishment—so she thinks—until she hears the father's verdict that it is disrespectful, and he shreds the papers into pieces. Her mother picks up the pieces, literally and figuratively, and, putting an end to her own dreams, symbolically passes on the torch of creativity to Yolanda.

Yolanda's imaginative storytelling and her curiosity, tools of trade for a writer, are highlighted in "The Human Body." Coveting her cousin's gift of modeling clay from their grandmother, Yolanda is willing to trade anything, even show her private parts, to get the clay. When caught in a prohibited area, Yolanda saves her and her cousin from the wrath of elders by an imaginative but credible tale. Yolanda makes an appearance in "The Drum," the final selection. An incident depicting a typical childhood obsession ends up revealing Yolanda's artistic temperament and her preoccupation with the life of imagination.

Another theme—the failure to communicate or the inability to deal with an unanticipated situation—is a prime concern of many immigrants and is the subject of Carla's recollections in "Trespass" and "An American Surprise." When a stranger exposes himself to Carla on her way home from school, she cannot come up with appropriate words to communicate with a police officer. The humiliation caused by one's inability to share thoughts seems an insurmountable hurdle to the newcomer. "An American Surprise" refers to a toy bank that Sandi gives to Gladys, the maid, without her parents' knowledge. Her failure to communicate ends in Gladys's dismissal on a charge of theft. Sandi also recalls another incident, the dinner with their father's benefactor, whose wife's inappropriate actions in a state of drunkenness unnerved Sandi's father.

Sofia's rebellion is a direct outcome of her being caught between cultures. She is fiercely independent and leaves home, not an unusual act in America but an unforgivable act for an unmarried Dominican daughter. Years later, she is a happily married woman with two children ("The Kiss") when she finally realizes that she will never earn her father's forgiveness. "A Regular Revolution" returns to the year when Sofia was brainwashed during her stay with her relatives in the Dominican Republic; but for the "betrayal" by her sisters, she might have been trapped in the Dominican macho culture.

"The Four Girls" and "The Blood of the Conquistadores," narrated through the perspective of the mother and father, provide the missing links in the plot. The mother's observations about each of her daughters in "The Four Girls" are insightful, and the father's narrative recreates the terror he experienced before his escape from the island.

The worlds of the García sisters in the Dominican Republic and in the first decade of their stay in New York come alive in these memories and shed light on the process of acculturation.

IN THE TIME OF THE BUTTERFLIES

First published: 1994
Type of work: Novel

Three Dominican sisters sacrifice their lives for the cause of resisting the tyranny of the dictator Rafael Trujillo.

Alvarez had long desired to learn more about the Marabel sisters revered in the Dominican Republic. They were murdered in 1960, the same year that the Alvarez family fled to New York. *In the Time of the Butterflies*, based on historical facts, is an imaginative rendering of the incidents that transformed three ordinary women into unrelenting fighters against oppression.

The plot is neatly framed by the visit of an American journalist of Dominican origin to Dedé, the surviving sister. Dedé, accustomed to a stream of curious visitors to her little museum, wearily responds to the journalist's questions. In the process, the past memories are revived and form the plot of the book. Dedé becomes the principal narrator in the story. Finally "A Postscript" by the journalist brings the narrative full circle.

Structured in three parts, with four chapters in each section and an epilogue, the narrative covers the incidents from 1938 to 1960, the year Patria, Minerva, and Maria Teresa were brutally murdered. Each part begins with Dedé's point of view

and is followed by each sister's version of events. This technique provides smooth continuity of events and a deeper understanding of each sister's thinking.

The first section of the book provides an overview of the Marabel household. Each sister is clearly distinguished by her traits: Patria, the eldest, is deeply religious; Minerva, the intellectual, is the most outspoken; Dedé, the no-nonsense pragmatist, is the solid rock for the household; and the youngest, Maria Teresa (Mate), the idealistic romantic, is the most immature initially.

As the details of each sister's life are revealed, the reader learns of their goals and desires. They go through the normal vicissitudes of growing up. Patria had no interest in politics, yet when she sees innocent children being murdered, she plunges into the resistance movement. Minerva is the most vividly drawn character. Her intelligence, her courage to defy the dictator, and her leadership abilities convey her strengths. After her prison experience, she confesses her fears and insecurities hidden behind her cheerful appearance. Her vulnerability makes her a thoroughly credible character. Similarly, Mate initially reveals her immaturity in her diary entries; however, as her sisters engage in plotting against the regime, she, too, rises to the occasion. Her sustained silence about her torture shows how far she has come.

In the epilogue, dated 1994, Dedé provides an account of the last trip of her sisters to visit their imprisoned husbands, their murder presented officially as an accident, the assassination of Trujillo six months later, the trial of the sisters' murderers, the second coup to replace the elected president, a civil war and more killings, another dictatorship, and Dedé's incessant struggle to hold the remaining family together. Dedé may not have been active in the resistance, but her practical common sense and devotion to her sisters and their children make her sacrifice no less important.

Alvarez has presented a very loving portrait of all the sisters without any attempt at hagiography. They come across as normal, happy young women who were interested in developing their minds as well as spirits. They did not set out to change the world; they changed themselves in response to events. A remarkable feature of the work is that although the United States' role in sustaining dicta-torship on the Dominican Republic is no point of pride, Alvarez opts to stay away from this topic, thus producing an effective historical novel and not a political tract.

SUMMARY

Alvarez takes her writing seriously; for her it is an important, life-saving activity. When she began her career, there were few authors in English writing about the Latino experience; she was inspired by Maxine Hong Kingston's renowned book *The Woman Warrior* (1976). With her first successful novel, Alvarez opened the door for others who have enriched American literature with insights into the Hispanic world.

Initially focusing on the individual experience, Alvarez has gradually expanded her horizon. Her portrayal of the Dominican American world has a wide-ranging appeal. With her vivid and poetic language, she has captured the hearts and minds of her readers.

Leela Kapai

DISCUSSION TOPICS

- Which character or characters in *How the García Girls Lost Their Accents* are most vividly portrayed?

- Is it essential for immigrants to relinquish old traditions in order to seek the American Dream?

- How does Julia Alvarez's inversion of chronology affect the structure of the narrative in *How the García Girls Lost Their Accents*?

- In *In the Time of the Butterflies*, why does Dedé experience a sense of guilt after her three sisters were murdered? Is her guilt justified?

- Who among the four sisters in *In the Time of the Butterflies* can be considered the most courageous?

- Does Dedé's failure to participate in the resistance movement make her a coward?

BIBLIOGRAPHY

By the Author

POETRY:
Homecoming: Poems, 1984, revised and expanded 1996 (as *Homecoming: New and Collected Poems*, 1996)
The Other Side/El otro lado, 1995
Seven Trees, 1998
Cry Out: Poets Protest the War, 2003 (multiple authors)
The Woman I Kept to Myself, 2004

LONG FICTION:
How the García Girls Lost Their Accents, 1991
In the Time of the Butterflies, 1994
¡Yo!, 1997 (sequel to *How the García Girls Lost Their Accents*)
In the Name of Salomé, 2000
The Cafecito Story, 2001

NONFICTION:
Something to Declare, 1998

CHILDREN'S LITERATURE:
The Secret Footprints, 2000
How Tía Lola Came to Stay, 2001
Before We Were Free, 2002
Finding Miracles, 2004

EDITED TEXT:
Old Age Ain't for Sissies, 1979

About the Author

Alvarez, Julia. "On Finding a Latino Voice." In *The Writing Life: Writers on How They Think and How They Work*, edited by Maria Arana. New York: Public Affairs Press, 2003.
Echevarria, Roberto Gonzalez. "Sisters in Death." *The New York Times Book Review* (December 18, 1994): 28.
Rifkind, Donna. "Speaking American." *The New York Times Book Review* (October 6, 1991): 14.
Sirias, Silvio. *Julia Alvarez: A Critical Companion*. Westport, Conn.: Greenwood Press, 2001.
Stavans, Ilan. "Daughters of Invention." *The Commonweal* (April 10, 1992): 23-26.
_____. "Las Mariposa." *The Nation* 259, no. 15 (November 7, 1994): 552, 554-556.

RUDOLFO ANAYA

Born: Pastura, New Mexico
October 30, 1937

Since the critical and popular success of his 1972 coming-of-age novel Bless Me, Ultima, *Anaya has become one of the most acclaimed Chicano writers whose groundbreaking works blend myth, folklore, mysticism, and social realism.*

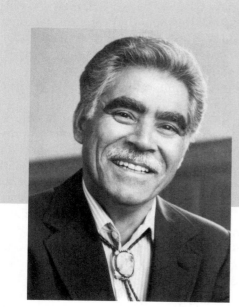

Michael Mouchette

BIOGRAPHY

Rudolfo Alfonso Anaya, son of Martin and Rafaelita Mares Anaya, was born on October 30, 1937, in Pastura, a small farming village in the eastern part of New Mexico. At sixteen, Anaya suffered a near-fatal spinal injury while diving into a shallow irrigation ditch, but he still managed to attend school in the neighboring town of Santa Rosa and ultimately, after his family relocated in 1952, in the barrios of Albuquerque. As a child, Anaya loved listening to the folktales, legends, and historic narratives of his grandparents. From 1956 to 1958, he attended the Browning Business School, but, finding the prospect of an accounting career unrewarding, he transferred to the University of New Mexico at Albuquerque, where he earned a B.A. in English in 1963. Within the university environment, Anaya first questioned his own cultural identity: a Latino for whom English was a second language suddenly surrounded by a culturally diverse community. He would later recall being disturbed by the absence of literature devoted to the Mexican American experience.

From 1963 until 1970, Anaya taught in the Albuquerque public schools but devoted his evenings to his own writing. During this time, he completed both an M.A. in English (1968) and an M.A. in guidance and counseling (1972) from the University of New Mexico. In 1971, he left the public

school system to become the director of counseling at the University of Albuquerque. He remained at this job for two years until the publication of his first novel.

His first novel, *Bless Me, Ultima,* was published in 1972 after considerable difficulty finding a publisher interested in a story that blended realism with mysticism, including a magic healer and a wicked witch. It tells the story of the relationship between Antonio, a young boy growing up in a small New Mexico village, and Ultima, his grandmother and spiritual guide, who helps him to understand his experiences. The book proved an enormous critical and commercial success and was translated into several languages. *Bless Me, Ultima* received the Premio Quinto Sol Award, Anaya's first national recognition and a forerunner of numerous later grants and fellowships. In 1974 on the strength of his new reputation, he was appointed an associate professor and in 1988 a full professor of English at the University of New Mexico. He remained on the faculty until 1993, when he retired to devote himself entirely to his writing. Shortly thereafter he was named professor emeritus.

His second novel, *Heart of Aztlán* (1976), was received much less enthusiastically. It portrays a year in the life of a Mexican family that moves from a small rural community to the barrio of Albuquerque. The family members respond very differently to the stresses of city life, and although Anaya uses some of the mystical, mythic elements of his earlier novel, the story relies heavily on traditional stereotypes.

His third novel, *Tortuga* (1979), won the Before Columbus Foundation American Book Award.

73

The book tells the story of a sixteen-year-old boy's initiation into knowledge during his recovery from a nearly fatal accident. Using traditional mythic symbolism, *Tortuga* continues in the mystical vein of the previous two novels. Indeed, they form something of a trilogy. Still Anaya struggled with the enormous burden of the success of his first novel—critical response did not find his follow-up works as rewarding.

With his emerging stature as the founding father of Chicano literature, Anaya began to experiment in other genres, including drama, children's books, short stories, epic poetry, travel journals, and even librettos for operas. Given his early love of stories told to him by his grandparents, Anaya was particularly drawn to children's books, introducing a generation of young readers to the legends and folktales of Mexican culture. His first foray into the field, a holiday tale called *The Farolitos of Christmas*, won the prestigious Tomas Rivera Mexican American Children's Book Award in 1987. He has since published more than a half dozen children's titles, each handsomely illustrated, including *Elegy on the Death of Cesar Chávez*, which lionizes the life of the Chicano activist who fought for civil rights for migrant farmworkers in California during the 1970's.

In addition to his writings, Anaya has tirelessly promoted Chicano literature, editing anthologies, translating works previously unavailable to an English-speaking audience, lecturing around the world, and writing reviews and essays for many magazines, both academic and nonacademic. He received National Endowment for the Arts fellowships in 1979 and 1980 and a Kellogg Foundation fellowship in 1983, as well as numerous regional and state awards.

Following his retirement from the University of New Mexico in the early 1990's, Anaya began his most ambitious writing project: a quartet of linked books set in New Mexico that, using the motif of the seasons, experimented with bringing together (audaciously) the grim realism of the murder mystery genre, the allegorical mysticism of folklore tales, and the stunning spectacle elements of Magical Realism. The results—*Alburquerque, Zia Summer, Rio Grande Fall,* and *Shaman Winter*—reestablished Anaya as the foremost Chicano writer of his generation. He received the 2001 Wallace Stegner Award, a lifetime achievement award for work devoted to

the American West. In April, 2002, Anaya was invited to the White House to receive the National Medal of the Arts from President George W. Bush.

ANALYSIS

With the 1972 publication of *Bless Me, Ultima*, Anaya became a popular writer and one of the most important voices in modern Chicano literature. In that novel, he succeeds in portraying the character of the Southwest's Mexican American people, with their myths, folklore, legends, and dreams. He also transcends these ethnic concerns so that the book appeals to many American readers. Because of the thematic universality of the coming-of-age story, its groundbreaking introduction of the Mexican-American experience, and its timeless allegorical vision of the struggle between good and evil, the novel has been widely read; in the age of canonical diversity, it continues to appear in the curricula of both colleges and high schools as a landmark work of Chicano fiction.

Since the publication of *Bless Me, Ultima*, Anaya has published works that similarly use ancient myth, the Mexican American heritage, and the conflicts caused by Mexican American attempts to fit into mainstream American society. Though each work presents a different story, his themes remain consistent. His central theme is, in the words of critic Antonio Marquez, that "life is sacred and the love of life is the greatest human achievement." To find the spiritual fulfillment necessary to see life as sacred requires understanding the harmony of all the forces in the universe. It is the search for this oneness and harmony that lies at the heart of much of Anaya's work.

Each work in the trilogy illustrates Anaya's concern with the search for personal spiritual harmony. In *Bless Me, Ultima*, Antonio finds self-knowledge and insight as a result of his relationship with his spiritual guide, Ultima. She provides him with the stability he needs as he proceeds through life, exploring intellectual and emotional situations. In *Heart of Aztlán*, a family searches for the answers posed by changes brought about by their move from a rural community to the barrio of Albuquerque. At the novel's end, the main character, Clemente, finds self-knowledge and begins to help other people who are not so fortunate. The last book in the trilogy, *Tortuga*, which Anaya patterned after a mythic journey, tells of a sixteen-year-old boy, nicknamed Tortuga (or "The Turtle" because of a body cast he must wear), who finds enlightenment during the desperately difficult time he spends recovering from a near-fatal accident.

To portray these themes, Anaya relies on mythopoetics, the art of mythmaking. He fuses mythic poetic images with images from his own childhood (from both the native traditions but as well from his schooling in Catholicism) and from the New Mexican landscape to connect the past and present so that the result is a completely new myth. Mythopoetics as an important element in understanding human nature is a belief Anaya shares with Carl Jung and other psychologists. In fact, Anaya's belief that all people share a collective memory of a time when there was more harmony in the universe is very similar to Jung's idea of the collective unconscious. Both Jung and Anaya have expressed the belief that people can make sense out of the fragmentation of the modern world through the use of certain archetypal symbols and images. Anaya works with many images and symbols: the turtle with its shell, representing alienation and a loss of faith; spiritual guides who lead the way to wisdom; and dreams that illuminate the past and foretell the future.

Dreams that reveal the collective unconscious and the path to self-knowledge appear frequently in Anaya's work. In *Bless Me, Ultima*, the boy Antonio gains wisdom from dreams that illustrate a tolerant attitude toward his father and from other dreams that help him to understand the troubled events of youth. In such short stories as "Iliana of the Pleasure Dreams," the dream symbolizes the harmony necessary for personal and spiritual fulfillment.

To integrate this material into his plots, Anaya frequently uses a favorite device, the epiphany, a moment when all things come together to reveal a truth. In *Heart of Aztlán*, the boy Clemente, in a moment of truth, can feel the rhythm of an ancient beat echoed in his own heartbeat. He can connect the dreams he has had with the reality around him. Doing this releases power into his life, and he can function because he understands. This synthesis of memory, dreams, and reality works best when the story is told in the first-person voice, as in *Bless Me, Ultima*. Even though it sometimes appears that the book's narrator is not mature enough to have such insights, the epiphanies succeed because the book

is a flashback told from an adult perspective. This moment of earned insight is a signature of Anaya's work, despite critical carping. At the end of Anaya's stories and novels, the characters find enlightenment and personal harmony as the result of their long searches. No alienation, irony, or uncertainty appears.

In the four books that make up the Albuquerque quartet, the defining literary achievement of his later career, Anaya treats contemporary sociopolitical issues that he had previously not addressed directly in his fiction through, improbably enough, the vehicle of the mystery/detective genre. The works are linked by the dramatic evolution of central character Sonny Braca, a contemporary Chicano detective whose ancestor is the flamboyant legendary nineteenth century law-and-order sheriff Elfego Baca. The novels parallels Sonny's difficult quest to define his identity—he is, he comes to discover, a powerful shaman—with the intricate (and absorbing) process involved in the solution of a crime. In addition to examining nearly four hundred years of cultural and historic evolution in New Mexico, the four novels treat contemporary issues, including Western environmentalism and irresponsible development (particularly the hot-button issue of where to bury nuclear waste), the drug crisis, the dilemma of urban decay, the corruption at the heart of the political process, the sorry state of public education, and the problematic future of cultural diversity. For all their contemporary feel, the works continued to introduce the supernatural: mythic elements, dream sequences, allegorical characters, and a profound spiritualism that draws on a cosmic conception of the universe as a battleground between good and evil.

In *Zia Summer*, for instance, the gruesome ritualistic murder of Sonny's cousin—her body is drained of blood and cut with ancient Pueblo Indian symbols—leads Sonny into a radical antinuclear activist underworld bent on blowing up a truck loaded with nuclear waste in order to demonstrate the dangers of its proposed burial. The fanatics are led by a charismatic activist known as Raven who will become Sonny's antagonist throughout the quartet. He is, befitting Anaya's cosmic dimension, a *brujo*, or sorcerer, a powerful entity bent on chaos and destruction and able to assume animal shapes. In *Rio Grande Fall*, the battle between Sonny and Raven escalates, as does the quartet's mystical component. Sonny seeks the help of a spiritual guide, a healer who helps him understand his progressively denser visions. In this volume, Sonny must contend with a Latin American cartel of drug smugglers (they kidnap his girlfriend), and to combat them he begins to tap into his own primitive spiritual identity, the spirit of the coyote with its cunning and its instinct for survival. He closes the novel grievously wounded after a pitched confrontation with Raven. However, in the final volume, *Shaman Winter*, the most dramatically mystical in the series—it takes place, in large part, in Sonny's dreams—he ultimately recovers his spiritual wholeness and his considerable powers as a shaman.

In the quartet, Anaya continued to foreground his longstanding concerns about cultural identity and the role of the past in both shaping the sense of self and determining where that self ultimately belongs in a contemporary multicultural world. These are not easy questions. In introducing the Chicano experience into mainstream American fiction, Anaya, in a prolific career that has spanned more than four decades, reveals the conflicts, contradictions, and concerns of Mexican American culture with uplifting narratives in which (as in the traditional folktales that he loved as a child) the self withstands its most difficult challenges and the forces of good triumph over evil.

"ILIANA OF THE PLEASURE DREAMS"

First published: 1989
Type of work: Short story

A spiritual experience reconciles a young woman's dreams and reality and awakens her to the fullness of her life.

"Iliana of the Pleasure Dreams" is the last story in *Tierra: Contemporary Short Fiction of New Mexico* (1989), a book edited by Anaya that also contains stories by writers such as Tony Hillerman, Ed Chavez, and Patricia Clark Smith. The story illustrates Anaya's methods in his short works. In the preface, he tells about the *tierra*, the land, of New Mexico, which is "an ingredient which dictates the natural pace of the stories in this collection" and

"nourishes our creativity." The story of a beautiful, newly married young woman, Iliana, is set in a rural mountain valley. Anaya combines realistic details of the land with the details of Iliana's dream to tell an initiation story that ends with people in harmony with the earth and themselves.

One summer night, Iliana awakens from a dream in which she is running across a field of alfalfa toward a beautiful young man. The dream is very real, and she quietly moves toward the window to contemplate its meaning while looking at the night landscape. Anaya describes this scene so that the details of the breeze and the crickets in the landscape mesh with the dream. Iliana thinks of her early life with her strict religious aunts, her timidity with her shy, silent husband, and her uneasiness about the pleasure that was so real in her dream. She recalls her intention to confess her dream to the priest, but on the way to the church, trees seem to overwhelm her like the arms of men. The landscape is the connection between the dream life and the real world.

The next day, Iliana and her husband, Onofre, go to the church to see a miracle, the face of Christ, which reportedly has appeared on the wall. As the young couple drives to the church, Anaya again describes the earth and the landscape. Iliana is excited and surrenders herself to the mood of tense expectation. She smells the damp, rich earth and remembers the horse she used to ride.

Iliana goes with her aunts to pray, remembering the pleasure of her dream as she kneels. Anaya describes the images again. The smells of the mountains, the prayers of the women—all are entangled. As Iliana prays to see the image on the wall, her dream image appears, and she sees not Christ but the man of her dreams. She is overwhelmed, and as she faints, she visualizes the rolling clouds, the red color of the earth, and the man.

When she awakes, it has grown cooler and darker, and Iliana wonders about what she saw, whether it was the devil tempting her or the answer to the dream. She cannot find Onofre right away and runs into a field of fragrant purple alfalfa, almost like her dream. This time, she sees the man in the field; it is her husband. Both confess that they did not see the face of Christ on the wall, but both have realized the meaning of their separate dreams. As they stand together, they speak of the dreams and the need to share them. They understand the meaning of dreams and go home, to new awakenings for each other and to their life connected to the land.

All through the story, the colors, shapes, and textures of the landscape blend into the texture of Iliana's life. The future relationship of the two young people will harmonize with that landscape, because the land nourishes the human spirit. By synthesizing the details of dream and reality, Anaya successfully communicates this creative energy throughout the story.

THE LEGEND OF LA LLORONA

First published: 1984
Type of work: Novella

A reimagining of the life of the legendary Doña Marina, known as La Malinche, who was interpreter and then lover of Spanish conquistador Hernán Cortés.

The Legend of La Llorona, part of Anaya's shift in the 1980's away from longer narrative to more restricted genres such as poetry, drama, children's stories, and short fiction, appropriates the story of one of Mexico's most reviled historic figures. In a slender narrative (barely seventy pages), Anaya examines the pre-Colombian culture at the very moment that marked its eventual extinction: the invasion by European conquistadores, from their arrival in 1519 to their entrance in November, 1521, into Tenochtitlán. In focusing on Malinche, the beautiful Aztec woman whose felicity with languages enabled her to serve as interpreter for the Spaniards, Anaya investigates thorny issues of assimilation and cooperation, specifically the massive influence of a brutalizing Anglo culture that simply dismissed an empire that had existed in Central America long before the conquistadores "discovered" it.

In Anaya's retelling, however, Malinche is no caricature villain. She is more than her culture's Eve-figure, deserving of the nearly five hundred years of contempt that she has received at the hands of both historians and folklorists who see in her cooperation with the marauding Cortés the unforgivable act of cultural betrayal. Rather Malinche is in part a victim of oppressive Aztec social customs: Despite her beauty and her intelligence, she is sold in the slave trade after the birth of a brother, who enjoys family favor only by virtue of his gender; Malinche is subsequently simply given to the Europeans at Tabasco. Adept at native languages, she quickly masters Spanish and serves first as translator but, ultimately, becomes Cortes's mistress, bearing him a son in 1522. When Cortés summons his own wife from Spain, however, Malinche and her son are no longer welcome. She is abandoned. Indeed, her son will later be killed while taking part in a doomed insurgency.

Dispensing with traditional historic investigation for a symbolic interpretation, Anaya recasts Malinche as tragic victim by fusing her story with that of the Mexican folklore figure of La Llorona (the crier). Although many versions of the story exist in Hispanic tradition, the general outline is consistent: A proud, beautiful woman seduced and then abandoned by a wealthy, dashing ranchero is driven to drown the children she had conceived with him. Immediately riven by inconsolable guilt, the woman runs along the river crying for her lost children. She is found dead by the river the next day. Generations of Hispanic children have been cautioned not too wander too far from home on the night of a full moon, as La Llorona still haunts the world looking for children to take. Interestingly, more than a decade after *The Legend of La Llorona*, Anaya published a children's version of the tale that softens this a bit—the woman does not kill her children but rather loses them to a sinister allegorical figure, Señor Tiempo, or Time.

In asserting Malinche as the historic prototype for the Weeping Woman, Anaya moves beyond the two traditional readings of the woman: on one hand, the long-held view of her as reviled figure whose name has become in Hispanic culture a slang term for prostitute and, on the other, the contemporary feminist reading of her as an empowered female undone by male duplicity. Rather Anaya sees Malinche with a poetic eye, allowing her as character to suggest a symbolic level, suspended between simplistic interpretations and left ambiguous, both victim and victimizer, a complex precursor of Anaya's own generation's struggle with the dilemma of accommodation and the profound sorrow over lost cultural identity.

BLESS ME, ULTIMA

First published: 1972
Type of work: Novel

Helped by the spiritual guidance of his grandmother, a young Mexican American boy endures the struggles of growing up.

Bless Me, Ultima, the book that established Anaya as an important writer, is often considered his best work. The novel tells the story of three years in the life of Antonio Marez, a young Mexican American boy living in the small New Mexico farm village of Guadalupe around the time of World War II. During these years, Antonio experiences tragedies and struggles. He emerges as a more mature person because of his relationship with his grandmother and spiritual guide, Ultima.

In exploring this relationship, Anaya uses a large variety of interesting materials and techniques. He interweaves legendary and mythic details into realistic descriptions of the New Mexican landscape to create a rich picture of the lifestyle of the characters. He tells the story from the point of view of the narrator, the boy Antonio, but endows him with insights too mature for a young person, thus creating a multiple point of view for the events. Moreover, Anaya frequently incorporates dreams into the story. The plot consists of the struggles Anaya considers the important ones in life, those concerning loss of faith and family problems. It examines Anaya's favorite theme: that harmony and reconciliation are necessary for self-knowledge and spiritual fulfillment.

Antonio's parents welcome Ultima, a *curandera* (spiritual guide), into their family in the first chapter. This begins Antonio's awareness of the passage of time. He comments that the time of childhood seemed to stand still. In the middle of the chapter, Anaya uses the boy's dream to accentuate the element of time as well as to introduce the conflict between his mother's desire for a stable life and his father's desire to keep the old ways of the *vaquero,* the traditional Mexican life for a man.

It is Ultima who helps Antonio through the family struggle between these two philosophies, as well as through his problems with his three brothers and two sisters and through the other conflicts in the book. Antonio excels in school and socially; however, he has problems with his relationship to the Church, because he cannot reconcile its spiritual teachings with the bureaucracy and artifice connected to it. He also experiences four deaths, including the drowning of a close friend. Through all these struggles, Ultima provides stability by satisfying Antonio's emotional and intellectual needs, thus enabling him to grow spiritually as well.

The story ends with Ultima's death. The book describes only three years in Antonio's life, but at the end, he is a different person.

To add dimension to Antonio's character, Anaya frequently includes dreams made up of legendary and mythic materials. Dreams influence his outlook and conduct. For example, dreams in which battles of mythic proportion appear often lead into real arguments with his parents. A complex nightmare involving ancient rituals and symbols of horror enables him to understand the real events of a friend's murder. At the end, when events affirm Antonio's growth and development, the dreams become a quieting, healing experience, paralleling the influence of Ultima upon him.

Even though the boy is only eight years old at the novel's end, the process and themes Anaya deals with are universal. The structure of the narration and the mingling of dream, legend, and reality make the work interesting. Anaya's vision of balance and wholeness and his ability to synthesize details from many sources to create myths make *Bless Me Ultima* an important work.

HEART OF AZTLÁN

First published: 1976
Type of work: Novel

Members of a Mexican American family react differently in confronting the problems they encounter when they move from a rural farming community to a barrio in a large city.

Heart of Aztlán is the second novel in a trilogy begun with *Bless Me, Ultima* and concluded with *Tortuga.* Each of the novels involves a seer, a spiritual guide to help the characters deal with the problems they face and to help structure the spiritual wholeness, peace, and harmony that bring them understanding of their identity and purpose. In *Heart of Aztlán*, this spiritual guide is Crispin, a blind poet who enters the life of the Chavez family as they encounter the hostile environment of the Albuquerque barrio.

The story takes place in 1950, when the family moves from the small rural community of Guadalupe to the barrio of the big city. There they encounter many problems, and each faces these differently. The family's eldest son manages to find work, but the youngest son becomes a drug addict and is eventually killed. The middle son, like his father, reveres the land they have left and cannot make the adjustment to new surroundings. Because his father becomes an alcoholic, the middle son must take over the leadership of the family. The women, who are portrayed stereotypically, face equal hardships. Two daughters become prostitutes, and the mother must take orders from her middle son. This is the family situation when Crispin enters.

Crispin's arrival brings changes, especially to the father, Clemente, who has not been able to cope with the technology, religion, or capitalism of the city. Crispin helps him to find the spiritual strength to see things clearly. Eventually, Clemente becomes a barrio leader. Anaya is working with social and

political issues in this novel, and he leaves many parts of the story line confused as he makes a statement about the exploitation of human beings.

The end of the novel is intended to be uplifting but has been seen as, rather, confusing and unsatisfying. The people, along with Clemente, "shout without fear." Even though they are not afraid, they have not succeeded in achieving the spiritual wholeness suggested by the appearance of the seer Crispin. Anaya uses a mixture of dreams and symbols to suggest such events as the death of the youngest boy, Benjie, and their place in the universe. As a whole, however, these also do not fit together.

Anaya himself said that his novel was an experiment in combining elements from myth with socioeconomic themes from barrio life. The resulting novel covers too much too simplistically. Even though *Heart of Aztlán* gives a picture of conditions facing Mexican Americans in the 1950's, Anaya was clearly not comfortable treating contemporary issues so directly.

ALBURQUERQUE

First published: 1992
Type of work: Novel

A twentyish boxer struggles to find his biological family amid a hotly contested mayoral election that will decide the future development of Albuquerque, New Mexico.

In *Alburquerque*, Anaya uses the old name for the city, arbitrarily changed, according to tradition, by a nineteenth century English-speaking train stationmaster in a move that Anaya sees as indicative of cultural intolerance. A former Golden Gloves boxing champion and now a first-year student at the University of New Mexico, Abrán González, is inexplicably summoned to the deathbed of renowned local painter Cynthia Johnson. She tells him that she, a wealthy Anglo, is in fact his biological mother. She dies, however, before revealing the name of González's father, only that he was Mexican. González must suddenly confront radical questions of his mixed identity—in the barrios, he had always been proud of his Mexican heritage.

With the help of his mother's nurse, the saintly Lucinda, he resolves to track down his father.

To help in his efforts, González agrees to return to the ring in a glitzy promotional fight designed to promote the mayoral campaign of the wealthy and influential Frank Dominic, who cagily promises to use his considerable influence to help González find his father. Dominic quickly emerges as a shady politico without any authentic cultural identity and loyal only to soulless materialism and ruthless self-promotion. The defining issue in the upcoming vote centers on delicate negotiations with the Pueblo Indians for their land (and specifically their access to water) as part of Dominic's grandiose plans for urban development. Inadvertently enmeshed in the divisive campaign, González comes under the spell of the current mayor (a sexually intriguing divorcée) and makes a single disastrous decision to spend the night with her. When González later agrees to visit Lucinda's parents in the mountains north of the city, Dominic, furious that the boxer is reneging on their deal, informs Lucinda of that sexual liaison. Lucinda, in love with González, is crushed and leaves him.

When a friend of González notices that a figure in one of Cynthia Johnson's paintings looks remarkably like one of his professors, he comes to discover that the professor, Ben Chávez, a successful teacher and writer, is in fact González's father. Years earlier, the professor, a poor kid from the barrio, had fallen in love with Cynthia. Her father, a country-club aspirant, had forbidden the relationship and thus Chávez had never known about the birth of their son and how Cynthia had been compelled to put him up for adoption.

González's friend and Lucinda, who has found her way to forgiveness, rush to the convention center the night of the exhibition fight to tell González about his father and thus prevent the big fight—they fear that Gonzàlez is far from his fighting prime. Indeed, when they arrive, González is taking a terrible beating. Inspired by finally meeting his father and by the generous forgiveness of Lucinda, however, he wins the fight. His new celebrity effectively ends Frank Dominic's shallow vision of modernization and returns the city to a celebration of its cultural roots.

Clearly, Anaya investigates questions of cultural identity by exploring those who struggle to conceal their ethnic makeup, those who have lost touch with their cultural heritage, and those who find the narrowest ethnic identity sufficient. Using the political story of Albuquerque's own identity crisis as an allegory for González's struggle with the new dimensions of his ethnic identity, Anaya reveals how the future belongs, ironically, to those willing to connect with the vanishing past. Abrán González—part fighter, part painter, part teacher—whose cultural identity draws from the rich reservoirs of both Jewish and Mexican traditions, becomes a sort of inspirational prototype of the future, the embodiment (literally) of racial cooperation and harmony.

SHAMAN WINTER

First published: 1999
Type of work: Novel

A detective confronts difficult issues of his cultural ancestry while attempting to find the kidnapped daughter of the mayor of Albuquerque.

Shaman Winter, the fourth volume in Anaya's Albuquerque quartet, represents the series' most experimental exploration of the intricate link that Anaya sees between sleuthing and discovering cultural and ethnic identity in a multicultural contemporary world.

As in the other volumes in the quartet, *Shaman Winter* centers on the confrontation between Sonny Braca, a heroic detective, and his nemesis Raven, an evil cult leader of radical environmental activists, a charismatic chameleon-like power broker who, with fanatic commitment, leads antinuclear protests in terroristic acts of mayhem to promote their agenda. He presents an imposing challenge to Braca: Articulate and intelligent, championing the defense of the New Mexico landscape (although through nefarious means), he is also a *brujo,* or shaman, able to assume the shape of a raven at will.

In this closing volume, however, the confrontation between the two characters turns decidedly metaphysical (to the dismay of many critics of the book who see the metaphysical elements as heavy-handed and didactic). There is a conventional thriller plot: The mayor's teenage daughter is kidnapped by white supremacists under the direction of Raven (four raven feathers are found on her pillow). Yet Anaya develops much of this narrative within the dreamworld of Sonny, who has been hospitalized from his showdown with Raven in *Río Grande Fall* and is now wheelchair-bound. Sonny is haunted by strange dreams that send him into a richly symbolic landscape of an ancient New Mexico, where he encounters both mythic characters of traditional folklore as well as a steady succession of historic figures who represent the incursion of the European settlers, from the arrival of the conquistadores to the establishment of the Anglo government in the mid-nineteenth century and the relocation of the indigenous peoples onto controlled reservations. Raven, who comes to assume the full potent powers of a mythic sorcerer-figure, determines that, to destroy his archenemy once and for all, he will enter Sonny's dreams and there destroy Sonny's ancestors, thus effectively removing Sonny from history. It is a provocative premise.

Sonny is led through the world of spirits by a wisdom-figure named Don Eliseo, who directs Sonny toward the realization that he descends from the union of an Anglo and a hauntingly beautiful native woman, herself the daughter of a shaman who comes to be threatened by Raven. Amid that complex narrative of capture and pursuit, Sonny accepts the reality of his mixed heritage, indeed affirming that cultural identity itself must transcend the stubbornly persistent boundaries of nationality and race. As such a multicultural figure, Sonny embodies what Anaya sees as a cosmic—rather than culture-bound—race. Sonny emerges as a figure of genesis and creation, while Raven serves as the embodiment of death and destruction. By the close of the novel, the wounded Sonny has recovered not only physically but spiritually as well and has emerged from the dense darkness of the metaphoric winter to the promise of becoming a shaman in his own right.

In the pitched mystical battle between Sonny and Raven (their names indicating their allegorical positioning), Anaya does more than recite the familiar grievances of indigenous peoples against the incursion of English-speaking cultures. Anaya opts for a far broader philosophical speculation on race and cultural identity itself through the metaphor of kidnapping as a vehicle for exploring the loss and recovery of identity. Using powerful symbols and allegorical figures drawn from Latino culture, Anaya affirms that the necessity of discovering historic heritage and cultural identity serves as a premise for ultimately transcending the limits of such identities to embrace a wider cosmic sensibility.

SUMMARY

Since the publication of his first work, *Bless Me, Ultima*, Rudolfo Anaya has brought into America's mainstream literary discussion the complex identity crisis facing the contemporary Mexican American. Anaya defined that spiritual and moral crisis in terms that see the Chicano experience in a much larger frame of reference, making the Chicano quest for identity and spiritual fulfillment a larger, twentieth century dilemma. Drawing on his background in Catholicism and his upbringing listening to the fabulous tales of his Spanish ancestry, Anaya melded elements of social realism, folklore, myth, and the supernatural that, in turn, pioneered an audaciously experimental kind of narrative that freely mingled the realistic and the magical.

Louise M. Stone; updated by Joseph Dewey

BIBLIOGRAPHY

By the Author

LONG FICTION:
Bless Me, Ultima, 1972
Heart of Aztlán, 1976
Tortuga, 1979
The Legend of La Llorona, 1984
Lord of the Dawn: The Legend of Quetzalcóatl, 1987
Alburquerque, 1992

Zia Summer, 1995
Jalamanta: A Message from the Desert, 1996
Rio Grande Fall, 1996
Shaman Winter, 1999
Serafina's Stories, 2004

SHORT FICTION:
The Silence of the Llano, 1982

DRAMA:
The Season of La Llorona, pr. 1979
Who Killed Don José?, pr. 1987
Billy the Kid, pb. 1995

SCREENPLAY:
Bilingualism: Promise for Tomorrow, 1976

POETRY:
The Adventures of Juan Chicaspatas, 1985 (epic poem)
Elegy on the Death of Cesar Chávez, 2000 (juvenile)

NONFICTION:
A Chicano in China, 1986
Conversations with Rudolfo Anaya, 1998

CHILDREN'S LITERATURE:
The Farolitos of Christmas: A New Mexico Christmas Story, 1987, 1995 (illustrated edition)
Maya's Children: The Story of La Llorona, 1997
Farolitos for Abuelo, 1998
My Land Sings: Stories from the Rio Grande, 1999
Roadrunner's Dance, 2000
The Santero's Miracle: A Bilingual Story, 2004 (illustrated by Amy Cordova; Spanish translation by Enrique Lamadrid)

EDITED TEXTS:
Voices from the Rio Grande, 1976
Cuentos Chicanos: A Short Story Anthology, 1980 (with Antonio Márquez)
A Ceremony of Brotherhood, 1680-1980, 1981 (with Simon Ortiz)
Voces: An Anthology of Nuevo Mexicano Writers, 1987
Aztlán: Essays on the Chicano Homeland, 1989
Tierra: Contemporary Short Fiction of New Mexico, 1989

MISCELLANEOUS:
The Anaya Reader, 1995

DISCUSSION TOPICS

- How do the magical elements in Rudolfo Anaya's fiction—visions, dreams, paranormal phenomena, allegorical characters—contribute to his themes? Do they help or hurt his fiction?

- Anaya's work is clearly interested in the relationship between personal identity and culture. What does Anaya see as the relationship between the individual and the individual's cultural and ethnic community?

- Frequently Anaya's characters set off on quests, most often a metaphor for spiritual searching. For what do Anaya's characters search?

- How is Anaya's vision of the contemporary spiritual crisis, the drift into materialism and selfishness, influenced by his own upbringing in and later abandonment of Catholicism? In what way is Anaya a religious writer?

- What does Anaya suggest about the role of the contemporary ethnic writer when it comes to questions of cultural and community identity?

- Anaya is known for uplifting, affirmative endings. Do you find his endings convincing? Are they intended to be realistic or inspirational?

- Anaya's fiction shows a deep and profound love of the land. How does Anaya react to the late twentieth century disregard for the sacramental holiness of the earth?

- Trace the influence of and evidence of Anaya's love of the tradition of oral storytelling.

About the Author

Augenbraum, Harold, and Margarite Fernández Olmos, eds. *The Latino Reader: An American Literary Tradition from 1542 to the Present.* Boston: Houghton Mifflin, 1997.
Bruce-Novoa, Juan. *Retrospace: Collected Essays on Chicano Literature.* Houston: Arte Publico Press, 1990.

_____. "Rudolfo A. Anaya." In *Chicano Authors: Inquiry by Interview.* Austin: University of Texas Press, 1980.

Candelaria, Cordelia. "Rudolfo Alfonso Anaya (1937-   )." In *Chicano Literature: A Reference Guide,* edited by Julio A. Martínez and Francisco A. Lomelí. Westport, Conn.: Greenwood Press, 1985.

Dick, Bruce, and Silvio Sirias, eds. *Conversations with Rudolfo Anaya.* Jackson: University Press of Mississippi, 1997.

González-Trujillo, César, ed. *Rudolfo A. Anaya: Focus on Criticism.* La Jolla, Calif.: Lalo Press, 1990.

Olmos, Margarite Fernández. *Rudolfo A. Anaya: A Critical Companion.* Westport, Conn.: Greenwood Press, 1999.

Taylor, Paul Beekman. "Chicano Secrecy in the Fiction of Rudolfo A. Anaya." *Journal of the Southwest* 39, no. 2 (1997): 239-265.

Vassallo, Paul, ed. *The Magic of Words: Rudolfo A. Anaya and His Writings.* Albuquerque: University of New Mexico Press, 1982.

SHERWOOD ANDERSON

Born: Camden, Ohio
    September 13, 1876
Died: Colón, Panama Canal Zone
    March 8, 1941

Though he wrote novels, autobiographies, and poems, Anderson is valued principally as a writer of short stories that penetrate the surface of undistinguished small-town characters unfulfilled in a materialistic society.

Library of Congress

BIOGRAPHY

Sherwood Anderson was born in Camden, Ohio, a small town near Dayton, on September 13, 1876; he was the third of seven children of Emma and Irvin Anderson. His mother was of Italian descent. His father was a sign painter who was far from being an economic success but who had been a cavalryman in the Union army during the Civil War, where his training as a harness maker was particularly valuable. Gradually the local, independent saddlery was superseded by the harness factories, and craftsmen such as Irvin Anderson became redundant and impoverished. Emma Anderson took in laundry to supplement the family income. The social and economic circumstances of his parents clearly influenced Sherwood's later thinking and his choice of themes for his stories. In 1884, the Anderson family moved from Camden to Clyde, Ohio, near the Lake Erie city of Cleveland, which is frequently mentioned in *Winesburg, Ohio* (1919).

For a time after 1896, Anderson worked in a Chicago warehouse before enlisting for service in the Spanish-American War, from which he was discharged with the rank of corporal. Thereafter, he enrolled in Wittenburg Academy at Springfield, Ohio, and graduated in June, 1900, becoming an advertising salesman and copywriter in Chicago. In 1904, he married Cornelia Lane, the first of the four wives whom, as he said, he tried "blunderingly

to love." During those years he became a professional success, writing what he called "rather senseless advertisements," but he was spiritually unsatisfied. Accordingly, he moved to Elyria, a small town on the periphery of Cleveland, and in 1906 founded the Anderson Manufacturing Company, which produced paint.

For a dozen years Anderson was rather successful economically, and he took satisfaction in his family; however, his success was not wholly fulfilling, and he engaged in extramarital affairs, overindulged in alcohol, and started writing a novel. One day he left his office, was found walking the streets of Cleveland, and was hospitalized for a mental breakdown. Upon his release he returned to Chicago to join the band of writers (including Ben Hecht, Floyd Dell, Theodore Dreiser, and Carl Sandburg) who were the leading spirits within the Chicago Renaissance.

Anderson showed the novel on which he had been working before his breakdown to his new acquaintances in Chicago. They recommended it for publication, and *Windy McPherson's Son* (1916), largely autobiographical, offered many indications of the nature of Anderson's subsequent writing, though it cannot be regarded as a major work of fiction. The character Windy McPherson is a thinly veiled portrait of Anderson's father; his son, Sam, gropes with the loneliness and oppressiveness of a small town (Caxton, Iowa) and tries to kill his father. He goes to Chicago, becomes successful, and marries advantageously—only to renounce the world of business and financial security in an endeavor to "find truth." In many ways the early episode imitates Huckleberry Finn's supposed killing of his father, Pap, which impels Huck's Mississippi River odyssey in Mark Twain's *Adventures of Huckleberry Finn* (1884), but the rest of the story, with its exploration of loneliness and aspiration, success and withdrawal, previews the very essence of *Winesburg, Ohio.*

In the same year, 1916, Anderson divorced Lane and married Tennessee Mitchell. Then, in 1917, he published *Marching Men,* a novel set in the central Pennsylvania coal mining region that highlighted the failure of a movement to organize the miners against the oppressiveness of cheerless, stultifying routine. In *Mid-American Chants* (1918), Anderson attempted his hand at poetry but with slight success. His models were *Spoon River Anthology* (1915), by Edgar Lee Masters, and the verse of Carl Sandburg, Vachel Lindsay, and Gertrude Stein. It was in the following year, 1919, that he first gained widespread recognition with the publication of *Winesburg, Ohio,* a series of frequently interconnected stories treating the unfulfilled potential, the unsatisfied craving for sexual satisfaction, and the tyranny of mediocrity and orthodoxy in small-town America.

During a trip to Europe in 1921, Anderson met writers Ernest Hemingway, Gertrude Stein, Ford Madox Ford, and James Joyce. During this year Anderson became the first recipient of the *Dial* award; the next year it was awarded to T. S. Eliot for *The Waste Land* (1922). *Many Marriages* (1923) shocked some readers by its sexual frankness, which was considered an element of the new realism of literature that was most apparent in the work of D. H. Lawrence and that resulted, in large part, from the emphasis placed by Sigmund Freud on the role of sex in human personality and behavior. Anderson saw his characters as suffering from thwarted emotions.

Anderson divorced Mitchell in 1924 and married Elizabeth Prall. They went to live for a time in New Orleans (he had been there earlier, when he was writing *Many Marriages*). There he met William Faulkner, who was then working as a newspaperman, and he influenced Faulkner in both subject matter and style, encouraging him to become a novelist. Anderson's *Dark Laughter* (1925), a novel that contrasts the spiritual sterility of the white population with the irrepressible optimism and endur-

ance of black people, is at once the most mature of his novels and the one closest in technique and philosophy to those of Faulkner, who was indubitably his superior in prose fiction technique and psychological exploration.

In 1927, Anderson settled in Marion, Virginia, and edited two local newspapers, one Democratic, the other Republican. In 1929, he divorced Prall. With the onset of the Depression, Anderson joined Dreiser, John Dos Passos, Edmund Wilson, Malcolm Cowley, and other distinguished leftist writers in advocating a new order based on workers' interests. His political interests were not new: In *Hello Towns!* (1929) and *Nearer the Grass Roots* (1929) he had sung the merits and shortcomings of the small towns of America, those sources of "every phase of life." *Perhaps Women* (1931), a polemical study, proposed that a solution to the problem of the mechanical sterility of modern life might be found in the political leadership of women.

In 1933, Anderson was married, for the fourth time, to Eleanor Copenhaver. That year he published a collection of short stories, *Death in the Woods, and Other Stories.* Subsequently he wrote *Puzzled America* (1935), social essays; *Kit Brandon* (1936), a novel showing characters still trapped in constraining environments; *Home Town* (1940), essays; and memoirs. In 1937, he was elected to the National Institute of Arts and Letters. He died in Colón, Panama Canal Zone, on March 8, 1941, while on a tour sponsored by the U.S. Department of State.

Hart Crane, John Steinbeck, Thomas Wolfe, and many other modern American writers were directly or indirectly influenced by Anderson. No less than Faulkner declared that Anderson was "the father of my generation of American writers and the tradition of American writing which our successors will carry on."

ANALYSIS

Winesburg, Ohio is dedicated to the memory of the author's mother, Emma Smith Anderson, who died when Sherwood was nineteen. She had exercised a crucial influence on her son's attitudes to life, for he wrote that her "keen observation on the life about her first woke in me the hunger to see beneath the surface of lives." This hunger persisted throughout Anderson's life and extended even to his attempts at autobiography. He continued to search for the wellsprings of the personality, the psyche, of all the characters in his grand drama of life, including himself.

In a prefatory sketch to *Winesburg, Ohio*, called "The Book of the Grotesque," Anderson offers an insight into his goal and method in the collection of stories that follows. An old writer offers an allegory about the early days of humankind, when there were many thoughts but no truths; people assembled thoughts and constructed their own tentative truths to live by, but in so doing each became a "grotesque," and "the truth he embraced became a falsehood." Anderson even enumerates some of the principal truths that made people into grotesques: "There was the truth of virginity and the truth of passion, the truth of wealth and of poverty, of thrift and of profligacy, of carelessness and abandon. Hundreds and hundreds were the truths and they were all beautiful."

What is intended by this account is not unequivocal but seems to suggest that by taking a truth out of context and without regard to other truths, a person can follow a false philosophy and become eccentric and even pitiable. The two dozen stories about small-town folk who fail to conform to the norms of society and are accordingly alienated from their fellows never satirize those forlorn and unsatisfied people, those solitaries, those loners. They explore the roots of their disquietude, which are frequently found to have had their origins in some apparently insignificant experience, affront, or rejection that has been long denied or forgotten but is recalled for the edification of Anderson's persona, the youthful George Willard, newspaper reporter for the *Winesburg Eagle*.

None of Anderson's characters is a representative of power, authority, or success in the traditional sense—even the schoolteacher, Kate Swift; the clergyman, the Reverend Curtis Hartman; and the town doctors, Dr. Reefy and Dr. Parceval, are individuals of neither achievement nor authority. Their sullenness and reclusiveness, their very attitudes toward themselves, their neighbors, and life itself demand explication, and Anderson finds in the slightest indication of emotional stress (a sign, a movement, or a look) a means for opening his story. One critic has noted that Anderson was preoccupied by a desire "to describe the agonies and the failures of the unsuccessful, the deprived, and the inarticulate," and it became apparent early in

the twentieth century that this could often be accomplished plausibly by the application of the insights of Viennese psychologist Freud, who placed stress on both the role of dreams and the suppression of sexuality.

Anderson's immediate precursors in American fiction, such as Dreiser, Frank Norris, Ambrose Bierce, and Sinclair Lewis, had worked against the popular mode of sentimental fiction and had led a "revolt against the village" in favor of realistic portrayals of the expanding industrial society. Their realistic and naturalistic fiction was putting an end to the romanticism that had survived into the twentieth century. They were less interested in the psychological than in the economic, political, and social influences on individuals, however. It was Anderson who undertook the development of this approach to characterization.

He sought, somewhat paradoxically, to do it within the modern equivalent of the village, the small town on the periphery of the great new industrial cities of the Midwest—the small towns that were the refuge of many of the former inhabitants of the cities.

The grotesques of Winesburg are not engaged in any grand enterprises or plots; rather, they are depicted in the smallest of human endeavors, and their traumatic experiences or socially disapproved actions in the past are—seen in proper perspective—either very minor aberrations or ones subject to multiple interpretations. Yet it seems that just such minor events, decisions, or traits are the ones that affect the lives of ordinary people. The focus of each story is not the solving of a complicated plot but rather the recognition of an epiphany, a special insight or revelation, that explains life's vicissitudes and failures. Action and plot are alluded to, but they are distant and merely set the stage for the discovery of the reasons for the inglorious lives of characters diminished by materialism and the mores of small-town provincialism and philistinism. Notwithstanding their epiphanies, none of Anderson's characters appear defeated and crushed; they all manage to continue, though much chastened and more philosophic.

The simplicity of Anderson's style has often been remarked upon, and many critics have supposed that it had a direct influence on the style of Hemingway and his many followers and imitators. At its best it has all the virtues of midwestern speech: straightforwardness, honesty of statement, freedom from artificial flourishes and rococo constructions, demotic vocabulary, and the predominance of the simple declarative sentence.

His language, though, is not without detail and vividness, as one can see in the opening of "An Awakening": "Belle Carpenter had a dark skin, grey eyes and thick lips. She was tall and strong. When black thoughts visited her she grew angry and wished she were a man and could fight someone with her fists." Anderson's simple vocabulary and syntax suit his subjects to perfection: He captures the very essence of simple lives in simple language. It was Gertrude Stein, the famous mentor of American writers and experimenter with language, who commented that no one in the United States could equal Anderson for "a clear and passionate sentence."

WINESBURG, OHIO

First published: 1919
Type of work: Short stories

A newspaper reporter recounts significant episodes in the lives of the interesting and sensitive residents of his small town.

Winesburg, Ohio offers detailed analyses of more than twenty of the residents of a fictional town in the region of Dayton, Ohio, and it introduces more than a hundred of the inhabitants of this community of some eighteen hundred people—the greatest number through incidental anecdotes and pointed, penetrating vignettes. The result is something akin to a novel, though there is no unifying story line and no central character or protagonist—George Willard, the young newspaperman, being merely the one through whose eyes the townsfolk are viewed.

The prefatory chapter, which concerns an old writer's dream of a procession of grotesques, sets the pattern for the sequence of twenty-two stories that follows; the writer's unpublished manuscript, "The Book of the Grotesque," set forth his theory that the moment one took a truth and tried to live by it, it became a falsehood. Anderson's book offers his implicit insight that any virtue that is

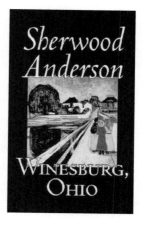

overindulged or pursued uncompromisingly degenerates into its antithesis, a vice.

Winesburg, with its three doctors, three saloons, several churches, large residential hotel (the New Willard House, an ancient establishment), school, farms, newspaper office, and several specialty stores adjacent to the railroad station, is the quintessential small town of American legend. It is a quiet, gentle little town built upon the fundamental Protestant virtues and populated by industrious, frugal neighbors—or so it seems. Anderson, however, shows that Winesburg, representative of most small towns, harbors mainly people who are far from happy, successful, and contented.

His stories explore the backgrounds and private aspirations or motivations of representative inhabitants—doctors, teachers, clergymen, retailers, and shop assistants. All of them are, in one way or another, "alone and defeated" and living lives that are unfulfilled. They quietly nurse their hurts and failures, trying to hide them from others.

Most of the characters stand, lie, or sit by windows and doors: Symbolically they are separated, set apart from the town. Almost all are shown trying to reach out to touch others. Their hands are described in particular detail, such as Dr. Reefy, with his "gnarled knuckles"; Elizabeth Willard, with her "long white hands," hands that are "white and bloodless"; and Tom Willy, the saloonkeeper, whose hands looked as though they had been "dipped in blood that had dried and faded." Kate Swift, the schoolteacher, desperately wants to touch her former student, George Willard, as she (now thirty) realizes that touching is a necessary preliminary to intimacy, and she realizes that sexual intimacy is an essential ingredient of a full and satisfying life.

Further, most of the characters at some point seek out George Willard as someone they believe will be interested in them as individuals and not only as sources of newspaper copy. Kate Swift sees him as "rapidly becoming a man," though he still has "the winsomeness of the boy"; that is, he has some of the qualities of the worldliness of age and some of the traits of the physically firm and attractive. It is this combination of characteristics—attractive mind and physique—that makes Willard appealing to many of the characters, even to the Reverend Curtis Hartman, the Presbyterian pastor whose wife is "afire with secret pride" in him. Hartman confesses, when he thinks about his wife, that he almost hates her because "she has always been ashamed of passion and has cheated me." Most of the other characters are aware of their lack of sexual fulfillment also; many obtain temporary satisfaction through illicit or occasional assignations in the woods beside Waterworks Pond.

Significantly, most are seen wandering the streets alone at night as they escape their confining homes and rooms: Almost all the houses in Winesburg seem to have back windows that look out on alleyways through which the lonely prowl, like scavenging animals, in their search for contact, companionship, and love.

One of the most interesting of the stories is "Hands," which offers a portrait of Wing Biddlebaum, a fat, bald little man with "nervous little hands" who had once been a teacher but had an innocent passion for caressing the hair or shoulders of his students. Biddlebaum has been a Winesburg resident for twenty years and is "the town mystery." As Adolph Myers, he had been run out of his Pennsylvania town when a half-witted boy misunderstood the motivation of his teacher's touching him, and he has since picked fruit and done farm labor to earn a livelihood. He is something of an enigma, for when he talks to George Willard, his eyes glow and his hands rise: He sees beauty, and he seeks to attach himself to it. Truly, as Anderson suggests in a phrase, this is "a story of hands"—as are many of the others.

Many of the characters in *Winesburg, Ohio* display outward signs of their inner conflicts and torments; they have nervous tics such as scratching an elbow until the coat sleeve is worn through, they chuckle incessantly, or they wear their clothes continuously for ten years. They have an irrepressible urge to talk to willing listeners; they run nude into the rain; they drink heavily; they use pillows as surrogate lovers. Even George Willard, after losing his virginity to Kate Swift, "courted" the young boy Seth Richmond. All the characters, as representatives of universal people, have their hidden, repressed desires, their stories of traumatic loss, their life-scarring memories of experiences that transformed their optimism, expectation, and potential satisfaction into failure, bitterness, and introversion.

SUMMARY

Of her husband, George Willard's mother says, "Nothing he had ever done had turned out successfully." This appears to be true, also, of the characters into whose lives Anderson's readers are allowed to peer. These characters all once had high hopes and expectations in life; through some quiddity, some misunderstanding, some quirk, their life plans were disrupted or destroyed. By means of the flashback and the introduction of minor players in the lives of the grotesques, the reader can appreciate the crucial weaknesses and decisions that have determined the present. Anderson's achievement is that he is not unrelievedly mechanical in his presentation: His simple prose style seems fully appropriate to the wide range of characters that he portrays, and Winesburg even today seems genuinely representative of America's small towns.

A. L. McLeod

BIBLIOGRAPHY

By the Author

LONG FICTION:
Windy McPherson's Son, 1916
Marching Men, 1917
Winesburg, Ohio, 1919
Poor White, 1920
Many Marriages, 1923

Dark Laughter, 1925
Beyond Desire, 1932
Kit Brandon, 1936

SHORT FICTION:
The Triumph of the Egg, 1921
Horses and Men, 1923
Death in the Woods, and Other Stories, 1933
The Sherwood Anderson Reader, 1947

DRAMA:
Plays: Winesburg and Others, pb. 1937

POETRY:
Mid-American Chants, 1918
A New Testament, 1927

NONFICTION:
A Story Teller's Story, 1924
The Modern Writer, 1925
Tar: A Midwest Childhood, 1926
Sherwood Anderson's Notebook, 1926
Hello Towns!, 1929
Nearer the Grass Roots, 1929
Perhaps Women, 1931
No Swank, 1934
Puzzled America, 1935
Home Town, 1940
Sherwood Anderson's Memoirs, 1942
The Letters of Sherwood Anderson, 1953
Sherwood Anderson: Selected Letters, 1984
Letters to Bab: Sherwood Anderson to Marietta D. Finley, 1916-1933, 1985

DISCUSSION TOPICS

- Sherwood Anderson is described as a man who, despite trying a variety of jobs, marriages, and locales, was dogged by a sense of living an unfulfilled life. Do the unfulfilled characters in his fiction generally have such an awareness? Or do they differ from their author in this respect?

- What does Anderson gain from using a newspaper reporter as his narrator in *Winesburg, Ohio*?

- Anderson calls his Winesburg characters "grotesques." Are his grotesques ever likable? Are they ever beautiful?

- Each of Anderson's characters is said to achieve an epiphany, "a special insight or revelation." What evidence do you see that these epiphanies actually do the characters any good?

- Do you see any instances of Anderson's style being less simple than it seems to be?

About the Author

Anderson, David D., ed. *Sherwood Anderson: Dimensions of His Literary Art.* East Lansing: Michigan State University Press, 1976.

Appel, Paul P. *Homage to Sherwood Anderson: 1876-1941.* Mount Vernon, N.Y.: Paul P. Appel, 1970.

Campbell, Hilbert H. "The 'Shadow People': Feodor Sologub and Sherwood Anderson's *Winesburg, Ohio.*" *Studies in Short Fiction* 33 (Winter, 1996): 51-58.

Campbell, Hilbert H., and Charles E. Modlin, eds. *Sherwood Anderson: Centennial Studies.* Troy, N.Y.: Whitston, 1976.

Ellis, James. "Sherwood Anderson's Fear of Sexuality: Horses, Men, and Homosexuality." *Studies in Short Fiction* 30 (Fall, 1993): 595-601.

Hansen, Tom. "Who's a Fool? A Rereading of Sherwood Anderson's 'I'm a Fool.'" *The Midwest Quarterly* 38 (Summer, 1997): 372-379.

Papinchak, Robert Allen. *Sherwood Anderson: A Study of the Short Fiction.* New York: Twayne, 1992.

Rideout, Walter B., ed. *Sherwood Anderson: A Collection of Critical Essays.* Englewood Cliffs, N.J.: Prentice-Hall, 1974.

Small, Judy Jo. *A Reader's Guide to the Short Stories of Sherwood Anderson.* New York: G. K. Hall, 1994.

Townsend, Kim. *Sherwood Anderson.* Boston: Houghton Mifflin, 1987.

Williams, Kenny J. *A Storyteller and a City: Sherwood Anderson's Chicago.* De Kalb: Northern Illinois University Press, 1988.

MAYA ANGELOU

Born: St. Louis, Missouri
April 4, 1928

Primarily known for her series of autobiographies, Angelou is also a poet, dancer, singer, actress, producer, director, and scriptwriter.

Courtesy, Central Arkansas Library

BIOGRAPHY

Born Marguerite Annie Johnson on April 4, 1928, Maya Angelou is the daughter of Vivian Baxter and Bailey Johnson. When her parents' marriage ended in divorce, she was sent to Stamps, Arkansas, to live with her paternal grandmother, Annie Henderson. Maya was three years old, and she was joined by her brother Bailey, who gave her the name Maya.

Angelou graduated with top honors from the Lafayette County Training School in 1940 and was sent to the San Francisco Bay Area, where her mother had moved. Continuing her education at George Washington High School, she also attended evening classes at the California Labor School, where she had a scholarship to study drama and dance. Shortly after receiving her high school diploma, she had a son, Guy Bailey Johnson. She began a career as a professional entertainer in the 1950's as a singer-dancer at the Purple Onion, a cabaret in California. She was invited to audition for a production of *Porgy and Bess* (1935) and did, in fact, receive a part in that George Gershwin musical, giving her the opportunity to travel widely with the cast in 1954 and 1955. In 1957, she appeared in the Off-Broadway play *Calypso Heatwave* and recorded "Miss Calypso" for Liberty Records.

Three years later, Angelou and her son moved to New York, where she joined the Harlem Writers Guild and collaborated to produce, direct, and star in *Cabaret for Freedom*, which raised funds for the Southern Christian Leadership Conference (SCLC). Upon the close of that show, she became Northern coordinator for the SCLC at the invitation of Martin Luther King, Jr., with whom she worked.

Inspired by King and other civil rights leaders, she decided to move to Africa, ostensibly so that her son could be educated in Ghana. While living there, she served as assistant administrator of the University of Ghana's School of Music and Drama and also worked for the Ghanaian Broadcasting Corporation and as a freelance writer for the *Ghanaian Times*.

In subsequent years, Angelou performed in various theater productions, adapted plays for the stage, and contributed to the performing arts in multiple ways. She performed in Jean Genet's *The Blacks* in 1960 (joining a cast of stars that included James Earl Jones and Cicely Tyson) and adapted Sophocles' *Ajax* for its 1974 premiere performance at the Mark Taper Forum in Los Angeles. She also wrote the screenplays *Georgia, Georgia* (1972) and *All Day Long* (1974). Her television appearances include playing the role of Kunta Kinte's grandmother in 1977's *Roots*, serving as a guest interviewer on *Assignment America*, and appearing in a special series on creativity hosted by Bill Moyers.

Her most important contributions, however, are her writings. In 1970, she began a series of autobiographies with her book *I Know Why the Caged Bird Sings*, which was followed by subsequent autobiographies and several volumes of poetry. In 1993, she became only the second poet to read at a presidential inauguration when she read her poem "On the Pulse of Morning" at President Bill Clinton's inauguration ceremony. Since then, she has written more poems and books, including children's books, a cookbook, and *Elder Grace: The Nobility of Aging* (2005). She has appeared in numerous television programs. Currently, she is a coveted speaker and gives numerous interviews in which she promotes her activism.

Angelou is the recipient of more than four dozen honorary degrees and numerous literary awards, among them the North Carolina Award in Literature and a lifetime appointment as the Reynolds Professor of American Studies at Wake Forest University in Winston-Salem, North Carolina. Other honors include an appointment by Present Jimmy Carter to the commission of the International Women's Year; her recognition by *Ladies' Home Journal* as Woman of the Year in communications in 1975; and her reception, in 1983, of the Matrix Award in the field of books from the Women in Communications. Her additional awards include the Medal of Distinction from the University of Hawaii Board of Regents in 1994; a Gold Plaque Choice Award from the Chicago International Film Festival in 1998 for *Down in the Delta*; an Alston/Jones International Civil and Human Rights Award in 1998; a Sheila Award from the Tubman African American Museum in 1999; recognition as one of the one hundred best writers of the twentieth century from *Writer's Digest* in 1999; a National Medal of the Arts in 2000; and a Grammy Award in 2002 for her recording of *A Song Flung Up to Heaven*. Various buildings have been named after her, including the Maya Angelou Public Charter School Agency in Washington, D.C., and the Maya Angelou Southeast Library in Stockton, California. On May 6, 2005, Angelou delivered the commencement address at Michigan State University's undergraduate convocation ceremony, at which she was also awarded an honorary Doctor of Humanities degree.

ANALYSIS

In an interview, Angelou described her autobiographical style in the following way: "I've used, or tried to use, the form of the Black minister in storytelling so that each event I write about has a beginning, middle, and an end. And I have tried to make the selections graduate so that each episode is a level, whether of narration or drama, well always dramatic, but a level of comprehension like a stair-

case." Angelou's autobiographies surely demonstrate this narrative and dramatic approach, and her poems also suggest the narrator and playwright at work.

Her six volumes of autobiography reveal a narrator's strong voice as well as a playwright's ability to set a stage, introduce characters, and portray the conflicts and tensions among those characters as they interact with one another and deal with their own internal conflicts and challenges. *I Know Why the Caged Bird Sings* was published in 1970 and has been followed by subsequent self-portraits, including *Gather Together in My Name* (1974), *Singin' and Swingin' and Gettin' Merry Like Christmas* (1976), *The Heart of a Woman* (1981), *All God's Children Need Traveling Shoes* (1986), and *A Song Flung Up to Heaven* (2002). Each volume has the Angelou touch of storytelling and dramatic rendition, and each also has the incremental sense of movement toward Angelou's idea of "a level of comprehension like a staircase."

Additionally, the volumes deal with an important theme for Angelou: survival. *I Know Why the Caged Bird Sings*, for example, narrates the placement and displacement of the author as a southern black girl and demonstrates that her experiences of racial discrimination, rape, and numerous other victimizations did not destroy her; on the contrary, they emboldened and strengthened her, thus committing her to survival at all costs.

In her second volume of autobiography, *Gather Together in My Name*, the scene shifts, but the message remains the same: Young mother though she is, seventeen-year-old parent though she is, she must survive and triumph over the various discriminations, mostly racial, that she endures. In a book that has a beginning, middle, and end—a structure that Angelou claims exists in all of her autobiographies—the end is an especially poignant reminder of survival. Learning a lesson from a drug addict, Angelou proclaims: "I had walked the precipice and seen it all; and at the critical moment, one man's generosity pushed me safely away from the edge. . . . I had given a promise and found my innocence. I swore I'd never lose it again."

The following four autobiographies continue this emphasis upon survival—whether it is viewed through Angelou's experiences traveling with the *Porgy and Bess* production throughout Europe, the Middle East, and North Africa, as narrated in

Singin' and Swingin' and Gettin' Merry Like Christmas; through her experiences in New York coordinating the Southern Christian Leadership Conference for Martin Luther King, Jr., as narrated in *The Heart of a Woman*; or through Angelou's quest to find her identity in Africa, as narrated in *All God's Children Need Traveling Shoes*. Seeking survival, physical, intellectual, emotional, spiritual, in all six volumes of autobiography, Angelou as narrator and playwright tells her stories and sets the stage for her dramatic productions.

While it might seem that Angelou's poetry departs from these narrative and dramatic impulses, as the volumes are, after all, verse and not prose, the opposite is actually true. Like her autobiographical narratives and dramas, the poems also tell stories and present scenes from human dramas. Perhaps the best example of this appears in Angelou's fourth volume of poetry, a collection of songlike poems published in 1983 titled *Shaker, Why Don't You Sing?* The poem "Caged Bird," an obvious echo of Angelou's best-known autobiography, *I Know Why the Caged Bird Sings*, narrates the story of a free bird and a caged bird, the latter singing a song of freedom and survival that is the same song sung by Angelou in all of her works. The caged bird's song is a protest, as are Angelou's autobiographies, and it is also a song of hope, still another characteristic of Angelou's self-portraits. Taken together, the ten volumes of prose and poetry are narrative dramas, portraits of a woman and her culture, songs of survival at all costs. In later years, Maya Angelou's role as "rags-to-riches" survivor has been spiced with outspoken activism regarding the disadvantaged of any race. She is no longer a singing caged bird, but one who swoops and dives in her efforts toward opening the cages for the rest of humanity.

I KNOW WHY THE CAGED BIRD SINGS

First published: 1970
Type of work: Autobiography

In this self-portrait, Maya Angelou narrates her childhood in Stamps, Arkansas, and her adolescent years in California.

I Know Why the Caged Bird Sings, Angelou's first autobiography, is a story of a child becoming an adolescent, a story of a victim who comes to realize that all people are, to some extent, victims, and a story of survival. It is a lyrical narrative—almost a prose poem in some places—in which the autobiographer's voice is strong and musical, just as the title conjures up musical imagery.

Maya Angelou as a child is a displaced person, separated from her mother and father at the age of three and moved around almost as frequently as a chess piece. Her earliest memories are of Stamps, where she and her brother Bailey are raised by their grandmother, a woman of remarkable strength and limitless love for her grandchildren. This grandmother, known as Momma, provides security for Maya and Bailey and also offers a role model for the young girl, who is beginning to understand the role of victim to which black children—and especially black girls—are subjected.

Momma owns the general store in Stamps and is respected as a businesswoman, a citizen of the community, and an honest and straightforward person. She represents the qualities that will eventually define her granddaughter, and she demonstrates those qualities on a daily basis, most especially when dealing with members of the white community. In a significant incident, she reveals the ability to survive that her granddaughter will eventually develop herself.

Three young white girls come to Momma's property to taunt Momma through various antics, including one of the rudest acts possible in the South of the 1930's: calling an adult by her first name. Throughout this series of insults, Momma does not react to the girls and, instead, stands on the porch, smiling and humming a hymn. While the granddaughter is outraged by this incident, wanting to confront the girls, the grandmother remains impervious and unwilling to demean herself by responding to her attackers—except when they leave, at which point she courteously bids them farewell, calling each by her first name preceded by

"Miz." The young Angelou comes to realize that Momma had won the battle by rising above the pettiness and rudeness of her inferiors. She was superior, and she had survived. She had also taught her granddaughter a lesson for all time.

Most lessons, however, need to be learned and relearned, and so Angelou faces that uphill battle when, at the age of eight, she is displaced again, this time to be returned to her mother in St. Louis. Whereas Stamps represents security and orderliness, St. Louis symbolizes its opposites. The most dramatic example of this insecure, disorderly, frightening world is the rape of eight-year-old Maya by her mother's boyfriend, Mr. Freeman. Confused and terrified by this act and the subsequent murder of Freeman—a murder that the child mistakenly thinks she has caused—Angelou becomes a voluntary mute and lives in a world of silence for nearly five years. She is healed by Bertha Flowers, a woman in Stamps, to which Maya returns. Flowers extends friendship to the mute Maya, a friendship that beckons the young girl to leave her self-imposed silence and embrace a new world of words, poems, songs, and a journal that chronicles this new stage in her life.

Moving to Oakland and then San Francisco in 1941, at the age of thirteen, Maya rejoins her mother and deals with dislocation and displacement still again. At this point in her life, however, she is maturing and learning that the role of victim, while still a role to which she is assigned, is also a role played by others—blacks and whites. She learns that the human challenge is to deal with, protest against, and rise above the trap of being victimized and exploited. In the final scene of the novel, Angelou is not merely a young woman coming to this realization for herself; she is a young mother who has just borne a son and who is therefore struggling to see how she can be responsible not only for herself but also for another. The book ends with this sense of mutual responsibility and mutual survival: Mother and child know why the caged bird sings, and they will sing their song together.

ALL GOD'S CHILDREN NEED TRAVELING SHOES

First published: 1986
Type of work: Autobiography

In her fifth autobiography, Angelou relates her pilgrimage to Ghana, where she seeks to understand her African roots.

All God's Children Need Traveling Shoes is about hopelessness and repeats the theme of displacement. However, in this instance, the sense of displacement is more complex than in *I Know Where the Caged Bird Sings.* In the 1960's, Angelou travels to what she believes is the place of her African roots, hoping that this country will fill the vacuum she feels for home. By returning to the land of her ancestors, where all are black regardless of color, she hopes to find and perhaps recognize "home." She joins other black Americans also questing for identity and security, and, like most of them, Angelou discovers that the geographical search is a misleading one. The source of security, she comes to learn, is not in a place but within oneself.

Angelou chooses to live in Ghana following the end of her marriage. Kwame Nkrumah is Ghana's beloved ruler five years after its independence from Britain, and there is a sense of pride in the new country. Angelou joins a group of black Americans who have come to Ghana to be part of the great experiment. Angelou hopes that she and her son will find a land freed of the racial bigotry she has faced wherever she has lived or traveled. Hopeful and idealistic, she sets herself up for disappointment and disillusion. During her three-year stay in Africa, she is not welcomed as she has expected to be; even more painful, she is frequently ignored by the very people with whom she thinks she shares roots, the Africans. As she tries to understand this new kind of pain and homelessness, she also struggles with the sense of having two selves, an American self and an African self.

A stunning example of this struggle occurs when the black American community in Ghana, together with some sympathetic Ghanaians, decides to support the August 27, 1963, March on Washington—the march led by Martin Luther King, Jr.—by leading a demonstration at the U.S. Embassy in

Accra. The march does not have the impact its participants hope it will have because the demonstrators, including Angelou, are ambivalent about who they are, where they are, and where their quest for security is leading them. This ambivalence is dramatized when one of the marchers jeers a black soldier who is raising the American flag in front of the American embassy, prompting Angelou to reflect on the fact that the Stars and Stripes was the flag of the expatriates and, more important, their only flag. The recognition of her divided self continues during the remainder of her stay in African, including during time spent with Malcolm X. The volatile activist has a profound impact upon Angelou, who had met him two years earlier but who sees him and hears his words from her current context of an orphan looking for a home and looking for reasons to stay in that home. As she observes the various personalities Malcolm X exhibits—from big-brother adviser to spokesperson against oppression and for revolutions—she reflects upon his commitment to changing the status quo in the United States. As she leaves, she observes that Malcolm's presence had elevated the expatriates but that his departure left them with the same sense of displacement with which they had arrived in Africa.

Ultimately, Angelou is compelled to return to the United States. She leaves, having become aware that home is not a geographical location but a psychological state. She leaves having learned that her survival depends upon finding herself within herself, wearing her traveling shoes, like all God's children.

A SONG FLUNG UP TO HEAVEN

First published: 2002
Type of work: Autobiography

Angelou experiences the Watts riots and the assassinations of Malcolm X and Martin Luther King, Jr., and finally learns to deal with them through writing.

A Song Flung Up to Heaven begins in 1964 with Angelou returning to the United States from Ghana in order to help with the Civil Rights move-

ment, specifically to write and organize for Malcolm X. Shortly after she lands in California, he is assassinated before her work with him can begin. Her brother takes his grief-stricken sister to Hawaii, where she sings in nightclubs, with no notable success. Returning to California, she works as a door-to-door surveyor in the Watts District of Los Angeles, thus getting to know the people's poverty and anger. Therefore, she is not surprised by the outbreak of violence and senses the riots before she learns of them.

> We smelled the conflagration before we heard it, or even heard about it. . . . Burning wood was the first odor that reached my nose, but it was soon followed by the smell of scorched food, then the stench of smoldering rubber. We had one hour of wondering before the television news reporters arrived breathlessly.

After a stormy encounter with her former lover, Angelou returns to New York, where she meets Dr. Martin Luther King, Jr., and agrees to promote the movement. However, history repeats itself. Before she can go south for the movement, King also is assassinated. Again devastated, Angelou becomes a recluse until writer James Baldwin invites her to a dinner with glittering New York literati that reawakens her passion for writing. Friends encourage her to write and to begin by writing her life. Eventually, Angelou moves back to California and, in an effort to make spiritual sense of and triumph over her experiences, begins to write. *A Song Flung Up to Heaven* ends with her writing the first few lines of *I Know Why the Caged Bird Sings*, opening the gate to her most important career and yet circling back nicely to her first, most beloved book.

A Song Flung Up to Heaven engrosses the reader with its portrait of a sensitive woman caught up in some of the most important events of the twentieth century. It is also compelling because of its simple yet poetic and intimate style. Angelou recounts her story as if confiding to a friend. She intersperses narration with heartrending scenes, such as when a phone caller indirectly reveals Malcolm X's assassination by remarking that New York blacks are crazy because they murdered one of their own kind. Her literary devices enliven the prose, such as when she personifies the strangling effect of hopelessness: "Depression wound itself around me so securely I could barely walk, and didn't want to talk . . . " Angelou's mundane yet refreshing similes are juxtaposed with tumultuous events, as in her response to her lover's remark that he needs her: "Needed? Needed like an extra blanket? Like air-conditioning? Like more pepper for soup? I resented being thought of as a thing. . . ."

By the time the book ends, the reader is touched and sad, yet inspired. *A Song Flung Up to Heaven* somehow suggests that if Angelou can transcend such dire circumstances, perhaps others can too.

"ON THE PULSE OF MORNING"

First published: 1993
Type of work: Poem

This poem speaks of the importance of human beings joining together, in hope, to create and greet the future.

"On the Pulse of Morning" was read at President Bill Clinton's inauguration ceremony in January, 1993. Only the second poet to read at a presidential inauguration, Angelou has said this about her poem: "In all my work, what I try to say is that as human beings we are more alike than we are unalike." This piece celebrates that sense of similarity, connectedness, and human solidarity.

Beginning with the recognition that rocks, rivers, and trees have witnessed the arrival and departure of many generations, "On the Pulse of Morning" proceeds to have each of these witnesses speak to the future, beginning with the Rock, which announces that people may stand upon its back but may not find security in its shadow. On the contrary, says the Rock, humans must face the future, their "distant destiny," boldly and directly.

The River sings a similar song, calling humans to its riverside but only if they will forego the study of war. If human beings will come to the River, "clad in peace," this ageless body of water will sing the songs given to it by the Creator, songs of unity and songs of peace.

The Tree continues this hymn of peace and

hope, reminding humankind that each person is a "descendant of some passed-on traveler" and that each "has been paid for." Pawnee, Apache, Turk, Swede, Eskimo, Ashanti—all are invited by the Tree to root themselves beside it. Thus united with Rock, River, and Tree, the poem announces, the human race can look toward a future of peace and connections and away from a past of brutality and discontinuity. In the final stanza, this paean of praise is most lyrical:

> Here on the pulse of this new day
> You may have the grace to look up and out
> And into your sister's eyes, into
> Your brother's face, your country
> And say simply
> Very simply
> With hope
> Good morning.

Like Angelou's autobiographies and like her volumes of poetry, "On the Pulse of Morning" speaks of survival. Lyrical and inspirational, it calls human beings to have the imagination and courage to build up instead of tear down, and it echoes the titles of Angelou's other works, especially *I Know Why the Caged Bird Sings*. If all caged birds sing together, this poem asserts, then the human race will indeed survive.

SUMMARY

Maya Angelou's many achievements in diverse fields testify to the breadth of her talent, the strength of her character, and the power of her vision. As an actress, singer, activist, playwright, poet, and, especially, a compelling autobiographer, she has succeeded in communicating her remarkable experiences and perspective to an appreciative and ever-growing audience. Now in speeches and in interviews, Angelou criticizes the class system that keeps its heel on the poor, and she exhorts people to action, both for themselves and for others. The bird, finally out of its cage, swoops toward those still caged with cries of protest and relentless pecking at the gates of oppression.

Marjorie Smelstor; updated by Mary Hanford Bruce

BIBLIOGRAPHY

By the Author

NONFICTION:

I Know Why the Caged Bird Sings, 1970 (autobiography)

Gather Together in My Name, 1974 (autobiography)

Singin' and Swingin' and Gettin' Merry Like Christmas, 1976 (autobiography)

The Heart of a Woman, 1981 (autobiography)

All God's Children Need Traveling Shoes, 1986 (autobiography)

Wouldn't Take Nothing for My Journey Now, 1993 (autobiographical essays)

Even the Stars Look Lonesome, 1997

A Song Flung Up to Heaven, 2002 (autobiographical essays)

Hallelujah! The Welcome Table: A Lifetime of Memories with Recipes, 2004 (cookbook)

Elder Grace: The Nobility of Aging, 2005

POETRY:

Just Give Me a Cool Drink of Water 'fore I Diiie, 1971

Oh Pray My Wings Are Gonna Fit Me Well, 1975

And Still I Rise, 1978

Shaker, Why Don't You Sing?, 1983

Poems: Maya Angelou, 1986

Now Sheba Sings the Song, 1987 (Tom Feelings, illustrator)

I Shall Not Be Moved: Poems, 1990

On the Pulse of Morning, 1993

The Complete Collected Poems of Maya Angelou, 1994

Phenomenal Woman: Four Poems Celebrating Women, 1994

A Brave and Startling Truth, 1995

SHORT FICTION:

"Steady Going Up," 1972

"The Reunion," 1983

DRAMA:

Cabaret for Freedom, pr.1960 (with Godfrey Cambridge; musical)

The Least of These, pr. 1966

Encounters, pr. 1973

Ajax, pr. 1974 (adaptation of Sophocles' play)

And Still I Rise, pr. 1976

King, pr. 1990 (musical; lyrics with Alistair Beaton, book by Lonne Elder III; music by Richard Blackford)

SCREENPLAYS:

Georgia, Georgia, 1972

All Day Long, 1974

DISCUSSION TOPICS

- Is there a shift in tone between Maya Angelou's early and late works? If so, what is it, and why do you think the change occurred?

- Strong women are portrayed in Angelou's works. Are there strong men too? If so, who are they? Are their strengths different from those of the women? If so, how?

- Trace the theme of transcendence in Angelou's works. How do her characters "rise above" their circumstances?

- Angelou has been criticized, sometimes by African American critics, that her works are simply "uplift" works and not genuine art. Do you agree or disagree? Why?

- At least three volumes of Angelou's autobiographies detail a loss of innocence. What are these major disillusionments? Which is the most complex?

- How is the mother figure enshrined in Angelou's works?

- Does Angelou's faith influence her work? How?

- Although Angelou writes almost exclusively about African Americans, her books and poetry are popular with all races. Why?

TELEPLAYS:
Black, Blues, Black, 1968 (ten episodes)
The Inheritors, 1976
The Legacy, 1976
I Know Why the Caged Bird Sings, 1979 (with Leonora Thuna and Ralph B. Woolsey)
Sister, Sister, 1982
Brewster Place, 1990

CHILDREN'S LITERATURE:
Mrs. Flowers: A Moment of Friendship, 1986 (illustrated by Etienne Delessert)
Life Doesn't Frighten Me, 1993 (poetry; illustrated by Jean-Michel Basquiat)
Soul Looks Back in Wonder, 1993
My Painted House, My Friendly Chicken, and Me, 1994
Kofi and His Magic, 1996
Renie Marie of France, 2004 (illustrated by Lizzy Rockwell)
Mikale of Hawaii, 2004 (illustrated by Rockwell)
Izak of Lapland, 2004 (illustrated by Rockwell)
Angelina of Italy, 2004 (illustrated by Rockwell)

About the Author

Coulthard, R. "Poetry as Politics: Maya Angelou's Inaugural Poem, 'On the Pulse of Morning.'" *Notes on Contemporary Literature* 28, no. 1 (January, 1999): 2-5.

Hagen, Lyman B. "Poetry." In *Heart of a Woman, Mind of a Writer, and Soul of a Poet: A Critical Analysis of the Writings of Maya Angelou.* Lanham, Md.: University Press of America, 1997.

Koyana, Siphokazi, and Rosemary Gray. "Growing up with Maya Angelou and Sindiwe Magona: A Comparison." *Safundi: The Journal of South African and American Comparative Studies* 7 (November, 2001).

McPherson, Dolly A. *Order Out of Chaos: The Autobiographical Works of Maya Angelou.* New York: Peter Lang, 1990.

McWhorter, John. "Saint Maya: *A Song Flung Up to Heaven.*" *The New Republic,* May 20, 2002.

Moore, Opal. "Learning to Live: When the Bird Breaks from the Cage." In *Censored Books: Critical Viewpoints,* edited by Nicholas J. Karolides, Lee Burress, and John M. Kean. Lanham, Md.: Scarecrow Press, 2001.

Neubauer, Carol. "Maya Angelou: Self and a Song of Freedom in the Southern Tradition." In *Southern Women Writers: The New Generation,* edited by Tonnette Bond Inge. Tuscaloosa: University of Alabama Press, 1990.

Saunders, James Robert. "Breaking Out of the Cage: The Autobiographical Writings of Maya Angelou." *The Hollins Critic* 28 (October, 1991): 1-11.

Sylvester, William. "Maya Angelou: Overview." In *Contemporary Poets,* edited by Thomas Riggs, 6th ed. New York: St. James Press, 1996.

Walker, Pierre. "Racial Protest, Identity, Words, and Form in Maya Angelou's *I Know Why the Caged Bird Sings.*" *College Literature* 22, no. 3 (1995): 91-105.

John Ashbery

Born: Rochester, New York
July 28, 1927

Recognized as one of the finest American poets of the last half of the twentieth century, Ashbery has been a major exponent and practitioner of the idea that poetry need not necessarily make sense or come to conclusions about philosophic problems.

Biography

John Ashbery was born in Rochester, New York, to Chester Frederick and Helen (Lawrence) Ashbery. He spent much of his childhood on his grandparents' farm in northern New York, close to the shores of Lake Ontario. He attended Deerfield Academy and went on to Harvard University, from which he graduated in 1949; his undergraduate thesis examined the poetry of the British writer W. H. Auden. During Ashbery's early years he had wanted to be a painter, but he studied English literature at college, and in 1951 he was granted an M.A. by Columbia University for his study of English novelist Henry Green. He did further graduate work at New York University, and later in France, on the experimental writer Raymond Roussel.

Between 1951 and 1954, Ashbery worked as a copywriter for the Oxford University Press in New York City and at McGraw-Hill in 1954 and 1955. During the 1950's he associated with a small group of young writers, including James Schuyler and Frank O'Hara, who attempted to bring the theories of abstract Impressionistic painting into literature and who came to be known as the New York school of poetry. Ashbery, however, has always rejected the suggestion that they were ever so cohesively organized as to be a "school."

In 1953, Ashbery published his first volume of verse, *Turandot, and Other Poems*. From the beginning critics were skeptical about the lack of clarity in his poems, although his enormous sophistication, his use of allusion, and his wittiness were quickly appreciated. In 1955, still pursuing his academic interests, he received a Fulbright scholarship to study in France at the university in Mont-

pellier. In the following year he moved to Paris; he also published his second volume of poetry, *Some Trees* (1956). While in Paris, his interest in art, which had led to his enthusiasm for abstract Impressionists such as Jackson Pollock and Willem de Kooning, drew him into writing art criticism for the Paris edition of the *New York Herald Tribune*, and he continued to do that work until 1965. He also formed a connection with *Art News*.

In 1962, Ashbery's poems in *The Tennis Court Oath* brought the skepticism about his work to its sharpest response, and this book has retained a reputation for being the least sensible of all of his works. Despite formidable opposition, however, Ashbery began to win prizes. As early as 1960, he won the Poets' Foundation Award; in 1962, he won the Ingram-Merrill Foundation award; in 1963, the Harriet Monroe Memorial Prize and the Union League Civic and Arts Foundation Prize. This pattern of public recognition and critical praise, tempered by considerable critical disdain from certain quarters, was to continue.

Ashbery reached his highest point of acceptance with *Self-Portrait in a Convex Mirror* (1975), which won the Pulitzer Prize, the National Book Award, and the National Book Critics Circle Award. The books of new poetry he has published since then have had his usual critical ups and downs over the matter of the poetry often not making sense. Ashbery seems unrepentant about this, and it is often a major theme in his work, as he wants his poems to reflect a world which he sees as lacking in coherence. He also wants his poems to have the formlessness, the nonrational element, which is common to abstract Impressionist painting.

In 1966, Ashbery returned from Paris to New

York and took up the post of executive editor with *Art News*. In the 1970's, he broadened his activities to include teaching English at Brooklyn College and the poetry editorship of the *Partisan Review*. In 1978, he joined *New York* magazine as its art critic, and from 1980 to 1985, he reached an even wider audience as the art critic for *Newsweek*. He has continued to teach and to write both art criticism and poetry. In 1985, he received a MacArthur Prize fellowship and the Lenore Marshall/Nation Poetry Prize. In 1987, he published *April Galleons*, a collection of poetry; in 1989, a collection of his art criticism written between 1957 and 1987 was published as *Reported Sightings: Art Chronicles, 1957-1987*. He is a regular poetry contributor to *The New Yorker*.

ANALYSIS

Ashbery's poetry is a battleground for literary critics: Some consider him the finest poet of the late twentieth century; some consider him an occasionally good poet whose work is often of questionable literary quality; some critics dismiss him as entirely worthless. The main reason for this is quite simple: His poems often do not make sense. Ashbery knows this; indeed, his work is deliberately impossible to paraphrase much of the time, and he willingly admits that many of his poems are meaningless, given the way in which readers and critics ordinarily try to turn poems into prose as an element of their value as art. It is possible, for example, to identify certain Ashbery poems as clearly nonsensical. What confuses the issue is the fact that many of his poems are a teasing combination of what looks like sensible prose or poetry mixed with passages of seemingly arbitrary confusion. It is not a matter, however, of Ashbery's being unable to speak clearly; it is a deliberate element in his work, which he not only defends but also espouses as having literary and intellectual merit.

Perhaps the best way to approach the matter is through two ideas: that art in the twentieth and twenty-first centuries, particularly the plastic and aural arts, has been strongly inclined to move toward the nonrepresentational, and that Ashbery has spent a considerable amount of his time as an art critic, supporting the most experimental members of the American school of abstract expressionism in painting. Throughout his career as a commentator on contemporary painting, he has been a great admirer of Willem de Kooning, Franz Kline, and Jackson Pollock, and he has had an equal enthusiasm for the radical musical compositions of Arnold Schoenberg, John Cage, and Anton von Webern.

The history of art in general shows a close alliance between the artistic object and the world as it is generally perceived. In the mid-nineteenth century, particularly in painting and sculpture, the idea developed that the artist need not necessarily attempt to represent reality but could elaborate on it. That movement, which begins in Impressionism and moves on to cubism and ultimately to variations on the abstract, had, by the time of Ashbery's coming of age, been fully manifested in many of the arts. The most difficult of the arts to so manipulate has been the literary art, simply because the basic materials—the word, the sentence, and the paragraph—are by their very nature rational. Color or sound may be used arbitrarily; words are another matter. The attempts to break the literary arts away from reality have been much more difficult—although not impossible, as the work of writers such as Franz Kafka and dramatist Samuel Beckett have shown.

Poetry, too, has had some success in repudiating sense. Poets such as T. S. Eliot, W. H. Auden, and Wallace Stevens, all of whom influenced Ashbery, are often very difficult to understand. The difference between them and Ashbery lies in the fact that there is some confidence in the fact that close study of these poets' work usually allows the reader to break the code to get at what the poet is trying to say, however densely it may be expressed. With Ashbery it is not quite so simple; often he is clearly not expressing himself in a way that can be turned into sensible prose.

Ashbery is a poet of philosophic concern. He writes about the problems of life as human beings live it. That kind of poet is traditionally expected to express metaphysical questions, large or small, in elegant verse form and complicated imagery in which one metaphor leads reasonably to another and another; they ultimately lead to some sort of insight into the problem. The aesthetic pleasure lies in the poet's use of language, metaphor, and structure, all eventually making sense, if often on a very specific plane of intelligence. Deciphering the secret, forcing the images to connect, leads to the secret in the center, and that has been the tradition of the poetry of ideas through the centuries (if somewhat more intensely formidable in the hands of twentieth century poets).

In Ashbery's case, however, the contemplation of the mysteries of life is complicated by the pose of diffidence, the not uncommon late twentieth century idea that one cannot know the truth. It is made even more difficult by Ashbery's constant determination to write poems about the diverse and devious experience of trying to discover truth in the making of a poem. Many of his best poems begin with the same kinds of questions about life which other poets address, but they quickly become studies of how difficult it is even to keep the subject straight. They usually conclude without the question being answered, and often with the clear suggestion that no answer is possible, at least through the medium of poetry.

An added difficulty lies in the way Ashbery uses figures of speech such as metaphors and similes. The trained reader expects that such poetic improvisations will illuminate the subject and will have some clearly logical connection to it. Ashbery often starts with figures that elaborate on the subject but quickly allows images into the poem that seem irrelevant. This practice is an aspect of his idea that his poems should be a record of how thoughts on the subject filter through his own mind and that the seemingly irrelevant images are legitimate because they are part of how his mind jumps in and out of the subject—how one thing leads, not necessarily logically, to another.

The poet bent on being clearly understood filters out the arbitrary thoughts, giving his or her readers an edited version of how the poetic flow operates. Ashbery leaves everything in, and as a result much of his material seems off the topic; indeed, much of it is, although there is often a crazy tonal logic about these maundering intrusions, just as there is in his sometimes maddening inclination to mix pronouns, shifting without any warning from "I" to "you" to "he" or "she." As a result, there is a feeling of constant flux, of spontaneity and witty vivacity, and a sense that the reader is implicated in the struggle to get things straight. Clarity, however, is only momentary and is often less important than the recording of the act of creation, however confused intellectually.

"THE SKATERS"

First published: 1964
Type of work: Poem

A poem about the difficulties and failures of the poetic process presented in the form of a confused journey through the alternatives open to the contemporary poet.

"The Skaters" has been sharply dismissed by many critics as being meaningless for the most part and being much less successful than the later poem "Self-Portrait in a Convex Mirror" (1975) as an attempt at dealing with the problem of the poem in the late twentieth century. Even its supporters are less enthusiastic about it than they are about "Self-Portrait in a Convex Mirror," in part because it is a much more difficult poem. On the other hand, it can be explicated, but only in part, and the reader must eventually accept Ashbery's refusal (stated more than once in the poem) to write what he considers the old-fashioned poem of sensible argument and appropriately obvious image.

If the best face is put upon the poem, as it has been by a few supporters of Ashbery, it can be read as his attempt to explain the difficulties of writing poetry of a new kind for an audience that expects philosophic poems to be clearly argued and intent on reaching sensible conclusions. The image of the skaters with which the poem begins can be seen as an example of the old style of art—graceful and skilled, but, significantly, going around in circles. This image will appear over and over in the poem as a reminder of how things used to be (at least for the poet), and against it is played out a search for a new way of dealing with reality.

The poem begins innocently enough, with a rather inflated description of the sight and sound of ice skaters. It may be a nod of compliment to the stylistic inclinations of Wallace Stevens, a poet much admired by Ashbery. It may, however, seem somewhat pompous in its fastidiousness, which would not be inconsistent with the main idea of the poem that art of that kind is no longer viable. Whatever the case (and with Ashbery much is left up to the reader), the skaters lead to a memory of childhood ribaldry and to the suggestion that little of the past is worth keeping, and very much less is retained.

Even music, however varied in form, has little long-lasting emotional purchase, and this statement leads to the virulent repudiation by the poet of any ability to express the emotional aesthetic that is so often expected of the poet: "'I am yesterday,' and my fault is eternal./ I do not expect constant attendance, knowing myself/ insufficient for your present demands/ And I have a dim intuition that I am that other 'I' with which/ we began."

Time is seen as constantly fleeting, and nothing has much meaning in the long run: "Thus a great wind cleanses, as a new ruler! Edits new laws, sweeping the very breath of the streets/ Into posterior trash." There are suggestions that these changes might make for a new optimism, but ultimately all fails. The section ends with the suggestion that the particular is irrelevant and that if there is to be poetry, it will be less perfect in its forms or conclusions:

> Hence, neither the importance of the individual flake,
> Nor the importance of the whole impression of the storm, if it has any, is what it is,
> But the rhythm of the series of repeated jumps, from abstract into positive and back to a slightly less diluted abstract.

Mild effects are the result.

The second section, however, continues the search into the romantic world of past poetry. For a time, it looks as if the imaginative dream might prevail, but difficulties occur, and the poet falls back into a kind of mild despair, recognizing that for him poetry is inadequate not only to discover meaning in life but also to deal with the serious social difficulties of the world. There are also problems with the poem of meaning, simply because Ashbery allows his mind to wander through a maze of images that may seem quite incomprehensible.

The third section reveals a strong stylistic change. A kind of stolid, commonsense, step-by-step approach to the problem is tried in order to discover the secret of life and its relation to poetry. Some critics have seen touches of travel literature in the material, and it is a section in which adventures are essayed, if kept on a lower level than those of the second section by the insistence that only one thing, death, exists. The excursion into nature leads into a widening of experience, with Romantic

implications, but it all ends with soaked clothing and the danger of the mundane head cold—the banality of real life. There is no room for the imagination; no one is interested in adventure, and the poet sees himself at the end "like a plank! Like a small boat blown away from the wind."

The fourth section is the easiest to understand, as it is a kind of short story of depressed country life, a metaphor for the dreariness, the increasingly unimaginative particularities, of common experience in which, significantly, the trout (like the skaters) are circling aimlessly and the pump, which might be seen as a source of refreshment, is broken. The ending is particularly flat; the constellations, if rising in perfect order, have an arbitrariness about that order that suggests a meaningless universe, one in which the old kinds of poetry of metaphysical optimism have no place.

Ashbery is trying to create something like an abstract poem in which the accumulation of images supports the occasional moments of clear statement but with the kind of free-form looseness of association that has been so successful in abstract painting, in which objects do not necessarily mean anything specific. Instead, they add up to a sense of rightness that has very little to do with logic but much to do with an emotion which cannot be quite expressed in any other way. The poem is, in that sense, a metaphor for the failure of the old kinds of poetry to express the state of contemporary life, and the form it takes, a kind of surging, swaying movement in and out of sense and nonsense, is an example of poetic form imitating poetic meaning. It could be said that, in part, the form of this poem is its meaning.

"SELF-PORTRAIT IN A CONVEX MIRROR"

First published: 1975 (collected in *Self-Portrait in a Convex Mirror*, 1975)
Type of work: Poem

Ashbery contemplates the nature of the work of art and its relation to truth, memory, human souls, and the world in general.

"Self-Portrait in a Convex Mirror" is Ashbery's most popular and most critically honored poem, and it

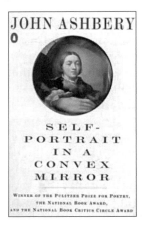

brings together some of the best and some of the most annoying elements in his work. From its beginning, it requires some basic knowledge of a specific painting that Ashbery (a well-known art critic) admires. Italian painter Parmigianino (1503-1540), whose real name was Francesco Mazzola, was one of the foremost mannerist painters. He produced a self-portrait, and in order to impress his Roman patrons with his technical prowess, he painted the likeness as it would appear in a convex mirror.

The poem begins with a charming, succinct description of the painting, rich with critical perception and including excerpts from comments that had been made about the work at the time of its presentation in the early sixteenth century. It is essential to remember that it is not a realistic portrait of the painter, as it is deliberately distorted as it would be in a convex reflection. This eccentric, tricky idea is consistent with the stylistic experimentations of mannerist painters, who often chose to present subjects in graceful distortion rather than attempt to record life with absolute accuracy.

The speaker in the poem is impressed in particular with the representation of the eyes, which are usually considered in art to give entrance to the soul. The eyes in this picture do not fully satisfy the speaker, however deftly they are painted, and it is this sense of failure to capture the soul which precipitates the main subject of the poem: How can one know reality, how does one record it in art or otherwise, given one's limitations as a human being?

It becomes clear that however much he enjoys the painting, he senses its inadequacy as a representation of reality. The flatness of the canvas, however cleverly manipulated, militates against the kind of three-dimensional experience of life: "But your eyes proclaim/ That everything is surface. The surface is what's there/ And nothing can exist except what's there." The problem of holding on to experience leads into a contemplation of past relationships and of how thin they are in the memory—how eventually everything sifts down into a kind of blurred mush without much significance. The poem juxtaposes the speaker's consideration of the painting (and that of other critics) with contemplation of day-to-day experience, attempting to come to some conclusion about the relation between art and life. The way in which the portrait, in its convexity, reaches out at the same time it recedes leads to the conviction that "art" may not necessarily be a satisfactory haven for truth about reality.

There is, as a result, an intellectual and tonal tussle in the poem as the speaker shuffles between the experience of the flux of life, in which constant accumulation never makes much sense, and his admiration for the world of art which is able to select and to idealize. That admiration is continually eroded by his uneasiness as to the truth of art, as the inexorable push of time and experience diminish any certainty that art has much to do with life as it is ordinarily lived:

> This always
> Happens, as in the game where
> A whispered phrase passed around the room
> Ends up as something completely different.
> It is the principle that makes works of art so unlike
> What the artist intended. Often he finds
> He has omitted the thing he started out to say
> In the first place.

Much of the poem is occupied with considering several different ways in which reality proves to be obdurate, not only in art but also in life. Ashbery tries to find some way in which the case for art can be made, and his comments upon the painting, and Parmigianino's work in general, are a kind of tour-de-force example of creating poetry and art criticism at the same time. More difficulty will be confronted in dealing with the examples of how life slips and slides about, because it is there, in the main, that the images are often incomprehensible. The reader must give up any attempt to understand fully what is being said and accept a vague, dreamy sense of emotional rightness. Clarity in those passages comes and goes as the poet allows his mind to roam about in and out of rational focus.

What does become cumulatively clear is that Ashbery is not simply concerned with the painting, but with all art, including poetry. This is a major theme in his work: the inability of poetry to discover truth and to fix it once for all, because reality is always in flux and the work of art is static. Yet the poem goes even further in suggesting that Ashbery is also talking about the peculiar state of humankind—always searching for truth and always at the whim of constant change. Such a conclusion could be depressing, but in Ashbery's poem there is a kind of genial, sophisticated acceptance. There is a celebration of humankind's incapacity to "know," which makes humans, in a sense, captives like the figure in the Parmigianino painting, slightly distorted and unable to escape.

"Mixed Feelings"

First published: 1975 (collected in *Self-Portrait in a Convex Mirror*, 1975)
Type of work: Poem

The poet seems to be looking at an old photograph of some young women and imagines what they are like and how they would speak to him.

Ashbery's finest work may be in his long poems, where the space gives him time to develop a sense of what it is like to attempt to deal with a specific, recalcitrant subject. A shorter poem, such as "Mixed Feelings" (from the volume *Self-Portrait in a Convex Mirror*), while being a good poem, provides a kind of five-finger exercise in understanding Ashbery's peculiar charms as a poet. The idea is a simple one. The poet either thinks he is smelling frying sausages while looking at an old photograph, or he is, in fact, doing so. It hardly matters. What does matter is his attempt to date the picture, which is not too difficult, because he recognizes the aircraft in the photograph as one used in World War II.

Some young women are leaning against it. He imagines their names, typically common names for women at the time, and thereby provides a perceptive confirmation of the fact that times change, as does the style in choosing names for children. He wonders how he would explain to them how much the world has changed in more than thirty years. Would they want to listen, he wonders, standing as they do with that smart knowingness of young women? Perhaps they would tell him to get lost, using the slang of the day. Perhaps they would rather go to a café for a cup of coffee. Ashbery is, in fact, slyly evoking the social world of wartime, when servicemen tried to pick up young women with a smart quip and were often rebuffed just as smartly.

Ashbery is not sure if his imagined setting is right. The picture reminds him of California, but his reference to the garment district suggests New York. The light looks western, and the idea of the aircraft is strongly allied to the Pacific Coast for him. The Donald Duck cartoon on the airplane is a lovely touch, and it was common for combat aircraft to carry some kind of cartoon on the fuselage. He wonders about the girls in the photograph, but he is not going to spend much time at it. In the end, he imagines that sometime he will meet young women like them in an airport lounge and that they will then chat with him just as trivially as the women in the photograph might have done.

It is a very modest poem, and it shows that Ashbery can make sense if he wants to. It possesses the sort of tender stillness that often appears in short passages in his longer poems, and it has that peculiar eye for detail which is a mark of his work. It makes even his most obscure metaphors ring with associations that are hard to place but difficult to forget. The easy informality, the simple conversational style, and the cogent, economical way in which a complicated idea is presented with little sense of trickiness are elements that come and go in his longer poems, but they have a life of their own in many of his shorter works, in which a quiet moment is captured. It is a clever poem, but it is difficult to tell that from a quick reading. The poem is based on the association of ideas, but it is the way those ideas are dropped into place—with such seeming innocence, starting with the homely idea of the smell of sausages, a common kind of food for the troops—which leads to the photograph and beyond.

"MORE PLEASANT ADVENTURES"

First published: 1984 (collected in *A Wave*, 1984)
Type of work: Poem

The poem appears to be about the history of a personal relationship, perhaps a marriage, and its eventual failure; it may be a metaphor for life in general.

"More Pleasant Adventures," a poem from *A Wave* (1984), is one of those small performances by Ashbery that tempt critics into presuming that it stands for something other than itself, sometimes with preposterous consequences. On the surface it seems simple enough. The first two lines, for example, with the idea of the wedding cake looming behind them, are very smart, very succinctly sophisticated in their summing-up of the way in which the romance settles down to living day by day. The following metaphors, tracing the gradual lack of mutual interest, round out the first verse with a poetic version of how couples stop communicating.

The second verse starts with a double example of how Ashbery makes use of nonpoetic language. "Heck" has a kind of down-home simplicity that is not expected in poetry. It is followed by an equally deflated idea, a line from the popular song from the 1940's, "Sentimental Journey." Serious poets are "supposed" to quote from opera, but Ashbery chooses the songs of the streets. There is a rightness about this; anyone who rationalizes a failed relationship with the word "heck" is hardly likely to possess a repertoire that transcends Tin Pan Alley. It surely places the failure as less than tragic, how-

ever, and the rest of the poem is a listing of minor failures, ending in a suggestion that whatever else the years have done, they have resulted in the accumulation of some property for the unhappy pair to fight over.

Ashbery is often distinguished from poets such as Robert Lowell and John Berryman because he is thought not to tell stories of human anguish and failure. Poems such as "More Pleasant Adventures," however, suggest the contrary. It may be possible to take this poem to a higher level of metaphorical gesture and claim that it makes a more portentous statement about human nature, but on its most obvious level it is a very wry, astringently cool, somewhat antiromantic look at the failure of love, written from the point of view of one of the participants thereto. There is, however, a common theme in Ashbery's work that suggests that life tends to be less and less romantic as it passes by.

SUMMARY

If art is to be, in part, a reflection of the time and place in which it is created, Ashbery's deliberate refusal to make meaning within a pleasingly complicated network of aesthetic and philosophic maunderings has a rightness about it. His digressions ask large questions but decline to answer them. The latter half of the twentieth century lost that certainty, that assurance in social, political, religious, and familial structures, which was previously the source and basis of art. At the same time, Ashbery has managed to link the verbal arts with music and with the plastic arts in producing works which cannot be paraphrased and which stand for themselves as pure aesthetic gesture.

Charles H. Pullen

BIBLIOGRAPHY

By the Author

POETRY:
Turandot, and Other Poems, 1953
Some Trees, 1956
The Tennis Court Oath, 1962
Rivers and Mountains, 1966
Selected Poems, 1967
The Double Dream of Spring, 1970

Three Poems, 1972
Self-Portrait in a Convex Mirror, 1975
Houseboat Days, 1977
As We Know, 1979
Shadow Train, 1981
A Wave, 1984
Selected Poems, 1985
April Galleons, 1987
Flow Chart, 1991
Hotel Lautrémont, 1992
Three Books: Poems, 1993
And the Stars Were Shining, 1994
Can You Hear, Bird: Poems, 1995
The Mooring of Starting Out: The First Five Books of Poetry, 1997
Wakefulness: Poems, 1998
Girls on the Run: A Poem, 1999
Your Name Here, 2000
As Umbrellas Follow Rain, 2002
Chinese Whispers, 2002

LONG FICTION:
A Nest of Ninnies, 1969 (with James Schuyler)

DRAMA:
Everyman, pr. 1951
The Heroes, pr. 1952
The Compromise: Or, Queen of the Carabou, pr. 1956
The Philosopher, pb. 1964
Three Plays, pb. 1978

NONFICTION:
The Poetic Medium of W. H. Auden, 1949 (senior thesis)
Reported Sightings: Art Chronicles, 1957-1987, 1989
Other Traditions, 2000
John Ashbery in Conversation with Mark Ford, 2003

TRANSLATIONS:
Murder in Montarte, 1960 (of Noel Vixon)
Melville, 1960 (of Jean-Jacques Mayoux)
The Deadlier Sex, 1961 (of Genevieve Manceron)
Alberto Giacometti, 1962 (of Jacques Dupin)
The Landscape Is Behind the Door, 1994 (of Pierre Martory)
Giacometti: Three Essays, 2002 (of Dupin)
The Recitation of Forgetting, 2003 (of Franck André Jamme)

EDITED TEXT:
Best American Poetry, 1988, 1988

DISCUSSION TOPICS

- How is John Ashbery's interest in art reflected in his poetry?

- Ashbery says his poetry is about a world lacking in coherence. Explain how one or more poems explore this theme.

- Ashbery is strongly influenced by W. H. Auden, T. S. Eliot, and Wallace Stevens. Compare one of his poems to a work by one of these poets.

- Explain how Ashbery introduces an important question about life without answering it. Within the context of his poetry, is such an answer necessary?

- Explain how Ashbery ignores logic in the structure of his poetry.

- How does "Self-Portrait in a Convex Mirror" address the nature of reality?

- How does Ashbery use geographical locations to suggest something other than themselves?

About the Author
Bloom, Harold, ed. *John Ashbery.* Philadelphia: Chelsea House, 2004.
Casper, Robert N. "Interview with John Ashbery." *Jubilat* 9 (Fall/Winter, 2004): 44-50.

Herd, David. *John Ashbery and American Poetry.* New York: Palgrave, 2000.

Lehman, David, ed. *Beyond Amazement: New Essays on John Ashbery.* Ithaca, N.Y.: Cornell University Press, 1980.

Moramarco, Fred. "Across the Millennium: The Persistence of John Ashbery." *American Poetry Review* 33 (March/April, 2004): 39-41.

Shapiro, David. *John Ashbery: An Introduction to the Poetry.* New York: Columbia University Press, 1979.

Shoptaw, John. *On the Outside Looking Out: John Ashbery's Poetry.* Cambridge, Mass.: Harvard University Press, 1994.

Vincent, John. "Reports of Looting and Insane Buggery Behind Altars: John Ashbery's Queer Poetics." *Twentieth Century Literature* 44 (Summer, 1998): 155-175.

Yau, John. "The Poet as Art Critic." *American Poetry Review* 34 (May/June, 2005): 45-50.

ISAAC ASIMOV

Born: Petrovichi, Soviet Union (now in Russia)
January 2, 1920
Died: New York, New York
April 6, 1992

First recognized for his science fiction, Asimov became more broadly known for his books of science popularization—and for being the most prolific author of his day, with 470 published books at the time of his death.

Library of Congress

BIOGRAPHY

Asimov was born in the village of Petrovichi, in the Soviet Union, on January 2, 1920, the first child of Judah Asimov and Anna Rachel Berman Asimov. The Asimovs emigrated to the United States in 1923 and settled in Brooklyn, where Asimov's father owned a series of candy stores. Asimov taught himself to read at the age of five and was regarded as a child prodigy, both for his ability to learn and for his prodigious memory.

After skipping several grades and completing junior high school in two years instead of three, Asimov enrolled in the Boys' High School of Brooklyn, a selective, prestigious school noted for mathematics. He entered at age twelve and a half, two and a half years younger than his fellow students, and continued to be sheltered from the lives of his fellows, particularly girls.

Asimov then entered Columbia University, intending to become a doctor. After he had to kill and dissect a cat in anatomy class, he switched to chemistry and after graduation continued the study of chemistry at Columbia. He had obtained his M.S. and was on his way to his Ph.D. when the United States entered World War II. Asimov interrupted his studies to work at the U.S. Navy yards in Philadelphia (with Robert A. Heinlein and L. Sprague de Camp). At that time he married Ger-

trude Blugerman, with whom he would have two children: David, born in 1951, and Robyn, born in 1955. He served less than a year in the Army before resuming his studies at Columbia, earned his Ph.D. in 1948, and after a year of postgraduate work accepted a position as instructor at the Boston University School of Medicine, teaching biochemistry.

Asimov's career in science fiction began in 1935, when he started writing letters to the editor of *Astounding Science Fiction*. In 1938 he visited editor John W. Campbell, Jr., in his office, taking with him his first story, which was rejected. "Marooned Off Vesta," his third story, was published in the March, 1939, issue of *Amazing Stories*. Asimov succeeded in selling his tenth story, "Trends," to John Campbell for the July, 1939, *Astounding Science Fiction*.

In the years to come, Asimov would visit Campbell once a week, suggesting an idea (or receiving a suggestion for one) and returning with a publishable story. His series of robot stories began with "Reason" in the April, 1941, *Astounding Science Fiction*. The following year he published "Foundation," the first of his Foundation stories eventually collected as *The Foundation Trilogy* (1963).

Asimov would write many more stories and novels, including novels of future "locked-room" crimes featuring Lije Bailey and his robot assistant/competitor R. Daneel Olivaw. Eventually, in the last decade of his life, Asimov became a best-selling author by returning to his robot and Foundation roots and combining them into a future history culminating in the creation of the Galactic Empire and the foundations that try to cushion its fall.

107

In 1958 he left teaching over a dispute about his academic research style (his writing was his research, he insisted) for full-time writing, which was providing more income than his teaching salary. The launch of the Soviet satellite *Sputnik* convinced him that he should pursue the science popularizations that he had begun in 1952 with *Biochemistry and Human Metabolism* and in 1957 with monthly science columns in *Fantasy and Science Fiction*. He would publish no more science fiction novels except the novelization of the film *Fantastic Voyage* (1966), *The Gods Themselves* (1972), and *Foundation's Edge* (1982). Instead he published hundreds of science books and became known as an erudite and entertaining public speaker.

Asimov separated from his first wife and moved back to New York in 1970. He was divorced in 1973 and married Dr. Janet Jeppson, a psychiatrist. He died April 6, 1992, from complications of acquired immunodeficiency syndrome (AIDS) acquired through a transfusion during earlier open-heart surgery.

ANALYSIS

Asimov's science fiction, like his science popularizations, was based on a cool rationality and a transparent style. When complimented by a scholar about a poetic passage near the end of his story "Nightfall," he insisted the passage was John Campell's editorial addition. Asimov's ability to describe complicated issues in understandable prose and appropriate analogies, carried over from his science-fiction writing, made his science articles and books successful, from *The Intelligent Man's Guide to Science* (1960) to *Asimov's Biographical Encyclopedia of Science and Technology* (1964) and *Asimov's Chronology of Science and Discovery* (1989). He also exhibited the playfulness of *Lecherous Limericks* (1975) and *The Sensuous Dirty Old Man* (1971) and began weaving personal references into introductions and headnotes with his editing of *The Hugo Winners*.

The breadth of his subjects was remarkable. He wrote mystery novels and stories as well as science fiction, edited more than a hundred anthologies, and published nonfiction books about general science, mathematics, astronomy, earth sciences, chemistry and biochemistry, physics, biology, history, the Bible, literature (including William Shakespeare), and humor and satire. He also wrote two massive volumes of autobiography as a way of celebrating the publication of his two hundredth book: *In Memory Yet Green* (1979) and *In Joy Still Felt* (1980). Some years later he put together a memoir, *I. Asimov* (1994).

Asimov's science fiction was shaped by his love for the genre's magazines, his admiration for Campbell, and his financial need. The amount he received for his stories was small at first (a penny a word at the beginning, two cents a word a bit later), paying for little more than his tuition. He also wrote, however, for the love of the genre, his satisfaction at his relationship with Campbell, and the admiration of editors and readers. His ability to get published regularly—forty-eight stories between 1939 and 1950 (with a gap during the War) meant that he published an average of almost five stories a year—he attributed in part to his chancing on two series ideas: the robot stories and the Foundation stories. He wrote an article about it for his fellow science-fiction writers: "There's Nothing Like a Good Foundation." During this period he published eleven robot stories and eight Foundation stories. He also reported income for those ten years of $7,821.75, a little more than $710 a year.

Asimov's science-fiction writing career significantly changed after he sold his first novel, *Pebble in the Sky* (1950), to Doubleday. Although he would continue to write stories, his focus would change to novels. Another major shift occurred when he began writing for Horace Gold after the creation of *Galaxy Science Fiction* in 1950. Although he would continue to publish in Campbell's *Astounding Science Fiction*, he did some of his best work for *Galaxy*, particularly *The Caves of Steel* (1954) and *The Naked Sun* (1957), which later were released in a single volume as *The Robot Novels* (1957). They were among the first successful blends of detective story and science fiction. In his Galaxy novels Asimov presented more rounded characters influenced by family, environment, and emotion.

Asimov's earlier work, and much of his fiction throughout his career, was played on a bare stage by characters who reasoned and behaved rationally. His villains generally were as rational as his heroes. He said in an interview, "It's not even a triumph of rationality over irrationality or over emotion, at least not in my favorite stories. It's generally a conflict between rationalities and the superior winning. If it were a western, where everything depends upon the draw of the gun, it would be very unsatisfactory if the hero shot down a person who didn't know how to shoot." Nevertheless, his two favorite stories, "The Ugly Little Boy" and "The Bicentennial Man," favored sentiment over rationality.

"NIGHTFALL"

First published: 1941 (collected in *Nightfall, and Other Stories*, 1969)
Type of work: Short story

A group of scientists gather to experience the fall of night, which, because the planet has six suns, occurs only every 2,049 years.

Asimov had been publishing stories for two years before he got his first story featured on the cover of *Astounding Science Fiction*. "Nightfall" was recognized almost immediately as a classic and represented a validation of the author's place in science fiction. When the first volume of the Science Fiction Writers of America's *The Science Fiction Hall of Fame* was published, "Nightfall" got more votes than any other story. Asimov looked back ruefully on the plaudits, because he felt he wrote better stories later. Nevertheless, when he incorporated himself, he chose the name of "Nightfall, Inc."

The story was suggested by Campbell, who quoted Ralph Waldo Emerson's statement in *Nature* (1836): "If the stars should appear one night in a thousand years, how would men believe and adore, and preserve for many generations the remembrance of the City of God." And he asked Asimov what he thought would happen. "I don't know," Asimov said. "I think they would go mad," Campbell said. "I want you to write a story about that."

Asimov made the story's daytime period 2,049 years (roughly comparable to the time between the height of the Roman Empire and the present, or between Greek democracy and Sir Isaac Newton). He invented (less plausibly) a planet, Lagash, with six suns so that one was never out of the sky, except in predictable situations in which all the suns but one were on the opposite side of the planet, and the remaining one was eclipsed by a moon.

The story takes place, like a one-act play, in the observatory set up to record the fall of night and the appearance of the stars. Most of what happens is related in the form of questions by a reporter, answered by the director of the university and a psychologist. The only action is when a cultist attempts to destroy the astronomical cameras set up to record the event. The cult has accumulated mythological writings and religious interpretations of the rise and fall of previous civilizations every two millennia and believes the stars are sacred and that they would be profaned, if not destroyed, by being filmed. At the end, a mob from the nearby city gathers to storm the university, night falls, the stars appear, and everyone goes mad.

The story works in spite of the lack of action and character development. The situation is totally unlike human experience, and yet the responses, like the history of scientific discovery, seem all too human. The attempt to understand the unknown by rational processes and its opposite, the emotional reaction to the mysterious, reside at the heart of the science-fiction enterprise. The built-in ironies contrast Lagashian accomplishment and expectations against those of humans on Earth. Additionally, the twenty-one-year-old Asimov was already skilled at presenting scientific concepts in understandable language and images and in a kind of Socratic dialogue.

I, ROBOT

First published: 1950
Type of work: Short-story collection

Asimov started his consideration of robots and their interaction with humans in these eight stories written and first published between 1940 and 1950.

I, Robot was published by a specialty publisher, Gnome Press, in 1950, the same year that Doubleday published Asimov's first novel, *Pebble in the Sky*. Neither sold well, but *Pebble in the Sky* did better than *I, Robot* because the former was a novel. Nevertheless, the publication of the collection was a signal event in attaching Asimov's name to the robot concept and in enhancing his aura of publication as well as presaging the many collections to come.

Stories about robots had been published before. Even the title was taken from Eando Binder's "I, Robot" in *Amazing Stories* for January, 1939. What Asimov brought to the concept was the notion of safeguards. In his 1964 collection *The Rest of the Robots*, Asimov explained that he had grown tired of the stories about humans creating artificial life that turns against its creators. Nothing, he said, is built without safeguards, from stairs to knives to steam engines, and robots would have safeguards built into them in the form of "the three laws of robotics" that Campbell derived from his stories. First, a robot cannot harm a human being or by inaction allow a human being to come to harm. Second, a robot must obey an order given by a human being unless this comes into conflict with the first law. Third, a robot must protect itself from harm unless that comes into conflict with the first two laws. Several attempts were made to film *I, Robot* before Will Smith starred in a film of that title in 2004 (which offended Asimov fans by flouting the three laws of robotics).

The first story in the collection, "Robbie," was published in Frederik Pohl's *Super Science Stories*. The rest were published in *Astounding Science Fiction*. "Robbie" describes human distrust of robots until a family learns that its daughter was saved from death by the instant, unthinking action of her robot servant. "Runaround" deals with the quandary of a robot circling a pool of selenium on Mercury because his law of self-preservation exactly balances, at that distance, his law to obey instructions. "Reason" reveals Asimov's two robot engineers, Powell and Donovan, putting together a robot intended to handle a beam of energy from the sun to the earth from a satellite. The robot does not believe inferior beings could create him and invents a religion based on the energy converter. The engineers leave him as he is because his religion makes his work even more reliable. In "Catch That Rabbit" Donovan and Powell discover that six sub-robots stress a robot's positronic abilities.

Susan Calvin, Asimov's favorite roboticist, tries to cope with a robot accidentally equipped with telepathic ability in "Liar!" and the conflict between obeying orders and telling a truth that will hurt a human. "Little Lost Robot" describes the problem of a too-sensitive first law that would keep scientists from danger, and how the law about obeying orders means that humans must be careful about casual comments (like "Get lost"). "Escape," which involves computers rather than robots, asks how a computer can be asked to solve a problem that might involve the death of a human being. In "Evidence" the question is raised as to how one can tell robots from humans when the people in question stand on their right not to have their privacy invaded. "The Evitable Conflict" takes up the question of robot superiority suggested in "Evidence" and the ambiguity of what constitutes harm or good for humans as the robots take over the human economy.

THE FOUNDATION TRILOGY

First published: 1951, 1952, 1953
Type of work: Short-story collections

Inaccurately titled a "trilogy," the Foundation Trilogy is a collection of eight stories published originally in Astounding Science Fiction *between 1942 and 1950, and a ninth written especially for the first book publication.*

The "trilogy" was published originally as *Foundation* in 1951, *Foundation and Empire* in 1952, and *Second Foundation* in 1953, first by Gnome Press and as individual paperback volumes by Avon and in 1963 by Doubleday as a single volume.

The first story in the book, "The Psychohistorians," reveals how Hari Seldon predicted the fall of the galactic empire through the use of psychohistory and set up two foundations, the first composed of 100,000 encyclopedists sent to Terminus, ostensibly to write the *Encyclopedia Galactica* (from which Asimov includes excerpts as epigraphs) but actually to provide the foundation for rebuilding and shorten the period of barbarism from twenty-five thousand years to one thousand.

"Foundation" (called "The Encyclopedists" in the book) and "Bridle and Saddle" (called "The Mayors" in the book) tell the story of the appearance of Hari Seldon in his "time vault" with a prediction about a Seldon crisis at hand. The galactic empire has fallen, and Terminus is threatened by two powerful neighboring systems because Terminus has atomic energy and the others do not. Mayor Hari Seldon works out an ostensible surrender to one of them but thirty years later reveals that the creation of an atomic religion protects Terminus from being taken over. In the two stories that follow, "The Traders" and "The Merchant Princes,"

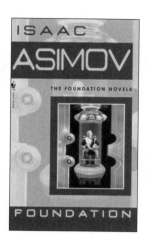

Asimov shows Terminus responding to new challenges and spreading its influences, through trade, throughout nearby systems.

Foundation and Empire is made up of two novellas, *The General* and *The Mule*. Both deal with challenges to Terminus as the initial vigor of the Foundation deteriorates into a dependence upon Seldon's predictions, a kind of psychohistorical determinism that some critics have called debased Marxism. (Asimov denied knowing anything about Marx and said, instead, that his concept of psychohistory was based on the theory of gases.) The general who attempts to take over the empire is thwarted by the historical principle that a weak general is no threat to the Foundation, and the emperor cannot tolerate a strong general lest he seize the throne. "The Mule," on the other hand, brings up the question of the unpredictable, in this case a mutation in the Mule, which allows him to influence people's attitudes and behavior. The Mule falters because of his affection for a young woman whom he cannot bear to influence because she liked him for himself.

Second Foundation also is made up of two novellas, *Search by the Mule* and *Search by the Foundation*. In the first of these, the Mule's search for the Second Foundation, ostensibly located at "Star's End," leads him in false directions until he finally is trapped, and adjusted, by a Second Foundation psychologist. In *Search by the Foundation*, the First Foundation searches for the Second and seems to find it, only to have adjustments at the end make the First Foundation's victory illusory.

Critically, the books should be approached as individual stories growing out of a single set of premises: the fall of the galactic empire and psy-

chohistory, which is the ability to foresee broad historical trends. After the first two stories, Asimov had no overall plan but built each new story on the open-endedness of the previous, like a set of Tinkertoys. Eventually he felt that the effort to review previous situations for the reader became too great, and he gave up writing more stories in this universe until he returned in 1982 to write *Foundation's Edge* and *Foundation and Earth* (1985), and then *Prelude to Foundation* (1988) and *Forward the Foundation* (1993) as prequels dealing with Hari Seldon's arrival on Trantor and experiences leading up to "The Psychohistorians."

Much of the historic relevance of the Foundation stories derived from the fall of the Roman Empire. Asimov recounted how he was going on the subway to visit Campbell and did not have an idea to discuss. He had a volume of the works of Gilbert and Sullivan in front of him open to a picture of the fairy queen in *Iolanthe* kneeling in front of Private Willis of the Grenadier Guards. Asimov's mind wandered to soldiers, to a military society, to feudalism, to the breakup of the Roman Empire. When he got to Campbell's office he was ready to discuss the fall of the galactic empire. To this he added not only psychohistory but a set of philosophic principles that play themselves out in the stories: that power lies behind the throne and that one generation's solution becomes the problem for the next generation. Thus the stories offer a series of smart assistants working behind the scenes to invent solutions to problems as they arrive and a series of solutions whose power lasts far behind their effectiveness.

THE GODS THEMSELVES

First published: 1972
Type of work: Novel

Two universes with different values for the strong nuclear reaction begin exchanging elements, to the benefit of each, until disaster looms in the human universe.

Samples of plutonium-186 begin appearing in a scientific laboratory in place of tungsten. Plutonium-186 can exist only in a universe in which the nuclear reaction is much weaker. The element is a source of energy in the human universe, as is the tungsten in the alien universe.

The novel consists of three novellas. The first, *Against Stupidity,* is a story of professional jealousy and scientific persistence in getting plutonium-186 accepted and used. The second novella, *The Gods Themselves,* takes place in the alien universe, where mating consists of the merging of three different nebulous creatures. One of them is uneasy about the transfer of material and the prospective mating and sends warnings to the human universe. This is the most engrossing of the three. The third novella, *Contend in Vain,* describes life on the moon and the effort to stop catastrophe to the human universe by constructing "cosmeg pumps" on the moon and using part of the energy to counteract the changes in field intensity that threaten to explode the sun and perhaps even the galactic arm.

"The Bicentennial Man"

First published: 1976
Type of work: Short story

A robot develops creativity and ability to learn and eventually wants to become a "man," even if it means his death.

By an accidental arrangement of positronic brain pathways, robot NDR ("Andrew") is artistic and can learn. His owners, the Martin family, treat him well, selling his art but depositing half the proceeds into his account and getting him every upgrade. Finally Andrew buys his freedom, wears clothes, writes a robot history, obtains legal rights for robots, replaces his body parts with organic ones, and becomes a robobiologist. Finally, his request to be declared a man is turned down because of his immortality. He then arranges for the potential of his immortal body to be slowly drained, and on his two hundredth anniversary the world president signs the act declaring the dying Andrew "a Bicentennial Man." "The Bicentennial Man" was filmed in 1999, with Robin Williams as Andrew.

The Robots of Dawn

First published: 1983
Type of work: Novel

Elijah Bailey is called to solve another crime, the "death" of a robot, on the planet Aurora.

The long-postponed sequel to *The Caves of Steel* and *The Naked Sun, The Robots of Dawn* is another locked-room mystery that detective Lije Bailey is called to the Spacer planet Aurora to solve. He is reunited with Gladia Delmarre, with whom he had a frustrated relationship in *The Naked Sun.* The novel devotes some time to discussing why destroying a robot is murder and sifting through a series of suspects until Bailey finally discovers that another robot (Giscard) caused the brain-death to shield the robot's creator, and that he himself is present to further the cause of space exploration. In the process, Asimov hints at the beginnings of psychohistory.

The Robots of Dawn was the beginning of Asmov's efforts to combine his robot stories and his Foundation stories into a single unified future history. Because there are no robots in the Foundation stories, this novel was the first stage in rationalizing their disappearance (or going undercover). The final stage was depicted in the sequel, *Robots and Empire. The Robots of Dawn,* more than twice as long as its two predecessors put together, was a best seller.

Summary

Professor George G. Simpson of Harvard University called Asimov "one of our natural wonders and national resources." Simpson was referring to Asimov's science popularizations, but Asimov always viewed himself as a science-fiction writer, and his science-fiction writing, noted for its clarity, rationality, and scope, was a foundation for later science fiction. It will be remembered and read long after his other works are forgotten.

James Gunn

BIBLIOGRAPHY

By the Author

LONG FICTION:
Pebble in the Sky, 1950
Foundation, 1951
The Stars Like Dust, 1951
The Currents of Space, 1952
Foundation and Empire, 1952
Second Foundation, 1953
The Caves of Steel, 1954
The End of Eternity, 1955
The Naked Sun, 1957
The Robot Novels, 1957 (includes *The Caves of Steel* and *The Naked Sun*)
The Death-Dealers, 1958 (also known as *A Whiff of Death*)
The Foundation Trilogy, 1963 (includes *Foundation*, *Foundation and Empire*, and *Second Foundation*)
Fantastic Voyage, 1966
The Gods Themselves, 1972
Murder at the ABA: A Puzzle in Four Days and Sixty Scenes, 1976
Foundation's Edge, 1982
The Robots of Dawn, 1983
Robots and Empire, 1985
Foundation and Earth, 1985
Fantastic Voyage II: Destination Brain, 1987
Prelude to Foundation, 1988
Azazel, 1988
Robot Dreams, 1989
Nemesis, 1989
Robot Visions, 1990
Nightfall, 1991 (with Robert Silverberg)
The Ugly Little Boy, 1992 (with Silverberg)
Forward the Foundation, 1993
The Positronic Man, 1993 (with Silverberg)

SHORT FICTION:
I, Robot, 1950
The Martian Way, 1955
Earth Is Room Enough, 1957
Nine Tomorrows, 1959
The Rest of the Robots, 1964
Asimov's Mysteries, 1968
Nightfall, and Other Stories, 1969
The Early Asimov, 1972
Tales of the Black Widowers, 1974
Buy Jupiter, and Other Stories, 1975

DISCUSSION TOPICS

- The common image of science fiction is rocket ships and atom bombs. How does Isaac Asimov's fiction fit that image?

- How do Asimov's robots differ from the robots usually encountered in works of science fiction?

- How could one improve upon Asimov's three laws of robotics? Would they work? What if they applied to humans?

- The Foundation stories have been compared to the fall of the Roman empire. What kind of resemblances are obvious? How does Asimov use them?

- Is psychohistory possible? Is it desirable? What does it predict? How does Asimov prevent it from limiting human initiative?

- In "Nightfall," the Lagashians and even the scientists go mad. Is Asimov's outcome believable? Would humans behave the same way? What comparable human reversal of experience would drive humans mad?

- Asimov makes human space exploration and colonization desirable, even imperative, in *The Robots of Dawn*. Why is it important to Asimov? Should it be important to humanity?

Isaac Asimov

More Tales of the Black Widowers, 1976
The Bicentennial Man, and Other Stories, 1976
Good Taste, 1977
The Key Word, and Other Mysteries, 1977
Casebook of the Black Widowers, 1980
The Winds of Change, and Other Stories, 1983
The Union Club Mysteries, 1983
Computer Crimes and Capers, 1983
Banquets of the Black Widowers, 1984
The Disappearing Man, and Other Mysteries, 1985
Alternative Asimovs, 1986
Isaac Asimov: The Complete Stories, 1990-1992 (2 volumes)

NONFICTION:

The Chemicals of Life: Enzymes, Vitamins, Hormones, 1954
Inside the Atom, 1956
The World of Carbon, 1958
The World of Nitrogen, 1958
Words of Science and the History Behind Them, 1959
Realm of Numbers, 1959
The Intelligent Man's Guide to Science, 1960
The Wellsprings of Life, 1960
Life and Energy, 1962
The Search for the Elements, 1962
The Genetic Code, 1963
The Human Body: Its Structures and Operation, 1964
The Human Brain: Its Capacities and Functions, 1964
A Short History of Biology, 1964
Asimov's Biographical Encyclopedia of Science and Technology, 1964
Planets for Man, 1964 (with Stephen H. Dole)
The Greeks: A Great Adventure, 1965
A Short History of Chemistry, 1965
The New Intelligent Man's Guide to Science, 1965
The Neutrino: Ghost Particle of the Atom, 1966
The Roman Republic, 1966
Understanding Physics, 1966
The Genetic Effects of Radiation, 1966
The Universe: From Flat Earth to Quasar, 1966
The Roman Empire, 1967
The Egyptians, 1967
The Dark Ages, 1968
Science, Numbers, and I, 1968
Asimov's Guide to the Bible, 1968-1969 (2 volumes)
The Shaping of England, 1969
Asimov's Guide to Shakespeare, 1970 (2 volumes)
Constantinople: The Forgotten Empire, 1970
The Sensuous Dirty Old Man, 1971 (as Dr. A)
Electricity and Man, 1972
The Shaping of France, 1972
Worlds Within Worlds: The Story of Nuclear Energy, 1972

The Shaping of North America from Earliest Times to 1763, 1973
Today, Tomorrow, and . . ., 1973
Before the Golden Age, 1974 (autobiography)
Earth: Our Crowded Spaceship, 1974
Our World in Space, 1974
The Birth of the United States, 1763-1816, 1974
Lecherous Limericks, 1975
Our Federal Union: The United States from 1816 to 1865, 1975
Science Past—Science Future, 1975
The Collapsing Universe, 1977
The Golden Door: The United States from 1865 to 1918, 1977
A Choice of Catastrophes: The Disasters That Threaten Our World, 1979
Extraterrestrial Civilizations, 1979
In Memory Yet Green: The Autobiography of Isaac Asimov, 1920-1954, 1979
The Annotated "Gulliver's Travels," 1980
Asimov on Science Fiction, 1980
Joy Still Felt: The Autobiography of Isaac Asimov, 1954-1978, 1980
Visions of the Universe, 1981
Exploring the Earth and the Cosmos: The Growth and Future of Human Knowledge, 1982
The Roving Mind, 1983
The History of Physics, 1984
The Edge of Tomorrow, 1985
Robots: Machines in Man's Image, 1985 (with Karen A. Frenkel)
Asimov's Guide to Halley's Comet, 1985
Exploding Suns, 1985
The Dangers of Intelligence, and Other Science Essays, 1986
Beginnings: The Story of Origins—of Mankind, Life, the Earth, the Universe, 1987
Past, Present, and Future, 1987
Asimov's Annotated Gilbert and Sullivan, 1988
The Relativity of Wrong, 1988
Asimov on Science, 1989
Asimov's Chronology of Science and Discovery, 1989
Asimov's Galaxy, 1989
Frontiers, 1990
Asimov's Chronology of the World: The History of the World from the Big Bang to Modern Times, 1991
Atom: Journey Across the Subatomic Cosmos, 1991
I. Asimov: A Memoir, 1994
Yours, Isaac Asimov: A Lifetime of Letters, 1995 (Stanley Asimov, editor)
It's Been a Good Life, 2002 (Janet Jeppson Asimov, editor; condensed version of his 3 volumes of autobiography, *In Memory Yet Green, Joy Still Felt*, and *I. Asimov*)
Conversations with Isaac Asimov, 2005 (Carl Freedman, editor)

CHILDREN'S LITERATURE:
David Starr: Space Ranger, 1952
Lucky Starr and the Pirates of the Asteroids, 1953
Lucky Starr and the Oceans of Venus, 1954
Lucky Starr and the Big Sun of Mercury, 1956
Lucky Starr and the Moons of Jupiter, 1957
Lucky Starr and the Rings of Saturn, 1958

About the Author

Goble, Neil. *Asimov Analyzed.* Baltimore: Mirage, 1972.

Gunn, James. *Isaac Asimov: The Foundations of Science Fiction.* Lanham, Md.: Scarecrow Press, 2005.

Hassler, Donald M. *Reader's Guide to Isaac Asimov.* Mercer Island, Wash.: Starmont, 1991.

Moskowitz, Sam. "Isaac Asimov." In *Seekers of Tomorrow: Masters of Modern Science Fiction.* Cleveland: World, 1966.

Olander, Joseph D., and Martin H. Greenberg, eds. *Isaac Asimov.* New York: Taplinger, 1977.

Patrouch, Joseph F. *The Science Fiction of Isaac Asimov.* Garden City, N.Y.: Doubleday, 1974.

MARGARET ATWOOD

Born: Ottawa, Ontario, Canada
November 18, 1939

One of the most prominent and prolific Canadian authors, Atwood is also one of the world's best-selling writers. Although Atwood is best known for her novels, she writes poems, short stories, children's fiction, and essays and has even worked in nonmedia, including film, television, and theater.

Courtesy, Vancouver International Writers Festival

BIOGRAPHY

Margaret Eleanor "Peggy" Atwood was born in Ottawa, Ontario, on November 18, 1939, the second of three children of Margaret Dorothy (Killam) and Carl Edmund Atwood. Her father was an entomologist who conducted research in the bush country of Quebec and Ontario. Therefore, Atwood spent many of her summers at the family cottage exploring the Canadian wilderness until her family would return to Toronto for the school year. This connection to and exploration of the natural world would have a dramatic effect on her later writing.

Atwood's passion for the creative arts began at a young age. Between the ages of eight and sixteen, she was more interested in painting and designing clothing than in writing. She jokingly calls this time her "dark period" because beyond these years, she was devoted to writing; however, she would go on to illustrate some of her books of poetry and to win respect as a painter.

Atwood wrote for the school paper during her teens at Leaside High School and contributed to the school magazine *Clan Call*. From 1957 to 1961, she attended the University of Toronto, where she pursued her B.A. in English. During her undergraduate career, she formed a bond with teacher and critic Northrop Frye. Her mentor introduced her to the poetry of William Blake, which would subsequently impact her own poetry. Even the ti-

tles of some of her books, such as *Double Persephone* (1961) and *Two-Headed Poems* (1978), reveal a double vision of mythic contradictions that stems from the influence of Blake's writings. Even more important was her friendship with professor and poet Jay Macpherson, whose irony and formal choices are also reflected in Atwood's work. After graduating with honors from her undergraduate studies and publishing numerous poems in the college's magazines, Atwood completed her master's degree in English at Radcliffe College, Harvard University, in 1963.

That year, Atwood took a position at a marketing research firm, which would give her context for her novel *The Edible Woman* (1969). During this period, she wrote poetry that would appear in various literary journals and would make her one of Toronto's new literary voices in the 1960's. At this time, she also worked on a novel, *Up in the Air so Blue*, which remains unpublished. In 1964 she provided CBC radio with *The Trumpets of Summer*, a choral composition with music by John Beckwith.

She then moved to Vancouver and taught English at the University of British Columbia for one year. This was the first of many temporary teaching positions and writer-in-residence positions she would hold, including those at Sir George Williams University (now Concordia University), the University of Alberta, York University in Toronto, and the University of Toronto. Also, in 1964 she wrote her novel *The Edible Woman* in six months, though mistakes made by her publishers would delay the novel's release for five years.

Atwood returned to Radcliffe from 1965 to 1967

to pursue her doctorate. During this time she proposed a thesis, "The English Metaphysical Romance," but never finished the degree. At Harvard, she met James Polk, an American. In 1967 the two married, and this relationship would be an influence on Atwood's love poetry. Nevertheless, they would separate in 1972 and eventually divorce. After separating from Polk, Atwood began a relationship with novelist Graeme Gibson. The couple moved to a farm near Alliston, Ontario, and their daughter, Eleanor Jess, was born on May 17, 1976.

In 1967 Atwood was awarded the General's Award, Canada's most esteemed literary honor, for her book of poems *The Circle Game* (1966). The poetry in this collection established major themes in Atwood's work including Canadian identity and the conflict between humans and nature. Atwood also gained recognition for *Survival: A Thematic Guide to Canadian Literature*, which she published in 1972. This piece became a work of importance for Canada's cultural nationalists. In 1973 she was made an officer of the Order of Canada; she was promoted to companion in 1981. Throughout Atwood's career, she has been active in the Writer's Union of Canada, having helped to establish the union in the early 1970's, and in the Anglophone Canadian division of PEN International; she has served as president of both. Also, she is a member of the Canadian Civil Liberties Union and the editorial board of the influential Toronto-based House of Anansi Press.

Atwood's writing has influenced readers across the globe. Her novel *The Handmaid's Tale* (1985) was noted as the most widely taught novel in America in 1996. Atwood has been the recipient of various literary awards, including honorary degrees from Smith College (1982) and the University of Toronto (1983), among many others. She has also received the City of Toronto Book Award, the Canadian Booksellers Association Award, and numerous other honors. Two of Atwood's novels have been selected for CBC Radio's *Canada Reads* competition: *The Handmaid's Tale*, supported by former prime minister Kim Campbell in 2002, and *Oryx and Crake* (2003), supported by Toronto city councillor Olivia Chow in 2005.

ANALYSIS

Atwood is known as the "Octopus" and as a "Medusa" by critics for her wit and her biting sense of humor. She is concerned with the creation and function of art as well as its importance in both the political and social worlds. For Atwood, art is an issue of morality; her writing provides a way to look at the world critically, to witness the world's shortcomings, and to offer solutions for redemption. Atwood believes that, ultimately, art must function as an agent of truth and that the artist should provide both knowledge and confrontation.

Often, Atwood teaches through negative example in her work. Many of her protagonists do not appear heroic at the start of her novels. Also, her narrators are usually not reliable, and they may even be mentally unstable. They are often fragmented and isolated from others and from their settings; they have mixed feelings about their pasts and about their connections to their homeland, Canada.

Thematically, Atwood explores the contradictions behind Canada as a nation and the identity of those who consider themselves Canadians. She has argued that Canadians have always felt victimized. This victimization is a result of the merciless nature that Canadians encountered when they first settled in the country's vast wilderness and of the colonialist forces that overpowered their political and cultural trends. Through her work, Atwood hopes to encourage Canadian writers and readers to create a more positive and independent view of themselves. This fresh self-image is rooted in identification with indigenous cultures such as Native American and French-Canadian rather than with British and American cultures.

Atwood's own contradictory feelings toward her native land are apparent in her work. Her negative feelings toward Canada mingle with nostalgia. Her Canadian heritage is the source of plentiful images and archetypes that are fundamental to her novels. Just as Atwood is constantly exploring her identity through her writing, each of her protagonists is fighting to find a new voice. Moreover, Atwood's Canada, a symbol of unexploited wilderness and innocence, is feminine in an otherwise masculine world. Atwood's attention to gender goes beyond her portrayal of Canada, for she is concerned with the power struggle between men and women on many levels.

Although by the early 1970's, many critics viewed Atwood as one of the most influential feminist writers, Atwood states that she is against the concept of power as a whole in the hands of men or women. Although she does not consider herself a feminist writer, her concern with feminist issues began with her early interest in the nineteenth century British novel. Many such novels were written by women, such as Jane Austen and George Eliot. Similarly, Atwood has chosen to write criticism on numerous contemporary female American and Canadian feminist authors; this is an indication of her interest in the content area.

In Atwood's fiction, her female characters are often exposed to abundant suffering. Atwood has stated that these characters suffer because they mimic the experiences of women in reality. Also, she exposes women's deepest fear of being used by those around them, unable to extricate themselves from their situations. Atwood's work presents the physical survival of women in terms of a sisterhood rather than on an individual level. Her feminist concerns are integral in many of her novels, specifically in *The Edible Woman, Surfacing* (1972), *Life Before Man* (1979), *Bodily Harm* (1981), and *The Handmaid's Tale.*

Just as Atwood does not identify herself as a feminist writer, neither does she consider herself a science-fiction writer. A majority of her fiction is set in the present day, with details that allude to North America. For this reason, she has been associated with realism: the way things are currently rather than how they might be. Her most popular novel, *The Handmaid's Tale,* was a blatant exception to this trend. The work won the Arthur C. Clarke Award in 1987 for the best science-fiction novel published in the United Kingdom. Additionally, a sprinkling of her short stories and poems, as well as her later novel *The Blind Assassin* (2000), illustrates a concern with the future and the fantastic. Atwood herself refuses to classify her own writing as science fiction because her work does not contain technological hardware. She deems futuristic gadgetry fundamental to science fiction, so she prefers the term speculative fiction in regard to her own writing.

As a writer of poetry, Atwood states that she has a distinct personality from that of a writer of prose. She views poetry as a lens through which one condenses and reflects. In her poetry, she often blurs the line between the real and the unreal. She accomplishes this to the degree that what the reader would view as reality becomes illusion and the unseen becomes more tangible and true. However,

Atwood's prose and poetry contain common thematic material and stylistic choices. Her novels and short stories are poetic in style, and her poems maintain a strong narrative strain.

Stylistically, Atwood chooses to incorporate irony, symbolism, self-conscious narrators, allegory, and bold imagery into her poetry and fiction in order to explore complex relationships between humans and the natural world, discomforting human characteristics, and power struggles between genders and political groups. Although her voice has been criticized as being overly formal and emotionally detached, she has been compared to writers such as George Orwell.

SURFACING

First published: 1972
Type of work: Novel

A young woman who is made mentally unstable by her oppressive social surroundings finds stability by shedding what those around her have deemed sanity.

Surfacing has been applauded for its characterizations, style, and themes. Thematically, the novel is about victimization and attempts to avoid victimization. The heroine of the novel battles the forces that suppress her, and at the end of the novel she gains confidence and a sense of freedom. In many ways, the novel is evocative of Sylvia Plath's *The Bell Jar* (1963).

Surfacing begins with the nameless heroine and her lover Joe traveling away from the city. They are accompanied by a married couple, David and Anna, and they are all visiting her family's cabin on an island in a Quebec lake. The heroine's father has disappeared, and the heroine is trying to find some answers as to his whereabouts. The men hope to take some photographs for a book they are creating together. Although the father, a botanist, is not found, they decide to remain at the lake.

The flaws and ugliness in each character surface while they are at the lake. Relationships between David and Anna and between the heroine and Joe begin to unravel. Problems in the marriage of David and Anna become apparent, while Joe be-

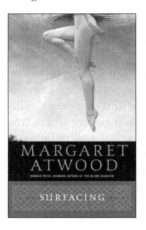

comes discontented with his lover because she seems to be obsessed with her search for clues in the cabin. The heroine believes that her parents have left her these clues in her childhood home.

Toward the end of the novel, the heroine runs from all of her companions; the wild island seems to have taken hold of her. Although this journey may seem like a nervous breakdown, it is a time for her to make peace with her past and her identity. Only after the heroine frees herself from society's influences and connects with her primitive self is she able to develop her true character and to recapture the many memories that she thought she had lost. She reconnects with her parents and with the spirits of indigenous people. She has saved herself by embracing the voice of nature that demands that she avoid all human constructs. Symbolically, the antagonist forces that destroy nature throughout the novel also represent the United States. The theme of anti-Americanism is present throughout the work; for example, American tourists overrun the previously unspoiled landscape.

Eventually, the heroine of *Surfacing* learns of her father's death. She must leave the cabin and the lake, for winter is approaching. When she returns, she will need to resume working and to attempt to better her relationship with Joe. A new woman, she is no longer a passive victim.

"FOOTNOTE TO THE AMNESTY REPORT ON TORTURE"

First published: 1978 (collected in *Two-Headed Poems*, 1978)
Type of work: Poem

A man who works in a torture chamber tries to avoid thinking about the atrocities that occur in the room.

The first stanza of "Footnote to the Amnesty Report on Torture" introduces the torture chamber. The voice in the poem describes how the chamber defies the human imagination; it does not resemble a dungeon, it is not reminiscent of a pornography magazine, and it is not futuristic. Instead, the chamber is compared to a dirty train station—a place that is all too familiar. The image of the train station includes a man who cleans the station's floor. This individual is the precursor to the unnamed man introduced in the third stanza who sweeps the floor in the torture chamber.

The man who cleans the torture chamber must deal with the grotesque smells and remove the remnants of the previous night's activity. He reminds himself that he is grateful for his job and that he is not the torturer. This man remains unnamed and generic; he could be any man in any country.

Other shocking images in the poem include limp bodies of those who refuse to speak thrown onto the consul's lawn. Bodies of children who have been killed in order to extract information from their parents are also described. Despite these atrocities, the anonymous man performs his job each day and does his best to dissociate himself. He completes his work because he must provide for his children and his wife; however, he is fear-ridden. In the back of his mind he cannot detach himself from this cruel world, and he knows that he and his family could be the government's next targets. The poem makes a bold statement about the harsh reality behind political systems.

THE HANDMAID'S TALE

First published: 1985
Type of work: Novel

A young woman is forced to become a potential "breeder" after Fundamentalist Christians impose a dictatorial government on the United States.

The Handmaid's Tale begins near Boston in the mid-1980's. A faction of right-wing Christians establishes a dictatorship after killing members of the United States government. The result is Gilead, an ultraconservative country that denies women power. Women are unable to hold jobs, use credit cards, or seek education. Also, massive pollution exists due to nuclear and biological warfare. Radioactive territory, known as the Colonies, becomes the home of Jews and of other minorities, because the new government wants only to propagate members of their own sect. Essentially, Atwood has created a dystopia which stands in direct opposition to an ideal world or utopia. Atwood drew upon research about present-day trends in environmental degradation and diseases to create an authentic setting.

Due to massive pollution and to the spread of sexually transmitted diseases, reproduction is difficult for women. Many babies are miscarried or born with defects. Women who cannot reproduce, as well as homosexuals, are considered worthless and are banished to the Colonies. Women are divided up into classes; colored clothing is used to separate the classes. The government establishes a secret police force to arrest fertile women, who become Handmaids. These Handmaids are breeders who must participate in sexual acts in order to create more members of the white race.

The women are given names that represent the men who control their lives; these names signify that women have lost their identities and that they are victimized by men. One such woman, named "Offred" is ripped away from her family. She is forced to be a Handmaid and is relocated to a center to receive the proper training for her new vocation. The Re-education Center is enclosed by barbed wire, and the conditions are rudimentary. Offred maintains her individuality, while acting as if she is conforming to the ways of the center and to the demands of her overseers, matrons such as Aunt Lydia and Aunt Elizabeth, who attempt to control the thoughts of their prisoners.

In secret, the Handmaids attempt to maintain relationships with one another and to maintain their morale. However, others adapt to the robotic ways and mental states required of them by their restrictive daily lives. Offred finishes her training at the center and is made a member of Gilead's Handmaids. Her first attempt at conception is fruitless, so she is sent to Commander Fred, for whom she is named. Her new routine consists of food shopping and seclusion in a protected room. Her only exposure to others consists of prayer sessions, birthing, medical procedures, and executions. In a monthly ceremony, Offred mates with the commander after a Bible reading in front of his wife, Serena.

While Offred is being inseminated by the commander, she lies on Serena's thighs. Although the commanders are considered high-ranking in the regime, they do not have much power over the household, for their aging wives govern the homes. This irony reinforces that the rigid nature of the government results in a lack of freedom for the commanders, too.

Unbeknownst to Serena, the commander develops a fondness for Offred beyond the ritualistic mating, and he calls Offred for evening visits. On such visits, they play forbidden games, such as Scrabble, and he allows her to look at his fashion magazines. Fred even gives Offred snippets of information about the world beyond her confinement. One particular evening, Fred gives her an ornate outfit of glitter and feathers to wear. Dressed provocatively, Offred accompanies him to an illegal nightclub where women of ill repute and lesbians work. The women at this club are also subject to the oppressive forces of men.

Serena learns about Offred's illicit relationship with her husband and confronts the Handmaid. As Offred is weighing her options—for Serena is accusing her of treason—a van appears. Offred meets the operatives of an underground group called "The Eyes." Although the commander objects, the two agents charge Offred with divulging the state's secret information, and she leaves in the van.

The reader learns more about Offred's fate in a speech delivered by an archivist in 2195, although the ending is ambiguous. The professor offers information about Offred's experiences, as found on cassette tapes. The professor suggests that the Handmaid escaped her fate. He believes that she made the tapes before she escaped the country and that she lived her life in isolation in order to save her family from repercussions. Offred's survival conveys the strength of the human spirit regardless of oppressive forces. In conclusion, Atwood refuses to call the novel a warning, even though she has alluded to current events; she says she has no political agenda of that sort.

CAT'S EYE

First published: 1988
Type of work: Novel

Elaine Risley, a reputable Canadian painter, returns to Toronto, where she revisits her childhood, her failed marriage, and her former relationships.

Cat's Eye focuses on a fifty-year-old protagonist, Elaine, who is revisiting the city of her childhood. Elaine is a controversial artist who is returning for an exhibition of her works. During her journey, she undergoes a transformation, for she learns about herself, her art, and her life at various stages in the novel.

Elaine's childhood begins with her traveling with her family across northern Canada. Her father is an entomologist who follows infestations; therefore, the family moves from motel to motel until she is eight years old. Elaine's early childhood contrasts the new existence she faces when her family relocates to Toronto. She is forced to adapt to suburbia, which includes learning a new vocabulary and local etiquette. The clothing, speech, and items Elaine encounters reflect the rigidity associated with the 1940's and 1950's that Atwood recalled from her upbringing.

Elaine must learn what it means to be feminine and to socialize with members of her own sex. She realizes that she is different from the others at school and that her parents are not wealthy. During this time, Elaine becomes fascinated by another girl her age, named Cordelia. Cordelia lives in a large home with a cleaning woman and with other extravagances that Elaine admires. Cordelia claims to befriend Elaine; however, Cordelia and her other friends constantly harass Elaine for her many shortcomings and submit her to torturous acts. Elaine does her very best to garner their approval, for she considers them her only friends and fears further isolation. Atwood is illustrating the cruelty that exists in little-girl behavior.

Miraculously, Elaine breaks away from Cordelia. As teens, the two rekindle a friendship, although of a different kind; Elaine has become the stronger of the two. Cordelia fails out of school, and independent Elaine develops a passion for art, which she

studies at university. During her studies, she has a love affair with a teacher and mentor and then meets another art student, Jon, whom she marries. Among other events, Elaine has a daughter and tries to commit suicide. During this time, she finds herself involved in the emerging feminist movement. In an ironic twist, Elaine encounters Cordelia as an adult. Cordelia is now the one who has attempted suicide and who is confined to a mental institution.

Unfortunately, Elaine is still haunted by Cordelia and plagued by insecurities. Although Elaine does not meet her friend when she revisits Toronto, she does return to the place where they were children together. By returning to this setting, Elaine undergoes a catharsis, and she makes peace with Cordelia by letting go of her past. The novel portrays the personal and social implications of evil and redemption.

Cat's Eye presents many similarities to Atwood's experiences. Critics have commented that Elaine's voice reflects Atwood's own. Elaine's travels in northern Canada, her passion for art, and her relationship with the feminist movement are all reminiscent of Atwood's life. The novel has received praise for its chronicle of memory through a weaving of the present and past. It has also been applauded for its electrifying imagery and poetic language.

"DEATH BY LANDSCAPE"

First published: 1991 (collected in *Wilderness Tips*, 1991)
Type of work: Short story

Middle-aged Lois has recently relocated to a condominium apartment; she reflects on her childhood summer camp and the mystery surrounding a particular canoe trip.

In "Death by Landscape" Lois, a widowed mother, displays her art collection on the walls of her new waterfront apartment. She spends time admiring the paintings, yet they do not fill her with peace. On the contrary, the paintings show landscapes that make her very uneasy. Lois fears the depiction of the wilderness.

She recalls her summers at Camp Manitou, which she experienced from the ages of nine to thirteen. She remembers the traditions associated with her camp experience. She can still sing the words to the songs and remember the spunky counselors. The head of the camp, Cappie, kept the camp running during the Depression and World War II, even when money was tight. The camp setting represents a domesticated wilderness, a human-made construction which hints at the true wilds.

At the beginning, Lois struggled to adapt to camp life. She did not like writing to her parents or sleeping in a room full of other girls. She then grew to enjoy herself, and she made a strong friendship with a camper named Lucy. The two maintained their friendship throughout the years and during the summers, but Lucy seemed to have changed by their last year at camp together. She grew disillusioned with her newly divorced parents and became involved in a relationship with a gardener's assistant.

The climax of the story occurs when the girls participate in a week-long excursion in the wilderness. They set out by canoe after a ceremonious departure. On the second day of the trip, the two girls separate from the other campers to climb a trail to a lookout point; it is a sheer cliff that overlooks the lake. Lucy says she is going to go urinate, yet she does not return. Instead, Lois hears a scream, although she cannot identify it. The campers head back to camp without Lucy; even the police cannot find her. When they return, Cappie insinuates that Lois pushed Lucy.

In retrospect, Lois realizes that Cappie merely needed someone to blame for the unfortunate event, but Lois struggles to let go of her friend. She is also haunted by the wilderness. The protagonist cannot believe that Lucy has died, and for this reason she has been living two lives. At the end of the story, Lois can finally accept the wilderness as part of herself.

ALIAS GRACE

First published: 1996
Type of work: Novel

Grace Marks has been accused of murdering her employer and his mistress; Dr. Simon Jordan attempts to unlock her story.

In her novel *Alias Grace*, Atwood explores the psychological mind-set of one of the most infamous Canadian women of the mid-nineteenth century. The author's fascination with the murderess began when the Canadian Broadcasting Corporation asked her to write a play about Grace in 1974. The protagonist is the historical figure Grace Marks, an Irish immigrant who worked in Toronto in the 1840's. The setting is established as The Kingston Penitentiary at the start of the novel, where Grace is carrying out her life sentence for the murder of her wealthy employer, Thomas Kinnear, and his pregnant mistress.

Grace is sentenced for the murder, along with James McDermott, her coworker and supposed lover. James, a stable hand, claims that Grace incited him to perform the gruesome murders; he is hanged for his part. There is much dissent as to Grace's guilt; she claims to have no recollection of the killings, which occurred when she was a scullery maid of sixteen. Among those who wish to exonerate Grace are a group of reformers who seek help from Dr. Simon Jordan. The reformers hope that by engaging the doctor, they can end Grace's fifteen years of imprisonment. Jordan, a reputable figure in the fledgling field of mental health, is sufficiently intrigued to help the prisoner. Jordan is riveted by Grace, yet he continues to find her an enigma.

As Jordan encourages Grace to reveal information about her experiences, the story of her impoverished life trickles to the surface. Jordan learns about her childhood, her brutal passage from Ireland to Canada, and her employment with Thomas Kinnear from the age of twelve. By the middle of the book, the tension heightens as the secrets of her employer's household come to light. Furthermore, Grace is haunted by flashbacks of the murder and by the memory of a friend who died during a botched abortion. As the mystery continues to unravel, antagonizing forces surface, such as gender roles, socioeconomic status, and the power of sexuality.

Still, Jordan does not know whether Grace is innocent or guilty. Despite the fact that *Alias Grace* is Atwood's first venture into historical fiction, the book has commonalities with her other works. Themes include the changes in women's morality and the power struggle between the sexes. Although a few critics noted that Atwood's attention to historical details strains the momentum of the novel, several marveled at the author's ability to provide Grace with a lyrical and authentic voice. They also noted the skill with which Atwood depicted the time and place in her haunting narrative.

ORYX AND CRAKE

First published: 2003
Type of work: Novel

Snowman appears to be the only human to survive a catastrophic event; he must struggle to find nourishment and other essentials in order to endure.

As in *The Handmaid's Tale*, Atwood creates a futuristic dystopia in which she places her protagonist, Snowman. Although Snowman has managed to survive some kind of catastrophe, the specifics surrounding the event are not revealed until the end of the work. The only other forms of life that Snowman meets on the barren seaside landscape are humanoids and animals that have resulted from bioengineering. The humanoids are called Crakers, innocent beings that are tractable and resistant to diseases. These green-eyed mutants manifest selected traits; they are uninterested in sex and violence, and their skin is impervious to ultraviolet light.

Along with the narrative of Snowman's daily existence, the reader learns of his youth via flashbacks. As a child he was called Jimmy (he has renamed himself Snowman), and his best friend was named Glenn, who later adopts the name Crake. Both lived in a compound built by a bioengineering firm for its employees. The compound was isolated from other cities. Crake, a scientific whiz, and Jimmy were raised in dysfunctional families. Jimmy's mother left the family because of her moral resistance to her husband's work; he was responsible for creating genetic hybrids.

Crake's father appears to have been murdered in the wake of a scandal with the firm. Crake grows from a youth who spends his time surfing the Web to a scientific mastermind in charge of a secret project. First he studies at the Watson-Crick Institute, which has a reputation like that of Harvard University—before Harvard ceased to exist. Jimmy attends Martha Graham Academy, a more liberal setting with a focus on the humanities. Even though Crake is fundamental to the story, his character is never fully developed, and he proves to be more of an instrument for the plot.

As the gap between the friends grows, and time passes, Jimmy does little more than hold menial employment and seduce women. The naïve Jimmy finally reconnects with Crake, who employs him. Crake reveals that he is altering human embryos to eliminate their faulty features; in a sense, Crake is playing a godlike role. Jimmy also comes into contact with Oryx, a captivating woman whom Jimmy recognizes from pornography. Oryx imparts snippets of her life to Jimmy, although she remains a hazy figure throughout.

Finally, it is revealed that the apocalyptic event was not a nuclear war; the cause was a potent and fatal plague. When the deadly virus took hold, it spanned the earth from Hong Kong to Toronto. Snowman perpetuates the myth of Oryx and Crake to keep the green-eyed mutants alive. At the end of the novel, there is a suggestion that a new humanity has evolved; the Crakers may be exhibiting some of the traits that Crake had attempted to eliminate in them, such as the desire to lead or to organize religion.

In this cautionary tale, Atwood manages to keep the reader riveted with her careful use of dark humor and asides. The author is known for her ability to create authentic female voices in her novels; in

Oryx and Crake, she manages to construct a realistic male voice and to convey both the twisted emotional environment in which he matured and a society propelled by commercialism, pornography, and technology.

SUMMARY

Atwood is a multitalented writer with a flare for sardonic humor. In her novels, poetry, and short stories, she makes bold stylistic choices which resonate with the reader. Her concerns with feminist issues, with the struggle between humankind and the natural world, and with Canadian nationalism are inherent in her work. She is a voice of magnitude in her native land and a critic of Canadian matters of trade, culture, and foreign policy. Atwood's pieces are studied in many secondary schools and universities worldwide. She has won a variety of prestigious awards throughout her career.

Jamie Sondra Sindell

DISCUSSION TOPICS

- In what ways do Margaret Atwood's early childhood experiences in the Canadian wilderness affect her works?

- Compare and contrast the dystopias in Atwood's novels *The Handmaid's Tale* and *Oryx and Crake.*

- In "Death by Landscape," why does the protagonist have trouble letting go of her friend?

- *Alias Grace* has been both praised and criticized for its attention to the details of Victorian life. How and why do such details affect the momentum of the novel?

- Chronicle Elaine's growth as an individual throughout her journey in *Cat's Eye.*

BIBLIOGRAPHY:

By the Author

LONG FICTION:
The Edible Woman, 1969
Surfacing, 1972
Lady Oracle, 1976
Life Before Man, 1979
Bodily Harm, 1981
The Handmaid's Tale, 1985
Cat's Eye, 1988
The Robber Bride, 1993
Alias Grace, 1996
The Blind Assassin, 2000
Oryx and Crake, 2003

SHORT FICTION:
Dancing Girls, and Other Stories, 1977
Bluebeard's Egg, 1983
Murder in the Dark: Short Fictions and Prose Poems, 1983
Wilderness Tips, 1991
Good Bones, 1992 (pb. in U.S. as *Good Bones and Simple Murders,* 1994)

POETRY:
Double Persephone, 1961
The Circle Game, 1964 (single poem), 1966 (collection)
Kaleidoscopes Baroque: A Poem, 1965

Margaret Atwood

Talismans for Children, 1965
Expeditions, 1966
Speeches for Dr. Frankenstein, 1966
The Animals in That Country, 1968
What Was in the Garden, 1969
The Journals of Susanna Moodie, 1970
Procedures for Underground, 1970
Power Politics, 1971
You Are Happy, 1974
Selected Poems, 1976
Two-Headed Poems, 1978
True Stories, 1981
Snake Poems, 1983
Interlunar, 1984
Selected Poems II: Poems Selected and New, 1976-1986, 1987
Selected Poems, 1966-1984, 1990
Poems, 1965-1975, 1991
Poems, 1976-1989, 1992
Morning in the Burned House, 1995
Eating Fire: Selected Poems, 1965-1995, 1998

NONFICTION:
Survival: A Thematic Guide to Canadian Literature, 1972
Second Words: Selected Critical Prose, 1982
The CanLit Foodbook: From Pen to Palate, a Collection of Tasty Literary Fare, 1987
Margaret Atwood: Conversations, 1990
Deux sollicitudes: Entretiens, 1996 (with Victor-Lévy Beaulieu; *Two Solicitudes: Conversations,* 1998)
Negotiating with the Dead: A Writer on Writing, 2002
Moving Targets: Writing with Intent, 1982-2004, 2004 (pb. in U.S. as *Writing with Intent: Essays, Reviews, Personal Prose, 1983-2005,* 2005)

CHILDREN'S LITERATURE:
Up in the Tree, 1978
Anna's Pet, 1980 (with Joyce Barkhouse)
For the Birds, 1990
Princess Prunella and the Purple Peanut, 1995 (illustrated by Maryann Kowalski)
Rude Ramsay and the Roaring Radishes, 2004 (illustrated by Dusan Petricic)

EDITED TEXT:
The New Oxford Book of Canadian Verse in English, 1982

About the Author

Cooke, Nathalie. *Margaret Atwood: A Biography.* Toronto, Ontario: ECW Press, 1998.
Hengen, Shannon. *Margaret Atwood's Power: Mirrors, Reflections, and Images in Select Fiction and Poetry.* Toronto, Ontario: Sumach Press, 1993.
Nischik, Reingard, ed. *Margaret Atwood: Works and Impact.* Rochester, N.Y.: Camden House, 2000.
Stein, Karen F. *Margaret Atwood Revisited.* New York: Twayne, 1999.
Wilson, Sharon, Thomas Friedman, and Shannon Hengen, eds. *Approaches to Teaching Atwood's "The Handmaid's Tale" and Other Works.* New York: The Modern Language Association of America, 1996.

LOUIS AUCHINCLOSS

Born: Lawrence, New York
September 27, 1917

In the tradition of Henry James, Auchincloss wrote realistic novels about the wealthy New Yorkers who thought of themselves as America's aristocrats, thus establishing his reputation as the outstanding novelist of manners of his time.

Inge Morath

BIOGRAPHY

Louis Auchincloss was born on September 27, 1917, at Lawrence, Long Island (later a suburb of New York City), the third among four children and the second of three sons. The Auchincloss family, Scottish in origin, had grown both numerous and prosperous in and around New York City, initially engaging in the wool trade but later branching out into the professions. Louis's father, Howland, a 1908 graduate of Yale University, practiced law on Wall Street. Howland and his wife, the former Priscilla Stanton, saw to it that their children were raised "comfortably" but without ostentation, in relative ignorance of how well-off their family might possibly be.

Howland Auchincloss, although highly successful in a rather arcane field of legal practice, appears to have been what later generations would describe as a "workaholic" and suffered frequent nervous breakdowns in his fifties. Well before that time, young Louis would seriously question the hold of Wall Street on his father's life and time. Priscilla Stanton Auchincloss was a strong, perceptive wife and mother despite numbing, often inexplicable inhibitions and "taboos," possibly deriving from guilt feelings over the death of a younger brother when Priscilla was no older than six. It is from his mother that Auchincloss claims to have derived his keen powers of observation and recall.

Beginning his education at the private Boyce School in Manhattan, Auchincloss enjoyed the companionship of such classmates as the future actors Mel Ferrer and Efrem Zimbalist, Jr., before Boyce closed its doors permanently just before the Wall Street crash of 1929. By then, Louis was old enough to follow in the footsteps of his father and elder brother by enrolling at the prestigious Groton School in Massachusetts, a training ground for diplomats and statesmen. Feeling ostracized by his classmates in the aftermath of a schoolboy prank early in his Groton career, young Louis worked hard to distinguish himself academically, earning the high grades he sought but, as he later recalled, almost missing the real point of education. Auchincloss credits Malcolm Strachan, hired to teach at Groton toward the end of his own stay there, with reorienting his reading habits toward enjoyment and away from simple achievement.

Enrolling at Yale in 1935, again following the pattern established by his father, Auchincloss read widely for pleasure both inside and outside class, in time attempting a novel of his own based upon his social observations. When the manuscript was rejected by Scribner's, not without some words of encouragement for the aspiring author, Auchincloss saw fit to read the rejection as an omen of sorts and to follow his father into the practice of law without wasting any time. Skipping his senior year at Yale, he actively sought the best law school that would accept him without benefit of a bachelor's degree, enrolling at the University of Virginia as he turned twenty-one in the fall of 1938.

Avoiding the "temptations" of literature, either as reader or as writer, with all the resolve of a recov-

127

ering addict, Auchincloss studied hard at Virginia, as he had done at Groton, soon discovering in legal prose and logic some of the same delights that he had found in literature. Determined to succeed both as student and as lawyer, he steered clear of the thriving "country-club" social scene but remained quite as observant of his surroundings as he had been during his "literary" days. In any case, his devotion to his studies soon paid off in high grades and honors; upon graduation in June, 1941, he was hired by the Wall Street law firm of Sullivan and Cromwell, where he had worked as a student clerk during the summer of 1940.

Auchincloss's seemingly impulsive decision to skip his senior year at Yale soon turned out to have been a wise one indeed: He was able to complete his studies and actually practice law for several months before the Japanese invasion of Pearl Harbor in December, 1941, with a secure job awaiting his return from military service during World War II.

Commissioned an officer in the Navy, Auchincloss was initially posted to an office job in the Canal Zone, a billet far removed from the war itself and, as he would demonstrate in both *The Indifferent Children* (1947) and some of his early short stories, an atmosphere conducive to petty politics and backbiting. Auchincloss later did see action in both the European and Pacific war theaters, eventually assuming command of an amphibious vessel. While at sea, he made good use of his enforced leisure by reading widely from volumes purchased while on shore leave or from books left to gather dust in the ship's library.

Upon his return to civilian life, Auchincloss took a brief vacation to complete *The Indifferent Children* before returning to his job at Sullivan and Cromwell. Still unmarried, he remained close to his parents and felt the need to accommodate their wishes even as he opposed them; he agreed that his first novel, once accepted, be published under a pseudonym in order to spare the family name. In its first editions, therefore, *The Indifferent Children* appeared under the byline "Andrew Lee"—ironically named for an Auchincloss ancestor. The book's reviews, although mixed, were generally favorable—enough so, at any rate, that Auchincloss would continue to turn out fiction after office hours at Sullivan and Cromwell: *The Injustice Collectors*, an anthology of short stories initially pub-

lished in magazines, appeared in 1950, followed by the novel *Sybil* in 1951. Still somewhat uncomfortable with his dual careers, Auchincloss felt obliged to choose between them and decided, toward the end of 1951, to devote his full time to his writing, supported by an allowance from his father.

At the end of two years, however, having produced one novel (*A Law for the Lion*, 1953) and the short stories collected in *The Romantic Egoists* (1954), Auchincloss was ready to resume his career as an attorney, writing fiction during his spare time as before. Barred by company policy from returning to Sullivan and Cromwell once he had resigned, he eventually found a position with the firm of Hawkins, Delafield and Wood. Elevated to partnership in 1958, he would remain with the firm for more than thirty-two years, from the spring of 1954 until his retirement in 1986.

In 1957, just before turning forty, Auchincloss married Adele Lawrence, a Vanderbilt descendant then in her mid-twenties with whom in time he would have three sons, John, Blake, and Andrew. Comfortable at last with the pursuit of two careers, Auchincloss proceeded to flourish in both, his elevation to partnership coinciding roughly with the publication of his generally well-received Wall Street novels, *The Great World and Timothy Colt* (1956; expanded from one of the longer short stories in *The Romantic Egoists*), *Venus in Sparta* (1958), and *Pursuit of the Prodigal* (1959). It was not until 1960, however, that Auchincloss would truly hit his stride with the remarkable efforts *The House of Five Talents* (1960), *Portrait in Brownstone* (1962), *The Rector of Justin* (1964), and *The Embezzler* (1966).

Thereafter, Auchincloss continued to turn out novels, short fiction, and essays at the approximate rate of one volume per year. His finest works are often said to be the four novels published between 1960 and 1966, though *I Come as a Thief* (1972), *The House of the Prophet* (1980), and *Watchfires* (1982) are also much admired. In 1986, Auchincloss retired from his legal practice, but he remained in New York City, living on Park Avenue in New York City and spending summers at a second home in Bedford, New York. He stayed active as a writer, not only producing more novels, among them *The Scarlet Letters* (2003) and *East Side Story* (2004), but also publishing important nonfiction works, including three impressive biographies: *J. P. Morgan: The Financier as Collector* (1990), *Woodrow Wilson* (2000), and *Theodore Roosevelt* (2001). With the appearance of *The Collected Stories of Louis Auchincloss* in 1994, critics were prompted to reassess the writer's short fiction, and they found it as finely crafted as his longer works. Although Auchincloss has long been considered the best novelist of manners of his time, because he has excelled in so many genres he is now often referred to as one of America's most distinguished men of letters.

ANALYSIS

In 1960, the year that he broke new literary ground with *The House of Five Talents*, Auchincloss published an article in *The Nation* titled "Marquand and O'Hara: The Novel of Manners," subsequently included in *Reflections of a Jacobite* (1961). Examining the work of both authors in considerable detail, Auchincloss concluded that the novel of manners, as developed by Henry James and Edith Wharton and refined by F. Scott Fitzgerald in *The Great Gatsby* (1925), had all but died at the hands of John P. Marquand and John O'Hara, whose works were then held in fairly high esteem. Both men, he argued, tended to invent social stratifications instead of merely observing them. More often than not, class distinctions exist only in the minds of individual characters, a tendency that caused Auchincloss to describe both authors as "psychological" as opposed to "social" novelists. Quite probably, he concluded, the social upheavals of the Depression and two world wars had rendered the convention more or less obsolete. Notwithstanding, Auchincloss was working even then to disprove his own suspicions, reaching back toward James and Wharton and even French novelist Marcel Proust for guidance as he sought to record and make sense of his own keen observations.

Although it was not until 1960 that Auchincloss reached full maturity as a novelist, he had spent most of the previous decade mapping out the fictional universe that his later characters would inhabit. Unlike O'Hara and Marquand, Auchincloss felt no need to invent social stratifications, finding them already in place. Of particular interest to Auchincloss, from his earliest novels onward, is the problematical question, or "myth," of an American "aristocracy"—an apparent contradiction in terms which has nevertheless been perpetuated in American society ever since the earliest settlers or their descendants began looking down their noses at

other settlers more recently arrived in the New World. During the twentieth century, as Auchincloss observes in his fiction, the notion of an American aristocracy has tended to persist, yet not without challenge and change. Increasingly, those born to what Thorstein Veblen described in 1899 as the leisure class have found themselves entering the workforce, often in direct competition with those born to "humbler" origins.

A persistent Auchincloss "myth" is that of the Protestant minister's son, most commonly a native of New England, whose work ethic combines with ambition to drive him ever upward in the business or professional world. By the time he reaches the top, such a man is virtually indistinguishable, except perhaps for his continued commitment to the work ethic, from the hereditary "aristocrats" against whom he has successfully competed. His Harvard or Yale education, although acquired with scholarship aid supplemented by odd jobs, has been much the same as that of his richer peers. If anything, the minister's son has earned higher grades and learned more, the better to realize his own American Dream. Meanwhile, his white, Anglo-Saxon Protestant status and name have provided the clergyman's son with the perfect "cover," allowing him to blend in as he moves from the meritocracy into the perceived aristocracy, joining country clubs and sending his children to private schools as he wisely invests the residue of a steadily increasing salary.

From the 1930's onward, both Marquand and O'Hara had focused much of their attention on the business world, purporting to show how careers are made and broken. During the 1950's, Auchincloss covered much the same territory, inevitably inviting comparison with the two older, already established novelists. On close examination, however, Auchincloss's novels of the period seem rather more authentic and credible than those of O'Hara and Marquand, and with good reason. Unlike the two older authors, Auchincloss lived and worked in the world that formed the subject of his novels; what is more, he was well versed in the "novel of manners" tradition, which Marquand and O'Hara were not.

Beginning with *The House of Five Talents*, Auchincloss broadened and deepened his portrait of society, having laid the foundation of his fictional universe with the "Wall Street" novels of the late

1950's. The Wall Street setting is still very much in evidence, often at the center of the action, but is complemented by historical and social background. Auchincloss began to experiment with viewpoint and narrative voice, producing convincing "eyewitness" accounts: The main narrators of *The House of Five Talents* and *Portrait in Brownstone* are elderly women, born during the nineteenth century; in *The Rector of Justin* and *The Embezzler*, the elusive nature of human "truth" is underscored by Auchincloss's skillful use of multiple narrators, both male and female, no two of whom recall what they have witnessed in quite the same way. Each narrator is fully delineated as a character in his or her own right, self-revealing by choice of words and turns of phrase as well as by selective recollection.

A frequent reader of Proust, Auchincloss in his strongest novels approaches the French author's remarkable blend of chronicle and art. In preparing *The Rector of Justin* and *The Embezzler*, for example, Auchincloss began with lawyerly research, reading thousands of pages of nonfiction dealing, respectively, with the history of prep schools and with the notorious Richard Whitney fraud case of the 1930's; he then proceeded to transform history into art, discarding or changing the "facts" as he sought to tease out the archetypal meaning behind them. Of *The Embezzler*, he recalls, "When I was sure I had my crime exactly right, I invented an entirely new criminal and gave him an entirely new family, plus an entirely new motivation."

A similar approach would characterize most of Auchincloss's mature fiction; unlike the historian, Auchincloss is concerned less with what happened than with why and how it might have happened. A case in point is *The House of the Prophet* (1980), Auchincloss's first and only true roman à clef, loosely but frankly based on the life and career of the columnist and pundit Walter Lippmann; upon learning that a Lippmann biography was in progress, Auchincloss resolved to tell the story in his "own" way, through art, altering certain facts and dates for dramatic effect, speculating upon the thoughts and motivations of "Felix Leitner."

Among the more remarkable features of Auchincloss's fictional universe, from the early 1950's onward, has been his thoughtful, credible portrayal of the changing role of women in American society during the twentieth century. His second and third novels, *Sybil* and *A Law for the Lion*, deal with the emergent female consciousness as lawyers' wives begin to question the inequities of marriage and of the divorce laws then on the books in the state of New York. In some novels, Auchincloss goes back in time to trace the emergence of the feminine consciousness among the economically privileged, showing how certain women deliberately refused to be liberated. However, in others, he reveals his sympathy with women who refuse to adopt stereotypical behavior. The heroines of *The Lady of Situations* (1990) and *Her Infinite Variety* (2001) remain very much their own persons, and in the end, both of them attain success in a male-dominated world, though in the process they have to become as ruthless as the men whose power they challenge.

Perhaps the most frequent criticism leveled against Auchincloss is that he writes exclusively about New York, and about New Yorkers of a certain social class. On reflection, however, such criticism tends to be shortsighted: For good or for ill, New York, even more than Washington, D.C., is where major decisions are made, often by people very like those of whom Auchincloss writes. Moreover, relatively few of his main characters are "natives." Most commonly, the Auchincloss protagonist has migrated to New York from New England or the Middle Atlantic region in search of fame and fortune, much as a provincial European would settle in Paris or London. Auchincloss's New York is, in fact, a microcosm of American civilization, at once rebellious against and nostalgic for its perceived European origins. Auchincloss's greatest achievement as a novelist would seem to be his credible, literate, and resonant portrayal of life behind the scenes of political and economic power.

THE HOUSE OF FIVE TALENTS

First published: 1960
Type of work: Novel

Writing in 1948, a rich, aging spinster recalls her life and times.

The House of Five Talents, announcing the full range of Auchincloss's skill as novelist and chronicler, is narrated in the first-person voice by Miss Augusta

Millinder, known familiarly as Gussie, a seventy-five-year-old heiress who, after the social upheavals of two world wars and a depression, sees fit to record her memoirs for posterity. Ostensibly penned during 1948, Gussie's testimony ranges from the gaslight era of her adolescence to the narrative present, providing an insider's view of society against the backdrop of history.

Unmarried by choice, having broken her engagement to a promising young architect for reasons best known to herself, Gussie Millinder emerges early in life as a keen observer and occasional meddler, using her spinsterhood as a vantage point from which to analyze and criticize the marital and parental misadventures of her relatives and friends. Gussie's meddling, however well-intentioned, fails more often than it succeeds, allowing the unseen Auchincloss to inject elements of plot into an otherwise linear narrative.

In her twenties, for example, Gussie tries, unsuccessfully, to thwart her parents' divorce and her father's subsequent remarriage to an actress. Later, in an incident presaging the plot of *The Embezzler,* she will offer to save a cousin's husband from bankruptcy and prison by covering his embezzlement with her own funds, on condition that the man retire permanently from business. Unhappy in retirement, the man pleads with Gussie to release him from his vow and soon reverts to his old ways, eventually disappearing abroad as a fugitive from justice. With the approach of old age, Gussie again intervenes to force a marriage between her scapegrace nephew Oswald, a Communist sympathizer, and the showgirl who is carrying his unborn child; the marriage predictably fails, leaving Gussie with little choice but to adopt the child herself.

Set mainly in New York City, with occasional excursions to such fashionable turn-of-the-century "watering places" as Newport and Bar Harbor, *The House of Five Talents* credibly evokes both tradition and transition as Gussie meets the twentieth century, already "liberated" by her spinster status from constraints that still bind her married female relatives. As she approaches forty, for example, Gussie supplements her self-education with college courses and teaches in a girls' school, although she does not need the money. With the approach of World War I, she volunteers for auxiliary service in Europe, proceeding upon her return to develop a career of active, if selective, community service, giving as freely of her time as of her money.

Notable for Auchincloss's effective exploitation of first-person narration, *The House of Five Talents* also presents his first full-scale portrait of American society, showing how the would-be aristocracy defines itself, whether in its choice of sports and resorts or in the marriage of such rich Americans as Gussie's sister Cora to impoverished but titled Europeans. Gussie Millinder herself, meanwhile, remains among Auehincloss's most memorable and entertaining characters.

PORTRAIT IN BROWNSTONE

First published: 1962
Type of work: Novel

A broker's wife discovers her true strengths as she transforms herself from matron into matriarch.

Combining the narrative approach of *The House of Five Talents* with the general subject matter of his earlier Wall Street novels, Auchincloss in *Portrait in Brownstone* explores both office politics and the emergent female consciousness through the eyes of one Ida Trask Hartley, who, around the age of sixty, begins at last to perceive the full extent of her experience and talents. Bookish and somewhat retiring, Ida has spent most of her life in the shadow of her hard-driving husband, Derrick, a minister's son from New England, and her glamorous cousin Geraldine Denison, Derrick's sometime mistress. Indeed, it is Geraldine's suicide, following a long slide into alcoholism and depression, that begins the process of Ida's awakening and liberation, a process that forms the true plot of the novel.

Like Gussie Millinder in *The House of Five Talents*, Ida Hartley is a keen observer and gifted storyteller. In search of self-discovery, she revisits her past, recalling her mother's close-knit extended family, the Denisons, and her uncle Linnaeus Tremain, a brilliant, perceptive financier. Although all the male Denisons are gainfully employed and most have been to college, it is Tremain's sustained generosity that enables them all to live in relative comfort and that allows Ida to attend college, the first woman in her family to do so.

Enrolled at Barnard College and interested in liberal politics, Ida soon finds herself debating political issues with Derrick Hartley, a Harvard graduate who, having made a small fortune with a Boston brokerage firm, has moved to New York with hopes of working for Linnaeus Tremain. Little deterred by Tremain's insistence that no vacancy exists in his firm, Derrick quite literally "dines out" on his accumulated savings while waiting for the older man to change his mind. It is at those dinners that Derrick makes the acquaintance both of Ida Trask, who will fall in love with him, and of Ida's mother, who will persuade her brother-in-law to give Derrick a job. As Tremain in time learns, much to his dismay, he has at last met his match.

Ida asks her cousin and perpetual rival Geraldine to entertain Derrick during a weekend in 1912 when she needs to be out of town. Derrick, studious and reserved, soon loses his heart and head to the flirtatious, fickle Geraldine, who does not return his love. In time, Ida wins Derrick back and marries him. A daughter and then a son are soon born to the Hartleys, whose marriage proceeds smoothly and without major incident until 1935, when Geraldine, recently widowed, entices Derrick into an affair with divorce and remarriage in mind. Derrick, meanwhile, has prospered in his work, somewhat at the expense of his chosen mentor Tremain. Having in effect forced Tremain's retirement, he goes so far as to have the older man's name removed from the firm's corporate name after his death, a gesture which deeply offends Ida.

Following Geraldine's death early in 1950, Ida at last takes stock of her life, noticing that her daughter Dorcas and Dorcas's second husband are about to do to Derrick what Derrick once did to "Uncle Linn." At the same time, she perceives that her son Hugo, still unmarried as he approaches forty, has embarked on a potentially dangerous affair with a divorce-bound married woman. Mustering all the accumulated resources of her intelligence, education, and experience, Ida moves quickly to intervene in both cases, assuming control of Derrick's firm after he suffers a sudden, provoked heart attack and buying for Hugo a sufficient share of stock in the company for which he works that he will be able to name himself president, thus ensuring his eligibility for marriage to a much younger distant cousin and removing the married woman from his life.

To be sure, Ida's sudden assertiveness stops somewhat short of "liberation" as perceived by later generations. Still, Auchincloss, through Ida, has successfully portrayed a moment of transition in American social history, when women of his mother's generation, at least the lucky ones, discovered at last the courage of their convictions.

Significantly, Ida is the only character in *Portrait in Brownstone* allowed to speak for herself; the sections of the novel devoted to Derrick and their children are narrated in an affectless third-person style reminiscent of the author's Wall Street novels, providing counterpoint as Ida seeks within herself the resources needed to assume the control for which she has been well trained.

THE RECTOR OF JUSTIN

First published: 1964
Type of work: Novel

The New England prep school, a uniquely American institution formed on British models, is here caught and portrayed in all its ambiguity.

The Rector of Justin continues Auchincloss's analytical portrayal of American society and its institutions, here focusing upon the type of boys' boarding school that he himself attended and that has furnished the United States with much of its business and political leadership since the end of the nineteenth century. Told from a number of viewpoints, the tale of Justin Martyr Academy and its founder, the title character Francis Prescott, remains tantalizingly incomplete even at the end, showing the basic anomaly of an institution that seeks to foster "democratic" ideals while charging high fees and adhering to a selective admissions policy.

The unifying narrator of *The Rector of Justin* is one Brian Aspinwall; too frail of health to join his fellow Americans in preparing to fight the Nazis, he arrives to teach at Justin Martyr Academy during the eightieth year of the legendary founder's life. At first merely keeping a diary of his impressions and encounters, as of his own possible vocation to the Episcopal priesthood, Brian finds himself drawn to the old man by what he perceives as the latter's unwavering moral courage. In time he goes on to project a full-scale biography of Prescott, assembling spoken and written testimony from a variety of witnesses. Proceeding with his chosen task, Brian discovers that others before him have tried, and failed, to produce a Prescott biography. Brian too will fail, for want of life experience and objectivity.

The book, as it stands, intersperses Brian's reflections with his steadily increasing, yet maddeningly inconclusive, documentation. Notably absent from the growing pile of written testimony is any word from Prescott himself; throughout his long life and career the old man has written little or nothing, preferring instead to be remembered by his actions. Yet it is precisely those actions, variously remembered and interpreted, that somehow fail to "add up," leaving even the elderly Prescott himself with the impression that he has somehow failed in his self-appointed mission.

Born during 1860 in New England, Prescott lost his father to the Civil War and his mother to disease while he was still a child, spending most of his youth in an early prototype of the type of school that would become his "dream." Completing his education at the University of Oxford, Prescott carefully studied the British "public schools" as potential models for his own academy, somehow missing the basic contradiction between British aristocratic ideals and the already ingrained democratic ideals of his New England boyhood. While at Oxford, moreover, Prescott momentarily lost interest in the religious studies that he deemed necessary for the founder/headmaster of an Episcopal school, instead reading deeply in the Greek and Latin classics.

Diverted from his dream, Prescott returned to the United States in 1881, embarking on a brilliant career with the New York Central railroad and planning marriage to a vivacious young woman from California, only to abandon both in great haste after a mysterious dream or vision during which his earlier ambition returned with a vengeance. Curiously, Prescott remains somewhat uninterested in theology, pursuing the prescribed course of study only to acquire what he sees as the teaching credential needed for his chosen task. While at Harvard, Prescott also met Harriet Winslow, an intellectually inclined "proper Bostonian" to whom he would remain married until her death

nearly sixty years later. His wife and three daughters, however, would assume a distinctly secondary importance in his life, overshadowed by the creation—and preservation—of the "perfect" boys' preparatory school.

As Brian Aspinwall proceeds with his research, it becomes increasingly clear—to the reader, if not to Brian himself—that Prescott's single-minded perfectionism, ironically founded on imperfect principles, has left many human casualties in its wake, including family, friends, and former students. The school's alumni and trustees, represented in the novel mainly by the Wall Street lawyer David Griscam, continue to draw inspiration from Prescott's dream even as they perceive its limitations, going so far as to lie to Prescott about the school's business affairs in order to keep the shared dream intact. In his eighties, Prescott at last begins to perceive some of the flaws in his ideal, lamenting the fact that his students and alumni are, in fact, aristocrats of the sort that he instinctively distrusts and dislikes. Still, he crucially fails to acknowledge, let alone examine, his own role in perpetuating those institutions that he professes to hold in contempt.

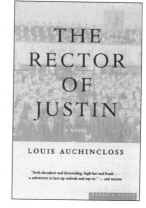

Thanks to the multiplicity of voices and viewpoints presented, *The Rector of Justin* emerges as both a readable, intriguing novel and a document of social history elevated to the dimension of myth. Although suspected of using his own alma mater, Groton, and its founder, Endicott Peabody, as his models, Auchincloss in fact cast his net considerably wider, studying the history of preparatory schools in general before concocting his own archetype, a school whose ingrained contradictions, embodied in the heart and soul of its founder, are all too plainly evident. For all of its implied criticism, however, *The Rector of Justin* is neither an exposé nor an indictment of the American prep school; throughout the narrative, the possible virtues of a prep school education are clearly delineated, showing that Prescott's vision, however flawed and unrealistic, is not without its merits.

THE EMBEZZLER

First published: 1966
Type of work: Novel

A notorious fraud case of the 1930's is recalled during the 1960's by its perpetrator, his former wife, and her current husband, once his best friend.

Building upon the strengths implicit in *The Rector of Justin*, Auchincloss in *The Embezzler* uses conflicting narrative voices and viewpoints to illuminate the mythical dimensions of recent American economic history. Departing from the recorded facts of the Wall Street fraud case that led directly to federal control of the American stock market, Auchincloss reinvents the case and its principal characters with credibility and skill, adding human dimension to an otherwise dry, if significant, historical event.

The Embezzler opens with the memoirs of Guy Prime, the title character, writing during 1960 to "set the record straight." Well into his seventies and living in self-imposed exile in Panama, Guy concedes the facts of his misdeeds but remains quite unrepentant, having paid his debt to society with a prison term; indeed, he reasons, the Franklin Delano Roosevelt administration could hardly wait for an excuse to enact laws already written, and Guy Prime just happened to provide that excuse.

Presumably discovered among Guy's effects after his death in 1962, his memoirs are subsequently read and commented upon by his former wife and her current husband in the two sections that complete the novel. As in *The Rector of Justin*, the confrontation of conflicting testimony concerning the same events and people casts considerable doubt upon the possibility of "truth" with regard to human nature; at the end it is doubtful indeed whether any of the characters involved could ever have understood the words or motivations of the others.

Recalling his youth in New York and later at Harvard University, Guy Prime evokes a setting and atmosphere similar to those of *Portrait in Brownstone*. At Harvard, Guy first meets Reginald "Rex" Geer, the industrious, ambitious son of an austere New Hampshire parson. Initially drawn to each other by the proverbial attraction of opposites, the sybaritic, gregarious New Yorker and the studious, reserved New England Yankee soon become close friends. When Rex is about to drop out of Harvard for financial reasons, Guy intervenes, unseen and unsuspected, to ensure for Rex the scholarship aid that he needs. Indeed, it is Guy's persistent meddlesome streak (reminiscent of Gussie Millinder and Ida Hartley) that will in time cause most of his problems with Rex, as with other people as well. Easygoing and affable, Guy often tries too hard to keep other people happy, little mindful that they might be happier, or better off, without his "help."

After Harvard, both Guy Prime and Rex Geer are hired by Marcellus de Grasse, a prosperous private banker and Prime family friend to whom Guy has introduced Rex. Rex rises quickly through the firm; Guy, although moderately successful, finds the work a bit too confining for his expansive temperament and draws on family connections to found his own brokerage house, inviting Rex to join him as full partner. When Rex, true to his own character, refuses, Guy simply cannot understand Rex's need to succeed on his own. Thereafter, the two men's differing needs and temperaments continue to strain their friendship, even as their professional relationship grows even closer. Guy's brokerage firm, soon prosperous, becomes a principal client of Rex's bank.

During World War I, the two Harvard graduates again find themselves at odds: Guy, among the first to volunteer for combat, is instead assigned to a staff job, presumably because of his skill at meeting people; Rex, late to volunteer because of the pressures of his job, joins the war at the last minute but nevertheless emerges as a true hero. Thereafter, Guy envies Rex the latter's combat experience, even as Rex remains convinced that Guy could have seen action had he so desired. During the decade to follow, the battle lines between Guy and Rex become even more sharply defined, as their respective approaches to finance come into conflict.

By Guy's own rueful reckoning, his own decade, the broker's decade, was that of the 1920's, an age of deals and speculation; Rex's decade follows, after the crash of 1929, when a banker's conservative instincts are needed to save whatever money might be left. A born salesman and trader, Guy is both ill-prepared and temperamentally ill-suited for the retrenchment of the Depression years. Still in good financial shape himself, he moves into the 1930's at full speed, investing in such then-risky ventures as tranquilizer pills and prefabricated housing. In order to keep his various ventures afloat, he borrows to the limit from a variety of institutions; once that limit is exceeded he becomes, in effect, the embezzler of the title, pledging securities that his firm holds in trust for various family members and for the Glenville Country Club, founded by Guy Prime himself. He intends to put the money back.

One fact upon which *The Embezzler*'s three narrators seem to agree is that Guy did not embark on the most reckless phase of his trading until after he discovered, or began to suspect, an affair between his wife, Angelica, and Rex Geer during 1934. Guy himself encourages Angelica to interest Rex in horseback riding as therapy for job-related stress. Whatever his suspicions may be, Guy soon begins borrowing heavily from Rex's firm, and then from Rex himself, to cover unanticipated losses in real estate and mining ventures.

The ultimate confrontation between the two men begins during the spring of 1936, when Guy asks Rex to "cover" some embezzled bonds belonging to the Glenville Country Club; Rex, whose son is by then engaged to Guy's daughter Evadne, agrees to do so, on condition that Guy liquidate his firm and retire from business, the better to protect trusting, unsuspecting clients. Left with little choice, Guy asks for a "reprieve" of several months to "set his affairs in order," proceeding instead with even riskier speculations in a desperate, reckless attempt to repair the damage himself and keep his firm in business. Predictably, he fails, and Rex, also predictably, refuses to bail him out; Guy's firm thus goes into bankruptcy, and Guy himself goes to prison, willingly and almost gleefully—he has not gone down without a fight.

A quarter of a century after the fact, Guy, Rex, and Angelica—whom Rex has married after her divorce from Guy and the subsequent death of Rex's ailing first wife—have widely differing interpretations of what happened, why, and to whom. Both Guy and Rex feel betrayed by each other, Guy because Rex stole not only his wife but also his good name, Rex because Guy in effect "sold out" the stock market to the government, forcing the imposition of federal controls in place of the gentlemanly code of honor that had previously sufficed on Wall Street.

Angelica Hyde Prime Geer, whose memoir closes the novel, attempts to strike a balance between her husbands, seeing their conflict of wills not in absolute terms but as a clash of idiosyncrasies. She tends to favor Rex's interpretation of events, having long since concluded that Guy is something of a mythomaniac, an incurable romantic who tends to lose contact with reality. In the end, however, it matters little who may be "right" or "wrong"; Auchincloss, through his skillful use of shifting narrative viewpoints, has illuminated an otherwise puzzling incident in recent American history, showing how hard it is to know exactly where the truth lies.

WATCHFIRES

First published: 1982
Type of work: Novel

A man who prides himself on ethical behavior finds that it is not as easy as he had thought to live a morally upright life.

Watchfires is set in New York during the Civil War period. When the protagonist of the novel, Dexter Fairchild, was sixteen, his father, a prominent Episcopal clergyman, left his wife, his children, and his parish to run off to Italy with a married woman. As a result, Dexter lost his faith, but he replaced it with a strict ethical code. Now a lawyer, Dexter Fairchild considers himself a model of probity and self-control.

As the novel begins, Fairchild, now forty, is deeply troubled. It seems increasingly unlikely that a compromise between the fire-eating Southerners and the fanatical abolitionists will be reached, even to save the Union. The conflict has reached into his own household: Fairchild's wife, Rosalie, has espoused the cause of the abolitionists, and the two Fairchild boys, Fred and Selby, have taken to debating the issues loudly all over the house.

However, Dexter has a more immediate problem. His cousin, Charles Fairchild, has discovered an amorous note that his wife, Annie, received from Jules Bleeker, a journalist. Since Annie is Rosalie's younger sister, Dexter considers it his moral obligation to put Bleeker in his place. He has

Bleeker fired by the newspaper where he works and ousted from society. Rosalie is furious; her husband, she says, is like a self-ordained priest, a watchman over everyone else's conduct. Ironically, like his father, Dexter proves unable to practice what he preaches. When Annie throws herself at him, they become involved in a passionate affair, which continues until she dismisses him for being too possessive.

The Civil War ends the political debates in the Fairchild household and gives both Dexter and Rosalie an opportunity to live purposeful lives. Dexter works with his father-in-law to raise money and acquire supplies for the troops. Rosalie nurses wounded soldiers until Dexter becomes ill from overwork, and then she cares for him. They do become closer. However, Rosalie needs another cause, and she finds it in women's rights. Again, Dexter is appalled, but by now the two of them have learned to ignore their basic incompatibility, which in their youth was not considered an impediment to marriage.

After the war, Fred seeks his fortune by becoming involved with the speculators around Cornelius Vanderbilt. When Selby is killed in a train wreck that was the direct result of their machinations, Fred is devastated. However, he recovers, marries a Vanderbilt, and succeeds in the field of law. The book ends in 1895 with Dexter Fairchild at the graves of his wife and his son Selby, who, he says, are still trying to keep him from making a fool of himself.

In *Watchfires*, Auchincloss tells the story of a past era through the eyes of two well-meaning but very different people who lived through it. As the story progresses, Dexter keeps trying to reason out what is right and then to do it, only to find himself in the wrong. By contrast, Rosalie lets her heart lead her but too often is disappointed in the people who share her beliefs. Throughout the book, Auchincloss never lets his readers forget that power and wealth can accomplish anything. During the war, there is some honest patriotism. Before the war, however, men such as Rosalie's powerful father and his friends own everyone around them, and after it the gospel of greed engulfs the nation.

DIARY OF A YUPPIE

First published: 1986
Type of work: Novel

In his journal, a lawyer justifies every unfeeling and unscrupulous act that marked his road to success.

Diary of a Yuppie is a candid first-person account of a crucial period in a young lawyer's life. The book is presented as a private journal but is unlike most such works in that it is surprisingly free of confessions of guilt or even expressions of regret. To Robert Service, the title character, the end always justifies the means.

The novel begins in 1979. At thirty-two, Service is happily married to Alice, a beautiful, intelligent woman whom he met at Columbia University, and they have two daughters. Service specializes in corporate takeovers, and he has done so well that at the beginning of the next year, he expects to be made a partner in his firm. With this achievement, he will have outdone his father, who never became a partner but settled instead for an inferior position. The respect that Service might otherwise have bestowed on his real father has gone to Branders Blakelock, a highly respected member of the firm and the young man's mentor and sponsor.

However, from Service's vantage point, Blakelock no longer deserves his respect or even his loyalty when, by criticizing the younger man's tactics, he proves to have what Service considers nineteenth century values. To Service, that criticism justifies his conspiring with Glenn Deane, another unscrupulous lawyer, and Peter Stubbs, a gifted and wealthy young man, to steal the most capable young men from their present firm and start their own. After Blakelock informs her as to what Service has done, Alice is so appalled that she moves out. Service cannot understand why she disapproves of his actions. He misses her, however, and is determined to do anything to get her back.

Six months later, the new firm has seventeen partners and thirty-nine associates. However, Service's conspirator Deane has gathered a little court around him that threatens Service's power. Again, Service strikes, but by expelling Deane from the

Louis Auchincloss

firm, he infuriates Alice, who had been about to return to her husband.

Although Service had always prided himself on his fidelity, he now becomes involved with another woman, Sylvia Sands, a professional fund-raiser, who proves to be both as clever and as unscrupulous as Service. At first, Service is dazzled by the circles in which she moves, but before long, he realizes that she is controlling both his social life and his professional commitments. When she tries to force him to divorce Alice and marry her, he breaks off the affair. Alice takes Service back, just as he is, and he resolves to act more like the man Alice wants him to be. When she turns out to be pregnant, he is ecstatic, for to him that is proof that the gods are truly on his side.

Throughout the novel, Service justifies every unethical act on the grounds that, because every human being is selfish and greedy, he is merely acting in self-defense. It is significant, then, that in the end he promises to "act" differently, not to "be" different. Moreover, since he will no longer be keeping a journal, he will not even have to contemplate what he truly is. Clearly, Auchincloss means Robert Service to represent modern man at his worst: a creature who glories in his freedom from all constraints, a creature without a soul.

The Lady of Situations

First published: 1990
Type of work: Novel

Battling financial obstacles, social stereotypes, malice, and scandal, a determined and sometimes ruthless young woman makes her way to success.

By entitling his book *The Lady of Situations*, Auchincloss points to the fact that his heroine, Natica Chauncey, attains success by treating every difficult situation not as an obstacle but as an opportunity. Her independent spirit and her clear-sightedness qualify Natica for her role as a heroine. However, her life story suggests that a woman such as Natica will often sacrifice others in order to fulfill her own potential.

The Lady of Situations is for the most part nar-rated by an omniscient author. However, the novel is framed by first-person narratives entitled "Ruth's Memoir," in which Natica's aunt, Ruth Felton, reports her observations, thus functioning much like a Greek chorus. A similar passage appears at three other points in the book.

The novel begins in the 1960's, with Ruth, now in her seventies, recalling the time three decades before when Natica's difficulties began. Natica's bankrupt father spends his time perfecting his fly-fishing technique; her mother refuses to admit that the Chauncey name no longer means anything. She is too obtuse to let Ruth pay Natica's way through a prestigious private school, where she could make the friendships that would serve her in later life.

The primary narrator now takes up Natica's story. After graduating from Barnard College, Natica meets and marries Thomas Barnes, an assistant rector at Averhill School. Unlike her naïve husband, Natica sees Averhill as it is, a hotbed of hypocrisy and malice. However, after autocratic headmaster Reverend Rufus Lockwood makes Natica his secretary, she enjoys feeling powerful and is almost happy. Unfortunately, when Lockwood's wife realizes that Natica has some influence over him, he is forced to fire her.

By now, Natica is so bored with her husband and the school that she embarks upon an affair with a new teacher, the wealthy, charming Stephen Hill. After she becomes pregnant, Hill insists on her divorcing Barnes and marrying him. Ever the pragmatist, Natica agrees. Though he is the innocent party, Barnes is dismissed from Averhill, becomes a military chaplain, and is later killed in wartime.

Meanwhile, Natica has miscarried. She is somewhat relieved, however, because she feared that the child would resemble Barnes, who was probably his father. Back in the United States, Hill's mother, who adores Natica, arranges for her to be accepted by society. However, Hill proves to be lazy and moody. Realizing that he resents her success in business, Natica quits her job and persuades Hill's mother to buy them a bookstore. When he learns from Barnes that he was not the father of the child Natica lost, Hill shoots himself.

Again, Natica makes the best of things. She persuades Hill's mother to pay her way through law school and then joins a law firm, where she finally meets a man she can both love and respect. When

137

she appears in the final "Memoir," set in 1966, Natica is happily married and has three children, as well as a flourishing law practice.

Ruth points out, however, that Natica has made her way to success by manipulating some people and destroying others, notably two husbands. Natica just laughs, but Ruth muses that she would rather be an old maid than have Natica's memories. Ruth fulfills the role of the Greek chorus, raising the moral questions that Natica does not choose to ask.

SUMMARY

Taken together, *The House of Five Talents, Portrait in Brownstone, The Rector of Justin,* and *The Embezzler,* constitute the keystone of Auchincloss's fictional universe, providing a credible, authoritative portrait of American society and politics from the late nineteenth century until well past the midpoint of the twentieth, a period encompassing two world wars and the Great Depression. In such later novels as *The Country Cousin* (1978) and *The Book Class* (1984), Auchincloss has often returned to the temporal setting of *Portrait in Brownstone* and *The Embezzler,* evoking the transitional period of the 1930's with rare insight and skill. Throughout his fiction, Auchincloss is sensitive to the dilemmas of intelligent women in a society that expects them to be pretty, docile, and not particularly bright. The quest of women for independence and self-fulfillment is the subject of both *The Lady of Situations* (1990) and *Her Infinite Variety* (2001). Perhaps Auchincloss's greatest achievement is that, although like Jane Austen, he limits his writing to his own experience,

in the lives of his wealthy New Yorkers he find examples of every virtue and vice, every strength and frailty, every hypocrisy and self-delusion of which the human race is capable.

David B. Parsell;
updated by Rosemary M. Canfield Reisman

DISCUSSION TOPICS

- What are the characteristics of upper-class New York society as Louis Auchincloss depicts it?

- How do his characters reveal their total selfishness?

- How do the parents in Auchincloss's novels relate to their children?

- How and why are certain marriages promoted in Auchincloss's novels?

- What does Auchincloss suggest makes for an unhappy marriage? A happy one?

- How do the women in Auchincloss's novels gain and keep power?

- Which men and women in Auchincloss's novels do you see as victims?

- What evidence is there in Auchincloss's novels that, although his characters believe themselves to be America's aristocrats, in reality it is only their money that has made them prominent?

BIBLIOGRAPHY

By the Author

LONG FICTION:
The Indifferent Children, 1947 (as Andrew Lee)
Sybil, 1951
A Law for the Lion, 1953
The Great World and Timothy Colt, 1956
Venus in Sparta, 1958
Pursuit of the Prodigal, 1959
The House of Five Talents, 1960
Portrait in Brownstone, 1962
The Rector of Justin, 1964
The Embezzler, 1966

A World of Profit, 1968
I Come as a Thief, 1972
The Partners, 1974
The Dark Lady, 1977
The Country Cousin, 1978
The House of the Prophet, 1980
The Cat and the King, 1981
Watchfires, 1982
Exit Lady Masham, 1983
The Book Class, 1984
Honorable Men, 1985
Diary of a Yuppie, 1986
The Golden Calves, 1988
Fellow Passengers, 1989
The Lady of Situations, 1990
Three Lives, 1993 (novellas)
The Education of Oscar Fairfax, 1995
Her Infinite Variety, 2001
The Scarlet Letters, 2003
East Side Story, 2004

SHORT FICTION:
The Injustice Collectors, 1950
The Romantic Egoists, 1954
Powers of Attorney, 1963
Tales of Manhattan, 1967
Second Chance: Tales of Two Generations, 1970
The Winthrop Covenant, 1976
Narcissa, and Other Fables, 1983
Skinny Island: More Tales of Manhattan, 1987
Fellow Passengers: A Novel in Portraits, 1989
False Gods, 1992 (fables)
The Collected Stories of Louis Auchincloss, 1994
Tales of Yesteryear, 1994
The Atonement, and Other Stories, 1997
The Anniversary, and Other Stories, 1999
Manhattan Monologues, 2002

NONFICTION:
Reflections of a Jacobite, 1961
Pioneers and Caretakers: A Study of Nine American Women Novelists, 1965
Motiveless Malignity, 1969
Edith Wharton: A Woman in Her Time, 1971
Richelieu, 1972
A Writer's Capital, 1974
Reading Henry James, 1975
Life, Law and Letters: Essays and Sketches, 1979
Persons of Consequence: Queen Victoria and Her Circle, 1979
False Dawn: Women in the Age of the Sun King, 1984
The Vanderbilt Era: Profiles of a Gilded Age, 1989
J. P. Morgan: The Financier as Collector, 1990

Love Without Wings: Some Friendships in Literature and Politics, 1991
The Style's the Man: Reflections on Proust, Fitzgerald, Wharton, Vidal, and Others, 1994
The Man Behind the Book: Literary Profiles, 1996
La Gloire: The Roman Empire of Corneille and Racine, 1996
Woodrow Wilson, 2000
Theodore Roosevelt, 2001

About the Author

Bryer, Jackson R. *Louis Auchincloss and His Critics: A Bibliographical Record*. Boston: G. K. Hall, 1977.

Dahl, Christopher C. *Louis Auchincloss*. New York: Frederick Ungar, 1986.

Gelderman, Carol. *Louis Auchincloss: A Writer's Life*. New York: Crown, 1993.

Parsell, David B. *Louis Auchincloss*. Boston: Twayne, 1988.

Piket, Vincent. *Louis Auchincloss: The Growth of a Novelist*. New York: St. Martin's Press, 1991.

Tuttleton, James W. "Louis Auchincloss at 80." *New Criterion* 16, no. 2 (October 1, 1997): 32-36.

_____. "Louis Auchincloss: The Image of Lost Elegance and Virtue." In *A Fine Silver Thread: Essays on American Writing and Criticism*. Chicago: Ivan R. Dee, 1998.

Vidal, Gore. "The Great World and Louis Auchincloss." In *United States*. New York: Random House, 1993.

PAUL AUSTER

Born: Newark, New Jersey
February 3, 1947

In his work, Auster has combined provocative themes with complex, troubled characters, brought to situations by coincidence or chance, to create fiction that is haunting, mysterious, and hypnotic.

© Jerry Bauer

BIOGRAPHY

The grandson of first-generation Jewish immigrants, Paul Auster was born in Newark, New Jersey, on February 3, 1947, to Samuel and Queenie Auster. He grew up in South Orange and attended high school in Maplewood, twenty miles southwest of New York City. His father was a landlord; his mother was thirteen years younger than her husband. Auster examines the complexities of his relationship with his parents and of their relationship with each other in *The Invention of Solitude* (1982) and *Hand to Mouth: A Chronicle of Early Failure* (1997).

In 1959 Auster's uncle, Allen Mandelbaum, a talented translator, left boxes of books in storage at the Auster home when he traveled to Europe. Auster discovered and read all of the books, and this sparked his interest in writing and literature. He began to write poems as a teenager and showed his poems to Mandelbaum, who was a tough but fair critic.

After Auster graduated from high school, he left to travel around Europe for the summer. He went to Spain, Italy, France, and Ireland. While traveling, he began work on a novel. He returned to the United States and enrolled at Columbia University in the fall. In 1967 he again left America to spend his junior year studying in Paris. Though he loved Paris, he became disillusioned with college and dropped out of the year abroad program, choosing

to live instead in a small hotel on the rue Clément. He returned to New York in November and was, fortunately, reinstated in Columbia.

A high lottery number in the Vietnam War draft kept Auster from serving. He went on to get both his B.A. and M.A. in English from Columbia. Instead of pursuing a Ph.D., he took a job with the U.S. Census Bureau. After that, he worked as a merchant seaman on the *Esso Florence* to fund a move to France. He lived in France for four years, working as a translator and as a caretaker of a farm in Provence.

He married the writer Lydia Davis in 1974, and they had a son, Daniel. When he returned to New York, Auster published his first two books of poetry, *Unearth* (1974) and *Wall Writing* (1976). He divorced Lydia in 1979 and married Siri Hustuedt, whom he had met at a poetry reading, in 1981. He and Hustuedt had a daughter, Sophie. Auster received Ingram Merrill Foundation grants in both 1975 and 1982, and he also received National Endowments of the Arts fellowships in 1979 and 1985. In 1979 and 1980 he worked on "Portrait of an Invisible Man" and "The Book of Memory," memoirs which would make up *The Invention of Solitude* (1982), his first major work of prose. He also, at this time, edited *The Random House Book of Twentieth-Century French Poetry* (1982).

Auster continued to write poetry and essays, and to translate French literature, until his breakthrough novel, *City of Glass* (1985), the first book of *The New York Trilogy* (1990), which was nominated for an Edgar Award for best mystery novel in 1986. The second volume of *The New York Trilogy*, *Ghosts* (1986), was also well received, and the third vol-

141

ume, *The Locked Room* (1986), was nominated for numerous awards.

Auster taught creative writing at Princeton University from 1986 to 1990. In 1994 he worked with director Wayne Wang on the films *Smoke* (1995) and *Blue in the Face* (1995). Coincidentally, Wang had become a fan of Auster when he read "Auggie Wren's Christmas Story," which appeared as an Op-Ed piece in *The New York Times* on Christmas Day, 1990. This tale of confused identities was eventually used in the moving last act of *Smoke*.

Auster also published the novels *In the Country of Last Things* (1987), *Moon Palace* (1989), *The Music of Chance* (1990), *Leviathan* (1992), *Mr. Vertigo* (1994), *Timbuktu* (1999), *The Book of Illusions* (2002), and *Oracle Night* (2003). Picador published his *Collected Prose* in 2003, and Overlook Press published his *Collected Poems* in 2004. Auster also wrote and directed the film *Lulu on the Bridge* (1998), edited and translated *The Notebooks of Joseph Joubert: A Selection* (1983, 2005), and edited and wrote an introduction for the collection *I Thought My Father Was God* (2001). Auster received the Morto Dauwen Zabel Award from the American Academy of Arts and Letters in 1990, the esteemed Chevalier de l'Ordre des Arts des et des Lettres in 1993, and the Prix Medicis for foreign literature, also in 1993, for *Leviathan*. His work has been translated into more than twenty languages. He lives in Brooklyn, New York.

ANALYSIS

A fan of hard-boiled detective novels, and of the humbleness with which many practitioners of that genre proceeded, Auster pseudonymously wrote one for money in 1978. The novel did not achieve its intended purpose, and Auster continued on as a well-regarded but struggling poet, translator, and essayist. He again turned to writing novels in the mid-1980's, this time under his own name. Still influenced by the sharpness and crispness of the best of the hard-boiled detective novels, Auster again drew from that genre to fashion a crafty and unusual twist on the detective story, *City of Glass*, the first volume of *The New York Trilogy* (1990). He followed this with two more curious and inventive detective stories, the second and third volumes of *The New York Trilogy*: *Ghosts* and *The Locked Room*.

It is apparent in these three books that Auster's style is heavily influenced by hard-boiled writers such as Dashiell Hammett, Raymond Chandler, and James Cain, writers who crafted sharp, clear, and economical sentences in the manner of Ernest Hemingway but ultimately cooked up complicated and cryptic potboilers. Auster, though, does not limit himself to the hard-boiled school. He is also deeply influenced by nineteenth century American authors like Edgar Allan Poe, Herman Melville, Nathaniel Hawthorne, and Henry David Thoreau, and the felt presence of these writers is plain—in fact, in the reader's face—in *The New York Trilogy* and later works.

On the surface, Auster's work—especially *The New York Trilogy*—is like Poe reimagined by Chandler (or some such combination). It is, however, never merely that, because Auster's trenchant prose only serves to derail the reader as Auster promptly reveals the literary tricks that he has up his sleeve. The first thing to know, then, is that an Auster story is almost never what it at first seems. Auster never gives presents anything that is exceedingly simple or too difficult to handle, and he is never too clever for his own good. His novels, instead, unfold as gracefully and seamlessly as a well-played baseball game.

Auster often employs metafictional narrative techniques and textual puzzles that allow his stories to traverse the landscapes of ostensibly dissimilar genres. Essentially, Auster allows characters who are equal parts gumshoe, silent-film comedian, and existentialist quester to run wild in a universe governed by chance and circumstance. In Auster's work one often meets worn-out, broken, and paranoid characters who must confront the problem of the past in order to move on. They often follow a series of clues which lead them away from their normal lives into worlds where order is disrupted, where time stands still, and where, to paraphrase Robert Penn Warren's discussion of the characters in Joseph Conrad's *Nostromo* (1904), they are perilously balanced in their humanity between the deep darknesses in themselves and the immense indifference of nature.

Nowhere is this more evident than in *The New York Trilogy*. In *City of Glass*, the protagonist, Daniel Quinn, literally disappears into the brutal anonymity of New York City, and in *The Locked Room*, the much sought-after Fanshawe disappears into the vastness of America and the world, only to reappear in a fantastical locked room in the nameless narrator's skull and, finally, in a literal locked room in Boston. Ultimately, in a strange twist, one learns that Quinn has pursued Fanshawe. Their identities blur, as do the identities of many characters in *The New York Trilogy*, canceling each other out, and speaking to the connectedness of things, to the recognition by these characters that the death of the self is the true source of selfhood.

Above all, Auster's work is concerned with themes of mystery and chance, of space and coincidence, of isolation and identity. He presents questions about what is real and what is imagined, but he is not an idealist. A typical character of his is likely to have a doppelgänger or a ghostly connection to a historical or literary figure. Auster also seems to have a preoccupation with the mystical and transformative power of notebooks. In this way, he is similar to the American filmmaker David Lynch, who, in *Mulholland Drive* (2001), placed a seemingly simple object, a blue box, at the center of his mystery. Auster, in fact, has more in common with Lynch than one might at first assume, namely a taste for whodunits that play out like surrealist noir and draw from a curious cabinet of potent symbolism and imagery. Both have created art that is simultaneously powerful, ambitious, and accessible. What seems to set Auster's characters apart is their understanding that if one does not cultivate the past—instead of choosing to misinterpret one's guilt about it—one is doomed. Auster's work teaches that there is nothing, no event, from which wisdom cannot be drawn. It is only after one accepts that everyone depends on everyone else, and everything that has come before and that exists today, that one can learn to live well in the world.

THE NEW YORK TRILOGY

First published: 1990
Type of work: Novels (includes *City of Glass*, 1985; *Ghosts*, 1986; and *The Locked Room*, 1986)

A mystery novelist assumes the identity of a real detective; a detective named Blue is hired by a client named White to follow a man named Black; a nameless narrator moves into the life of a childhood friend who has disappeared and is presumed dead.

The New York Trilogy comprises Auster's first three novels, *City of Glass* (1985), *Ghosts* (1986), and *The Locked Room* (1986). It introduces the themes that Auster would continue to explore in novels for years to come. Drawing on the style of hard-boiled detective fiction and the imagery of film noir, Auster sets these three intricate mysteries in New York in different time periods. Essentially, each of these three books tells the same story, as the nameless narrator confesses at the end of *The Locked Room*, related at different stages of the narrator's awareness. They are tales about the nature of identity and language and the role that coincidence and chance plays in forming the human character. Auster uses concise language to reveal the pieces of a complicated textual puzzle. Never perplexing just for the sake of it, Auster remains focused and accessible throughout.

The first of these books, *City of Glass*, was published in 1985 by Sun and Moon Press, a small Los Angeles company, after being rejected by other publishers seventeen times over the course of two years. It is the story of Daniel Quinn, a mystery novelist who writes a series of detective novels about a private eye named Max Work, under the pseudonym William Wilson. One day Quinn, devastated by the death of his wife and son, receives a call from someone looking for Paul Auster of the Auster Detective Agency. Ultimately, Quinn, anxious and bored, assumes Auster's identity and pretends to be a private detective. He accepts the case and begins trailing a man named Stillman, a linguist who had been confined to a mental institution for locking up his son alone in a room for nine years.

It is immediately apparent how much fun Auster is having with names: "William Wilson" is taken from an Edgar Allan Poe short story of the same name, and it is also the real name of New York Mets center fielder "Mookie" Wilson. Daniel Quinn's initials are not insignificant, nor is the "Mrs. Saavedra" that the reader learns is waiting for Peter Stillman after he first talks to Quinn, as Miguel de Cervantes's *Don Quixote* (1605) plays a major role in the text. There is also "Paul Auster," the character—later in the book, one learns that "Paul Auster" is not a detective at all but a writer with a wife named Siri and a son named Daniel. Daniel Quinn and Auster's son joke about having the same name, just as Quinn marvels early on that Peter Stillman, the son of the man Quinn is hired to track, has the same name as his dead son. The story is all about shifting identities, about characters who melt and mold into one another.

Such dynamics carry into the subsequent volumes, *Ghosts* and *The Locked Room*. In *Ghosts*, a detective named Blue, a student of Brown, is hired by White to follow a man named Black. Coincidentally, the story begins in Brooklyn on February 3, 1947, the day that Auster was born in Newark. What, then, to make of this? Though one knows that *Ghosts* is a twist on the stories told in *City of Glass* and *The Locked Room*, one gets the feeling that Auster began the story with a simple question: "What might have been happening in New York on the day that I was born, and how is it connected to my life?" Auster, like Blue, who reads *True Detective* magazine religiously, is concerned with the possibilities of chance, with the way that lives weave and intersect. He knows that the present is equally as mysterious as the past and the future.

In *The Locked Room*, a nameless narrator is called by the wife of his childhood best friend, Fanshawe. (The name Fanshawe is also that of the title character of Nathaniel Hawthorne's first book, *Fanshawe: A Tale* [1828].) Fanshawe's wife, Sophie, tells the narrator that her husband has been missing for more than six months, that she presumes he is dead, and that he left instructions that, if anything should ever happen to him, the narrator should become his literary executor. Fanshawe, it turns out, was a reclusive genius, leaving behind a closet full of extraordinary novels, poems, and plays. The narrator accepts the task and, slowly, moves into Fanshawe's life: He publishes his work, marries his wife, adopts his son, and begins work on a biography of him.

Again, Auster is examining the frailty of human existence—how, almost by chance, one can move into an altogether different life and become another person. For Auster, detective work—following ambiguous clues and lousy leads—is the stuff of the human story: the search for character, for identity, and, ultimately, for death. Auster is also concerned with why and how people create art, and nowhere does he meditate on this subject more poignantly than in *The Locked Room*. The true artist, Auster knows, must submit to necessity.

THE MUSIC OF CHANCE

First published: 1990
Type of work: Novel

In order to pay off a debt, a former firefighter and a tempestuous gambler are forced to build a stone wall in a Pennsylvania meadow.

The Music of Chance begins with Jim Nashe, a former firefighter from Boston, coming to the end of a year-long road journey. In this way, the novel is reminiscent of Jack Kerouac's *On the Road* (1957), but the similarities end there. Nashe, one learns, is on the road thanks to a $200,000 inheritance from a father he never really knew, which has allowed him to leave behind his everyday life and drift around the United States. His trip is a series of chance encounters, and, just as the money is about to run out, he meets a seedy character named Jack Pozzi, a gambler who inducts him into the "International Brotherhood of Lost Dogs." Nashe gambles away the last of his inheritance by bankrolling a poker game that Pozzi has put together. The game is with two Pennsylvania millionaires named Flower and Stone, who demand that Nashe and Pozzi work off their debt by building a stone wall on their estate.

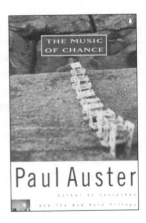

Another strong outing by Auster, this book differs significantly from his others. It is a road narrative, but, as always in Auster's world, chance is an authoritative force. Auster explores the roles of security and serenity, the restraints of freedom and solitude, the power of language and randomness in a violently apathetic world, and the nature of the true quest for justice. *The Music of Chance* is a thrilling story told in clean and exact prose.

THE BOOK OF ILLUSIONS

First published: 2002
Type of work: Novel

A grieving Vermont professor studies the life of a silent film comedian who vanished from sight in 1929 and embarks on a journey when he finds out that the comedian has resurfaced.

In *The Book of Illusions*, David Zimmer has lost his wife and two sons in a tragic car crash. Left wealthy by the insurance settlement, the grieving Zimmer quits his job as an English professor at a Vermont college and becomes a reclusive alcoholic. Flipping through television channels one night, Zimmer happens upon a film clip of the silent come-dian Hector Mann, who disappeared under mys-terious circumstances in 1929. Suddenly, Zimmer's life has purpose again, as he becomes enthralled by Mann's work and writes a book about him. Some time later, after the book has been published, Zim-mer receives a letter from someone in New Mexico claiming to be Mann's wife. The woman tells Zimmer that Hector has read his book and would like to meet him. Zimmer is obviously confused, presuming that Mann has long been dead, and he writes the letter off as a fraud. A visit from an unusual and remarkable woman named Alma Grund, however, changes Zimmer's mind.

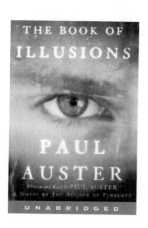

The Book of Illusions takes Auster's relationship with risk and chance to a new and exciting level, as Auster examines, in great depth, the life of a van-ished man. We learn where Hector Mann went, what he did, and why he remains in hiding. Like François-René de Chateaubriand in his *Mémoires d'outre-tombe* (1849-1850; memoirs of a dead man), which Zimmer translates, Mann seemingly com-municates from a world beyond. He meditates on life, art, and love, as does Zimmer himself, and this sets the uniformity of mood pervading the novel. Like Hawthorne, whose "The Birthmark" is al-luded to by Alma, Auster has a spirit of introspec-tive memory and moral consciousness. *The Book of Illusions* is, in a way, a high-wire act, a reflection on the thin line between madness and sanity, and, ar-guably, the finest achievement of Auster's career.

SUMMARY

Auster is often viewed as an experimental writer, but in the end, he has a very traditional take on how stories should be told. His narratives are straightforward, and everything—the textual puz-zles, the conventional detective motifs, the labyrin-thine logic, and the noir imagery—serves the story. He writes in lucid prose and is often referred to as a metaphysical detective novelist because of his deep concern with issues of self-invention and doubt. Auster's work is organized around themes of syn-chronicity and chance, of randomness and causal-ity, but he never alienates the reader by sacrificing the inherent pleasures of storytelling.

William Boyle

BIBLIOGRAPHY

By the Author

LONG FICTION:
City of Glass, 1985
Ghosts, 1986
The Locked Room, 1986
In the Country of Last Things, 1987
Moon Palace, 1989
The New York Trilogy, 1990 (includes *City of Glass, Ghosts,* and *The Locked Room*)
The Music of Chance, 1990
Leviathan, 1992

Mr. Vertigo, 1994
Timbuktu, 1999
The Book of Illusions, 2002
Oracle Night, 2003
Auggie Wren's Christmas Story, 2004

SCREENPLAYS:
"Smoke" and "Blue in the Face": Two Screenplays, 1995
Lulu on the Bridge, 1998

POETRY:
Unearth, 1974
Wall Writing, 1976
Disappearances: Selected Poems, 1988
Ground Work: Selected Poems and Essays, 1970-1979, 1990
Collected Poems, 2004

NONFICTION:
The Art of Hunger, and Other Essays, 1982 (also as *The Art of Hunger: Essays, Prefaces, Interviews,* 1991)
The Invention of Solitude, 1982, 1988
Hand to Mouth: A Chronicle of Early Failure, 1997
The Red Notebook: True Stories, 2002
The Story of My Typewriter, 2002

TRANSLATIONS:
The Notebooks of Joseph Joubert: A Selection, 1983, 2005
A Tomb for Anatole, 1983 (of Stéphane Mallarmé's poetry)

EDITED TEXTS:
The Random House Book of Twentieth-Century French Poetry, 1982
I Thought My Father Was God, and Other True Tales from NPR's National Story Project, 2001

MISCELLANEOUS:
Collected Prose: Autobiographical Writings, True Stories, Critical Essays, Prefaces, and Collaborations with Artists, 2003

DISCUSSION TOPICS

- Where does Paul Auster generally draw the names of his characters from, and why are his choices relevant?

- How does Auster employ elements of horror and mystery?

- What is the importance of place in Auster's work?

- Consider the general symbolic significance of Auster's work. What comment on American society is he making?

- How does Auster examine the connectedness of things?

- Auster, like Fanshawe in *The Locked Room,* shows a fondness for little anecdotes or parables in his work. How do these asides, which often deal with historical and literary figures, help one to understand the characters?

- Auster seems to be preoccupied by chance, circumstance, and choice. Do his characters follow realistic paths, or is what happens to them represented in a fantastic way?

- What, in Auster's work, is the relationship between the actual world and the world of the imagination?

About the Author

Alford, Steven E. "Spaced-Out: Signification and Space in Paul Auster's *The New York Trilogy.*" *Contemporary Literature* 36 (1995): 613-632.

Barone, Dennis, ed. *Beyond the Red Notebook: Essays on Paul Auster.* Philadelphia: University of Pennsylvania Press, 1995.

Bloom, Harold, and Amy Sickels, eds. *Paul Auster.* New York: Chelsea House, 2003.

Chénetier, Marc. *Paul Auster as the Wizard of Odds: Moon Palace.* Paris: Didier Erudition, 1996.

Lavender, William. "The Novel of Critical Engagement: Paul Auster's *City of Glass.*" *Contemporary Literature* 34 (1993): 210-239.

Little, William G. "Nothing to Go On: Paul Auster's *City of Glass.*" *Contemporary Literature* 38 (1997): 133-163.

Rowen, Norma. "The Detective in Search of the Lost Tongue of Adam: Paul Auster's *City of Glass.*" *Critique: Studies in Contemporary Fiction* 32 (1991): 224-235.

Saltzman, Arthur. *Designs of Darkness.* Philadelphia: University of Pennsylvania Press, 1990.

JIMMY SANTIAGO BACA

Born: Santa Fe, New Mexico
January 2, 1952

Through his autobiographical poetry, Baca has gained wide recognition as a spokesman for Chicano culture, particularly its poor and underprivileged.

Lawrence Benton/
Courtesy, New Directions Publishing

BIOGRAPHY

Jimmy Santiago Baca, born in 1952 to Chicano parents in Santa Fe, New Mexico, had a deprived and unsettled childhood. He spent his early childhood first with grandparents, until he was five, and then in an Albuquerque, New Mexico, orphanage. He ran away from the orphanage when he was eleven and for the next nine years lived on the streets and in various detention centers.

In 1972, Baca was arrested and convicted for possession of heroin with intent to sell. He was sent to prison in Florence, Arizona, where he stayed for the following seven years. There, according to the Arizona Supreme Court, which ordered his release in 1979, he was subjected to cruel and unusual punishment, including electric shock therapy.

Despite its harshness, however, Baca's prison experience turned him around as a person and set his life on a new course. Poetry became his savior. In prison, he began reading and writing, first a journal and then poetry. He was encouraged by several people, including Will Inman, former publisher of *New Kauri* poetry magazine, who visited Baca in prison. He also submitted poems to *Mother Jones* magazine, where the distinguished poet Denise Levertov was poetry editor. Describing Baca as "an

extraordinarily gifted poet," Levertov published three of his prison poems in *Mother Jones* and began a correspondence with him.

Louisiana State University Press, noted among academic presses for its support of poetry, published Baca's collection *Immigrants in Our Own Land* (1979). The poems in *Immigrants in Our Own Land* center mostly on Baca's prison experience. After he left prison, Baca expanded his subject matter to include his whole autobiography and his identification with Chicano culture. His next major work, *Martín: &, Meditations on the South Valley* (1987), represented those expanded interests in a dramatic fashion. Introduced by Levertov and published by a prominent New York publisher, New Directions, *Martín: &, Meditations on the South Valley* won the Before Columbus Foundation American Book Award.

Thereafter, Baca's literary reputation blossomed. Although some Chicano critics described his poetry as prosy and self-engrossed, Baca's fame spread rapidly beyond Chicano circles. His poetry readings and workshops became popular across the United States. He received a Ludwig Vogelstein Foundation Award, the 1989 International Hispanic Heritage Award, and a Wallace Stevens Yale Poetry Fellowship. He attracted media coverage, appearing on *The Today Show* and National Public Radio. He also began working on a number of film scripts, including scripts for actor Edward James Olmos and *La Bamba* (1987) producer Taylor Hackford.

Despite such national attention, Baca remains rooted in the Chicano culture of the Southwest. He has said, "Foremost and always until my last breath I'm going to be a Chicano." He has also closely identified with the region around Albuquerque, as some of his titles indicate; the collection *Poems Taken from My Yard* (1986) was incorporated into *Black Mesa Poems* (1989). Baca, with his wife and two sons, lives on a ranch in the Black Mesa area south of Albuquerque. Besides writing, he takes a strong interest in being a parent and in the Atrisco Land Rights Council, which represents claimants to the seventeenth century Spanish land grant. He earned his Ph.D. in literature from the University of New Mexico in 2003.

ANALYSIS

The charges that Baca's poetry is prosy and self-engrossed are, to some extent, justified; he has also been accused of misspelling the Chicano Spanish that his poems include. Some readers might also feel that Baca's empathy for convicts and members of youth gangs overlooks an important factor: What about their victims?

These criticisms should not be allowed to obscure Baca's achievements. He is largely a self-taught poet who has shown tremendous development, and indicated the capacity for more, over his career. It has been said that Baca taught himself to read and write in prison. He got his schooling primarily from the streets and prison, so it is not surprising that his early work should reflect this background. Nor is it surprising that his early work should be prosy, documentary descriptions of his experiences.

The remarkable advances made by Baca are apparent in *Martín: &, Meditations on the South Valley.* There are prosy passages, especially when Baca provides exposition and narrative transitions, but the description is sharper, more selective, and filled with striking, even surrealistic, metaphors:

> The lonely afternoon in the vast expanse of llano,
> was a blue knife
> sharpening its hot, silver edge on the distant
> horizon of mountains, the wind blew over
> chipping red grit, carving a pre-historic scar-
>   scaled
> winged reptile of the mountain.

His subject matter, while still grounded in his own life, has also become more inclusive. It has even assumed, as Levertov notes in the introduction, a mythic quality.

Black Mesa Poems shows development in other directions. Here Baca takes on machismo, the cult of aggressive manliness, and redefines it. He depicts a man who grows out of his violent concept of machismo, exemplified by killing a bull, and accepts a nurturing, caring role, represented by fatherhood. In an interview in the *Albuquerque Journal*, Baca stated that "I see a sort of feminism permeating the Chicano male now."

In the same interview, Baca said that in raising his children he was "learning how to reparent myself because I was so brutalized" by growing up on the streets. Baca's efforts to reparent himself and to redefine machismo are part of his overall poetic project to reclaim himself, his heritage, and the Chicano culture.

In this context, Baca's autobiographical poetry is not simply self-engrossed; it takes on wider, even archetypal, meaning. The efforts of Baca and his hero Martín to reclaim themselves necessarily include identification with their culture, the Chicano culture, which must also be reclaimed. Therefore, the work of reclamation is interrelated, occurring along a spectrum that involves individuals, language, culture, history, and land.

IMMIGRANTS IN OUR OWN LAND

First published: 1979
Type of work: Poetry

Baca surveys his thoughts and experiences in prison.

Immigrants in Our Own Land provides samples of Baca's early work, which is indeed prosy. The collection includes a number of so-called prose poems, description divided into prose paragraphs. Other poems are in free-verse lines. In both kinds of poems, however, the description is somewhat flat, including too much direct statement and metaphors which are commonplace or trite.

Similarly, the point of view in the poems is limited. Centered on Baca's prison experience, the poems dwell on the plight of the inmates—on how Baca and the other inmates are ground down—but there is remarkably little concern with how they got

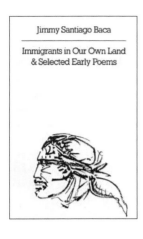

Jimmy Santiago Baca

Immigrants in Our Own Land
& Selected Early Poems

there in the first place. It is as if readers are to assume that all these men are victims of mistakes and injustices. Baca may have even thought so at the time; he repeatedly expresses his solidarity with the other inmates and condemns the forces that oppress them.

The point of view, however limited, does have a positive side: "This is suffering, pain, anguish, and loneliness,/ but also strength, hope, faith, love, it gives a man/ those secret properties of the Spirit, that make a man a man." There is a determination in Baca to endure and remain "strong enough to love you,/ love myself and feel good." Despite harassment—in "It's Going to Be a Cold Winter," new guards ransack Baca's cell and subject him to a strip search—a healing process occurs, encouraged by the passing time, moments of quietness, the prison routine, and a new warden who brings reforms and new activities, including "a poetry workshop where the death house had been."

In "So Mexicans Are Taking Jobs from Americans," perhaps the best poem in the volume, Baca also extends his sympathies outside the prison. He reaches out to feel solidarity with poor Mexicans whose children are starving and to mock the economic fears of complacent, overfed "gringos":

> Mexicans are taking our jobs, they say instead.
> What they really say is, let them die,
> and the children too.

The volume's title poem, "Immigrants in Our Own Land," is also effective. It presents prison as a kind of reverse Ellis Island, where convicts are processed into a new land of "rehabilitation" that proves to be illusory. The title also seems to allude to Chicanos whose families have lived in the Southwest since the original Spanish land grant, but who are sometimes still treated like immigrants, legal or illegal. The poem thus connects prison to the Chicano situation, with the prison experience becoming a metaphor for the denial of Chicano land, language, culture, and identity.

MARTÍN: &, MEDITATIONS ON THE SOUTH VALLEY

First published: 1987
Type of work: Poetry

After life on the streets, Martín builds a home for himself and his small family.

Martín: &, Meditations on the South Valley consists of two long narrative poems that form a sequence: They relate the story of Martín, a generic or mythic poor Chicano. In writing these poems, Baca came into his own as a poet. Although the poems are somewhat prosy, particularly at narrative junctures, he manages his language well: Chicano folk life is described in memorable, original metaphors and diction (including some Chicano Spanish) that form pictures like punched art in old tin. His style has developed considerably since *Immigrants in Our Own Land*, becoming what Denise Levertov called Gongoresque, with touches of native Hispanic surrealism: "The highway was a black seed split/ petals of darkness blossomed from."

The two poems are also peopled with a gallery of vivid characters, including Martín's grandmother, parents, and pals (mostly gang members). Inhabitants of barrios come forth with old stories about his parents—one-armed Pepin, blind Estela Gomez, Señora Martinez, Melinda Griego, Pancho Garza, and Antonia Sanchez, Ia bruja de Torreón. There are also stories of Martín's friends, who have suffered their separate fates—"Johnny who married,/ Lorenzo killed in Nam,/ Eddie en la Pinta,/ Ramon who OD'd in Califas." The main story, however, is Martín's, based on Baca's autobiography but freely changed and shaped to mythic purposes.

Like Baca, Martín is a deprived child from a broken family. Martín's parents abandon him; later, his mother is killed by her jealous second husband, and Martín's father dies of alcoholism. Martín himself lives first with his grandmother and then in an orphanage, but at the age of ten he runs away. He becomes an uprooted person, living a dissolute and sometimes violent life on the streets. In the first section of *Martín*, he says, "I have been lost from you Mother Earth," but he promises to return.

Most of *Martín* recounts his wanderings and his

efforts to return to his roots. He questions people about his parents, trying to reconstruct memories of them. He has a pleasant image of his mother "dancing in front of the mirror/ in pink panties, . . . / Her laughter rough as brocaded cloth/ and her teeth brilliant as church tiles." He also remembers some friendly visits with his father, but mostly the memories are bad. His mother, sexually abused by her own father, could never form close emotional ties: She left her husband and the newborn Martín and "ran away to California" with her lover. Martín also well remembers his last meeting with his father: His drunken father cuffed and cursed him, and "I kicked you down/ vomiting whiskey/ to the ground."

Martín's search for roots continues, and he finally finds them in Burque (Albuquerque), where he moves in with a good woman, Gabriela. They eventually buy "a small house/ along the river, in Southside barrio." Martín's rebuilding of the dilapidated home and clearing of trash from the "half-acre of land in the back" symbolize the reestablishment of his Chicano roots, and these are solidified by the birth of a baby, Pablito. In the poem's last lines, Martín cradles the baby and promises, "you and all living things,/ I would never abandon you."

In *Meditations on the South Valley*, the saga of Martín and his little family continues. Disaster strikes: Their home burns to the ground, and they are forced to move into a suburban apartment with middle-class tenants who have "ceramic faces" and walk manicured poodles. A test of how well Martín's roots are established, the experience only deepens his appreciation for the barrio: "I don't want/ to live here/ among the successful. To the South Valley/ the white dove of my mind flies,/ searching for news of life." With all its dirt and disorder, the barrio contains a vitality for which Martín longs:

> People live out real lives in the South Valley.
> Tin can lids patch adobe walls,
> the moon through a window
> smolders at St. Francis' statue feet
> on a dresser,
> and there is a quietness heavy as blood
> that spills over into each afternoon.
> and brims like flame over the fields.

Meditations on the South Valley reaffirms the richness of Chicano culture, even among the poor. It has substance and solidity, a rootedness in place and history and old things. In this spirit, Martín, with the help of his pals, sets about rebuilding his home, but even better this time around. In the poem's conclusion, Martín sums up his motivation: "I was stripped down to the essential/ force in my life—create a better world, a better me,/ out of love."

SUMMARY

Baca has developed into a powerful spokesman for Chicano culture, enshrining life in the barrio and writing in a style with a distinctively Hispanic flavor. Embodying his vision in the character Martín, a down-to-earth man with mythic qualities, Baca urges Chicanos to reclaim and hold on to their culture.

Baca's vision is one that all readers can share and ponder. Like Wendell Berry, Gary Snyder, and the Appalachian poet Jim Wayne Miller, Baca provides a critique of mainstream but diluted American culture. Like those other writers, Baca speaks for an alternative way of life that is rooted in the land, a distinct culture, and loving relationships.

Harold Branam

BIBLIOGRAPHY

By the Author

POETRY:
Jimmy Santiago Baca, 1978
Immigrants in Our Own Land, 1979

Swords of Darkness, 1981
What's Happening, 1982
Poems Taken from My Yard, 1986
Martín: &, Meditations on the South Valley, 1987
Black Mesa Poems, 1989 (includes *Poems Taken from My Yard*)
Immigrants in Our Own Land, and Selected Early Poems, 1990
In the Way of the Sun, 1997
Set This Book on Fire, 1999
Que Linda la Brisa, 2000 (with Benjamin Alier Sáenz; photographs by James Drake)
Healing Earthquakes: A Love Story in Poems, 2001
C-Train (Dream Boy's Story) and Thirteen Mexicans, 2002
Winter Poems Along the Rio Grande, 2004

SHORT FICTION:
The Importance of a Piece of Paper, 2004

SCREENPLAY:
Bound by Honor, 1993 (with Floyd Mutrux and Ross Thomas)

DRAMA:
Los tres hijos de Julia, pr. 1991

NONFICTION:
A Place to Stand: The Making of a Poet, 2001

MISCELLANEOUS:
Working in the Dark: Reflections of a Poet of the Barrio, 1992 (essays, journal entries, and poetry)

DISCUSSION TOPICS

- What portrait of convict life is painted by Jimmy Santiago Baca's prison poems?

- Does Baca's poetry glamorize crime and violence?

- Discuss how Baca's use of Chicano Spanish adds flavor to his poetry.

- Denise Levertov has said that Baca's works have a mythic quality. Explain in what ways they present a mythic view of Chicano life and the American Southwest.

- Discuss the theme of parenthood or need for family in Baca's poetry.

- How is Baca's poetry a commentary on the concept of machismo?

- In *Martín: &, Meditations on the South Valley*, is Martín a fully developed character like those found in fiction?

About the Author

Coppola, Vincent. "The Moon in Jimmy Baca." *Esquire* 119 (June, 1993): 48-52.

Fuss, Adam. "Jimmy Santiago Baca." *BOMB* 84 (Summer, 2003): 58-63.

Harris, Marie, and Kathleen Aguero, eds. *A Gift of Tongues: Critical Challenges in Contemporary American Poetry.* Athens: University of Georgia Press, 1987.

Keene, John. "'Poetry Is What We Speak to Each Other': An Interview with Jimmy Santiago Baca." *Callaloo: A Journal of African-American and African Arts and Letters* 17 (Winter, 1994): 33-51.

Levertov, Denise. Introduction to *Martín: &, Meditations on the South Valley.* New York: New Directions, 1987.

Lynch, Tom. "Toward a Symbiosis of Ecology and Justice: Water and Land Conflicts in Frank Waters, John Nichols, and Jimmy Santiago Baca." *Western American Literature* 37 (Winter, 2003): 405-428.

Meléndez, Gabriel. "Carrying the Magic of His People's Heart: An Interview with Jimmy Santiago Baca." *The Americas Review* 19 (Winter, 1991): 64-86.

Moore, George. "Beyond Cultural Dialogues: Identities in the Interstices of Culture in Jimmy Santiago Baca's *Martín and Meditations on the South Valley.*" *Western American Literature* 33 (Summer, 1998): 153-177.

Olivares, Julián. "Two Contemporary Chicano Verse Chronicles." *The Americas Review: A Review of Hispanic Literature and Art of the USA* 16, nos. 3/4 (Fall/Winter, 1988): 214-231.

Shirley, Carl R., and Paula W. Shirley. *Understanding Chicano Literature.* Columbia: University of South Carolina Press, 1988.

Stahura, Barbara. "The *Progressive* Interview: Jimmy Santiago Baca." *Progressive* 67 (January, 2003): 26-30.

JAMES BALDWIN

Born: New York, New York
       August 2, 1924
Died: St. Paul de Vence, France
       December 1, 1987

Through his novels, essays, plays, and poetry, Baldwin boldly and articulately documented the dilemma of race in the United States.

© John Hoppy Hopkins

BIOGRAPHY

James Baldwin was born in New York City on August 2, 1924. His mother, Emma Berdis Jones, was unmarried at the time, and his illegitimacy would haunt him throughout his life. In 1927, Emma married David Baldwin, a former slave's son who had come north from New Orleans filled with bitterness toward whites. David worked in factories, preached on weekends, and raised his ten children with iron discipline and little warmth.

James grew to hate his father for constantly criticizing and teasing him. As a teenager, he rebelled in many ways, first by becoming a Young Minister at a rival congregation, then by rejecting the church to pursue writing. At the same time, he watched his father slowly descend into a mental illness borne of anger. Days before Baldwin's nineteenth birthday, his father succumbed to tuberculosis.

From the first, Baldwin loved to read, and by the time he graduated from the prestigious De Witt Clinton High School in the Bronx, he had written essays for his school and church papers and made friends, black and white, who later became important professional contacts. In 1942, to help support his family, he went to work laying railroad track for the Army in New Jersey. It was his first experience outside New York, and the bigotry he faced there infuriated him. He spent several years moving from job to job, exploring his sexual nature in brief affairs with other men, and writing his first novel.

In 1945, Baldwin received a Saxton Fellowship for the manuscript, but its rejection by publishers devastated him: He went into hiding and started a lifetime career of heavy drinking. He turned to writing smaller pieces—stories, articles, reviews—and by 1948, he was being taken seriously in periodicals such as *New Leader* and *Commentary*. The strains of being black among whites and homosexual among heterosexuals (he was at one point engaged to be married) were too oppressive, however, so he left to join friends in exile in Paris. For the rest of his life he would frequently cross the Atlantic Ocean.

In Paris he lived a penniless, bohemian life and met such writers as Truman Capote, Saul Bellow, and Jean Genet. Black novelist Richard Wright, whom Baldwin had known in New York and both revered and resented, was also in Paris. The rift between them, the old champion and the new, continued to grow. An article by Baldwin criticizing Wright's *Native Son* (1940) was published simultaneously in Paris and New York and attracted much attention.

Baldwin became great friends with a Swiss national named Lucien Happersberger, and it was in Lucien's Alpine village that he completed *Go Tell It on the Mountain* (1953), his first published novel. Returning to New York, he found readjustment difficult, again facing the racism he had crossed the ocean to escape. He wrote steadily, compiling topical essays into a collection called *Notes of a Native Son* (1955). His second novel, *Giovanni's Room,* published in England in 1955 and a year later in the United States, established his literary standing and identified him as an openly homosexual novelist.

With his mounting success, Baldwin remained deeply sensitive to the plight of blacks. In 1956, he covered a conference of black writers and artists in Paris and made his first trip into the Deep South, where he met the Reverend Martin Luther King, Jr., Rosa Parks, and other civil rights activists. These experiences confirmed his commitment to civil rights and led to a second volume of essays, *Nobody Knows My Name: More Notes of a Native Son* (1961). Two years later, he published *The Fire Next Time*, a piece about the extremist Black Muslims and Baldwin's own more moderate views. By virtue of his essays, he came to be considered a spokesman for his race. In 1963, Attorney General Robert Kennedy invited Baldwin and other prominent blacks to discuss the nation's racial situation. Despite goodwill on both sides, no common language could be found, and the meeting reminded Baldwin how far the nation still had to come.

Baldwin continued writing fiction. *Another Country*, his most candid and ambitious novel, appeared in 1962 to mixed reviews; his plays *Blues for Mister Charlie* (1964) and *The Amen Corner* (1954) were recognized for their vivid passion but faulted for poor structure; his sole volume of short stories, *Going to Meet the Man* (1965), and the novel *Tell Me How Long the Train's Been Gone* (1968) evoked the criticism that Baldwin was getting stale. He was accused by activist and writer Eldridge Cleaver of race hatred in *Soul on Ice* (1967), and he spared no mercy in an ongoing rivalry with novelist Norman Mailer. In many ways he was caught on the fence separating art and politics, and his articulateness and artistic vision were waning.

The final straw was the assassination of King on April 4, 1968. The loss, on both personal and political levels, profoundly affected Baldwin. Years of hope and struggle had only brought him back to the bitterness that had killed his father. In 1970, at the age of forty-six, he settled permanently in southern France. He still returned frequently to the United States, was still as devoted to friends and family as he had always been, and still wrote. None of his later works, however—*No Name in the Street* (1971), further essays on race; a novel, *If Beale Street Could Talk* (1974); essays on film, *The Devil Finds Work* (1976); his last novel, *Just Above My Head* (1979); a book of poetry, *Jimmy's Blues: Selected Poems* (1983); and other articles, collections, and collaborations—garnered the praise of his earlier works. While he had myriad projects in mind, it became more and more difficult to write. He lectured and taught widely, but decades of liquor, cigarettes, constant travel, casual romance, publicity, and loneliness were taking their toll.

Baldwin developed cancer of the esophagus, and it claimed his life on December 1, 1987, in his home in France. His brother David, who had always been a close friend and support, was at his bedside when he died. A week later, more than five thousand people attended the funeral service held for him at New York's Cathedral of St. John the Divine, on the edge of his native Harlem.

ANALYSIS

Baldwin's turbulent and passionate life informs all of his writings. His life and art were inseparable; he wrote to understand the trials of the past and to articulate principles for the future. In his essays, he constantly depicted and expanded upon personal experiences, and in his fiction he drew on autobiographical events, issues, and characters, building dramatic situations that closely reflected his intimate experience of the world. He refused to lie, to shield, or to "prettify" reality.

Though Baldwin limited his fictional settings to those he knew—a poor, religious Harlem home, the expatriate community in France, New York's jazz scene—he explored them deeply and critically. His experience with his friend Tony Maynard's legal battle against a false murder conviction inspired *If Beale Street Could Talk*, in which a young woman searches for the truth that will acquit her fiancé of rape, and Baldwin's last novel, *Just Above My Head*, treats the anguished life of a homosexual gospel singer, a life not unlike his own.

Baldwin's early exposure to writers and writing helped him to become a skilled craftsman: His favorite childhood novels were Charles Dickens's *A Tale of Two Cities* (1859) and Harriet Beecher Stowe's *Uncle Tom's Cabin* (1852). His acquaintance with black writers Richard Wright, Countée Cullen, and Langston Hughes forced him to consider the particular problems of the black writer in the United States. Later, he was strongly influenced by the novels of Henry James—especially *The Ambas-*

sadors (1903), *The Portrait of a Lady* (1881), and *The Princess Casamassima* (1886). Though writing about wealthy white New Yorkers, James explored the same questions of individuality and nonconformity in a conformist society.

Baldwin was a precise writer: He chose words carefully and connected images with emotions in ways calculated to achieve maximum effect. His love of jazz music and appreciation of art infused his writing with evocative rhythms, colors, and textures, and his early training in the church is evident not only in the religious aspects of his stories but also in language replicating the simplicity, poetry, and ardor of the Bible and the traditional sermon. *The Fire Next Time*, perhaps his most renowned work, employs the biblical image of God's wrathful fire, as interpreted through a popular Negro spiritual song, to predict America's fate in the absence of meaningful progress toward a new racial order.

Race was always a crucial issue to Baldwin but never a simple one. Though he often felt pure rage at the legacy of white supremacy, he strove in his life to speak to and treat black and white people in the same manner, and this determination to deal with people first as individuals helped him to create a language that is brutal but not unjust, objective but not detached. Baldwin never fully blames or exonerates anyone; as members of the human race, everyone is both guilty and innocent of shared history. For Baldwin, the color problem was not a problem for blacks alone but for all members of society; the suppression of blacks and black culture has been a result of white fear and confusion, and it has inhibited the development not so much of black identity but of a truly integrated and fulfilled American identity. Though keenly aware of both his African American roots and his frequent voluntary exile, Baldwin considered himself American through and through, and he sought to express himself in American terms to an American audience.

In a similar fashion, though himself a homosexual, Baldwin tried to avoid all bias or prejudice in his treatment of sex, sexuality, and love. His curiosity and candor allowed sex and love to be used as meaningful modes for the expression of uniquely personal identity, and not simplistic ways of limiting or pigeonholing character.

Ultimately, the issues of race and sexuality become issues of identity and individuality. Baldwin,

though a black homosexual, felt free to express himself through white, female, or heterosexual characters, and his voice, whether it be as the authoritative social observer of *Notes of a Native Son* and *Nobody Knows My Name*, the third-person narrators of *Go Tell It on the Mountain* and *Another Country*, or the intimately confessional protagonists of *Giovanni's Room* and *Tell Me How Long the Train's Been Gone*, is always searching for meaning, for a solution to the problem of expressing oneself forcefully and honestly in an imperfect world that bombards the individual with preordained roles and assumptions. While ostensibly writing about "exiles," "bisexuals," or "artists," all of which terms may have applied to Baldwin at points, he reserved for his characters the right to go beyond such labels and the freedom to feel and act according to the entire range of possible human behavior.

GO TELL IT ON THE MOUNTAIN

First published: 1953
Type of work: Novel

A young black man in Harlem begins to confront the legacy of anger and guilt that he is inheriting from his family.

Go Tell It on the Mountain, Baldwin's first published novel, tells a passionate story closely paralleling the author's own family background. It focuses on John Grimes, a black boy growing up in a religious home in Harlem under the stern hand of his preacher father, Gabriel. The action of the novel takes place in 1936, on John's fourteenth birthday, with sections detailing previous events in the lives of John's aunt Florence, his father, and his mother, Elizabeth.

Florence is a strident and bitter woman who left her ailing mother and irresponsible younger brother to come North. She married a man named Frank, who abused and abandoned her, and now she approaches old age feeling empty, living alone, and sharing in the life of her brother's family.

Gabriel, her brother, had been a wild young man, but he repented, became a preacher, and married a fallen woman named Deborah. Succumbing to temptation, however, he impregnated a young woman he worked with and then refused to acknowledge his paternity. He watched his son Royal grow before his eyes and heard of the boy's violent death in a knife fight. Gabriel drifted in despair, his wife passed on, and he came to New York to begin a new life. There he met Elizabeth.

Elizabeth was nine when her mother died, and, because her father ran a brothel, she went to live with her aunt in Maryland. There she fell in love with a young man named Richard; they moved to New York. Richard, wrongly accused of robbery, took his own life, leaving Elizabeth behind, alone and pregnant with John. Through Florence she met Gabriel, newly arrived from the South. They married, and Gabriel promised to treat John as his own. He preferred their other children, however, above all the fiery Roy, to his docile and pensive stepson, John.

The character of Gabriel is a sharper version of Baldwin's own father, and, accordingly, his sternness and coldness elicit John's hatred. Everyone assumes that John will become a preacher like Gabriel, but, approaching manhood, John is having deep religious doubts. He is also feeling guilt over the sin of masturbation and is subtly becoming aware of his admiration for and attraction to Elisha, another young man in the church.

During the course of the day depicted in the novel, John's younger brother Roy is slashed in a fight, Gabriel strikes Elizabeth in anger, and Florence confronts Gabriel with his past in the form of a pained letter from his long-dead first wife. The novel's central action, however, is John's personal journey, culminating in the climactic third part titled "On the Threshing Floor." Through a long night in the family's church, the Temple of the Fire Baptized, John experiences a frenzy of fear, inspiration, and awakening, a spiritual rite of passage before his family and congregation, in which he gives himself over to powers outside himself, infused as they are with familial and racial history, and begins to see the road he must travel.

The action of *Go Tell It on the Mountain* is not ex-

pansive; rather, it focuses on inner turmoils and private moments. Time moves slowly, and the interspersed flashbacks elucidate present moments or events. Through the accumulation of information, Baldwin slowly brings into focus how centuries of racial oppression—slavery, injustice, rape, violence—have shaped the lives of one Harlem family and how the complex family picture affects a sensitive young man at a crucial juncture in his life.

GIOVANNI'S ROOM

First published: 1956
Type of work: Novel

The inability of a young American in Paris to confront his bisexuality leads to his male lover's tragic downfall.

Giovanni's Room is an intimate, confessional narrative of an American named David who looks back on his turbulent experiences in France on the eve of his return to the United States. The novel works through two time frames simultaneously, for as past events are recounted, the relevance of the present moment gradually emerges. By the end, night has become morning, and only then does the story being told reach its conclusion.

Months earlier, David came to France with his girlfriend Hella, but uncertainty in their relationship and her wanderlust sent her traveling solo to Spain. David, with little money and none forthcoming from his father in the United States, befriends and exploits the generosity of a middle-aged homosexual, a Belgian American businessman named Jacques. With Jacques he moves through the world of Paris gay bars, and at one of them he meets a handsome Italian bartender named Giovanni. David and Giovanni have an immediate rapport, and on the night of their meeting they stay out until dawn under the patronage of Jacques and Giovanni's boss Guillaume; they end up alone back at Giovanni's room, where they embark on a sexual relationship.

Having little money, David moves in with his new lover. Though David has had homosexual feelings and experiences before, the intensity of his fascination for Giovanni, and his own position in life—

nearing thirty, and, ostensibly, marriage with Hella—make his relationship with Giovanni new and threatening. As so often has happened in the past, David ignores the possible consequences of his actions and continually reminds himself of his freedom, at any point, to abandon this new situation.

Giovanni's room, as the title suggests, has metaphorical significances for the story David is telling. It is cluttered with the debris of Giovanni's life—an unhappy past in Italy, an uncertain future in France, a superficial present of drinking and pandering among a subculture characterized by gossip, jealousy, and scandal. Just as Giovanni satisfies David's repressed desires, so does he find in David meaning and hope, and his room becomes, alternately, a haven or a prison, an Eden or a hell, a passageway to truth or a dead end, for both young men.

Throughout the telling of this history, the narrative returns to David's present in a rented house in southern France, alone, without either of his lovers. Time passes slowly; he measures the hours of the night drinking, preparing to leave, thinking mournfully of Giovanni, and waiting for morning to come. He recounts his panic and denial at Giovanni's growing dependence on him. Upon receiving news of Hella's imminent return from Spain, he cavalierly seduces a woman acquaintance, for whom he feels no desire, to prove his independence and control. When Hella arrives, David abandons Giovanni; though they run into each other, he never admits to anything more than a casual friendship. Hella is puzzled but attributes David's behavior to the ambiguities of life in exile.

Meanwhile, Giovanni falls out of favor with Guillaume and loses his job. He has become "passe," a trifle no longer worth the attentions of the older men who frequent the bar. Without a job and without David, he becomes desperate; one night he comes to the bar drunk to demand his job back and, in a moment of fury, murders Guillaume. He takes to the streets and is covertly aided by David but eventually is caught, tried, and condemned to the guillotine.

With Giovanni's crime, David becomes aware of how irresponsibly he has behaved and how much he has been evading the truth. He takes Hella to the south to escape the horrors of Paris, which for him has taken on the dimensions and associations

of Giovanni's tiny room, but he cannot face Hella and runs away, only to be found by her days later among the homosexual subculture of Nice. His secret is revealed, and Hella departs for the United States, leaving David alone to face Giovanni's execution, which seems also to be his own, with the coming dawn.

In *Giovanni's Room,* Baldwin colorfully depicts the life of certain Paris milieus, but his focus is primarily on the three characters in the lovers' triangle. The dialogue is peppered with phrases of French that add atmosphere and reinforce the sense of anonymity and ambiguity so crucial to David's sensibility. Baldwin explores his chosen themes—bisexuality, exile, self-deceit, and guilt—with candor and boldness, remarkably so, given the age in which he wrote. The tone of the novel is one of rigorous self-examination and honest resignation; David has come to accept, although too late, responsibility for his actions. As such, his growth through the novel is a passage into maturity, a painful and tragic loss of innocence.

ANOTHER COUNTRY

First published: 1962
Type of work: Novel

A young black jazz drummer's suicide subtly affects the lives and loves of those he leaves behind.

Another Country is an intricate novel about a diverse group of idealistic but often troubled individuals in New York City. The novel is unified by the character of Rufus, a young black musician who commits suicide early in the novel but remains a vital presence in the awareness and memory of others.

Book 1, "Easy Rider," follows Rufus on the night of his suicide. Memories tell his history: growing up in Harlem and learning about racism, becoming a successful jazz drummer, meeting and falling in love with a simple, good-hearted southern woman named Leona, feeling impotent against society's view of their interracial relationship, letting anger and alcohol inhibit his music, distrusting and abusing Leona, driving her to a mental hospital, losing his sense of worth, and, ultimately, jumping off the

George Washington Bridge. The first book ends with Rufus's death.

The second book, "Any Day Now," follows the people closest to Rufus as they go on without him. His best friend, Vivaldo, an aspiring writer of Irish Italian descent, loves him and feels guilty for not saving him. At Rufus's funeral, Vivaldo is drawn to Rufus's younger sister Ida, and they soon become lovers. Ida is quiet, beautiful, proud, and bitter. Whereas Vivaldo can accept individuals without regard to color or gender, Ida can never escape, even as she becomes a successful singer, awareness of her limited position as a black woman.

Losing Rufus brings Vivaldo and Ida closer to Vivaldo's friend and former teacher Richard and his wife, Cass. Richard has just sold his first novel, a popular murder mystery, and Cass is realizing the limits of his artistic vision. It is Cass who sends news of Rufus's death to Eric, an American actor in Paris who was once his closest friend. After three years abroad, Eric is returning to New York to appear on Broadway, with Yves, his young French lover, soon to follow.

Another Country is unified not so much by a single action as by an interwoven pattern of events and themes. The story often jumps abruptly from scene to scene, and the narrative voice enters the minds of the characters—especially Vivaldo, Cass, and Eric. Seeking honest means to express themselves, they engage in parties and discussions, arguments and sex, with the mystery of Rufus always nearby. Vivaldo is plagued by jealousy when Ida spends time with her fast-talking producer, but she accuses him of making the racist assumption that all black women are whores. Eric, anxious about his future with Yves and somewhat dazed to be back in New York, becomes a haven for the disillusioned Cass; she comes to him, and they begin an affair. As the weeks pass, Vivaldo's jealousy becomes more isolating, Cass's infidelity more frivolous, and Eric's future with Yves more certain.

In the culminating book 3, "Toward Bethlehem," Vivaldo comes to Eric for friendship and comfort and, both filled with the memory of Rufus, they spend a night of passion together. Meanwhile, Richard has confronted Cass, and she must face her actions. Soon thereafter, Ida confesses to Vivaldo that she has indeed been unfaithful and realizes that, in trying to vindicate her brother's death by exploiting the white system, she has become a whore after all. Ida and Vivaldo come to a precarious understanding, and Cass predicts that she and Richard will do the same. The novel ends as Yves arrives from Paris to Eric's welcoming embrace.

Baldwin's careful structuring of his plot elements employs simultaneous action—different scenes occurring at the same time—and discrepant awareness—knowledge available to the reader but not to individual characters—to highlight the self-absorption, misunderstanding, and folly endemic to human interactions. Parallel situations, such as Vivaldo's courtship of Ida and Eric's courtship of Yves, Rufus's mistreatment of both Eric and Leona, Richard's and Ida's professional successes, and Ida's and Cass's infidelities, illuminate the complexity of Baldwin's world.

In *Another Country*, conventional racial and sexual assumptions are rejected, and the characters struggle on equal terms to make the connections they need. The novel's cryptic title functions on several levels, referring to exile (Eric's experience in France), to oppression (the black experience in America), to idealism (the yearning for a land free of social evils), and, most important, to the experience of love—entering, conquering, possessing, and inhabiting another person, tenderly or violently, emotionally or physically, with all that such otherness offers to the one who dares to love.

NOTES OF A NATIVE SON

First published: 1955
Type of work: Essays

Black people hold a precarious position in American political and artistic life, and their validation is essential to the fulfillment of the American identity.

Notes of a Native Son is a collection of essays published previously in various periodicals. Though not originally written to be published together, they share Baldwin's concerns over the resolution of the United States' racial dilemma and the question of American identity.

The first group of essays focuses on the black person as artist and on his or her image within the cultural canon. In "Everybody's Protest Novel,"

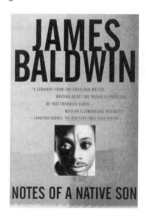

Baldwin, once an enthusiastic fan of Harriet Beecher Stowe, labels her an "impassioned pamphleteer" and criticizes *Uncle Tom's Cabin* and other "protest novels," including Richard Wright's *Native Son*, for falling short of their lofty aims, abusing language, and overtaxing credibility. Baldwin goes on in the second essay, "Many Thousands Gone," to recognize *Native Son* as a literary landmark but questions its actual power, given the depersonalization and mythification of blacks as Uncle Tom and Aunt Jemima. In essence, the "native son" is a monster created by American history, and it is American history that must confront and re-create him. The third essay in the group, "Carmen Jones: The Dark Is Light Enough," criticizes an all-black production of a theatrical standard for perpetuating racial stereotypes.

The second group focuses on the sociopolitical scene. "The Harlem Ghetto," the earliest of the essays, documents the congestion and claustrophobia of 1948 Harlem. Baldwin considers token civic improvements—playgrounds and housing projects—to be at best superficial and at worst injurious. The position of black leaders is impossible, the black press merely models itself on downtown counterparts, and the popularity of churches only reflects the pervasive hopelessness.

This hopelessness is evidenced in "Journey to Atlanta," which recounts the experiences of a group of black singers, including Baldwin's brother David, as guests of the Progressive Party in Atlanta. The Melodeers, anticipating a week of open artistic exchange in the Deep South, encounter only disappointment and failed promises. They are coerced into canvassing for the party, have little opportunity to rehearse or perform, and are finally abandoned without support or return bus fare.

In the title essay, "Notes of a Native Son," Baldwin juxtaposes his feelings upon his father's death—the end of a lifetime of racial bitterness—with images of Harlem in August, 1943, despoiled from widespread rioting after the controversial shooting of a black soldier. The private and public worlds merge to reflect the cycles of life in a tormented community. As Baldwin's father lay on his deathbed, Baldwin's mother lay waiting to give birth to her last child. Before the rioting, Harlem also lay in wait—tense, sweltering, and crowded with white policemen ready to strike and uniformed black soldiers heading off to war in Europe. With the passage of time, death, life, and rage came to fruition, and Baldwin surveys the results. He recalls first becoming aware of his violent feelings against whites, and he knows that with his father's death he must confront his filial hatred, just as Americans, black and white, must confront their shameful history.

The last group draws on Baldwin's experiences in exile. "Encounters on the Seine: Black Meets Brown" depicts the relations between American blacks and Africans—relations that are not automatically warm and fraternal—and the simplistic and pitiful attitude Baldwin met among the French. In "A Question of Identity," he analyzes what Americans such as himself seek in voluntary exile—an anonymity that expresses a longing for identity. Baldwin says that only by rejecting American values can one eventually affirm them, that the self-alienated discovers America by going to Europe.

The collection ends with two anecdotal essays. "Equal in Paris" relates Baldwin's false arrest for the theft of hotel bedsheets and his comic but demoralizing adventures in Parisian prisons and courts. Finally, "Stranger in the Village" tells of the summer Baldwin spent in his friend Lucien's Swiss village, a community that had never before seen a black person. The villagers approached him with curiosity and a bit of fear; he felt no malice, but he detected in their ignorance traces of the imperial and missionary traditions. Baldwin compares his experience there with the larger experience of blacks as supposed "strangers" in the "village" of the United States.

Notes of a Native Son demonstrates Baldwin's ability to connect disparate experiences and images—emotional and political, abstract and concrete, past and present—into persuasive arguments. His prose is full and textured, and ideas have the force of weight. At times, Baldwin speaks though the first-person singular voice of African American history, an "I" that endured displacement, slavery, and all that followed. The tone becomes bitter, stubborn, and accusing. At other times, he adopts an empowered first-person plural voice, a "we" that assumes a white audience and refers to blacks from a distance. Yet Baldwin's characteristic objectivity, a more precise and color-free voice, is always available, and in these essays he acknowledges the complexity of these issues, the partial truth of cultural assumptions, and the shared responsibility for social transformation.

SUMMARY

Baldwin was very much a man of his era. By the time of his death, his message had been received and digested by the American populace; yet his vision, so passionate and articulate at its inception, will not lose relevance so long as prejudice and bigotry—oppression of those perceived as "other," "inferior," or "different"—persist. As a spokesman and activist, he helped to bring about the social transformation of his nation, to the benefit of all races, genders, and sexualities. As an artist, he found a unique and personal idiom for expressing the anguish and joy of his life.

Barry Mann

BIBLIOGRAPHY

By the Author

SHORT FICTION:
Going to Meet the Man, 1965

DRAMA:
The Amen Corner, pr. 1954, pb. 1968
Blues for Mister Charlie, pr., pb. 1964
A Deed from the King of Spain, pr. 1974

LONG FICTION:
Go Tell It on the Mountain, 1953
Giovanni's Room, 1956
Another Country, 1962
Tell Me How Long the Train's Been Gone, 1968
If Beale Street Could Talk, 1974
Just Above My Head, 1979

SCREENPLAY:
One Day, When I Was Lost: A Scenario Based on "The Autobiography of Malcolm X," 1972

POETRY:
Jimmy's Blues: Selected Poems, 1983

DISCUSSION TOPICS

- Why does James Baldwin find it so difficult to endorse the work of writers such as Harriet Beecher Stowe and Richard Wright, who would seem to be his colleagues in the struggle against racism?

- Baldwin is described as having been influenced by Henry James, a white novelist whose characters tend to be part of the upper crust of society and whose style is very sophisticated and elaborate. Considering Baldwin's background and typical subject matter, what could Baldwin expect to learn from James?

- In what ways, other than in his identity as an African American, did Baldwin feel himself to be an outsider? Did his writing benefit from this outsider status?

- In his essay "Notes of a Native Son," Baldwin concludes that he must accept life and people as they are but that he must not accept injustice. Since injustice is always caused by human beings, how is this possible?

- Can a white American ever be as conscious of his or her own race as Baldwin was of his?

- What evidence is there that Baldwin abandoned his early refusal to read the Bible?

NONFICTION:
Notes of a Native Son, 1955
Nobody Knows My Name: More Notes of a Native Son, 1961
The Fire Next Time, 1963
Nothing Personal, 1964 (with Richard Avedon)
No Name in the Street, 1971
A Rap on Race, 1971 (with Margaret Mead)
A Dialogue, 1975 (with Nikki Giovanni)
The Devil Finds Work, 1976
The Evidence of Things Not Seen, 1985
The Price of the Ticket, 1985
Conversations with James Baldwin, 1989
Collected Essays, 1998

CHILDREN'S LITERATURE:
Little Man, Little Man, 1975

About the Author

Fabré, Michel. "James Baldwin in Paris: Love and Self-Discovery." In *From Harlem to Paris: Black American Writers in France, 1840-1980.* Chicago: University of Illinois Press, 1991.

Hardy, Clarence E. *James Baldwin's God: Sex, Hope, and Crisis in Black Holiness Culture.* Knoxville: University of Tennessee Press, 2003.

Kinnamon, Keneth, comp. *James Baldwin: A Collection of Critical Essays.* Englewood Cliffs, N.J.: Prentice-Hall, 1974.

Leming, David. *James Baldwin: A Biography.* New York: Alfred A. Knopf, 1994.

Miller, D. Quentin, ed. *Re-viewing James Baldwin: Things Not Seen.* Philadelphia: Temple University Press, 2000.

O'Daniel, Therman B., ed. *James Baldwin: A Critical Evaluation.* Washington, D.C.: Howard University Press, 1981.

Porter, Horace A. *Stealing the Fire: The Art and Protest of James Baldwin.* Middletown, Conn.: Wesleyan University Press, 1989.

Standley, Fred L., and Nancy V. Burt, eds. *Critical Essays on James Baldwin.* Boston: G. K. Hall, 1988.

Sylvander, Carolyn Wedin. *James Baldwin.* New York: Frederick Ungar, 1980.

Tomlinson, Robert. "'Payin' One's Dues': Expatriation as Personal Experience and Paradigm in the Works of James Baldwin." *African American Review* 33 (Spring, 1999): 135-148.

Troupe, Quincy, ed. *James Baldwin: The Legacy.* New York: Simon & Schuster, 1989.

Weatherby, W. J. *James Baldwin: Artist on Fire.* New York: Donald I. Fine, 1989.

Toni Cade Bambara

Born: New York, New York
   March 25, 1939
Died: Philadelphia, Pennsylvania
   December 9, 1995

Bambara produced several notable collections of short fiction and two novels exploring the African American experience in the latter half of the twentieth century, most revealingly through the eyes of young girls and activist women.

Joyce Middler

BIOGRAPHY

Born Toni Cade in New York City in 1939 to Helen Brent Henderson Cade, the author would legally add Bambara to her surname in 1970. She claims to have stumbled across the word in her grandmother's sketch pad, and it is the name by which she is recognized as an influential African American writer of the latter twentieth century. Bambara's mother, Helen, attracted to the artistic wellspring of the Harlem Renaissance of her day, encouraged her daughter to partake of the cultural resources available in New York City during the 1940's and 1950's, including museums, galleries, and performance spaces.

Following this enriching childhood, Bambara attended Queens College, majoring in theater and English and earning her bachelor of arts degree in 1959. Employment as a social worker followed, and she wrote fiction in her spare time, publishing her first piece at the age of twenty. Bambara left for Europe in 1961 to continue her arts training; in Paris, she practiced mime at the Ecole de Mime Etienne Decroux and studied commedia dell'arte at the University of Florence in Italy. Returning to New York, Bambara earned her M.A. from City College in 1964, where she first taught courses in English. By 1969, she was an assistant professor at Rutgers

University. In addition to her classroom activities, Bambara continued to write and to serve her community through various arts outreach programs.

In 1970, Bambara began her work as an editor of ethnic anthologies. *The Black Woman: An Anthology* contained works by established writers such as Toni Morrison and Alice Walker alongside emerging voices. A second edited collection, *Tales and Stories for Black Folks*, followed in 1971. By now a number of Bambara's stories had appeared in print, and interest was expressed by Random House to publish a collection of her short fiction. *Gorilla, My Love* appeared in 1972 to critical acclaim. A second volume of her collected stories, *The Sea Birds Are Still Alive* was published in 1977. Both collections presented stories about the African American experience as told from the perspective of women.

Bambara's academic career became more fluid in the 1970's as she accepted visiting professorships, first at Stephens College in Columbia and later at Spelman College in Atlanta, where she relocated with her daughter, Karma. She traveled abroad during this decade, expanding the venue for her social activism. She visited both communist Vietnam and Cuba in order to meet with women's collectives and discuss their goals for empowerment. The end of the decade saw her completing her first novel, *The Salt Eaters* (1980). The new genre allowed more room for experimentation with form, a decision that garnered mixed critical responses.

During the 1980's, Bambara moved to Philadelphia to work as a television production consultant.

She turned to film as a new outlet for her political views. In 1989, she produced *The Bombing of Osage Avenue*, documenting the Cobb's Creek bombing of the MOVE headquarters. The bomb ignited an entire neighborhood, killing five children and six adults and depriving more than sixty families of their homes. Bambara thought it was important for black filmmakers to claim their stories. The support she had shown emerging African American writers by including them in her edited anthologies in the 1970's she aimed to extend to emerging filmmakers in the 1980's.

In the early 1990's, Bambara experienced unaccustomed fatigue and was diagnosed with advanced colon cancer. Though she would not recover from her illness, she continued to be productive, working on new film projects, including *W. E. B. Du Bois—A Biography in Four Voices* (1995, with Amiri Baraka, Wesley Brown, and Thulani Davis). The documentary was released shortly before her death in Philadelphia on December 9, 1995. Two posthumous works, a collection of her essays and stories titled *Deep Sightings and Rescue Missions: Fiction, Essays, and Conversations* (1996) and the novel *Those Bones Are Not My Child* (1999) are testimony to her continuing legacy.

ANALYSIS

In fulfilling her roles as teacher, social worker, filmmaker, editor, and author, Bambara always considered herself first and foremost a social activist, an agent for positive change, so it is no surprise that her characters take up this clarion call. Most of the women and many of the men who populate her stories are oppressed by the social institutions and attitudes that surround them, but few are beaten down. In situation after situation, they rise above their circumstances and triumph.

The character of Hazel "Squeaky" Parker who appears in the stories "Gorilla, My Love" and "Raymond's Run" is a case in point. A lanky black girl at odds with conventional standards of femininity, she does not hide her supposed eccentricities but flaunts them. Her long legs, the source of her incredible speed, are an embarrassment to her mother, who wishes she would hide them behind a skirt. Instead Squeaky glories in them:

> I'll high-prance down 34th Street like a rodeo pony to keep my knees strong even if it does get my

mother uptight so that she walks ahead like she's not with me, don't know me, is all by herself on a shopping trip, and I am somebody else's crazy child.

The importance of knowledge for both individual growth and the collective good is often stressed in Bambara's stories, even if the intended recipients are reluctant learners. In the widely anthologized short story "The Lesson" from *Gorilla, My Love*, a community activist mistakenly believes a tour of F. A. O. Schwarz, the New York toy giant, will edify the neighborhood children. As they gawk at overpriced toys, what is meant to be a lesson in the evils of conspicuous consumption backfires; instead the children realize how marginalized they are and how deep the divide is that separates the privileged from the underprivileged in the United States.

Love is the core value in Bambara's stories about families and community. Rarely is romantic love the goal, but rather an intrinsic human love that values the dignity of neighbors, family members, and self. When the faith healer in *The Salt Eaters* attempts to bring a suicidal woman back to mental equilibrium, her aim is not just to cure the individual, but to bring wholeness to the entire community. A fragmented community spawns broken individuals; cure the social ills, Bambara suggests, and produce whole individuals.

Empowerment is the central theme of Bambara's work. Empowered people have more control over their lives than those who accept the status quo. Change is positive energy in Bambara's stories, particularly when it is the agent for expanding ideas of normalcy and broadening the scope of social acceptance. Bambara's three constants—knowledge, love, and empowerment—are weapons in an assault on the racial, sexual, and class prejudices that divide people by diminishing their value and limiting their opportunities. Ethnic pride derives from a blending of these values. When Candy in "Christmas Eve at Johnson's Drugs N Goods" (from *The Sea Birds Are Still Alive*) finds herself disillusioned by the season's commercialism, the African American festival of Kwanza presents itself as an alternative celebration, one that she is curious to pursue.

Critics generally laud Bambara's nontraditional structure and her experiments with form and language. She circumvents linear storytelling by allowing episodes to play in mental rather than chronological time. As characters recall situations, those events are conjured up, and readers are witness to the ebb and flow of human thought and emotion. The oral traditions of ethnic storytelling are evident in Bambara's works. Acutely she records the sounds of the human voice and its cadences. The vibrant pulse of street talk and the nuances of intimate conversation become musical notes running through her works, rhythms and tones at once familiar and unique.

"RAYMOND'S RUN"

First published: 1971 (collected in *Gorilla, My Love*, 1972)
Type of work: Short story

A younger sister finds herself the caretaker of her mentally challenged brother in a story about defying limitations and achieving victories.

"Raymond's Run" appears in the collection *Gorilla, My Love* and has been published independently as a work of young-adult fiction. The story features twelve-year-old Hazel Elizabeth Deborah Parker, who narrates the story. Nicknamed Squeaky for her high-pitched voice, she is a competitive runner, as is her older brother, Raymond, her unofficial training partner. Because he has Down syndrome, neither the community nor his family expects him to succeed in life. The Parkers seem to have accepted Raymond's limitations, but Squeaky is cognizant of her parents' embarrassment over her tomboyish activities. A connection is implied between Raymond's developmental disability and Squeaky's supposed gender deviance, both apparently aberrations of nature.

Squeaky's independent spirit refuses to bow to social constraints, however, and she ignores maternal advice that would retard her pace. Recalling how she danced in a school pageant, Squeaky critiques her parents and the social norms they attempted to enforce: "You'd think they'd know better than to encourage that kind of nonsense. I am not a strawberry. I do not dance on my toes. I run. That is what I am all about." Confident in her

self-knowledge, Squeaky pushes the boundaries of socially prescribed norms.

Readers are privy to the thoughts, emotions, and attitudes of the unabashed Squeaky, a skinny black girl whose sole ambition is to cross the finish line first. Among the challenges she faces preparing for the annual May Day event are sexist notions of appropriate behavior, particularly as they apply to a young girl on the verge of adolescence. Squeaky is encouraged to trade her gym shorts for a skirt and to adopt a slower, less assured stride. Even her school principal suggests she let another student win the race, perhaps the nice new girl whose dress and demeanor the principal approves. However, false modesty is a virtue that Squeaky rejects. In her eyes, girls should not diminish their abilities but work as ambitiously as boys to develop their talents.

Running is a metaphor for transcending limitations of race, gender, and disability. In the act of crossing the finish line a mere step ahead of the new girl, Squeaky notices that Raymond, in a lane of his own devising on the other side of the playground fence, has beaten them both. For the first time she shifts her vision away from her own goals and expands it to include those of another. She realizes that Raymond can be a competitor in life, and Squeaky vows to help him in his personal race. Ultimately this is a story about dismantling barriers to form a more inclusive and tolerant society.

"GORILLA, MY LOVE"

First published: 1971 (collected in *Gorilla, My Love*, 1972)
Type of work: Short story

A passenger in her grandfather's car, a young girl navigates the lies adults tell children and the untrustworthiness of words in general.

Hazel is a reappearing character in Bambara's collection *Gorilla, My Love*, and in this title story, she is perturbed that her Hunca Bubba is getting married and changing his name back to its original Jefferson Winston Vale. The source of her dismay is delayed until the end of the story when it is revealed that Hunca Bubba had vowed to wait for Hazel to grow up in order for the two of them to marry. Whether the young girl ever took her uncle's proposal seriously is unclear, but the deception has consequences. The sole female passenger in the company of three generations of male relatives, Hazel spends the drive time skeptically reexamining all the promises that adult males make to female children and all their specious claims, including religious ones.

She recalls an outing to a movie theater with her brothers in tow, again the lone female in a male group. In place of the thriller "Gorilla, My Love" advertised on the marquee, a film about the life of Jesus is projected onto the screen. Feeling swindled, the children scream their displeasure in the dark auditorium. Caught in the halo of the theater matron's flashlight, they are escorted outside. Unable to recoup their money, a vengeful Hazel sets fire to the concession stand. Threatened with a beating, Hazel talks her father out of administering her punishment by proclaiming "if you say Gorilla My Love, you suppose to mean it."

Hazel is assigned the task of guiding the men's drive home after a day of pecan picking, but it is an adult responsibility she rejects. Positioned in the passenger seat beside her grandfather who steers, she holds the map but offers no directions. The adult males call her pet names like "Peaches" and "Scout" in an effort to get her to assist them, but she dismisses their efforts at appeasement. Instead she claims her own identity and independence by pronouncing herself "Hazel" and lets them drive where they will.

Trust is a central issue in this story about the disillusionment of youth. When lies are commonplace and deceit practiced openly, adults and their sugar-coated words cannot be trusted. Hazel's extreme anguish at story's end is her response to the news of her uncle's impending marriage and to her perceived abandonment, but it indicates her greater loss of faith in men's honor. Skeptical of their promises, she plots a new course through their world, proceeding cautiously and navigating solo.

THE SALT EATERS

First published: 1980
Type of work: Novel

A woman suffers a severe emotional breakdown, the result of sexist and racial oppression, and a faith healer attempts a cure.

The Salt Eaters chronicles the mental crisis of Velma Henry, a community activist, and efforts to restore her to health. Minnie Ransom is the faith healer who employs nontraditional methods to mend her disturbed client. The treatment takes place in a medical facility where skeptical interns and traditional medical professionals witness the healing as if in attendance at a theatrical performance. Velma, shaky, dirty, vulnerable, and underdressed in a hospital gown, is seated before the aged healer Minnie, who is swaddled in flowing robes and adorned in handcrafted ornaments. Face to face they appear in stark contrast: young and old, naked and clothed, insane and sane. The initial response of their audience to the scene is one of boredom as changes do not occur quickly enough for them to record on their clipboards, but the slow pace of the healing allows Velma, in a series of flashbacks, to review events leading up to her breakdown.

Renowned for its experimental form, the novel avoids a strict chronological approach to narration. Instead it allows portions of random events to appear, some coherent and indicative of Velma's earlier cogent sensibility, and some verging on the incomprehensible, revelatory of her break with reality. It is a journey through, and a record of, the mental landscape of a woman whose life's mission

is noble (to revive a black community through positive social action) but who faces opposition so brutal and destructive that she chooses to withdraw from reality rather than face its oppressive stasis.

While Velma struggles to regain her sanity, other citizens fear a different illness. They live in dread of nuclear residue, chemical poisons, and other industrial pollutants that may filter down into their community. In an attempt to stave of disease, some members of the community have taken to eating soil, the salt eaters of the novel's title. However, the source of Velma's illness is not hazardous waste; she has been poisoned by social maladies: Racial prejudice and sexual oppression have infected her body with abuse so severe that her mind cannot filter the toxins.

Events occur in the fictional southern town of Claybourne, a predominantly black community where tensions exist between the genders. Women are the workhorses in a community center where the men receive all of the political power and most of the acclaim. It is this dual oppression (beaten down as a woman and denied opportunity as a person of color) that contributes to Velma's malady. Even as Minnie conducts her healing, a male doctor supervises from the margins, often interrupting her art with his belittling asides. In the end, however, the women triumph. Having successfully processed memories of events that led to her suicide attempt, the broken woman wills herself back to life under the encouragement of Minnie. Velma rises off her stool, spreads her fingers, and surveys her hands as if to assess their readiness for the work ahead. Whether they are the wings she will need to carry her on her journey is left ambiguous; Bambara notes only that she has shed her cocoon.

THOSE BONES ARE NOT MY CHILD

First published: 1999
Type of work: Novel

Zala Spencer struggles to survive the disappearance of her son during an outbreak of child slayings in the city of Atlanta.

Published posthumously and edited by her friend, writer Toni Morrison, *Those Bones Are Not My Child* is a fictional account of the actual epidemic of child killings that plagued residents of the city of Atlanta in the early 1980's. The plot of this historical novel is based on events surrounding the murders of those forty children by a serial killer or killers and the resultant investigation.

The central characters, Zala Spencer and Nathaniel (Spence) Spencer, are estranged when they learn that the first of their three children, Sonny, is missing and presumed a victim of the killing spree. Their shock at his disappearance reunites them as they search for answers. Initially too overcome with grief to function, Zala refocuses her sorrow into outrage, becoming a community activist in her efforts to know the truth about her son's fate.

In addition to the personal story about a mother's plight, the novel is also a broad critique of a city, one that held the promise of a brighter future for all it residents with its election of a black mayor in 1980. However, the number of dead children begins to mount, and rumors circulate in African American communities, murmurs about child pornography and suspected Ku Klux Klan activities. A pall hangs over the black community whose residents fear the vulnerability of their children and resent the apparent indifference of white authorities.

Central to the novel is the troubling question of unequal protection. Justice may be blind, but injustice seems to see color with great clarity. Speculation that officials delayed their investigation of the crimes because the victims were young, black, and poor leaves communities distraught, divided, and suspicious. When Wayne Williams, a black man, is charged with the murders, many are skeptical that the actual killer has been caught. They suspect Williams is the wrong man at the right time, a convenient scapegoat for the heinous crimes.

Epic in scope, the work is Bambara's most ambitious at 669 pages. A mixture of styles, including journalistic and confessional, lends the novel its realism. However, unlike traditional historical novels that seek to provide a factual tableau upon which to unfold fictionalized versions of real events, Bambara does the opposite. In *Those Bones Are Not My Child*, the supposed facts of the case (information culled from newspaper accounts and legal records) are in dispute. It is the fictional Spencers who are all too real.

Toni Cade Bambara

SUMMARY

Bambara writes powerfully about the varied experiences of African American women across three decades of change: the 1960's, 1970's, and 1980's. In her stories and novels, characters' expectations for a shared social consciousness are grounded by the realities of racial prejudice, sexual oppression, and class divide. However, her characters never abandon hope to embrace despair; instead, they take action. By imaginatively re-creating the patterns and sounds of ethnic speech, Bambara extends the range of voices heard in late twentieth century American literature.

Dorothy Dodge Robbins

BIBLIOGRAPHY

By the Author

LONG FICTION:
The Salt Eaters, 1980
Those Bones Are Not My Child, 1999

SHORT FICTION:
Gorilla, My Love, 1972
The Sea Birds Are Still Alive: Collected Stories, 1977
Raymond's Run: Stories for Young Adults, 1989

SCREENPLAYS:
The Bombing of Osage Avenue, 1986 (documentary)
W. E. B. Du Bois—A Biography in Four Voices, 1995 (with Amiri Baraka, Wesley Brown, and Thulani Davis)

EDITED TEXTS:
The Black Woman: An Anthology, 1970
Tales and Stories for Black Folks, 1971
Southern Exposure, 1976 (periodical; Bambara edited volume 3)

MISCELLANEOUS:
"What It Is I Think I'm Doing Anyhow," *The Writer on Her Work*, 1981 (Janet Sternburg, editor)
Deep Sightings and Rescue Missions: Fiction, Essays, and Conversations, 1996

DISCUSSION TOPICS

- Discuss how Velma's mental illness in *The Salt Eaters* is the product of sexual bias and racial prejudice.
- How does the African American tradition of oral storytelling feature in Toni Cade Bambara's works?
- Through what specific actions do young girls in Bambara's stories demonstrate their resistance to social norms?
- Explore how truth telling is an important aspect of Bambara's work.
- Who are the social activists in Bambara's fiction, and what problems are they trying to remedy?

About the Author

Alwes, Derek. "The Burden of Liberty: Choice in Toni Morrison's *Jazz* and Toni Cade Bambara's *The Salt Eaters*." *African American Review* 30, no. 3 (Fall, 1996): 353-365.
Bone, Martyn. "Capitalist Abstraction and the Body Politics of Place in Toni Cade Bambara's *Those Bones Are Not My Child*." *Journal of American Studies* 37, no. 2 (August, 2003): 229-246.
Butler-Evans, Elliott. *Race, Gender, and Desire: Narrative Strategies in the Fiction of Toni Cade Bambara, Toni Morrison, and Alice Walker*. Philadelphia: Temple University Press, 1989.
Collins, Janelle. "Generating Power: Fission, Fusion, and Post Modern Politics in Bambara's *The Salt Eaters*." *MELUS* 21, no. 2 (Summer, 1996): 35-47.
Heller, Janet Ruth. "Toni Cade Bambara's Use of African American Vernacular English in 'The Lesson.'" *Style* 37, no. 3 (Fall, 2003): 279-293.
Kelley, Margot A. "'Damballah Is the First Law of Thermodynamics': Modes of Access to Toni Cade Bambara's *The Salt Eaters*." *African American Review* 27, no. 3 (Fall, 1993): 479-493.
Muther, Elizabeth. "Bambara's Feisty Girls: Resistance Narratives in *Gorilla, My Love*." *African American Review* 36, no. 3 (Fall, 2002): 447-459.

Library of Congress

AMIRI BARAKA

Born: Newark, New Jersey
October 7, 1934

A founder of the Black Arts movement, Baraka is acknowledged to be a major influence upon experimental poetry and drama.

BIOGRAPHY

Born Everett LeRoi Jones in Newark, New Jersey, in 1934, Imamu Amiri Baraka was raised in the urban middle-class environment against which he has since rebelled. His father, Coyette (Coyt) LeRoi, was a postal employee, and his mother, Anna Lois Russ Jones, a social worker. Educated in the Newark public schools, Baraka began cartooning in junior high school and writing science fiction for the school publication in high school before graduating at the age of sixteen.

Although he had once considered the ministry as a career, Baraka accepted a science scholarship to Rutgers University. His experiences at Rutgers for one year, at Howard University where he did not complete his studies, and as an enlisted gunner in the Air Force (from 1954 to 1957) catalyzed his awareness of what he believed to be the illness of assimilation—that is, of black acquiescence and adaptation to white oppression. Consequently, after his discharge from the armed services, Baraka sought the supportive countercultural atmosphere of Greenwich Village in New York.

There, Baraka founded Totem Press and cofounded the avant-garde magazine *Yugen* with Hettie Cohen, a Jewish woman who would be his wife for seven years, from 1958 to 1965. In those years, he achieved recognition as a jazz and blues critic, worked as a poetry and small-press magazine editor, and took graduate courses in philosophy and comparative literature at Columbia University. Under the influence of such bohemian experimental poets as Allen Ginsberg, Gregory Corso, and William Carlos Williams (as well as Ezra Pound), Baraka established his early poetic voice with his first volume of poetry, *Preface to a Twenty Volume Suicide Note* (1961). This collection reflected his resistance to the debilitating effects of white stereotyping and black assimilation, suggesting his eventual movement to a separatist philosophy.

Throughout his literary career, Baraka has served as a role model of his philosophy that art must lead to greater awareness and stimulate its audience to action. A small sampling of his activities from 1959 to 1967 includes the following: 1959, compiling and publishing a pro-Castro anthology; 1960, touring Cuba with other artists at Fidel Castro's invitation; 1961, cofounding an experimental poetry group and magazine; 1963, seeing *The Toilet*, his first play, produced Off-Broadway and publishing *Blues People*, a book of music criticism; 1964, founding Black Arts Repertory Theatre and School; 1966, founding Spirit House, a black community theater with ongoing student workshops; and 1967, founding Jihad Publications for black nationalist writers.

Baraka's nationalism was fostered by repeated arrests in which charges were dropped or, as in one case, a judge's decision was reversed by the United States Supreme Court on appeal. At the same time, recognition of Baraka's literary achievements was both national and international. The author was awarded a John Hay Whitney Foundation Fellowship for fiction and poetry in 1962, the Obie Award for best Off-Broadway play (*Dutchman*) in 1964, a Yoruba Academy Fellowship in 1965, a Guggenheim Fellowship for 1965-1966, and second prize at the Dakar International Arts Festival as well as a grant from the National Endowment for the Arts in 1966. Certainly, the dichotomy between the positive responses of the literary community and the negative responses of the legal professions served to fuel his anti-assimilationist beliefs.

In 1965, his marriage was dissolved; in 1967, he married Sylvia Robinson, a black woman. The following year, LeRoi Jones became Imamu Amiri Baraka, thereby erasing his white heritage with Muslim and African words meaning "blessed poet/philosopher warrior"; his wife became Bibi Amina Baraka. For the next seven years, Baraka was to become increasingly active in nationalistic ventures and more fervid in his denunciations of white society. He called for nonpacifistic black attitudes and even for mass exterminations of whites, white organizations, and white culture, so that blacks could create a totally independent country—in essence a black utopia. He endorsed black candidates in local elections, helped to found organizations for the protection and enhancement of black civil liberties and culture, and held high offices within both local and national activist groups.

Although he continues to be a fierce advocate of black rights, in 1974 Baraka dropped Imamu from his name in favor of the title "Chairman" when he adopted Marxism and socialistic beliefs. He also began to advocate a coalition of white and black proletariat against their middle- and upper-class oppressors. The need for a separate black state has been superseded by what Baraka perceives to be the capitalistic and imperialistic threat to the uninformed, disorganized masses. Consequently, Baraka in all of his writings shifted to a more didactic and less emotional function and content. What some critics have essentially termed rambling propaganda Baraka sees as rallying cries (predominantly to his black audience) for revolution.

ANALYSIS

Baraka's writings divide into three distinctive patterns according to both form and content. His first literary period, although sometimes unconventional in dramatic subject matter, is his most conventional in form. Written under the name LeRoi Jones, the work of this early period is distin-

guished by a preoccupation with self-identity as well as a nascent concern for the lack of a collective black consciousness.

The work of his second literary period, during which he had begun to write as Imamu Amiri Baraka, is more experimental in form and is marked by strong advocacy of black separatism. A romantic with a profound belief in humankind's spiritual potential, the Baraka of this period sees whites as having distorted their spiritual capacities into materialistic oppression; therefore, he advocates the extinction of the white race (and its cultural artifacts) and the creation of a new black world. To that end, Baraka seeks to raise his readers' consciousness of history amid racial identity so that, through dramatic involvement, they will be moved to active resistance.

The characteristics of this period (Baraka's most universally acclaimed) are based upon his belief that art is a dynamic, utilitarian process that must have an integral role in any "living" black community by virtue of the experiences it offers for growth. The white culture, according to Baraka, has already self-destructed from a pervasive, incurable emotional and spiritual paralysis.

Consequently, Baraka rejects white American English through the re-creation of black speech patterns, whose words and sounds combine synergistically to produce a challenging syntax and a lyrical dramatic rhythm. Unlike his goal during his first literary period, Baraka's intent at this stage is predominantly ethnocentric. He employs inflammatory and obscene language to startle his readers, to force their emotional awareness. Perceiving violence as the only viable means to black rebirth, Baraka consciously chooses a multisensory, surrealistic style that can assault his audience. His dramatization of historical injustices is uncompromising, as are his solutions. Furthermore, his consuming hatred of whites exacerbates the violence he advocates. His concern for the black oppressed is balanced to some degree by his affirmation that blacks, as the superior race, can overcome their oppressors and can establish self-sufficiency.

Baraka's need to disavow the deceit and the deadliness he believes to be inherent in white English gradually leads to increased literary experimentation. Generally, his punctuation and his capitalization become extreme; for example, he uses open parentheses and diagonals for pauses. He may capitalize every letter of a word for emphasis, spell phonetically, invent abbreviations, and pun. Another characteristic is his extensive use of present participles to connote the dynamic process of living.

In Baraka's nonfiction prose, he intermittently breaks the convolutions of his lengthy sentences with sentence fragments and asides addressed to the reader. His fiction is associational rather than chronological in content. In his poetry, he seeks the purest expression of his "beingness" by extending his verbal inventiveness, at times to the point of unintelligibility. His inversion of traditional symbols is particularly noteworthy. For example, the white god-figure and his dictums are false, created by the white race to victimize others; therefore, the sun, traditionally life-giving, becomes a symbol of black spiritual energy and a mortal threat to whites.

Slave Ship: A Historical Pageant (1967) is representative of his separatist ritual drama. As is typical of black nationalist theater, physical and emotional violence is portrayed in a series of evocative slave images meant to draw audience response on an emotional level. With little dialogue, the playscript depends heavily upon music, dance, sounds, and lighting to build—through horrifying black experiences—to the final affirmation of black beauty and power. When cast and audience unite, however, Baraka's script calls for a disembodied head to be thrown amid the celebration, a graphic reminder that the struggle has not ended.

Baraka's third literary phase is characteristically Marxist; he no longer uses Imamu as a part of his name. He seeks an intellectual rather than an emotional response to his writing. His style is didactic and propagandizing, and he has enlarged the scope of his concern from a focus on black cultural victimization and racial identity to a socialistic focus on the world's oppressed. Instead of denouncing whites as the cause of America's ills, Baraka defends all who have been victimized, regardless of race, and blames the world's "dis-ease" on capitalists and imperialists. This does not, however, mean that he has abandoned his active participation in creating a unified black world of self-determination and nonoppression; in his third literary period he sees black nationalism being achieved as only one consequence of an inevitable socialist revolution.

DUTCHMAN

First produced: 1964 (first published, 1964)
Type of work: Play

On the New York subway, Lula, a thirty-year-old white woman, seduces and murders Clay, a twenty-year-old black man.

Dutchman, winner of the 1964 Obie Award for best Off-Broadway production, is a riveting dramatization of psychosexual, interracial tensions. The title bears mythical implications, supported by Baraka's own stage directions, which indicate a subway setting filled with modern myth. Despite Baraka's insistence that the two main characters are individuals, not allegorical creations, he confines them within this subterranean set. The Dutch sailed the first slave-bearing vessel to the American colonies. The legend of *The Flying Dutchman* is one of a ship cursed to sail the seas eternally without ever finding safe harbor. Even if the first were a simple allusion, together these suggest that white America has doomed itself through its nonrecognition of blacks as human. If so, Lula, as the white representative, will inhabit the subway, preying upon her black victims until one galvanizes himself into action, freeing himself and both races through her murder.

Lula, the protagonist, controls scene 1. She enters from behind Clay, initiates their confrontive conversation, and sits beside him. Even though he is uncomfortable, she makes seductive overtures. Her accurate assessment of his middle-class background and assimilationist behavioral mask also fascinates him into continuing their conversation. Lula, the oppressor, condescendingly sees Clay as a stereotype and commands the topics with which they essentially talk at each other. By admitting that she is a liar—and later, that she is insane—Lula forces him into the untenable situation of having to process each of her statements as fact or fiction. Furthermore, it is she who offers Clay an apple that he accepts; critics have made much of the possible Adam and Eve analogy. Lula is also the initiator of physical aggression, first running her hand along Clay's leg and later harshly grabbing and shaking his wrist.

Clay, in suit and striped tie despite the summer heat, has assimilated into the white world. He does

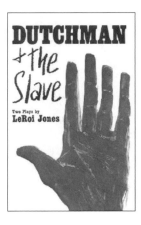

not wish to call attention to himself. Clay sees Lula also as a stereotype—of the liberal white woman fascinated by fantasies of interracial sexual intercourse. Momentarily excited by her, he allows himself to become vulnerable by adapting to her mercuric emotional shifts.

In scene 2, as Lula describes her party plans in seductive detail, Clay begins to make physical advances. Their dialogue, strikingly fast-paced from the play's opening lines, intensifies into a dueling rhythm as they both become more openly confrontational. They even capture the attention of normally apathetic fellow subway riders, who watch their interaction with some interest. A major shift occurs when Lula unmasks Clay, accusing him of having escaped to her (the white) side. Clay assumes control, and Lula defends herself with hysterics, singing and dancing in the train aisle. Clay refuses every invitation to join her until she goads him to restrain her by warning him that he is dying because of his assimilation, that he must release himself from his self-imposed bonds. He wrestles her (as well as the drunk who attempts to defend her) into submission, slapping her with full strength.

Baraka sees dance as an ultimate expression of life. Lula's hysterical invitation, however, assumes a double meaning. Even though she may be offering Clay an apparent passageway out of his self-victimization, she is simultaneously inviting him into a new bondage: life on her terms. With no viable means of regaining his mask or escaping, Clay is finally free to expunge his rage. He erupts into a devastating diatribe that avows his contempt for those who surround themselves with illusions to avoid reality, his homicidal hatred of whites, and his need to assimilate so as not to commit mass murder. According to Clay, black art and music are escape valves that would be unnecessary if the artists would simply exterminate whites: "A whole people of neurotics, struggling to keep from being sane. And the only thing that would cure the neurosis would be your murders."

Clay defeats himself, however, by retreating tiredly from an insistence upon action to the safety of words. He concludes with a warning not to trust assimilated blacks because someday they will embark on a genocidal rampage, using as their justification the same white rationalizations they have been taught.

As Clay bends to gather his books, Lula stabs him twice; after he has destroyed her illusions of him, she must destroy him. Whether her actions are premeditated can be interpreted dramatically through her interactions with the other passengers. Her earlier admission that she knows them even more intimately than she knows Clay and their easy acquiescence in disposing of his body suggest either complicity or a compelling fear. That their presence as her "crew" is prearranged is in keeping with the Dutchman myth. Her preparation to start the cycle once more with another young black who enters the car further supports the mythical interpretation.

In *Dutchman*, Baraka dramatizes two of his major themes. The first is that dehumanizing sexuality, in any form, leads to death. Clay and Lula's sexual interaction is simply another layer of masking. It is sterile, with no spiritual or emotional intimacy. Baraka's second theme is that psychic paralysis leads to annihilation. Clay has the opportunity to survive until he is caught in his own self-destructive trap. As a poet, he retreats into words and poetry when challenged because they are safe and comfortable, even when he recognizes the need for action. He does not see his art's potential as a motivating agent for change, and he reverts to passive resistance, giving up. Consequently, his art, too, is sterile. It is Lula who survives, by committing the extreme guerrilla action in murdering him.

"AN AGONY. AS NOW."

First published: 1964 (collected in *Transbluesency: The Selected Poems of Amiri Baraka*, 1995)
Type of work: Poem

From within a white metal shell, the poet views nature and remembers himself.

In "An Agony. As Now," from *The Dead Lecturer* (1964), Baraka describes in sensuous phrases his emotional and spiritual paralysis. The title of this poetry collection is a reference to the attempted suicide of the speaker. His sense of dissociation from the self who hates him is a normal part of the recovery process; however, Baraka adds another level of meaning. The inverted symbolism of white implies that assimilation, voluntary or involuntary, is a significant factor of the imprisonment.

Openings in the mask allow the persona to see, but the metal prevents any human contact. Introspectively addressing his ruminations to the soul he has sightlessly abandoned, he recalls a woman who ran from him to the forest of white "civilization" and a man decaying from psychic paralysis, "never beautiful." The speaker's mind races unencumbered to the sun in a series of associational images that offer a brief hope for resurrection with fragmented water imagery. Nevertheless, the torment escalates as he recognizes the corruption surrounding him. The sun is love, self-actualization, God, but the poet is trapped within himself and does not know how to reach the love, despite his need. Therefore, the sun reaches out to him, heating his white metal shell and burning awareness into him. His final scream is a scream of self-realization, a moment of truth, in which he relinquishes his detachment and accepts himself.

Baraka's characteristic devices include the use of open parentheses and commas to stop his reader and to increase the associational possibilities of his phrasing. Inverted symbolism and the repetition of key words and phrases reinforce his meaning as he guides his reader on a journey from mind, through sun, God, and soul, to beauty. The speaker's shell is the corrupting veneer of white civilization. To acknowledge his true identity, the black poet must reject the easy answers and accept his black consciousness as beautiful. Only after he destroys the facade will he again feel.

"MONK'S WORLD"

First published: 1993 (collected in *Funk Lore: New Poems, 1984-1995*, 1996)
Type of work: Poem

The poet recalls his encounter with Thelonious Monk and his music in the jazz quarter of Manhattan.

One cannot fully understand "Monk's World" without knowing about jazz. To Amiri Baraka, poetry is a form of music guided first by rhythm, without which words, which are rhythmic themselves, do not even exist. To look at "Monk's World," therefore, references to the background and the virtuosity of black music are indispensable. Originally appearing in a bilingual Italian publication *Morso Dal Suono* in 1993, the poem is a dedication to Thelonious Monk, the "High Priest of Bebop" in the 1940's, and to his music, which has continued to inspire Baraka throughout his career.

Written in avant-garde language and free form, the poem begins with one of Monk's most enduring jazz ballads, "Round Midnight," where readers are brought into the jazz scene with Monk improvising the "hot" bebop music—the fire engine solo—in the Village Vanguard, a renowned Manhattan jazz club. Adding to the fervor and musicality of the poem are the terms that Baraka uses: "spaced funk" ("spaced" suggesting the state of being "spaced out" associated with drug taking, particularly marijuana, of which jazz musicians have been fond), "numbers & letters" (musical composition and improvisation), "black keys signifying" (the underlying messages or criticism on which the music plays), "weird birds" (bebop, which is "weird" because it is still new, radical, and somewhat oppositional compared to traditional jazz, and "bird" referring to the great American jazz musician Charlie "Bird" Parker).

Baraka described the music that he encountered with Monk as an "intimate revelation" in which the "black keys" answered his questions, in which the piano collected one's feelings into its "diary." The music speaks not only the words that one uses to communicate but also the unspeakable emotions that one desires to share. The atmosphere of the jazz quarter was brought to great intensity when Monk "dipped" and "spun" the music with which he "danced" at the audience, who in response want to get up and dance. "What's happening?" appears twice as a question, or rather as an exclamation in the sixth stanza, to convey the celestial state of mind brought about by the music of "every googolplex" (immense quantity) of a second. John Coltrane, another great American jazz musician, was introduced onto the scene when Monk played with him. The second-to-last stanza makes references to Monk's composition "Straight, No Chaser" and to *Interstellar Space*, in which Coltrane recorded compositions named after the planets.

The poem ends as an echo to the opening stanza where the fire engine solo becomes screaming blues and "cats" standing around turn into scatted flying things, bringing the music to its height and filling the night and the empty street with vigor and vibrancy—this is Monk's world.

SUMMARY

Baraka is a crucial figure in American literature. His indomitable insistence that the oppressed be freed and that art be an active factor in the process has led him to the creation of versatile forms of expression in poetry, drama, fiction, and nonfiction prose. A leading black aesthetician, he consistently extends his art into action. A critical concern, however, has been that he fails to reach his intended audience, the black masses. As his experimentation continues, his writing grows ever more esoteric and may become accessible to smaller and smaller audiences.

Kathleen Mills; updated by Selina Lai

BIBLIOGRAPHY

By the Author

POETRY:
Spring and Soforth, 1960
Preface to a Twenty Volume Suicide Note, 1961
The Dead Lecturer, 1964
Black Art, 1966
A Poem for Black Hearts, 1967
Black Magic: Sabotage, Target Study, Black Art—Collected Poetry, 1961-1967, 1969
It's Nation Time, 1970
In Our Terribleness: Some Elements and Meaning in Black Style, 1970 (with Fundi [Billy Abernathy])
Spirit Reach, 1972
Afrikan Revolution, 1973
Hard Facts, 1975
Selected Poetry of Amiri Baraka/LeRoi Jones, 1979
Reggae or Not!, 1981
Transbluesency: The Selected Poems of Amiri Baraka, 1995
Wise, Why's, Y's, 1995
Funk Lore: New Poems, 1984-1995, 1996
Somebody Blew Up America, and Other Poems, 2003

DRAMA:
The Baptism, pr. 1964, pb. 1966
Dutchman, pr., pb. 1964
The Slave, pr., pb. 1964
The Toilet, pr., pb. 1964
Experimental Death Unit #1, pr. 1965, pb. 1969

DISCUSSION TOPICS

- How would you describe the interaction between Lula and Clay in *Dutchman*? What does it suggest about the relationship between the black and white races?

- Amiri Baraka considers violence as the ultimate means to bring about a black rebirth. How does violence function in *Dutchman*?

- How is racism addressed and dealt with in *Dutchman* and "An Agony. As Now."?

- What are the changes that the poet has experienced in "An Agony. As Now."? What is the significance of these changes?

- What are the two selves presented in "An Agony. As Now."? Can they coexist? Why or why not?

- Identify some of the avant-garde techniques that Baraka employs in "An Agony. As Now." and "Monk's World."

- What is "jazzification"? Draw examples from "Monk's World" to illustrate such elements in the poem.

- What do you think Monk is "signifying" with the "black keys" in "Monk's World"?

Jello, pr. 1965, pb. 1970
A Black Mass, pr. 1966, pb. 1969
Arm Yourself, or Harm Yourself, pr., pb. 1967
Great Goodness of Life (A Coon Show), pr. 1967, pb. 1969
Madheart, pr. 1967, pb. 1969
Slave Ship: A Historical Pageant, pr., pb. 1967
The Death of Malcolm X, pb. 1969
Bloodrites, pr. 1970, pb. 1971
Junkies Are Full of (SHHH . . .), pr. 1970, pb. 1971
A Recent Killing, pr. 1973, pb. 1978
S-1, pr. 1976, pb. 1978
The Motion of History, pr. 1977, pb. 1978
The Sidney Poet Heroical, pb. 1979 (originally as *Sidnee Poet Heroical*, pr. 1975)
What Was the Relationship of the Lone Ranger to the Means of Production?, pr., pb. 1979
Weimar, pr. 1981
Money: A Jazz Opera, pr. 1982
Primitive World: An Anti-Nuclear Jazz Musical, pr. 1984, pb. 1997
The Life and Life of Bumpy Johnson, pr. 1991
General Hag's Skeezag, pb. 1992
Meeting Lillie, pr. 1993
The Election Machine Warehouse, pr. 1996, pb. 1997

LONG FICTION:
The System of Dante's Hell, 1965

SHORT FICTION:
Tales, 1967
The Fiction of LeRoi Jones/Amiri Baraka, 2000

NONFICTION:
"Cuba Libre," 1961
The New Nationalism, 1962
Blues People: Negro Music in White America, 1963
Home: Social Essays, 1966
Black Music, 1968
A Black Value System, 1970
Strategy and Tactics of a Pan-African Nationalist Party, 1971
Kawaida Studies: The New Nationalism, 1971
Raise Race Rays Raze: Essays Since 1965, 1971
Crisis in Boston!, 1974
The Creation of the New Ark, 1975
The Autobiography of LeRoi Jones/Amiri Baraka, 1984
Daggers and Javelins: Essays, 1984
The Artist and Social Responsibility, 1986
The Music: Reflections on Jazz and Blues, 1987 (with Amina Baraka)
Jesse Jackson and Black People, 1994
Conversations with Amiri Baraka, 1994 (Charlie Reilly, editor)
Eulogies, 1996
Bushwacked! A Counterfeit President for a Fake Democracy: A Collection of Essays on the 2000 National Elections, 2001
The Essence of Reparations: Afro-American Self-Determination and Revolutionary Democratic Struggle in the United States of America, 2003

EDITED TEXTS:
The Moderns: New Fiction in America, 1963
Black Fire: An Anthology of Afro-American Writing, 1968 (with Larry Neal)
African Congress: A Documentary of the First Modern Pan-African Congress, 1972
Confirmation: An Anthology of African-American Women, 1983 (with Amina Baraka)

MISCELLANEOUS:
Selected Plays and Prose, 1979
The LeRoi Jones/Amiri Baraka Reader, 1991

About the Author

Benston, Kimberly W. *Baraka: The Renegade and the Mask*. New Haven, Conn.: Yale University Press, 1976.
_____, ed. *Imamu Amiri Baraka (LeRoi Jones): A Collection of Critical Essays*. Englewood Cliffs, N.J.: Prentice-Hall, 1978.
Brown, Lloyd W. *Amiri Baraka*. Boston: Twayne, 1980.
Fox, Robert Elliot. "LeRoi Jones/Amiri Baraka: A Scripture of Rhythms." In *Conscientious Sorcerors: The Black Postmodernist Fiction of LeRoi Jones/Amiri Baraka, Ishmael Reed, and Samuel R. Delany*. New York: Greenwood Press, 1987.
Harris, William J. *The Poetry and Poetics of Amiri Baraka: The Jazz Aesthetic*. Columbia: University of Missouri Press, 1986.
Hudson, Theodore R. *From LeRoi Jones to Amiri Baraka: The Literary Works*. Durham, N.C.: Duke University Press, 1973.
Lacey, Henry C. *To Raise, Destroy, and Create: The Poetry, Drama, and Fiction of Imamu Amiri Baraka (LeRoi Jones)*. Troy, N.Y.: Whitston, 1981.
Watts, Jerry G. *Amiri Baraka: The Politics and Art of a Black Intellectual*. New York: New York University Press, 2001.
Woodard, Komozi. *A Nation Within a Nation: Amiri Baraka (LeRoi Jones) and Black Power Politics*. Chapel Hill: University of North Carolina Press, 1999.

DJUNA BARNES

Born: Cornwall-on-Hudson, New York
      June 12, 1892
Died: New York, New York
      June 18, 1982

Best known and most frequently celebrated for her dense, lyrical prose, Barnes was an important contributor to American expatriate culture of the 1920's and a significant modernist novelist.

Courtesy, New Directions Publishing

BIOGRAPHY

Djuna Barnes was born into an eccentric, bohemian family at Cornwall-on-Hudson, New York, on June 12, 1892. Her mother, an amateur violinist who wrote poetry throughout her life, was perhaps the most conventional figure in the Barnes family. Barnes's father, Wald Barnes, rarely held any substantial employment, and he was a notorious philanderer. He adopted his mother's surname as a reaction against his own father, and his first name was merely one of many he employed throughout his early life. Wald's mother, Zadel, also lived with the family, and supported her son's interests in spiritualism. During her late childhood, Barnes moved with her family to a farm on Long Island, but her parents soon separated, the eccentric and self-indulgent Wald having exceeded even his wife's amazing tolerance of his selfish behavior.

Partly as a consequence of her family's eccentric opinions, Barnes never attended public school, but she did move to Manhattan to attend art school. Her first book, a collection of poems and drawings titled *The Book of Repulsive Women*, was published in 1915, and Barnes for a time considered the careers of artist and writer to be equally open to her. During much of World War I, Barnes lived in Greenwich Village and earned a living as a freelance journalist for various small New York and Brooklyn newspapers.

With her expatriation to Europe in 1919, Barnes's life began a new chapter; no longer simply a member of an artistic community in the United States, she became a celebrated figure of international, although predominantly American, bohemian culture. It was in Europe that Barnes initiated longtime friendships with Natalie Barney, the famous lesbian advocate, and Peggy Guggenheim, the wealthy heiress, gallery owner, and patron of innumerable artists, including Barnes.

Barnes also interviewed James Joyce, the great modernist novelist, and carried on distant acquaintanceships with such luminaries as author Ernest Hemingway. In 1923, Barnes published *A Book*, a critically successful collection of poems, short stories, plays, and drawings. This text was subsequently republished with some alterations as *A Night Among the Horses* (1929), but it is best known by its earlier title. While living in Paris, Barnes began a love affair with the American artist Thelma Wood; this relationship, which lasted throughout the 1920's, was traumatic for Barnes emotionally, and it ultimately formed the basis for her novel *Nightwood* (1936).

Barnes's next book, *Ryder* (1928), was a best-selling novel in the United States, and it became the focus of post-office inquiries because of its sexual frankness. Like *Nightwood*, it is also biographical and draws upon Barnes's early familial experiences.

In the following year, Barnes published a satire on the Paris lesbian community titled *Ladies' Almanack* (1928), which was privately printed and not widely available until a Harper & Row reprinting in

1972. During the 1930's, Barnes lived in England, first in Guggenheim's household and later on her own in London. Her most important novel, *Nightwood*, was published during this period, and it gained for her the support of the profoundly influential poet T. S. Eliot.

Having briefly returned to France in 1939, Barnes was almost trapped by the advancing German armies in their summer advance of 1940; however, she managed to escape with the financial aid and encouragement of Guggenheim, and she arrived in New York later that year. Returning to Greenwich Village, she settled into a small studio apartment on Patchin Place, where she resided for the rest of her life. Initially, Barnes experienced extreme financial difficulties in New York and for a time returned to painting. She published a verse drama, *The Antiphon*, in 1958 and continued to work at various literary projects until her death.

In her later years, Barnes became increasingly isolated, partly as a consequence of ill health and partly as the result of her alienation from a world which paid her small attention. She was, however, awarded a National Endowment for the Arts grant in 1981, and her *Creatures in an Alphabet* (1982), a collection of brief animal alphabet rhymes, was published shortly after her death on June 18, 1982, at the age of ninety.

ANALYSIS

Eliot once described Djuna Barnes's *Nightwood* as a novel that in its stylistic prowess and its preoccupation with horror and fate very much resembles an Elizabethan tragedy. Although Barnes herself was widely read in the literature of the English Renaissance, the motivation for the preoccupation with decay and emotional trauma in her work stems from sources much nearer than the Elizabethans. Barnes insisted (in a 1919 interview with the American bohemian publisher Guido Bruno) that life was fundamentally morbid, particularly if one considers the life that goes on beneath the surface of everyday life.

Although she was not a serious student of depth psychology, Barnes's work reveals a passing acquaintance with Freudian notions, and her concern with the morbid character of psychological experience is largely a consequence of her decision to explore the often possessive and aggressive aspects of the family dynamic and of romantic relationships. In this respect, the Freudian influence in her work only substantiates the impact of the other major influence in Barnes's fiction—fin de siècle literature.

In Barnes's early journalism, there are frequent references to Irish poet and playwright Oscar Wilde and to the drawings of English artist Aubrey Beardsley. Both figures are connected with the aura of exotic decadence that is commonly associated with European culture at the turn of the twentieth century, and Barnes's early poems and art definitely demonstrate the impact of the languid and often strangely animalistic figures that one characteristically finds in Beardsley's drawings.

The Book of Repulsive Women is perhaps the best example of such influence in Barnes's work, but it can also be found in the grotesque imagery that pervades her late verse drama, *The Antiphon*. Thematically, one might consider Barnes to be preoccupied with the process of decay and emotional estrangement, and this concern with impending doom and dissolution has led critics to consider her otherwise possibly eccentric fiction as very much in the mainstream of American fiction that runs from Herman Melville's tortured mariners to the apocalyptic vision of Hollywood that one finds in the fiction of Nathanael West.

While the thematic concerns in Barnes's work are very tightly focused, her stylistic and technical achievements are extravagant and wide-ranging. In this respect, Barnes is also very much in the mainstream of the spirit of literary experimentation that characterized the modernist movement of the 1920's. Her own interest in the work of Joyce is well known, and, as her novel *Ryder* demonstrates, Barnes is able to imitate effectively virtually every major writer in the history of English prose. In *Ryder*, this rhetorical exuberance is often entertaining and occasionally dazzling, but in *Nightwood* it is the motor that drives the novel.

In *Nightwood*, Barnes largely eschews any interest in plot in favor of a detailed representation of the consciousnesses of the major figures. In her preoccupation with motivation and with the associative patterns that preoccupy her characters, Barnes's writing in *Nightwood* parallels what is often described as stream-of-consciousness prose, most frequently associated with the fiction of James Joyce and with the psychologically motivated passages in the work of William Faulkner.

Barnes's subsequent interest in verse drama reflects a further rhetorical development in her work, and it looks forward to her late return to poetry and short lyrics. In this respect, Barnes's career may be thought of as describing a circle that begins with short verse, passes through the prose experiments of the 1920's and 1930's, and returns to verse via the very demanding form of blank verse drama. It should not be forgotten, of course, that throughout her life Barnes continued to pursue visual art; her drawings form an essential part of novels such as *Ryder* and collections such as *A Night Among the Horses*, and they may well be studied for insights into the prose that they illustrate.

Finally, Barnes must also be read as an important example of lesbian writing and for her efforts to write a women's modernism and to use experimental techniques to explore the estranged and oppressed roles of women. Her world of gay women in *Nightwood* is doubly distanced from the white heterosexual norms of modernist fiction, and as such this novel represents an important oppositional voice in the history of twentieth century literature.

RYDER

First published: 1928
Type of work: Novel

The eccentric and philandering Wendell Ryder attempts to assert patriarchal control over his family, but he ultimately fails.

Barnes's first novel, *Ryder,* is most significant for its display of technical virtuosity; it contains Elizabethan lyrics, audacious drawings, and enough ribald prose passages to have made it a minor scandal when it was first published. The plot describes the efforts of Wendell Ryder to found his own dynasty, but Wendell's successes are achieved largely at the expense of the women in the text; his wife, Amelia, and his mistress, Kate Careless, are ruthlessly exploited to fulfill Wendell's selfish ends. What impresses one most about Barnes's first popular success, however, is her early feminism and her ability to manipulate the novel form.

While many of her compatriots were celebrating

the triumph of male sexuality, Barnes was concerned with exploring the ways in which women were exploited by men. Chapter 5 in this novel, "Rape and Repining," demonstrates her interest in early feminism in its mocking attack on women for their own misfortune. In addition, Barnes's novel reflects the influence of Joyce in its use of a narrative that abandons strict chronology in favor of digressive commentaries upon the various women and their roles in the novel. For example, Barnes devotes a considerable amount of space to Kate Careless, one of Wendell's mistresses and one of the most important figures in the text. At the same time, she recounts at great length the checkered career of Wendell Ryder, who is extravagantly indulged by his mother, Sophia.

Ryder is particularly significant for its narrative excesses, but it is also an important example of early feminist fiction. Perhaps most significant for the subsequent development of Barnes's career is the appearance in this novel of Dr. Matthew O'Connor, a figure that she would use to advantage in *Nightwood.* In contrast to the aggressively patriarchal and yet ineffectual Wendell, Dr. O'Connor embraces both the insight of a patriarch and the compassion traditionally associated with the feminine psyche, making his sexual ambivalence an important part of the novel's thematic concerns. The example of Dr. O'Connor does little to mitigate Wendell's excesses, however, and the novel concludes with Wendell alone and bewildered by the effects of his dominance.

Barnes also suggests throughout the novel that the history of the Ryder family is indicative of a larger malaise, of which Wendell Ryder is only the latest manifestation. The first chapter, "Jesus Mundane," confirms this view by parodying the rhetoric of the Old Testament to insist upon humankind's fundamental ignorance and mediocrity. This first chapter is also indicative of the stylistic virtuosity and wit of the novel, which foregrounds language and style, frequently at the expense of plot development. In its bawdy imitations of Elizabethan lyrics and its allusive prose, the novel presents a series of different perspectives on the Ryder family, and these verbal portraits are accompanied by Barnes's illustrations.

Ryder is primarily significant as an example of the influence of Joycean experimentation upon modernist American literature; although it has not received extensive critical attention, its concern with male dominance also makes it an important anticipation of the direction of much later feminist writing.

NIGHTWOOD

First published: 1936
Type of work: Novel

Robin Vote, a young, mysterious woman, is pursued by a series of lovers, particularly by an emotionally tortured American, Nora Flood.

Nightwood is Barnes's most important work and the one most frequently read and discussed. Although it has a reputation as a difficult novel, it has been widely and enthusiastically admired by important literary figures, most notably perhaps Eliot, who was instrumental in securing its publication, and the Welsh poet Dylan Thomas. The primary focus in *Nightwood* is not plot but rather psychology, in that the narrative focuses upon the emotional reactions of its characters and their responses to Robin Vote. The novel's prose is dense and richly metaphorical, and two of its eight chapters consist solely of long conversations on the nature of lesbian love and sexuality.

The novel begins by considering the familial background of Felix Volkbein, the son of a Jewish Viennese merchant, who feels estranged and excluded from the snobbish world of European culture and society. Volkbein meets Robin Vote in the company of Dr. Matthew O'Connor, who is called to assist Robin after she has collapsed in a Paris hotel. Barnes's description of Robin consistently emphasizes her lack of volition; in this instance, for example, she is surrounded in her hotel room by exotic plants, and her skin is said to have a texture that is normally associated with plants.

Mistakenly reading Robin's lack of volition as a sign of malleability, Volkbein later marries Robin in order to fulfill his aspiration of founding a familial dynasty. After the birth of their child, however, Robin withdraws into a solitary life of travel and immerses herself in Catholicism. Abandoning her child and husband, she reappears some months later in Paris with her lover, Nora Flood. Two features of these events are particularly significant for an overall understanding of the novel. The first is the notion of decline, as marked by Felix Volkbein's failed familial ambitions; the second is the use of religious imagery in connection with the unconscious, a connection that Barnes exploits throughout the novel.

The next section of *Nightwood* describes the tempestuous relationship of Robin and Nora and the disintegration of that relationship as Robin is wooed away from Nora by the flighty and neurotic figure Jenny Petherbridge. Nora is distraught at this turn of events, and, in order to discuss her situation, she pays a visit to Dr. O'Connor. At this point, O'Connor emerges as a figure of great rhetorical prowess. An impoverished transvestite, O'Connor displays a profound understanding of Nora's dilemma, but his disquisitions on sexuality and love go far beyond Nora's emotional situation and become in themselves brilliant rhetorical exercises, full of wit and self-mocking irony. Barnes based the character of O'Connor upon an actual figure from the expatriate milieu in Paris in the 1920's, but his conversation best recalls the rhetorical wit of *Ryder*, where he appears in a much more subdued form.

Consistent with the thematic concerns of *Nightwood*, O'Connor's soliloquies revolve around the notions of decay and the psychodrama of sexuality, and his often grotesquely humorous but dark pronouncements foreshadow many of the subsequent events in the novel.

In the later sections of *Nightwood*, the narrator reveals that Felix Volkbein's child is physically and mentally weak, and the reader catches a final glimpse of Volkbein, drunkenly nodding to aristocrats in a Viennese café. O'Connor is similarly last seen in a drunken collapse after a tirade in a Paris café, and Nora despairingly returns to America. There she encounters Robin Vote for the final time in a decaying chapel on her estate. As Nora looks on helpless, Robin bows before an altar to the Madonna and then sinks to her hands and knees to confront Nora's dog, which retreats, whimpering, at Robin's animal intensity. At the end of the novel, after a hysterical fit of laughing and weeping, Robin lies exhausted on the floor of the chapel.

Nightwood, through its often obscure associative patterns, demonstrates powerfully the dark and destructive side of emotional relationships; it is equally important for its consideration of love within a lesbian context. Barnes also reflects the intellectual climate of her contemporaries in her use of Freudian dream patterns to illustrate the preoccupations of her characters, and, as is her earlier work, the novel is filled with striking lyrical prose.

SUMMARY

Barnes is perhaps the most important woman writer to emerge from the American expatriation in Paris in the 1920's. Her rhetorical mastery of a variety of prose forms and her concern with the unconscious enabled her to execute novels that are held together by their metaphoric associations rather than by the demands of plot or chronology. In this respect, her work is an important example of the modernist development of the novel form. In addition, her exploration of the roles of women, both through lesbian love and through the oppressive nature of patriarchal culture, make Barnes's work an important anticipation of the issues to emerge from later feminist writing.

Thomas Carmichael

DISCUSSION TOPICS

- Djuna Barnes came from a very eccentric family. Do any aspects of her subject matter or style reflect this background?

- Like a number of other talented young writers, Barnes seemed to be trying to shock her readers. To what pitfalls is such an approach liable?

- Barnes applied a demanding technique—stream of consciousness—to the explication of characters who are themselves unconventional and difficult to fathom. Was she expecting too much of her readers, or might they regard these difficulties as a compliment?

- Barnes's work is called "an important example of lesbian writing." Explain who you think can profit most from her writing: gays or straight people?

- Was Barnes "ahead of her time" in the 1920's or 1930's, or more attuned to her time than her critics?

BIBLIOGRAPHY

By the Author

LONG FICTION:
Ryder, 1928
Nightwood, 1936

SHORT FICTION:
A Night Among the Horses, 1929
Spillway, 1962
Smoke, and Other Early Stories, 1982
Collected Stories, 1996

DRAMA:
Three from the Earth, pr., pb. 1919
The Antiphon, pb. 1958
At the Roots of the Stars: The Short Plays, pb. 1995

POETRY:
The Book of Repulsive Women, 1915 (includes drawings)

NONFICTION:
Interviews, 1985 (journalism)
New York, 1989 (journalism)

CHILDREN'S LITERATURE:
Creatures in an Alphabet, 1982

MISCELLANEOUS:
A Book, 1923 (enlarged edition published as *A Night Among the Horses*, 1929; abridged as *Spillway*, 1962)
Ladies' Almanack, 1928
Selected Works, 1962

About the Author

Field, Andrew. *Djuna: The Formidable Miss Barnes*. Austin: University of Texas Press, 1985.

Galvin, Mary E. "Djuna Barnes' Use of Form and the Liminal Space of Gender. " In *Queer Poetics: Five Modernist Women Writers*. Westport, Conn.: Greenwood Press, 1999.

Grobbel, Michaela M. *Enacting Past and Present: The Memory Theaters of Djuna Barnes, Ingeborg Bachmann, and Marguerite Duras*. Lanham, Md.: Lexington Books, 2004.

Harris, Andrea L. "'The Third Sex': Figures of Inversion in Djuna Barnes's *Nightwood*." In *Other Sexes: Rewriting Difference from Woolf to Winterson*. Albany: State University of New York Press, 2000.

Kannenstine, Louis F. *Duality and Damnation: The Art of Djuna Barnes*. New York: New York University Press, 1977.

Marcus, Jane. *Hearts of Darkness: White Women Write Race*. New Brunswick, N.J.: Rutgers University Press, 2004.

Messerli, Douglas. *Djuna Barnes: A Bibliography*. Rhinebeck, N.Y.: David Lewis, 1975.

Parsons, Deborah. *Djuna Barnes*. Tavistock, Devon, England: Northcote House in association with the British Council, 2003.

Scott, James B. *Djuna Barnes*. Boston: Twayne, 1976.

JOHN BARTH

Born: Cambridge, Maryland
May 27, 1930

Widely recognized for the formal ingenuity of his novels, Barth is a major novelist whose work superbly demonstrates the development of postmodern fiction in the United States.

Teturo Maruyama

BIOGRAPHY

John Barth was born in Cambridge, Maryland, in the second year of the Great Depression. After graduating from local public schools, Barth spent the summer of 1947 studying theory and orchestration at New York's Juilliard School of Music. At the time, Barth's aspiration was to become a big-band jazz arranger in the tradition of Billy Strayhorn, but he soon felt that in comparison with the sophistication of his influences his own talents were limited, so he abandoned music as a career.

Returning to Maryland's Eastern Shore at the end of the summer of 1947, Barth found that he had been awarded a scholarship to The Johns Hopkins University, and he elected to attend Johns Hopkins in the fall of that year to pursue a major in journalism. Although Barth has suggested that his interest in working with past literature, particularly myth and historical narrative, is a by-product of his interest in musical arrangement, he first became seriously interested in writing fiction in the creative writing classes he took at Johns Hopkins. There he was also introduced to the world of literature and criticism, and by the time he had completed his A.B. degree, which was awarded to Barth in 1951, he had effectively decided to devote himself to writing fiction.

His first extended work of fiction, a novel titled "The Shirt of Nessus" (unpublished), was Barth's master's project, for which he received an M.A.

from Johns Hopkins in 1952. He then enrolled in the Ph.D. program in literary aesthetics at Johns Hopkins, but financial constraints forced him to abandon his studies and seek steady employment. In 1950, Barth had married Harriet Ann Strickland, and by 1953 they had two children, a daughter, Christine, born in 1951, and a son, John, born in 1952. A third child, David, was born in 1954. Barth joined the English faculty at Pennsylvania State University as an instructor in the fall of 1953, and he remained there until 1965.

While teaching, Barth continued to hone his craft, and he began to produce quickly; his first two novels were both written in 1955. *The Floating Opera* (1956), written during the first three months of that year, was nominated for the National Book Award, and his second novel, *The End of the Road* (1958) was made into a (very unsuccessful) film in the late 1960's. Although the sales of these novels were not large, Barth was encouraged by their critical success, and he followed them in 1960 with his third novel, *The Sot-Weed Factor.* This extravagant mock-historical fiction was praised effusively by Leslie Fiedler and others, and it marked Barth's arrival as a major contemporary writer, which was subsequently acknowledged by the "citation in fiction" Barth received from Brandeis University in 1965.

At the same time, Barth was becoming sought-after professionally; after working his way up the ladder of academic promotion at Pennsylvania State, he accepted an appointment in 1965 to the English department at the rapidly expanding State University of New York, Buffalo, where he was the Edward H. Butler Professor of English from 1971 to 1973.

In 1966, Barth published his perhaps best-known and most successful novel commercially, *Giles Goat-Boy: Or, The Revised New Syllabus* (1966). For a time, Barth was celebrated in popular weekly magazines such as *Time,* and his novel was highly placed on the national best-seller lists; however, Barth's fiction is often demanding and difficult, and *Giles Goat-Boy* was no exception. The novel has often been referred to as a largely unread best seller, but *Giles Goat-Boy* nevertheless established Barth in the forefront of audacious American writing and placed him in the company of contemporary figures such as Thomas Pynchon. Barth's next volume of fiction, *Lost in the Funhouse* (1968), is a collection of often experimental short narratives, and these marked a further step for Barth into the field of metafiction, or the literature of extreme narrative self-consciousness.

Barth was divorced from Harriet Ann Strickland in 1970, and in 1971 he married Shelly Rosenberg. He published *Chimera* (1972) in the following year, for which he was chosen as cowinner of the National Book Award. In 1973 Barth returned to Baltimore and Johns Hopkins, this time as a faculty member in The Johns Hopkins University Writing Seminars. His next novel, *Letters: A Novel* (1979), was followed by *Sabbatical: A Romance* (1982), then *The Tidewater Tales: A Novel* (1987), *The Last Voyage of Somebody the Sailor* (1991), *Once upon a Time: A Floating Opera* (1994), and *Coming Soon!!!* (2001). In 2004 he published *The Book of Ten Nights and a Night: Eleven Stories.* Barth has also been an important spokesman for experimental fiction, and his most significant essays have been published together in *The Friday Book* (1984) and in *Further Fridays* (1995). His other awards include the F. Scott Fitzgerald Award (1997), the PEN/Malamud Award (1998), and the Lannan Literary Awards lifetime achievement award (1998).

ANALYSIS

In his 1987 introduction to the Anchor Literary Library editions of his early novels, Barth remarks that his first novel, *The Floating Opera,* reflects the influence of French existentialist thought in post-World War II American culture. Most conspicuous in Barth's assimilation of existentialist influence is the notion of the world's absurdity, or what Barth describes elsewhere as the ultimately arbitrary nature of existence and the accompanying human recognition that this absurd existence is the ground of human experience. This view is repeated throughout Barth's fiction: In his first novel, *The Floating Opera,* it finds its expression in Todd Andrews's despairing reflection over his inability to exclude any fact from the vast research he has amassed in preparation for the writing of his own narrative. For Andrews, every fact has significance, but none has any ultimate importance because the world itself is finally without any absolute principle of order.

Similarly, Ebenezer Cooke, the protagonist of Barth's third novel, is plunged into spiritual paralysis by his awareness that every choice is equally valid but that no choice is necessary or compelling. These same dilemmas haunt George, the central figure in *Giles Goat-Boy,* and Ambrose, the protagonist of one series of stories in *Lost in the Funhouse.* Thematically, these ideas are most significant in Barth's fiction for their impact upon his consideration of questions of value and the motive for action in the world.

In Barth's first novel, his protagonist is able to avoid suicide in part by his own incompetence; however, his subsequent principled rejection of suicide is more significant. Reasoning that nothing has intrinsic value, Todd Andrews concludes that all decisions based upon value judgments about the world are ultimately matters of opinion, including the decision to take his own life. Each of Barth's subsequent protagonists confronts this dilemma in some form, and, while his novels are often ribald and extravagantly humorous, Barth finally endorses what he describes as a "Tragic View" in his work. This view can be said to be tragic in the sense that it posits death and fragmentation as the horizon against which existence is plotted; it also entails an acknowledgment of the absence of any final answers to the questions that Barth poses, together with a refusal to give in to resignation in the face of uncertainty.

Barth's fiction is consistently organized so that these ideas are also suggested by the formal strategies of narration, structure, and representation in each novel. For example, Barth frequently employs a self-conscious narrator in his later work who calls attention to the facts that the text is a work of fiction, not a simple transcription of the real world, and that fictional narration is itself governed by conventions that have nothing to do with reality. In this way, the self-conscious in Barth's fiction suggests that language reveals the way that reality, or representations of it, are inventions and have little to do with what is actually the case. Self-conscious narration is thus always for Barth a representational strategy, designed to signal all forms of order as impositions upon a fundamentally arbitrary world.

Barth's landmark 1967 essay, "The Literature of Exhaustion," presents his most cogent description of the relationship of fictional technique to these thematic concerns, and the same view is restated in his later essay, "The Literature of Replenishment" (1980). In both essays, Barth insists that the novel must affirm the artificial elements in art, but he also asserts that fiction does represent the world in approximate ways. For many, the questioning of the authority for values and the interrogation of language in Barth's fiction have made his work exemplary of the postmodern aesthetic, and Barth's use of parody and elaborate structural devices has reinforced this view. Barth himself is acutely aware of the relationship between literary history and the history of civilization and ideas. He has suggested, tor example, that the Chartres cathedral or Beethoven's Sixth Symphony would be embarrassing if they were created today. For Barth, literary techniques live in history and are subject to historical change, but change simply reflects the ways in which culture is a direct consequence of the ideas that motivate it.

In addition to exploring the relationship between fiction and reality and the question of value in individual action, Barth's work has exhibited recurring patterns and motifs. The role of the love triangle, for example, is central to Barth's first three novels, as well as the notion of twinship as the metaphorical representation of opposites that yearn to be united. Barth's work from *The Sot-Weed Factor* on also demonstrates a singular preoccupation with the pattern of ritual heroic adventure; again, this pattern is employed as a metaphor for the path of individual life experience, often ironically so. This ironic use of ritual or legendary material is also conspicuous in Barth's retelling of classical myths in *Lost in the Funhouse* and *Chimera*. In these stories, the principal concern is very much one of self-doubt and the stability of individual identity. This is consistent with Barth's insistence upon the absurd nature of the world outside the

self, but it is also part of Barth's consideration of the nature of love and the ground for human relationships.

What finally impresses one most in Barth's fiction are his technical virtuosity and his willingness to pursue the implications of his dramatized ideas relentlessly.

THE FLOATING OPERA

First published: 1956
Type of work: Novel

An Eastern Shore lawyer confronts the absurdity of existence and is driven to attempt suicide.

Barth's first published novel, *The Floating Opera*, anticipates much of his subsequent development in its playful devices and tone and in its thematic preoccupation with absurdity. The first-person narrator and protagonist, Todd Andrews, recounts the experiences of his life leading up to his decision not to commit suicide in 1937; although Todd is currently fifty-four and the present time of the narration is 1954, the novel is principally concerned with the events leading up to his fateful decision on June 21 or 22, 1937. Todd has been living with the possibility that he may die at any moment as a consequence of his chronic heart condition, a subacute bacteriological endocarditis with a tendency to myocardial infarction, first diagnosed when he was released from the Army at the end of World War I. This fact, the unpredictable nature of his own continued existence, prompts Todd's recognition of his inability to order and control his own experience, but this alone does not lead to suicide.

Todd also becomes convinced that there is no rational basis for human values and actions as a consequence of his conviction that sexuality is simply hilarious and his experience of killing a German soldier who had befriended him during the battle for the Argonne Forest. In Todd's view, humankind is literally a species of animal; at the same time, he insists that there is no justification for any action. Any line of questioning, he argues, maintained long enough eventually ends in an unanswerable question which reveals that there is no ultimate reason for the opinions and values people hold.

Consistent with this view, Todd's narration signals repeatedly that his ordered story is simply a fabrication, put together from any number of possible interpretations and orderings of the facts of his life. In the chapter titled "Calliope Music," for example, he begins with two columns of print, placed side by side on the page. The left column comments upon the absurd law case that Todd is currently considering, while the right column comments upon the rational basis for suicide. Though Todd excuses this device as a symptom of authorial ineptitude, this typographical arrangement demonstrates that no single account is definitive or conclusive in arranging all the facts relevant to his experiences. At the same time, it emphasizes Todd's awareness of his role as the narrator of his own story. In addition, Todd repeatedly refers to the indeterminate nature of his experiences; frequently, he is unable to remember an exact date or precise time.

Despite these assertions of indeterminacy, Todd persists throughout *The Floating Opera* in attempting to impose a rational order on his own existence and to find a rational basis for a single human action. This latter endeavor is represented in his "inquiry" into the causes of his father's own suicide, the result of his financial ruin in the stock market crash of 1929. In the same spirit, he adheres to a principle of limited inconsistency in his daily habits. He breaks daily habits as a matter of principle and maintains others for their sheer absurdity. In a similar vein, he adopts a series of masks to govern his life, but when his final mask, that of cynicism, collapses, his awareness of the absence of any ultimate rational justification for moral actions and values presses in on him, and he decides to commit suicide.

Ironically, it is only through a rigorous application of his philosophical insight that Todd is able subsequently to reject suicide. His original plan is to blow up a visiting showboat, Captain Adam's *Original and Unparalleled Floating Opera*, with its entire cast and audience aboard. As his name aptly suggests, Captain Jacob Adam fulfills a patriarchal role in presiding over a metaphorical image of life and the world. It is certainly significant that Hamlet's "To be, or not to be" soliloquy from William Shakespeare's *Hamlet* (1600-1601) and Jacques's

enumeration of the seven ages of man ("All the world's a stage") from *As You Like It* (1599-1600) are part of the performance. The importance of these speeches is belittled by the audience's hostile reaction to the second-rate actor who performs them; however, Todd appropriates the latter speech as a felicitous metaphor to substantiate his assertion that Hamlet's question is meaningless. In strict point of fact, Todd does not reject suicide; his attempt is thwarted for reasons he never discovers, but he does mark this failed attempt as a provisional turning point. After this event, Todd suggests that in the absence of absolutes of any kind, relative values might be lived by; it is with this tentative assertion that the novel closes.

The formal ingenuity in *The Floating Opera* and its mixture of bawdiness, low comedy, and intellectual seriousness identify it as a typical Barth novel. Although less extravagant than his subsequent large fictions and less involved technically than *Lost in the Funhouse*, *The Floating Opera* is essential to any understanding of Barth's development, and it is perhaps the most concise presentation of the ideas that form the dramatic and formal motivation for much of his later work.

THE SOT-WEED FACTOR

First published: 1960
Type of work: Novel

In the early eighteenth century, a young immigrant tobacco planter loses and then regains his Maryland estate.

Barth's third novel, perhaps his most widely acclaimed critical success, is written as a flamboyant imitation of an eighteenth century novel. His narrator adopts the tone and the locutions of eighteenth century narrators, and his descriptions of early colonial life in Maryland and of life in the London of the period are designed to recall the descriptions known of those places from contemporary literature. The importance of this narrative strategy is twofold: On one hand, the parodic imitation of an earlier novelistic style draws the reader's attention to the ways in which this narrative is purely a product of fictional conventions; on the other hand, the density of authentic historical detail in the text consistently suggests to the reader that Barth is re-creating a plausible, although wildly humorous, colonial milieu. By exploiting the tension between these competing claims, Barth is able to suggest the absence of any but a fictional order and at the same time present a compelling necessity for choice and action, as suggested by the realistic aspects of the novel.

One of the most conspicuous features of *The Sot-Weed Factor* is its immensely complicated plot, itself a feature of the assertion of artifice in Barth's fiction; like Barth's earlier fiction, *The Sot-Weed Factor* demonstrates his preoccupation with value and action. Ebenezer Cooke, the novel's protagonist and the son of a Maryland "sot-weed factor," or tobacco planter, is raised as an orphan in England together with his twin sister, Anna. After an education at home supervised by the family's tutor, Henry Burlingame, himself educated at the University of Cambridge but without familial connections, Ebenezer goes off to Cambridge, where his wild imagination and inability to take the world seriously make him an indifferent student at best. Ebenezer's disposition here recalls the problems of Todd Andrews in Barth's first novel and will be the source of many of his future difficulties.

After returning from Cambridge, Ebenezer embarks on a career as a poet in London. Hopelessly naïve, he takes his own innocence and literal virginity as a sign of his calling, and he obtains a commission as the poet laureate of Maryland before he is sent to that colony to oversee his father's estate. Again, Cooke's career as a poet is significant: There was a historical Ebenezer Cooke, who wrote well-known satires on life in colonial Maryland, including one that shares the title of Barth's novel. Parts of these poems are included in this narrative.

Cooke and his scheming servant are intercepted by pirates while crossing the Atlantic Ocean, and, after being taken prisoner, they are forced to walk the plank. They manage to swim to shore and make their way to Maiden, the site of Cooke's father's estate. Ebenezer then manages to lose his estate in a bizarre afternoon of impromptu colonial justice, and he only regains it with great difficulty, with the considerable help of Burlingame, his former tutor, who is embroiled in dark political intrigues in the American colonies involving Lord Baltimore, William Penn, the French, and the Indians. These political schemes are an important part of Barth's thematic concern with the absence of any sure knowledge in the world and with the often obscure effects of any single human action. These political machinations are complemented in the novel by the presence of Barth's rewriting of the journal of Captain John Smith, the early Virginia explorer and adventurer, which calls into question the Pocahontas legend—and, by implication, much early American history.

Ebenezer's sister, Anna, follows him to America, largely to pursue her passion for Burlingame, and these three are reunited at Maiden after the estate has been wrestled away from those who had turned it into a brothel and an opium den. In large part, Ebenezer's successful reclaiming of his plantation is dependent upon the good graces and legal authority of Joan Toast, a former London prostitute (and Ebenezer's first near-mistress). Although syphilitic and dying, she marries Ebenezer, and it is his consummation of this marriage that allows him to regain legal title to his inheritance. At the end of the narrative, Burlingame disappears into the machinations of political life, and Joan Toast dies along with her infant son, but Ebenezer's sister's son, Andrew, lives and is raised by Ebenezer and his sister at Maiden.

With the publication of his satire upon Maryland, Ebenezer's laureateship is withdrawn, but it is offered again later in his life by one of Lord Baltimore's heirs. Ebenezer declines this offer, however, and dies with little recognition. Barth's narrator uses this ending to assert the distance between fiction and fact by drawing attention to the regaining of Ebenezer's estate, which should be the natural conclusion to the story, and the ambiguous and inconclusive events that he describes at the end of the narrative. In this way, the structure of Barth's narrative and the narrator's commentary upon that structure are employed to reinforce the thematic preoccupations so consistently found in his fiction.

The Sot-Weed Factor marks an important advance in Barth's fiction. The use of parody, the elaborate structural devices in the novel, and the self-conscious narrator all point to strategies that Barth subsequently found increasingly congenial to his aesthetic program.

GILES GOAT-BOY: OR, THE REVISED NEW SYLLABUS

First published: 1966
Type of work: Novel

A young boy, raised among goats, attempts to transform the allegorical world/university in which he lives.

One of the attractions that *Giles Goat-Boy* held for its initial readers and that certainly contributed to its early commercial success was its sustained allegory. Barth employs the metaphor of the university as the ground of his setting so that the Cold War world is divided into Eastern and Western campuses, and the various quads are identified with the major powers of post-World War II politics.

For example, the United States corresponds to New Tammany, Germany to Siegfrieder College, Asia to the monastic world of T'ang, and the Soviet Union to Nikolay College. In Barth's novel, New Tammany is lead by Lucius Rexford, also known as "Lucky," a thinly disguised portrait of President John F. Kennedy. In addition, various political ideologies are presented in allegorical fashion: For example, communism is described as Student-Unionism. Events of twentieth century history are also represented in Barth's allegory so that, for example, World War II becomes Campus Riot II. The Eastern and Western campuses of Barth's world-as-university are each controlled by a separate computer, which is known by the acronym of WESCAC in the west, and Barth's novel is presented as a transcription of tapes from WESCAC's files.

Like the manipulation of eighteenth century novelistic conventions in *The Sot-Weed Factor,* the use of allegory in *Giles Goat-Boy* is designed to assert the fictional nature of Barth's narrative and to suggest at the same time a correspondence between this elaborate fiction and the historical world of the early 1960's.

Into this world Barth injects George, a young man who is raised by Max Spielman in the New Tammany goat barns. Max was essential to the New Tammany effort in Campus Riot II, but he has since been blacklisted and expelled from any place of power. George spends his early life as a goat, and his narrative gains much of its humor from its caprine perspective. After realizing his true calling, however, George sets off to pursue a human career in the world of New Tammany. He becomes convinced that his mission in life is to become Grand Tutor of the Western Campus and to achieve his own education, or commencement, with the ultimate aim of discovering his true identity and of setting New Tammany straight.

In his quest, George follows loosely the pattern of heroic adventure outlined by Joseph Campbell, the comparative mythographer, in his study *The Hero with a Thousand Faces* (1949). According to Campbell's pattern, or monomyth, the typical hero traces a course that leads him from initiation to illumination to disillusionment, and while Barth's George conforms to this course, he often does so ironically. This elaborate structural pattern is mocked, in part, to demonstrate the very limits of all imposed order. Despite the efforts of the False Tutor, Harold Bray, to thwart his education, and although often misled by his own misunderstandings, George does achieve a moment of mystical transcendence in the belly of WESCAC, the computer. Yet, like all mystical moments, this one is short-lived, and although George enjoys some brief notoriety, little changes in New Tammany. By the end of the novel's epilogue (or "Posttape"), George is saddened by his experiences, despairs of the future, and has withdrawn from active life in New Tammany.

Among the more interesting narrative devices in Barth's novel is the self-conscious commentary provided by the text's various framing devices. *Giles Goat-Boy* begins not with the story of George but with letters from various readers in a publishing house commenting upon the quality of this novel and upon the character of its author. This "Publisher's Disclaimer" is followed by a "Cover-Letter to the Editors and Publisher" written by a "J. B.," who then describes how he received his manuscript, titled *The Revised New Syllabus*, from one Stoker Giles. This series of frames suggests the confusion surrounding the question of authorship of the transcriptions, and it thereby echoes the preoccupation with truth and the impossibility of arriving at absolute certainty that haunts George's quest.

These frames also provide a self-conscious commentary on the narrative that they introduce; much the same effect is achieved when, at the height of George's quest, he asks a librarian for directions to Tower Clock. The librarian complies, but her response is read from a book, which appears to be *Giles Goat-Boy*—thus Barth's novel itself appears as an object in his narrative. This narrative moment dramatizes the thematic preoccupation with patterns and the struggle for the knowledge of order in the world.

While *Giles Goat-Boy* has not maintained the large reputation it enjoyed when it was published, it was an important book for Barth's career because it first signaled his growing interest in the ironic possibilities of myth, and it demonstrated a further step in his manipulation of structure and narrative techniques as formal correlatives for his thematic concerns.

LOST IN THE FUNHOUSE

First published: 1968
Type of work: Short stories

Through a series of stories that range from Homeric Greece to the contemporary United States, successive artist figures question their lives and their vocations.

The most experimental of Barth's works, *Lost in the Funhouse* employs an extreme narrative self-consciousness and the manipulation of narrative voices to dramatize Barth's continuing concern about values, action, and the absence of sustaining order in the world. At one point, Barth considered including a tape of his readings of these short narratives along with the book itself; this idea was abandoned, but it does suggest the extent to which Barth was exploring the limits of written narrative in the late 1960's. *Lost in the Funhouse* is a series of short narratives designed to be read together, like a novel, in the order that they are arranged. This notion is graphically represented by the first narra-

tive, a Möbius strip titled "Frame Tale," which, when cut and pasted according to the instructions, is emblematic of the cy-

cle. As the protagonists grow older in this series, the actual settings recede into the past, from twentieth century Maryland to classical Greece to the Homeric Greece of the Trojan War. The quest to understand the self and achieve a basis for value and action, however, remains a central concern.

An early series in *Lost in the Funhouse* describes the childhood experiences of Ambrose Mensch in Maryland immediately prior to and during World War II. Ambrose is a sensitive child whose keen awareness and nagging doubts recall the disposition of Ebenezer Cooke in *The Sot-Weed Factor*, and three stories describe the ironic circumstances of his naming, his call to become an artist, and his great moment of existential doubt as he is lost in the funhouse of the collection's title during a family vacation. As Ambrose's awareness and doubts grow, Barth's narrative techniques also become increasingly self-conscious, mirroring on the formal level the concerns he presents thematically. This pattern is repeated in the other narratives in the collection and perhaps reaches its climax in the convoluted frame structures of his "Menelaiad," a story about the self-doubts that plague the Greek hero Menelaus and his love for Helen of Troy.

Some of the narratives in this collection are quite gimmicky, while others are either extremely short or wildly complicated, but there is an overall unity in *Lost in the Funhouse* that revolves around the questions of individual identity, the possibility of value, and the limits of human knowledge. It is also significant in that it suggests the audacious climate of experimentation that characterized advanced American literature of the late 1960's.

SUMMARY

As perhaps the most sophisticated practitioner of postmodern fiction in the United States, Barth is a central figure in the literary history of the contemporary period. Each of Barth's books is consistent with the others in its pursuit of ideas and problems that Barth first considered, in their nascent form, very early in his career. Each Barth novel or short story is also distinctive in demonstrating a distinctive aspect of his technical prowess as a writer. While experimentation in and for itself has never been Barth's aim, his success as a novelist, in large part, has depended upon his willingness to take risks and to experiment—and to do so with a keen sense of the literary tradition in which he writes.

Thomas Carmichael

BIBLIOGRAPHY

By the Author

LONG FICTION:
The Floating Opera, 1956
The End of the Road, 1958
The Sot-Weed Factor, 1960
Giles Goat-Boy: Or, The Revised New Syllabus, 1966
Chimera, 1972 (three novellas)
Letters, 1979
Sabbatical: A Romance, 1982
The Tidewater Tales: A Novel, 1987
The Last Voyage of Somebody the Sailor, 1991
Once upon a Time: A Floating Opera, 1994
Coming Soon!!!, 2001

SHORT FICTION:
Lost in the Funhouse, 1968
On With the Story, 1996
The Book of Ten Nights and a Night: Eleven Stories, 2004

NONFICTION:
The Friday Book: Essays, and Other Nonfiction, 1984
Further Fridays: Essays, Lectures, and Other Nonfiction, 1995

DISCUSSION TOPICS

- John Barth once studied to become a jazz arranger. Does his literary technique have anything in common with jazz?

- Todd Andrews in *The Floating Opera* cannot bring himself to exclude any fact gathered in his research, presumably a consequence of the world lacking any ordering principle. Could this failing be explained in any other way?

- Explore the suggestions of the "alternative" title of *Giles Goat-Boy*, which is *The Revised New Syllabus*.

- Discuss the following assertion: Barth's novels frequently contain bawdy elements, but the novels themselves are not bawdy.

- Is there a contradiction involved in judging the world "absurd" and working as hard and long at educational and literary pursuits as Barth has?

- Although Barth's successive works have provoked surprise—it has never been easy to predict what he will do next—does not a careful study of his work reveal strikingly consistent features?

About the Author

Bowen, Zack R. *A Reader's Guide to John Barth*. Westport, Conn.: Greenwood Press, 1994.

Fogel, Stan, and Gordon Slethaug. *Understanding John Barth*. Columbia: University of South Carolina Press, 1990.

Harris, Charles B. *Passionate Virtuosity: The Fiction of John Barth*. Urbana: University of Illinois Press, 1983.

Morrell, David. *John Barth: An Introduction*. University Park: Pennsylvania State University Press, 1976.

Schulz, Max F. *The Muses of John Barth: Tradition and Metafiction from "Lost in the Funhouse" to "The Tidewater Tales."* Baltimore: Johns Hopkins University Press, 1990.

Scott, Steven D. *The Gamefulness of American Postmodernism: John Barth and Louise Erdrich*. New York: Peter Lang, 2000.

Waldmeir, Joseph J., ed. *Critical Essays on John Barth*. Boston: G. K. Hall, 1980.

Walkiewicz, E. P. *John Barth*. Boston: Twayne, 1986.

Ziegler, Heide. *John Barth*. New York: Methuen, 1987.

DONALD BARTHELME

Born: Philadelphia, Pennsylvania
April 7, 1931
Died: Houston, Texas
July 23, 1989

One of the most influential of the American avant-garde fiction writers of the post-World War II era, Barthelme produced four novels and a children's book but became most widely known for his highly distinctive short stories.

Bill Wittliff

BIOGRAPHY

Donald Barthelme was born in Philadelphia, where his parents had been students at the University of Pennsylvania. His father was an architect; his mother had studied English. A few years later, the family moved to Houston, where his father became a professor of architecture at the University of Houston.

Texas may seem an unlikely place for one of the most-discussed writers of nonlinear, "experimental" fiction to have developed, but Barthelme credits his father's interest in what, for the time, were advanced architectural styles with fostering his interest in the avant-garde. The house they lived in was designed by his father, and it was remarkable enough for Houston that, Barthelme has said, people used to stop their cars and stare at it. It was this interest of his father that Barthelme credited with being the most influential clement of his early years on his later development. In high school, Barthelme wrote for both the newspaper and the literary magazine. In 1949 he entered the University of Houston, majoring in journalism. During his sophomore year (1950-1951) he was the editor of the college newspaper, the *Cougar*. During this year he also worked as a reporter for the *Houston Post*.

In 1953, Barthelme was drafted into the U.S. Army, arriving in Korea the day the truce ending the Korean War was signed, at which point he became the editor of an Army newspaper. Upon his return to the United States, he once again became a reporter for the *Houston Post* and returned to the University of Houston, where he worked as a speechwriter for the university president and attended classes in philosophy. Although he attended classes as late as 1957, he ultimately left without taking a degree.

Barthelme has said that he read extensively during this period in a number of fields that he later integrated into his fiction: literature and philosophy as well as the social sciences. In 1956, he founded a literary magazine called *Forum*, where he developed an interest in the layout and design of the magazine as well as its literary content. This interest became evident in later years, when he began to incorporate graphics, usually nineteenth century lithographs, into his short stories. At the age of thirty, he became the director of Houston's Contemporary Arts Museum.

In 1962, Barthelme moved to New York to be the managing editor of the arts and literature magazine *Location*. His first published story, "The Darling Duckling at School" (later revised and printed as "Me and Miss Mandible"), appeared in 1961. His first story for *The New Yorker*, titled "L'Lapse," appeared in 1963. Since then, most of his works have appeared first in this magazine, to the point where Barthelme's name became almost a synonym for an ironic, fragmentary style that characterized its pages in the late 1960's and early 1970's. Erudite, brief, fragmentary, disjointed: His stories seemed to many to epitomize a certain New York (or *New Yorker*) attitude toward life in general. Barthelme also wrote film criticism for that magazine.

Barthelme's first collection of short stories, titled *Come Back, Dr. Caligari,* appeared in 1964. His first novel, *Snow White,* a modern takeoff on the fairy tale, appeared in 1967. Further short stories were collected in *Unspeakable Practices, Unnatural Acts* (1968), *City Life* (1970), *Sadness* (1972), *Amateurs* (1976), *Great Days* (1979), and *Overnight to Many Different Cities* (1983). Many critics see the height of his short-story production in the volume *City Life,* noting a tendency of his later stories either to repeat the techniques of the earlier ones or to become more like traditional short stories. Barthelme published two other novels before his death, *The Dead Father* (1975), which some commentators regard as his masterpiece, and *Paradise* (1986). A fourth novel, *The King,* appeared posthumously (1990). The first of two anthologies of previously published stories, titled *Sixty Stories,* appeared in 1981; a companion volume, *Forty Stories,* appeared in 1987.

Barthelme married twice. His only child was a daughter, Anne Katharine, born in 1965 to his first wife, Birgit. It was for Anne that he wrote his children's book, *The Slightly Irregular Fire Engine: Or, The Hithering Thithering Djinn,* which won a National Book Award in 1972. At his death from cancer on July 23, 1989, he was survived by his second wife, Marion.

Barthelme was a member of the American Academy and Institute of Arts and Letters, the Authors League of America, the Authors Guild, and PEN (International Association of Poets, Playwrights, Editors, Essayists, and Novelists). In addition to the National Book Award for his children's book, he was the recipient of a Guggenheim Fellowship in 1966 and the PEN/Faulkner Award for Fiction for *Sixty Stories.* Barthelme taught for brief periods at Boston University, the State University of New York, Buffalo, and the College of the City of New York, at the last of which he was Distinguished Visiting Professor of English from 1974 to 1975.

ANALYSIS

For the reader new to Barthelme, the most productive way to approach his works is in terms of what they are not: what they avoid doing, what they refuse to do, and what they suggest is not worth doing. Nineteenth century literature, and indeed most popular ("best-seller") literature of the twentieth and twenty-first centuries, is structured according to the two elements of plot and character. These two Barthelme studiously avoids, offering instead a collage of frequently amusing fragments whose coherence is usually only cumulative, rather than progressive.

The typical Barthelme story is brief and is based on an intellectual idea rather than an emotional one. Its plot is inevitably interrupted by seemingly unrelated subplots (or fragments of them) and contains elements whose presence is not immediately explicable—and indeed, whose only justification is precisely that they are without explanation. Its characters are usually little more than names attached to strings of talk, and the talk usually changes character many times during the course of the piece so that these hollow personages express themselves in a bewildering array of contents and tones of voice. Many times they are quoting, implicitly or explicitly, well-known philosophers who were much discussed in the 1960's and 1970's or mouthing the empty phrases of the advertising media. Several commentators have pointed to Barthelme's training in journalism and speechwriting to explain his fascination with the verbal detritus of modern society.

Barthelme's works are not for those whose formal education is deficient, nor are they for those who have lived in ignorance of the philosophical currents of Western thought in the second half of the twentieth century. For example, the title of "Kierkegaard Unfair to Schlegel" plays on the names of two nineteenth century European thinkers; "A Shower of Gold" refers to the way in which, according to the classical poet Ovid, Zeus appeared to a woman named Danae. "The Abduction from the Seraglio" quotes the title of an opera by Wolfgang Amadeus Mozart, and "The Death of Edward Lear" introduces as a character the author of nonsense verse. Barthelme's works, moreover, may not be for those from areas of the world untouched by New York's peculiar brand of edgy energy. Commentators have pointed out that Barthelme's works presuppose and celebrate a position of ironic distance from the demands of a competitive society. They will probably speak most directly to readers who have noted the debased status of words in Western industrial nations and noticed that the most widely disseminated utterances of the early twenty-first century seem to be the most trivial.

Barthelme is frequently classified as a postmodernist author, one of a generation of writers who came to international prominence in the late 1960's and the 1970's. Among other things, this label means that his most immediate predecessors are the modernist authors of the early years of the twentieth century such as T. S. Eliot, James Joyce, and Franz Kafka. Critics have split regarding whether Barthelme is doing fundamentally the same things as the earlier modernist authors or whether his works represent a significant development of their method. A number of the modernist authors, Gertrude Stein and Virginia Woolf among them, also rejected the nineteenth century's linear plot, with its development of characters and a definable beginning, middle, and end. Stein, for example, joined fragments into seemingly random strings or structured them by the sounds of the words themselves or by the associations they created in her mind. Woolf emphasized the individual fragmentary moment of perception and the associations of the minds of her characters instead of the development through societally determined factors. Eliot wrote a poetry of fragments (especially in *The Waste Land*, 1922) structured, according to some commentators, by contrast with a mythical world that had been lost. Joyce's *Ulysses* (1922) is certainly structured on this principle.

In addition, it is usually asserted with respect to Barthelme that his works evoke the fragmentary nature of modern urban life or the alienation of consciousness that such nineteenth century thinkers as Karl Marx and Friedrich Engels thought inevitable in industrial societies. This, too, was suggested by the modernists as a reason for the nature of their own works, most notably by Eliot. Yet, at the same time, Barthelme diverges from the modernists in that he seems to lack their belief in the power of art to change the world: His stance is ironic, self-deprecating, and anarchistic. The only reaction to the "disassociation of sensibility" of which Eliot spoke that is now possible, Barthelme seems to say, is the cackle of laughter. If there is a "message" in Barthelme's fiction, it would surely have to be that the problems of the late twentieth century lie (in William Wordsworth's phrase) too deep for tears and are, at any rate, beyond the capacities of the artist to affect them.

"A SHOWER OF GOLD"

First published: 1963 (collected in *Come Back, Dr. Caligari*, 1964)
Type of work: Short story

A young artist appears on a television quiz show and suffers a series of strange intrusions into his life.

"A Shower of Gold," one of the works from Barthelme's first collection of short stories, is a meditation on themes developed most fully by the existential philosopher Jean-Paul Sartre, whose influence on American thought was especially strong in the 1950's and 1960's. The story has more of a plot than do many of Barthelme's works, and it has a somewhat recognizable situation; its departures from reality are in the twists of situation and in the episodic interruptions by seemingly unconnected characters and plot developments.

The protagonist, a struggling New York artist named Peterson, is trying to get on a television program called *Who Am I?* The only qualification necessary is that he have strong opinions about some subject—a criticism on Barthelme's part of the premium that contemporary society placed on novelty over depth, and on the emphasis on the individual implied by making the fact of belief so important. Peterson gets on the show by citing surprising factual data as his opinion, and he is praised by the woman running the program, Miss Arbor, to the extent that he mouths the platitudes of Sartrean philosophy.

Miss Arbor eagerly asks Peterson if he is alienated, absurd, and extraneous: all the depressing things that Sartre held to define humankind's position in the universe. Nothing is so negative or weighty, Barthelme is saying, that it cannot be turned into glossy ad hype. Peterson resists Miss Arbor's attempt to pigeonhole him but agrees to go on the show. While waiting to do so, he has run-ins with a number of people: his exploitative manager, who wants him to compromise his artistic integrity by sawing his artworks in half so that they will sell better; his barber, who continues the flow of prepackaged Sartre; the president (whose secret-service agents invade Peterson's loft and attack him); the player of a "cat-piano" (made by pulling the tails of cats held fast in a frame); and three young women from California who preach a philosophy of "no problem" but exploit his kindness, as do all the others.

Despite these flickering, clearly absurd, and dreamlike happenings, Peterson continues to look for meaning in life. However, he sees the error of his ways when finally he does appear on the show and listens to the monologues of the other contestants. He then begins to free-associate, trailing off in the middle of a fairy-tale version of the tale of Zeus and Danae from which the story's title is derived and which constitutes Barthelme's simultaneous evocation of and brushing away of the myth of wholeness that will forever evade Peterson.

"THE INDIAN UPRISING"

First published: 1965 (collected in *Unspeakable Practices, Unnatural Acts,* 1968)
Type of work: Short story

Comanche Indians are attacking a city that seems to be Paris; the situation has echoes of an insurrection in a developing nation.

"The Indian Uprising" is Barthelme's vision of a world under siege, of civilization defined as perennially under attack from the forces of disorder that have entered into its very streets and define its mode of existence. The characters alternate an artistic café life with moments in which they torture and interrogate the Indians. The unnamed protagonist, referred to only in the first-person voice, asks a woman identified as Sylvia whether she thinks they are leading a good life. Her answer is in the negative, yet neither the protagonist nor the story suggests a means by which that life could be altered.

While the siege continues, the protagonist, whose descriptions of cafés and nightlife echo those of Ernest Hemingway writing of Paris, discusses the situation with a number of people, mixing battle reports with references to the nineteenth century French composer Gabriel Fauré, echoes of the so-called hyacinth girl in Eliot's *The Waste Land*, and quotations from William Shakespeare. He

stops to analyze the composition of one of the barricades (which results in a lengthy list of detritus); his conclusion is that he knows nothing. His main occupation, however, seems to be making a table.

One of his companions, a Miss R., echoes the Austrian philosopher Ludwig Wittgenstein and discourses on the nature of words. A cavalry regiment plays music from a series of Italian composers in streets named for American military heroes (in the fashion of streets and squares in Normandy). At the end, the Indians may have completely penetrated the city, but it seems as if the protagonist is readying himself to enter prison (he is asked for his belt and shoelaces), and in any case it may not matter.

This mixture of places and times seems intended to focus attention on the only thing that ties them all together: the fact that for the inhabitants of this city, torture and battle have become normal and are integrated into daily existence. Life has become defined as the response to a threat and would have no meaning without it. On a general level, this can be read as a repetition of Sigmund Freud's insistence that civilization is founded on repression. On a more specific level, it may be a portrait of a society that could not exist without its mobilization in war.

"AT THE END OF THE MECHANICAL AGE"

First published: 1973 (collected in *Amateurs,* 1976)
Type of work: Short story

An unnamed narrator weds a woman he meets at the grocery store. God comes to their wedding, but the couple divorces before their child is born.

"At the End of the Mechanical Age" is Barthelme's teasing meditation on the necessity and impossibility of conceptualizing human existence in the inhuman terms of "age" or "era." His point of departure is certainly the suggestion, first developed in the 1960's and 1970's, that industrial society was evolving into a state that would be fundamentally different from that which had defined it for the previous two centuries—what some commentators have called postindustrial society. Barthelme pokes fun at this notion without fundamentally overturning it, by having the two main characters, the unnamed "I" and his eventual wife, "Mrs. Davis," speak of "the end of the mechanical age" as if it were the same thing as talking about the end of the day, a precise thing with a particular nature and schedule.

They speculate on what will come after the mechanical age, as if an "age" were like a day or a season, but Barthelme's feelings come through in their agreement that whatever it will be, the age to follow will not be pleasant. In response to the question of whether there is anything to be done about all this, Mrs. Davis replies that the only solution is to "huddle and cling." Clearly, whatever will happen to humankind, it is not something that can be controlled, at least not by the average citizens that make up middle-class society.

The protagonist has met Mrs. Davis at the grocery store in front of the soap display; they hold hands before they speak, and when they do talk, it is for Mrs. Davis to express an opinion, as if on a television commercial, regarding one of the brands of soap. Later, they converse by singing songs of male and female savior figures named Ralph and Maude, who will redeem the world after the mechanical age has come to an end. Before it does, there is a flood, which echoes the end of the world that Noah survived; the two pass the time by drinking drinks of "scotch-and-floodwater" in their boat.

Even marriage as an institution is part of the mechanical age, which is why theirs must end. God, as much a character in all these developments as either of the human beings, comes to their wedding. The protagonist tries to get a clear view of the situation by asking God about the state of things, but he does little besides smile and disappear. Predictably, neither their marriage nor their child has had an effect on the alteration of ages, and at the end each leaves in search of his or her savior.

"THE EDUCATIONAL EXPERIENCE"

First published: 1973 (collected in *Forty Stories*, 1987)
Type of work: Short story

Students wander about a great fair, where the products of Western civilization are being offered in slipshod profusion.

"The Educational Experience" offers Barthelme's view not only of what current education consists—random facts with no coherence—but perhaps also of the worth of the entire sum of humankind's history: nothing. Barthelme's theory of history is contained in a fractured quotation from Wittgenstein that is offered by the "group leader" toward the end of the story: "The world is everything that was formerly the case." People are nothing but the bodies of their predecessors, which do not form into a coherent whole, as the chunks of citation and reference remain undigested. This past ranges from the Fisher King of the Holy Grail quest legends (whom T. S. Eliot claimed to have included in *The Waste Land*) to the television character Sergeant Preston of the Yukon.

Time has itself changed all those things from the past of which education consists. Another of the grail motifs that Eliot appropriated, the Chapel Perilous, has been turned into a bomb farm, and Antonio Vivaldi's concerto *The Four Seasons* has become *The Semesters*. Education is clearly no fun. The students are not allowed to smoke, but the narrator reflects that this is undoubtedly "necessary to the preservation of our fundamental ideas." Both the pretensions of the educators and the disinterest of the students are criticized: The students are told that they will be both more beautiful and more employable, but they are only in a hurry to get back on the bus that has brought them to this exposition. Those doing the educating are similarly in the dark: Several of the students are "off in a corner, playing with the animals," and the professors are unsure whether to "tell them to stop, or urge them to continue." As the narrator concedes, "perplexities of this kind are not infrequent, in our business."

Neither the students nor the teachers believe

what is being said, but both groups bravely play along as if they do. Both, it is clear, have lost touch with the real history of Western civilization, given that it has to be visited on a whirlwind tour. At the same time, however, this history has become both more trivial and more threatening, so that recovering it may not be as simple a thing as merely a change of method.

SNOW WHITE

First published: 1967
Type of work: Novel

A modern-day retelling of the German fairy tale of Snow White that ends badly.

Snow White is the first of Barthelme's four novels and is one of his most lucid works of any length, largely by virtue of the clarity with which he indicates to the reader at all points what it is that he is doing—or rather, what he is avoiding. The work includes references to what is being avoided so that the reader is aware of the avoidance.

Every reader knows the characters of the standard version of the fairy tale: Snow White, the handsome prince of whom she dreams, the wicked stepmother, and the seven dwarves who live in the forest and with whom Snow White finds refuge. Indeed, all of these have their equivalents in the characters of Barthelme's version, along with several others not in the fairy tale. In this version of the story, Snow White is twenty-two, lives with seven men with whom she regularly has unsatisfying sex in the shower, and seems to have confused herself

with Rapunzel from another fairy story, as she continually sits at her window with her hair hanging out. Her dwarves have modern names such as Bill (the leader), Clem, Edward, and Dan, and they suffer from a series of ailments, of which the most important seems to be that Bill no longer wishes to be touched. Dur-

ing the day, the seven men work in a Chinese baby-food factory.

The closest thing this retelling of the tale has to a prince is a man named Paul, who does not seem to want to fulfill his role of prince. Avoiding Snow White, he puts in time in a monastery in Nevada, goes to Spain, and joins the Thelemite order of monks. Ultimately he does end up near Snow White but only as a Peeping Tom in a bunker before her house, armed with binoculars. The story's version of the wicked queen is named Jane; she writes poison-pen letters and ultimately makes Snow White a poisoned drink, which Paul drinks instead. He dies. There is another character named Hogo (for which there is not a prototype in the fairy tale), who makes a play for Snow White. She rejects him, but he ends up taking on the role of chief dwarf, which Bill has vacated.

The underlying point of the contrast generated by these modernized versions of the fairy-tale characters is clearly that which was the point of Joyce's version of *Ulysses*, namely, that there are no heroes today. This, in fact, forms the center of the personality problem both of Paul, who does not want to act like a prince although he is one, and of Snow White, who is unsure about the nature of her role as Snow White: She continues to long for a prince, but at the same time she feels it necessary to undertake the writing of a lengthy (pornographic) poem that constitutes her attempt to "find herself."

Snow White is a somewhat more accessible work than many of Barthelme's short stories, partly because its greater length dilutes the quotations and echoes of philosophers, and partly because the use of the well-known story as a prototype gives the reader a sense of a larger structure. This frame also clears some space for Barthelme to fill with his verbal jokes, most of which are directed at pointing out to the reader how language constructs that which people take to be reality. The book also abounds in the same kind of mindless repetition of stock phrases by characters that characterizes "A Shower of Gold" and which was partly explained by "The Educational Experience."

SUMMARY

Barthelme was one of the most innovative and original writers of the second half of the twentieth century, drawing on and developing the themes and techniques of the modernists who preceded him. Avoiding plot and developed characters, his works are collages of the high and low, the sublime and ridiculous, of which modern society is constituted. In his short stories and novels, the fragmentary nature of modern society is both exemplified and exploited for comic effect, becoming both subject matter and technique of his writing.

Bruce E. Fleming

BIBLIOGRAPHY

By the Author

SHORT FICTION:
Come Back, Dr. Caligari, 1964
Unspeakable Practices, Unnatural Acts, 1968
City Life, 1970
Sadness, 1972
Amateurs, 1976
Great Days, 1979
Sixty Stories, 1981
Overnight to Many Distant Cities, 1983
Forty Stories, 1987

LONG FICTION:
Snow White, 1967
The Dead Father, 1975
Paradise, 1986
The King, 1990

CHILDREN'S LITERATURE:
The Slightly Irregular Fire Engine: Or, The Hithering Thithering Djinn, 1971

MISCELLANEOUS:
Guilty Pleasures, 1974
The Teachings of Don B.: Satires, Parodies, Fables, Illustrated Stories and Plays of Donald Barthelme, 1992 (Kim Herzinger, editor)
Not-knowing: The Essays and Interviews of Donald Barthelme, 1997 (Herzinger, editor)

About the Author

Barthelme, Helen Moore. *Donald Barthelme: The Genesis of a Cool Sound*. College Station: Texas A&M University Press, 2001.
Gordon, Lois. *Donald Barthelme*. Boston: Twayne, 1981.
Hudgens, Michael Thomas. *Donald Barthelme: Postmodernist American Writer*. Lewiston, N.Y.: Edwin Mellen Press, 2001.
Klinkowitz, Jerome. *Donald Barthelme: An Exhibition*. Durham, N.C.: Duke University Press, 1991.
McCaffery, Larry. *The Metafictional Muse: The Works of Robert Coover, Donald Barthelme, and William H. Gass*. Pittsburgh: University of Pittsburgh Press, 1982.

DISCUSSION TOPICS

- Donald Barthelme's father's architectural achievements strongly influenced him. What features of the son's literary work might be considered analogous to architectural ones?

- Assess the suitability of several of Barthelme's short story titles.

- Plot and character are not particularly important to Barthelme. How does this fact relate to his concentration on the short story form rather than on the novel?

- What other characteristics of Barthelme's philosophy of literary composition suit his predilection for the short story?

- Judging from the story "The Educational Experience," what has gone wrong with the study of history? Does the story contain suggestions as to how it might be better taught?

- The tale of Snow White has often been ridiculed and parodied. What elements of this fairy tale does Barthelme appear to take most seriously?

- What are some of the targets in Barthelme's attack on modern culture?

Donald Barthelme

Molesworth, Charles. *Donald Barthelme's Fiction: The Ironist Saved from Drowning.* Columbia: University of Missouri Press, 1982.

Olsen, Lance, ed. *Review of Contemporary Fiction* 11 (Summer, 1991).

Patteson, Richard F., ed. *Critical Essays on Donald Barthelme.* New York: G. K. Hall, 1992.

Roe, Barbara L. *Donald Barthelme: A Study of the Short Fiction.* New York: Twayne, 1992.

Stengel, Wayne B. *The Shape of Art in the Short Stories of Donald Barthelme.* Baton Rouge: Louisiana State University Press, 1985.

Trachtenberg, Stanley. *Understanding Donald Barthelme.* Columbia: University of South Carolina Press, 1990.

Waxman, Robert. "Apollo and Dionysus: Donald Barthelme's Dance of Life." *Studies in Short Fiction* 33 (Spring, 1996): 229-243.

ANN BEATTIE

Born: Washington, D.C.
September 8, 1947

Sometimes called a voice of the "Woodstock generation," Beattie writes indirect short stories and novels that depict "numbed" characters struggling to find happiness.

Sigrid Estrada

BIOGRAPHY

Ann Beattie was born in Washington, D.C., on September 8, 1947, the only child of Charlotte Crosby Beattie and James A. Beattie. She attended the Lafayette Elementary School and graduated from high school in Washington, D.C., in 1965. Her father was a grants management specialist for the Department of Health, Education, and Welfare. If Beattie did not find her early schooling very stimulating, she seems to have been preparing in some fashion for writing even during her childhood. In an interview with Patrick H. Samway, Beattie explained:

> I was an only child. . . . It is often true of only children that they become watchers because they belong to small families and are tightly bonded to those units. . . . I am continually squirreling away situations that I don't consciously realize are registering.

It was in college that she began to take literature seriously. She took a course with Frank Turaj, who, she says, "taught me how to read." She received a B.A. degree from the American University in 1969 and matriculated as a graduate student in English at the University of Connecticut. It was there that she started submitting stories for publication; she received her master's degree in 1970. "A Rose for Judy Garland's Casket" was her first story pub-

lished, and in the same year, 1972, she withdrew from the doctoral program. Beattie later explained that she was miserable and that she simply decided to write instead of "reading criticism about writing all day."

In 1973, she married David Gates, a fellow University of Connecticut graduate student and a musician and writer as well. Beattie published "Victor Blue," in *The Atlantic Monthly*, that same year, and her first story to appear in *The New Yorker*, "A Platonic Relationship," came out a year later.

Beattie has been a visiting writer as well as a lecturer at the University of Virginia. At Harvard University she held a Guggenheim Fellowship and was a Briggs Copeland lecturer. Doubleday brought out the short-story collection *Distortions* and Beattie's first novel, *Chilly Scenes of Winter*, almost simultaneously in 1976. United Artists released *Chilly Scenes of Winter* as a film in 1979, calling it *Head Over Heels*. *Falling in Place*, a second novel, received an award from the American Academy and Institute of Arts and Letters when it appeared in 1980, and Beattie was again invited to be a visiting writer at the University of Virginia. Not surprisingly, her alma mater, the American University, recognized her as one of its distinguished alumni.

A second short-story collection, *Secrets and Surprises* (1978), was followed by the collections *Jacklighting* (1981) and *The Burning House* (1982). In May of 1982, Beattie and Gates were divorced. *Love Always*, her third novel, was published in 1985, and a fifth short-story collection, *Where You'll Find Me, and Other Stories*, was published in 1986. With her fourth novel, *Picturing Will* (1989), Beattie extended her literary domain dramatically; the novel was well received, gaining a front-page review in the book review section of *The New York Times*. Beattie has homes in Charlottesville, Virginia, and Key West, Florida, with her second husband, painter Lincoln Perry.

ANALYSIS

Critic Christina Murphy has called Beattie a neorealist who uses an equivocal voice. Unlike the univocal narrator, the equivocal narrator does not offer the reader a particular perspective or interpretation; the equivocal narrator simply offers accumulated detail. Therefore, readers must approach Beattie's works actively—they must be acutely aware of Beattie's fine distinctions of character and circumstance.

Critics do not challenge Beattie's characters' credibility; an occasional critic, however, challenges her interest in her milieu. If many of Beattie's characters closely resemble a select segment of her generation's college graduates, some certainly do not. "Dwarf House," one of the short stories in *Distortions*, provides one example. Unlike his self-pitying mother, his confused brother, and several other miserable characters outside the Dwarf House, James accepts his physical limitations and his options realistically. Although he must stand on a chair to meet people of normal height eye to eye, he has found work, friendship, and love. James can be happy.

Even before she gave readers a small clue to her complex irony and seeming detachment by using as her copyright "Irony and Pity, Inc.," Beattie revealed an extraordinary understanding of human personality and the dynamics of human relationships. Engaging readers by forcing them to verify behavior and events with their own experiences before they can understand her fiction seems to be Beattie's technique. The reader need not be as nonjudgmental as Beattie seems to be.

Most of Beattie's characters are engaged in some kind of struggle for happiness. Often they are self-alienated. A great number of characters in *Distortions* seem to think and function inappropriately; they are doomed to struggle and fail. None of the lovers in "Four Stories About Lovers" seems happy; few are faithful. "The Lifeguard" is the story of the drowning of four children whose boat is set afire by one who has brought along gasoline.

It is only those characters like the dwarf James and his bride in "Dwarf House" who may love and marry in anything near ecstasy. There is some gift in a capacity for love. Sam, in "Snakes' Shoes" in the same collection, can help the child of estranged parents by using the magic of imagination and love to transform antagonists into friends. Like Sam and James, Noel in "Vermont" empathically consoles the narrator when her husband leaves her. "You're better off," he reassures her, and she is certainly better off when Noel is ready to love her. A young Georgetown student, Sam, in "A Platonic Relationship," can give Ellen, a music teacher, a fulfilling, if not a permanent or conventional, relationship.

In the collection titled *Secrets and Surprises*, the struggles continue. For the main character in "Shifting," for example, happiness is synonymous with independent movement and eventual sexual freedom. In *The Burning House*, several key characters learn to recognize their own pain, a certain requisite to alleviation of suffering. In those instances they are far more aware of the reality of their own experience than are all the characters in *Falling in Place*, who probably terrify more than one reader (and critic) by their disengagement.

In more recent writing, such as *Where You'll Find Me*, a short-story collection, and *Picturing Will*, a novel, Beattie retains her equivocal narrative stance, but her important characters show courage in finding and losing love; they act as foils distinguishing responsible nurturing from wanton irresponsibility in their behavior.

"DWARF HOUSE"

First published: 1975 (collected in *Distortions*, 1976)
Type of work: Short story

A dwarf and his new bride seem to have found the happiness that eludes the "normal" members of his family.

"Dwarf House," which first appeared in *The New Yorker* magazine, was included in the first collection of Beattie's short stories, *Distortions*, the following year. Because in this story James and his bride, both little people, are the only characters to have found happiness, Beattie seems to pose a question about the essentials for contentment. In contrast to James and his bride-to-be, MacDonald, the so-called normal brother, returns from a visit to the "dwarf house" (inhabited by one of his brothers, several other dwarves, and a giant) to report to his self-pitying mother not only that James refuses to return to the home of his previous misery but also that James is working, he is in love, and he plans to be married. When MacDonald telephones his own wife from his office with the usual "late-night meeting" excuse, after which he takes his secretary for a drink, he discovers that more things are askew. His secretary manages to smile only with the help of drugs, and she has recently had an abortion.

When the family assembles for James's wedding, the minister releases a bird from its cage to symbolize "the new freedom of marriage and the ascension of the spirit." This is marvelously apt, for the bride's true radiance challenges all the "normal" characters—MacDonald, his wife, MacDonald and James's mother—to a painful awareness, but only if they can perceive it.

"VERMONT"

First published: 1975 (collected in *Distortions*, 1976)
Type of work: Short story

A woman whose husband has just left her ponders whether she loves a male friend enough to move in with him.

In "Vermont," characters in a typical Beattie milieu are revealed in intimate relationships. Noel, whose wife, Susan, has finally had to tell him that she has been having an affair, comforts the narrator when her own husband, David, announces his imminent departure. Although Beattie seldom describes her characters physically, Noel, the more generous and understanding lover, appears to be physically awkward and unattractive compared with David, who, early in the story, pities Noel for his "poor miserable pajamas."

Noel tells the narrator that she "will be better off" without David, and he does his best to take David's place as a friend and a father to her young daughter. When he eventually suggests that she

and her daughter move in with him, she considers and finally protests that she cannot say that she loves him. He answers, "Nobody has ever loved me and nobody ever will. What have I got to lose?" If the narrator really does not love him, however, she has much to lose. When she later reveals that she has been considering his comment carefully, possibly because she does not find him unlovable (and cannot accept the bleak outlook he has for himself), he comments, "Well, I've told you about every woman I ever slept with. Which one do you suspect might love me?" They are speaking by telephone, and the narrator whispers to herself, "Me!"

David appears again at the story's end to visit his former wife and his daughter and to reveal the extent of his confusion in his current relationship; he is not happy with his new girlfriend.

"SHIFTING"

First published: 1978 (collected in *Secrets and Surprises*, 1978)
Type of work: Short story

A teenage boy teaches a woman married to a controlling husband how to shift.

"Shifting," in the collection *Secrets and Surprises*, is about the focal character's need for emotional change as well as her means of finding it: being taught to drive a standard transmission Volvo by a teenager who likes and perhaps understands her.

Natalie is in a bind: She has a rigid, controlling husband who does not even laugh at her jokes. Although both she and her husband have agreed to sell the old Volvo left to them by Natalie's uncle, she puts prospective buyers off and secretly learns to drive the car. Sharing her husband's car has been too restrictive.

Michael is a local teenager who delivers the evening newspaper to the old lady next door and is puzzled that Natalie's husband has not taken the trouble to teach his wife to "shift." Telling her, "You can decide what it's worth when you've learned," he charges her four dollars after her fourth and final lesson. She has allowed him, not herself, to assess a value for her lessons. Natalie finds the money she gave him neatly folded on the floor mat when she returns to the car two hours after entering Michael's house for a drink: Shifting need not apply exclusively to driving.

"LEARNING TO FALL"

First published: 1979 (collected in *The Burning House*, 1982)
Type of work: Short story

Ruth, a single parent, and a friend of hers contemplating a new relationship are both learning that grace is an aspect of courage.

Characters in two of the short stories in *The Burning House* represent definitive types that appear in Beattie's novels. Ruth in "Learning to Fall," the collection's first story, is a loving, nurturing, single parent and friend. She is "learning to fall"—literally, in a dance class, but figuratively as well—to accept the inevitable. Her husband left her while she was pregnant, and her lover admires her but does not want any of the responsibility of Ruth, whose son, Andrew, was damaged in the process of being born.

The narrator of the story, a friend of Ruth, has a sometime lover, Ray, who visits with Andrew and the narrator, showing great gentleness to the two; they regularly take the excursion to New York so that Ruth can entertain her lover in Westport. In a restaurant with Andrew and the narrator, Ray patiently tries to help Andrew locate his gloves. When all three leave the restaurant to return to the street, the narrator sees herself with Ray and Andrew and imagines the possibility of the inevitable relationship. Perhaps she is falling. She decides that at least she can be like her friend Ruth and "aim for grace."

In "The Burning House," the title story of the collection in which "Learning to Fall" appears, there is a character who may be called a second definitive type. Frank behaves in a way that suggests to the narrator, his wife, that her frustrating marriage is deteriorating. Frank has made the important decisions: He has even "chosen the house," and the house is burning. In the final scene, with the couple in bed, Frank delivers to his wife what some critics have recognized as the ultimate insult—his conception of the difference between the sexes:

Men think they're Spiderman and Buck Rogers and Superman. You know what we all feel inside that you don't feel? That we're going to the stars. . . . I'm looking down on all this from space. . . . I'm already gone.

FALLING IN PLACE

First published: 1980
Type of work: Novel

A frustrated teacher of summer school gets to know an unhappy family in which the father and mother are separated and the young son wounds his sister with a gun.

In Greek myth, Icarus's exuberantly beating wings hurl him toward the sun, where they melt, and he plunges to his death in the sea. The Icarian figure adorning the cover of *Falling in Place* suggests the downside of youthful aspiration; the major characters in *Falling in Place* do not take control of their lives. Instead, they seem to fall numbly into place through indirection.

Of all the major characters in the novel, only Cynthia Forrest seems fully aware of how disappointing she finds her own life. From her standpoint, she is wasting a very good mind trying to teach summer-school students about literature. Perhaps ironically, her students dub her "Lost-in-the-Forrest"; from their standpoint, the name is apt. Cynthia does not usually concern herself with students as individuals, and she is using an anthology of excerpts, so the literature may seem unreal and the students' personal experience irrelevant. The students' welfare does not seem to be a concern for Cynthia. She becomes involved with one student, Mary, only when Mary's father, John Knapp, expresses concern about Mary's summer-school work and makes a date to talk to her teacher.

The conference between parent and teacher is not without some sexual overtones, and it takes place in a restaurant. If Mary's welfare is really at issue here, it is lost in the dynamics of multiple protocols: the protocol of the business lunch, the protocol of the relationship between parent and teacher, and the unstated protocol between a young, attractive woman and an ostensibly successful man.

The summer-school class has disturbed Cynthia.

One of her common nightmares, dreamed often after teaching, is that she is falling. Cynthia (realistically) believes that she is not reaching her students. She does not seem to realize that she has failed to help them link literature to their lives. The best Cynthia can do is to keep herself minimally functional. Her own love life is disappointing until the very end of the novel, when her whimsical, immature lover, Spangle, returns from Madrid, where he had rescued his wayward brother, and New York, where he failed to rekindle an old flame.

Most of the characters in *Falling in Place* are dying in their tracks. At the instigation of a friend who has proved himself monstrous in many respects, John Knapp's ten-year-old son, John Joel, shoots his sister Mary. He had not known the gun was loaded.

John Knapp has been living with his mother in Rye, New York, where he is close to work and to his mistress, Nina. The family remains in Connecticut to be visited on weekends. The youngest of the Knapp children was brought to his paternal grandmother's house to cheer her when the family first learned that she may have cancer. Louise, who is John's wife and the children's mother, did not attempt to keep her child. She even relinquishes John Joel after the shooting, and she accepts her divorce from John with philosophical stoicism.

The one time the readers see Louise in close contact with one of her children is when she takes John Joel berry-picking and picnicking. On that occasion, Louise and John Joel speak of intimate things. Included in the heavy baggage that John Joel needs to unload is the revelation that his friend Parker has found his mother's diaphragm and put a pinhole in it. Parker is hardly a good friend for John Joel, but there are no others available; Mary does not have a choice of friends either. Except for one unsatisfactory friend each, the Knapp children are alienated from other kids. The shooting, although it is technically an accident, is the climax of a great deal of mutual hostility.

John Knapp is having an affair with Nina, who not very much older than his daughter. She is stronger than he is in many ways, but she is dissatisfied with her job, as well as her home—a small, womblike apartment, where John feels safe and she feels cramped. Nina cannot understand how John can be materially rich and yet so dissatisfied. Nina believes that money will make her happy.

By the novel's end, John Knapp has left his family to be with Nina, John Joel has joined his baby brother at their grandmother's house, Louise is helping Mary recover, and Cynthia is greeted by the returned Spangle. No problems have been resolved, and it is not likely that anybody will be very happy. On the very last page of the novel, however, there is an upbeat answer to what seems to be a trivial question. Greeted by her old boyfriend, Spangle, and hearing about his brother's lost keys and money, Cynthia asks what was wished for when everything was thrown into the fountain. Spangle's answer is, "The usual, I guess."

PICTURING WILL

First published: 1989
Type of work: Novel

A photographer whose husband has left her raises her son, Will; the reader learns that her second husband, Mel, is the most nurturing "parent" in the novel.

Will's mother, Jody, is a professional photographer; the novel's title is eventually seen to be both apt and ironic. Human growth certainly requires love and devotion more than it does the commercial virtues of glitz and promotion. In the opening chapter of the section, titled "Mother," the reader is told, "Only a baby—someone who truly needed her care—could have made [Jody] rise to the occasion" when Wayne leaves her. Jody does become a famous and gifted photographer who shows extraordinary insight, a sense of drama, and an unusual capacity for composition. She is a successful wedding photographer as well. It is significant, however, that the picture of Will that she carries with her is actually rubbed out and almost indecipherable; the real picture is an internal one. It is with intuitive accuracy that Jody chooses the right community for her early success, the suitable parent (not the biological one) for her son, and the agent who (though a child molester) successfully promotes her artistic career. In this novel, one good apple, Mel, the adoptive father, decontaminates the bunch.

If petty, vain, irresponsible men are unfit fathers, then Wayne has done both his wife and son the greatest service by abandoning them. Originally having met Jody by accident, Wayne is inca-

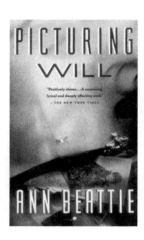

pable of growth: "Wayne read books—not to expand his horizons . . . but to reinforce the limits of what he believed." Wayne finds purpose neither in work nor in close, trusting relationships.

The final portion of the novel describes Wayne's life: his relationship with his third wife, his attitude toward his male coworkers and bar chums, and his affairs with other women. He is "lucky" with other women, but he otherwise feels sorry for himself. His resentment of Jody's refusal to have an abortion and his consequent resentment of Will is made clear in his relationship with Will when he visits with him in Florida. Corky, Wayne's third wife, and Zeke, his work associate, are far more supportive and nurturing of Will than is Wayne.

Wayne's affairs are given sexually explicit treatment—unusual in Beattie's works. The details emphasize Wayne's vanity and selfishness, no less his immaturity. When one of his lovers allows Wayne to use her estate for a pool party, he entertains Will and all of his own friends. His ultimate act of bravado is to urinate in the pool.

When Wayne's luck with women turns, he is erroneously charged with drug dealing, a charge appropriate only to his former girlfriend. As Will is being prepared for an early return flight to New York to pose with his mother in a picture for *Vogue*, he looks out a bathroom window to see his father being taken into custody by two policemen. This, a strange experience involving Haveabud, the man who becomes his mother's agent, and his disap-

pointment in not being able to see his dear friend, Wag, are heavy childhood agonies.

Mel is an intellectually as well as an emotionally sustaining force in the novel. In what Christina Murphy calls "inner narratives" in *Picturing Will*—italicized whole chapters are found finally to be journal entries of Mel—he beautifully describes the parent's plight. One often-quoted passage is worth repeating:

> Do everything right, all the time, and the child will prosper. It's as simple as that, except for fate, luck, heredity, chance, the astrological sign under which the child was born, his order of birth, his first encounter with evil, the girl who jilts him in spite of his excellent qualities, the war that is being fought when he is a young man, the drugs he may try once or too many times, the friends he makes . . . and animals with rabies.

Mel is a true lover and a devoted father. It is he who drives Will to Florida to visit his natural father, Wayne, and who willingly works for Haveabud because he will promote Jody's artwork in New York. In the last section of the novel, "Child," the reader sees that Mel's faith that he and Will can "stand firm" and make it is justified. The now happily married Will is coaxing his own son to continue the cycle as he urges, "Come on, baby. Throw me the ball."

SUMMARY

Beattie's stories and novels demonstrate that she is, as she has said she hoped to be seen as, "astute about human behavior." Her stories about people struggling to make their peace with the world and find contentedness have struck a strong chord with a generation of readers who came of age in the 1960's and 1970's. In her novel *Picturing Will*, she moved beyond her indirect portrayals of alienation to a depiction of a nurturing parent, a universal father.

Judith Schnee

BIBLIOGRAPHY

By the Author

SHORT FICTION:
Distortions, 1976
Secrets and Surprises, 1978
Jacklighting, 1981
The Burning House, 1982
Where You'll Find Me, and Other Stories, 1986
What Was Mine, and Other Stories, 1991
Park City: New and Selected Stories, 1998
Perfect Recall: New Stories, 2001

LONG FICTION:
Chilly Scenes of Winter, 1976
Falling in Place, 1980
Love Always, 1985
Picturing Will, 1989
Another You, 1995
My Life, Starring Dara Falcon, 1997
The Doctor's House, 2002

NONFICTION:
Alex Katz, 1987

CHILDREN'S LITERATURE:
Goblin Tales, 1975
Spectacle, 1985

DISCUSSION TOPICS

- Ann Beattie is said to be nonjudgmental about her characters. Does this detachment makes her characters more or less realistic and complex?

- How does Beattie create ironic distance between her narrators and the characters and events being described?

- Show how Beattie's treatment of the struggle for happiness differs in two of her short stories.

- How does "Dwarf House" question the idea of normality?

- How is driving a metaphor for the complexities of life in "Shifting"?

- Is *Falling in Place* only the story of a dysfunctional family or does it say something about such themes as individuality and responsibility?

- What does *Picturing Will* seem to be saying about the nature of parenthood?

About the Author

Centola, Steven R. "An Interview with Ann Beattie." *Contemporary Literature* 31 (Winter, 1990): 405-422.
Friedrich, Otto. "Beattieland." *Time* 135 (January 22, 1990): 68.
Hill, Robert W., and Jane Hill. "Ann Beattie." *Five Points* 1 (Spring/Summer, 1997): 26-60.
McCaffery, Larry, and Sinda Gregory. "A Conversation with Ann Beattie." *Literary Review* 27 (Winter, 1984): 165-177.
Montresor, Jaye Berman, ed. *The Critical Response to Ann Beattie*. Westport, Conn.: Greenwood Press, 1993.
Murphy, Christina. *Ann Beattie*. Boston: Twayne, 1986.
Plath, James. "Counternarrative: An Interview with Ann Beattie." *Michigan Quarterly Review* 32 (Summer, 1993): 359-379.
Schneiderman, Leo. "Ann Beattie: Emotional Loss and Strategies of Reparation." *American Journal of Psychoanalysis* 53 (December, 1993): 317-333.
Young, Michael W., and Troy Thibodeaux. "Ann Beattie." In *A Reader's Companion to the Short Story in English*, edited by Erin Fallon, R. C. Feddersen, James Kurtzleben, Maurice A. Lee, Susan Rochette-Crawley, and Mary Rohrberger. Westport, Conn.: Greenwood Press, 2001.

SAUL BELLOW

Born: Lachine, Quebec, Canada
June 10, 1915
Died: Brookline, Massachusetts
April 5, 2005

Critically recognized as one of the most significant American novelists of the twentieth century, Bellow has depicted the hero as a sensitive sufferer pitted against the values of a materialistic age.

© The Nobel Foundation

BIOGRAPHY

Saul Bellow's parents were Russian Jews who had emigrated to Canada. A precocious, intelligent child, he had learned not only English but also Yiddish, Hebrew, and French by the time the family moved to Chicago in 1924. Bellow always considered Chicago his spiritual birthplace. In 1933, he graduated from Tuley High School and enrolled in the University of Chicago, where, by his own account, he was peripatetic in his studies, drifting from one course to another, registering for one but finding another more interesting. Among novelists, Theodore Dreiser and Joseph Conrad were particular favorites, though Bellow seems to have read widely, especially in sociology. He received his bachelor's degree with honors in sociology and anthropology in 1937.

During those years before World War II, Bellow was living in Chicago and learning his art, writing on a bridge table in a back bedroom of his apartment during the day. His first wife, Anita Goshkin, was a social worker, and she helped support him while he wrote. By 1938 he had gotten a job with the Works Progress Administration (WPA) as a biographer of local novelists and poets, a position that not only paid some of the bills but also satisfied

his intellectual appetite for wide reading, which included the works of such novelists as Sherwood Anderson and "homespun" poets such as Edgar Lee Masters and Vachel Lindsay. Bellow's interest in Anderson is significant, as the grotesque, alienated characters of Anderson's works can be seen as being transmuted into the suffering human beings seeking meaning that appear in Bellow's novels.

Bellow's first story, "Two Morning Monologues," appeared in 1941; it is a short, slight tale in which Bellow clearly showed that he was still an apprentice. He served a brief term in the U.S. Merchant Marine, and, like Joseph, the main character in his first novel, *Dangling Man* (1944), Bellow waited out World War II. His intellectual breadth secured for him a job on the editorial staff of the "Great Books" project of the *Encyclopedia Britannica*; he also taught English briefly at the University of Minnesota in 1946. *Dangling Man* is a self-consciously austere work, tracing its hero's growing disaffection from society, his wife, and himself as he waits to be drafted. The diary format, reflective of Joseph's thoughts and tensions, is skillfully handled and allows Bellow to portray Joseph's conflicts in psychological rather than chronological time.

Set in New York City, *The Victim*, Bellow's second novel, was published in 1947. It focuses on Asa Leventhal, a Jew, who tries to come to terms with the guilt imputed to him by his Gentile friend Allbee, who accuses Asa of complicity in Allbee's failure in life. The themes of guilt and responsibility intertwine and deepen the character of Asa as "sufferer with dignity," one of the characteristics of the so-called Bellovian hero. The book brought its author a more solid reputation and helped earn for him a Guggenheim Fellowship in 1948. Bellow went to live in Paris. For the next few years, he traveled about Europe and began work on his third novel.

The Adventures of Augie March (1953) won the National Book Award and established Bellow as one of the United States' most important novelists. Augie became a new kind of literary cult hero—the intellectual vagabond whose travels across the United States revealed him to be a sensitive soul driven to find a higher reality amid the soul-killing materialism of modern society.

Throughout the 1950's, Bellow lived in New York City, teaching at several universities and publishing a number of short stories, articles, and book reviews. Another marriage came and, in 1955, another Guggenheim award. In 1956 Bellow brought out his fourth novel. *Seize the Day* is recognized as one of its author's most important works. Powerful in its economy, the book is a forceful account of a day in the life of Tommy Wilhelm, a loser with a soul. Like Gimpel the Fool, the hero in Isaac Bashevis Singer's classic short story (which Bellow had translated from the Yiddish in 1953), Tommy engages the reader's sympathy in spite of his foolishness and his failures because of a capacity for turning his suffering into a meaningful form of endurance. Tommy prevails, saddened and chastened, the representative of mid-twentieth century man.

By the time of his fifth novel, *Henderson the Rain King* (1959), Bellow had achieved that rare distinction of being both popularly acclaimed and critically recognized. In that novel, the theme of success, already treated in *Seize the Day*, is reworked. Eugene Henderson is a success—a millionaire who sets out for Africa in an attempt to find spiritual coin as a replacement for the tedium of his personal affluence.

In the early 1960's, Bellow served as coeditor of a short-lived periodical, *The Noble Savage*, an intellectual journal of human culture. He also continued to teach, now at the University of Chicago, an institution with which he became regularly associated throughout the 1960's and 1970's. *Herzog* (1964), his sixth novel, is often regarded as his best. It won the National Book Award, and with it Bellow came to be regarded as America's foremost contemporary novelist. Moses Herzog, whose letters to the world-at-large are both a plea for understanding and a commitment to life, spoke to the world of the 1960's, as Augie and Tommy had to the world of the 1950's.

The mid-1960's saw also the production of several plays, notably *The Last Analysis* (1964), which had a short run on Broadway. Three one-act plays in 1965 met with failure. Dramatically confusing, the plays drift from heavy-handed portentiousness to farce. This brief experience as dramatist was Bellow's last attempt at writing for the stage.

By contrast, his next novel, *Mr. Sammler's Planet* (1970), became a best seller and won for Bellow a third National Book Award. In spite of critical acclaim, however, the novel was puzzling to many readers because of its "metaphysical" cast—it contains long passages of philosophical speculation by its protagonist, Mr. Sammler, an old man whose main interest is the study of a thirteenth century mystic, Meister Eckhardt. With the publication of *Humboldt's Gift* (1975), Bellow reached the pinnacle of his literary career. This comic novel of great zest and insight garnered the Pulitzer Prize for 1975; in the following year, Bellow, then sixty-one, received the highest accolade in literature, the Nobel Prize.

Bellow's first nonfiction work also appeared in 1976. *To Jerusalem and Back: A Personal Account* describes the novelist's visit to Israel, and it deals with the special problems of survival faced by that nation. *The Dean's December* (1982) is viewed as a disappointing novel. Void of the comic gusto that marks Bellow's best work, the book is a novel of ideas in the spirit of *Mr. Sammler's Planet*, recording the philosophical meditations of its protagonist as he contends with the destructive political and social forces represented in the Communist city of Bucharest, to which he travels, and the American city of Chicago, to which he returns.

Him with His Foot in His Mouth, and Other Stories appeared in 1984, and the 1980's concluded with three more novellas. *More Die of Heartbreak* (1987) features, once again, one of Bellow's intellectual heroes, this time a college professor of Russian literature who comes to the United States from Paris in search of his visionary uncle. Written when Bellow was in his early seventies, the book typifies the author's continuing affirmation of human values amid the crushing dysfunction of modern life. A

Theft and *The Bellarosa Connection* appeared in 1989. Though lacking the scope of his earlier work, these novellas, especially the latter, probe the connection between guilt and responsibility and insist, finally, on the primacy of the human spirit.

Bellow's last novel, *Ravelstein*, was published in 2000. This book can be seen as a kind of farewell, in which Bellow voices the same concern about the survival of the human spirit amid the luxurious entanglements of contemporary life. Abe Ravelstein has achieved personal success, wealth, and fame, but his cynicism has made him basically a lonely, alienated man.

ANALYSIS

What sets Bellow's novels apart from those of his major contemporaries, such as Thomas Pynchon, John Barth, and Norman Mailer, is primarily the treatment of the hero. The critical consensus is overwhelming in its assessment of the Bellow protagonist as a sensitive, thinking being who contends with the soul-destructive forces of modern society. Though often a victim and a spiritual alien in a materialistic world, Bellow's protagonist is nevertheless capable of dignity, sympathy, and compassion.

In his critical essays as well, Bellow calls for a more positive vision of humans as glorious sufferers wounded by their own aspirations and ideals in a world that has lost its belief in both. Bellow's vision of humankind's conflict with the world is not presented as a journey into chaos, as such a conflict is often portrayed in contemporary works. Unlike his contemporaries, Bellow does not locate his hero in a world where meaning and purpose are nonexistent or, at best, random. In Pynchon's *Gravity's Rainbow* (1973) or Barth's *Giles Goat-Boy* (1966), for example—or even in the works of the South American Magical Realists such as Julio Cortázar and Jorge Luis Borges—reality is a virtual factoid, a fabulous construction, an existential hall of mirrors against which the hero or antihero bumps his psyche.

By contrast, Bellow's world has substance. The settings of his novels—New York, Chicago, or even the countryside—are fully realized, authentically felt places. These environments, in fact, thrust the hero into a kind of moral laboratory in which to test his or her own values and gradually come to terms with life. For Bellow, it is not the world that is illusory but the hero's ability to achieve certainty of comfort and intellectual ease. The hero, in fact, must always strive to understand his or her place in the order of things. "The fault, dear Brutus," as William Shakespeare wrote, "is not in our stars, but in ourselves, that we are underlings."

The hero as underling, what Bellow himself called the greatness of humankind's "imbecility," is explored in the novels not with naturalistic gloom but rather from a point of view that is, above all, genuinely comic. Bellow is one of America's supreme comic novelists. His vision of humankind's plight entails an awareness of the contradiction between desire and limitation, between aspiration and ability. Such a contradiction has been, throughout Western literature, a vital source for the comic temper. It is interesting to note that among the novelist's other pursuits is his translation from the Yiddish of Isaac Bashevis Singer's "Gimpel Tam" (1945; "Gimpel the Fool," 1953), a work spiritually akin to Bellow's own point of view. Gimpel is the schlemiel, the loser with the soul whose place in heaven is assured by the genuine humility of his earthly naïveté, a humility amounting to a holiness through submission. The Bellovian hero is the intellectual schlemiel, aggrieved by the madness of contemporary life but unable to submit with Job-like serenity, as Gimpel does.

Bellow is thus at odds with the naturalistic writers who preceded him and from whose tradition he emerged. Those writers, such as Dreiser, saw humans as basically victims, creatures irredeemable by any imaginative aspirations because the weight of social forces—dramatized as economic imperatives or as ethical and emotional bankruptcy—keeps them down.

The problem for Bellow's heroes is not the lack of imagination or the inability to feel but the reverse. Protagonists such as Tommy Wilhelm in *Seize the Day*, for example, suffer—like Gimpel—not only because the world is a pitiless place but also because they refuse to submit to the pitilessness, striving instead for some humanistic ideal. Tommy Wilhelm wants sympathy; he demands it as a human being. Yet his expectations lie fallow in the stony ground of his father's heart and in the heartlessness of Tamkin and the commodities exchange.

Another intellectual schlemiel, Moses Herzog, whose name in German suggests the word "heart," is a scholar of Romanticism who writes letters to the world to keep from going mad. His alienation from the world can only partly be explained as neurosis. Much of it stems, as does Tommy Wilhelm's, from his own moral insight, which places him above the world while keeping him enthralled by the demands of the world.

Ultimately, what places Bellow in the mainstream of classic novelists—if one can label a contemporary as "classic"—is his concern with a theme common in the work of the great novelists: the inherent contradiction between the hero's potential as a human being and the moral value of his actual experience. Such a theme, sometimes expressed as the conflict between illusion and reality, has been characteristic of great literary works from Miguel de Cervantes' *Don Quixote de la Mancha* (1605; *Don Quixote of the Mancha*, 1612), whose hero jousts with windmills in the belief that they are giants, to Gustave Flaubert's *Madame Bovary* (1857; English translation, 1886), whose heroine finds the illusion of romance stronger than the reality of daily life.

All of Bellow's protagonists joust, metaphorically, with windmills. A seeker such as Charlie Citrine in *Humboldt's Gift* has a romantic, imaginative point of view which is counterpoised by the hardened realism of his mistress and of his mentor, Humboldt. The huge, corporeal reality of Sorella Fonstein in *The Bellarosa Connection* contrasts ironically with her own spiritual delicacy; even the freneticism of Augie March betrays at ground level Augie's sense of human decency.

Finally, Bellow is one of the great wordsmiths of the American novel. His prose style varies with the nature of the protagonist and the dilemma. The euphoric, Whitmanesque breathlessness of *The Adventures of Augie March* simmers into the quiet restraint of *Seize the Day*, expands into Moses Herzog's tempered frustrations, and dilates into the metaphorical considerations of *Mr. Sammler's Planet*. In each work the prose is often a startling mix of erudition and slang, of the analytically precise and the casually colloquial; yet it is also effective and always right. His work is irresistibly entertaining, containing accurate portrayals of contemporary life dramatized by dialogue of unerring naturalness.

THE ADVENTURES OF AUGIE MARCH

First published: 1953
Type of work: Novel

Through a skein of events from Chicago of the Depression to postwar Paris, Augie March experiences life as an affirmation of the human spirit.

Bellow's third work is not only a picturesque novel of great zest but also a kind of *Bildungsroman*, an autobiographical record of physical experience as it relates to intellectual and emotional growth. Augie's own exuberant narration of his life, beginning in Chicago during the Great Depression, reveals a personality who is in some ways a reckless and amoral character reminiscent of the rogue-heroes of the Spanish picaresque novel of the sixteenth and seventeenth centuries. Yet he is also a man who must define himself by his relationship to others and who views the world at large as basically sound. Many critics have likened the book, and Augie in particular, to *Adventures of Huckleberry Finn* (1884), and certainly Augie's status as folk hero, his take-the-world-as-it-is attitude, and his earthy narrative "talk" are very much influenced by Mark Twain's classic American novel.

Yet Augie is deeper than Huck because he is less naïve and, because of his origins, more cynical. He is not easily drawn into others' sphere of influence, as, by contrast, Huck was credulously drawn to the Duke and the King. Augie's adventures—his various jobs as stock boy, coal salesman, petty thief, prize-fight manager, union organizer, and even eagle trainer—are attempts to taste all of life. Augie is the embodiment of nineteenth century American poet Walt Whitman's belief in the value of all people and professions. All labor is valuable in a democracy; all occupations play a part in the positive force that is life itself. The various

jobs are also, for Augie, a means to an end, the end being, as he says, "a better fate."

A better fate was also what the heroes of a previous literary generation sought for themselves. Clyde, in Dreiser's *An American Tragedy* (1925), however, climbed the social ladder only to end a literal prisoner to his own ambition: That there was no way out but death was the naturalistically logical conclusion to Clyde's ambition. Unlike Clyde, Augie is not merely a product of his environment, not only the sum total of his experiences (equaling zero). The "better fate," as Augie implies, is, indeed, worldly success but success tempered by insight. Though he ends his story in Paris, involved in some international business ventures of questionable legitimacy, Augie comes to understand the value of commitment to humanity, the need for involvement with life.

This sense of commitment is ultimately missing in Augie's life. He is a hero the reader can admire for his individuality and sense of independence, but he does not learn by the novel's end to cease his wandering ways—emotional, intellectual, or physical. His major love affairs, first with Thea, then with Stella, whom he marries, are largely failures. Even his ability to accept people as they are—Einhorn, for example, whose crippled body Augie carries about—does not encourage him to commit himself to a creed or code.

Augie can see people objectively; he is capable of giving them the benefit of the doubt. The world is thus not a valley of despair. Beyond this passive acceptance of people for what they are in a world clearly teeming with life, however, Augie has no goal, no plan. Lacking commitment, he drifts from one adventure to another, hoping for the right "feel." He is akin to a latter-day knight-errant, seeking adventures in the vague hope of discovering the Holy Grail.

SEIZE THE DAY

First published: 1956
Type of work: Novella

Like a Greek tragedy, this novella is an intensely compact work examining one day in the agonized life of loser Tommy Wilhelm.

Set in the Gloriana Hotel on Broadway during one morning and in the commodities exchange on Wall Street later in the day, *Seize the Day* begins with its suffering hero, Tommy Wilhelm, seeking the company of his father, Dr. Adler. Dr. Adler does not love his son and views him as a failure and a dreamer. Adler disdains his son's misery: Tommy's marriage has failed, and his career at Rojax Corporation has floundered. In seeking out his father, Tommy does not so much want financial help, though he needs it and even expects it. What he really seeks is his father's approval and love. At the very least, he seeks understanding from the old man, a compassion that Tommy has not found from anyone—especially his wife, who is stonily demanding further alimony. Adler is pitiless, disdainful, and sententious, One of Bellow's most consummately realized villains, he is a soulless creature who is himself ironically effete, living in tight-fisted retirement in a second-rate hotel.

Broke and desperate, Tommy turns to another father figure, a wily, fast-talking con man, Dr. Tamkin. Tamkin wearies Tommy with his incessant talk, an overwhelming mixture of Emersonian bromides on self-reliance and psychoanalytic jargon about money as a type of aggression. He convinces Tommy to invest the last of his money on the commodities market—ironically, in futures.

Tommy's inevitable failure is depicted in a brilliant scene in which he anxiously watches the exchange board for signs of profit, while Tamkin, ever talking, preaches on the evils of greed. When Tommy is wiped out, Tamkin disappears and Tommy is left a pathetic victim. He is, in his father's words, a slob. In the final scene, the broken Tommy wanders into a funeral chapel. There, unknown to the mourners, he weeps aloud for the dead, a gesture symbolizing his own dead end and suggesting his deeper, personal loss of love, compassion, and human sympathy.

Seize the Day is rich in character portrayal. Reminiscent of Einhorn in *The Adventures of Augie March*, Tamkin is a characteristic mix of the comic and the villainous. Fast-talking, full of trite sayings, and even shrewdly understanding of his victims' needs, Tamkin is the con man par excellence because he has almost convinced himself of his own sincerity in preaching against the evils of materialism. He cheats Tommy not only out of his money but also out of his beliefs, his ideals. Dr. Adler, whose name means "eagle" in German, is indeed a predator of sorts. Like Tamkin, he preys on his son's weakness as a way of preening himself. Lofty, aristocratic, and fiercely aloof, Adler has become ignoble by divorcing himself from human feelings.

The novella's title provides a final ironic commentary on the story's central idea. The carpe diem theme—literally, "seize the day"—was a classical pronouncement that urged humans to make the most of their time, to extract from each moment the joy of life that time was ever stealing away. Tommy's dilemma is that he cannot subscribe to that pronouncement. His failed investment in futures is an ironic assertion of Tommy's need to live beyond the day, beyond the commercial grind—to seek for a deeper meaning of life and its sufferings.

HENDERSON THE RAIN KING

First published: 1959
Type of work: Novel

A millionaire goes to Africa in search of meaning, eventually finding it in sympathy for humankind.

Henderson the Rain King is a mad, antic fantasy, perhaps the most comic of Bellow's novels. Rich, world-weary Eugene Henderson, like the heroes of myth, seeks escape from the burden of the world and embarks on a journey to unknown lands in search of meaning and peace. The unknown land is Africa, and Henderson arrives there in poverty of spirit, having, like Ishmael in Herman Melville's *Moby Dick* (1851), the need to find purpose in his life. Henderson is a kind of Tommy Wilhelm in reverse, except that Henderson, a graduate of an Ivy League university, has a broader perspective, a core of reference that is beyond Tommy's imagining. Whereas Tommy seeks meaning in the financial markets and then in the urbanized coldness of his father's disapproval, Henderson, already financially secure, seeks meaning in the pastoral and the primitive. Where Tommy seeks relief in futures, Henderson seeks salvation in a kind of past, a land primeval and innocent.

His first adventure is in the land of the Arnewi, in a village in the midst of mountains and clean air.

The landscape suggests a primordial world of Edenic innocence, and Henderson at first is a kind of Adam, ready to start fresh. The novel, in fact, is rich in suggestive allusions to biblical and secular literary characters. As a new Adam, however, Henderson is a failure. As Moses, armed with his faith, had parted the waters of the Red Sea to save his people, so Henderson, armed with the weapons of technology, attempts to rid the life-giving well of an infestation of frogs. His role as savior backfires: He blows up the well, bringing destruction rather than life. Like Mark Twain's "Sir Boss" in *A Connecticut Yankee in King Arthur's Court* (1889), Henderson has tried to improve humankind by the beneficence of civilization; he has tried to impose a modern system of values on a primitive but honest culture.

In this first adventure, however, the destruction that Henderson wreaks teaches him little about his own place in the world. Continuing his quest for meaning, he comes next to the Wariri, among whom his most telling lessons in self-wisdom occur. Though he has become a "rain king" by the notable feat of moving a stone rain goddess, his exalted position comes only at the price of his physical humiliation—he is flayed and thrown into the mud of a cattle pond.

Additionally, Henderson comes under the influence of the tribe's philosopher-king, Dahfu, who ponders metaphysics and is convinced that his destiny is to return in the afterlife as a lion. King Dahfu is a puzzling character. He seems genuinely humble in the face of universal mysteries revealed to him in his philosophy, yet his incessant talking reminds the reader of the stream of con men who appear in Bellow's novels, from Einhorn and Tamkin to the gangster, Rinaldo Cantabile, of *Humboldt's Gift.* Dahfu's effect on Henderson is both serious and wildly comic. Convinced that Henderson must free himself from his fears of inadequacy, Dahfu prescribes a therapy entailing Henderson's confrontation with a lioness. The scene in which the rain king finally learns to imitate the courage of the lioness, even to the point of getting down on all fours and roaring, is both comic and pathetic. Again, Henderson is humiliated, this time spiritually, but he has learned the meaning of humanity's noble fragility in a crazy world.

The novel ends with one of those physical epiphanies typical of Bellow's work. Henderson is at an airport in Newfoundland—the place name reflects Henderson's newfound self. He has escaped from the Wariri and from the "past" of Africa, and he has taken under his wing an American child who is flying back to the United States, alone and frightened. He cares for the child, gives it comfort, and embraces it. He has found his meaning: sympathy for the family of humankind.

HERZOG

First published: 1964
Type of work: Novel

A student of Romanticism, Moses Herzog, tries to come to term with the material, unromantic world.

Considered by many to be Bellow's masterwork, *Herzog* may well be his prototypical novel, and Herzog the prototypical Bellovian hero. Like Emily Dickinson, who wrote poems as a means of opening a communion with the world, Moses Herzog, sensitive student of Romanticism, writes letters to the world-at-large in an attempt to keep his sanity and to measure his need for compassion and empathy in a world devoid of both. Like Gimpel the Fool, Herzog is a true schlemiel, a loser by the standards of the world but a noble spirit.

Though capable of anger and self-pity at the breakup of his marriage, and of lust in his relationship with his mistress, Ramona, Herzog can still yearn for a deeper, richer life. Like the great thinkers to whom he writes his imaginary letters, he seeks meaning and peace. Even amid the bustle of the urban life of New York and Chicago, Herzog is withdrawn into the private bustle of his mind, remembering events from his broken marriage and formulating rebuttals to the negative, spirit-killing philosophies of men such as Sandor Himmelstein, whose surname means "stoney heaven," and even seventeenth century philosopher Baruch Spinoza. His letters come to him like bursts of inspiration and serve as antidotes to his own fears that he is out of his mind.

The novel thus represents a form of psychoanalysis: Herzog's remembrances are transferred into the actual world of his letters. The direction of the plot is thus not chronological but psychological: Events have meaning not in relation to time but in their associations with other events or ideas. The main action of *Herzog* is not physical but mental, and despite brilliant evocations of city life, the real power of the book is the revelation of Moses Herzog's mind.

The incisive treatment of the effects of the urban experience on a sensitive, troubled spirit, however, is finely contrasted in *Herzog* with scenes of almost idyllic calm. Scenes of Herzog enjoying the pleasures of his country retreat in the Berkshires serve both to reinforce the traditional aspects of Bellow as a novelist—his use of nature as a corrective to Herzog's troubled mind, for example—and to strengthen the psychological truthfulness of his hero. Herzog is, after all, a student of Romanticism, and nature for the Romantic was curative, an agency or force by which people, by attuning themselves to its power, could find inspiration, illumination, and genuine spiritual sustenance.

Nowhere is the redeeming force of nature more explicit than in the scene in which Herzog, from his country retreat, recalls the time Valentine Gershbach (his former wife's lover) was bathing Herzog's child. The scene is presented with the feeling of a pastoral. The purity, the gentleness implicit in Gershbach's action, gives pause to Herzog's anger. Herzog sees his rival as a human being, a fellow creature, as much to be pitied as condemned. He releases his anger and comes to terms with Gershbach; Herzog thus survives not by hating but by forgiving.

MR. SAMMLER'S PLANET

First published: 1970
Type of work: Novel

Old, one-eyed Mr. Sammler, survivor of the Holocaust, is both horrified and philosophically resigned to the cultural nightmare of 1960's America.

Mr. Sammler's Planet explores the typical Bellovian conflict of accepting the world on its own terms while recognizing and adhering to higher spiritual values. The "planet" of Mr. Sammler is not the moon—a plan for the colonization of which has been proposed by his scientist friend—but the very earth itself. Moreover, Mr. Sammler, an aged, one-eyed Polish Jew now living in New York with his daughter, is not an astronomer by profession but by a philosophical state of mind. With his one good eye he peers through the telescope of history, exploring the cultural landscape of a planet which has just sent a man to the moon yet which is rife with social and political cant and a spiritual emptiness. Having escaped death in a concentration camp during World War II, Sammler is disillusioned, even horrified by the violence around him. The novel presents a dreary, hellish picture of New York of the late 1960's. Surrounded by muggers, pickpockets, and an assortment of hollow intellectuals, Sammler is convinced that the world has gone mad, that the human race has deteriorated into barbarism.

An indictment of the radicalism of the era, the novel is Bellow's bleakest, and Mr. Sammler his most despairing hero, a survivor of the Nazis who finds an almost cosmic indifference in the prevailing violence and decay. For Mr. Sammler, New York City is representative of the demise of culture, of humanism.

In the course of his three-day adventure that constitutes the heart of the plot, Sammler experiences fear of death at the hands of a "Negro" deviant, engages in a philosophical conversation about biology and human will with his scientist friend, and makes an abortive attempt to visit his dying nephew. Each day presents one aspect of the endemic cultural decline.

The last scene of the novel is crucial in understanding Mr. Sammler's ultimate resignation. Too late to say good-bye to his dying nephew, Sammler stands at the bedside of the corpse and mutters a kind of prayer for the dead. The scene is reminiscent of the final act of an earlier Bellovian hero: Tommy Wilhelm in *Seize the Day*, broke and desperate, visits a funeral chapel and weeps for the unknown dead. Sammler's prayer is a similar act, a personal mourning for dead humanity.

HUMBOLDT'S GIFT

First published: 1975
Type of work: Novel

Two writers try to reconcile their poetic ideals with the demands of the world of popular taste and the lure of success.

Humboldt's Gift is a kind of gothic novel in the sense that its protagonist is haunted by a ghost. The ghost is both a living man and the spirit or ideals that the man, an older writer named Von Humboldt Fleisher, represents.

Humboldt is a writer whose talent—or genius—has been corrupted by the American vision of success. The protagonist is modeled closely on Bellow's recollections of a friend, poet Delmore Schwartz, who in the late 1930's produced a first book of poetry that was hailed as a work of promising genius but who died with the promise unfulfilled. Humboldt has also produced a first volume of poems, *Harlequin Ballads*, but has since lived off his early reputation. Humboldt had "made it big," as the narrator remarks, but had produced nothing since. Instead, he had lived the good life, which included fast cars, women, and other trappings of materialistic success.

Yet Humboldt was aware of his entrapment by the overpowering world of things. Sensing his own surrender to materialism, he had taken to playing the role of the great Romantic nonconformist. The paradox of Humboldt's condition was that, as a poet, he was an example of unfulfillment and failure, but as a man and public figure he represented the idea of poetry as a spiritual, revivifying force capable of saving a sick society.

It is this paradox that haunts the narrator, Charlie Citrine. He too is a writer, but unlike Humboldt, his idol, he has not produced any significant work—he has written histories, biographies, and political essays, the residue of others' ideas. Citrine dreams of producing his own great work, a philosophical treatise on the human mind; like Humboldt, however, he gives in to the demands of public taste. He writes a Broadway play which becomes a smash hit and secures a lucrative motion-picture contract. Now wealthy, Citrine has become another Humboldt of sorts. When Humboldt dies and becomes, in Citrine's words, one of his "significant dead," Citrine renews his aspiration, believing that he has been singled out to produce a great work.

Ironically, Citrine's aspiration remains largely unfulfilled. He falls to the lure of the flesh. His mistress, Renata, is flesh personified, and his passionate enjoyment of her is his only genuinely poetic experience. In fact, the poetry of Charlie Citrine is in his natural zest for the physical quality of living, a total, rhapsodic immersion in *things*.

This expression of the intensity of life is one of the hallmarks of the novel. The villains, for example, are depicted with a Dickensian verve and sprightliness. Rinaldo Cantabile, the gangster who ensnares Citrine into subjection by a gambling debt, is portrayed with such fearsome energy that he is wonderfully comic in his wickedness. Charlie Citrine's "adventures" amid the likes of Cantabile and Renata and her gorgonic mother can be viewed as latter-day depictions of the hero in the underworld, a hell of soulless materialism.

Humboldt's Gift is thus the most gothic of Bellow's novels. Just when Charlie has met defeat—broke, dejected, and deprived even of the luscious Renata, who has married an undertaker (perhaps from the underworld)—he is visited by a final ghost: Humboldt's gift, a legacy of a film script from the dead poet. Citrine submits the script to a producer, makes a fortune from the sale of the rights, and once again is on his feet, independent, ready to continue the pursuit of the good life. The old Romantic dream, however, is gone. Citrine realizes that he will never produce art, that he is too addicted to the popular taste and the world of the flesh. In the final scene, Citrine is at Humboldt's gravesite. He has buried his idol and, with him, the dream of producing poetry in the materialistic land of America.

THE BELLAROSA CONNECTION

First published: 1989
Type of work: Novella

Sorella Fonstein hounds showman Billy Rose into an interview during which she hopes Billy will admit his responsibility—and thus admit his humanity—in saving Sorella's husband from the Nazis.

As Bellow had used the traditional, even old-fashioned narrative structure of the picaresque for his first major work, *The Adventures of Augie March*, so thirty years later the author shows his interest in more modern narrative forms. *The Bellarosa Connection* is an example of the so-called new journalism, in which real events and people are treated in broadly fictional ways. E. L. Doctorow, for example, had used such historical personalities as Harry Houdini, Henry Ford, and J. P. Morgan in the fictional tapestry of his *Ragtime* (1975).

In *The Bellarosa Connection*, Bellow creates a series of events based on the historic atrocity of the Holocaust during World War II. The action centers on Sorella Fonstein's persistence in gaining an interview with impresario Billy Rose, who was responsible—through his anonymous underground railroad—for bringing a number of Jews to America as they escaped from the Nazis. Among those who were saved was Sorella's husband, Harry. Fonstein is snubbed by Billy Rose (the European Jews had called their savior "Bellarosa"), but Sorella herself, with tigerlike tenacity, ultimately succeeds in confronting Billy and blackmailing him, through her knowledge of a scandal, into meeting with Harry.

Billy's ignorance and crudity as a human being are portrayed with insight, for if human character is fraught with contradiction, then Billy's character is contradiction personified. His motive for underwriting his sole example of generosity and unselfishness in a life of hustling selfishness is never fully explained; Billy himself is not really sure of his motive. As a Jew, Billy may have truly acted in sympathy with his fellow Jews, as if (as the narrator points out) "the God of his fathers still mattered." For one time in his life, this obsessively vulgar person begrudgingly freed the font of human goodness within him.

In spite of his complexity, however, Billy Rose is not the main character. He is seen by the reader only in the climactic interview with Sorella. It is, in fact, Sorella who commands the reader's—and the narrator's—attention. Like many of Bellow's women, she is fierce, tenacious, and in absolute command over her husband. With an animal obesity to match, she is bright and yet oddly gentle, even humble. What Sorella achieves by the interview is not only Billy's consent to meet with her husband so that Harry can thank him. At bottom lies Sorella's extorting from Billy a sense of responsibility for the life he had saved, a responsibility that extends to all humanity. Billy thus shares kinship with Harry, with Jews, and with all humankind. Sorella seems to have understood this connection—the real Bellarosa connection—the chain of mutual responsibility, of recognition of human suffering, of compassion for the human condition.

This connection is ultimately clarified by the novella's point of view. The narrator is a distant relation of Sorella, who tells the story in an effort to purge his memory. He is the founder of Mnemosyne Institute, a company engaged in training businessmen and government leaders in memory techniques. Like Billy Rose, the narrator is a self-made millionaire. His working motto being "memory is life," he is now on the eve of retirement, about to pass on the business to his son. His recollections of the Fonstein and Billy Rose story thus close the circle of relationship. The narrator's memory forms the link connecting the participants of the drama with the rest of humankind. Like the narrator, the reader is vicariously involved. Humanity, through memory, is being tested and vindicated.

RAVELSTEIN

First published: 2000
Type of work: Novel

The narrator recalls the larger-than-life acts and opinions of Abe Ravelstein, professor, best-selling author, and political philosopher.

Ravelstein, like its title character, is a puzzling work. At once a mass of fact and observations on history, philosophy, and the world-at-large, the book ap-

pears to be composed of a series of discontinuous scenes and repetitive pronouncements affirming the genius of Abe Ravelstein, professor, best-selling author, and would-be celebrity. Yet when the narrator, Chick, reveals that as Ravelstein's friend and admirer he has been selected by the professor to write his memoirs, the scheme of the novel's structure becomes clear, the apparent disjointedness a mark of the narrator's admiration and puzzlement. *Ravelstein* is thus a tribute to a great man and a cautionary tale illustrating his weaknesses.

Though Ravelstein is a worldly success, a big man with big appetites, almost a kind of cult leader among young intellectuals, he is, as his name implies, a "complicated" fellow whose real sympathies lie "knotted" and "tangled" amid the blandishments of the physical world. Seduced by success and fame into pursuing an extravagant lifestyle, Ravelstein enjoys all the pleasures of the modern world while pontificating to Chick in a tone of hardened cynicism.

Chick is amused, even impressed by the breadth and seeming wisdom of Ravelstein's knowledge, from the political origins of twentieth century Germany to the courtship rituals of native South American headhunters. Ravelstein's opinions permeate Chick's life, and Abe Ravelstein himself is the last of a long line of fast-talking hustlers and con men who fill Bellow's books, characters such as Einhorn in *The Adventures of Augie March* and Tamkin in *Seize the Day*.

Though there is a bit of the charlatan in Abe Ravelstein, he is not spiritually bankrupt. While he gently mocks what he considers Chick's conventional idealism and his capacity for hope, he insists that Chick write his biography, thus revealing his own yearning for immortality, for the human need to be remembered. Throughout this final novel, Abe Ravelstein, this "raveled" human being who is both "complicated" and at "loose ends," admits to Chick that he is a confirmed nihilist. Ravelstein dies of acquired immunodeficiency syndrome (AIDS), and Chick himself survives a near-fatal illness near the end of the book. Chick realizes that his friend's hard-core reliance on pleasure and materialism actually disguised his basic human empathy. When he tells Chick, for instance, that the Jewish people are living witnesses to the absence of redemption, Ravelstein is confronting the great question that all of Bellow's heroes face: How does a human being come to terms with the allurements of the physical world and still preserve a spiritual integrity?

SUMMARY

Bellow summarized his own literary goals as well as his achievement in his 1976 Nobel Prize acceptance speech. In it, he declared that the novelist's duty essentially is to affirm the value of the human soul, to record the ultimate triumph of the spirit in the midst of materialism. Indeed, Bellow's novels insist on the primacy of the hero—suffering, questioning, doubting, and yearning—always central to the plot, not a peripheral element subject to its randomness.

Bellow's distinction as a novelist is precisely his concern for character in conflict with society. His insistence on human values puts him at odds with many latter-day novelists and places him, instead, in the tradition of the great nineteenth century novelists who saw character as the central focus of the novel.

Edward Fiorelli

BIBLIOGRAPHY

By the Author

LONG FICTION:
Dangling Man, 1944
The Victim, 1947
The Adventures of Augie March, 1953
Seize the Day, 1956
Henderson the Rain King, 1959
Herzog, 1964
Mr. Sammler's Planet, 1970
Humboldt's Gift, 1975
The Dean's December, 1982
More Die of Heartbreak, 1987
A Theft, 1989
The Bellarosa Connection, 1989
The Actual, 1997 (novella)
Ravelstien, 2000
Novels, 1944-1953, 2003 (includes *Dangling Man, The Victim,* and *The Adventures of Augie March*)

SHORT FICTION:
Mosby's Memoirs, and Other Stories, 1968
Him with His Foot in His Mouth, and Other Stories, 1984
Something to Remember Me By: Three Tales, 1991
Collected Stories, 2001

DRAMA:
The Wrecker, pb. 1954
The Last Analysis, pr. 1964
Under the Weather, pr. 1966 (also known as *The Bellow Plays*; includes *Out from Under, A Wen,* and *Orange Soufflé*)

NONFICTION:
To Jerusalem and Back: A Personal Account, 1976
Conversations with Saul Bellow, 1994 (Gloria L. Cronin and Ben Siegel, editors)
It All Adds Up: From the Dim Past to the Uncertain Future, 1994

EDITED TEXT:
Great Jewish Short Stories, 1963

DISCUSSION TOPICS

- What qualities characterize the typical Bellovian hero?

- What qualities characterize the Bellovian antagonist or villain?

- Discuss the role of the thinker in Saul Bellow's novels.

- Discuss the treatment of the "loser" or the "failure" in Bellow's novels.

- What is Bellow's attitude toward modern culture?

About the Author

Bradbury, Malcolm. *Saul Bellow.* New York: Methuen, 1982.

Braham, Jeanne. *A Sort of Columbus: The American Voyages of Saul Bellow's Fiction.* Athens: University of Georgia Press, 1984.

Cronin, Gloria L., and Leila H. Goldman, eds. *Saul Bellow in the 1980's: A Collection of Critical Essays.* East Lansing: Michigan State University Press, 1989.

Cronin, Gloria L., and Ben Siegel, eds. *Conversations with Saul Bellow.* Jackson: University Press of Mississippi, 1994.

Goldman, L. H. *Saul Bellow: A Mosaic.* New York: Peter Lang, 1992.

Hyland, Peter. *Saul Bellow.* New York: St. Martin's Press, 1992.

Newman, Judie. *Saul Bellow and History.* London: Macmillan, 1984.

Siegel, Ben. "Simply Not a Mandarin: Saul Bellow as Jew and Jewish Writer." In *Traditions, Voices, and Dreams: The American Novel Since the 1960's.* Newark: University of Delaware Press, 1995.

Trachtenberg, Stanley, comp. *Critical Essays on Saul Bellow.* Boston: G. K. Hall, 1979.

© Jerry Bauer

THOMAS BERGER

Born: Cincinnati, Ohio
July 20, 1924

Concerned more than perhaps any other American writer of his time with the control exerted over the individual by language, Berger has written novels exploring the banality and violence of existence.

BIOGRAPHY

Thomas Louis Berger was born in Cincinnati, Ohio, on July 20, 1924, the only child of Charles and Mildred Bubbe Berger. He grew up in the nearby suburb of Lockland, where his father was business manager of the local school system. Encouraged by both parents, especially his mother, young Berger read incessantly.

While in high school, Berger held jobs as hotel desk clerk and theater usher and worked in a branch of the Cincinnati Public Library. After briefly attending Miami University in Oxford, Ohio, and the University of Cincinnati, he enlisted in the Army in 1943. Berger served as a medic in England, France, and Germany, and was stationed with the Occupation forces in Berlin following the end of World War II.

Berger graduated with honors from the University of Cincinnati in 1948 and moved to New York City. He became a graduate student at Columbia University in 1950, took Lionel Trilling's famous course in modern American literature, and began a thesis on George Orwell but never finished. He also studied at Charles Glicksberg's writers' workshop at the New School for Social Research, at the same time as Jack Kerouac, Mario Puzo, and William Styron. Berger had decided to become a writer when he was sixteen, having been inspired by the urbane, erudite commentators on the radio

program Information Please. At the New School workshop, he wrote a story a week for three months, beginning with melancholy, maudlin, simple stories in the manner of Ernest Hemingway before coming under the influence of William Faulkner. On June 12, 1950, he married Jeanne Redpath, an artist he had met at the New School.

During the late 1940's and early 1950's, Berger worked as a librarian at the Rand School of Social Science, as a staff member of *The New York Times Index*, and as a copy editor for *Popular Science Monthly*. In this period, he wrote reviews for *New Leader* and *Institute of Social Studies Bulletin* and published his first short story, the Hemingway-influenced "Dependency of Day and Night," in *Western Review* in 1952.

In 1954, the Bergers moved to Rockland County, New York, on the Hudson River so that he could devote more time to his writing while working as a freelance copy editor for publishing houses. After rejections from four publishers, Berger's first novel, *Crazy in Berlin*, was published in 1958. This novel and its sequel, *Reinhart in Love* (1962), sold a meager forty-five hundred copies. His third novel, *Little Big Man* (1964), sold ten thousand copies and won the Western Heritage Award and the Richard and Hinda Rosenthal Foundation Award, presented by the American Academy and Institute of Arts and Letters for a notable work of fiction not considered a commercial success. Berger began receiving more public attention with the release of the 1970 film version of *Little Big Man*, directed by Arthur Penn and starring Dustin Hoffman.

Sales of the film rights to several of his novels al-

216

lowed Berger the freedom to move about while he continued to practice his craft. He and his wife have lived in England, California, Maine, and New York. In addition, Berger has taught at the University of Kansas, Southampton College, Yale University, and the University of California at Davis. Berger retired from writing after *Suspects* (1996) and again after *The Return of Little Big Man* (1999), only to return to his craft each time.

ANALYSIS

While his novels have been generally well-received by reviewers, and while he is regarded by his colleagues as a writer's writer, Berger's overall critical reputation has suffered somewhat because of the difficulty of categorizing his work, which does not fit into any standard literary movement or school. Critics often misunderstand Berger's intentions or lazily lump him into a misleading category. Because of the humor, violence, and absurdity in most of his novels, he has sometimes been grouped with the black humorists, yet his fiction lacks the anger and delight in the grotesque associated with black humor. While there are strong satirical elements in his novels, Berger similarly rejects the label of satirist. He has little interest in overtly criticizing society; he is too pessimistic to believe it can change its ways.

Because several of his novels exploit the conventions of fictional genres, Berger has also been called a parodist—yet in these books, he is not making light of genres but lovingly paying homage to their conventions. *Little Big Man* is a Western; the futuristic *Regiment of Women* (1973) has science-fiction elements; *Who Is Teddy Villanova?* (1977) is a detective novel; *Arthur Rex* (1978) is an Arthurian romance; *Nowhere* (1985) resembles a spy thriller; *Being Invisible* (1987) is an antiutopian novel; *Orrie's Story* (1990) retells the Orestes legend, updating Greek tragedy to small-town America at the end of World War II; *Robert Crews* (1994) is a survival tale in the tradition of Daniel Defoe's *Robinson Crusoe* (1719); and *Adventures of the Artificial Woman* (2004) revisits the Frankenstein myth. In interviews, Berger has expressed his disgust at reviewers' labeling of these works as parodies. His goal has been, rather, to celebrate these genres by identifying and applauding their characteristic plots, protagonists, themes, and other devices.

Although Berger is also uncomfortable with being called a comic novelist, he is clearly a comic writer in the tradition of Charles Dickens (a major influence on his work), Mark Twain, and Franz Kafka. Lacking the moral fervor of the true satirist, Berger exposes his characters' foibles with compassion. He stands out from other American novelists of his time by writing about ordinary people with acceptance of their deficiencies and without condescension. Despite the almost complete absence of sentimentality in his fiction and despite his constant illustration of negative aspects of his characters' behavior, Berger displays an unusual tolerance for human weaknesses. Nevertheless, his characters are presented with strong irony. Their interpretations of the reality they encounter are never entirely accurate or reliable.

Resisting both idealism and despair, Berger is among the least didactic of novelists. He apparently agrees with Dr. Otto Knebel in *Crazy in Berlin*, who says, "If you think I shall tell you what is right or wrong, my friend, you are mistaken. That is your own affair. I care only for practical matters." While his characters may believe in causes, they learn, often painfully, that such beliefs are not beneficial to their individuality, as with the devotion of the knights to the chivalric code in *Arthur Rex*.

Despite his claim that his fiction is not thematic, Berger's novels do say something about the problem of identity, the uncertainty of human relationships, the prevalence of violence in all societies, and the elusiveness of truth and happiness. Still, readers will best appreciate his work if they heed his warning to approach it "without the luggage of received ideas, a priori assumptions, sociopolitical axes to grind, or feeble moralities in search of support."

While a major subject in Berger's fiction is victimization, his characters are enslaved primarily by perceptions bounded by language. His books are about the characters' efforts to free themselves from someone else's definition of reality, a necessarily verbal definition. In *Killing Time* (1967), Berger shows how perceptions of violent crime are influenced by the language used to describe it, whether journalistic, legalistic (varying from police to lawyers), or sensationalistic, as in the tabloid press. *Killing Time*'s Joe Detweiler, a murderer, says, "The act is the truth, really. Everything else is language." By cutting himself off from language, Detweiler loses touch with reality.

Berger shows how language can be a weapon with varying degrees of effectiveness. In *Neighbors* (1980), Earl Keese foolishly attempts to protect himself from the assaults of his obnoxious neighbors, Harry and Ramona, with conventionally polite phrases and clichés. Rejecting the apparent advances of the seductive Ramona, Earl conducts a conversation through a keyhole: "If you'd act right for once, then maybe I could perform as a decent neighbor. My intent is good—in fact it has been since the first—but you and Harry have always succeeded in alienating me, I don't know why." Ramona replies, "Have you got gonorrhea or something?" After Earl expresses outrage at this suggestion and Ramona fails to respond, he modifies his position: "But maybe I didn't hear you correctly, so skip my criticism. I really would like to begin with a clean slate." Ramona unsettles this conventional man by saying the unexpected, and Earl's inherent decency, which is not being mocked, makes him think he may be the one in the wrong. Such failures to communicate are central to Berger's humor.

In *Who Is Teddy Villanova?*, detective Russel Wren constructs plausible theories to explain everything that transpires in the novel, only to have the theories finally explain nothing. Berger overturns the expectations of the typical reader of mysteries who expects logical explanations for everything by offering another set of explanations to offset those imagined by Wren. Berger illustrates how many human problems result from errors in communication and from confusion created by the inexact use of language, showing how, in a world of words, language determines the quality of experience.

CRAZY IN BERLIN

First published: 1958
Type of work: Novel

A naïve, somewhat idealistic young American soldier in post–World War II Berlin is initiated into the moral ambiguity and violence of life.

Crazy in Berlin, which opens on Carlo Reinhart's twenty-first birthday, is Berger's only remotely autobiographical novel, a coming-of-age tale in which his protagonist learns something about the com-

plexities of the modern world. As an Army medic in Berlin following the end of World War II, Reinhart meets a wide variety of Americans, Germans, and Russians who introduce him to love, chaos, and madness. He spends much of the novel wandering from one lying or misinformed person to another as he acquires some sense of his identity.

The other characters include the idealistic Lieutenant Schild, a Jewish communist who leaks military secrets to the Russians; Lichenko, a Red Army deserter and would-be capitalist harbored temporarily by Schild; Bach, a giant, philosophical invalid who presents a case for anti-Semitism even though he hid his Jewish wife from the Nazis for four years; Dr. Otto Knebel, a former communist, tortured and blinded in a Russian concentration camp, who becomes a fascist after the fall of the Nazis; and Schatzi, a former supporter of Adolf Hitler imprisoned in Auschwitz for his criminal activities and now a cynical Soviet agent. Then there are the three women in Reinhart's life: Lori, Bach's wife and Knebel's twin sister, who represents for Reinhart an unattainable romantic ideal; Trudschen, Lori's whorish, masochistic, sixteen-year-old cousin, who appeals to Reinhart's irrational side; and Veronica Leary, a flirtatious, buxom Army nurse, who represents vulgar American normality.

After Schild, betrayed by Schatzi, is abducted by two communist agents, Reinhart attempts to rescue him. He kills one of the abductors, but Schild is murdered by the other. Reinhart, who receives a serious head wound, undergoes six months of therapy in a psychiatric ward. He obtains revenge for Schild by betraying the treacherous Schatzi.

Reinhart tells his psychiatrist that Schild was insane for believing in the King Arthur stories he read as a boy and that he is himself crazy for sharing Schild's romantic idealism. Reinhart senses that traditional values are without philosophical justification, yet he remains loyal to them in the name of decency and civilized behavior. Constantly musing on what it means to be Jewish, consumed by guilt over his German ancestry, aware of his potential for evil, Reinhart sees all sides to every argument and feels responsible for any injustice. He is on a seemingly endless quest to understand what cannot be understood.

Reinhart's often comic quest continues in *Reinhart in Love*, in which he returns to what passes for normality in the United States, finishes college, and marries a shrew; *Vital Parts* (1970), in which he has become a middle-aged failure at marriage, fatherhood, and business; and *Reinhart's Women* (1981), in which he keeps house for his daughter, a successful model, becomes a gourmet cook, and finally loses his grand expectations for himself, shedding his guilt and self-pity in the process. Reinhart has been called one of the most original heroes in American fiction because he embodies so many aspects of the American character in his journey through confusion and despair and because he maintains his integrity and humanity in an increasingly materialistic, nihilistic world. A good-hearted man in a corrupt society, he is a victim of his virtues.

LITTLE BIG MAN

First published: 1964
Type of work: Novel

A white man is adopted by Indians but eventually fits into neither white nor Indian societies.

Little Big Man is 111-year-old Jack Crabb's account of his life from 1852, when he is ten and most of his family is killed by drunken Indians, to 1876, when he becomes the only white survivor of the Battle of the Little Bighorn. During these twenty-four years, Jack is adopted first by Old Lodge Skins, chief of a small band of Northern Cheyenne, and later by the Reverend Mr. Pendrake and his beautiful, unfaithful young wife. Leaving the Pendrakes, Jack alternates between white and Indian societies, never fitting in comfortably with either. He longs for middle-class comforts, but circumstances and his restless nature block his success.

Jack is constantly being victimized. His white wife and child are stolen by Indians and later killed by the cavalry, as are his Cheyenne wife and their newborn son. Except for Old Lodge Skins, all

Jack's Indian friends are killed—one, ironically, when he is unknowingly about to kill Jack. Jack is shot on four occasions, and only his roguish trickery saves him from being killed in a gunfight by Wild Bill Hickok. The novel builds to General George Armstrong Custer's fiasco at the Little Bighorn and to the death of Old Lodge Skins, who chooses to die when he recognizes that the destruction of the Indian way of life is inevitable. Despite Berger's presentation of the American West as violent, melodramatic, and absurd, *Little Big Man* has lighter moments stemming from a multitude of colorful characters and a plethora of coincidences recalling those in the novels of Dickens.

Always concerned with the differences between reality and the various ways it is perceived, Berger debunks the myth of the West. Legendary heroes are not that heroic: Kit Carson denies hardluck Jack a handout, Wyatt Earp knocks him out for belching, and Hickok is tired, sad, and paranoid. Berger's Indians are hardly noble savages: Their camps stink, they eat dogs, and their women and children mutilate wounded enemies. The West is so beclouded by myth, however, that the truth can never be known. Even eyewitness accounts such as Jack's are untrustworthy because of the way matters are distorted to fit preconceptions and fulfill stereotypes.

Despite considerable evidence to the contrary, Berger's characters adhere to their romantic illusions. After their wagon train is attacked and members of her family are raped and murdered, Jack's sister Caroline follows the Cheyenne because she thinks they lust after her and because she wants to be an Indian princess. The savages dispel her misconceptions by failing to recognize that she is a woman. Years later, she reminds Jack of how the Indians "brutally stole" her "maidenhood." Since the truth is embarrassing, she has created her own myth.

Most important is *Little Big Man*'s presentation of Jack as the American innocent in search of his identity and the meaning of America. He is modern man trapped in a chaotic, often meaningless universe. The natural order of the Indian world is attractive but unrealistic when confronted by rampaging progress, but the more artificial order of the white world, in which all that can be aspired to is respectability, seems superficial. The only true order or meaning is that created by the individual, but he must recognize its limitations.

The Return of Little Big Man (1999) follows Jack's story for the seventeen years after Little Bighorn, as he meets more historical figures, including Buffalo Bill Cody, Bat Masterson, Annie Oakley, Sitting Bull, and Queen Victoria. Working as Hickok's bodyguard, a bartender, an interpreter at an Indian school, and several positions in Cody's Wild West, Jack again finds himself explaining Indian culture to whites. Berger continues to contrast how Indians and whites see and often misinterpret each other's behavior and motivations. His main satirical target is the ways Americans romanticize the past, as with Jack's eyewitness account of the O.K. Corral shootout, which differs considerably from the legend. Jack's fondness for show business illustrates Berger's view of how reality is transformed into art.

The Feud

First published: 1983
Type of work: Novel

In small-town America during the Depression, a series of misunderstandings result in a feud between two families.

The Feud is perhaps Berger's best example of what he has called "pure fiction"—relatively free of journalistic, sociological, and other thematic concerns. The novel's deliberately complicated plot and large cast of characters serve primarily to support its stylistic concerns, which, more than anywhere else in Berger's work, center on the way in which people manipulate language to justify outrageous behavior.

The dispute between Depression-era families somewhere in middle America begins when Dolf Beeler goes to Bud Bullard's hardware store for paint remover and, when he refuses to dispose of

his unlit cigar, gets into an argument with Junior Bullard (Bud's teenage son) and Reverton Kirby (Bud's cousin). When the store burns down that night, Dolf is blamed. Bud, who has no insurance, then attempts suicide and later has a breakdown. Events soon escalate; Dolf's car blows up, and Dolf bloodies the nose of kindly Walt Huff, Bud's brother-in-law, before having a heart attack. The endless series of disasters in this comedy of errors is complicated by a misguided love affair between Dolf's son and Bud's daughter, making the novel a blend of the legendary Hatfield-McCoy feud and William Shakespeare's *Romeo and Juliet* (1595).

As usual, Berger's characters are searching, blindly and ineptly, for freedom and self-respect and are hindered primarily by the foolish limitations they impose upon their perceptions of the world. The ironically named Rev considers himself a man of principles because of his faith in such beliefs as "*Worship the Lord, but never trust a preacher any farther than you can throw him.*" *The Feud* is a catalog of such twisted clichés, which the characters employ as a way of ordering their chaotic universe. Berger does not condemn them but celebrates their faith in the American vernacular and the energy of their language: "Don't give me any lip, you runt. You want somepin t'eat, you just gimme your order." Berger also indulges himself occasionally by blending all of his linguistic devices into a frenzy, as when Rev comes upon Dolf's daughter Bernice engaged in sex with fireman Ernie Krum: "You think you can come up here where innocent women and children are living and corpulate like unto animals of the field, make a spectacle of yourself, hold up to mockery all the principles of God-fearing men, roll in slime and throw it in our face? I'd like to see you both kestrated."

Despite such excesses, Berger seems genuinely to like his foolish creations. They are always distinctive individuals, never types. The guardians of the Pulitzer Prize overruled their committee's selection of *The Feud* as the best work of fiction for 1983, probably because of an inability to understand the concept of pure fiction, because Berger's novel lacks the obvious thematic content expected of "serious" fiction. Yet in presenting the chaos created in part by language, Berger cannot escape such content, and he paints a loving tribute to contemporary paranoia.

CHANGING THE PAST

First published: 1989
Type of work: Novel

An unhappy, unfulfilled middle-aged man is given several chances to change the life that he has led.

Berger's interests in science fiction, popular culture, and the ordinary lives of middle-class Americans all come together in *Changing the Past*. A mysterious stranger claiming to work for a government agency gives an unhappy New Yorker a chance for a different identity. Walter Hunsicker, copy editor at a large publishing house, has been chosen because he is seemingly satisfied with his wife, son, and job. Walter is a variation on the copywriter of *Being Invisible* (1987), who can disappear at will but remains at the mercy of the forces raging around him.

After one day as Jack Kellog, ruthless business tycoon, Walter wants to try again because that identity is too remote from how he sees himself. Berger then presents lengthy narratives with Walter as Jackie Kellog, vulgar nightclub comedian; John Kellog, novelist; and Jonathan Kellog, radio psychologist. In each life, Walter experiences setbacks before achieving success and fame, only for a decline to follow. He desperately wants love and sexual fulfillment, but things somehow never work out.

Berger satirizes topics such as show business, literary jealousies, self-help, politics, and fame as Walter/Kellog flails away at each of his lives. Jackie cynically uses people on his way to the top, and when his popularity wanes, he just as cynically resorts to religion in an attempt to regain favor. John becomes his unappetizing agent's lover as a means of getting published. Initially uncomfortable with dealing with sexual questions on his radio program, Jonathan slowly becomes a sexual adviser to the nation. Berger is constantly amused at how Americans seem to be both lascivious and puritanical at the same time.

Berger suggests that Walter's need to change the past is indicative of his problem. Anyone who wants such a change is destined for unhappiness. While such a moral judgment may be more blatant than is usually the case for Berger, he is still more interested in narrative for its own sake and has Walter stand by objectively without interfering with the follies of his different selves. Seeing how Kellog will slowly rise and fall is fascinating. Each version of Kellog finds a different way in which to fail, with Berger adopting a different tone and structure each time. While Jackie and John are followed from their youth, Jonathan's success is revealed at the beginning of his story, with the account of his rise coming in the middle. Such variations are fitting for a novel examining the nature of time. Jonathan's inevitable collapse is the most surprising, especially since he is the most humane of the vain Kellogs, though each eventually wants to do better. This last quality illustrates Walter's essential nature, because he wants each Kellog to be someone of whom his wife and son could be proud. Walter painfully learns that the nature of happiness involves more than fate and free will.

MEETING EVIL

First published: 1992
Type of work: Novel

When an ordinary man offers to help a driver in distress, a series of uncontrollable events leads him to be suspected of murder.

Meeting Evil combines the characters and situations of *Killing Time*, *Neighbors*, and *The Houseguest* (1988) to darkly comic effect. John Felton, married and the father of two, is an unsuccessful real estate salesman in a small community. Like many of Berger's Everyman protagonists, John is an essentially good person motivated by a sense to do right and to seem considerate of others. His benign tolerance is severely tested when a stranger comes to his door on John's day off and asks for help in pushing a stalled car. Richie turns out to be John's complete opposite and the embodiment of a typical civilized American's worst nightmares.

A much more dangerous version of Harry and Ramona of *Neighbors* and the visitor in *The Houseguest*, Richie is a psychopath who sincerely believes that he is not a bad person. Violence just happens to erupt wherever he goes, though he insists that it is the police who commit most crimes. John is unable to break away from Richie as he steals cars, kidnaps other innocents, and carries out more mayhem. John escapes only to be charged with Richie's crimes. The often hilarious novel's denouement plays out when John finally returns home to find his wife entertaining Richie, whom she thinks is his client.

Richie's acts cause John to reevaluate his values, though he corrects himself every time that he feels he is giving in to Richie's cynical view of human nature. Despite one violent act after another, John remains terrified of being thought rude and is shocked that strangers might be wary of him. More than anything, John wants the unfair views that others take of him because of Richie to stop. Berger suggests that there is a subtle distinction between civilized behavior and the perception of such behavior. John's civility is sincere yet is an ineffective weapon against the chaos surrounding him.

The ironic relationship between the characters is underscored by Richie's admiration for the person he considers his only friend. Although Richie, an escapee from a mental institution, constantly mocks John's bourgeois views, he likes John's refusal to sway, his insistence upon sticking to his principles in the face of overwhelming reasons to do otherwise. John's sense of responsibility wavers but never disappears, while Richie accepts no responsibility for his actions. In this world of misconstrued motivations and perverted morality, John's essential decency is an ineffective weapon. This point becomes even clearer when John goes from being Richie's victim to being victimized by the foolish police. John comes to realize that what is most important is not how others perceive him but what he thinks of himself. Before he can arrive at this view, he must face what he and Richie have in common, that the criminal represents his darker side.

Berger, as always wanting to keep his reader off-balance, briefly shifts to Richie's point of view midway through the novel. Richie's insistence that he lives by a code and that he detests immorality makes his antics even more ironic. Berger follows this interlude with John's recognition that this extreme situation has brought out previously hidden qualities, an opportunity to make up for earlier failures, an awareness that he has enclosed himself in a "convenient moral armor." He actually needs a

monster such as Richie to goad him into changing his complacent life, to recognize that his life has been as aimless as Richie's own.

SUSPECTS

First published: 1996
Type of work: Novel

When a young woman and her daughter are murdered, the police suspect her ineffectual brother-in-law.

While several of Berger's novels have been considered genre parodies by critics, *Suspects* seems to be an almost straightforward police procedural in the tradition of Ed McBain, shifting back and forth between the police investigating a brutal murder and the aimless life of their prime suspect. The novel lacks the irony and humor of most of Berger's efforts while demonstrating his interest in storytelling as an end in itself. The seemingly effortless, realistic, often mundane dialogue recalls such crime writers as George V. Higgins.

Donna Howland and her three-year-old daughter are killed while Larry Howland is at a motel with his boss's wife. After initially suspecting Larry, the police turn their attention to his younger half brother, Lloyd, fired from his job at a supermarket shortly before the murders. The narrative follows the unstable Lloyd on his rambles as he is befriended by Molly, a long-distance truck driver. When he learns of the deaths, Lloyd confronts Larry, whom he suspects, but is arrested himself.

Berger also follows the investigation of Moody, a suggestively named homicide detective, with glimpses of his personal life, including heavy drinking and two failed marriages. Moody is disgusted to learn that LeBeau, his partner, is having an affair with Daisy O'Connor, a police officer whom Moody has known since she was a child because her father was his partner. That the Howland murders, as well as a string of violent robberies, are solved less by painstaking police work than by sheer chance is the closest Berger comes to his usual irony, though he is clearly sympathetic to the police and their struggle to avoid cynical views of human nature. The unlikely friendship that develops between Lloyd and

Moody offers some sentimentality atypical of the ever-evolving Berger.

Though Berger probably intends *Suspects* to be an example of pure fiction, it does comment on the hypocrisies of small-town life. The neighbor who kills the Howlands thinks that a murderer is less evil than what he terms a sex maniac. Many of Berger's men fear and mistrust sex. Lloyd is confused by his feelings for Donna and is capable of having sex only with prostitutes, never with "nice" women. Another Berger target is the American obsession with the media. The killer, who sees himself as an exemplary citizen, wants to confess to a television news team rather than to Moody and LeBeau. The killer's defense of his actions represents one of Berger's best explorations of how language can be distorted into the banality of evil. The matter-of-fact tone of *Suspects* makes the revelation of the killer and his motives all the more shocking. The novel's greatest strengths are the sharply drawn characters, especially with the complicated motivations of Lloyd, who is preoccupied with not seeming phony, and Moody, who retreats from the chaos of life by allowing his work to engulf him.

SUMMARY

Style and content are inseparable in Berger's distinctively American novels that explore the mysteries of daily existence. His characters assert their identities through language. Speaking to his friend Reinhart in *Vital Parts*, Splendor Mainwaring, who defines himself in part by changing his name, says of his son, who also changes his name several times, "Raymond will say almost anything. He has discovered the technique of bold assertion, in which the content is almost irrelevant. He is American to the core: to *say* is to *be*. You and I make a distinction between rhetoric and reality." This distinction between reality and the way in which language is used

DISCUSSION TOPICS

- How is violence essential to Thomas Berger's work?

- In what ways is Berger commenting on the typical lives of ordinary Americans?

- Berger's novels are often inspired by other literary works or genres. In what ways are such novels commentaries on fiction itself?

- Berger has denied that his novels are parodies. In what ways is he right or wrong?

- How is language the central element of Berger's novels?

- How are Berger's novels examples of "pure fiction," in which storytelling is more important than character and theme?

- How does the character of Carlo Reinhart evolve in the course of Berger's novels?

- Compare the ways in which the American West is presented in *Little Big Man* and *The Return of Little Big Man*.

to create or distort it is the essence of Berger's fictional world. He has said that he writes to amuse himself and looks for himself through the English language: "Language is tremendously important to me. It's a morality and a politics and a religion. I really believe that if you write well you're a 'good' man." Berger's novels deal uniquely and entertainingly with how language and morality are intertwined.

Michael Adams

BIBLIOGRAPHY

By the Author

LONG FICTION:
Crazy in Berlin, 1958
Reinhart in Love, 1962
Little Big Man, 1964
Killing Time, 1967
Vital Parts, 1970
Regiment of Women, 1973
Sneaky People, 1975
Who Is Teddy Villanova?, 1977
Arthur Rex, 1978
Neighbors, 1980
Reinhart's Women, 1981
The Feud, 1983
Nowhere, 1985
Being Invisible, 1987
The Houseguest, 1988
Changing the Past, 1989
Orrie's Story, 1990
Meeting Evil, 1992
Robert Crews, 1994
Suspects, 1996
The Return of Little Big Man, 1999
Best Friends, 2003
Adventures of the Artificial Woman, 2004

DRAMA:
Other People, pr. 1970

About the Author

Barr, Marleen. "Men in Feminist Science Fiction: Marge Piercy, Thomas Berger, and the End of Masculinity." In *Science Fiction Roots and Branches: Contemporary Critical Approaches*, edited by Rhys Garnett and R. J. Ellis. New York: St. Martin's Press, 1990.

Chapman, Edgar L. "'Seeing' Invisibility: Or, Invisibility as Metaphor in Thomas Berger's *Being Invisible*." *Journal of the Fantastic in the Arts* 4 (1992): 65-93.

Landon, Brooks. *Thomas Berger*. Boston: Twayne, 1989.

_____. "Thomas Berger: Dedicated to the Novel." *World & I* 18 (October, 2003): 208-209.

_____. "Thomas Berger's *Arthur Rex*." In *King Arthur Through the Ages*, edited by Valerie M. Lagorio and Mildred Leake Day. New York: Garland, 1990.

Sinowitz, Michael Leigh. "The Western as Postmodern Satiric History: Thomas Berger's *Little Big Man*." *Clio* 28 (Winter, 1999): 129-148.

Stypes, Aaron. "Thomas Berger and Sheer Incongruity." *South Dakota Review* 32 (Winter, 1994): 34-43.

Wallace, Jon. "A Murderous Clarity: A Reading of Thomas Berger's *Killing Time*." *Philological Quarterly* 68 (Winter, 1989): 101-114.

Zimmerman, Brett. "The Linguistic Key to Crabb's Veracity: Berger's *Little Big Man* Revisited." *Western American Literature* 38 (Fall, 2003): 270-288.

WENDELL BERRY

Born: Henry County, Kentucky
August 5, 1934

Dan Carraco

As a poet, essayist, and novelist, Berry has become widely recognized as an advocate of responsible farming and environmental practices.

BIOGRAPHY

Wendell Berry was born in rural Henry County, outside Port Royal, Kentucky, on August 5, 1934. His father, John Berry, was a respected lawyer and attorney for the Burley Tobacco Growers Association. The Berrys—Wendell's mother, two sisters, and brother—were all readers, and they were a lively and well-informed family. His father was a keen judge of farmland and often spoke with his sons about the merits of various local farms.

Wendell attended local public schools and entered the University of Kentucky in Lexington, where he earned his B.A. in 1956 and his master's degree in English in 1957. He married Tanya Amyx in May, 1957, and taught for a year at Georgetown College, a small liberal arts school in Georgetown, Kentucky. Deciding to pursue a career as a writer, he applied for a Wallace Stegner Writing Fellowship at Stanford University, studying under Stegner in 1958-1959, and then serving as E. H. Jones Lecturer (in creative writing) in 1959-1960. Berry's first novel, *Nathan Coulter,* was published by Houghton Mifflin in 1960. A Guggenheim Foundation Fellowship allowed him to travel with his wife and family in France and Italy for a year in 1962.

Berry returned to accept an appointment as assistant professor at New York University, where he directed the freshman English program from 1962 to 1964. By this time he was actively publishing po-

etry, earning the Vachel Lindsay Prize from *Poetry* magazine in 1962. His elegy on John F. Kennedy's death, "November Twenty-six, Nineteen Hundred Sixty-three," first published in *The Nation* and reprinted with illustrations by Ben Shahn, won special recognition.

In 1964, Berry made a momentous decision to leave the New York literary scene and return to Kentucky, where he purchased a run-down farm near his boyhood home of Port Royal and joined the English department at the University of Kentucky. Berry describes the complex reasons behind this decision in his autobiographical essay, "The Long-Legged House." He rebuilt a small summer house on the banks of the Kentucky River as a study and began to restore Lane's Landing Farm as a working farm. By that time, he was well into his second novel, *A Place on Earth* (1967), which he completed with the assistance of a Rockefeller Foundation Fellowship. He also published his first poetry volume, *The Broken Ground* (1964), that same year. Berry's return to Kentucky marked a reaffirmation of local family ties that stretched back five generations to when his great-grandfather had emigrated from Ireland and settled in Port Royal in 1803.

Though his New York friends warned him against returning home, Berry has never regretted his decision. In returning to his native community to reclaim his heritage, Berry made a decision to write about what he knew best: the land and people of his native Kentucky hill country. His fictional Port William was his "undiscovered country," but he had to discover how to write about his native region, how to free himself from the southern romantic clichés and to see things clearly. In *The Hidden Wound* (1970), Berry writes about the crippling legacy of slavery and the destructive attitudes toward the land that it fostered. The book is also a meditation on race relations and a tribute to Old Nick and Aunt Georgie, black tenants on his father's farm who had influenced Berry as a boy. In a broader sense, the book is about how Americans have exploited both people and land.

Writing and organic farming became twin vocations for Berry. He consciously decided to restore his hillside farm by farming it organically. He claims that his training as a poet helped him to become an organic farmer, to view farming as a way of life and not merely as an exploitation of the land for profit. He views both a farm and a poem as a complex of living structures that "mutually clarify and sustain each other."

Berry was clearly inspired by his return home, publishing numerous poetry volumes in the following decade—such as *Openings* (1968), *Farming: A Hand Book* (1970), *The Country of Marriage* (1973), and *Clearing* (1977)—as well as a third novel, *The Memory of Old Jack* (1974), and the essay collection *A Continuous Harmony: Essays Cultural and Agricultural* (1972).

Along with his teaching at the University of Kentucky, Berry periodically accepted visiting appointments, returning to Stanford University in 1968-1969 as a visiting professor of creative writing and subsequently serving as writer in residence at the University of Cincinnati in the winter of 1974, at Centre College in the winter of 1977, and at Bucknell University in 1987.

In 1977, Berry published his fourth essay collection, *The Unsettling of America: Culture and Agriculture.* He resigned his professorship at the University of Kentucky in order to accept a position as contributing editor for two of the magazines at Rodale Press, *Organic Gardening* and *New Farm.* He has continued to be a leading spokesman for small-scale family farming and sound conservation practices, opposing the wastefulness of large-scale corporate farming. His essays have appeared in publications as diverse as *The Hudson Review, Harper's Magazine,* and *The Nation* on one hand, and *Blair and Ketchum's Country Journal* and *Organic Gardening* on the other.

In 1980, Berry changed publishers and went to North Point Press, a small, well-respected West Coast publisher in Berkeley, California, which published his work until 1991. The 1980's were an active decade for Berry, with two poetry volumes appearing, *A Part* (1980) and *The Wheel* (1982), as well as an essay collection, *The Gift of Good Land* (1981), and a book of literary essays, *Standing by Words* (1983). North Point Press also published another essay collection, *Recollected Essays, 1965-1980* (1981), and Berry's *Collected Poems, 1957-1982* (1985). A collection of Port William stories, *The Wild Birds* (1986), appeared the next year, followed by *Sabbaths* (1987), a poetry volume; *Home Economics* (1987), another essay collection; *Remembering* (1988), a novella; and *What Are People For?* (1990), an essay collection. Berry returned to teach part-time at the University of Kentucky, but he guards his privacy as a writer and is reluctant to accept engagements that will take him away from his writing or farming.

ANALYSIS

Stegner has written of Berry's work, "It is hard to say whether I like this writer better as a poet, an essayist, or a novelist. He is all three, at a high level." What connects all of Berry's work is a tough-minded regional vision whose constituents are not the traditional southern pieties but the integrity of language, farming, marriage, labor, and place. His regionalism is more akin to that of William Carlos Williams than that of William Faulkner. It has less to do with mythologizing a region than with the complex cultural memory of a particular place that comes from many generations of continuous settlement in that place. He is not interested in evoking a mythic past or recounting the decline and fall of a planter aristocracy but rather in describing an ethic and a way of life based upon devotion to land and place.

Berry's decision to return to his native region was based on his desire to avoid the rootless, urban nomadism of modern American life. In *A Continuous Harmony,* he criticizes the restless mobility of modern motorized culture. Deserts may produce nomadic cultures, but for the rich, fertile, well-watered land of Kentucky to do so is preposterous. Berry's regionalism might almost be described as ecological:

> The regionalism that I adhere to could almost be described simply as *local life aware of itself.* It would tend to substitute for the myths and stereotypes of a region a particular knowledge of the life of the

place one lives in and intends to *continue* to live in. It pertains to living as much as writing, and it pertains to living *before* it pertains to writing. The motive of such regionalism is the awareness that local life is intricately dependent, for its quality but also for its continuance, upon local knowledge.

All of Berry's writing has derived from this vision of stubborn loyalty to a particular place. It has its roots in Thomas Jefferson's ideal of the intelligent yeoman farmer and in the Southern Agrarian ideals articulated by Allen Tate and others in *I'll Take My Stand* (1926). To these political and literary antecedents, Berry brings a keen ecological awareness along with a profound respect for the culture of farming—in the root sense of "agriculture." His interest is in developing long-term sustainable methods of agriculture that will not exhaust the land or harm the environment and will allow a rural village culture to reestablish itself in the United States. He is opposed, therefore, to the powerful economic and social forces that have combined to disrupt rural American life since the end of World War II.

In his novels, Berry celebrates three families of his fictional Port William community—the Coulters, the Feltners, and the Beechums—who farm the rolling hillsides and rich bottomlands of the Kentucky River Valley region, west of the Appalachians. In a carefully controlled, meticulously detailed style, he recounts the small triumphs and disappointments of their lives. They are all small tobacco farmers with mixed livestock and grain crops who struggle from year to year, sustained by the pride and discipline of their work. Berry evokes the strengths and continuities of the community that sustained this way of life until recently. Economic issues often pit the greed and indifference of outsiders against local farmers who struggle to produce a livelihood and preserve their farms.

In his first novel, *Nathan Coulter,* Berry recounts the growth of a young Kentucky farm boy whose loveless home is dominated, after his mother's death, by a harsh father driven to overworking his farm and himself. In this brutal, male environment, young Nathan Coulter finds nurturance in his carefree Uncle Burley, who is not driven by the obsession to own and dominate the land.

In Berry's next novel, *A Place on Earth*, Mat Feltner tries to come to terms with the loss of his only son, Virgil, during World War II. In the seasonal idylls of work and family, Mat struggles to continue working his land in memory of his son. *The Memory of Old Jack*, Berry's third and perhaps most accomplished novel, traces the life of Jack Beechum, a retired farmer of ninety-two, who relives his life as farm boy, husband, father, lover, farmer, and community figure on a radiant day in September, 1952. A short-story collection, *The Wild Birds*, recounts six more stories of the families of the Port William fellowship, and a novella, *Remembering*, tells the story of a crisis of faith experienced by farmer Andy Catlett after he loses his right hand in a corn picker. In all these works, Berry's fictional style is spare and deliberately understated, in the formalist tradition, with carefully chosen narrative and symbolic incidents.

Berry's poetry celebrates the lyrical dimensions of his agrarian vision of the farmer as husband to farm and land as well as to wife and family. Stewardship is the major unifying theme—between the farmer and his family, community, land, and region. As a pastoral poet, Berry writes about the land, the seasons, the cycle of the agricultural year. His root metaphor is husbandry—caring, rearing, nurturing, growing, and harvesting what the land yields. In the vision of his poems, the mythos of male generativeness finds its response in female receptivity. The voice in his poems is, in turn, pensive, meditative, celebratory, and affirming. One of his chief personae, "the Mad Farmer," sometimes voices radical or whimsical agrarian social or political positions that reflect the more polemical arguments in Berry's essays, but there is a quiet, elegiac mood in his poetry as well, one that celebrates the richness of the moment in the poetic perception and gives thanks for his marriage, his land, and his community.

Berry's essays are his most assertive genre; in them he voices most directly his concerns about the ravages of strip mining, corporate farming, agribusiness, racism, and consumerism, balancing these against the virtues of small, self-contained farms and rural communities. His *The Unsettling of America: Culture and Agriculture* has become a basic text of the environmental movement.

For Berry, environmental responsibility begins with personal frugality, careful land use, and intact farming communities. The environmental crisis, he argues, is at heart a human problem, rather than an economic or technological one. It is a problem of optimal scale, of knowing how to farm in a sustainable manner, rather than exploiting and ruining the land. The healthiest farms and rural economies are the most diverse; they are not the huge, one-crop monocultures encouraged by corporate farming. Such diversity depends upon the kind of family farms that survived in the United States until the end of World War II.

In his essay collections, Berry traces the social and economic decline of the family farm and its environmental consequences. Water pollution, pesticide contamination, and topsoil runoff are but a few of the adverse consequences of poor farming practices. With the demise of small, carefully run farms and the subsequent loss of farm labor, corporate farmers were forced to adopt wasteful practices. Berry's Kentucky countryside was once a good farming region, with many small farms lovingly tended. Now there are abandoned farms and rural poverty. In *What Are People For?*, Berry concludes that "we have nearly destroyed American farming, and in the process have nearly destroyed ourselves."

NATHAN COULTER

First published: 1960 (revised, 1985)
Type of work: Novel

Nathan Coulter, a young Kentucky farm boy, faces a harsh, demanding father and the loss of his mother and as he grows to maturity.

Berry's first novel, *Nathan Coulter,* is a spare, lean *Bildungsroman* that traces the development of the young protagonist, Nathan, as he grows from childhood to adulthood in a Kentucky farming family. Narrated by Nathan in the first-person voice, the novel recounts the working lives of the Coulters, who raise tobacco on a hill farm outside Port William. The action is set in the early part of the twentieth century, when the farm work was done by hand and with mules. Each person's value was known by his labor. Nathan and his older brother, Tom, are slowly initiated into this work of farming. The novel re-creates the mythos of a pre-World War II farming community.

Nathan Coulter is the story of a male-dominated family, of a father who drives himself and his sons too hard in a continual struggle to force his farm to yield. Jarrat Coulter is competitive and driven, as was his father, and he tries to instill in his sons the same stern discipline of work. Unfortunately for him (and for them), there is no joy in his labor or his land, nor any real nurturing for his sons or his farm.

Jarrat unconsciously blames his sons for their mother's death. He leaves them in the care of their grandparents and withdraws into sullen resentment. This resentment of his children culminates in a terrible fight with his older son, Tom, during the tobacco harvest, after he has driven his help beyond endurance. Beaten and humiliated, Tom leaves home, and Nathan is left in the care of his Uncle Burley, who has refused the burden of landownership. Burley is virtually the only kind and humane figure in this bleak novel.

In his portrait of Jarrat Coulter, Berry reveals the limitations of this harsh work ethic. Jarrat has attempted to dominate both his land and his family, to the detriment of both, without any compassionate attachment to either. In his "severe and isolated manhood," he has closed himself off from healing relationships with his sons or his land. When the break comes with his children, it is complete. Jarrat's brother Burley, on the other hand, lacks the ambition to farm, preferring instead to hunt and fish when he is not working for others. Burley has a gentler nature, however; each brother has something that the other lacks, and each is, by himself, incomplete.

There is much cruelty in this novel—much agrarian violence—toward men, animals, and the land. The two boys blow up a friend's pet crow with a dynamite cap and fuse, Uncle Burley shoots the heads off live ducks at a carnival, fish are blown out of the river with a stick of dynamite, and Burley's hunting dogs tear apart a live raccoon. This cruelty seems to emerge from a masculine agrarian culture that is bent on dominating the land rather than living within its limits. Women are scarcely mentioned in the novel except as background figures, and there are few community customs or celebrations to soften this harsh frontier ethic.

Berry writes about the succession of generations on the land, but the Coulters are too competitive to work the same land, so Jarrat buys the farm adjoining his father's land. In the original 1960 version of the novel, Berry traced Nathan's maturation until he starts to farm himself. In the condensed version of the novel, published in 1985, he cut the work considerably, ending it with the death of Nathan's grandfather after the fall tobacco harvest. Unable to live with his father, Nathan's older brother, Tom, has already left to farm elsewhere, and the novel ends with the hope that Nathan and his father will eventually be reconciled.

THE COUNTRY OF MARRIAGE

First published: 1973
Type of work: Poetry

Berry's fourth volume of poetry contains thirty-five lyric poems that celebrate farming, marriage, and nature.

The lyric poems in *The Country of Marriage* celebrate Berry's rich and complex sense of place through the interlocking relationships of birth, marriage, livelihood, and heritage. The quiet, contemplative poems collected in this volume celebrate the land in its different moods and seasons. Through the dominant metaphors of marriage and husbandry, Berry invokes the deep and enduring relationship of his poetic persona, the "Mad Farmer," to family, land, and place. Berry's poems recall another poetic commitment to a particular place: the growth of William Carlos Williams's poetry from his lifelong service as a pediatrician in Paterson, New Jersey.

In the opening poem, "The Old Elm Tree by the River," Berry proclaims: "In us the land enacts its history." These sentiments are later echoed in his lyric tribute to Agrarian writer Allen Tate, "The Clear Days," in which Berry intimates that the poet and lover will remain distracted "Until the heart has found/ Its native piece of the ground." In the final selection, "The Anniversary," he concludes, "What we have been becomes/ The country where we are." These poems are about Berry's multiple marriages of commitment: to a region, a human relationship, a vocation, and a vision. The firmness and certainty of his commitment are reflected in the quiet, contemplative serenity of his lines.

Berry's commitment to place is reinforced in his adulatory "To William Butler Yeats," which celebrates the Irish poet's loyalty to his native region: "Poet, you were but keeping faith/ With your native truth and place." In "The Wild Geese," the poet affirms that "What we need is here." Another lyric, "A Homecoming," concludes, "Show me/ my country. Take me home."

The title poem, "The Country of Marriage," is a long, intimate courtship poem, written in the first-person voice and presumably addressed to the poet's wife. His promise to her provides him, like a wanderer, with "the solace of his native land/ under his feet again and moving in his blood." The common life shared by the poet and his wife renews him, like the hospitable welcome of a house, orchard, and garden. She is the one to whom he always returns. The bond of their relationship is much more than a pragmatic exchange of love and work; it is a partnership of loving mutuality. They drink the renewing waters of their relationship, planting their lives together in the place they have consecrated by their marriage. Its abundance survives their thirst, for "like the water/ of a deep stream, love is always too much."

The discerning reader may hear in this lovely marriage poem faint echoes of Edmund Spenser's great Elizabethan nuptial poem, "Epithalamion" (1594), particularly in the theme of marriage standing as a firm bulwark against the mutability of time. A companion piece, "A Marriage, an Elegy," contains echoes of the classical myth of Baucis and Philemon, the faithful old couple whose hospitality was rewarded by the gods, who granted their wish that they never be separated even after their death.

The nurturing care of farming husbandry is celebrated in such poems as "Planting Trees," "The Gathering," "Planting Crocuses," and "The Asparagus Bed." Farming is seen as an honorable livelihood, worthy of being passed on from father to son. Other poems reflect a Frostian response to the various moods of nature, as in listening to a song sparrow singing in the

fall, admiring the wild geese flying overhead, or marveling at the mist rising from a river in the bitter cold of winter.

The mood of Berry's poems is not always lyrical or meditative, however; some poems take on a more strident or polemical tone, particularly those spoken by his Mad Farmer persona. "The Mad Farmer Manifesto: The First Amendment" celebrates responsible land ownership as an antidote to the abstract greed of consumerism. "Testament," a poem calling for a simple death and burial, echoes William Carlos Williams's "Tract," a poem on the same topic. The triptych "Inland Passages" recalls the frontier transition from hunting to homesteading, farming, and finally a settled rural culture, contrasting restless wandering with contented settlement in one place. The closing poem in the volume, "An Anniversary," recalls in the cycle of the seasons the Edenic myth of innocence, fall, loss, and redemption.

THE GIFT OF GOOD LAND

First published: 1981
Type of work: Essays

Twenty-four essays explore the relationships between culture and agriculture.

Berry's fourth essay collection, *The Gift of Good Land*, continues to address many of the same issues that he has touched upon in earlier volumes. Many of these essays first appeared in *The New Farm* or *Organic Gardening* during Berry's period of association with Rodale Press. These essays nicely balance theory and practice, both reflecting Berry's criticism of prevailing assumptions of modern American agriculture and offering cultural alternatives to large-scale, mechanized, single-crop farming. A more sensible economy of scale, according to Berry, would favor small, diversified farms such as those of the Amish and of others who practice traditional or alternative farming methods.

One must defend the small farm, Berry argues in his foreword, on more than economic terms. One must judge economic health according to the overall health and vitality of human and natural households:

Like a household, [the small farm] is a human organism, and it has its origin in both nature and culture. Its justification is not only agricultural, but is a part of an ancient pattern of values, ideas, aspirations, attitudes, faiths, knowledge, and skills that propose and support the sound establishment of a people on the land. To defend the small farm is to defend a large part, and the best part, of our cultural inheritance.

Throughout the volume, Berry stresses the indivisibility of culture and agriculture: A culture's farming methods will invariably reflect the values and assumptions of that culture. The United States has tended to stress bigness, impersonality, mechanization, and exploitation of the land. For Berry, however, small is better. Emphasizing the interconnectedness of humans, land, climate, animals, and local culture, Berry values small-scale, labor-intensive agricultural techniques that allow the land to be used continuously while still maintaining its fertility and yield.

Berry cites a number of diverse examples of local, native farming cultures that are admirably suited to their local soil and climate conditions—those of the Indians of the Peruvian Andes, the Hopi of the southeastern Arizona desert, and the Amish farmers of Pennsylvania. In each of these diverse examples, the scale, balance, diversity, and quality of the agriculture are appropriate for the local environment. Good farming, Berry emphasizes, involves communal techniques, craftsmanship, and artistry evolved over long periods of time, not merely drudgery. Each of these is a small-scale solution, markedly in contrast with the factory system of modern American agriculture.

In his essays, Berry stresses small-scale solutions for agricultural problems. He asks how much technology is enough and what is too much. He advocates a wise restraint in the use of large-scale farm machinery, preferring instead to work with hand tools or with horses at a slower, more deliberate pace. Berry praises the homestead, the garden, the small, intensively worked farm as best achieving the ideal of long-term sustainable yield. The best farms imitate nature in their variety. The organic farm, according to Sir Leslie Howard, is one whose structure is formed in imitation of a natural system. Soil fertility can best be studied by understanding the nutrient cycle of a woodland. In "Solving the Pattern," Berry lists fourteen critical standards for solving agricultural problems that are equally valid as general ecological principles.

In his title essay, "The Gift of Good Land," Berry attacks the traditional notion of land ownership, suggesting that the land is lent to humanity and brings with it the responsibility for good steward-ship. He compares the Judeo-Christian legacy with the Buddhist doctrine of "right livelihood" or "right occupation," his purpose being to establish a biblical argument for ecological and agricultural responsibility.

To practice good stewardship, Berry argues, is to imitate God's love for his creation and to respect that creation as something that exists beyond hu-man understanding and exclusively human pur-poses. To attempt to dominate and exploit the land is to commit exactly the same kind of sin of hubris or pride that was exemplified in Satan's rebellion against God's order. To calculate the success of modern agribusiness solely in economic terms, apart from the long-term health of the land and the human community, is to commit the equally se-rious sin of abstraction.

By this, Berry means the reduction of a greater good, the continued vitality of the land, to a lesser good: short-term economic profit. The economics of agribusiness, Berry charges, ignores the com-plex disciplines necessary to traditional farming practices and ultimately destroys the land, the farming communities, and the culture on which they are based. He defends the small farm because its smallness is a prerequisite of diversity, which is, in turn, a prerequisite to the care and nurture of the world as God's creation.

"PRAY WITHOUT CEASING"

First published: 1992 (collected in *That Distant Land*, 2004)
Type of work: Short story

A grandson recalls how his grandfather found the moral strength to forsake revenge for his father's murder by his best friend.

In "Pray Without Ceasing," the first of five stories in *Fidelity* (1992), Andy Catlett recounts the day in July, 1912, when his great-grandfather, Ben Feltner,

was shot by his friend and kinsman, Thad Coulter, over an imagined slight. An old newspaper article about the murder stimulates Andy's recollection of how his grandfather Mat Feltner, Ben's son, was able to break the cycle of violence and revenge.

Thad's problems began when he learned that he would lose his farm, heavily mortgaged to fi-nance his son Abner's grocery in Hargrave. Abner defaulted on the loan, and Thad could not repay the bank. Drunk and belligerent, Thad went to Ben Feltner's farm early one morning to ask for help. When Ben showed him to the door and told him to return when he was sober, Thad felt insulted and cursed his friend.

Their paths converged later that Saturday in Port William. Ben had come to seek advice from Thad's kinsmen, and Thad had come seeking re-venge. Thad shot Ben down in front of his son, Mat, who was physically restrained from pursuit by his friend, Jack Beechum. Mat's hard-won moral re-straint contrasts with Thad's physical and moral degradation after the murder, as he sank into self-loathing and abused his wife, daughter, and mule. Thad's daughter, Mary Elizabeth, pursued her fa-ther as he fled before finally surrendering to the sheriff in Hargrave. Despite Mary Elizabeth's con-soling efforts, Thad hanged himself in his prison cell that night.

At Ben Feltner's wake, Jack Beechum supported Mat's nonviolence. Miss Della Budge, Jack's for-mer teacher, advised them to "pray without ceas-ing" (1 Thessalonians 5:17). When a mob ap-peared outside the Feltner house to organize a lynching, Mat renounced vengeance and instead invited them either in to eat or to disperse.

"Pray Without Ceasing" illustrates the power of nonviolence and forgiveness to break the cycle of violence and revenge. Mat's moral courage heals the wounds of violence and restores family ties bro-ken by a rash, impulsive act. Mat's peacemaking re-unites two families, first in friendship and later in marriage. Grandson Andy Catlett is the child of that forgiveness.

SUMMARY

"My work has been motivated," Berry has writ-ten, "by a desire to make myself responsibly at home in this world and in my native and chosen place." This theme of a responsible and self-sufficient regionalism, rooted in the skills and knowledge of Berry's native Kentucky farming communities, is at the heart of his vision. As a poet, novelist, and essayist, Berry has celebrated the virtues of farming as a vocation, of the dignity of marriage, and of the rich diversity of local communities. His moral vision is based on the enduring Jeffersonian ideal of a nation of independent yeoman farmers, and Berry is a wise and perceptive cultural critic. His works range beyond agriculture and regionalism to offer a commonsense prescription for restoring the wholeness and vitality of rural American communities.

Andrew J. Angyal

BIBLIOGRAPHY

By the Author

POETRY:
November Twenty-six, Nineteen Hundred Sixty-three, 1963
The Broken Ground, 1964
Openings, 1968
Findings, 1969
Farming: A Hand Book, 1970
The Country of Marriage, 1973
An Eastward Look, 1974
To What Listens, 1975
Horses, 1975
Sayings and Doings, 1975
The Kentucky River: Two Poems, 1976
There Is Singing Around Me, 1976
Three Memorial Poems, 1976
Clearing, 1977
The Gift of Gravity, 1979
A Part, 1980
The Wheel, 1982
Collected Poems, 1957-1982, 1985
Sabbaths, 1987
Traveling at Home, 1989
Sabbaths, 1987-1990, 1992
Entries, 1994
The Farm, 1995
The Selected Poems of Wendell Berry, 1998
A Timbered Choir: The Sabbath Poems, 1979-1997, 1998
Given, 2005

LONG FICTION:
Nathan Coulter, 1960, revised, 1985
A Place on Earth, 1967, revised, 1983

DISCUSSION TOPICS

- Can Wendell Berry be considered a "spiritual" writer despite his disavowal of formal Christianity?

- What are the larger thematic implications of the biblical allusion in the title "Pray Without Ceasing"?

- Why does Thad Coulter shoot Ben Feltner? Why does Mat Feltner not avenge his father's death?

- How does "Pray Without Ceasing" fit into the thematic and narrative structure of *Fidelity*? What are the implications of the title of that short-story collection? "Fidelity" to what?

- How is Berry's southern Agrarian orientation reflected in his agricultural and cultural essays in *The Gift of Good Land*?

- What is the role of women in Berry's agrarian world? What is Berry's view of marriage? How is that view reflected in the poems of *The Country of Marriage*?

- Is Berry's regional vision ultimately nostalgic or elegiac? Does he witness the passing of an older order or celebrate a legacy of enduring agrarian values? Is it significant that most of his stories are set before World War II? What began to happen to the small family farm after the war?

The Memory of Old Jack, 1974
Remembering, 1988
A World Lost, 1996
Jayber Crow, 2000
Hannah Coulter, 2004

SHORT FICTION:
The Wild Birds, 1986
Fidelity, 1992
Watch with Me, 1994
Three Short Novels, 2002
That Distant Land: The Collected Stories, 2004

NONFICTION:
The Long-Legged House, 1969
The Hidden Wound, 1970
The Unforeseen Wilderness, 1971
A Continuous Harmony: Essays Cultural and Agricultural, 1972
The Unsettling of America: Culture and Agriculture, 1977
Recollected Essays, 1965-1980, 1981
The Gift of Good Land, 1981
Standing by Words, 1983
Home Economics, 1987
What Are People For?, 1990
Harland Hubbard: Life and Work, 1990
The Discovery of Kentucky, 1991
Standing on Earth, 1991
Sex, Economy, Freedom, and Community, 1993
Another Turn of the Crank, 1995
Life Is a Miracle: An Essay Against Modern Superstition, 2000
The Art of the Commonplace: The Agrarian Essays of Wendell Berry, 2002 (Norman Wirzba, editor)
In the Presence of Fear: Three Essays for a Changed World, 2002
Citizenship Papers: Essays, 2003

About the Author

Cornell, Robert. "*The Country of Marriage:* Wendell Berry's Personal Political Vision." *Southern Literary Review* 16 (Fall, 1983): 59-70.

Ditsky, John. "Wendell Berry: Homage to the Apple Tree." *Modern Poetry Studies* 2, no. 1 (1971): 7-15.

Freyfogle, Eric. "The Dilemma of Wendell Berry." *University of Illinois Law Review* 1994 (2): 363-385.

Hass, Robert. "Wendell Berry: Finding the Land." *Modern Poetry Studies* 2, no. 1 (1971): 16-38.

Hicks, Jack. "Wendell Berry's Husband to the World: *A Place on Earth.*" *American Literature* 51 (May, 1979): 238-254.

Merchant, Paul, ed. *Wendell Berry*. Lewiston, Idaho: Confluence Press, 1991.

Morgan, Speer. "Wendell Berry: A Fatal Singing." *Southern Review* 10 (October, 1974): 865-877.

Nibbelink, Herman. "Thoreau and Wendell Berry: Bachelor and Husband of Nature." *The South Atlantic Quarterly* 84 (Spring, 1985): 127-140.

Pevear, Richard. "On the Prose of Wendell Berry." *Hudson Review* 35 (Summer, 1982): 341-347.

Smith, Kimberly K. *Wendell Berry and the Agrarian Tradition: A Common Grace*. Lawrence: University Press of Kansas, 2003.

_____. "Wendell Berry's Feminist Agrarianism." *Women's Studies* 30 (2001): 623-646.

JOHN BERRYMAN

Born: McAlester, Oklahoma
October 25, 1914
Died: Minneapolis, Minnesota
January 7, 1972

Berryman's The Dream Songs *(1969) reconciles features of the long poem and the short lyric in an idiom which is tragicomic, classically formal, yet idiomatic.*

Daniel A. Lindley

BIOGRAPHY

John Berryman was born John Allyn Smith, Jr., on October 25, 1914, in McAlester, Oklahoma, the elder son of John Allyn Smith, Sr., and Martha Shaver Little Smith. The Smiths would have one other child, Robert Jefferson Smith, born September 1, 1919. Between 1914 and 1926, the Smith family moved about every two years to various Oklahoma farming communities, the elder Smith holding a series of banking positions. In 1924, a scandal involving the senior Smith's brother's theft of funds forced Berryman's father to resign from the First State Bank in Anadarko, Oklahoma. By 1925, Berryman's parents and grandmother had moved to Tampa, Florida. The boys remained in Oklahoma at a Roman Catholic boarding school, St. Joseph's Academy. Tempted by cheap land and quick profit, Berryman's father began to speculate in Florida real estate. By mid-1926, however, the land boom collapsed, Smith went bankrupt, and the entire family, including the boys (by this time recalled from Oklahoma), moved to Clearwater, Florida. It was there that they rented an apartment in a building owned by John Angus McAlpin Berryman.

The Smiths' marriage was by then all but ended. Smith, increasingly despondent over his business failures and his wife's obvious romantic involvement with their landlord, threatened suicide. On June 26, 1926, Smith was found shot dead outside their apartment, apparently a suicide. By September 8, 1926, his wife had married Berryman and had changed her own first and middle names to Jill Angel. She also changed her elder son's name to John Allyn McAlpin Berryman, though this was not done legally until 1936, when Berryman filed for a passport to study in England. Thus it was that at the age of twelve, the future poet had to abandon the name of his father and assume that of his mother's lover. His stepfather, whom he called "Uncle Angus," was a distant but never cruel man; even so, his father's apparent suicide continued to affect Berryman throughout his life. It certainly contributed to his preoccupation with death by suicide and foreshadowed his own manner of death.

After a generally unhappy stay at South Kent School in South Kent, Connecticut, Berryman had the good fortune to attend Columbia University, starting in 1932. It was there that he studied under Mark Van Doren. Van Doren, himself a poet as well as a scholar, encouraged Berryman to write verse, took him as a protégé, and was instrumental in helping him obtain the Euretta J. Kellett Scholarship for two years of study in England at Clare College, University of Cambridge. Berryman spent 1936 through 1938 at Clare College, pursuing his studies in the alternately brilliant, erratic, and lackadaisical way that typified his entire school career.

The two most important events of this period of his life were his engagement (despite a previous commitment to American Jean Bennett) to Beryl Eaman, a young English actress (for whom he would write a verse play, *Cleopatra*, in 1937) and his winning of the Oldham Shakespeare Prize. Eaman would stay with the Berrymans in 1938 and early 1939, but her doubts, coupled with the onset of World War II, led to her breaking the engagement.

The war years were difficult for Berryman. His mother had separated from his stepfather. Though Berryman had managed to place several poems with *The Southern Review* in 1938, he was without any work until the fall of 1939, when he managed (through Van Doren) to obtain an instructorship in English at Wayne University, Ann Arbor, Michigan. By December, however, he was having fainting spells, misdiagnosed as petit mal, a form of epilepsy. Things seemed better in the fall of 1940 but only for a short time.

He obtained an instructorship at Harvard University and published some of his poems in *Five Young American Poets* (1940), but he was not generally liked by his Harvard colleagues because of his irascible temperament and his firm refusal to pursue doctoral studies. He did not endear himself to James Laughlin, publisher of the poetry anthology, when he objected to his work being published with other poets, despite the fact that the others were Elizabeth Bishop, Randall Jarrell, W. R. Moses, and George Marion O'Donnell.

Berryman's poor eyesight and medical history meant exemption from military service, but with the United States' involvement in the war, college classes were small. He married his first wife, Eileen Patricia Mulligan, in 1942, but Harvard did not renew his contract, so at the end of spring term in 1943 he was without a teaching post and had little hope of finding one. He accepted a temporary position teaching English and Latin at Iona Preparatory School in New Rochelle, New York, in the fall of 1943 but resigned three weeks after the term had begun, to accept an instructorship in English at Princeton University.

Largely on the strength of his promise, for he had as yet published relatively little and nothing of a scholarly nature, Berryman obtained a two-year Rockefeller Foundation Research Fellowship in 1944 to prepare an edition of William Shakespeare's *King Lear* (1608). It was at this time that he first met the American poet Robert Lowell and Lowell's wife, author Jean Stafford.

Berryman never would complete his Shakespeare text, but the postwar years would bring a series of works which would dramatically illustrate his evolving style: *The Dispossessed* (1948), an anthology of verse that resembles the poetry of William Butler Yeats and Robert Frost; *Homage to Mistress Bradstreet* (1956), a long poem in which the poet attempts to seduce an unhappy and frustrated Anne Bradstreet (an American Puritan poet); and *Seventy-seven Dream Songs* (1964), later supplemented, rearranged, and published as *The Dream Songs* (1969). This last is his masterwork, and it introduced "Henry," a Berryman persona, as its antihero.

Despite the steadily increasing fame he won through these works and the tenured position he held as Regents Professor of Humanities at the University of Minnesota, Minneapolis, Berryman's personal life grew ever more chaotic. His second marriage, to Elizabeth Ann Levine, the mother of his only son, Paul, lasted less than three years (from 1956 to 1959). His third marriage, in 1961, to Kathleen Donahue, was more stable; his two daughters, Martha and Sarah Rebecca, were born in 1962 and 1971, but Berryman's drinking and despondency threatened even this relationship in the months before his death. Lukewarm critical reaction to *Love and Fame* (1970), which is a sober view of Berryman's pursuit of both as avenues to happiness, raised fears concerning his power to create verse. Though the critics had been kinder to *Berryman's Sonnets* (1967), those were twenty-year-old poems about a 1947 love affair.

Amid fears that his creative life was over, that his third marriage was failing, and that he was no longer effective as a teacher, Berryman closed the covenant that much of his poetry indicates he believed he had with his father. On a bitterly cold morning in Minneapolis, January 7, 1972, he leaped from the Washington Avenue Bridge, which connects the University of Minnesota's east and west campuses. His life thus ended as violently as had those of several poet colleagues he most admired: Hart Crane, Randall Jarrell, and Sylvia Plath.

ANALYSIS

Berryman sought a distinctive poetic voice throughout his career. As a young man, he particularly admired Yeats's ability to make poetry intensely personal yet mythic. He also admired Frost as a distinctly American and nonacademic poet who believed that what a poem implied was as important as what it literally expressed. Consequently, in the beginning of his career, Berryman was wary of T. S. Eliot's objective universal themes and characterizations. He also considered Eliot's use of learned allusions artificial. Neither was Berryman fond of Eliot's mentor Ezra Pound or "new poets" such as William Carlos Williams. He loved the gaudy imagery and eclecticism of Wallace Stevens.

Berryman would modify such negative positions considerably in the latter half of his career. Even late in his life, he obliquely criticized Williams's understanding of the function of narrative and history in a typically outspoken interview published in the *Harvard Advocate*. He also wrote a never-published, scholarly introduction to the poems of Pound, came to love Pound's *Hugh Selwyn Mauberley* (1920) and *Cantos* (1917-1970) as forerunners of his own *The Dream Songs*, and was himself admired by Pound as a new voice in American poetry.

Berryman's contacts with Eliot became more amicable over the years as well. His intense dislike for Eliot's poetry when Berryman was a student at Cambridge was still apparent in 1953, when Berryman wrote that he considered *Homage to Mistress Bradstreet* a reaction to long poems as they were then written—a veiled thrust at Eliot's *The Waste Land* (1922) and Williams's *Paterson* (1946-1958). Berryman courted Eliot's approval in the late 1940's when both were residents at Princeton University, but it is noteworthy that Eliot disliked Berryman's introduction to the Berryman anthology as originally submitted to Faber & Faber, where Eliot held a directorship, and that Eliot rejected *Seventy-seven Dream Songs* outright.

Clearly, Berryman identified most consistently with poets who were social outcasts, whose verse, like his own, was intensely personal and guardedly self-revelatory. He often began his literature courses with Walt Whitman's "Song of Myself" (1855, 1881). He had lifelong empathy with fellow suicide Crane and the flamboyant style and way of life of drinking companion Dylan Thomas. He pitied but also admired Delmore Schwartz and Jarrell, and he wished that he had met Plath, whose life so closely resembled his own.

Berryman's early verse, written before and during World War II, is personal but derivative. An attentive reader will note echoes of Whitman, Frost, Pound, Eliot, and even Williams in *The Dispossessed*. The sonnets to Lise, written to a woman named Chris with whom Berryman had a love affair during the late 1940's while at Princeton, are in the Petrarchan mode. They were published in the late 1960's, and in reprintings the name Chris appears instead of the Petrarchan echo (Lise for Laura). These poems are important in Berryman's oeuvre primarily because they show his turning toward specific personalities as well as actual locations and events. They also reveal something of the poet's chaotic life, his frantic and tawdry attempts to keep the affair secret, yet his decided attempt to couch every rendezvous in terms of high art.

The Berryman persona also appears as seducer in *Homage to Mistress Bradstreet*. Berryman received guarded critical approval for this long poem. He took the American Puritan poet Bradstreet as its subject, primarily because he considered her personal frustrations overwhelming and her poetry mediocre. In this sense, she represents the way Berryman saw his own life and art at the time. That he was having an affair with his own "Ann," the woman who would become his second wife, allows the poet's attempt at the seduction which frames the poem a personal level of meaning.

The Dream Songs, begun in 1955 and continued through 1968, represents the full realization of Berryman's style. Its 385 lyrics, which Berryman insisted should stand as a single poem, tell in disjointed narrative the life story of "Huffy Henry," a Berryman persona. Henry is an antihero, invariably thwarted by the circumstances of his life but inevitably rising to meet a new challenge, only to be struck down again. Berryman injects various details from both small and major incidents of his life, though a reader unacquainted with the poet's private life will miss many of the details. That Berryman successfully mixes various styles and achieves a distinctive tone which is simultaneously tragic and comic is a measure of the degree to which the poet had refined his style and altered his methods of composition.

The Dream Songs came to be a curse as well as a blessing for Berryman. It catapulted his verse to international attention, and fellow writers such as Saul Bellow, Adrienne Rich, and Ralph Ellison helped circulate the individual poems as they appeared. Berryman's old friend, publisher Robert Giroux, encouraged the poet at every turn, publishing *Seventy-seven Dream Songs* as an interim text and promising publication of the larger collection once Berryman had determined the number and final arrangement of poems he wanted to include. The literary world realized that Berryman's most important work was imminent, and by 1966 even *The New Yorker,* which had repeatedly rejected most of Berryman's submissions, was accepting new dream songs as soon as they came from his pen. The Guggenheim Foundation provided two year-long grants, in 1966 and 1967, specifically to free Berryman from teaching and to hasten completion of *The Dream Songs.*

Unfortunately, Berryman had by this time fallen so completely into the distinctive style of this verse that he became unable to write in any other manner. What is more, he became unable to stop writing. In the desperately manic way that characterized so much of his literary life, Berryman would telephone fellow writers in the early morning hours to read the poem he had just written. Ellison bore the brunt of many of these telephone calls, almost always for advice on the poems employing black dialect, but Bellow and Rich also had to render immediate critical opinions on matters of arrangement and choices for inclusion in the final edition. Berryman came to fear that he would never finish, so he arbitrarily closed the collection at 385 songs. His fear that he would never be able to write in other styles led him to rush his next two collections into print; the consensus of critical opinion holds that this was a mistake.

His Toy, His Dream, His Rest (1968) and *Love and Fame,* published two years later, represent Berryman's attempts to deal with larger, more serious subjects inappropriate to the format of *The Dream Songs.* Berryman's struggle with alcoholism was greatest at this time; despite his involvement with Alcoholics Anonymous, he never permanently conquered his addiction. Similarly, his return to Roman Catholicism, nominally the religion of his boyhood, was short-lived. General despondency over indifferent reaction to his last works, widespread student dissatisfaction with his teaching, and a third marriage nearing collapse because of his alcoholism likely hastened the suicide that he had feared would inevitably conclude his life.

THE DISPOSSESSED

First published: 1948
Type of work: Poetry

The best example of Berryman's early style, this volume's poems are solidly written and of good quality but derivative.

Many of the poems in *The Dispossessed* date from Berryman's student days. Their method of composition is conservative, betraying adaptations from Yeats, Frost, and Eliot. This is not to imply, however, that they stand outside Berryman's thematic canon. The title of the collection, followed by the dedication to his mother, imply the themes of estrangement and alienation which would become familiar elements in Berryman's later verse. The dedication ironically reveals Berryman's bitterness at never having known his father and, legally as well through a changed name, having effaced his father's memory. The poetry, as a collection, implies that, all attempts notwithstanding, no genuine rebirth is possible in the world of the 1930's and 1940's.

The opening poem, for example, "Winter Landscape," establishes the scene of a weary, frozen world in which "three men . . . in brown" return from the hunt and are at once frozen in time. Like the figures of John Keats's Grecian urn, they are unaware of "the evil waste of history/ outstretched." Some readers will recognize in Berryman's setting the details of Pieter Brueghel's painting *Hunters in the Snow* (1565), but the poet also allows the reader to see the men as Adolf Hitler's brownshirts. Human beings participate in the march of history, continuing the cycle from epoch to epoch, but history is forever on a demoralized and degraded course. Even worse, the actors in Berryman's human comedy have neither the consolations of art and civilization, which one finds in the gyre poems of Yeats, nor the power to act as interpreters of the cause of their malaise. No hidden spiritual life, which was Eliot's solution for the same problem, ever appears as an avenue of escape.

More telling is the resemblance of "Winter Landscape" to "The Return," a poem from Pound's early collection *Ripostes* (1912); Pound's poem was itself inspired by a poem of Henri de Régnier. It was written on the eve of World War I and is a prophecy of the ennui and exhaustion felt by hunters returned from the hunt. Berryman's poem was written immediately before the beginning of World War II. Like Pound, Berryman was experimenting with symbolism at the early stage of his career, and this variation, twice removed from Régnier's original, underscores Berryman's conviction, derived via Yeats, that Western civilization is doomed to repeat its mistakes in ever more degraded variation.

Both poems use the same setting, that of weary hunters returning in the snow. Pound's imagery is more overtly classical—the invincible hunters were "Gods of the winged shoe," recalling Hermes, the swift messenger. Berryman's image is that of the invincible Fascist brownshirts. A stanza drawn from each poem reveals quite clearly the degree of Pound's influence. Pound's second stanza reads:

> See, they return, one, and by one,
> With fear, as half-awakened;
> As if the snow should hesitate
> And murmur in the wind,
>   and half turn back;
> These were the "Wing'd-with-Awe,"
> Inviolable.

Pound's stanza may be compared with the first stanza of Berryman:

> The three men coming down the winter hill
> In brown, with tall poles and a pack of hounds
> At heel, through the arrangement of the trees,
> Past the five figures at the burning straw,
> Returning cold and silent to their town.

Consequently, disfigurement and distortion are recurring images, particularly in the poems of the first part of the collection. "The Statue" of the volume's second poem is "tolerant through years of weather," and it cynically looks at passersby though it is never considered by those who glance at it. The person it commemorates is long dead, and no one knows or cares that it immortalizes someone named Humbolt. "A Point of Age" marks the start of a life's journey in a world where all the travelers are uncertain of their destination. "The Ball Poem," literally about a boy's lost ball, sets forth Berryman's epistemology of loss: that one can replace missing elements in life, but these replacements never duplicate what is gone. Berryman saw life as a series of losses, the first and most significant for him being the death of his father.

"Fare Well," written in December, 1946, represents Berryman's attempt to lay the ghost of his father to rest. The poem juxtaposes the mysterious rebirth imagery of Yeats (the phoenix, the tree of life, and fire) with the warm snow of Eliot's *The Waste Land*.

> O easy the phoenix in the tree of the heart,
> Each in its time, his twigs and spices fixes
> To make a last nest, and marvelously relaxes,—
> Out of the fire, weak peep . . .
> Father I fought for Mother, sleep where you sleep!
> I slip into the snowbed with no hurt
> Where warm will warm be warm enough to part
> Us. As I sink, I weep.

The poems of parts 2 through 4 continue these themes. "Canto Amor," a love song written when Berryman was thirty, expresses the poet's hope that his marriage will survive the uncertainties of the world. "The Lightning," which concludes part 4, reproduces the terza rima of "Canto Amor," the three-line rhymed-verse form of Dante's *La divina commedia* (c. 1320; *The Divine Comedy*, 1802). The poet's sister-in-law, Marie Mabry, fears a violent lightning storm, but the poet sees the lightning as simply one manifestation of the violent chance of nature. The title poem of *The Dispossessed* ends part 5. Part of the poem dates from August 6, 1945, the day of the U.S. bombing of Hiroshima, Japan. The new dawn of the nuclear age is as lifeless as the winter landscape of the collection's opening poem. The child of the nuclear age is deformed and grotesque, a "faceless fellow."

HOMAGE TO MISTRESS BRADSTREET

First published: 1956
Type of work: Poem

A long poem that uses the figure of Anne Bradstreet to portray human temptation, guilt, grief, suffering, and pain.

It was irrelevant to Berryman whether on not the historical figure represented in his *Homage to Mistress Bradstreet* ever actually experienced the discontent described in the poem. The Bradstreet it describes is a montage of frustrations, temptations, and feelings of guilt, very much like those of the poet who created hen. Though Berryman had written the poem's first stanza and several lines of the second in March, 1948, he set them aside for nearly five years until the tone of Saul Bellow's *The Adventures of Augie March* (1953) gave him inspiration for the idiom he sought. Using notes he had made on the historical Bradstreet during this hiatus, Berryman wrote fifty new stanzas during the first two months of 1953, completing the entire poem on March 22 of that year. He was fond of saying that he finished the poem five years to the day after he had started it.

Berryman had been fascinated with Bradstreet as early as 1937. He read her poems and letters to her husband, and examined as much historical detail as he could find about daily life in Puritan Massachusetts. Bradstreet's mediocrity as a poet, coupled with the severe moral code of the society in which she lived, predisposed him to see an affinity with his own circumstances. To a degree, then, she is a mask for Berryman, whose guilt for his marital infidelity was strong following the affair he described in his sonnets; however, Bradstreet is also "Lise" herself and at least one other lover. By 1953, these distinctions had become relatively unimportant: Bradstreet had become every person who doubts or feels guilt, frustration, and estrangement.

Berryman considered both himself and Bradstreet to be poets in societies hostile to their art. He portrays her as rejecting both her husband and father and the Puritan deity that sanctions their view of life. Even so, Berryman knew that this was taking great liberties with the historical evidence available. The historical Bradstreet's letters portray her as a model of devotion to her husband; members of her family encouraged her writing of poetry and (without her knowledge) saw to the first publication of her poems. This is likely the reason Berryman chose to have his heroine's dilemma resemble that of the woman in the Scottish ballad "The Demon Lover." His Bradstreet also faces a demonic tempter, the male poet persona, another mask for Berryman himself. Such temptation, never acted upon but remaining wholly within the mind of the woman tempted, allows the poem to remain within the realm of historical possibility.

The structure of the poem is distinctive, though its stanza form resembles the eight-line configuration Yeats favored. The poet tempter's voice blends with Bradstreet's thoughts, and the tension is unremitting. Bradstreet mentally renounces family, faith, and life in Puritan Massachusetts; she desires to yield to her poet tempter, and realizes that in the very thought she has sinned. Even so, she does nothing overtly; to those who know her, she remains among the elect and is destined for salvation. That she lives for many years after the temptation, though she has privately succumbed, adds the burden of hypocrisy to guilt.

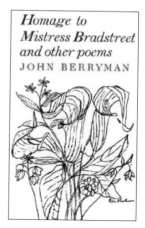

Homage to Mistress Bradstreet represents the poet's final departure from the Poundian symbolism of his earlier verse. He sought in its movements from formal rhetoric to low idiom a means of personalization that would yet allow him to mask the individual he personified. The result allows his Bradstreet to function simultaneously as unfulfilled wife, unfulfilled poet, and vicarious lover who sins in thought though not in deed. She is, therefore, a more particularized creation than Eliot's J. Alfred Prufrock; she is associated with the strictures of her Puritanism yet is also a reflection of the same moral scruples in which Berryman was raised.

Berryman's Bradstreet is, like her creator, the domesticated but sorely tempted poet. She is heroic because, unlike her creator, she never succumbs to her temptation; yet, because she never actually experiences forbidden love, she never rises above mediocrity. Her tragedy is that she bears all the burdens but reaps none of the artistic rewards of her sin. She remains, like Berryman himself, tied to her unhappy domestic conventions in an environment hostile to creativity.

Berryman's marriages and love affairs became, to his own mind at least, a means of pursuing fame through love. At the latter stage of his career he admitted this openly, but in the early 1950's he still required a mask. The Bradstreet poem allowed him to explore his personal situation from a nominally feminine point of view. His discussions with William Carlos Williams, a personal friend with whom he largely disagreed on matters poetic, clearly show his amusement at Williams's belief that historical references needed to be scrupulously faithful to documented facts. Though Berryman knew Bradstreet's background and the history of American Puritanism in astonishing detail, he believed that his verse portrait need only be consonant with what might have been.

Berryman intended *Homage to Mistress Bradstreet* as his response to the theological underpinnings of Eliot's long poems, particularly *The Waste Land*. He also objected to the anonymity of Eliot's characterizations, what Eliot would have considered correlative objectivity. Aiming for a tone never before produced in long poetry, Berryman sought possible historicity, while avoiding Williams's strict understanding of the historical, such as one finds in *Paterson*. Though she is sorely tempted and guilty in her own eyes, Berryman clearly considers his Bradstreet a heroine, if only because she has endured life.

BERRYMAN'S SONNETS

First published: 1967
Type of work: Poetry

These poems constitute an important shift in Berryman's style, away from a rhetorical mode and toward a sustained nervous idiom.

Berryman's Sonnets, a cycle that traces a five-month love affair that began in April, 1947, contains poems that were written in 1947 while Berryman was teaching at Princeton University. The cycle was not published until 1967, primarily because of its explicit references to persons, places, and events of that time. The woman who is its subject was called "Lise" in the first printing of the work, perhaps a Berryman equivalent for the "Laura" of Petrarch's sonnets. In reprintings which followed upon the success of *The Dream Songs*, however, Berryman restored his subject's actual name and changed the title of the collection to *Sonnets to Chris*.

In isolation from Berryman's other works the cycle is not impressive; it follows the predictable pattern of meeting, anticipation, love, and loss that one finds in Petrarch. What makes it important is Berryman's discovery of the "nervous idiom" he would develop in *Homage to Mistress Bradstreet* and, still more successfully, in *The Dream Songs*. Berryman uses this technique to describe the poet's increasingly agitated state of mind as his mistress first yields, then rejects her lover's advances, and ultimately abandons him. Berryman's sonnets mark the poet's movement toward the greater use of idiom and what he had called as early as 1934 "a more passionate syntax." They betray a young poet still searching for his voice and indicate a veering away from Poundian symbolism.

Berryman clearly used the discipline that the sonnet form imposed as a means of tempering his tendency to expand relentlessly and to control the jarring effects of the idiom he was coming to prefer. He candidly admits as much in sonnet 66 when he "prods our English" to "cough me up a word" that will "justify/ My darling fondle."

Readers of *The Dream Songs* will recognize in the sonnets several characteristics of Berryman's fully realized style. First, there appears a fascination with the method of composition. Language becomes a lexicon or thesaurus from which the poet, in vestigial homage to Pound, must select mot juste ("precise word"). The French phrase, which Pound repeatedly used to describe his own process of composition, becomes anglicized in Berryman's sonnet as "justify." Then too, the process by which the proper word arrives is fundamentally unattractive, fitful, and spasmodic; in this case, the language expectorates it. Clever as it is, the imagery is fundamentally ugly, with the lover's word becoming so much phlegm. On the other hand, the poet is aware that the adulterous meetings the sonnets commemorate are also ugly. Thus, in this roundabout way, the poet justifies his "darling fondle."

Berryman's real fascination with Lise/Chris was perhaps the new direction in which it took his poetry. Even as the relationship destroyed his marriage, it gave rise to new opportunities to explore the tormented mind of the lover. Lise/Chris was no Dantean Beatrice, nor was she a Petrarchan Laura. The Berryman anima inspires lust and infidelity. In the final analysis, Lise/Chris provides a poet whose greatest fear is creative infertility with the opportunity to write. If there were any doubts that the process of composition underpins the entire cycle, they are dispelled by sonnet 117, the last in the collection. As fall turns to winter and the attraction, too, begins to chill, the poet waits in the grove—with more than a hundred sonnets in his pocket—for his mistress to appear. When "my lady came not/ . . . I sat down & wrote."

As in a classical sonnet sequence, development of the love relationship is keyed to the changing seasons: the beginnings in spring, with reference to "all the mild days of middle March"; an awareness of death, even at the affair's zenith in July (sonnet 65); bitterness in the aftermath of dying love (sonnet 71), written in September. The concluding poems, written in 1966 specifically for publication, note the acute, unhappy aftermath of the experience but settle upon another beginning, "free . . . of the fire of this sin" (sonnet 111).

THE DREAM SONGS

First published: 1969
Type of work: Poetry

The life, misfortunes, and utter optimism of Henry, Berryman's most original creation, are presented.

The Dream Songs, a work that Berryman always maintained is one poem in 385 parts, is the poet's tragicomic view of his chaotic existence. Its distinguishing features are its humor and its idiom, both portrayed by Henry, the Berryman "I and not I" of all the songs (Berryman identified Henry this way in the *Harvard Advocate* interview). Berryman chose the name Henry precisely because he did not like it, which allows Henry's occasional identification as "Henry Pussycat," the compliant one on whom the world unloads all its woes, as well as "Huffy Henry," who sulks, is arrogant, but ultimately accepts every calamity. The only other character in *The Dream Songs* is "Mr. Bones," who appears as minstrel interlocutor in the black dialect poems. All the particulars of the individual songs refer to specific events in Berryman's life. Often these are obscure or seem relatively unimportant in themselves—a film he sees, the weather, a trip to Ireland—but even these neutral or happy events

reveal Henry's predisposition to sadness and depression. Significant events, such as the birth of a child or the death of a friend, elicit the same serious doubts and questions.

Berryman sought to represent in modern form many of the elements one finds in classical heroic epic. For this reason, *The Dream Songs* presents skewed time sequences and a heroic prospectus that is the tragicomic counterpart of the typical mythic hero. For example, Henry dies in section 4, approximately a quarter of the way into the songs; the entire section, written as fourteen posthumous poems (numbers 78 through 91), tells of his struggle toward heroic resurrection. Henry being what he is, he naturally never achieves a classical heroic apotheosis; if anything, his despair appears more pronounced in the episodes that follow. The best he manages, though he does so with relative consistency, is a small spark of hope, most often in the poems which concern his daughter's birth and growth.

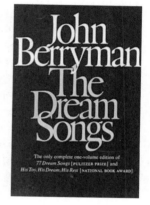

The poems written in black minstrel dialect, which employ jazzlike rhythms and sometimes a minstrel show format with Mr. Bones as interlocutor, are especially effective in maintaining the tragicomic tone. Bones is not only the classic minstrel show figure, he is also a tragicomic persona of death and reveals the bitterly comic features of life, as in the final lines of song 50:

> —Mr. Bones, your troubles give me vertigo,
> & backache. Somehow, when I make your scene.
> I cave to feel as if
>
> de roses of dawns & pearls of dusks, made up
> by some ol' writer-man, got right forgot
> & the greennesses of ours.
> Springwater grow so thick it gonna clot
> and the pleasing ladies cease. I figure, yup,
> you is bad powers.

Though Berryman's break with symbolism was complete by the time he began composition of *The*

Dream Songs, he retained to the end of his career the conviction (shared by Robert Browning, another poet he admired) that life is action and that the best verse portrays not character but character in action. For this reason, Berryman tells his readers relatively little about Henry as a person. It is enough that his subject bears a name the poet dislikes intensely. It is equally revealing that Henry lives his life on a much more mundane level than Pound's mask, Hugh Selwyn Mauberley. Mauberley, like Pound, is Ulysses, a heroic figure who relentlessly combats Philistinism in all its forms. Henry, on the other hand, is a lovable nonentity who is usually defeated before he begins. The fact that neither character is an accurate self-portrait of its creator is unimportant.

Berryman saw the writing of poetry as a practical matter, as a process whose primary purpose was to dispel fear. For him, as for Stephen Crane, the subject of a Berryman biographical study, verse was an "anti-spell," a kind of word magic. Berryman's fears, like those of Crane, were essentially three in number: abandonment, uncertainty, and death. This view of poetry as ritual is a consistent element in Berryman's development. It explains his fascination from boyhood with the Roman Catholic liturgy, his admiration for Yeats's verse plays, and his relentless pursuit of his created persona, Henry.

As happened with almost everything Berryman did, *The Dream Songs* became an obsession, so much so that he feared he would never again be able to return to writing more conventional forms of poetry. His fears are understandable, as there are clearly poetic subjects that do not yield to a tragicomic mode. Also, Berryman came to realize the limitations of Henry as a recurring presence in his work. It was largely for this reason that Berryman wrote *Love and Fame*, which details his personal search for what he considered the only rewards of life, and *Delusions, Etc. of John Berryman* (1972), whose first section is structured according to the hours of the Roman Catholic liturgical office. This last work is his most overtly spiritual, and it coincides with his return to Roman Catholicism in the year before his death.

DISCUSSION TOPICS

- Walt Whitman begins his great poem "I celebrate myself and sing myself." John Berryman certainly sings himself. To what extent can he be said to celebrate himself?

- What features of Berryman's poetry seem calculated to overcome the modern reader's resistance to long poems?

- What does Ann Bradstreet represent to Berryman—an alter ego, a fantasy lover, an afflicted fellow poet, a victim of Puritan culture, or some blend of these and/or other possibilities?

- The sonnet cycle has been practiced and its conventions explored and exploited for centuries. What distinctive techniques and content does Berryman bring to *Berryman's Sonnets*?

- Contrast "Huffy Henry" of *The Dream Songs* and T. S. Eliot's J. Alfred Prufrock as antiheroes.

- In some writers creativity and self-destructiveness seem to be like two sides of a coin. To what extent is this true of Berryman?

SUMMARY

Berryman sought to achieve a distinctly American idiomatic style which, nevertheless, maintained the structures of classical verse forms. He moved toward this goal steadily in the years following World War II, and by the early 1950's he believed that American rather than British poets constituted the last great hope for poetry written in English. The disorder of his personal life inspired the themes of his poems, but it never affected their craftsmanship. Berryman came from a different tradition from that of academic poets such as Eliot or W. H. Auden; he was an irascible maverick from birth to death, a genius who was at once pitiable and admirable.

Robert J. Forman

BIBLIOGRAPHY

By the Author

POETRY:
Five Young American Poets, 1940 (with others)
Poems, 1942
The Dispossessed, 1948
Homage to Mistress Bradstreet, 1956
His Thought Made Pockets and the Plane Buckt, 1958
Seventy-seven Dream Songs, 1964
Short Poems, 1967
Berryman's Sonnets, 1967
His Toy, His Dream, His Rest, 1968
The Dream Songs, 1969
Love and Fame, 1970, 1972
Delusions, Etc. of John Berryman, 1972
Henry's Fate, and Other Poems, 1977
Collected Poems, 1937-1971, 1989

LONG FICTION:
Recovery, 1973

NONFICTION:
Stephen Crane, 1950
The Arts of Reading, 1960 (with Ralph Ross and Allen Tate)
The Freedom of the Poet, 1976
We Dream of Honour: John Berryman's Letters to His Mother, 1988

EDITED TEXT:
The Unfortunate Traveller: Or, the Life of Jack Wilton, 1960

About the Author

Bloom, Harold, ed. *John Berryman.* New York: Chelsea House, 1989.
Haffenden, John. *John Berryman: A Critical Commentary.* New York: New York University Press, 1980.
_____. *The Life of John Berryman.* Boston: Routledge & Kegan Paul, 1982.
Haffenden, John, ed. *Berryman's Shakespeare: Essays, Letters, and Other Writings by John Berryman.* New York: Farrar, Strauss and Giroux, 1999.
Halliday, E. M. *John Berryman and the Thirties: A Memoir.* Amherst: University of Massachusetts Press, 1987.
Hirsch, Edward. "One Life, One Writing! The Middle Generation." *The American Poetry Review* 29, no. 5 (September/October, 2000): 11-16.
Kelly, Richard J., and Alan K. Lathrop, eds. *Recovering Berryman: Essays on a Poet.* Ann Arbor: University of Michigan Press, 1993.
Linebarger, J. M. *John Berryman.* New York: Twayne, 1974.
Mariani, Paul. *Dream Song: The Life of John Berryman.* 2d ed. New York: William Morrow, 1996.
Thomas, Harry. *Berryman's Understanding: Reflections on the Poetry of John Berryman.* Boston: Northeastern University Press, 1988.
Travisano, Thomas. *Midcentury Quartet: Bishop, Lowell, Jarrell, Berryman, and the Making of a Postmodern Aesthetic.* Charlottesville: University Press of Virginia, 1999.

AMBROSE BIERCE

Born: Horse Cave Creek, Ohio
   June 24, 1842
Died: Mexico (?)
   January, 1914 (?)

One of American literature's most overlooked writers, Bierce has earned limited recognition for a small number of bizarre and much-anthologized short stories, many of which are set against the backdrop of the Civil War.

BIOGRAPHY

Ambrose Bierce was born in Horse Cave Creek, in Meigs County, Ohio, on June 24, 1842, to Laura and Marcus Aurelius Bierce. When Bierce was four years old, the family moved to northern Indiana, and it was there that the writer grew up. He inherited an interest in books from his father and was instructed in religion by his mother.

A career in journalism and an involvement and interest in things military began early for Bierce. He left home at fifteen and worked as a printer's devil for two years for a local newspaper. At seventeen he entered the Kentucky Military Institute. Shortly after he left the institute, the Civil War broke out, and Bierce was one of the first to enlist in the Ninth Regiment of the Indiana Volunteers, which he served, off and on, for three years. During his service he received numerous citations for bravery, was wounded in the head, and rose to the rank of first lieutenant.

After being discharged, Bierce tracked down confiscated Confederate cotton for the federal government and then accompanied his former commander, General W. B. Hazen, a hot-headed leader whom he admired, on a mapping expedition to the West. It was on this trip that Bierce settled in San Francisco, where he was able to begin his writing career in earnest. In 1868 he took a job with a newspaper called the *News-Letter,* for which he wrote a column titled "Town Crier." In it, he employed satire and wit to expose and attack both public figures and institutions he deemed guilty of hypocrisy. The column was a rousing local success.

Bierce married Molly Day in 1871, and a honeymoon trip to Europe (courtesy of Molly's father) took the writer to London, where he went to work for Tom Hood's *Fun* and for *Figaro,* writing under the pen name Dod Grile. He also published three collections of columns, sketches, and fiction under this name while in London: *The Fiend's Delight* (1873), *Nuggets and Dust Panned out in California* (1873), and *Cobwebs from an Empty Skull* (1874). The cynicism displayed in the pieces that make up these books and the articles he wrote for the London papers earned the writer the nickname "Bitter Bierce."

Bierce returned reluctantly to San Francisco in 1877 and wrote for and edited various newspapers during the following nine years, all the while producing articles that enhanced his reputation as a witty, even cruel social satirist. During this period he became the mentor of several aspiring writers and put together a collection of pessimistic and satirical definitions which he titled "The Devil's Dictionary." In 1886, he went to work for the San Francisco *Examiner.* His marriage dissolved in 1888.

The high point of Bierce's career in terms of his fiction writing came in 1891 with the publication of *Tales of Soldiers and Civilians* (subsequently altered and published under the title *In the Midst of Life* in 1898). It is the bizarre, even supernatural, violent, and cruelly ironic stories of this collection that have earned for Bierce his place, limited as it is, in American literature. The stories, much to the author's chagrin, inspired comparisons with those of Edgar Allan Poe. Though captivating reading, they did not fit into the mold of the realist, local color literature of the time.

Other creative collections followed (*Black Beetles in Amber,* a book of satirical poems, in 1892, and *Can*

Such Things Be?, a varied collection of stories, in 1893), but Bierce continued his journalistic writing, in part because he enjoyed it and in part because his creative work did not win the national attention he believed he deserved. Bierce moved to Washington, D.C., in 1896. Between 1896 and 1913, he wrote for the *Examiner* and later for the magazine *Cosmopolitan*, while assembling the various volumes of his collected works. During this period, part of his "Devil's Dictionary" was published under the title *The Cynic's Word Book* (1906).

In 1913, Bierce left Washington, D.C., and headed to Mexico, where he planned to observe the Mexican Revolution before moving on to Europe. He attached himself to Pancho Villa's revolutionary army and, in December of 1913, sent a letter from Chihuahua, Mexico, concerning his experiences with Villa's company. By most accounts, this letter was the last that anyone ever heard of the American writer. A number of obituaries appeared over the years, all providing different details concerning the author's demise. It is not certain, however, when, where, or how Bierce died.

ANALYSIS

Bierce wrote almost all of his fiction during the height of the realist movement of American literature. Bierce, however, was emphatically nonrealist, rejecting virtually all tenets of the movement, particularly that concerning the use of "local color." Bierce believed that fiction, in the tradition of great literature, should make use of and engage the imagination rather than merely attempt to paint a detailed picture of contemporary reality. It is precisely this belief and the exercise of it in his works that placed him outside the mainstream of American literature during his lifetime. It is also precisely this belief that makes his stories seem ahead of their time and which makes them so much more appealing to the post-Sigmund Freud reader than they were to late nineteenth century readers.

The majority of Bierce's stories are intense, detailed, and objectively told. They are sharply focused narratives which present protagonists faced with a psychologically challenging situation. Bierce penetrates the inner world of his characters and often places them in a macabre, even supernatural, and often cruelly ironic world (frequently set against the backdrop of the Civil War) both remi-niscent of Edgar Allan Poe and anticipating a host of twentieth century writers, from Franz Kakfa to Jorge Luis Borges. At their best, the stories both captivate and surprise the entranced reader. At their worst, they are marred by coincidences so improbable that even the reader capable of the most profound suspension of disbelief finds them impossible to accept, even within the context of their fictional world.

No collection of Bierce's stories so vividly displays both the strengths and the weaknesses of the author's fiction (often within the same story) as does *Tales of Soldiers and Civilians* (or *In the Midst of Life*, as it is more commonly known). "An Occurrence at Owl Creek Bridge" and "Chickamauga" are included in this collection, as are "The Affair at Coulter's Notch," in which a Civil War artillery captain fires, unknowingly, on his own plantation; "The Man and the Snake," in which a man dies of fright of what turns out to be a stuffed snake with shoe buttons for eyes; and "The Suitable Surroundings," in which a man dies after reading a ghost story in a haunted house.

Beyond fiction, Bierce's literary writings, from essays to poetry, are characterized by the pessimism, cynicism, and wit for which Bierce the journalist was more known than was Bierce the short-story writer. It is his stories, however, particularly the much-anthologized "An Occurrence at Owl Creek Bridge" and, to a lesser degree, "Chickamauga," that have earned for Bierce his place in the history of American literature.

"AN OCCURRENCE AT OWL CREEK BRIDGE"

First published: 1891 (collected in *Tales of Soldiers and Civilians*, 1891)
Type of work: Short story

During the Civil War, a Confederate spy is about to be hanged; he seems to escape, but his escape is only a dream.

"An Occurrence at Owl Creek Bridge" is by far Bierce's most widely read story, and it may also be his best. It focuses on Peyton Farquhar, a Southern planter and part-time Confederate conspirator,

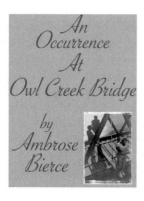

who, as the story opens, is about to be hanged on the Owl Creek bridge for having attempted to burn it. As Farquhar is being hanged, the reader is told, the rope breaks and he plunges alive into the water below. The rest of the story recounts his escape down the creek and then through the forest toward his home. Just as he reaches his house, where his wife awaits him, he feels a sharp blow to the back of his neck. In reality, he is not home at all: He hangs dead, of a broken neck, beneath the Owl Creek bridge. The rope has not, in fact, broken. Farquhar's escape has been only a momentary illusion.

What makes this plot so successful, as it lures the reader into the story, and what makes the whole story so captivating, is the technical brilliance of the narration. Bierce begins the story, for example, with a very objective, unadorned, strikingly dispassionate, and minutely detailed description of both the soldiers and Farquhar on the bridge as the former prepare for the latter's execution. The objectivity of the prose lends an official air to the narrative, almost as though it were not a piece of fiction at all but a military report. This objectivity combines with the detail with which the scene is set, including everything from an explanation of the various postures of the soldiers to the exaggerated ticking of the prisoner's watch, to lend a profound degree of realism to the story. The reader is thus led to believe from the beginning of the story that what is being told is minutely accurate.

Once Farquhar is in the water, the tone is far less dispassionate, however, as the narrator enters the head of the fleeing prisoner, focusing on Farquhar's reactions both to the soldiers who pursue him and to the task of escape. Details abound here as well, though, ironically, it is through these details that the reader is provided with hints (extremely subtle ones, almost certainly imperceptible to the first-time reader) that Farquhar's escape is but a dream and not real at all. Farquhar's senses as he escapes, for example, are heightened beyond those of a normal human being, as he can even see the insects on each leaf of the trees on the creek bank from his position in the water.

Later, Bierce's description of the forest as Farquhar heads homeward becomes dreamlike. The reader is told that the road Farquhar takes "was as wide and straight as a city street, yet it seemed untraveled." Elsewhere, the narrator reports that the forest "on either side was full of singular noises, among which—once, twice, and again—he distinctly heard whispers in an unknown tongue." As Farquhar gets closer to home, he feels pain and swelling in his neck. While much of this description may be attributed to a prisoner actually fleeing from his near execution by hanging, some of it is plainly nonrealistic in nature. The reader thus has the information necessary to decipher the story but is, in all likelihood, unable to do so, lured into Farquhar's compelling tale of flight.

Another element of the story's presentation that merits mention is its structure. Bierce divides the story into three numbered sections, the content and division of which serve to intrigue the reader. The first section describes the setting of the execution right up to the point when the plank below Farquhar's feet is removed. The second section abruptly shifts to background information on Farquhar and how he came to commit the act for which he is being executed. The narrator reveals that a Confederate soldier had told Farquhar of the vulnerability of the bridge, thus planting the seed for Farquhar's action. The last line of the section reveals that the Confederate soldier was, in fact, a Federal scout. The third and final section picks up where the first section left off, with Farquhar apparently plunging into the water, and it concludes with the abrupt and surprising ending.

"An Occurrence at Owl Creek Bridge" is, in both content and presentation, a tour de force, a story that lures, captivates, and surprises its reader. It is a perfect Biercean story in that it is an intense and detailed narrative that mixes both real and unreal and ends in violent death and cruel irony. Whether Bierce is a master of the short story genre is debatable. This story, however, is undoubtedly a masterwork.

"CHICKAMAUGA"

First published: 1891 (collected in *Tales of Soldiers and Civilians*, 1891)
Type of work: Short story

During the Civil War, a small boy plays at war, gets lost in the woods, falls asleep, and awakens to a macabre and horrifying reality.

Like "An Occurrence at Owl Creek Bridge," "Chickamauga" possesses classic Biercean features, including the violence of war and a bizarre version of reality. The chief difference in this story, however, is that the bizarre reality, for all its appearance as such, is no dream; it is all too real.

The story tells of a small boy, who, with toy wooden sword in hand, wanders off into the woods to fight invisible foes, just as his ancestors have battled real ones. The boy strays too far and becomes lost. Finally, he lies down to rest and sleeps for several hours. Soon after he awakes, he is joined by hundreds of wounded and dying soldiers making their way in macabre fashion through the twilight near where the boy lies. Rather than being frightened by them, he is entertained. He even tries to play with them and eventually, sword in hand, takes a position in front of the group and "leads" them.

Soon he and the soldiers come upon a fire. He then recognizes the buildings of his own plantation and runs in search of his mother, whom he finds, her

white face turned upward, the hands thrown out and clutched full of grass, the clothing deranged, the long dark hair in tangles and full of clotted blood. The greater part of the forehead was torn away, and from the jagged hole the brain protruded, overflowing the temple, a frothy mass of gray, crowned with clusters of crimson bubbles—the work of a shell.

The child attempts to scream, but it is revealed that he is a deaf-mute, a fact which explains how the soldiers have managed to lay waste to his family's plantation, fight throughout the area where he lay, and begin their retreat, all while he slept.

The most intriguing aspects of "Chickamauga" concern the bizarre world it creates and the fact that this bizarre world is not illusion but reality. Ironically, the story begins almost as a story for children, as the narrator tells of the boy's innocent foray against make-believe enemies. When the boy does encounter a real "foe"—a rabbit—he begins to cry and flees. The innocence that pervades this section, however, is accompanied by a dark, or at least more serious, underside, as both the boy's motivation in his play and his actions are described in military terms, if only in mock fashion. Once the boy awakens, however, the story becomes dreamlike—or more accurately put, nightmarelike—as the hundreds of wounded soldiers stumble their way through the "ghostly mist." Even more bizarre is the playful manner with which the boy regards the soldiers. The reader is even told that the boy "laughed as he watched them. But on and ever on they crept, these maimed and bleeding men, as heedless as he of the dramatic contrast between his laughter and their own ghastly gravity."

The chief irony in all of this is that as bizarre as the reality painted by the narrator is, it is indeed reality. This is particularly surprising to the reader familiar with "An Occurrence at Owl Creek Bridge." Certainly the reader of that story would expect the child to awaken or in some other way reveal that he has only dreamt the horrifying scenes described by the narrator, but the dreamlike scenes are worse than any nightmare because they are real. It is an interesting irony, and almost certainly one that Bierce, the staunch opponent of realism, appreciated, that one of his most bizarre stories, in spite of its apparent nonrealist qualities, turns out to be one of his most coldly realistic tales.

SUMMARY

Bierce's fiction never earned the fame that he believed he deserved. A nonrealist writing during the realist movement, he wrote in the shadows of more famous and more mainstream writers, such as Mark Twain and William Dean Howells. The lack of fame accorded Bierce, however, in no way detracts from the quality of his stories, some of which have appeared in numerous anthologies. While it is quite easy to find writers in American literature more celebrated than Bierce, it is difficult to find stories that can captivate and surprise the reader more than those of Bierce, whose works will be more appreciated, particularly for their portent of nonrealist, psychological fiction, as more readers discover this overlooked writer.

Keith H. Brower

BIBLIOGRAPHY

By the Author

SHORT FICTION:

Cobwebs: Being the Fables of Zambri the Parse, 1884

Tales of Soldiers and Civilians, 1891 (also known as *In the Midst of Life,* 1898)

Can Such Things Be?, 1893

Fantastic Fables, 1899

My Favourite Murder, 1916

Ghost and Horror Stories of Ambrose Bierce, 1964

The Collected Fables of Ambrose Bierce, 2000 (S. T. Joshi, editor)

POETRY:

Vision of Doom, 1890

Black Beetles in Amber, 1892

How Blind Is He?, 1896

Shapes of Clay, 1903

Poems of Ambrose Bierce, 1995

NONFICTION:

The Fiend's Delight, 1873

Nuggets and Dust Panned out in California, 1873

Cobwebs from an Empty Skull, 1874

The Dance of Death, 1877

The Dance of Life: An Answer to the Dance of Death, 1877 (with Mrs. J. Milton Bowers)

The Cynic's Word Book, 1906

The Shadow on the Dial, and Other Essays, 1909

Write It Right: A Little Blacklist of Literary Faults, 1909

The Devil's Dictionary, 1911

The Letters of Ambrose Bierce, 1922

Twenty-one Letters of Ambrose Bierce, 1922

Selections from Prattle, 1936

Ambrose Bierce on Richard Realf by Wm. McDevitt, 1948

A Sole Survivor: Bits of Autobiography, 1998 (S. T. Joshi and David E. Schultz, editors)

The Fall of the Republic, and Other Political Satires, 2000 (Joshi and Schultz, editors)

A Much Misunderstood Man: Selected Letters of Ambrose Bierce, 2003 (Joshi and Schultz, editors)

TRANSLATION:

The Monk and the Hangman's Daughter, 1892 (with Gustav Adolph Danziger; of Richard Voss's novel)

MISCELLANEOUS:

The Collected Works of Ambrose Bierce, 1909-1912

Shadows of Blue and Gray: The Civil War Writings of Ambrose Bierce, 2002 (Brian M. Thomsen, editor)

About the Author

Berkove, Lawrence I. *A Prescription for Adversity: The Moral Art of Ambrose Bierce.* Columbus: Ohio State University Press, 2002.

DISCUSSION TOPICS

- Is Ambrose Bierce an "overlooked" writer because he was a nonrealist in a realistic literary era, because his output was too small, or for some other reason?

- What virtues of good journalistic writing did Bierce bring to the composition of short stories?

- Was "An Occurrence at Owl Creek Bridge" designed to lead to a "surprise ending," or is the story's ideal reader expected to perceive that Peyton's "escape" is an illusion?

- Discuss Bierce's "Chickamauga" as a striking fictional fulfillment of the following statement: The Civil War was a conflict in which contacts between soldiers and civilians were frequent and keenly felt.

- Bierce's fiction is referred to as psychological rather than realistic. Justify or challenge this assertion by reference to several of his stories.

Blume, Donald T. *Ambrose Bierce's "Civilians and Soldiers" in Context: A Critical Study*. Kent, Ohio: Kent State University Press, 2004.

Davidson, Cathy N. *The Experimental Fictions of Ambrose Bierce: Structuring the Ineffable*. Lincoln: University of Nebraska Press, 1984.

_____, ed. *Critical Essays on Ambrose Bierce*. Boston: G. K. Hall, 1982.

Fatout, Paul. *Ambrose Bierce, the Devil's Lexicographer*. Norman: University of Oklahoma Press, 1951.

Gale, Robert L. *An Ambrose Bierce Companion*. New York: Greenwood Press, 2001.

Grenander, Mary Elizabeth. *Ambrose Bierce*. New York: Twayne, 1971.

Hoppenstand, Gary. "Ambrose Bierce and the Transformation of the Gothic Tale in the Nineteenth-Century American Periodical." In *Periodical Literature in Nineteenth-Century America*, edited by Kenneth M. Price and Susan Belasco Smith. Charlottesville: University Press of Virginia, 1995.

McWilliams, Carey. *Ambrose Bierce: A Biography*. 1929. Reprint. Hamden, Conn.: Archon Books, 1967.

Morris, Roy, Jr. *Ambrose Bierce: Alone in Bad Company*. New York: Crown, 1996.

O'Connor, Richard. *Ambrose Bierce: A Bibliography and a Biography*. Boston: Little, Brown, 1967.

Schaefer, Michael W. *Just What War Is: The Civil War Writings of De Forest and Bierce*. Knoxville: University of Tennessee Press, 1997.

West, Richard. *The San Francisco Wasp: An Illustrated History*. Easthampton, Mass.: Periodyssey Press, 2004.

J. L. Castel

ELIZABETH BISHOP

Born: Worcester, Massachusetts
February 8, 1911
Died: Boston, Massachusetts
October 6, 1979

Highly praised for a small oeuvre of carefully crafted poems, Bishop is known as an accessible modern poet with an eye for detail.

BIOGRAPHY

Elizabeth Bishop was born in Worcester, Massachusetts, the daughter of Thomas and Gertrude Bulmer Bishop. Both of her parents were of Canadian heritage, but her paternal grandfather had left Prince Edward Island to establish a well-known building firm in Worcester that was responsible for such landmark buildings as the Boston Public Library and Museum of Fine Arts.

Bishop's father died a few months after her birth, and as a result of this her mother suffered a breakdown and was treated in a sanatorium in Boston. In 1916, her mother returned to Canada for further treatment in proximity to her family, but the result was another breakdown that required her confinement in a mental hospital in Nova Scotia, where she remained until her death in 1934. Effectively an orphan, therefore, Elizabeth passed her early childhood with her mother's family in Great Village, Nova Scotia; some of her poems reflect memories of this time.

At the age of six, Bishop was taken to live with her paternal grandparents in Worcester. Some critics have suggested that she sensed the move as something like an expulsion from paradise and that images of simplicity and family affection such as she had known in Great Village continued all of her life to represent life's highest good. In Worcester she began to be frequently ill, suffering again

from the bronchitis she had contracted in Great Village, to which were added asthma and a number of other diseases. In order to give her happier surroundings, her grandfather arranged for her to live with her mother's sister in Boston. From the age of eight, she began to read poetry and fairy tales; she has mentioned Walt Whitman and Gerard Manley Hopkins as early poetic favorites.

Bishop entered boarding school at the age of sixteen, at the Walnut Hill School in Nantick. There she read the works of William Shakespeare and the English Romantic poets. She entered Vassar College with the intention of studying music, but later she told an interviewer that she was so terrified by the thought of recitals that she gave up the idea. In college she founded a literary review, called *Con Spirito*, with other literary-minded students, among them Mary McCarthy and Eleanor Clark, both of them subsequently well-known novelists. Bishop's first poems appeared there and later in the *Vassar Review*; many of these appear in the standard volume of her life work, *The Complete Poems, 1927-1979* (1983). During her time at Vassar, Bishop began bouts of heavy drinking that affected her writing output and her health for the rest of her life.

The greatest poetic mentor of Bishop's early years was Marianne Moore, who helped to get some of Bishop's poems published in an anthology called *Trial Balances* (1935). Bishop's first volume was *North and South* (1946), which was chosen for the Houghton Mifflin Poetry Award and which includes her most anthologized single poem, "The Fish." That same year she met poet Robert Lowell, with whom she maintained a lifelong friendship based on their mutual admiration for each other's works. In 1949, Bishop moved to Washington, D.C., in order to accept the post of poetry consultant to the Library of Congress. It was then that she visited the poet Ezra Pound, incarcerated in St. Elizabeths Hospital; the result of this was the poem "Visits to St. Elizabeths." Further awards came soon after, including the American Academy of Arts and Letters Award in 1950 and the Lucy Martin Donnelly Fellowship from Bryn Mawr College in 1951.

With the money from her prizes, Bishop set out for a trip to Brazil, where allergic attacks forced her to stay for a number of months. Once cured, she decided to stay on and, in fact, lived in Brazil for most of the rest of her life, returning to the United States only a few years before her death. During her time there, she met and fell in love with a Brazilian woman, Lota de Macedo Soares. The two lived together until Soares's suicide in 1967. In 1955, she published her next book, which included *North and South*, by then out of print, as well as her newer poems; the volume was titled *Poems: North and South—A Cold Spring*. Among the new poems was the widely acclaimed "At the Fishhouses." Much of her subsequent work, until the mid-1970's, touched upon her life in Brazil, including the volume *Questions of Travel* (1965). This was followed, in 1976, by *Geography III*. The prematurely titled *The Complete Poems* of 1969 won the National Book Award, and *Geography III* won a National Book Critics Circle Award. Bishop was the recipient of honorary degrees from Rutgers University and Brown University. She died of a cerebral aneurism in Boston in 1979.

ANALYSIS

Bishop held a unique place in American poetry during her lifetime, and after her death she has come to seem one of the few truly durable and original voices of twentieth century poetry. An accessible voice in a period of frequently puzzling poets, Bishop's style was marked by precision and clarity, so that many critics have spoken of her work as a logical development of Imagism, the short-lived school of precise observation and clipped phrases of Pound and F. S. Flint in the early years of the century. The single most frequently evoked model, however, is Moore, with whom Bishop was friends, and whom she addressed directly in one of her poems, "Invitation to Miss Marianne Moore," in

A Cold Spring. Certainly the link between the two comes readily to mind, not only because of the biographical connection between the two poets but also because of Moore's equally effective choice of precise words to evoke unitary states of things. Recently, however, some critics have challenged this linking.

The particular qualities of her poetry aside, it certainly added to Bishop's mystique that during the period of her greatest fame she lived in Brazil and was rarely seen in the United States. Another factor contributing to her reputation, perhaps paradoxically, was the fact that she wrote relatively little, a factor in part of her recurrent bouts of alcoholism. Her complete poems are contained in a single volume, like those of T. S. Eliot, and can conceivably be read through in a single sitting. In the glut of print in the modern world, the very parsimony of her production came to seem a virtue, as did her insistence on continual revision of the poems.

The impression that an initial reading of Bishop's poetry makes is certainly that of the polished surface. Her words are carefully chosen, her evocations of the physical world precise, ranging from the description of scales on the floor of the fish house ("At the Fishhouses") to the sensations of a child reading *National Geographic* in a dentist's waiting room ("In the Waiting Room," from *Geography III*). Her poems lack an easy moral; critics tend to agree that they avoid coming to overall, or perhaps overly pat, answers about the great themes of human existence. The reader must tease out the meaning, if indeed there is such, from under the shining surface.

As a result, some critics have found that Bishop's poetry lacks substance, an accusation more frequent with respect to her earlier, pre-Brazil poetry (which nevertheless contains many of her most celebrated single works). It is a refusal to disclose secrets, if secrets there be, that the reader senses in these early poems, or an unwillingness on the part of the author to get involved with the world. This changed to some degree when Bishop began to write about Brazil, from whose culture she evidently felt sufficient distance to allow herself to characterize it from the outside, as she was not able to do with North American culture. From the poems about Brazil, as a result, a number of more elemental, slightly less intellectualized human themes emerge, longing for other climes and satisfaction with daily living among them.

A number of critics have therefore seen the theme of Bishop's poetry taken as a whole to be that of involvement or noninvolvement with the world. By and large, the earlier poems are perceived as remaining within the bounds of the self, and the later poetry as being willing to step outside these bounds. Such easy dichotomies are not satisfactory, however, as there are early poems that clearly do take stands on human issues and later ones that do not seem to do so at all.

Critical stances such as these underline the curiously negative quality of most attempts to place Bishop in a larger context, whereby what she does not do becomes more important than what she does. Many social critics understand the twentieth century to be a time when previously hard-and-fast moral and social values were questioned, and they see relativity as the rule not only in physics but also in the world at large. Such critics praise Bishop precisely for having had the taste and sensitivity to avoid giving easy answers. In short, they praise Bishop for not committing certain faults or (as a variation) see the slight air of authorial absence in her poems as itself an indication of the built-in alienation or fragmentation of modern thought. One critic has suggested that she successfully subverts the now outmoded heroic/masculine vision of the hero, substituting for it a more rational female version. Other critics, more accustomed to poems that contain what has been called "the reek of the human," fault her poems for seeming to have been written by a "lady" (as well as a woman)—they seem too gentrified, too rarefied. What is certain is that her works avoid vulgarity of surface and vulgarity of message as well, itself an accomplishment of no mean measure.

"THE FISH"

First published: 1946 (collected in *North and South*, 1946)
Type of work: Poem

The narrator catches an old fish, then later lets it go.

"The Fish" is Bishop's most anthologized poem. The work is popular because it avoids the surrealism that makes puzzling some of the other poems published in Bishop's first collection. It is devoted in large part to a description of a fish that the narrator catches and, in the last line, lets go. The moral suggested is somewhat closer to the surface than is usual for Bishop; in addition, the slight but undeniable sententiousness of the narrator may make it easier for the reader to identify with him or her than with the less characterized and virtually invisible narrators of many of Bishop's other poems.

The work opens with a simple statement: The narrator has "caught a tremendous fish." The fish immediately comes to seem somewhat noble, or perhaps resigned: "He didn't fight./ He hadn't fought at all." The reader sees the fish immediately as humanized, both through the male pronoun as well as through the author's ascription to it of the adjective "venerable." The narrator clearly reacts to this creature as an equal to an equal, on one hand totally within his or her power, on the other hand a creature into whose eyes he or she looks. The reader is told that the fish's eyes are "far larger" than those of the narrator, "but shallower, and yellowed." The most intimate communication with another person frequently takes place through the eyes—so too this contact of fisher and fish.

This fish, however, is the veteran of many previous combats; from his lip hang the remains of five fishhooks. As a result, it seems that the narrator has been victorious where others have failed; the reader is told that "victory filled up/ the little rented boat." Yet this victory may perhaps be that of the fish, whose hooks have been referred to as "medals"—the fruits of military victory.

The last line reads: "And I let the fish go." Why "and," the reader may wonder. This suggests that the narrator's letting the fish go is the anticlimactic natural result of the fish's victory, an acknowledgment of the greater nobility of the natural world with respect to the human one. This reaction seems a bit extreme for the situation described; indeed, the slight discomfort the reader may feel with this poem lies in precisely this self-effacement of the narrator before the minutely described denizen of the deep. One may wonder whether human beings are nothing more than creatures to plague a fish.

"VISITS TO ST. ELIZABETHS"

First published: 1950 (collected in *The Complete Poems, 1927-1979*, 1983)
Type of work: Poem

This work describes a visit to a hospital for the mentally ill and to a poet (known to be Ezra Pound) who is incarcerated there.

"Visits to St. Elizabeths" is the result of Bishop's visits, while in Washington, D.C., as the poetry consultant to the Library of Congress, to see the great modernist poet Ezra Pound, who had been incarcerated in this mental hospital as an alternative to conviction for treason; he had made purportedly pro-Fascist radio broadcasts on Italian radio during World War II. Bishop's reaction, characteristically enough, has nothing to do with politics and focuses only on the man in the hospital, who is never named. Yet the poem seems to lose a great deal if the reader is unaware of the poetic stature of Ezra Pound (for some literary historians, the single most original figure of Anglo-American modernism, and at any rate a figure without whom the shape of twentieth century literature would have been vastly different). It helps to have a sense both of Pound's literary grandeur and stature and of the circumstances to which he had been reduced. The narrator's meditation involves a realization of both these extremes, of both the splendors and miseries of the poem's central figure.

The poem is stylistically somewhat peculiar in that it takes a particular metrical prototype as the model which it adopts and then varies, namely the childhood add-on song, "The House That Jack Built." The echo is made clear by Bishop's repetition of its basic structure of one line, separated by a blank line from the next group of two, separated in turn from the next group of three, and so on to the final stanza of twelve lines. For example, the first reads, "This is the house of Bedlam," the second, "This is the man/ that lies in the house of Bedlam." Already the reader can recognize the reference to the British hospital for the insane at Bethlehem, called Bedlam, whose chaos before the reforms of the nineteenth century has been preserved in the lowercase use of the noun "bedlam." The evocation is of lack of order; the man "lies" in this house, rather than, say, living there, as if slumped or quiescent, clearly not a fully functioning human.

As the poem progresses, details are added, but the adjectives applied to the man alter. At first he is "honored," then he is "old," "brave," then "cranky," "tedious," and "busy," and he ends up simply "wretched." The crazy round of the madhouse is evoked in this alteration of adjectives, as it is in the repetitive, sing-song rhythm of the increasing numbers of lines and details. In reacting to one specific person's situation, the narrator in this poem (essentially Bishop herself) seems to express a sense of human empathy that is sometimes lacking in Bishop's more cerebral poems, a realization both of the heights to which individual humans can rise and of the depths to which they can sink. The reader may be left thinking that the wretchedness of this person is not totally unmerited, a situation that may or may not correspond to one's understanding of the historical Pound but which at any rate makes the contemplation of the situation described in the poem possible rather than merely unbearable.

Elizabeth Bishop
The Complete Poems
1927-1979

"AT THE FISHHOUSES"

First published: 1955 (collected in *The Complete Poems, 1927-1979*, 1983)
Type of work: Poem

An unnamed narrator describes a visit to fish houses and talks with an old man.

Although "At the Fishhouses" consists largely of description, it also seems to offer a formulation of the relation between humans and nature, or humans and truth, which approaches that achieved by some of the poems of Robert Frost, in which daily occurrences are made to yield deeper meanings through a juxtaposition with larger themes. In this poem, furthermore, the precise descriptions that in many of Bishop's works are simply a fact of style come to take on the quality of content, being put in context by the sudden shift to abstraction of the work's final six lines.

The self-effacing narrator begins by description, sketching the old man who sits mending his nets, until nearly halfway through, where he or she appears for the first time in a possessive pronoun: The reader is told that this man "was a friend of my grandfather" (the word "I" is not used until even further down). The reader is given the silver surface of the sea, the benches, the lobster pots; even the tubs are lined with iridescent scales on which walk iridescent flies. Suddenly the man becomes real: He accepts a cigarette, a Lucky Strike. A line break introduces the reader to the theme of the water, that element from which come all these silvery riches and that forms the source of this man's life and livelihood. This separate section of six lines is tied to the first through the theme of color: In the water lie silver tree trunks.

The next section starts again with the water, an "element bearable to no mortal." The narrator waxes whimsical with memories of singing hymns to a seal, then returns to the water. This is the same sea that the narrator has seen all over the world, yet here it is so cold that no one would even want to put in a hand, for it would make one's bones ache; if one tasted it, the water would burn the tongue. This, the narrator reflects finally, "is like what we imagine knowledge to be." The narrator then enumerates the qualities ascribed to knowledge that, in fact, are possessed by this water:

> dark, salt, clear, moving, utterly free,
> drawn from the cold hard mouth
> of the world, derived from the rocky breasts
> forever, flowing and drawn, and since
> our knowledge is historical, flowing, and flown.

Knowledge, one imagines, is all around, but at the same time it is an element in which one cannot live or even dip one's limbs. Knowledge, furthermore, is inherently historical: a great stream of time that surrounds humankind, relative to an individual's own precise situation.

The suggestion seems to be that knowledge, paralleled to this translucent and inviting—but, in fact, inhospitable—element, is ultimately unreachable. The best one can do is live on the land, scrap-

ing the scales from fish that have been taken from this medium. One may imagine knowledge to flow all around, and in fact it is the font of those things necessary for human sustenance. Yet at the same time one can never attain it; indeed, it is a medium too fine for such corporeal creatures as humans to experience directly.

"QUESTIONS OF TRAVEL"

First published: 1965 (collected in *Questions of Travel*, 1965)
Type of work: Poem

As a meditation taking a tropical scene as its point of departure, the poem comments on the merits and disadvantages of travel.

"Questions of Travel" provided the title for Bishop's third volume of poetry, and it comes from a group of works that were written in, and take as their theme, Brazil. The poem is at once a series of very precise observations and, obliquely, a meditation on movement in place that suggests movement in the imagination. The dichotomy that is thereby set up between mind and body comes perhaps from the French philosopher René Descartes and echoes earlier literary treatments of the question of travel in works by Emily Dickinson, Ralph Waldo Emerson, and Marcel Proust.

In this poem, the narrator remains submerged, emerging only briefly in the pronoun "we" in the poem's second group of lines and then again before the final, italicized section as "the traveller," who (like Romantic poet John Keats's Grecian urn) writes his or her own motto, on which neither the narrator nor the author comments further. The result is that the reader is left with the ambiguity of knowing merely that this is what the traveler thinks, without knowing whether this is what the reader is to think. As the final section consists largely of questions, it may be precisely these questions that are the final "answer."

The poem's first line situates the reader immediately in an alien place, identified only as "here." All things are relative: From the narrator's point of view, the streams seem to be waterfalls, but from the point of view of the streams (if one can imagine this) the mountains become far away and tiny. In the second section begin the questions: Is it better to think of there from here? Would it have been better to think of here from there? Why do people travel? What, after all, are they looking for?

The ultimate decision of the poem seems to be for travel, enumerating as it does the strange, tiny details that can be perceived only outside the frames of one's normal life. The last of these details is the rain, which produces a silence during which "the traveller" writes the question which closes the poem: "Is it lack of imagination that makes us come/ to imagined places, not just stay at home?" Is there a point, that is, to physical displacement? Should one travel only in the mind? Is the imagination not better than reality? Though the poem ends on this question, Bishop's skill at evoking the details that precede it somehow suggests that travel in reality is better, or at least more interesting, than travel in imagination. Nevertheless, her vote remains somewhat hesitant, with the final image one of the person thinking of the inherent limitations of the human body: "Continent, city; country, society:/ the choice is never wide and never free."

"IN THE WAITING ROOM"

First published: 1976 (collected in *Geography III*, 1976)
Type of work: Poem

The poet recalls a childhood epiphany in a dentist's waiting room.

"In the Waiting Room" is a frequently anthologized poem which describes a moment of awakening consciousness in the poet's early life. The speaker sets the scene with Bishop's characteristic attention to minute detail. She has accompanied her Aunt Consuelo to the dentist's office and waits for her through the dark afternoon or evening of Massachusetts in February. While she waits, she reads a copy of *National Geographic*, observing the pictures of naked women, a dead man "slung on a pole," and a volcanic eruption. The pictures of the women both fascinate and horrify the child; she stares at their naked breasts and at the wire adornments binding their necks. At that moment, she

hears her aunt's soft gasp from the dentist's office, and she is moved by a series of understandings. One is that somehow all of us are united—the child viewer, the aunt, the women in the magazine. "I— we—were falling, falling. . . . " In fact, she feels everyone is falling off the world, and to stop that sense, she asserts her own identity. She is Elizabeth; she will be seven years old in three days. Still she is moved by the mystery of identity. Why should she be who she is? What binds her to her aunt, her family, the women in the picture? Why should the two of them be here at this particular moment? Bishop often writes about perceptions of time. Here, she pictures it as a black wave about to swallow the waiting room and all its inhabitants. As the poem ends, she feels restored to the ordinary order of things: the place, the time, herself—a February night in Worcester, Massachusetts, during the wartime, 1918.

"THE MOOSE"

First published: 1976 (collected in *The Complete Poems, 1927-1979*, 1983)
Type of work: Poem

A bus travels across Nova Scotia into a forest, where its progress in stopped by a moose in the road.

"The Moose" is a careful description of a bus journey through Nova Scotia. Its twenty-eight six-line stanzas employ an irregular pattern of slant rhyme which links two, sometimes four, end words in each stanza. Through most of the first half of the poem, the bus's journey is described in terms of the landscape that the bus traverses. The riders are scarcely mentioned at all. Instead, readers see the changing scenery. The bus moves from "narrow provinces/ of fish and bread and tea" past the Bay of Fundy, with its enormous tides, and then past the mud flats and the farmhouses and neat white churches. The battered old bus itself is not described until the fifth stanza. Stanzas six and seven picture the bus waiting for a passenger to say good-bye to the relatives he or she is leaving behind. Even the collie is noted here, and then the landscape reasserts itself in a description of flower gardens and little communities. In the thirteenth stanza, a woman enters the bus with some small fragments of conversation. At that point the bus is traveling by moonlight into the forest. The passengers fall asleep, and Bishop pictures them entering a world of dream filled with the comfortable voices of home and the details of daily life which, as the poet reminds her reader, also involves death. In the twenty-second stanza, the bus jolts to a stop, and the driver cuts the lights so that the passengers can look at a moose that has wandered into the road. Huge and homely and harmless, she sniffs at the bus while the passengers marvel and share a sudden sense of joy. Then the bus resumes its journey, leaving the moose on the dreamy moonlit road.

"ONE ART"

First published: 1976 (collected in *The Complete Poems, 1927-1979*, 1983)
Type of work: Poem

In this ironic villanelle, the poet muses on learning the art of losing things.

In "One Art," Bishop, who was always interested in using formal techniques, uses the villanelle to give form to her thoughts on loss. The form requires that the first and third lines of the first stanza be used alternately as third-line refrains for the succeeding stanzas until the last stanza, which contains four lines, the last two of which repeat the refrain lines. As in this poem, the line length is commonly iambic pentameter, and the rhyme scheme for each triplet is *aba*. As with many writers of villanelles, Bishop alters some of the repeated lines instead of repeating precisely. Throughout much of the poem, her voice is flippant about the ease with which things get lost, things ranging from keys to time. In the fourth stanza, however, as she notes that she lost her mother's watch and a loved house, she sounds less willing to accept the loss. In the fifth, she says that losing two cities and an entire continent (probably a reference to her leaving Brazil) still was not a disaster, although such losses sound enormous to the reader. The last stanza is often taken to refer to the suicide of Bishop's Brazilian lover, Lota de Macedo Soares, the "you" the speaker says she has lost. However, when the speaker says that this shows that the art of losing is "not too hard to master," her understatement suggests the opposite, as the poem concludes that the loss "may look like (Write it!) like disaster." The parenthetical "Write it!" suggests one way to cope with disastrous losses—through art.

SUMMARY

Bishop carved a secure niche for herself in twentieth century poetry through the careful crafting of her few meticulously polished works. If some of her poems seem to evade involvement with the world in favor of a highly polished surface that will be most attractive to those who find refuge from action in words, others pose more centrally the very questions and problems that the more distant ones seem to avoid. Critics are united in their praise for her technique, and admiration for her understatement in an age of loudness continues to grow.

Bruce E. Fleming; updated by Ann D. Garbett

BIBLIOGRAPHY

By the Author

POETRY:
North and South, 1946
Poems: North and South—A Cold Spring, 1955
Questions of Travel, 1965
Selected Poems, 1967
The Ballad of the Burglar of Babylon, 1968
The Complete Poems, 1969
Geography III, 1976
The Complete Poems, 1927-1979, 1983

SHORT FICTION:
"In the Village," in *Questions of Travel*, 1965

NONFICTION:
The Diary of "Helena Morley," 1957 (translation of Alice Brant's *Minha Vida de Menina*)
Brazil, 1962 (with the editors of *Life*)
One Art: Letters, 1994

EDITED TEXT:
An Anthology of Twentieth Century Brazilian Poetry, 1972 (with Emanuel Brasil)

CHILDREN'S LITERATURE:
The Battle of the Burglar of Babylon, 1968

MISCELLANEOUS:
The Collected Prose, 1984 (fiction and nonfiction)

About the Author

Bloom, Harold, ed. *Elizabeth Bishop: Modern Critical Views.* New York: Chelsea House, 1985.

Boland, Eavan. "An Unromantic American." *Parnassus: Poetry in Review* 14 (Summer, 1988): 73-92.

Fountain, Gary. *Remembering Elizabeth Bishop: An Oral Biography.* Amherst: University of Massachusetts Press, 1994.

Kirsch, Adam. *The Wounded Surgeon: Confession and Transformation in Six American Poets: Robert Lowell, Elizabeth Bishop, John Berryman, Randall Jarrell, Delmore Schwartz and Sylvia Plath.* New York: W. W. Norton, 2005.

MacMahon, Candace, ed. *Elizabeth Bishop: A Bibliography, 1927-1979.* Charlottesville: University Press of Virginia, 1980.

Millier, Brett C. *Elizabeth Bishop: Life and Memory.* Berkeley: University of California Press, 1993.

Motion, Andrew. *Elizabeth Bishop.* Wolfeboro, N.H.: Longwood, 1986.

Parker, Robert Dale. *The Unbeliever: The Poetry of Elizabeth Bishop.* Urbana: University of Illinois Press, 1988.

Schwartz, Lloyd. *That Sense of Constant Readjustment: Elizabeth Bishop "North & South."* New York: Garland, 1987.

Schwartz, Lloyd, and Sybil P. Estess, eds. *Elizabeth Bishop and Her Art.* Ann Arbor: University of Michigan Press, 1983.

Travisano, Thomas J. *Elizabeth Bishop: Her Artistic Development.* Charlottesville: University Press of Virginia, 1988.

Wylie, Diana E. *Elizabeth Bishop and Howard Nemerov: A Reference Guide.* Boston: G. K. Hall, 1983.

DISCUSSION TOPICS

- Look at any of Elizabeth Bishop's poems for evidence that she pays careful attention to detail. What sort of detail can you find?

- Some of Bishop's poems, such as "The Moose" and "First Death in Nova Scotia," draw on Canadian settings. What specifically Canadian details do you find in her work?

- How does Bishop portray time in her work?

- Bishop is sometimes seen as a writer who keeps a distance between herself and her reader. What evidence can you see of that in her poems?

- What stanza forms can you find in Bishop's poems?

- What do Bishop's poems reveal about her feelings about travel?

- What kinds of landscapes seem to have interested Bishop in her many descriptions of them?

Edward Bloor

Born: Trenton, New Jersey
October 12, 1950

In innovative young-adult novels, Bloor creates a provocative picture of contemporary adolescence, specifically focused on the dynamic of the family, the role of education, the problem of intolerance, and the difficult process of self-discovery.

BIOGRAPHY

Edward William Bloor was born and raised in the working-class neighborhoods of Trenton, New Jersey, an ethnically diverse community. In school, Bloor played soccer and learned not only the intensity of competition but also enlightening lessons on cooperation across ethnic lines. He loved the upbeat sports novels of Clair Bee. After graduating with a B.A. from Fordham University in 1973 and working briefly in Boston and in England, Bloor accepted a position teaching middle-school language arts in Fort Lauderdale, Florida.

In 1986, he began work as a language arts textbook editor for Harcourt School Publishers near Orlando. In that capacity, as he evaluated submissions of young-adult novels, he decided to try writing one of his own. He had long been interested in writing—as a child, he had written plays and stories that had been well received by his family and teachers. Bloor began work on what would become his first novel, *Tangerine* (1997), while commuting to Harcourt. *Tangerine* would break new ground in young-adult fiction, rejecting the Harry Potter-style fantasy genre and preferring to treat thorny subjects such as school cliques, environmental mismanagement, the pressure of bigotry, and the complex human capacity for mayhem and evil. Such themes led reviewers to describe Bloor's work as dark, even gothic. *Tangerine*, however, hailed for its willingness to engage difficult contemporary themes as well as for its complex young-adult characters and multiple plot lines, was selected for numerous best-of-the-year lists of young-adult fiction, including the prestigious American Library Association listing.

Two years later, Bloor released his landmark work, *Crusader* (1999). Set in a failing family video arcade business in a Fort Lauderdale mall, the work is as much a probing look into the violence of hate crimes and the crooked politics of land development as it is a powerful story of a girl struggling to make peace with the murder of her mother seven years earlier and a difficult estrangement since from her father. *Story Time* (2004), a wickedly funny, Swiftian satire on public education and specifically the trend of standardized testing, took Bloor's writing in an entirely new direction. *London Calling*, a planned Bloor follow-up, involves time travel and draws on the experiences of children in World War II London during the Blitz.

ANALYSIS

Owing to Bloor's classroom experience, his novels resist the clichés of young-adult escapist fiction by creating central characters who, despite being "only" in middle school, exhibit a precocious sensibility, curiosity, rich vulnerability, and driving determination to discover truth amid the hypocrisies and easy lies of friends and adults. Bloor's realistic novels take place in a recognizable world of malls and soccer fields, overcrowded classrooms and hastily built housing developments. Bloor deploys the intimacy of first-person narration, allowing the plot to be revealed by adolescent characters, thus creating a sustaining seriousness to their predicaments. His central characters tend to be misfits who struggle within fractured families. Unable to fit within the precarious social environment of public schools, these characters rely on their own sensibilities and find that honest confrontation with who they are leads to a sustaining peace and, finally, to the challenge of accepting others.

Thus, Bloor's novels are tales of moral growth, nuanced and symbol-rich parables of adolescents earning redemption in a world crossed by the heavy pressure of evil. Unlike the cartoon evil that defines contemporary young-adult fiction, Bloor insists that evil, the menacing logic of violence and brutality, is a stubborn element of people who appear otherwise unexceptional. In novels set ironically amid the wash of the bright Florida sun, characters reveal a dark propensity for mayhem. Parents, friends, teachers, politicians, neighbors—each, in turn, betrays an inexplicable willingness to lie, to cheat, to steal, to hurt, and ultimately even to kill. Trust becomes a precarious investment, loyalty a risk, friendship rare and always defined against its own fragility. Such truth does not terrify in Bloor's fiction—the problematic reward of awareness is the best strategy to gain the maturity necessary to accept others. Bloor's upbeat vision, confident in the ability of the heart to grow and change, counsels education as the only way to combat closed-mindedness.

Structurally, Bloor challenges reader expectations by multiplying plot lines and splicing genres to create new reading experiences, essentially new genres. *Tangerine* is as much a sports novel as a searing family drama, *Crusader* as much a murder mystery as a probing social polemic, *Story Time* as much a burlesque of public education as a terrifying tale of demonic possession. Cinematic in their generous use of plot, with Bloor's pitch-perfect ear for adolescent conversation (no doubt from his years in the classroom), the novels surely entertain but serve ultimately to return their young readers to the world around them with new awareness.

There is a clear-eyed immediacy to Bloor's fiction—despite a reputation for gothicism, these novels do not indulge in such ornamental (and simplistic) excess. Bloor understands that the world is a complex of apparently good people doing evil things and apparently evil people doing good things. In that way, Bloor, ever the teacher, treats his readers, despite their young ages, much as he treats his central characters: as tough, reasonable minds whose tender hearts need to be coaxed toward important, if difficult, truths.

TANGERINE

First published: 1997
Type of work: Novel

A precocious, legally blind seventh-grader comes to understand his relationship with a violent older brother and the effects of bigotry during a championship soccer season.

Paul Fisher is an outsider. Transplanted at the beginning of his seventh-grade year from Houston to Florida, where his father has accepted a position as county engineer and where his older brother, Erik, a talented place-kicker, can pursue options for scholarships in a state fanatic about football, Paul does not easily fit in. Told that during an eclipse when he was five he foolishly stared directly into the sun and permanently damaged his eyes, he is now legally blind and wears thick glasses that have made him both self-conscious and introspective. Indeed, his lengthy journal entries form part  of the book. Paul is bothered by recollections that suggest that there might be more to his eye injury than he had been told. He resists the implications, preferring to live uneasily in the shadow of his older brother—and ever in eclipse. Erik is routinely cruel to Paul, unbeknown to his parents, particularly his father, who dotes on his older son's football talent and largely ignores Paul's considerable skills as a soccer goalie.

Adjustment to life in Florida is difficult for the Fishers. Their development community, plagued by the effects of its irresponsible construction (entire groves of citrus trees were hastily bulldozed, leaving new homes susceptible to termite infestations and the heavy stink from underground muck fires that continuously burn), symbolizes how long-ago mistakes inevitably take their toll until they are resolved. The middle school is a dreary row of portable classrooms, wooden shacks threaded by muddy walkways. Paul tries out for the school's soccer team, only to be dismissed when transfer paper-work listing him as handicapped makes him ineligible to serve in any spot except manager. Crushed, Paul is given a second chance when, during a heavy rainstorm, a fifty-foot sinkhole swallows a chunk of the school. He transfers to nearby rival Tangerine Middle School where, for the first time, he finds himself a minority student.

When Paul goes out for the school's soccer team, he begs his mother not to file his handicapped papers. He earns a spot as backup goalie to a girl—whose considerable skills give Paul his first lesson in expanding his perspective. The real impact of his transfer to Tangerine, however, centers on Paul's adjustment to the school's minority presence, particularly that of the tough Latino students who work as citrus farmers. Paul gets to know the Cruz family through Tino, who plays soccer. The older brother, Luis, is a maverick citrus grower who has developed a new strain of seedless tangerine, called Golden Dawn, which promises a wide market appeal. Paul visits their nursery, with its crude Quonset huts and its minimum appointments—a vivid contrast to his gated community where residents fret over matching mailboxes and uniform Tudor trim.

Unlike at his home, riven by unspoken hostilities and buried secrets and terrorized from a series of unexplained break-ins, Paul finds the Cruz family generous and open and the farm inviting and invigorating. The friendship is further nurtured when Paul works with Tino and his friends on a science paper about Luis's new tangerine. During the visit, Luis explains the work of a citrus nursery, how different varieties of tangerines are spliced into the same rough tree stock; in short, how such a beautiful abundance of fruit must be grown by transplanting seedlings into an unpromising host, suggesting Paul's own maturation within the rough world of Tangerine Middle School. When the soccer season closes in a dramatic tie with Paul's old school, Paul finds himself in tears on the bus on the way back to Tangerine, feeling at last part of a team.

When a freak Thanksgiving ice storm threatens the citrus crop, Paul volunteers to help stoke the smudge pots for a long, harrowing night during which he bonds in a most profound way with the Cruz family. Even as Paul grows into tolerance across race, gender, and ethnic divisions, his brother fights with Tino over insensitive slurs Erik

had made when Tino visited Paul's house to work on the science project. When Luis comes to the football practice field to teach Erik a lesson, Erik has a friend blindside Luis with a blackjack. Luis's resulting head injury triggers an aneurysm, and within days he is dead. Paul, waiting to pick up Erik after practice and out of sight under the stadium bleachers, had witnessed the cheap hit and also knew his brother's culpability. The police blame Luis's death on a branch that had fallen during the night of the freeze. Only Paul knows the truth. He is haunted—after he attends Luis's burial, he collapses, sobbing, in his backyard and digs deeply into the sugar sand until he hits the rich soil that the developers had so carelessly covered. It is then that Paul bonds with the dead citrus farmer, Luis, whom he decides is now part of him.

During an awards night to recognize his brother's undefeated football team, Tino and his friends come into the gym and begin a fight with Erik. At a dramatic moment of decision, Paul helps his friends from Tangerine and jumps the football coach who had grabbed one of them. When the Tangerine kids make their escape from the school, Paul as well runs out into the night, where he is confronted by his brother, swinging a metal baseball bat. Paul tells him what he knows—but Erik and his friend dismiss it because Paul is "blind." A chance remark by Erik triggers a flood of clarifying memory—Paul recalls the circumstances of his eye injury, how his brother had vandalized a wall with spray paint and had been caught, how he had blamed his little brother, and how Erik had held Paul's eyes open while a friend sprayed paint directly into them. Paul is stunned by the implications of his memory—specifically how his parents had protected their golden boy and how they had let Paul suffer, hating himself for stupidly staring into an eclipse.

Quickly Erik's malevolence is revealed. It is he and his friend who are behind the neighborhood break-ins. When Erik's friend is arrested for the death of Luis, Paul tells the arresting officers what he saw under the bleachers, including his brother's responsibility. The parents begin to see that the pampered Erik needs help. When Paul is expelled for the rest of the school year for jumping the coach, he transfers to a nearby Catholic school and, in a ritual assertion of his new identity, throws out his old clothes and outfits himself in the new school's uniform. Paul is ready now to begin the most difficult challenge of his adolescence, restoring a relationship with his father. In the closing scene, the father is driving Paul to the new school. It is a beautiful Florida morning, and the hanging muck fires have been, at least temporarily, lifted by a sweet morning breeze. The air clear, scented with citrus, Paul heads at last into a golden dawn of his own.

CRUSADER

First published: 1999
Type of work: Novel

A journalism student, haunted by her mother's unsolved murder during a robbery, exposes local political corruption and investigates hate crimes at the mall where she works; in the process, she learns the truth about her mother's death.

As *Crusader* opens, Roberta Ritter is at work, assembling an imposing "Crusader" figure as a promotion for the newest interactive video experience for her family's struggling video arcade. In this virtual-reality game, players score points by "killing" hordes of "Muslims." When one of the mall-shop owners, a Muslim, objects to the premise of the game and explains the actual history of the Crusades, Roberta confronts the difficult truth that good and evil are inextricably bound in the human character, that ignorance breeds prejudice, that prejudice leads to hate, and that hate expresses itself in violence. It is the beginning of her education into the wisdom of tolerance. It is also a lesson in the need to confront even the most painful realities. Roberta herself has spent seven years insulating herself from the implications of her own mother's death—knifed during a robbery of the family's previous arcade—by telling herself that her mother had died from a heart attack.

In a novel whose multiple plot lines hinge on the deception of surfaces and the complex reality of good and evil, Bloor tests the need to confront, the ease with which difficult realities are ignored, and the disparity between appearances and realities. Nothing is as it appears—Roberta, as an intern for

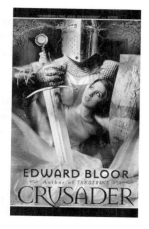

the local television station, learns techniques for splicing videotape in ways that create entirely new "realities." The mall where she works struggles to stay open while pretending to be prosperous, even launching an interior renovation centering on a showy fountain that is ironically connected with ancient, rusted pipes that end up leaking sewer gas. Dawg, a muscle-bound football lunkhead, is blamed for the rash of hate crimes because the police are certain that he "looks" like a redneck. Railroaded, Dawg is outfitted with an electronic monitoring device but, refusing to be framed for something he did not do, he runs deliberately into highway traffic in a stunning act of suicide. His friend, called Ironman because of his bulk and his T-shirts bearing Satanic legends, reveals an unexpected depth of feeling over his friend's death, grieving so deeply that he is driven to a suicide attempt of his own.

In short, Roberta's world stays stubbornly contradictory. Every assumption she makes about people eventually shatters. Her beautiful cousin, so focused on her own photogenic looks, is afflicted by chicken pox. Scarred and devastated, she undergoes a spiritual transformation and reveals a genuine compassion for others, particularly Ironman, and ultimately decides to become a police officer. A local rising political star promises to help the mall, while his son negotiates to have it torn down and replaced by a swanky golf course. More distressing, Roberta comes to understand that the hate crimes against the Muslim shop owner have been perpetrated by her own uncle, a decorated Gulf War veteran who struggles with a secret drinking problem, all in an attempt to close the mall to protect the family from losing everything if the arcade has to declare bankruptcy.

Honesty is even more painful when it comes to Roberta's father, who ignores Roberta (and the arcade's considerable financial dilemma) to pursue a romance with the mall's manager. Roberta's friendship with a police detective investigating the hate crimes, however, gives her access to long-filed evidence from her mother's murder, including the gruesome surveillance tape showing the knifing. Roberta's investigation of a snake tattoo on the assailant's arm leads her ultimately to determine that the killer, once a street addict, is now a charismatic televangelist whose cable show, which Roberta watches during long nights she is left alone by her father, celebrates forgiveness. Roberta discovers that her father had once been a cocaine addict and had hired the man to rob the family video store to pay off a loan shark, whom the father had used to pay for drugs. Although the father never intended the killing, Roberta cannot forgive him.

Mrs. Weiss, a survivor of the Nazi Holocaust who now owns a card shop in the mall and who serves as the novel's uncompromising moral conscience, had taken a keen interest in Roberta's upbringing. Upon her death, Mrs. Weiss leaves Roberta the shop and her home. Thus, Roberta is in a position to estrange herself from her father, which she does.

In the powerful closing scene, Roberta goes to the spot where her family arcade had stood and lays a wreath made of objects she had kept from her mother—photos, her arcade smock, her beloved Dr. Seuss books. She is overcome with unexpected compassion for those street kids whose tough lives make violent crime inevitable and hope difficult. Roberta's heart expanded, her compassion evident, she prays for them. It is a deeply spiritual closing. In a world of political spin-doctoring, phony "reality" talk shows, hate crimes that scapegoat minorities, virtual reality games, videotape faux-realities, and expensive cosmetic makeovers (all elements of Bloor's intricate plot), Roberta emerges as an uncompromising point of moral honesty, at last a crusader of her own.

DISCUSSION TOPICS

- In what ways are both Paul Fisher and Roberta Ritter crusaders?

- In what way are they both "tangerines"?

- How does Edward Bloor define a healthy parent-child relationship?

- What does Bloor suggest is the price for lying and hypocrisy?

- Both *Tangerine* and *Crusader* have a "happy" ending, but how does Bloor avoid sentimentality?

- What is gained by Bloor having his main characters speak for themselves?

- What are the advantages and disadvantages of being an outsider?

- How does Bloor define adulthood?

SUMMARY

Serious story lines that compel young readers to confront difficult truths have never been the mainstay of young-adult fiction. As a career educator, however, Bloor sees the role of writer as one of coaxing readers toward realizations that, while troubling in their implications, prepare those readers to engage a morally ambiguous world and to triumph over it by dint of an uncompromising commitment to honesty.

Joseph Dewey

BIBLIOGRAPHY

By the Author

LONG FICTION:
Tangerine, 1997
Crusader, 1999
Story Time, 2004

About the Author
Atkins, Kathy. "Welcome to Tangerine, and Be Careful: An Interview with Edward Bloor." *St. Petersburg Times*, February 18, 2002.
"Edward Bloor." In *Contemporary Authors*. Vol. 166. Detroit: Gale, 2003.

JUDY BLUME

Born: Elizabeth, New Jersey
February 12, 1938

Employing a steady mixture of humor and pathos, Blume constructs novels designed to traverse traditionally difficult, if not highly controversial, subject matter which empathizes with her largely female audience through the first-person perspectives of her young protagonists.

AP/Wide World Photos

BIOGRAPHY

Judy Sussman was born February 12, 1938, in Elizabeth, New Jersey, to Jewish parents: Esther, a quiet, book-savvy housewife, and Rudolph, a dentist. Much of Blume's fiction finds itself rooted in this family, particularly her father, who provided the model for many of his fictional counterparts in his strong joviality and support for his daughter's imagination.

As in many of her novels, though, physical distance between father and daughter proved to be problematic. In one instance, the family was forced to move to Florida for two years out of health concerns for Judy's older brother, David; her father remained in New Jersey, working to support them. Both siblings would experience severe illness in their youth. Her father's death in 1959 at the relatively young age of fifty-four, coupled with the death of two of his brothers in their forties, would haunt Blume's prose with a preoccupation with parental separation, mortality, and isolation.

Blume attended New York University (NYU), after mononucleosis arrested her start at Boston University during her first year there. She graduated with a B.S. in Early Childhood Education in 1960, which she never utilized, as she wished to stay at home with her children. In fact, she attributed much of her impetus to be an educator to her mother's pragmatism that she have a career in the

event that marriage did not work out for her. Esther Sussman's anxieties were quite prescient.

Judy Sussman became Judy Blume when she married John Blume, a lawyer, in 1959, during her junior year in college. Blume has stated that their sixteen-year marriage constituted a period during which she was expected to fulfill the role of a domestic homemaker: raising children, Randy Lee in 1961 and Larry in 1963, and attending to her husband, whom she divorced in 1975. Blume claims that her parents had instilled within her a need for a successful career, and she felt that her development was being arrested in such a marriage as hers. She would revisit this scenario with her short-lived marriage to Thomas Kitchens in 1976; they divorced in 1979.

It was during her marriage to John Blume that Judy began her preoccupation with storytelling and returned to her educational roots. She began writing her fiction in 1966 when her children entered nursery school. While she met with some success early on (two short stories were published over a three-year period), she encountered far more failure, receiving up to six rejections a week from publishers. Undeterred, though, after finding limited success, Blume enrolled in a graduate course at NYU titled "Writing for Children and Teenagers." The class would lead to her first books, *The One in the Middle Is the Green Kangaroo* (1969) and *Iggie's House* (1970) and predated her revolutionary 1970 opus, *Are You There God? It's Me, Margaret.*

Though met with a mixed reception because of its incredibly frank verisimilitude in dealing with both Margaret's menarche and her internal struggle to find a voice for her religious beliefs, the novel was praised as one of the outstanding books of 1970 by *The New York Times*. The book also marked Blume's first forays into censorship, as numerous groups sought to have it banned for its controversial exploration of familial and sororal bonds, religion, and the emergence of a nascent sexuality in women. While critically mixed, the novel was popularly acclaimed, particularly after it went into paperback, where its seventy-five-cent cover price made it widely more accessible to children.

Further notoriety followed with the publication of *Freckle Juice* and *Then Again, Maybe I Won't* in 1971 and *It's Not the End of the World* in 1972. Since that time Blume has written or edited more than twenty books and placed seventy-five million copies into print. She has expanded her canon to include a few distinctly adult novels. She also adapted her 1972 children's novel *Otherwise Known as Sheila the Great* into a stage musical produced in Millburn, New Jersey, in 2001, which Blume co-produced with her son Lawrence Blume.

The year 1987 proved to be landmark for Blume on a variety of levels including the publication of *Just As Long As We're Together*, her third marriage (to nonfiction writer George Cooper), and the death of her mother from pneumonia at the age of 83. Cooper and Blume are still married, with three children and one grandchild. Some of Blume's works are housed at the University of Minnesota, in the Kerlan Collection.

ANALYSIS

When Blume writes works of young adult fiction, she often aims for a target audience between the ages of eleven and fifteen. Her books operate as problem novels, works which are associated with hot-button issues keyed to that audience and the protagonist of the novel, such as Margaret's speculations on her own religion in *Are You There God? It's Me, Margaret* and Karen's all-consuming focus on her parents' pending divorce in *It's Not the End of the World*. The limited perspective allotted to the first-person internal narrative voice of her protagonists allows Blume to construct their struggle through each novel's issue seemingly in isolation. Each girl works through the problems of her world in her own mind, as only the reader is given access to her thoughts, fears, and, more often than not, self-

deprecating humor and embarrassment at the situation.

This narrative contrivance is a masterstroke within Blume's stories. It allows her young protagonists the opportunity to speak almost directly to the audience, drawing the reader into a conversation as both try to understand the world as a sociocultural phenomenon they share. In effect, Blume's books operate as a surrogate for the parents whom Blume feels may be ill-equipped to discuss sensitive matters with their children. She has noted that in her younger years, she tried to discuss sensitive topics, such as menstruation, with her father and found it confounding and unhelpful.

Blume's childhood experiences taught her that she did the best learning when she was among friends or simply being introspective; her characters follow suit. For example, in *Just as Long as We're Together*, Stephanie's narrative voice speaks directly to the audience when she considers why her new best friend, Alison, is so popular. That she takes the time to list all of Alison's attributes as if she were compiling them as evidence for the reader adds to the realism of her dilemma by providing the audience with a working blueprint of her deepest anxieties.

It is the frankness of Blume's characters which allows them to transgress from the novel into reality. As each of her protagonists must resolve a larger problem, they work through their worlds vis-à-vis interaction with other textual characters with similar problems. For example, Margaret discovers through her friend Nancy Wheeler's reaching menarche in a New York steakhouse that menstruation is not the badge of honor their clique assumed it to be, particularly given that Nancy had earlier lied about getting her period, before she had actually done so. Margaret reasons that while menstruation is an important step in her development as a woman, she also must own the maturity to wait for it to occur naturally, without prevaricating for the social boost.

In her works, Blume does not skirt the issue or use euphemism to lessen its blow; she writes with the boldness and precociousness of the children she is describing. When Nancy's period arrives, she is mortified, and she hides in the bathroom until her mother comes to help her. This very private event occurs before Margaret, who even must assist

Mrs. Wheeler in aiding Nancy. Margaret feels the embarrassment for Nancy's situation: her mother unmasking her lies, having difficulties with her period, and Nancy's betrayal of the confidences of the other members of their group. Margaret also feels sympathy for her situation. All of this is told to the reader through Margaret's internal narrative, to which only the audience is privileged. The resultant effect is therapeutic to the reader—while Margaret sympathizes with Nancy, the audience empathizes with Margaret and her responsibility with Nancy's trust.

In effect, Blume's works are *Bildungsromane*—novels whose principal subject matter deals with the moral, psychological, and intellectual development of the youthful hero who comes of age through the events of the novel. Blume's novels complicate that tradition by going to great lengths not to be didactic or preach to the reader. Blume's stories almost always arrive at open-ended conclusions, such as when Stephanie and Rachel *possibly* rediscover their best-friendship at the end of the novel, but Blume cuts the story short of establishing that conclusion, leaving the reader with an open interpretation of what to take from the story's message.

In the end, the humor undercutting the harsh, controversial subject matter of her work is Blume's forte. She breaks the tensions between these difficult trials and protects the reader from the garish realities of topics such as divorce, physical maturation, and even death with situational humor which often brings a little saccharine to the sour of her characters' lives. Blume's characters are wholly three-dimensional, complete with anxieties, absurdities, and the constructed naïveté similar to that of her reader; these attributes often humanize the characters and bring the hope out of their seeming hopelessness, even when a total resolution is deferred.

ARE YOU THERE, GOD? IT'S ME MARGARET

First published: 1970
Type of work: Novel

Having recently changed schools, a pre-teen girl must learn to navigate new social, physical, and religious spheres as she tries to determine who she is.

Are You There, God? It's Me Margaret was Blume's first weighty novel attempting to tackle a major problem (or problems) she associated with her own childhood: moving to a new community, separating from family, and coming into physical maturity. Margaret, the story's protagonist, relocates from New York City to a new town and school in suburban New Jersey. Though skeptical about her new surroundings, she quickly makes friends—an assemblage of girls who come to identify themselves as the Pre-Teen Sensations. It is among these girls that Margaret discovers the complex relations surrounding a variety of prepubescent issues including boys, menstruation, and petty jealousies surrounding girls who have had greater success with either of the former.

As the title indicates, the focus of the book centers around Margaret coming to terms with herself and her heritage as she tries to discover in what religious community she wishes to participate: Judaism or Christianity. Margaret's mother, recovering from trauma at the hands of her proselytizing Christian parents, and Margaret's father, shunned by his in-laws because he is Jewish, have decided that Margaret could choose her own religion when she is old enough to decide for herself.

Unfortunately for Margaret, "old enough" comes about through an assignment from her new teacher, Mr. Benedict, who assigns the individual class members a year-long study of something meaningful to them. Torn between two faiths and two sets of grandparents hoping she will choose their religion, Margaret decides that she will investigate the possibilities available to her.

It is therein, that Margaret's repeated canto of "Are you there, God? It's me, Margaret" gains multiple valences of possible meaning. Often used as a diary of her daily travail, Margaret prays to God for a variety of reasons, ranging from invoking him as a confidant to whom she can tell her secrets to calling out to him as a higher power with whom she can bargain (as when she asks him for larger breasts in exchange for cleaning her plate at supper every night for a month). When God apparently does not respond to her immediate need for divine intervention as an unexpected visit from her mother's parents derails her trip to Florida to see her other grandmother, Margaret forsakes God as unreliable and threatens never to speak to him again.

Margaret's notions of God operate on a personal level. She is still divided at the novel's end as to her religious inclinations, and she addresses God not with the reverence due a deity but more with an interest toward personal survival and naïve inquiry. At the story's end, when she reaches the menarche that she has been so desperate for, she feels that God has heard her. Only then does she address him with reverent thanks for making her feel as if she has arrived into physical maturity and closer connection to members of her social group.

IT'S NOT THE END OF THE WORLD

First published: 1972
Type of work: Novel

Faced with the impending divorce of her parents, young Karen Newman desperately tries to save her family from dissolution.

It's Not the End of the World might be characterized as Blume's most personal, almost autobiographical, early novel, given the events of her first marriage. Though she was yet to divorce her husband John Blume, the author found herself consumed with anxiety as she researched families going through divorce. In later years, she admitted that she had

not been honest with herself concerning her own failing marriage. She came to find that this novel is as much, if not more, about the feelings a child must experience as her parents go through divorce as the topic of divorce itself.

The plot, though much more singular in scope than *Are You There, God? It's Me, Margaret*, covers the complex emotions sixth-grader Karen Newman explores while watching her parents' marriage disintegrate day by day. In an effort to catalog the experience, she keeps a brief journal in which she grades each day by how its events affect her. When a boy she is attracted to in class chooses her as a spelling partner, the day rates an A+; when her brooding brother, Jeff, returns home after running away, C-.

Karen's confessional narrative in her journal expands upon a running commentary she keeps with the reader, who becomes a passive participant in the conversation. Although Karen has been best friends with Debbie since kindergarten, she forms an apprentice-like relationship with Val, whose mother is a recent divorcée.

Karen's narrative speaks of her constant feelings of loneliness and exile from anyone who can help her handle the conflicting emotions and responsibilities arising from the divorce. Much of this behavior is self-inflicted, as Karen intentionally tries to withhold this information from her schoolmates. What becomes interesting is that she compensates for this by directly addressing the reader as a confidant to her most sensitive secrets: her resentment of her mother's shaky attitude and lack of strong parental mores during the divorce, her desire for support from Jeff, and her desperate need for substantive, tangible advice from anyone concerning divorce.

It is in Karen's journal, revealing her unmitigated feelings and anxieties concerning her role within the marriage, where the divorce manifests itself as both a character and an adversary to be defeated in the novel. Karen tries anything she can think of to undermine the inevitable. As all attempts fail, Karen notices her mother and father's growing independence of each other (her mother takes on a new job at Global Insurance, and her father seeks a quicker divorce in Nevada). Karen's desperation increases, and her romantic delusions concerning reunification between more intense.

Tensions escalate to a climax, though, in the

novel's penultimate event: Jeff's running away. To this point in the story, as the divorce becomes more and more of a reality, Jeff's relationship with his mother becomes increasingly strained. He begins to ignore her more simple requests, reinterpreting them as assaults against him. He threatens to move out with his father, and he becomes increasingly reclusive from the family, retreating to his private space, *Jeff's Hideaway*. When his mother questions his expensive choice of a meal at a dinner out one evening, he strongly resists and orders the shrimp anyway. When it turns out that he does not enjoy the shrimp, a public argument between the two arises, resulting in Jeff leaving the table and running away—without any intervention from his mother, who thinks he is merely sulking.

When Jeff does not return later in the evening, mother and father are forced into each other's company. As Karen witnesses her parents' reaction to the situation, where concern for Jeff falls to the wayside in lieu of vitriol and blame for his actions, she finally comes to the realization that her parents sincerely dislike each other and reconciliation will be impossible.

JUST AS LONG AS WE'RE TOGETHER

First published: 1987
Type of work: Novel

Tensions mount between two friends when a popular third girl joins their group and threatens their long-held friendship.

Tensions within *Just as Long as We're Together* come from two sources: the separation between Stephanie Hirsch's parents and that between Stephanie and her best friend, Rachel Robinson. The main theme of the novel revolves around the awkwardness of identifying oneself with and within relationships, both marital and sororal.

Though the story is told dominantly from Stephanie's perspective, she often plays a supporting role within the story's subplots: the surprise and awkwardness surrounding her parents' separation; the welcome intrusion of Alison, a Vietnamese adoptee to a famous Hollywood couple who

have just moved into the neighborhood and into Stephanie's group of friends; and the resultant strain upon Stephanie's friendship with Rachel, a self-professed perfectionist who is the toast of the seventh grade.

As might be expected in the narrative of a young girl entering her teen years, Stephanie experiences a mix of burgeoning traumas. She has discovered boys as sexual objects worthy of her attention, she has discovered her own inadequacies in juxtaposition to the instantly popular Alison and irrepressible overachiever Rachel, and she even must deal with acting as a surrogate parent to her younger brother, Bruce, himself an overachiever yet slightly neurotic concerning global issues such as nuclear devastation.

Such pressures begin to take a physical toll upon Stephanie. She compensates for her inability to rectify her parents' relationship (her father is perpetually on business in California, and her mother approaches the trial separation with a calm that unnerves her further) by overeating, to the extent that both friends and family notice. This only compounds her self-criticism. Worse, she cannot confide in her friends because of the shame she feels and becomes mortified when word of the separation begins to spread. When the news finally reaches Rachel, who sees that Stephanie did not tell her about her parents' separation, Rachel overreact and disavows her friendship with Stephanie, on the basis that best friends do not keep secrets from each other.

The long-simmering pressure between Rachel and Stephanie reaches a boil only when Rachel's personal stresses become more than she can withstand. The arrival of Alison, someone whom Rachel and Stephanie view as so well-adjusted and popular that she threatens their own self-esteem, and the fact that Stephanie's life has become so convoluted that she unconsciously becomes distant to her, Rachel feels threatened and becomes defensive at what appears to her from her limited perspective as abandonment. Only at novel's end do both Stephanie and Rachel discover that they have had similar situations arise when they are forced to consider whether their friendship is salvageable or not.

As is customary within Blume's work, she denies the reader conclusion. Whether the girls' friendship can survive being a trio remains a mystery at the book's close. Likewise, though Stephanie's father returns from California to live in New York, the trial separation remains in place. The only real conclusion at which Stephanie arrives involves the transitory nature of romantic relationships, as she watches her parents consider other partners and her girlfriends, including herself, experience loves found and lost with boys who are as socially maladroit as are they themselves.

SUMMARY

The plurality and complexity of a child's life lies at the heart of most of Blume's works. Her greatest contribution to children's literature may come in her uncanny ability to capture the emotions of a child in print, without deference to adult perspective. Blume's young protagonists are as pockmarked and precocious as their real-world equivalents. Therein lies the charm, wit, and humor of her prose. Her unwavering admiration of the struggles of childhood parallels her consistent refusal to diminish, simplify, or condescend to youthful anxieties, joys, and imagination.

Joseph Michael Sommers

BIBLIOGRAPHY

By the Author

CHILDREN'S LITERATURE:
The One in the Middle Is the Green Kangaroo, 1969
Are You There God? It's Me, Margaret, 1970
Iggie's House, 1970
Freckle Juice, 1971
Then Again, Maybe I Won't, 1971
It's Not the End of the World, 1972
Otherwise Known as Sheila the Great, 1972
Tales of a Fourth Grade Nothing, 1972
Deenie, 1973
Blubber, 1974
Starring Sally J. Freedman as Herself, 1977
Superfudge, 1980
Tiger Eyes, 1981
The Pain and the Great One, 1984
Just as Long as We're Together, 1987
Fudge-a-mania, 1990
Here's to You, Rachel Robinson, 1993
Double Fudge, 2002

YOUNG ADULT FICTION:
Forever . . ., 1975

ADULT FICTION:
Wifey, 1978
Smart Women, 1984
Summer Sisters, 1998

DISCUSSION TOPICS

- How does Judy Blume's biography supplement a reading of her greater themes in children's fiction?

- How does humor operate within Blume's works?

- Blume's works often portray girls making the transition into puberty. What is it about this period in someone's life that offers such a wealth of material?

- What is the purpose of Blume's narrators addressing their readers directly, almost as if within a conversation with them?

- The anxieties encountered by young adults are ubiquitous within Blume's fiction: Religion, biology, relationships, generational conflict, marriage, divorce, and separation are all grist for her mill. How does such controversial subject matter aid the plots of her stories?

- Most of Blume's narratives are left without conclusive resolution. What is gained by withholding closure from the reader?

- What is "God's" function to a girl struggling to discover her own religion in *Are You There God? It's Me, Margaret?*

EDITED TEXT:

Places I Never Meant to Be: Original Stories by Censored Writers, 1999

MUSICAL DRAMA:

Otherwise Known as Sheila the Great, 2001

NONFICTION:

Letters to Judy: What Your Kids Wish They Could Tell You, 1986

About the Author

Blume, Judy. "Places I Never Meant to Be: A Personal View." *American Libraries* 30 (1999): 62-67.

Garber, Stephen. "Judy Blume: New Classicism for Kids." *English Journal* 73 (April 1984): 56-59.

Gleasner, Diana. *Breakthrough: Women in Writing.* New York: Walker, 1980.

Lee, Betsy. *Judy Blume's Story.* Minneapolis: Dillon Press, 1981.

Naylor, Alice Phoebe, and Carol Wintercorn. "Judy Blume." In *American Writers for Children Since 1960: Fiction,* edited by Glenn Estes. Vol. 52 in *Dictionary of Literary Biography.* Detroit: Bruccoli Clark, 1986.

Weidt, Maryann. *Presenting Judy Blume.* Boston: Twayne, 1990.

ROBERT BLY

Born: Madison, Minnesota
December 23, 1926

Bly is respected as one of the principal architects of postmodern American poetry, rejecting New Criticism and seeking a more politically active role for the generation of poets that emerged after 1945.

© Jerry Bauer/Courtesy, HarperCollins

BIOGRAPHY

Robert Elwood Bly was born in Madison, Minnesota, on December 23, 1926, to Jacob Thomas Bly and Alice Aws Bly, second-generation Norwegian immigrants. He grew up on his family's farm and, after completing high school in Madison, enlisted in the Navy, serving in a special radar program until the end of the war. According to Bly, one of the few positive memories he had of his experience in the Navy was the purchase of his first books of poetry, especially Carl Sandburg's *Chicago Poems: Poems of the Midwest* (1946) and Walt Whitman's *Leaves of Grass* (1855-1892).

After the war, using the G.I. Bill, Bly attended St. Olaf's College in Northfield, Minnesota, and studied writing under Arthur Paulson. Wanting to pursue his studies in a more concerted way, Bly transferred from St. Olaf's after only one year and entered Harvard University in 1947, where he majored in English. His education consisted of traditional English literature, augmented by courses in Latin, Greek, and German; however, he also read the works of respected contemporary poets, such as Robert Lowell (especially *Lord Weary's Castle*, published in 1946) and Richard Wilbur. Bly's interest in modern poetry led to an appointment during his junior year as literary editor of *The Harvard Advocate*, where he met other young writers and po-

ets, among them Donald Hall, John Ashbery, Kenneth Koch, Frank O'Hara, Adrienne Rich, and John Hawkes. Bly graduated from Harvard magna cum laude in 1950, and he delivered the class poem.

After spending seven months in a cabin in northern Minnesota, Bly decided to begin his career as a poet by moving to New York City, where he supported himself with a series of part-time jobs. At night, alone in his rented room, he read works of the Austrian poet Rainer Maria Rilke and classical poets Horace, Vergil, and Pindar; he also began work on his first book, *Silence in the Snowy Fields* (1962).

Tired of New York and eager to continue his academic studies, Bly enrolled in the University of Iowa's M.F.A. program in creative writing in 1954, under the direction of the midwestern poet Paul Engle. While there, Bly met several young, emerging poets, such as W. D. Snodgrass, Kim Yong Ik, and Marguerite Young. Also while at Iowa, Bly married Carolyn McLean, whom he had met while editing *The Harvard Advocate* in Massachusetts. The couple moved to a farm in Minnesota in June, 1955, while Bly continued working on his master's thesis. Completed in 1956, his collection of poems titled *Steps Toward Poverty and Death* fulfilled the thesis requirement for the M.F.A. in Creative Writing from Iowa.

The following year, Bly received a Fulbright Grant to translate Norwegian poetry and traveled to Oslo, Norway, where he read for the first time the works of poets such as Pablo Neruda, Georg Trakl, Juan Ramón Jimenez, and Gunnar Ekelof, all of whom he would later translate into English and publish in the United States. Not only did the translations serve Bly as a means of income upon his return to Minnesota in the late 1950's, but the poetry itself also influenced his work, invigorating it with new ideas on form and a new understanding of the poet's role in society. Bly's poetics began to take shape as early as 1958, when he and a friend, William Duffy, founded the literary journal (and subsequent publishing house) *The Fifties*. Bly's journal began by publishing works by poets such as James Wright, Donald Hall, and Louis Simpson, placing it among the most avant-garde of academic journals at that time. Changing its name to the Sixties Press in 1961, Bly began to publish translations of Trakl, Selma Lagerlöf, and others, collections of poems by emerging American poets, and his own *Silence in the Snowy Fields*.

In the early 1960's, after an extensive stay in Europe financed by an Amy Lowell Traveling Fellowship, Bly returned and became politically active against the Vietnam War. He organized antiwar poetry readings at many colleges and universities and organized American Writers Against the Vietnam War, which sponsored an anthology, *A Poetry Reading Against the Vietnam War* (1966). The Sixties Press continued to publish antiwar anthologies, such as *Forty Poems Touching on Recent American History* (1967), most of which were edited and introduced by Bly. His own activities became increasingly public, as he read at demonstrations and draft-card burnings. Academically, he continued to gain notice, however, receiving a Rockefeller Grant in 1967 and winning a National Book Award for his 1967 collection, *The Light Around the Body*. Even these academic honors, however, Bly turned into political statements, donating all prize money to the draft resistance movement and using his acceptance speeches as opportunities to denounce the publishing world for not taking a more active role in the antiwar movement.

During the 1970's, the Seventies Press continued to publish translations, and Bly continued to publish volumes of his own poems. His poetry readings took on a softer quality, with Bly reciting poems from memory and accompanying them on the dulcimer. When he was not reading or writing, Bly was founding and directing symposia on various topics, such as the Annual Conference on the Great Mother, later called the Conference of the Great Mother and the New Father. In the late 1970's, he began to travel to poetry festivals and gatherings all over the world.

By the late 1970's, Bly's family had grown to include two daughters, Mary and Bridget, and two sons, Noah and Micah. Despite his love of family and the close ties he had with his children, Bly and his wife, Carolyn, were divorced in 1979, after twenty-four years of marriage. In 1980, Bly married Ruth Ray and moved to Moose Lake, Minnesota. Bly's activities during the 1980's centered on his conferences for men, which he has sponsored at various universities around the United States. His purpose has been to counterbalance the tendency of modern society to do away with appropriate role models for men. His readings and symposia have been well attended and well received.

With the publication of *Iron John* (1990), subtitled *A Book About Men*, Bly's attraction as a public speaker on the recently dubbed men's movement quickly outdistanced his steady but relatively smaller draw as a reader of his own poetry, mostly on college campuses and in small bookstores. As he approaches his eighth decade, he continues to maintain a national and international speaking engagement agenda, both as a published poet and as a continuing leading figure of the now-established men's movement. His authorized Web site lists scheduled poetry readings on college campuses and at literary festivals as well as appearances at the Great Mother Conference and the Minnesota Men's Conference, among other professional and casual gatherings of men's groups. Bly continues to manifest the insights of a poet but with the zeal of a political or social reformer. He truly believes that if he is able to show men not only how to accept their "interior feminine" but especially the wildness or "un-niceness" that the Wild Man or Iron John represents in part as well, then men will be more self-actualized, and there is greater hope for human understanding and permanent relationships.

ANALYSIS

Rejecting the rather bleak view of T. S. Eliot's *The Waste Land* (1922), which set the tone for a generation of modernists, and further rejecting the obsessive, confessional writing of others in his own generation, Bly has chosen to write poetry that is inclusive, expansive, and, he believes, conducive to psychic healing. His career seems dedicated to offering opposition to the New Critics and their tendency to separate the artist's life from the art itself. Bly believes that such separation allows the art to be amoral and destructive—choking its ability to speak in the present tense about the great issues that society faces and will continue to face. For him, the modern desire to take an objective stance, to view the world from a comfortable distance, is dangerous. He has argued, therefore, for an approach to experience that has been called subjectivism—that is, an attempt to do away with the barrier between the subject and the object, to merge the two so that people can once again participate in the world in a more responsible and more spiritual way.

In his collection *News of the Universe: Poems of Twofold Consciousness* (1980), Bly elucidated his position that one could divide Western literature using the philosopher René Descartes as a marker. Prior to Descartes, according to Bly, Western literature reflected a people whose sensibility was not divided, a people who did not separate themselves from nature or from those elements in their own individual natures that they could not explain rationally, such as intuition, superstition, and spirituality. He cited the epic Anglo-Saxon poem *Beowulf* as an example, showing that when the poet describes the monster Grendel, he does so without having to explain its existence and without doubting that his audience will believe in such a creature; the *Beowulf* poet had complete "faith in nighttime events."

This proximity to the darker side of the human psyche, this lack of separation from nature, was destroyed, said Bly, when Descartes declared in 1619, "I think, therefore I am." After Descartes, Western literature would forever divide the autonomous self from nature. As Bly described it in his preface to *News of the Universe*:

> What I've called the Old Position puts human reason, and so human beings, in the superior position.... Consciousness is human, and involves reason. A serious gap exists between us and the rest of nature. Nature is to be watched, pitied, and taken care of if it behaves. In such language the body is exiled, the soul evaporated, the mind given executive power.

The danger of this philosophical stance in the West is that humans have become alienated from nature, alienated from that part of the psyche which participates in nature at the unconscious level, and alienated from an understanding of spirituality, which Bly maintained was also, for the most part, unconscious. This alienation leads to an amoral position regarding the natural world; people become observers merely, not participants.

Bly saw this tendency in the Western tradition culminating in the philosophy of the New Critics, a group of literary critics who sought to view art as artifact—that is, to view it aesthetically, without considering its historical or cultural context. What mattered to the New Critics was a work's position in the ongoing dialogue of literary achievement—its place in the established canon—and its allusions to the earlier traditions. Another important consideration for the New Critics was form—the existence of an identifiable, aesthetically satisfying form. Bly believes that New Criticism drew the lifeblood from poetry, causing it to be uninspired, even dead. He opposes the view that one can separate the artist, or the artist's world, from the art itself: The artist's overriding goal, after all, is to integrate the two. He objects to what he considers the New Critics' obsession with form. Bly himself is conscious of form changing form often, after lengthy deliberation and study, but views a concern with form as a natural function of the process of writing, rather than as the imposition of some preselected frame upon which one hangs one's work to please the makers of canons.

Mostly, however, Bly has objected to the absolutely amoral position of New Criticism when it comes to evaluating literature in its historical context. Bly believes that literature (and literary criticism) has a responsibility to face its political implications, to argue politically charged issues, and ultimately to take a stand on those issues. His propensity to do just that has been perhaps his single greatest achievement for those poets who have come after him; they have almost uniformly confronted political issues, refusing to shy away from the dialogue of the present, and this is true largely because of Bly's championing of the writer's political obligations during the 1960's and 1970's.

Unwilling to take as his literary models the traditional form and language of English literature as it descended to him via the established canon, Bly has chosen to find his models from pre-Cartesian sources, such as fairy tales, Anglo-Saxon and Norse poetry, and poetry from other cultures, especially more primitive (that is, non-Western) cultures. What he has searched for in these works has been referred to as the "deep image" archetypal images that speak on a level beyond the cultural, beyond the superficial. Bly's understanding of the deep image and its significance came from his reading of the philosopher Carl Jung, with his theory of a collective unconscious to which all humans have access via these mythic, archetypal images. Using such images as darkness, water, and death to represent experiences common to everyone, Bly attempts to write poetry that will ultimately heal, on the level of the psyche, Western society's tendencies toward alienation and destruction that he finds so unnecessary. In his poem "Sleepers Joining Hands," he writes of the healing power of poetry, using an archetypal image of optical illusion: "For we are like the branch bent in the water . . . / Taken out it is whole it was always whole."

THE TEETH MOTHER NAKED AT LAST

First published: 1970 (also collected in *Sleepers Joining Hands*, 1973)
Type of work: Poem

Using surrealistic images of destruction and bits of political speeches, Bly angrily denounces the Vietnam War as a manifestation of the United States' psychic disintegration.

Published separately in 1970, then later incorporated into *Sleepers Joining Hands* (1973), *The Teeth Mother Naked at Last* has been described as one of the best antiwar poems written in the twentieth century. Bly's strategy in the composition of the poem was to undermine somehow the sterility of the language the United States used—both in its nightly news broadcasts and on its political lecterns—when discussing the Vietnam War and the issues surrounding it. He did this by revealing these familiar phrases and familiar political statements to be false.

After a series of descriptive images from the war in Indochina, descriptions which move from the striking—almost beautiful—to the increasingly bloody and grotesque, Bly tells his reader, "Don't cry at that." Would one cry at other natural phenomena, he asks, such as storms from Canada or the changing of the seasons? The language used publicly to discuss the war was similar to the language reserved for inevitable, natural things. Bly forces the reader to admit that fact by exposing the harsher reality of war.

The language Bly uses was drawn from many sources: the phrases of the military ("I don't want to see anything moving. . . . [T]ake out as many structures as possible"); the standard phrases of columnists and television commentators; and the rhetoric of politicians, especially President Lyndon B. Johnson, whose Texas drawl Bly mimics by using hyphens. Then Bly, almost in a rage, warns that all such language conceals the truth. He catalogs those who lie, from the ministers to the reporters to the professors to the president, equating their willingness to lie with a kind of societal death wish. Bly sees in Americans' capacity to kill, and to kill in such a sterile, casual way, a profound psychic rift, a demonstration of their own spiritual inadequacy.

The myth embodied in the title of the poem is also the myth by which Bly understood that spiritual poverty. The myth of the Great Mother, first discussed at length by Jung, and later by several prominent anthropologists including Claude Levi-Strauss, reveals the Western attempt to disavow the more feminine aspect of the psyche and embrace the masculine, that is, logical, instead.

In an essay titled "I Came Out of the Mother Naked," which appears as a section of *Sleepers Joining Hands*—the section immediately after *The Teeth Mother Naked at Last*—Bly argues that the Great Mother, the embodiment of feminine consciousness in mythology, actually has four manifestations, which he lists as the Good Mother, the Death Mother, the Ecstatic Mother, and the Teeth Mother. He validates these aspects by taking examples from archaeology, mythology, and primitive poetry. The Good Mother is the image of the hearth, the one most familiar to the West; the Death Mother Bly describes as the mother figure responsible for evil and for evil witch and hag images; the Ecstatic Mother Bly equates with the muse of Greek literature, the feminine part of the consciousness that grants creativity; and the Teeth Mother, her opposite, is the aspect that destroys the spirit and forces people into a catatonic state, depriving them of the joy of life.

Robert Bly

This aspect of the feminine had perhaps the most importance for Bly, because he saw in her image the spiritual bankruptcy of the American psyche—to him, the war in Vietnam revealed that, as a people, Americans had chosen the Teeth Mother over the Ecstatic Mother; they had chosen to destroy rather than create. Bly's poem *The Teeth Mother Naked at Last* is perhaps the most remarkable antiwar poem of the Vietnam War era, precisely because it argues against the war on this most psychological, most fundamental level.

"SLEEPERS JOINING HANDS"

First published: 1973 (collected in *Sleepers Joining Hands*, 1973)
Type of work: Poem

Using autobiographical images, Bly embarks on a psychic journey into the darkness of his own consciousness to reveal the development of his inner personality.

"Sleepers Joining Hands," the title poem of Bly's 1973 collection, marks a departure from the type of poetry for which Bly had been known previously. His antiwar poetry, remarkable for his energetic, manipulative handling of the language of politics and political thought, had served as a training ground for the more mature, more personal poetry that distinguished this volume. Here language is used to uncover the truth of the psyche on a personal level. The use of Jungian psychology becomes more than a mere feature of the poetry; it becomes a central impetus—a tool for digging into the unconscious to discover the self.

The imagery of the poem is essentially autobiographical—recounting Bly's days in New York reading poems by Rilke in solitude, recalling his relationship to his mother and his father, describing his life at home with his wife and children. To say that this poem is autobiographical is misleading, however, because the poem is not written in normative language but written instead in a crazy-quilt juxtaposition of images in a tone Bly calls psychic. The language in the poem is like the language of dreams—bits and pieces of memory alongside half-thoughts and inner, often unvoiced, fears.

The poem has been described by the critic Richard Sugg as an epic quest seeking selfhood, but to understand this quest, one must first turn to the ideas of Jung. Jung believed each personality was made of three features: the individual consciousness (experiences and memory, of which one is aware), the individual unconscious (experiences and memory one has suppressed or forgotten), and the collective unconscious (inherited, universal experiences and memories of ancestors that are passed down to each individual). Archetypes, or images which reveal or reflect the collective unconscious, function as indicators of that part of the personality that is most strong but usually inaccessible. Jung believed (as does Bly) that an individual who could integrate the three aspects of personality would obtain an enlightened state (Jung's examples were Jesus Christ and Buddha) whereby his or her personality would be whole and intact.

It was this sort of integration Bly seeks in the lines of his poem, which uses images from his memory (consciousness); images from his dreams, fears, and unspoken feelings (unconscious); and archetypal images from mythology and religion (collective unconscious) to fuse the three into an overall understanding of the self. He often uses images of digging, of plunging down beneath the surface, of seeking the roots of the self. The journey takes place at night, and images of night prevail—owls, other nocturnal animals, and moonlight. It is a journey taken when one is in a dreamlike, unconscious state. What one finds at the end of the journey, at the core of the self, is communion with all other selves—full participation in the collective unconscious: One becomes the night creature, one becomes the archetypal image, one becomes a "sleeper," joining hands with "all the sleepers in the world."

Bly's poem "Sleepers Joining Hands" attempts this participation in the collective unconscious. The poem, and the other poems in the volume, marks a new plateau for Bly's achievement, not so much in form but in terms of poetic subject. Rather than seeking a more mature political voice, Bly turns his attention inward, writing what some critics have called psycho-spiritual poetry. Of this kind of poetry, which seeks to heal psychic wounds and regain the unconscious that has been lost, Bly has been recognized as an undisputed master.

274

"THE ANT MANSION"

First published: 1975 (collected in *The Morning Glory*, 1975)
Type of work: Poem

Coming upon a piece of wood inhabited by ants, the poet speculates on the mystical and metaphoric significance of the objects of human labor.

"The Ant Mansion," one of the longer prose poems included in Bly's volume *The Morning Glory* (1975), contains a short narrative in which the poet, after waking in his sleeping bag, takes a walk through the forest. He comes upon a "wood chunk" that has started to decay, providing a home to a colony of ants. He takes the object home and, after studying it, begins to speculate on its significance as a metaphor for human existence.

This poem, as well as the entire collection *The Morning Glory*, was the culmination of a series of poems Bly began in the early 1970's. After his psychological journeys in *Sleepers Joining Hands*, Bly began to experiment with the form he called the "prose poem," a form the French poet Charles-Pierre Baudelaire claimed would be the major poetic form of the twentieth century. The prose poem offered Bly several new options, introducing new elements into his poetry. First, it introduced the element of plot—the poems became more narrative in nature. Second, the emphasis was not on the form at all but on the content—not on the language, but on the thought. Third, it allowed Bly the best medium in which to write what had been called, for lack of a better phrase, the "thing poem," or the object poem.

In his essay "The Prose Poem as an Evolving Form" (1986), Bly points out that the main difference between usual poetic forms and the prose form is that the basic unit of the usual poem is the line. In the case of the prose poem, the basic unit is the sentence. According to Bly, the sentence allows the poem to proceed at a calmer, more relaxed pace; the prose poem establishes a more intimate, more natural, state for contemplation. According to Bly, the form's closest antecedent—although it resembles the fable, the short story, and the essay—is the haiku. Like the haiku, the prose poem (or ob-

ject poem) "is evidence that the poet has overcome, at least for the moment, the category-making mentality that sees everything in polarities: human and animal, inner and outer, spiritual and material, large and small." The prose poem allows a kind of participation in nature that more structured poetry does not allow.

Bly begins "The Ant Mansion" by describing a dream in which the rubbing of his sleeping bag causes him to dream of being bitten by a rattlesnake. This wakes him, and he heads to the pasture, veering into some nearby woods. There he discovers the chunk of wood; he takes it back to his house, placing it on his desk. He begins to study the object, noting its many cavities, the color of each various shade of brown or black. He speaks of the wood as an apartment house for ants, speaking of the cavities as floors and the bark strips as roofs.

In the second half of the poem, Bly remarks that the "balconies" created by the half-decayed wood would make excellent "places for souls to sit" and begins to consider inviting all those souls he has known that are now dead to come and live in the ant mansion. He includes villagers he has known, his brother, his grandmother, and eventually such large masses as those who died in the Civil War. By the end of the poem, it becomes clear that the ant mansion has become a symbol for the objects of human labor, the fruit of human life on earth, which no one (or very few) is ever likely to see or use. Bly ends the poem thinking of his father's labor and wishing that it, too, could be found by a pasture and somehow validated.

"FIFTY MALES SITTING TOGETHER"

First published: 1981 (collected in *The Man in the Black Coat Turns*, 1981)
Type of work: Poem

Employing dark, shadowy images, the poet descends into the psyche to unlock the mechanism that invigorates personality on the level of gender.

Bly's poem "Fifty Males Sitting Together," first published in *The Man in the Black Coat Turns* (1981), embodies a theme that occupied him throughout most of the 1980's and beyond: the significance and inadequacies of being male in Western culture. In a preface to *The Man in the Black Coat Turns*, Bly claims that in its poems he had "fished in male waters, which [he] experienced as deep and cold but containing and nourishing some secret and moving life down below." Bly's concern with maleness stems from his anthropological study of the Great Mother. It is Bly's contention that for the first forty thousand years or so of human existence, humans lived primarily in matriarchal cultures in which women retained the bulk of social, political, and religious power. These primitive cultures worshiped the Great Mother, symbol of the forces in nature and of life itself.

According to Bly, recorded history began when men began to fight against the Great Mother, asserting their superiority instead, the superiority of masculine thinking (logic and reason) over more natural (even more divine) patterns. This movement away from the Great Mother has left humans detached from nature, unsure of their strength, and intensely alone.

How this historical process manifests itself in modern life has preoccupied Bly since early in his career. He writes often of the male's relationship to the father, writing of it in terms of frustration, incongruity, and disunity. His own relationship with his father had been nonexistent, remarked Bly during an interview with Bill Moyers for a 1988 Public Broadcasting Service documentary titled "A Gathering of Men," until he realized—later on in life—that he had been involved in a sort of conspiracy with his mother to exclude his father. Once he realized this, he began a dialogue with his father that continued until his father's death. The problem, according to Bly, was that older males have very few ways in which to initiate younger males into society. Initiation—the integrating of the younger generation into the mainstream of cultural life—has become so haphazard and arbitrary in modern society as to be nonfunctioning. Part of the purpose of the seminars and symposia Bly organized across the United States was to enlist older males to be initiators of their younger brethren; he also sought to encourage younger males to understand their shared dilemma.

In the poem "Fifty Males Sitting Together," Bly describes a young male witnessing a ritual of descent—shadowy in nature—which takes place by a dark lake at night. Fifty males participate in the ritual, while the wives wait at home. Because he is of the woman's world, and because the darkness of the masculine ritual frightens him, the young male cannot participate in the older males' descent into the darker regions of the psyche; he "loses courage" and turns to nature instead. Using poetic irony, Bly refers to this turn as an ascent, but in the world of Bly's imagery, ascent is a defeat—true self-awareness and knowledge can come only from the psychic descent. When the young man turns away, he moves far away from the world of men and feels cut off from them, alone. Yet in a last line, characteristic of Bly, the young man looks back and sees the night descending on the other shore, as if to say that even though he cannot participate, he is at least aware of what he needs to heal his wounded psyche.

Iron John

First published: 1990
Type of work: Essays

Bly uses a legend collected by the Grimm brothers as a means to structure the eight essays or chapters of his text to show the cultural importance of initiation and risk-taking in the lives of men.

In what is arguably his most culturally significant publication, Bly reprints a pre-Christian northern European folktale, "Iron John," and addresses each and all of the major plot elements in the tale in chronological order over the course of eight chaptered essays, which is followed by an epilogue and then the entire text of the folktale. Bly uses the folktale to show how the fully developed, fully realized adult man is a combination of personae which can be identified at successive points in the tale.

Bly posits that the self-actualized adult male is in fact an entire community of beings—to be exact, seven distinct beings: King, Warrior, Lover, Wild Man, Trickster, Mythologist or Cook, and Grief Man. Bly criticizes the aspects of modern culture which do not allow for the adult male who has taken risks, been wounded, and even temporarily defeated. Bly argues that every man needs to en-

gage in a personal journey of risk-taking and initiation. He argues that one of the problems of contemporary postindustrial culture lies in the fact that the father works but the son does not usually see him work or learn from his professional experiences and competencies. When the father arrives home in the evening barely in time for dinner, "his children receive only his temperament, and not his teaching," and the temperament is likely to be problematic due to the technocratic daytime existence in which many fathers toil.

Bly uses the circumstances and conflicts of the folktale to delineate each of the beings that populate the fully realized adult male. The King figure initially represents the father figure, then a secondary tutelary figure after the protagonist leaves the original home. The various iterations of the King (Sacred King, Earthly King, Inner King) represent the will to power and the characteristics of the individual. The nobility of spirit is expressed in this being, though its potentiality can allow it to become the Poisoned King as easily as the Sacred King. Just so, the Sacred Warrior has a blessed side and a poisoned side, a Constructive Warrior and a Destructive Brutal Warrior. Just as modern bifurcated life has truncated and attenuated the impact of the father, so the ancient Sacred Warrior has often in modern times disintegrated into the mindless soldier, a casualty of mechanized warfare, from Bly's perspective. Bly is troubled by the ways that he sees contemporary society encouraging warriorhood among women, while discouraging the very same elements in boys and men. Respecting one's inner warrior is one of the ways that a man comes into a better understanding of the weighty forces involved in making and maintaining human relationships.

Bly identifies the lack of consistent, widespread, cultural initiation by older men and ritual elders in Western society. He emphasizes the importance of developing the Lover, a central element in maintaining what Bly calls one's "garden." Connected to the controlling metaphor of the Wild Man is his representation of the positive side of male sexuality; the Wild Man is the male protector of the earth, and his qualities of spontaneity, association with wilderness, honoring of grief, and respect for risk represent elements that Bly considers essential to the fully developed contemporary man. The Trickster, common in North American Indian folklore, provides counterpoint, irony, and insight, his very existence a critique of norms and complacencies. The Mythologist or Cook determines how long "cooking" should continue and the timing between stages or beings. Finally, the seventh being is the Grief Man; Bly emphasizes the value of being able to grieve deeply, to suffer a wound and always to remember it yet to recover from it. Bly investigates the Greek notion of *Katabasis*, the "Drop" involving the notion of disaster or extreme reversal of fortune towards the negative. Bly realizes that "A wound allows the spirit or soul to enter," and he seeks to facilitate the process of renewal and insight through loss. In articulating the seven beings of the ideal contemporary man, Bly throws down the gauntlet in creating a new courtier's handbook for the millennial male.

SUMMARY

Perhaps more than practically any other poet of his generation, Bly has sought to enact what he believes is the proper role for the poet in society: a consciousness-raising, outspoken advocate for change and a moral conscience for a society often too willing to be morally and spiritually complacent. Bly believes that as a culture, the Western world, particularly the United States, tends to shirk its responsibilities to humanity and to its own future generations. New Criticism and the poetry it championed encouraged this lack of responsibility through its emphasis on exegesis of the text without reference to author or context. Bly's criticism offers an effective counterstatement, to borrow a term from Edmund Burke, to formalistic theory, and his poetry offers a highly convincing, alternative voice.

Edward W. Huffstetler; updated by Richard Sax

BIBLIOGRAPHY

By the Author

POETRY:

The Lion's Tail and Eyes: Poems Written out of Laziness and Silence, 1962 (with James Wright and William Duffy)

Silence in the Snowy Fields, 1962

The Light Around the Body, 1967

The Teeth Mother Naked at Last, 1970

Jumping out of Bed, 1973

Sleepers Joining Hands, 1973

Point Reyes Poems, 1974

Old Man Rubbing His Eyes, 1974

The Morning Glory, 1975

This Body Is Made of Camphor and Gopherwood, 1977

This Tree Will Be Here for a Thousand Years, 1979

The Man in the Black Coat Turns, 1981

Out of the Rolling Ocean, and Other Love Poems, 1984

Loving a Woman in Two Worlds, 1985

Selected Poems, 1986

The Apple Found in the Plowing, 1989

What Have I Ever Lost by Dying: Collected Prose Poems, 1992

Meditations on the Insatiable Soul, 1994

Morning Poems, 1997

Eating the Honey of Words: New and Selected Poems, 1999

The Night Abraham Called to the Stars, 2001

NONFICTION:

Leaping Poetry: An Idea with Poems and Translations, 1975

Talking All Morning, 1980

American Poetry: Wildness and Domesticity, 1990

Iron John: A Book About Men, 1990

The Spirit Boy and the Insatiable Soul, 1994

The Sibling Society, 1996

The Maiden King: The Reunion of Masculine and Feminine, 1998 (with Marion Woodman)

TRANSLATIONS:

Twenty Poems of Georg Trakl, 1961 (with James Wright)

Forty Poems, 1967 (of Juan Ramón Jiménez)

Hunger, 1967 (of Knut Hamsun's novel)

Twenty Poems of Pablo Neruda, 1968 (with James Wright)

I Do Best Alone at Night: Poems, 1968 (of Gunnar Ekelöf)

Neruda and Vallejo: Selected Poems, 1971

Ten Sonnets to Orpheus, 1972 (of Rainer Maria Rilke)

DISCUSSION TOPICS

- The titles of Robert Bly's poems range from the rather general ("Night") to the overly specific ("After Drinking All Night With a Friend, We Go Out in a Boat at Dawn To See Who Can Write the Best Poem"). Consider how allusively or specifically Bly introduces his poetic subject matter through titles.

- How effectively and compellingly does Bly convey his antiwar beliefs, both in general and specifically about the Vietnam conflict?

- Is it disingenuous to suggest that the simple act of writing or reading poetry or prose can result in the psychic healing that Bly attests?

- Do the male-centric observations in *Iron John* and elsewhere have relevance for readers of both genders?

- How would Bly's poetry fare via a Formalist or New Critical reading? What new insights about his work might such a noncontextual reading provide?

- How well has Bly articulated the challenges of being a translator of poetry? How much influence from Pablo Neruda or Rainer Maria Rilke is there in the translations and how much from Robert Bly?

- How does Bly use rhyme, meter, and stanzaic configuration to convey his intended meaning, especially in his earlier poetry?

- Are some of Bly's early observations about the Jungian Mother consistent with his later assertions in *Iron John*?

Lorca and Jiménez: Selected Poems, 1973
Friends, You Drank Some Darkness: Three Swedish Poets, Harry Martinson, Gunnar Ekelöf, and Tomas Tranströmer, 1975
Twenty Poems, 1977 (of Rolf Jacobsen)
The Kabir Book: Forty-four of the Ecstatic Poems of Kabir, 1977
Truth Barriers: Poems, 1980 (of Tomas Tranströmer)
Selected Poems of Rainer Maria Rilke, 1981
Times Alone: Selected Poems of Antonio Machado, 1983
The Half-Finished Heaven: The Best Poems of Tomas Tranströmer, 2001
The Roads Have Come to an End Now: Selected and Last Poems of Rolf Jacobsen, 2001 (with Roger Greenwald and Robert Hedin)
Horace: The Odes, 2002 (with others; J. D. McClatchy, editor)
The Winged Energy of Delight: Selected Translations, 2004

EDITED TEXTS:

A Poetry Reading Against the Vietnam War, 1966 (with David Ray)
News of the Universe: Poems of Twofold Consciousness, 1980
The Winged Life: The Poetic Voice of Henry David Thoreau, 1986
The Rag and Bone Shop of the Heart: Poems for Men, 1993
The Soul Is Here for Its Own Joy: Sacred Poems from Many Cultures, 1995

About the Author

Altieri, Charles F. "Varieties of Immanentist Experience: Robert Bly, Charles Olson, and Frank O'Hara." In *Enlarging the Temple: New Directions in American Poetry During the 1960's.* Lewisburg, Pa.: Bucknell University Press, 1979.

Davis, William Virgil. *Understanding Robert Bly.* Columbia: University of South Carolina Press, 1988.

Friberg, Ingegard. *Moving Inward: A Study of Robert Bly's Poetry.* Goteborg, Sweden: Acta University Gothoburgensis, 1977.

Harris, Victoria. *The Incorporative Consciousness of Robert Bly.* Carbondale: Southern Illinois University Press, 1992.

Lensing, George S., and Ronald Moran, eds. *Four Poets and the Emotive Imagination: Robert Bly, James Wright, Louis Simpson, and William Stafford.* Baton Rouge: Louisiana State University Press, 1976.

Malkoff, Karl. *Escape from the Self: A Study in Contemporary American Poetry and Poetics.* New York: Columbia University Press, 1977.

Nelson, Howard. *Robert Bly: An Introduction to the Poetry.* New York: Columbia University Press, 1984.

Peseroff, Joyce, ed. *Robert Bly: When Sleepers Awake.* Ann Arbor: The University of Michigan Press, 1985.

Robert Bly Web site. www.RobertBly.com.

Smith, Thomas R. *Walking Swiftly: Writings and Images on the Occasion of Robert Bly's 65th Birthday.* New York: Perennial, 1991.

Sugg, Richard P. *Robert Bly.* Boston: Twayne, 1986.

PAUL BOWLES

Born: Jamaica, Queens, New York
     December 30, 1910
Died: Tangier, Morocco
     November 18, 1999

With powerfully surreal, sensual images taken from his expatriate experiences, Bowles portrays the landscapes and people of North Africa and Central and South America as well as the drifters who encounter them.

Cherie Nutting

BIOGRAPHY

Paul Bowles was born to Rena Winnewisser Bowles, a homemaker, and Claude Dietz Bowles, a dentist, on December 30, 1910, in the borough of Queens, New York City. His father was, as Bowles later recalled, a bad-tempered man, easily given to child beatings to enforce his will. Perhaps it was fortunate, then, that Paul's father was so addicted to his golf game that he was away from home on weekends whenever the weather permitted. Rena Bowles excused her husband's child abuse, but she showered attention on her son, devoting considerable time to reading poetry and playing music for him. She realized Paul had artistic proclivities and wanted to encourage them.

Like many creative young people who are abused, however, Paul retreated into himself, refusing to socialize with other children and, out of spite, beating weaker classmates symbolically to get revenge on those who beat him at school. His life was hellish, but it did encourage him to develop his creative powers.

After finishing secondary school in New York in 1928, he attended New York's School of Design and Liberal Arts for a matter of months, then went on to the University of Virginia; he stayed there only six months, however, before leaving for Paris in 1929. He went to Paris at the behest of famous com-poser Aaron Copland, and in Paris he discovered not only what pursuits he would follow but also where he would spend most of the remainder of his life: in Morocco. It would take another trip home to New York, then another semester of studies at the University of Virginia before he would become a true expatriate. The restless young man traveled to Berlin in 1931 and 1932, where he studied music under another great composer, Virgil Thomson.

Nevertheless, it was Bowles's return to Paris in 1933 (he would stay there for a year) that gave him his twin missions in life: He would compose serious music and he would write. While he was there, either Gertude Stein, American expatriate novelist, or her lover, Alice B. Toklas (the story varies), advised him to find the perpetual summer weather he craved as well as the splendid isolation from Western ways he also sought by moving to Morocco. In 1937, he turned to writing music in Tangier, Morocco, a small but highly international city across from Spain on the Mediterranean Sea. Although he turned his attention to composing scores for Tennessee Williams's *Summer and Smoke* (pr. 1947, pb. 1948) and *The Glass Menagerie* (pr. 1944, pb. 1945), among other plays, he never forgot what he was advised to do with his life when he lived in Paris: to write.

Though he had written reviews for the *New York Herald Tribune* as well as experimented with poetry, Bowles did not do any sustained writing until 1938, when he married another talented writer, Jane Auer, who as a girl had spent several years abroad. It was her encouragement and example that enabled

Bowles to focus upon writing rather than musical composition. Their relationship lasted until her death in 1973. It was apparently a combination of opposites—she, the emotional one and he, the cool, distant one.

In 1949, Bowles created the work for which he is best known, *The Sheltering Sky,* a magnificent depiction of the lack of real communication between people that brought Bowles significant recognition from critics such as Gore Vidal, who became a staunch advocate of Bowles's prose. *Let It Come Down* (1952), another novel, furthered Bowles's preoccupation with the horrors of life lived inauthentically and the drugged ennui of Western urbanites faced with life as it is lived in Morocco. Upon its publication, comparisons were made between his work and that of French existentialists Albert Camus and Jean-Paul Sartre.

A third novel, *The Spider's House* (1955), is a lament for a vanishing way of life and a celebration of the Morocco that was passing away under Western influence, influence which Bowles despised.

The novella *Up Above the World* (1966), which deals with the brutal murder of North Americans by a South American psychotic bent on getting rid of any witnesses to a murder he perpetrated, also included what was by now becoming Bowles's literary signature: a depiction of the violent meeting between the oversophisticated, soft Westerner and the life-hardened, primitive native of a developing nation.

An autobiography, *Without Stopping* (1972), followed; its title gave succinct testimony to the pattern of Bowles's life, a life in motion and a life in flight. This work explained his preoccupations, but it did not clarify much about his private life. Along with his acclaimed novels, Bowles wrote short stories and novellas after he moved to Morocco in the 1930's, and some of them have received as much attention as his longer works. In 1950 came his short-story collection *The Delicate Prey, and Other Stories,* followed by a novella, *The Time of Friendship* (1967), and two more collections of stories, *Pages from Cold Point, and Other Stories* (1968) and *Midnight Mass* (1981). In these strange tales of life in lands far distant from the United States, he deepens his development of the thesis that there is no real order in the natural world—that people are usually prey to one another and to natural forces beyond their control.

The Collected Stories of Paul Bowles, 1939-1976 (1979) offers readers many of his best tales, all of which demonstrate the cruel ferocity of nature and those living closest to it. His naïve Westerners pay heavily for their ignorance about or condescension toward such people. In addition, Bowles published a collection of poems titled *Next to Nothing: Collected Poems, 1926-1977* (1981).

Throughout his life's work, Bowles explored the terrain of the countries about which he wrote, carefully interweaving sights, smells, and sounds in ways one might expect from a person with so much musical talent. Certainly, Bowles showed no remorse in having abandoned American life, which he considered no life at all. It was primarily Morocco that gave him the raw material of his art.

ANALYSIS

Though widespread acclaim eluded Bowles, his impact upon contemporary fiction has been a lasting one and a significant one. More than any other American writer, he introduced existentialist concepts to American fiction. His main themes are those of existentialist fiction: the isolated self, the impossibility of meaningful communication between people, and the terrifying void beyond this world which can drive people insane.

Bowles's writing concerns, for the most part, people of frail identity searching for something to relieve the intense monotony that comes from being caught up in the self. These ennui-ridden searchers come to developing countries to have something to do, somewhere to go, even if they do not find meaning in this flight from familiarity.

The professor of "A Distant Episode," for example, a linguist with all the cultural sophistication and pride of the educated Westerner, wants to do a language survey in Morocco. What he finds is not what he seeks. Captured by wild, cruel Reguibat tribesmen, his tongue is cut out, and he is further mutilated so he can be sold as a comic curiosity piece. In order to survive, he soon learns to do what his captors say. Finally, however, a French soldier, thinking him a mad religious character, tries to shoot him. The story closes with him running toward the desert sun and certain death; the professor's personality disintegrates in the Sahara.

So, too, the personality of Kit Moresby of *The Sheltering Sky* falls apart under the harshness of imprisonment, and she adopts a new identity: helpless Arab concubine. Like Kit's, her husband's identity is destroyed by the filth, misery, and horrifying isolation he finds in the town of El Ga'a. Dying of typhus, he is completely alone: The natives of El Ga'a do not care whether he lives or dies because he is an outsider and a Nazarine (Christian). In his final moments he forgets who he was and turns into something without past or future.

Certainly, Bowles's characters talk to one another, but real communication is lacking. Their talk is fragmented, superficial, transitory. People in Bowles's stories do not say what they mean because they do not know anything important about themselves or the wider world around them. It is not that they do not wish to communicate but that words fail them, leaving them locked in anguish.

Cruelly projected behind the merciless white sky of Bowles's stories is the void. This meaninglessness he envisions hides just behind the "sheltering sky" and terrifies those who are aware enough to sense its presence. It is the same void that haunts the fiction of existentialist writers Albert Camus, Jean-Paul Sartre, and Samuel Beckett. The void is mirrored on earth by Bowles's terrible jungles and deserts, the places most hostile to human beings, with their cliffs, bad weather, and deadly creatures: scorpions, vipers, and poisonous lizards. The meaningless quality of the void is also found in the labyrinthine streets of the villages and towns of North Africa and Central and South America, where boredom and terror breed.

The flight of Bowles's characters from this void brings them no rewards, no respite—only frustration and a sense of futility, fragility, and absurdity. The only exception seems to be Fraulein Windling of *The Time of Friendship*, whose strong Christian beliefs give her an inner sense of purpose and integrity missing in most of Bowles's drifters. Bowles's people are never satisfied, and this dissatisfaction leads them to dissipation, crime, and death. The sterility within them grows until it overtakes them. They try to amuse themselves as they drift downward toward death, never connecting with others, never understanding how special life really is.

THE SHELTERING SKY

First published: 1949
Type of work: Novel

An American couple's travels in North Africa lead to the husband's death from typhus and the wife's sexual enslavement by a wealthy African.

The Sheltering Sky, arguably Bowles's best work, has as its setting his terrible yet hauntingly lovely depiction of the Sahara Desert. The chief protagonist could be said to be like the desert itself: an aloof, indomitable, compelling, disorienting, killer landscape—a killer waiting for new victims. All is mystery, despite the clarifying sunlight. A kind of anarchy reigns in the chaotic towns on the desert's periphery, and the farther one travels from coastal cities, the more anarchic and mysterious things become for Bowles's dissolute, bored characters.

Into this strange part of the world Bowles introduces his Americans, Port and Katherine (Kit) Moresby, a young husband and wife from New York, wandering aimlessly, supported by considerable funds. Port, whom Kit likes to insist is a writer, actually is no such thing: He really does nothing with his life.

Cynical and jaundiced by fruitless years spent in the United States, Port begins his African sojourn at the Café d'Eckmühl-Noiseux in a town somewhere close to the coast of Morocco.

Kit, his intelligent, attractive wife, is not quite as dissatisfied with life as is he, for she has lingering expectations of some kind of life illumination to come from this exile of theirs. She is alert to the people she encounters; her lively interest in her surroundings counters her husband's boredom, yet she also struggles to find meaning in her life and sometimes falls into a bored silence.

A fellow American simply called Tunner meets the Moresbys, then attempts to befriend them. He turns traitor to his new "friend," Port, when he seduces Kit on a train ride to the interior. Like Port and Kit, Tunner is a drifter drawn to North Africa by restless yearnings not quite identifiable. Also entering the picture are the Lyles, a bizarre couple supposedly composed of a mother and her spineless son who, it is found out, sleep together (whether they are incestuous is not stated). The boy, Eric, is a liar, a cheat, and a thief, and his mother is a loud-mouthed, obscene, overly aggressive woman, proud of herself to the point of narcissism.

The Lyles, however, serve only as distractions. The main focus of the novel is upon the contest of wills between Port and Kit, a contest which results first in Kit's committing adultery with Tunner, then later in her leaving Port's deathbed in order to rediscover personal freedom as well as escape his dying from typhus in an ugly, dirty hotel room. Port, though one to proclaim his insularity and self-sufficiency, relies to a marked degree on Kit for companionship. Any strength in their relationship comes from them finding themselves stranded in a strange land, one that is both intriguing and hateful.

Death, often veiled in the United States, here stalks the streets openly and conspicuously. Among stinking hotel patios and filthy, disease-bearing alleyways disguised as city streets, Port and Kit come to a temporary understanding. Yet, when temptation comes (in the banal form of Tunner), their self-serving relationship begins to fall apart; when Port is felled by the typhus, it is in ruins. Kit, having cuckolded her husband, deserts him completely, heading for the high desert outside of El Ga'a. Here, with the great blank sky surrounding her, she wanders lost and alone in the desert, realizing that death will surely come if no one rescues her.

Rescuers do appear: an old man and a young man, riding across the wastes on camels on the caravan route. The young, virile man, Belqassim, who has twenty-two wives and many servants, gives her a ride in exchange for sexual favors, their lovemaking taking place first in the evening after a long ride, then by day. Slowly but surely, Kit loses her mental bearings, bewitched by sand and distance; she comes to depend upon her "benefactors" despite the fact that they see her as no more than an exotic white slave. She realizes that her part of their unspoken bargain is to be an unprotesting concubine, paid in gold bracelets and big rings for her services.

Taken, disguised as a boy, into Belqassim's house, Kit is installed as a mistress (unbeknown to his wives, who accept this "young man" as a pathetic case shown kindness by their husband). Kit, depressed over her servitude and her sexual humiliation, plans a daring escape, which is foiled by Belqassim; he beats her to the point where she begins to lose her mind. Crazed and desperate, she tries again, and she succeeds in escaping. She makes her way to a French outpost, where she is placed in touch with the American legation.

Delivered against her will out of North Africa, she flies to an unnamed Western country—possibly France—and once again is surrounded by the wave of violent noise that is the hallmark of the West. Her mind distraught and her personality severely altered by the trials she endured abroad, she irritates the legation official sent to pick her up at the airport. It is painfully obvious that the desert and its inhabitants have stolen away her mind and soul and that she will live out her life in a place she hates.

LET IT COME DOWN

First published: 1952
Type of work: Novel

A dark tale of an antiheroic expatriate's descent into corruption, theft, and murder.

Let It Come Down greatly reinforced Bowles's reputation as a consummate "writer's writer," a craftsman who could capture the ambiguity, tenor, and dangerous fascination of developing foreign countries. This novel, his second, has as its setting Tangier, Morocco, prior to its loss of International Zone status in the early 1950's. Like many locales featured in Bowles's novels and stories, Tangier appears dirty, divided (into a slovenly native sector and a prosperous Western one), and sinister as a haven for drug addicts and smugglers. The physical division mirrors a political, economic, cultural, and spiritual division, for the city represents not only Moorish Morocco but also the whole Muslim culture of Africa. Its streets wind sinuously, like intricate designs in the mosaics of the sultan's palace, and the city echoes to the sounds of distant calls to prayer from minarets.

To Bowles, Muslim Tangier has a mysterious presence lacking in the Christian part of town; in a sense, it defies Western understanding. The isolation of people seems, to outsiders, more intense than it is in the cities of the West, and death hovers closer. The smells of Tangier are a violent assault: a mixture of garbage, urine, open-air meat and vegetable stands, and the perfume from exotic plants. Bowles's old Tangier, a city behind walls, retains the imprint of past conquerors, both Phoenician and Arab. Europeans have also left an impression upon the city, bringing with them what the author sees as a dangerous materialism represented by seedy, neon-lit night spots, big cars, and drunken, raucous public conduct. To Bowles, this new Tangier has a soullessness about it, its bourgeois comforts partially protecting Westerners from thoughts of death and destruction.

Let It Come Down tells the story of Nelson Dyar, a former New York City bank clerk. A self-acknowledged loser, misfit, and victim, Dyar spends the first half of the novel trying to lay claim to a beautiful, illiterate peasant girl, the prostitute Hadija. Hadija, however, is also pursued by another American expatriate living in Tangier, Eunice Goode, a lesbian who (like Dyar) has enough money to get by without doing much work. Goode (her surname as much an intended pun as Dyar's) is furious over Dyar's "interference" in her life; she intends to possess Hadija totally and make her a kind of slave. She plans to involve Dyar with a known Soviet agent, Madame Jouvenon—and the plan works. Goode suggests to Jouvenon that she enlist Dyar's services, as he, as an American living in Tangier, is bound to have contacts valuable to Soviet spymasters. Jouvenon, convinced, easily manages to convince the bankrupt Dyar to betray his country by offering him regular paychecks in exchange for information.

Goode calls the American Legation of Tangier and informs them of Dyar's perfidy. No immediate steps are taken to apprehend him, and events keep him from being apprehended by the legation.

Then, in an interesting twist of plot, Dyar's sometime employer, Wilcox, wants Dyar to exchange some currency for him on the black market. Sensing an opportunity to elude the Soviet spies who now employ him as well as a chance to be (temporarily, at least) rich, the larcenous Dyar joins with a young Morrocan, Thami, a thoroughly dissipated ne'er-do-well whose hashish habit frequently takes him away from his neglected wife and abused children. Thami spirits Dyar away in a leaky boat, and Thami's partner leaves them on a narrow strip of deserted beach below high cliffs, a locale not far from Thami's home village and his ancestral cottage, perched on a cliff above the sea.

When the ravenous Thami goes after food in his old village, the equally ravenous Dyar, out of boredom, takes up Thami's hashish pipe. Drugged and in a dream, he then wanders away from the house on the cliff. At the nearest town, Dyar accidentally meets Thami. Thami appears not to blame Dyar for stealing his pipe and its contents, so together they go back to the abandoned house on the cliff. After both take up heavy hashish smoking, Dyar, driven by unknown demons, accidentally (or possibly intentionally, Bowles does not make it clear which) kills Thami by sticking a nail in his ear as he sleeps and pounding the nail into his skull with a hammer stolen in the village.

Morning arrives, and Dyar, dazed and somewhat disconcerted rather than overwhelmed by guilt, attempts to move the corpse so that curious villagers will not find it, only to be interrupted by the unexpected arrival of a nymphomaniacal former lover from Tangier—Daisy, the Marquesa de Valverde. She is horrified after discovering the corpse of Thami and, leaving Dyar to fend for himself, returns to Tangier. The novel ends as rain comes down. Dyar, standing in the ruined patio of the deserted house, confronts his imminent death from starvation or angry villagers.

In his characteristically meticulous way, Bowles has created yet another of his visions of a Western exile bereft of purpose or morality who is destroyed in the cruel desert of North Africa. Yet Bowles does not want his characters—in this case, Dyar—to elicit reader sympathy, for there is nothing with which to sympathize. Instead, Bowles wants his readers to see their own baseness and spiritual vacuity mirrored in the plight of the characters.

Dyar loses himself in the surreal chaos of Tangier; it is his choice to do so. A pathetically inert figure, he acknowledges the fathomless emptiness of his existence, finding solace in alcohol, hashish, and fly-by-night affairs. Dyar is at once victim (of drugs, of his own stupidity and lack of insight, of circumstances) and victimizer. He victimizes young Hadija as if he were a predator and she were prey, yet finds himself the prey of another of Tangier's predators, the man-hungry Daisy. Dyar is victimized by Wilcox, whose promises of an easy life in Tangier turn out to be as meaningless as anything else he tells his "friend." Yet Dyar entices Thami to help him escape Tangier with Wilcox's money by pandering to his greed and then, accidentally or intentionally, kills him. Though Dyar has a chance to show internal fortitude by turning down the offer to spy for the Soviets, he forfeits it. He lives solely for himself, with no regard for the needs or feelings of others, and in this he is a typical Bowles character.

Nothing is resolved in *Let It Come Down*; Bowles permits no satisfying, neat conclusion. The reader is left with ambiguity and questions as well as a sense of dread. Bowles leaves a character living in a universe that neither wants him nor needs him. The earth is, in Bowles's radical estimation, much like the claustrophobic place depicted by French poet Charles Baudelaire, who envisioned earth as having a gigantic, smothering pan cover above it, sealing in humankind. To speak of plot, then, is difficult, because, as Bowles might say, "Everything happens, yet nothing happens." His people do not have meaningful experiences that somehow lead to a catharsis. Instead, they lurch from accident to accident. Things happen to people, in a dislocated way, but nothing connected to purpose can occur in this limbo of defeat.

"THE DELICATE PREY"

First published: 1950 (collected in *The Delicate Prey, and Other Stories*, 1950)
Type of work: Short story

Hideous deaths come to a young desert traveler and the tribesman who kills him.

Bowles's most celebrated short story is a brutal, ironic tale of fatal misjudgment, of deceit, of appalling cruelty, and of the destruction of a destroyer. Nature, in the form of the Sahara Desert, is as much a protagonist as is young Driss, the tale's victim.

"The Delicate Prey" revolves around three members of the Filala tribe, two brothers and Driss, the son of their sister, who make a fateful journey to the desert town of Tessalit. Driss is a young, virile man who enjoys the brothels of the town in which he resides. His uncles decide to take a short route to Tessalit through country that comes perilously close to the dreaded Reguibat warriors, a bloody-minded group of land pirates known for their horrible murders of those traveling through their domain.

On the journey, the three meet a lone camel rider who becomes their guide. No one seems to suspect the man except Driss, who questions his motives in serving as their guide. Driss remains quiet about his fears. The man identifies himself as a Moungari, a man from a supposedly peaceful, well-respected place. On a pretext of going hunting for gazelle, the Moungari lures one brother, then the next, to their deaths, shooting each in turn. Imagining the distant shots to be harbingers of a feast to come, Driss meanwhile drifts off to sleep. He awakens in horror when he finally realizes what the earlier shots signified. He sets off toward distant Tessalit, only to stumble across the camp of the Moungari and his friends.

As he hails them, they shoot him in the arm; as he tries to rise and shoot his enemies, he is suddenly pushed to the ground. The Moungari ties his hands, binds his feet, then, to Driss's horror—and the reader's—castrates him and makes a deep incision in his stomach, in which he places the testicles. Driss is then raped and, after a time, his throat is cut.

The rapacious Moungari makes the mistake of taking the wares he has stolen to Tessalit, where he is apprehended by French authorities, then handed over to the Filali merchants for punishment. They bind him, drink all of his water, giving him none, then take him to the desert, where they place him, bound, into a pit from which only his head emerges. One day later, the head, maddened by the heat, is portrayed as singing.

In this dark story, Bowles captures both the bleak hostility of the Sahara and the even more bleak nature of humans, creatures given to heinous deeds done in the spirit of celebration. The Sahara may be a killer, but it kills without malice. The Moungari and the Filali, on the other hand, are deliberate in their cold, astonishing acts of cruelty—true monsters from a desolate land.

THE TIME OF FRIENDSHIP

First published: 1967
Type of work: Novella

A platonic friendship between a North African boy and a middle-aged European woman ends as war approaches.

The Time of Friendship is a marked departure for Bowles, for instead of his usual bleak assessment of human nature, readers are given a glowing tale of mutual respect and love between two very different people. The story ends without betrayal, cruelty, or death. Yet death does hover just beyond the story's horizon as the two main characters, Fraulein Windling and her platonic love, the young desert dweller, Slimane (Arabic for Solomon), enjoy time together.

One winter, this middle-aged Swiss woman and this Muslim youth form a mutual attachment. She enjoys his rapt attention to her stories, and he enjoys hearing her tell them. When she, a devout Christian, indirectly challenges his Muslim assumptions about Jesus Christ, he reacts without anger; instead, he tells her an apocryphal story about Jesus, a man he regards as a Muslim prophet. Sensing her young protégé's religious nature and wanting to set him straight about Christ's true identity, she lovingly creates a crèche scene, carving Mary and baby Jesus, wise men, and shepherds from native clay, creating a floor from chicken feathers, and decorating the scene with candies from Switzerland.

While Fraulein Windling's back is turned, however, her friend inadvertently beheads the camels and other figures while trying to get at the candy. Deftly, subtly, Bowles uses the devastated manger scene as an omen of the future. War is coming: The French occupiers of the area are engaged in battle against local patriots, a lopsided conflict in which the heavily armed French are almost certain to prevail. When Fraulein Windling leaves her North African friend behind as a result of her forced repatriation home to Europe, she leaves with real grief in her heart, for she realizes that when she returns—if she ever will—he may be dead, a victim of the conflict. Thus, the last meeting is a sad one. Unspoken feelings speak the loudest as the two try to make conversation. As the train moves, she impulsively kisses Slimane's forehead and, by so doing, offers him evidence of her love.

In this story, Bowles's ability to convey stifled emotion and lost hopes with an astonishing economy of words is on full display; character and situation are carefully delineated. *The Time of Friendship* reverberates with loss but also with a kind of wild joy as two people share moments of intimacy and understanding.

SUMMARY

Paul Bowles is an innovator of the first order, whose masterful works deserve far more critical attention than has been given them. This slighting of Bowles, as some critics suggest, may be attributable to his strong anti-American bias, to his choice of locales ("too foreign," some say), or to his pessimistic view of human nature and human destiny. His works, while difficult and painful to read at times, offer readers a window on a strange, bizarre world that no other writer has offered.

John D. Raymer

BIBLIOGRAPHY

By the Author

SHORT FICTION:
The Delicate Prey, and Other Stories, 1950
A Little Stone: Stories, 1950
The Hours After Noon, 1959

A Hundred Camels in the Courtyard, 1962
The Time of Friendship, 1967
Pages from Cold Point, and Other Stories, 1968
Three Tales, 1975
Things Gone and Things Still Here, 1977
Collected Stories of Paul Bowles, 1939-1976, 1979
Midnight Mass, 1981
In the Red Moon, 1982
Call at Corazón, and Other Stories, 1988
A Distant Episode: The Selected Stories, 1988
Unwelcome Words, 1988
A Thousand Days for Mokhtar, and Other Stories, 1989
The Stories of Paul Bowles, 2001

LONG FICTION:

The Sheltering Sky, 1949
Let It Come Down, 1952
The Spider's House, 1955
Up Above the World, 1966

POETRY:

Scenes, 1968
The Thicket of Spring: Poems, 1926-1969, 1972
Next to Nothing, 1976
Next to Nothing: Collected Poems, 1926-1977, 1981

NONFICTION:

Yallah, 1957
Their Heads Are Green and Their Hands Are Blue, 1963
Without Stopping, 1972
Points in Time, 1982
Days: Tangier Journal, 1987-1989, 1991
Conversations with Paul Bowles, 1993 (Gena Dagel Caponi, editor)
In Touch: The Letters of Paul Bowles, 1994 (Jeffrey Miller, editor)

TRANSLATIONS:

The Lost Trail of the Sahara, 1952 (of R. Frison-Roche's novel)
No Exit, 1958 (of Jean-Paul Sartre's play)
A Life Full of Holes, 1964 (of Driss ben Hamed Charhadi's autobiography)
Love with a Few Hairs, 1967 (of Mohammed Mrabet's fiction)
The Lemon, 1969 (of Mrabet's fiction)
M'Hashish, 1969 (of Mrabet's fiction)
The Boy Who Set the Fire, 1974 (of Mrabet's fiction)
The Oblivion Seekers, 1975 (of Isabelle Eberhardt's fiction)
Harmless Poisons, Blameless Sins, 1976 (of Mrabet's fiction)
Look and Move On, 1976 (of Mrabet's fiction)
The Big Mirror, 1977 (of Mrabet's fiction)
The Beggar's Knife, 1985 (of Rodrigo Rey Rosa's fiction)
Dust on Her Tongue, 1989 (of Rey Rosa's fiction)
Chocolate Creams and Dollars, 1992 (of Mrabet's fiction)

DISCUSSION TOPICS

- What do Paul Bowles's isolated Westerners discover about themselves when confronted by alien civilizations?

- Why do Bowles's characters travel so far from home to go to such isolated places?

- Characteristically, when and how does violence make its entrance into Bowles's tales?

- How does Bowles portray the North African desert in *The Sheltering Sky*?

- In any Bowles story or novel, does foreign travel bring about a new state of mind in his main characters? If so, what is it?

- How are nomadic tribesmen portrayed in *The Sheltering Sky*?

MISCELLANEOUS:
Too Far from Home: The Selected Writings of Paul Bowles, 1993
The Paul Bowles Reader, 2000

About the Author

Bertens, Johannes Willem. *The Fiction of Paul Bowles: The Soul Is the Weariest Part of the Body.* Amsterdam, Netherlands: Humanities Press, 1979.

Caponi, Gena Dagel. *Paul Bowles.* New York: Twayne, 1998.

Carr, Virginia Spencer. *Paul Bowles: A Life.* New York: Scribner, 2004.

Miller, Jeffrey. *Paul Bowles: A Descriptive Bibliography.* Santa Barbara, Calif.: Black Sparrow Press, 1986.

Pounds, Wayne. *Paul Bowles: The Inner Geography.* Berne, Switzerland: Lang, 1985.

Review of Contemporary Fiction 2 (1982). Special Bowles issue.

Sawyer-Laucanno, Christopher. "An Invisible Spectator." *Twentieth Century Literature* 32 (Fall/Winter, 1986): 259-299.

Stewart, Lawrence D. *Paul Bowles: The Illumination of North Africa.* Carbondale: Southern Illinois University Press, 1974.

Kay Boyle

Born: St. Paul, Minnesota
February 19, 1902
Died: Mill Valley, California
December 27, 1992

The author of novels, short stories, children's books, essays, and articles, Boyle received several major awards for her fiction.

Library of Congress

Biography

Kay Boyle was born in St. Paul, Minnesota, on February 19, 1902, the daughter of Howard Peterson Boyle and Katherine Evans Boyle. Her father was a rather dim but well-intentioned figure in her life, while her paternal grandfather, Jesse Payton Boyle, was described by Kay as brilliant, reactionary, domineering, and destructive. Boyle's mother was active in the radical labor movement and other political causes, while her grandfather consistently criticized and opposed both mother and daughter. In Robert McAlmon's memoir *Being Geniuses Together*—a collaboration with Boyle once she revised and expanded it in 1968—she credited her mother with being the dominant influence in her life. It was her mother who instilled in her daughter social, political, and artistic values that permeated Boyle's work.

Boyle's formal schooling was sketchy: a few terms at two private girls' schools, a short time at the Cincinnati Conservatory of Music, and two years at the Ohio Mechanics Institute in Cincinnati, Ohio, where the family had moved in 1916. Travel took the place of conventional education in Boyle's life; while still a girl, she accompanied her family to Europe as well as to several cities in America. Indeed, travel became a constant factor in her life as she moved from one place to another; at various times, she lived in France, England, Austria, Germany, and Spain.

Before going off on her own, Boyle worked in her father's Cincinnati office for a short while, then moved to New York, where she found a job working on *Broom*, one of several avant-garde literary publications with which she was to become associated in America and Europe. The 1920's and 1930's were the era of the "little magazines," which promoted literary experimentation and innovation.

In June, 1922, Boyle married Robert Brault, a Frenchman, and the couple went to France in June, 1923, to spend the summer with Brault's family in St. Malo. Afterward, they moved to Paris, Le Havre, and the village of Harfleur, where, in 1924, Boyle began her second novel (the manuscript of the first was lost in the mail). As was to be the case with almost all of her novels and much of her short fiction, Boyle drew heavily upon events and persons in her own life for her material. *Plagued by the Nightingale*, a novel published in 1931, grew out of the period that she and her husband spent with his family in St. Malo.

Their marriage was shaky, and after meeting Ernest Walsh in 1925, Boyle became deeply involved with him and with his new magazine, *This Quarter*. Her early short fiction and poetry appeared in this review. Walsh died in October, 1926, and in March, 1927, Boyle gave birth to his daughter, Sharon. Briefly, she rejoined her husband, but the marriage came to an end in 1928.

Boyle was one of the many expatriate writers living and working in Paris in the period between the two world wars. Men and women who came of age during this time would later be known as the "lost generation." Boyle's work began to appear in a new

289

magazine, *transition*, in which also appeared the work of such writers as James Joyce, Gertrude Stein, Hart Crane, and Archibald MacLeish. Her poems, stories, reviews, a translation, and the preliminary drafts of a novel, *Year Before Last* (1932), appeared in this review. Her first book, a collection of short stories, was published in 1929, followed by *Wedding Day, and Other Stories* in 1930.

In the following ten years, Boyle's published work included six novels, three short-story collections, three translations, two ghostwritten volumes, a book of three short novels, a book for children, a collection of poems, and an anthology. During the same period, she won two O. Henry Awards for best short story of the year, and three of her stories appeared in the annual O. Henry anthologies. Forty of her stories were named in Edward O'Brien's annual collection of *Best American Short Stories*.

In 1931, Boyle married Laurence Vail, and the couple had three daughters. The Vails were divorced in 1943, after which Boyle married Baron Joseph von Franckenstein and had two more children. Franckenstein died in 1963.

In the years between 1942 and 1975, eight more Boyle novels appeared. Her short stories and short novels were published in ten collections. She also published five volumes of poetry and numerous translations, essays, articles, and other works of nonfiction.

Despite her prolific output, Boyle was not able to make enough money by her writing, and she supplemented her income by teaching. Although she had never graduated from college, she taught writing at a girls' school in Connecticut and at San Francisco State College (later San Francisco State University). She lectured and served as writer-in-residence at several colleges and universities and was made a fellow of Wesleyan University and the Radcliffe Institute of Independent Study. Boyle won two Guggenheim Fellowships, two honorary doctorates, a National Endowment for the Arts Fellowship for her "extraordinary contribution to American literature over a lifetime of creative work," and many other awards.

Following the example of her mother, Boyle was active in political causes all her life, in both Europe and America. Among the issues with which she was concerned were the rise of Nazism, the French Resistance movement during World War II, the occupation of Germany, the Joseph McCar-

thy hearings, and the movement against the Vietnam War. An outspoken and passionate champion of the poor and oppressed and a strong spokeswoman for the rights of individuals, Boyle reflected her concerns in her prose and poetry. Her personal life formed the substance of her fiction, and her political views permeated her work as well. For example, *Death of a Man* (1936) included material from her life in Austria, and her last novel, *The Underground Woman* (1975), concerns the experiences of a middle-aged woman who is arrested for taking part in an anti-Vietnam War demonstration, reflecting an experience that Boyle herself had undergone.

Because of her prodigious production over the years between 1931 and 1984, Boyle was recognized as a chronicler of the twentieth century, a popular author who occupied an indisputable place in the roster of important writers of her time. When she died in 1992, at the age of ninety, not all critics accorded her a place in the first rank of American writers, but it was universally acknowledged that she had made a worthy and valuable contribution to American literature.

ANALYSIS

Boyle's belief in the moral responsibility of the writer is clearly evident in everything that she wrote. Writing in *Story* in 1963, she expressed her conviction that a writer is "a moralist in the highest sense of the word" whose responsibility is "to speak briefly and clearly of the dignity and the integrity of individual man." The strongly autobiographical element in most of her work is apparent. The theme running through all of her work is the absolute necessity of love and the many obstacles and failures that prevent its fulfillment, such as narrow-mindedness, social conventions, bigotry, misunderstandings, and the tragedies of ordinary lives caught in war and other insuperable obstacles. The assertion of her moral convictions and the dependence on personal experience for her narrative sources characterize Boyle's fiction, which is consistently concerned with the importance of love in its many guises, manifestations, and frustrations.

That Boyle's life was extraordinary cannot be denied; thus, her use of her own experiences is understandable. As Sandra Whipple Spanier pointed out in a study of Boyle's life and work, Boyle was:

a fascinating woman who, in addition to writing over thirty books, had three husbands and six children and managed to be in the important places at the important times, participating actively in many of the major movements and events of our century. The effects of war—of defeat and occupation—were therefore prominent in her work.

Avalanche (1944), Boyle's most popular novel, highlights the bravery of the French Resistance. *A Frenchman Must Die* (1946) also focuses on the Resistance as it describes how a former Resistance fighter brings to justice a French aristocrat who collaborated with the Nazis. Other novels deal with the problems faced by the French and Germans as they rebuild their war-ravaged countries. The short story "The White Horses of Vienna" also deals with the issue of the rise of Nazism in Austria.

Other stories, such as those in *Life Being the Best, and Other Stories* (1988), concentrate on the search for love and meaning in individual lives. The novel *Monday Night* (1938) is an examination of two men on a quest for a prominent scientist whose false testimony has led to the conviction of several innocent men. In her last novel, *The Underground Woman,* Boyle capped her long career with an account of an event in her own life. The book tells of some women who were arrested and jailed for participating in a protest demonstration at an induction center during the Vietnam War. In her final fictional work, Boyle was thus true to the issues and ideals that had concerned her throughout her writing life.

Boyle received considerable attention and praise for her innovative and original style, especially in the early years, when she was a prominent member of the group of writers who in the 1920's and 1930's were rebelling against prevailing literary conventions. Boyle's style has been called poetic; it is intense, colored by strong images, trenchant metaphors, and telling details. Often, she writes in the stream-of-consciousness style that the modernists invented, expressing the thoughts and feelings of her characters through their own words, often in interior monologues, keeping herself as narrator in the background, even offstage.

One of the most notable of Boyle's literary characteristics is the way in which she tells her stories on two levels. The explicit events and descriptions are concerned with vividly drawn characters speaking in their own voices. She tends to use dialogue much more than narration. Beneath the surface, however, is the implied significance of what she is really writing about, the larger world stage on which individual lives are played out. Thus the focus, especially in her short stories, is highly concentrated—on, for example, a particular situation or an intense conversation that actually illustrates a larger theme, such as the human spirit in adversity or the disappointment of unfulfilled love. Boyle's tone is often rueful, even sad, revealing her compassion and concern for her characters.

Some critics have found Boyle melodramatic and self-conscious, her plots contrived, and her style affected. Her overriding aim, to transform society, has struck some as blatant and intrusive, and her emphasis on the necessity of love has been criticized as sentimental and overdrawn. Nevertheless, many other critics have admired her for the complexity and sensibility of her work and for the beauty and poignancy of her style. Certainly, the many awards and honors that she received indicate that Boyle deserved, and received, recognition as an important and distinguished writer.

"ANSCHLUSS"

First published: 1939 (collected in *Nothing Ever Breaks Except the Heart,* 1966)
Type of work: Short story

A young American woman is deeply affected by the changes in Austria resulting from the unification of that country with Germany.

"Anschluss" was regarded by many readers as one of Boyle's best stories about the effects of the rise of Nazism before World War II. Boyle's so-called war stories never take place on the battlefield. Instead, she shows how individuals' lives are touched by the events leading up to and during the larger conflicts. The characters are usually civilians, but some are military personnel caught by Boyle's observant eye away from the war front.

The heroine of "Anschluss" is a young woman named Merrill who works in Paris as an assistant to a fashion editor. Twice a year, Merrill takes a trip to her favorite vacation place, the village of Brenau in

Kay Boyle

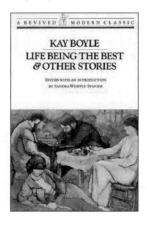

the mountains of Austria. The time is the 1930's. Boyle draws a sharp contrast between the trivialities of Merrill's life in Paris and the desperate straits of her two Austrian friends, Fanni and her brother Toni. Because of worldwide Depression, the two young Austrians are struggling to survive in a place where there are only occasional small jobs and little money.

Merrill remembers meeting Fanni on her first visit, two years before, in 1936. Her brother Toni had been arrested for engaging in political activities deemed treasonous. On this night, Fanni is celebrating Toni's release from jail. His appearance at the guest house marks the beginning of Merrill's romance, in which she abandons herself to the casual, careless life of the young Austrians, who manage to enjoy themselves despite their poverty and the uncertainty of their future, "as if they all knew that something else was going to happen in a little while." Merrill tries to persuade Toni to return with her to Paris, but he refuses, saying that he belongs in his own country.

In 1938, the Anschluss (Germany's annexation of Austria) takes place, and Merrill, returning to Brenau, expects that Toni is still rebelling and agitating. However, the change that has taken place in Austria has changed Toni as well. He now has a real job, as director of the Austrian Youth Local. When Merrill goes to the lake where Toni is the sports organizer, she feels awkward and self-conscious in her two-piece bathing suit, as she is surrounded by large, plainly dressed Germans on vacation, the "invading cohorts," as Boyle calls them. Toni criticizes Merrill for looking like an actress in a musical comedy. Clearly, he has changed. His carefree manner has disappeared, and he speaks gratefully of the Germans, who respect the Austrians. He sees no irony in the fact that the Germans regard Austria as a vacation ground, just as the bitterly resented Americans and English had formerly done.

The next day, Merrill sees Toni for the last time. At the train station, he is on the platform with several other young people in uniform. She is on the train; through the window, she sees him step to-

ward her as if to speak, but instead he clicks his heels together and lifts his hands in a salute. She cannot tell whether he is saying "Heil Hitler" or wishing her farewell.

It is characteristic of Boyle that she draws no morals in this story, nor does she point out the obvious concerning Fanni and Toni's acceptance of the Nazis. The bleak, simple ending is also typical of Boyle's style; having presented three appealing young characters and their situations in vivid, concise terms, she knows when to stop.

MONDAY NIGHT

First published: 1938
Type of work: Novel

Two men, searching for a famous toxicologist whose evidence has led to the convictions of several men, discover the shocking truth about him.

Monday Night, Boyle's sixth novel, is the only one that does not have an autobiographically based American woman as its heroine. Wilt, the main character of *Monday Night*, is an expatriate newspaperman who has lived in Paris for twenty years. He dreams of writing a great novel, if he can only find the right subject. A seedy, alcoholic, physically repulsive, single-minded, middle-aged man, he believes that he has finally discovered the story that will enable him to realize his dream. He has been led to this conclusion by his chance meeting with Bernie, a young, naïve American doctor who has come to Paris to pay homage to the famous Monsieur Sylvestre, the toxicologist whose testimony has resulted in the conviction and imprisonment—and sometimes execution—of several men.

Wilt is captivated by Bernie's quest, but he is much less interested in helping the younger man fulfill his goal than he is in his own thoughts, fantasies, and thirsts. Bernie, bewildered and tired, cannot resist Wilt, who drags him from one bar to another looking for leads to the famous scientist. They find his house; Sylvestre is not there, but a strange butler shows them around and obliquely reveals the truth about his employer. As they meet several people who know Sylvestre through various connections, Wilt begins to suspect that the man they are looking for is actually a criminal who has falsified his evidence in order to make up for his own failures in love and life.

Wilt becomes more and more excited, convinced that he now has the material to write the great novel of which he has dreamed. As the sinister and sordid story is revealed, Wilt is quite unconcerned about its effect on Bernie, who, after traveling all the way to Paris to express his admiration of his hero, has seen his ideals shattered.

At a train station, Wilt catches sight of Sylvestre alighting from a train. At the same time, Wilt sees a newspaper headline indicating that several murder cases involving Sylvestre's testimony have been reopened. Bernie has disappeared. It is clear that no one will ever know of Wilt's independent search and discovery.

This is not a pleasant story. Boyle seems to be saying that Wilt is doomed to failure, just as Bernie is fated for disappointment. Their quest was worthy, but they were not able to meet the challenge. The fault lies not in their ideals but in their own weaknesses.

The larger political and social issues that concerned Boyle so urgently in her other fiction are not emphasized here; perhaps as a result, *Monday Night* is one of her most popular novels. It is also the one that Boyle said was her favorite. It is not typical of her writing, but with its concentrated focus, its original characters, and its suspenseful plot, it is quite possibly not only her most popular but also her best novel.

THE UNDERGROUND WOMAN

First published: 1975
Type of work: Novel

A woman caught up in two of the major American issues of the 1960's reconciles the two roles that she has played in her life.

In *The Underground Woman*, Boyle's last novel, the author characteristically draws upon her own experiences for her basic framework. Like her heroine, Athena Gregory, Boyle was jailed for participating in a demonstration against the war in Vietnam;

likewise, her daughter rejected her family and joined a religious cult; similarly, Boyle was a professor at a San Francisco university.

The book opens with Athena and fifteen other protesters in a patrol wagon on their way to jail because they blocked the entrance of an induction center. Slightly more than half the book is taken up with Athena's observations of the personalities and actions of three groups of women: her fellow demonstrators, the long-term prisoners, and those who work in the jail. Boyle describes in detail the routine of the monotonous days, the vile food, the various jobs the prisoners are given, and their ugly clothing. She learns about the oppression of black and Latina women and is confirmed in her conviction that older people must share the responsibility of all Americans to fight for liberty and justice for everyone.

The second part of the book finds Athena returning home after her ten-day stay in jail. Again she experiences a kind of imprisonment, as her home has been taken over by members of the cult of Pete the Redeemer. Her daughter, Melanie, is not among them, and Athena feels sure that their promise of her return is false. With the help of a black neighbor, the cult people are forced out of her house. Melanie has been in Athena's mind throughout the book, but she never actually appears or takes any part in the action. As the book ends, Athena is once again in a patrol wagon, being taken off to jail for demonstrating against the draft. With her are some of the women with whom she had been imprisoned before. Athena has made her choice; in silence, she prays for connection with reality as she and the other demonstrators reenter the jail.

All of her life, Athena has tried to play two roles. In one, she has tried to live up to the ideal represented by the name her father gave her, that of the Greek goddess of war and reason. She speaks of this role as "that ancient unreality." The other role is that of a woman who wants to participate in modern life: marrying young, having children, being involved in issues such as the war. She feels that she has always been two women, one visible and understandable and the other "functioning underground," bravely enduring and working out her conflicts and troubles alone.

In this final novel, Boyle once again expressed her lifelong commitment to the struggle for justice and freedom, "pleading for the exercise of conscience." Not long before her death, Boyle described herself as "a dangerous 'radical' cleverly disguised as a perfect lady." Clearly, Boyle saw herself as "an underground woman," and it was that self-awareness and dedication to her ideals that enabled her to produce her last novel at the age of seventy-three.

SUMMARY

Among the women writers who were finding their voices and gaining increased recognition in the years between the two world wars and afterward—a time of great turmoil and upheaval—Boyle earned a place as one who was true to her ideals and principles throughout her writing life. One of her most interesting and revealing books was *Being Geniuses Together, 1920-1930*, a memoir of the "Lost Generation" written by her friend McAlmon

that she revised and greatly expanded in 1968. In this book, Boyle told of wanting to write of "the unseen world" of the poor and oppressed, which in her mind was too often ignored or belittled. She admitted that she had come to demand a great deal of women, and even more of women writers. To her, "It was an actual pain in the heart when they failed to be what they themselves had given their word that they would seem to be." Whatever her faults and weaknesses as a writer might have been, no one ever questioned her integrity and dedication in a time when these qualities were maintained only with the greatest steadfastness.

Boyle lived and wrote in challenging and interesting times. Her life was a reflection of those qualities, and she did not hesitate to put her experiences and principles to use in the service of her craft.

Natalie Harper

BIBLIOGRAPHY

By the Author

LONG FICTION:
Process, wr. c. 1925, pb. 2001 (Sandra Spanier, editor)
Plagued by the Nightingale, 1931
Year Before Last, 1932
Gentlemen, I Address You Privately, 1933
My Next Bride, 1934
Death of a Man, 1936
Monday Night, 1938
Primer for Combat, 1942
Avalanche, 1944
A Frenchman Must Die, 1946, 1939, 1948
His Human Majesty, 1949
The Seagull on the Step, 1955
Three Short Novels, 1958
Generation Without Farewell, 1960
The Underground Woman, 1975

SHORT FICTION:
Short Stories, 1929
Wedding Day, and Other Stories, 1930
The First Lover, and Other Stories, 1933
The White Horses of Vienna, and Other Stories, 1936
The Crazy Hunter, and Other Stories, 1940
Thirty Stories, 1946

DISCUSSION TOPICS

- What facts of Kay Boyle's early career contributed to her development as a novelist focused on political themes?

- Boyle seems to have learned more from travel experiences than from early domestic routine and formal schooling. To what extent can the same be said of Merrill in the short story "Anschluss"?

- Literary style is preeminently the effective use of language elements such as diction, phrasing, metaphors, and details generally. Examine carefully the style of a passage (a page or so) in Boyle's writing that you think deserves praise for its style and cite particular instances.

- Examine carefully a conversation in a Boyle short story that both reveals the speakers' characters and illustrates a larger theme.

- In what respects was Boyle herself, like Athena in the story of that name, an "underground woman"?

The Smoking Mountain: Stories of Postwar Germany, 1951
Nothing Ever Breaks Except the Heart, 1966
Fifty Stories, 1980
Life Being the Best, and Other Stories, 1988

POETRY:
A Glad Day, 1938
American Citizen Naturalized in Leadville, Colorado, 1944
Collected Poems, 1962
Testament for My Students, and Other Poems, 1970
This Is Not a Letter, and Other Poems, 1985
Collected Poems of Kay Boyle, 1991

NONFICTION:
Breaking the Silence: Why a Mother Tells Her Son About the Nazi Era, 1962
Being Geniuses Together, 1920-1930, 1968 (with Robert McAlmon)
The Long Walk at San Francisco State, and Other Essays, 1970
Words That Must Somehow Be Said: The Selected Essays of Kay Boyle, 1927-1984, 1985

CHILDREN'S LITERATURE:
The Youngest Camel, 1939, 1959
Pinky, the Cat Who Liked to Sleep, 1966
Pinky in Persia, 1968

EDITED TEXTS:
365 Days, 1936 (with others)
The Autobiography of Emanuel Carnevali, 1967
Enough of Dying! An Anthology of Peace Writings, 1972 (with Justine van Gundy)

About the Author

Austenfeld, Thomas Carl. *American Women Writers and the Nazis: Ethics and Politics in Boyle, Porter, Stafford, and Hellman.* Charlottesville: University Press of Virginia, 2001.

Bell, Elizabeth S. *Kay Boyle: A Study of the Short Fiction.* New York: Twayne, 1992.

Carpenter, Richard C. "Kay Boyle." *English Journal* 42 (November, 1953): 425-430.

_____. "Kay Boyle: The Figure in the Carpet." *Critique: Studies in Modern Fiction* 7 (Winter, 1964/1965): 65-78.

Chambers, M. Clark. *Kay Boyle: A Bibliography.* New Castle, Del.: Oak Knoll Press, 2002.

Elkins, Marilyn, ed. *Critical Essays on Kay Boyle.* New York: G. K. Hall, 1997.

Ford, Hugh. *Four Lives in Paris.* San Francisco: North Point Press, 1987.

Lesinska, Zofia P. *Perspectives of Four Women Writers on the Second World War: Gertrude Stein, Janet Flanner, Kay Boyle, and Rebecca West.* New York: Peter Lang, 2002.

Mellen, Joan. *Kay Boyle: Author of Herself.* New York: Farrar, Straus and Giroux, 1994.

Moore, Harry T. "Kay Boyle's Fiction." In *The Age of the Modern and Other Literary Essays.* Carbondale: Southern Illinois University Press, 1971.

Porter, Katherine Anne. "Kay Boyle: Example to the Young." In *The Critic as Artist: Essays on Books, 1920-1970,* edited by Gilbert A. Harrison. New York: Liveright, 1972.

Spanier, Sandra Whipple. *Kay Boyle: Artist and Activist.* Carbondale: Southern Illinois University Press, 1986.

Yalom, Marilyn. *Women Writers of the West Coast: Speaking of Their Lives and Careers.* Santa Barbara, Calif.: Capra Press, 1983.

T. CORAGHESSAN BOYLE

Courtesy, Allen and Unwin

Born: Peekskill, New York
December 2, 1948

Boyle is widely recognized for his comic picaresque novels and his satiric absurdist short stories.

BIOGRAPHY

T. Coraghessan Boyle was born in 1948, in Peekskill, New York, a small town on the banks of the Hudson River in the area made famous by Washington Irving in such stories as "Rip Van Winkle" and "The Legend of Sleepy Hollow." The middle name, pronounced kuh-RAG-is-son, is an admitted affectation; his real name is Thomas John Boyle. His father was a school bus driver, and his mother was a secretary. Boyle's grade school and high school education gave no indication of his future as a writer; in fact, he has said, in a typically facetious exaggeration, that he never read a book until he was eighteen, that he mostly read comic books and watched television. Music was his primary interest.

Boyle went to the State University of New York at Potsdam as a music major, studying the clarinet and saxophone. He has said that he really was not good enough to be a professional musician and did not have the discipline to practice. He drifted into a creative writing class, where he discovered writers such as John Barth, Thomas Pynchon, Donald Barthelme, and Gabriel García Márquez, all of whom have influenced his work.

When Boyle graduated from college, the Vietnam War and the pressure of the draft made him decide to become a teacher to qualify for a military deferment. Although he has characterized himself as a "wild, radical hippie" at the time, he got a job

teaching English at a junior high school in Peekskill in what Boyle has described as a tough slum school, where he often had to get violent to maintain discipline. It was during this time that he says he began taking drugs.

Feeling himself at a dead end and having gained some encouragement by publishing a story in *The New American Review,* he applied to the creative writing graduate program at the University of Iowa and was accepted on the basis of his work. At Iowa he studied under such writers as John Cheever, Vance Bourjaily, and John Irving, receiving his Ph.D. in 1977. Boyle also won a Creative Writing Fellowship from the National Endowment for the Arts in 1977, and his dissertation creative project, *Descent of Man,* was published in 1979. The book was well enough received to give Boyle a significant underground reputation and to earn for him a job as a creative writing professor at the University of Southern California (USC) in Los Angeles. The stories also won the Coordinating Council of Literary Magazines Award for Fiction and the St. Lawrence Award for Fiction.

Boyle's first novel, *Water Music* (1981), a picaresque work based on the adventures of Mungo Park, an eighteenth century Scottish explorer, was received by critics as a virtuoso performance. Boyle's delight in playing with the language was infectious, and the book was admired more for its exuberant style than for its thematic depth. Turning to a more realistic approach and a contemporary setting in his second novel, Boyle published *Budding Prospects: A Pastoral* (1984), a satiric treatment of the American Dream in which hippies growing marijuana in the Northern California backwoods are presented as modern models of Benjamin Franklin and Henry David Thoreau.

Boyle continued to write short stories during this period, publishing his collection *Greasy Lake, and Other Stories* in 1985, which was widely praised for its satire and humor. A particularly ambitious work is *World's End* (1987), a sprawling picaresque novel covering several generations of Hudson Valley families; the book won the PEN/Faulkner Award for American Fiction and was called Boyle's "peak achievement" in *The New York Times Book Review.* Boyle's third collection of short stories, *If the River Was Whiskey* (1989), was less enthusiastically received, with critics complaining that it did not contain any stories equal to some of the masterpieces in Boyle's first two collections. *East Is East* (1990), about a young half-Japanese man who jumps ship and lands on a small island near Georgia, similarly received only lukewarm response.

Boyle continued to garner awards and accolades. He received O. Henry Awards in 1988 for "Sinking House," in 1989 for "The Ape Lady in Retirement," in 1999 for "The Underground Gardens," in 2001 for "The Love of My Life," and in 2003 for "Swept Away." His *T. C. Boyle Stories: The Collected Stories of T. Coraghessan Boyle* (1998) won the Bernard Malamud Prize in Short Fiction from the PEN/Faulkner Foundation. In 2003, he was a National Book Award finalist for *Drop City.* In 2004, "Tooth and Claw" was a Best American Stories selection.

Boyle has said more than once that he yearns to be famous. Every book he writes he expects will end up on the best-seller list and make people forget the name of millionaire horror writer Stephen King forever. It is not the money that interests him, he claims. "I want to be read," insists Boyle. He lives near Los Angeles with his wife and his three children. Although he still presents himself for publicity purposes as a latter-day hippie, complete with shaggy hair and beard, a metal clip in his ear, and voodoo bracelets on his wrist, Boyle lives a hardworking middle-class life in the suburbs; he continues to teach at USC and to write books that he hopes will become best sellers.

ANALYSIS

Boyle's most pervasive fictional theme is the importance of history; his most predominant fictional method is satire. His two most ambitious novels to date, *Water Music* and *World's End*, are both sprawling picaresque novels deeply rooted in history. *Water Music* is based on the actual adventures of Mungo Park, a Scottish explorer who became the first white man to explore the Niger River in Africa and who published a best-selling account of his adventures titled *Travels in the Interior Districts of Africa* in 1799. *World's End* begins with seventeenth century native Indians and Dutch and American settlers of the Hudson River Valley of New York and traces the descendants of three families into the twentieth century. *The Road to Wellville* (1993) uses the historical character of John Harvey Kellogg, while *The Inner Circle* (2004) employs Dr. Alfred Kinsey to show additional permutations of the American Dream and its corrupting influence.

Whereas *Water Music* is modeled after both the eighteenth century picaresque novels of Laurence Sterne and the twentieth century send-ups of the picaresque novel by such writers as John Barth, *World's End* builds on the American mythmaking tradition originated by Washington Irving as well as such modern American mythmakers as Thomas Berger. Even Boyle's least mythic novel, *Budding Prospects*, a satiric send-up of the American Dream and the male escape fantasy, is deeply rooted in both the history of the Founding Fathers and the history of the hippie movement of the 1960's.

Boyle's stories, as is typical of the short story in general, are less dependent on history than are his novels. His short stories stand alone as independent satires, mostly on modern society and popular culture. Boyle's first collection, *Descent of Man*, features such absurd situations as the canine film star Lassie leaving her master Timmy for a love affair with a coyote, a woman falling in love with a brilliant chimpanzee who is translating Charles Darwin and Friedrich Nietzsche into Yerkish, and a group of teenagers who are so stoned on drugs that they do not notice that it is literally raining blood.

Boyle continued this kind of absurdist satire and parody in his second collection, *Greasy Lake, and Other Stories*, but some of the stories in this collection have such control and achieve such a powerful significance that they go beyond simple satire. Although the collection contains parodies of Sherlock Holmes and Nikolai Gogol's famous story "The Overcoat," as well as such absurd stories as one about a secret love affair between Dwight D. Eisenhower and the wife of Nikita Khrushchev and a story about the mating of whales, it also contains such surrealistically sublime pieces as "The Hector Quesadilla Story," about a baseball game that goes on forever, and such classic tragicomic nightmares as the title story. Critical response to Boyle's 1989 collection of stories, *If the River Was Whiskey*, and his novel *East Is East* indicated that Boyle had not moved much beyond his earlier works. According to several critics, these stories often seem self-parodies and do not have the scope of his earlier picaresque efforts.

WATER MUSIC

First published: 1981
Type of work: Novel

The lives of Mungo Park, a Scottish explorer, and Ned Rise, a thief, intertwine in eighteenth century England.

Water Music is based on the real-life adventures of eighteenth century Scottish explorer Mungo Park as told in his book *Travels in the Interior Districts of Africa*. It also focuses on the imagined adventures of Ned Rise, a member of Park's final exploration party, who uses his wits to survive on the streets of London. Both men are classic picaros, one in the mode of the adventuring nobleman and the other in the mode of the unscrupulous rogue. In the first part of the novel Boyle moves back and forth between Park's harrowing adventures in Africa as he escapes mutilation and death at the hands of savages and Ned Rise's exploits as he evades the clutches of fellow criminals and the gallows on the no-less-dangerous streets of London. Each chapter ends in a traditional cliff-hanger as the reader is whisked from the Niger to the Thames and then back again until the twin picaresque streams of the story merge, when Park returns to England a hero and Rise narrowly escapes death. Both feel the need to escape England and civilization, such as it is, which they do when Park makes his final (for him, fatal), disastrous expedition to the Niger River.

The novel has much purely visceral appeal; it is filled with sufficient sex and violence to hold the interest of even the most superficial and adolescent reader. Boyle is only following in a tradition,

however; such violence and degradation were the stock and trade of the picaresque novel, which constituted the pulp literature of the eighteenth and nineteenth centuries. Boyle uses the picaresque mode only as the means by which he can play with fictional conventions in an exuberant way. It is the language of the book that most catches the discriminating reader, combining as it does high-flown eighteenth century rhetoric with the flat and slangy language of the twentieth century. Other writers, such as John Barth and Donald Barthelme, have tried this technique with more success, but Boyle seems to take a great delight in his play with language, a delight the reader often shares.

Water Music is black humor at its blackest and most humorous. Called "High Comic Book Fiction" by one reviewer and a virtuoso performance on a grand scale by another, the book was both hailed for its inventive use of the picaresque/experimental mode and blasted for its comic-strip bathos and superficiality. Regardless of this mixed response, it is the book that made T. C. Boyle a name to reckon with in American literature.

"GREASY LAKE"

First published: 1985 (collected in *Greasy Lake, and Other Stories*, 1985)
Type of work: Short story

Three young men looking for adventure on a Saturday night find more than they bargained for.

"Greasy Lake," the title story of Boyle's best-received collection of stories, takes its title and its epigraph—"It's about a mile down on the dark side of Route 88"—from Bruce Springsteen's song "Spirit in the Night." The story focuses on three nineteen-year-old men living in a time (probably the 1960's) when, the narrator says, it was good to be bad, when young people cultivated decadence like a taste. Driving the narrator's family station wagon, they search for some escape from their suburban shopping-center lives at Greasy Lake, where, on the banks of festering murk, they can drink beer, smoke marijuana, listen to rock and roll, and howl at the moon.

On the particular occasion of this story, however, at 2:00 A.M., these extremely "bad" characters meet someone more "dangerous" than they are. When they try to embarrass a friend in a parked car, they find out too late that it is instead a "bad, greasy" stranger, who begins beating them up. Things go from bad to worse when the narrator loses the key to the station wagon and cracks the greasy stranger on the head with a tire iron. When the three, caught up in the violence, begin tearing the clothes off the girl in the car, they are interrupted by the arrival of another man, who threatens to kill them.

All this intense physical action is described in a combination of fear-filled seriousness and silly slapstick—that is, until the narrator, trying to escape, is driven into the primeval swamp of Greasy Lake, only to find himself stumbling over a floating dead body. As he crouches there in the shallow water, he listens to the greasy stranger taking the tire iron to his mother's Bel Air station wagon like an avenging demon. The story ends when the three boys start to leave and are stopped by the arrival of two young women in a silver Mustang who ask them if they want to party. By this time, however, they have had enough of "being bad" and drive

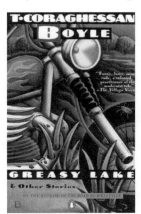

away in the wrecked car, leaving one of the girls standing there in the dirt road with her drug-filled hand outstretched.

"Greasy Lake" is a realistic, yet surrealistic, story about the posturing efforts of young men wanting to be tough. Boyle has said that it is about strutting around thinking you are bad and then finding someone who is tougher than you are. The proposition the story raises, says Boyle, is where is the bottom and does one really want to get there? The metaphor for the bottom is Greasy Lake itself, the ultimate end of the basic ironic dichotomy in the story between the suburban clean-cut and greasy primitivism. Although there is a distinction between the pretense of danger and real danger, the story suggests that the pretense can itself be dangerous. The progression from comic posturing and slapstick comedy to

gothic horror and final bathos is handled so deftly that the reader is irresistibly carried along by it.

"THE HECTOR QUESADILLA STORY"

First published: 1985 (collected in *Greasy Lake, and Other Stories*, 1985)
Type of work: Short story

An aged, overweight Mexican baseball player yearns for a final heroic gesture but gets caught in a game that lasts forever.

The hero of the slightly surreal "The Hector Quesadilla Story" is a typical Boyle antihero. Although the story is in the tradition of mythic tales of Babe Ruth and Joe DiMaggio, Hector Quesadilla, in his fifties, is no Sultan of Swat—he has shin splints, corns, and hemorrhoids. He is not only old, but he is also fat, a man who eats as though there were some creature inside him made of nothing but jaws and guts. He has not played regularly in ten years, but he wants one more season; he refuses to admit that he is old. In baseball, Hector believes, the grass is always green and the lights are always shining, for it is a game that never ends.

The story focuses on one particular day late in the season; it is Hector's birthday, and there is a home game at Dodger Stadium in Los Angeles. His entire family attends—his wife, his grandchildren, even his son, Hector, Jr., who studies English at USC and is writing a thesis on a mystical British poet, of whom Hector has never heard. Hector's own mystic adventure begins when the game is tied up at 5 to 5 at the bottom of the ninth inning and seems headed for extra innings. As the game goes into its twenty-second inning, Hector begins to feel, with a sense of wonder, that he is destined to be the hero of the longest game in history.

The story moves toward its transcendent climax at the top of the thirty-first inning, when finally Hector is sent up to bat and thus, it is hoped, to bring the game to an end. However, it is not to be. Although he connects with the ball, sending it over the center fielder's head to slam off the wall, his legs give out, and he is cut down at third base. Stunned and humiliated, he staggers to the dugout, to the jeers of the remaining crowd. Still it is not over, however, and Hector goes in again. The story (but not the game) ends with him stepping up to the plate, the bat flashing in his hands like an archangel's sword; the game goes on forever.

Although this story begins in Boyle's typical comic play, this time as a parody of the baseball hero biography, the magic of the game takes over. Instead of a comic parody, what results is a truly transcendent hymn to the national pastime and an objectification of the yearning in the heart of everyone to have that one moment in the sun. What makes the story work is its metaphoric objectification of the mythic ideal of "the game that goes on forever." The language moves from satiric flippancy to a poetic evocation of those countless Sunday afternoons on baseball fields all across the United States, where American children look for heroes, and old men try to hold on to youth.

WORLD'S END

First published: 1987
Type of work: Novel

The history of two families, the Van Brunts and the Van Warts, is told against the backdrop of the history of the Hudson Valley

World's End begins at the end of a workday in 1968 with the twenty-two-year-old Walter Van Brunt drinking beer at the Throbbing Elbow, a local bar, accompanied by wild-haired Hector Mantequilla and the sexy Mardi. From there, the book moves to explore the history of Van Brunt's family, which begins at a Hudson Valley trading post three centuries earlier, as well as the history of Walter's boss, Depeyster Van Wart.

The book moves back and forth in history, but themes emerge that apply to any era: the struggle of fathers to make a better life for their sons; the perils of disengagement with the world; power and its mutations, and the nature of treachery; the inability of the powerful to feel empathy or remorse; the rage of the powerless; and the failure to live up to impossible standards.

Two pivotal events occur in the course of the novel, one actual, one fictional. The first is the

Peekskill riots of 1949, when angry locals attacked outsiders who came from the city to hear a Paul Robeson concert; the other is an attempt to sabotage the Arcadia, a fictional countercultural shop moored in the Hudson River. Representatives of both families play key roles in both events. Over and over in the course of history, the Van Brunts encounter horrible physical disasters, many involving the loss of limbs. Harmanus Van Brunt dies after going mad as a result of witnessing the amputation of his son's leg. Lightning strikes his home while his wife and son are inside. Wouter Van Brunt betrays his cousins and allows them to be hanged, drawn, and quartered. Walter Van Brunt loses both feet in a motorcycle accident. The characters exploit, betray, and repeatedly fail one another as they either try desperately to control their lives or numbly give over that control to fate.

In the book, Boyle demonstrates that he is much more than a satirist; his prose is drunk on language and beautifully crafted, while the multigenerational cast of characters is complex and credible, portrayed against a vivid historical background. The sheer number of characters requires a three-page list at the beginning of the novel in order to explicate them. Boyle demythologizes sentimental images of early American history while showing, through their demasking, the actual injustices that have taken place throughout American society from the colonial era to the modern era.

THE ROAD TO WELLVILLE

First published: 1993
Type of work: Novel

John Harvey Kellogg, founder of Kellogg Cereals, develops a sanatorium to showcase his beliefs in a scientific diet.

Set in Battle Creek, Michigan, in the winter of 1907, *The Road to Wellville* explores the phenomenon of the rise of breakfast cereals and how the national rage for them made and lost fortunes.

John Harvey Kellogg, a scientist and showman who is both an early diet devotee and the inventor of cornflakes, runs a spa where the cream of American society and business comes to regain their

health and lose weight. In the winter of 1907, his clients include Will Lightbody, an alcoholic who has been prescribed alcoholic tonics, and his wife, a firm adherent of the spa's philosophy, who surreptitiously regularly slips an opium-based cure into his evening coffee. Over the course of the book, Will must save his marriage and fight his addiction, despite the hindrance of well-wishers.

At the same time, wealth seekers—including Charlie Ossining and his partner Goodloe H. Bender, who plan to sell the same product as Kellogg, but with a different name, "Per-Fo" (perfect food)—make their way to Battle Creek to attempt to con their way into the boom of the breakfast business. Despite the fact that Charlie is more victim than con artist, he is arrested, escapes, and eventually becomes the president of the "Per-To" (perfect tonic) Company four years later.

Kellogg (the child of a broom maker who accordingly believes that roughage "sweeps out" the system) does not just touch on diet but preaches on child rearing as well, using his forty-two adopted children as case studies. He has adopted the scores of orphans in order to transform them into testimonies of the sanatorium's healthy lifestyle. One of these children, nineteen-year-old George Kellogg, rebels and rejects Kellogg's lifestyle, extorting money by threatening to reveal his parentage and wallowing in dissipation. Showcasing the physical and spiritual corruption that Kellogg's regimen tries to arrest, George firmly rejects the identity Kellogg seeks to force on him and colludes with Ossining and Bender in an unsuccessful attempt to blackmail Kellogg.

Eventually as the details of the ritualized lifestyle of the sanatorium—five daily enemas, inspirational meetings, laughing exercises, a diet of vegetables and whole grains, sinusoidal baths, radium vapors, vibrotherapy, and forswearing coffee, among other practices—emerge, demonstrating that the sanatorium is as excessive as the lifestyles it attempts to address and that moderation, common sense, taking responsibility for one's own actions,

and accepting human frailties emerge as a cure that seems more likely to succeed. In this farcical novel, Boyle's comic genius emerges, animating characters that are realistic and as ridiculous as human beings can be. Over and over, pompousness is deflated and pretension shown for what it is: In the end, Kellogg is attacked by the chimpanzee and wolf that he has raised as vegetarians.

THE INNER CIRCLE

First published: 2004
Type of work: Novel

Indiana University zoology professor Dr. Alfred Kinsey maintains that the human need for sex equates to animal instinct while testing the bounds of his own marriage and establishing a circle of disciples.

In the late 1940's and early 1950's, the Kinsey Report, compiled by Dr. Alfred Kinsey, documented the results of a scientific study of male and female sexuality. The novel explores Kinsey's influence on American sexual and social mores through the voice of John Milk, Kinsey's assistant and first disciple, who assists Kinsey both in the office and in bed and with both Kinsey's wife and his own in group sex.

The fictionalization of Kinsey's story provides a lens through which the book examines the sexual revolution in sharp, provocative detail, especially as Kinsey's research grows increasingly voyeuristic and exhibitionistic. As Milk becomes part of the "inner circle" of researchers, he and his wife are drawn into experiments that become increasingly uninhibited and increasingly problematic for his marriage. The shyness regarding sexuality that permeates the era in which the book is set makes the research both alluring and alarming to Milk, whose sensibility reflects that of the readers of the Kinsey Report and chronicles the transformation of public attitudes and private behavior.

The book's primary theme is sex, marriage, and jealousy and the difficulties of attempting to quantify or classify personal interactions. Boyle explores the division between human pride and human animal natures and whether the act of sex can be separated from its emotional and spiritual context. In Kinsey's crusade to separate sex and morality, his attempt is doomed by his own uncompromising idealism. The novel also serves as a case study of what it means to become another person's apostle as it explores the impact of Kinsey's methods on Milk and his marriage.

SUMMARY

Boyle has arguably become one of the most ambitious and enthusiastic American authors writing today. Both in the scope of his picaresque novels and in the perception of his satiric short stories, he has carved out a place for himself in the comic experimental tradition of Barth and Barthelme. He is not a slavish imitator of those writers, however; he has a unique voice that manages to hover delicately between the serious and the satiric, and he has his own vision of the importance of history in the American psyche.

Charles E. May; updated by Catherine Rambo

BIBLIOGRAPHY

By the Author

LONG FICTION:
Water Music, 1981
Budding Prospects: A Pastoral, 1984
World's End, 1987
East Is East, 1990
The Road to Wellville, 1993
The Tortilla Curtain, 1995
Riven Rock, 1998
A Friend of the Earth, 2000
After the Plague, 2001
Drop City, 2003
The Inner Circle, 2004
Tooth and Claw, 2005

SHORT FICTION:
Descent of Man, 1979
Greasy Lake, and Other Stories, 1985
If the River Was Whiskey, 1989
Without a Hero, 1994
T. C. Boyle Stories: The Collected Stories of T. Coraghessan Boyle, 1998
After the Plague: Stories, 2001

EDITED TEXT:
Doubletakes: Pairs of Contemporary Short Stories, 2003

DISCUSSION TOPICS

- What place do you think "fad" medicine such as the Graham diet plays in T. Coraghessan Boyle's *The Road to Wellville*? Are there comparable modern-day diets or treatments?

- In *The Road to Wellville*, are the patients of the sanatorium looking for physical cures? What ailments are they really trying to address?

- Why does Boyle draw so often on history in his works? What does he accomplish by using American history?

- What recurrences and echoes occur in *World's End*? What cycles is Boyle trying to explore, and what does their repetition say about the nature of history?

- Boyle's work often manages to combine humor and pathos. How do they influence and enhance each other?

- Boyle has noted that he likes to defeat the expectations of readers, particularly ones that have read other pieces of his work. How does he actively work to defeat reader expectations and do the unexpected in his novels?

- One of the central themes of *Drop City* is the desire of the hippies to remain in a state of innocence, like children. What is Boyle trying to say about the desire to postpone adulthood, and how does it connect to his view of American culture?

About the Author

Abrams, Garry. "T. C. Boyle Would Be Famous." *Los Angeles Times,* October 7, 1987, B13-B14.

Adams, Michael. "T. Coraghessan Boyle." In *Dictionary of Literary Biography Yearbook: 1986,* edited by J. M. Brook. Detroit: Gale Research, 1987.

Ang, Audra. "Author, Professor, Eco-Conscious." *Associated Press* 18 (October, 2000).

Carnes, Mark. *Novel History: Historians and Novelists Confront America's Past (and Each Other).* New York: Simon & Schuster, 2001.

DeCurtis, Anthony. "A Punk's Past Recaptured." *Rolling Stone,* January 14, 1988, 54-57.

Shelden, Michael. "T. Coraghessan Boyle: The Art of Fiction CLXI." *Paris Review* 155 (Summer, 2000): 100-126.

"T. Coraghessan Boyle." In *Contemporary Literary Criticism,* edited by Dan Marowski. Vol. 36. Detroit: Gale Research, 1986.

Vaid, Krishna Baldev. "Franz Kafka Writes to T. Coraghessan Boyle." *Michigan Quarterly Review* 35, no. 3 (Summer, 1996): 53-57.

Ray Bradbury

Thomas Victor

Born: Waukegan, Illinois
August 22, 1920

Bradbury played a leading role in winning a large readership for science fiction in the 1950's by producing works with well-developed characters, provocative themes, and an attractive literary style.

Biography

Ray Bradbury was born in Waukegan, Illinois, on August 22, 1920, the son of Leonard Bradbury and Esther Moberg Bradbury. One of his older twin brothers died before his birth, and a younger sister, Elizabeth, died in infancy when he was seven.

Despite economic problems that took his family twice to Arizona in search of work, and despite the deaths of two siblings, Bradbury's memory of his early years is positive. In *Dandelion Wine* (1957) and other works, his boyhood home in Waukegan becomes Green Town, an idyllic if somewhat fragile midwestern town, where children enjoy the pleasures of playmates their age balanced with the opportunity for solitary explorations of a surrounding countryside.

In 1934, the family moved permanently to Los Angeles, where Bradbury soon adapted to his second beloved home. Los Angeles attracted him, in part, because it was a center of the entertainment industry which Bradbury had loved since at least the age of three, when he saw the 1923 film *The Hunchback of Notre Dame.* Throughout his life, Bradbury devoured the fiction of wonder and adventure: radio, motion pictures, comic books, pulp and slick magazines, and the novels of such authors as Edgar Rice Burroughs and Jules Verne. At the age of twelve, he and a friend found themselves unable to await the next sequel in Burroughs's Mars series and, therefore, wrote their own.

Bradbury had begun writing stories and poems as soon as he learned how to write. He made his first sale as a teenager, contributing a sketch to the George Burns and Gracie Allen radio comedy show. In high school, he also developed an interest in theater that continued throughout his writing career.

After finishing high school, Bradbury plunged into writing, trying to make himself quickly into a professional. He joined a science-fiction organization, studied with science-fiction writer Robert Heinlein, and worked with several other successful pulp fiction and screenwriters. He set himself the task of writing a story a week, while living at home and earning money selling newspapers. His first published story was "Hollerbochen's Dilemma," which appeared in *Imagination!* in 1938. He wrote his first paid science-fiction story, "Pendulum," in collaboration with Henry Hasse, and it appeared in *Super Science Stories* in 1941. Soon Bradbury was publishing regularly in pulp magazines such as *Weird Tales.*

When he married Marguerite McClure in 1947, he was a well-established writer, publishing more than a dozen stories each year. "The Big Black and White Game" appeared in *Best American Short Stories* in 1945, and "Homecoming" was selected for the O. Henry Awards *Prize Stories of 1947.* In the year of his marriage, Arkham House published his first story collection, *Dark Carnival* (1947); many of these stories were reprinted in the highly regarded collection *The October Country* (1955). From then on, his fiction was regularly recognized with awards and selected for anthologies. In 1949, the year the first of his four daughters was born, the National

Fantasy Fan Federation selected him best author of the year.

Bradbury's career continued to advance and then to diversify after 1949. *The Martian Chronicles* (1950) became one of the first science-fiction works to receive serious attention from the mainstream literary establishment when reviewer Christopher Isherwood praised it highly. (In 1977-1978, the play version would receive five Los Angeles Drama Critics Circle Awards.) Then followed a pattern of publishing collections of stories interspersed with new novels and other activities that included screenplays, musical theater, drama, and poetry. His best-known fiction appeared before 1963: *The Martian Chronicles, Fahrenheit 451* (1953), *Dandelion Wine, Something Wicked This Way Comes* (1962), and five collections of short stories. Each of the novels either grew from earlier published stories or was constructed of earlier stories worked together into a longer work. During this period, he also traveled to Ireland, where he worked on the screenplay for director John Huston's 1956 film version of Herman Melville's classic novel, *Moby Dick* (1851).

After 1963, Bradbury continued to publish short-story collections, but he devoted more of his energy to other areas, especially drama. His first collection of short plays, *The Anthem Sprinters and Other Antics* (1963), grew out of his six months in Ireland. He produced two shows based on his own works: *The World of Ray Bradbury* (1964) and *The Wonderful Ice Cream Suit* (1965). His other works in the 1960's included a cantata and a film history of America for the 1964 New York World's Fair. Though his interests in fiction and drama continued into the 1970's, he also turned his attention more decisively toward poetry, publishing three volumes and then collecting them into a single volume, *The Complete Poems of Ray Bradbury* (1982). During this period, he wrote much nonfiction prose for magazines ranging from *Life* to *Playboy*.

Film productions of Bradbury's works include *Fahrenheit 451* (1966), *The Illustrated Man* (1969), *The Martian Chronicles* (1980), and *Something Wicked This Way Comes* (1984). Of these adaptations, only French filmmaker François Truffaut's *Fahrenheit 451* was widely praised by film critics. Many of Bradbury's short stories have been adapted for television, some with great success. His own ani-

mated short film, *Icarus Montgolfier Wright*, was nominated for an Academy Award in 1962.

After 1980, Bradbury collected some of his early detective stories in *A Memory of Murder* (1984) and then published a detective novel, *Death Is a Lonely Business* (1985), and a gothic thriller set in Hollywood, *A Graveyard for Lunatics* (1990). In 1985, he began a series of adaptations of his own stories for a cable television series, *The Ray Bradbury Television Theater*. His awards include a life achievement award from the World Fantasy Convention (1977), a Gandalf "Grand Master" award at the Hugo Award Ceremonies of 1980, the Jules Verne Award (1984), the PEN Body of Work Award (1985), a Star on the Hollywood Walk of Fame (2002), and the National Medal of the Arts (2004). His wife of fifty-six years, Marguerite, died in 2003, survived by Bradbury and their four daughters.

Bradbury's achievements are mainly in fantasy and science fiction. His drama and film scripts have been well received, but his poetry has not. Continuing attention from literary scholars and cultural historians suggests that he will surely be remembered for the powerful and thoughtful storytelling that brought him to prominence in the 1950's. Bradbury's achievement opened a generation's hearts and minds to the worlds of imagination and wonder in fantasy and science fiction, beginning an era of wide popularity for and of scholarly interest in genres that had been on the fringe of modern culture.

ANALYSIS

Literary critic David Mogen has characterized well the central motif of Ray Bradbury's fiction: joyous absorption in the experience of living. In each of his major works, this joy in living plays a crucial role. Mogen sees this attitude in Bradbury's own life—in his prolific career with its many directions and in his nonfiction accounts of his life and career. One could guess this about Bradbury merely by looking at his book titles, not only those that recommend enthusiastic exploration or offer medicines for melancholy but also those that are drawn from visionary poets such as Walt Whitman and William Butler Yeats.

The dominant thematic note in Bradbury's fiction is a kind of hopefulness for humanity. Mogen and another critic, Gary K. Wolfe, have noted that Bradbury's optimism has roots in two major Western myths that have been important to many American writers: the frontier and the Garden of Eden. For Bradbury, the stars are the new frontier, humanity's next field of exploration and expansion. The stars also become a new Eden, an extension of the hope for new beginnings that idealistic explorers saw in America and that F. Scott Fitzgerald so eloquently captured in his description of the "fresh, green breast of the new world" at the end of a novel Bradbury admired, *The Great Gatsby* (1925).

Mogen sums up Bradbury's hopefulness by describing him as a visionary "who believes the human race will conquer death through spiritual rebirth in unearthly new frontiers." Bradbury's readers are aware of the dark elements in his fiction, however: the tales of terror collected in *The October Country*, the threatening ravine that cuts through Green Town, and the technological dystopias (of which *Fahrenheit 451* is the main example). Bradbury is acutely aware that human beings are capable of evil and contain darkness. He seems to see humanity as destined ultimately for transcendence of the kind described by nineteenth century American Romantic authors such as Whitman and Ralph Waldo Emerson, in which humanity approaches becoming godlike. Yet Bradbury also sees humanity in the present as blind to its best interests, selfish, turning technology to destructive rather than creative and imaginative ends, in continuous danger of self-destruction.

In a discussion of *The Halloween Tree* (1972), a lesser-known fable for young readers, Mogen illustrates what Bradbury sees as one of the greatest dangers facing modern humanity, the paralysis of imagination before the fear of death. This is also one of the main themes of *Fahrenheit 451*, and it appears in many of Bradbury's works. The purpose of the tale of terror, for Bradbury, is to help the individual human imagination symbolically confront its mortality. If people fail to face and deal with their deaths, they become the victims of terror, and the results of this victimization often include a drive for meaningless power and the impulse to impose a single order upon human experience.

In several of his works, this imposition of order appears as attempts to turn off the imagination, which is a source of multiple ideas of order. *Fahrenheit 451* offers a vivid picture of a society so afraid of death that it attempts to be a happiness machine, filling people's lives with empty, supposedly pain-less electronic stimuli and censoring all the great ideas and great books in the history of civilization. While such a society believes that it is escaping death somehow, it is in fact running directly toward death in the form of a military holocaust. The two major Green Town novels, *Dandelion Wine* and *Something Wicked This Way Comes*, show individuals facing death and the temptation to grasp evil power to evade death.

Bradbury's works show his optimistic faith in a fulfilling human destiny in some future time and place, and they also show his understanding of the barriers that humanity must overcome on its journey to this destiny and of the human limitations people are likely to carry with them into any future.

THE MARTIAN CHRONICLES

First published: 1950
Type of work: Short stories

Americans explore and colonize Mars, then abandon the colony. When atomic war breaks out on Earth, a few refugees return to Mars after Earth civilization is destroyed.

In the 1940's, Bradbury had established himself as a highly popular short-story writer. When a Doubleday editor encouraged him to try connecting some of his stories into a unified, novelistic collection, Bradbury quickly responded with *The Martian Chronicles*, a group of stories about people from Earth colonizing Mars.

The idea of the colonization of Mars had long fascinated Bradbury. When he produced *The Martian Chronicles*, he had published more than ten Martian stories, and he continued to produce more after the book was published. This book became the first of several Bradbury works that are called novels not because they have the traditional plot characteristics of the novel but because they are somewhat unified collections of related stories, rather like Sherwood Anderson's *Winesburg, Ohio* (1919). Bradbury repeated this form with varying success in *The Illustrated Man* (1951) and *Dandelion Wine*.

The Martian Chronicles is an apt title. Bradbury structured the book as a loose chronicle, begin-

ning in 1999 with the first expedition to Mars and ending in 2026, with what is probably the last. The chronological ordering establishes a strong forward movement in the first one-third of the book, which deals with four exploratory expeditions from 1999 to 2001. Roughly the middle one-third contains stories and episodes which, though placed from 2001 to 2005, are not very sequential. They seem more like a gathering of incidents illustrating aspects of a colonial period. The final third of the book, though it spans 2005 to 2026, really concentrates on the beginning and the end of this period. In 2005, atomic war begins to destroy Earth civilization, draws most of the Martian colonists back to their home planet, and effectively brings an end to space travel. In 2026, Earth is devastated, but a remnant of idealists from Earth escapes to Mars, hoping to start over.

While the overarching structure of a chronicle binds the book together at the beginning and end, there are other important unifying elements. One major element is the metaphor of the frontier. Bradbury repeatedly returns to the idea of Mars as a new frontier. The planet is a new world (like America), populated at first by predominantly peaceful, intelligent beings much like humans, though they have telepathic powers and a slightly different technology. The Martians find themselves playing the role of Americans Indians in the frontier metaphor, resisting invasion somewhat haphazardly until almost completely wiped out by a plague of chicken pox accidentally brought from Earth. There are no "Indian wars," but the abandoned cities and artifacts of Martian civilization become objects of interest, wonder, exploitation, and wanton destruction by the later colonists. The Martians, after their demise, produce converts, people who believe that the Martian civilization was better than their own and set out in various ways to imitate what they believe it was. This motif of conversion into Martians remains important throughout the book and becomes its final note.

The colonial phase begins with a Johnny Apple-seed character who dreams of the desert world becoming a green world and sets out on foot to plant trees over large areas. Bradbury's episodes and sketches present positive and negative aspects of the United States' colonial history. On the negative side are exploiters and materialist dreamers who ignore the spiritual significance of this new beginning and seize upon the dross—the chances for wealth and power available on a comparatively free frontier. On the positive side are those who come to Mars in search of spiritual freedoms denied on Earth. Among them is a large group of southern blacks who see in Mars the chance to gain what the United States has denied them. Their story, told in "Way in the Middle of the Air," may seem rather naïvely conceived when read by twenty-first century readers, but sketches such as this one gave Bradbury a reputation for radicalism in 1950. Among the spiritual questers is William Stendahl, who in "Usher II" prefigures themes in *Fahrenheit 451*, using Mars to escape from anti-imagination book censors on Earth and to take a poetically just revenge upon some of them.

In the last third of the book, Bradbury complicates the frontier metaphor by foregrounding the Eden myth that stands behind it and mixing in the new terror that existed during the period following World War II when he produced this book—the threat of atomic holocaust. In long years of war, Earth finally reduces itself to rubble, and at the last a small group of people flees to Mars, determined to start over and do things right this time. The image of a remnant of the spiritually pure leaving behind a hopelessly corrupt civilization to start anew is, of course, at the center of the American myth of the frontier.

"Pioneers" bringing their purity to an innocent and empty place evokes the idea of Eden regained, where a truly new start is possible. Added to these elements, however, is a feature that points to the profundity of the optimism behind this book that so vividly portrays humanity's failures and weaknesses. Remaining on Mars are the remnants of an ancient and wise Martian civilization and perhaps even some actual Martians. For humans to be converted into Martians, to become products of the place and its native spiritual presences, may lead to a true advance for humanity beyond the blind and selfish passions that have once again produced holocaust.

The idea of a saving remnant of the spiritually chosen pervades the Bible and the Judeo-Christian tradition. It also is important to Bradbury and appears regularly in his stories. This mythic pattern is one of the more important indications of optimism in Bradbury's fiction. He often tells stories such as this one, in which civilization dies because of its failures of wisdom, compassion, and imagination. Nearly always, however, the pattern includes a small new beginning by those whose vision is cleansed by suffering and who vow to preserve the best of the past and leave the worst behind, and this pattern converts Armageddon into a step toward salvation.

As the first work of American science fiction to gain a truly broad reading public, this book is of considerable historical importance in modern American literature. Although literary critics disagree about the book's artistic merits, *The Martian Chronicles* promises to remain in print as a popular favorite.

FAHRENHEIT 451

First published: 1953
Type of work: Novel

In a future United States, a man dedicated to burning all of humanity's great writings discovers he has been mistaken.

Fahrenheit 451—named for the temperature at which paper ignites and burns—is Bradbury's best-known novel and is probably also his best. Based on an earlier story, "The Fireman" (1950), and developing the censorship theme that appears in several other Bradbury works, this novel presents the dystopia that Bradbury may fear most.

In a future United States, the lowest common denominator of culture has imposed its ideas of happiness upon the whole culture. The universal idea of happiness has become an extrapolation of sitting in front of a television with a six-pack of beer, free of hard work, of complex human relationships, and of the disturbing stimulation of the ideas and images of the great artists and thinkers. In the future, television screens can be all four walls of a room. There, the viewer participates in the families and adventures that appear on "the walls" by subscribing to and then acting out a viewer script. When the walls fail to interest, one places receivers in the ears and blankets the mind with pleasant sound that blocks out awareness of self and world.

Montag, the protagonist, is a "fireman." His team's job is to burn books and arrest their possess-ors. Not all books are outlawed—only those that stimulate the imagination with their complex ideas or vivid images of human possibility, those books that encourage people to aspire toward thought and experience beyond the ordinary.

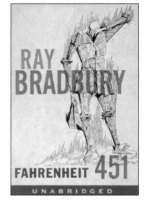

Though this story is often compared with George Orwell's dystopia *Nineteen Eighty-Four* (1949), the two books differ significantly. An especially important difference is the role of government. The tyranny of an oligarchy in *1984* is matched by the tyranny of the anti-intellectual majority in *Fahrenheit 451*. Bradbury's novel partakes of the atmosphere of anticommunism following World War II. The government seems distant, unconcerned with life in Montag's city, involved instead in the threat of atomic war that hangs over the nation. Beatty, Montag's boss, in a series of lectures on the history and theory of the firefighters' work, makes clear that the firemen act on behalf of ordinary people who know what happiness is, who want to be sure that everyone is happy, and who want to extirpate any who fail to conform to this idea of happiness. Book collectors are discovered and exposed by their neighbors, acting from a sense of civic duty; no secret police are required.

Montag's story develops rapidly and inexorably in three stages. Part 1, "The Hearth and the Sala-mander," presents a series of discoveries that lead Montag to steal and read from the books he is supposed to burn. He meets an imaginative young girl, Clarisse, who opens him to ways of seeing that he finds attractive. He discovers that his wife, Mildred, is not happy, despite her self-deluding assertions to the contrary, and that he is not happy either. Their lives are empty and teeter on the edge of self-destruction, held back only by the constant vacuous stimulation of electronic media and drugs. Montag is the salamander, the dragon of dangerous fire, but he discovers that his hearth is cold, that his home lacks spirit and love; it has no central animating principle. When he sees a woman who prefers to be burned with her books rather than to give them up, he realizes that they must contain something of great importance. He begins to read the books that he has almost unconsciously been hiding away in his home.

In part 2, "The Sieve and the Sand," Montag tries to understand the wisdom he believes is in his books, which include the Bible and poems such as Matthew Arnold's "Dover Beach" (1867). He finds that, in several ways, his mind is like a sieve; he does not know how to make sense of what he reads without any intellectual training or context. Frustrated at the futility of his efforts, he takes dangerous risks. He contacts Faber, an unemployed professor in whom he once confided, and becomes aware of the possibility of rebellion. He finds himself bursting to talk about what he has read and tries communicating with his wife. These activities bring him increasingly to the attention of Beatty, who has long suspected that Montag does not fit the fireman mold. Part 2 ends when Montag's team answers an alarm that brings them to his own house.

Part 3, "Burning Bright," tells of Montag's escape from his job and the imprisoning city. He becomes a fugitive when he kills Beatty rather than betray Faber. Montag concludes that Beatty wanted to be killed, that he manipulated the crisis before Montag's burning home in order to bring about his own death. This observation highlights one of the more puzzling aspects of the novel, which is how to read Beatty's character. Beatty is the spokesman for the majority point of view, yet the arguments he offers for keeping literature out of people's hands and destroying those who insist upon reading are filled with references to and quotations from the very works he opposes. Montag's final realization seems to suggest that Beatty, like Mildred, deludes himself into believing he is happy. Beatty, however, unlike Mildred, may come to understand his duplicity, leading him actively to seek death.

Montag's harrowing flight brings him finally to a hearth, where vagrants gathered around a fire warm themselves and form a community. He soon learns that they have met there to receive him into their fragile underground—a group of rebels who survive relatively unmolested in the countryside and whose rebellion consists essentially of memorizing great books in preparation for the day when they can be written down again. These people can help him understand the books they remember, and he himself can become a "book" by sharing what he has managed to remember from Ecclesiastes and the Book of Revelation. As he joins this community, atomic war comes to the nation, and the city he has left behind is consumed in flames. They believe that all the other cities are also being destroyed and therefore that their rebel group represents the phoenix, the new civilization to arise from the ruins of the old.

Bleak as this novel may appear, emphasizing as it does some of the worst things people can do, it nevertheless ends with an expression of hope that goes beyond the idea of the biblical saving remnant suggested by the phoenix image. One of the rebels speaks for them all, and probably for Bradbury, when he says, "We know all the damn silly things we've done for a thousand years and as long as we know that and always have it around where we can see it, some day we'll stop making the goddam funeral pyres and jumping in the middle of them." In order to know what those silly things are and where they lead, one must have the books that tell about them. One of the reasons the society of *Fahrenheit 451* fails is that it made a happiness machine that erased the past and prevented people from imagining the future. With their minds locked in the present, they could do nothing to stop the fiery holocaust from falling upon them.

DANDELION WINE

First published: 1957
Type of work: Novel

Twelve-year-old Douglas Spaulding and his friends in Green Town, Illinois, in the summer of 1928 have adventures that teach them about the joys and the pains of living.

Dandelion Wine, like *The Martian Chronicles*, was constructed from previously published stories. Bradbury made a significantly greater effort to turn these stories into a unified book, however, by revising the stories with care and by writing connecting material. He also provided a greater impression of unity than in *The Martian Chronicles* by dropping the stories' original titles and using no table of contents. *Dandelion Wine* is perhaps the most autobiographical of his novels. Elements of Bradbury can be seen in both Douglas Spaulding and his younger brother, Tom. Green Town, on Lake Michigan, is similar to Bradbury's childhood home, Waukegan, Illinois, and the Spaulding family is like the Bradbury family.

Readers have noticed the similarities between *Dandelion Wine* and Sherwood Anderson's *Winesburg, Ohio*. Bradbury's book differs in that the predominant point of view is preadolescent, so that the spiritual anguish and the problems of sexuality that are important in Anderson's book are virtually absent in Bradbury's. The childish exuberance in the feeling of being alive that is a central theme both exceeds the energy and falls short of the profundity one sees in George Willard, Anderson's youthful protagonist. Bradbury presents a vivid picture of a boy's life in a small midwestern town early in the twentieth century.

In the summer of 1928, Doug awakens to the momentous sense that being physically and spiritually alive is a great gift, and he begins to keep a written record of his life. This consists of two lists: One contains events that happen every summer like rituals—"Ceremonies"; the other contains new and unprecedented events—"Revelations."

Once Bradbury has established Doug as a boy awakening to a sense of the wonder of life and wanting to understand it in his imagination, the structure of the book falls into a collection of sketches and stories, roughly chronological. Each story is well-connected to the overarching structure, often in several ways. The story may contain a ceremony, a revelation, or a combination of the two, and it may contribute as well to one of several thematic patterns that structure Doug's awakening.

One of the main patterns is that of loss. Doug, his brother, and their friends interact with a number of very old people during this summer. One ancient man becomes their time machine, transport-ing them to the wonderful places he has been by telling stories. A Civil War veteran who cannot remember which side he was on, Colonel Freeleigh can nevertheless still picture and describe vividly the day he saw a giant herd of bison on the prairie or a battle in the war. Before the summer is over, he dies. So does Doug's great-grandmother, who loved to repair the shingle roof each summer. His best friend moves away. A pair of elderly ladies permanently park their electric car after hitting a pedestrian. The trolley makes its last run and is replaced by a bus. Doug is almost present at two killings. The arcade's ancient mechanical prophetess, the Tarot Witch, finally breaks down. Great and small, parts of Doug's world slip away, and with the realization that he is richly alive comes the realization that he must die.

At the end of the summer, Doug becomes mysteriously ill. His brother, Tom, realizes that Doug wants to die because he has lost so much during the summer. This will-to-death also arises from a deeper source, Doug's fear of facing and accepting his own mortality, an experience that Bradbury says he had when he was thirteen: "I discovered I could die, and that scared the hell out of me. And I thought, 'How do you escape *that* knowledge? Well, I'll *kill* myself.'"

Doug is cured by a kind of magic, when his friend the local junk man gives him two bottles of fragrant air to breathe in. Like the bottles of dandelion wine that the boys and their grandfather produce throughout the summer, these bottles contain reminders of the richness of life to be enjoyed in those moments when it might be forgotten. Doug realizes this; he also comes to feel an obligation to live in order to pass on to others the wonderful, if temporary, gift of life that he has received. His first success at passing on this gift comes when he restores his grandmother's magical power to produce delicious meals out of a chaotic kitchen after the too-orderly Aunt Rose ruins her cooking by organizing her. *Dandelion Wine* is a particularly rewarding novel for younger readers, but its fanciful humor and vivid portrait of small-town life can be enjoyed by older readers as well.

SOMETHING WICKED THIS WAY COMES

First published: 1962
Type of work: Novel

Jim Nightshade, Will Holloway, and his father, Charles Holloway, must face their deepest fears and desires when a dark carnival tempts them to surrender their souls in exchange for meaningless power.

"By the pricking of my thumbs,! something wicked this way comes." In William Shakespeare's *Macbeth* (c. 1605), the witches speak these lines as Macbeth approaches for his second meeting with them. He has come because he has found his ill-gotten power empty and insecure. The witches speak out of sympathy for the evil they have cultivated in him. When Charles Holloway quotes these lines in *Something Wicked This Way Comes*, he is also speaking of the sympathy of the evil that lurks always in the hearts of the good for the greater evil in the hearts of those who have given in—who have agreed to trade something for nothing, thus converting themselves into grotesques who feed on the pain and fear of others.

Quasi-allegorical in form, this novel, like *Dandelion Wine*, is set in Green Town and seems aimed at young readers. Two boys deal with the temptations of evil presented by Cooger and Dark's Pandemonium Shadow Show. Will Holloway and Jim Nightshade are best friends and neighbors. Will, son of Charles, was born just before midnight, Jim, just after midnight on Halloween Day. Will seems the natural child of reason and goodness, but fatherless Jim finds in himself an attraction to danger, to power, and to evil. Their friendship binds them together in mutual dependence and defense.

The novel is divided into three parts. In the first, "Arrivals," the Cooger and Dark carnival comes to Green Town at 3 A.M. on a Friday, the week before Halloween. No sooner does it arrive than impossible things begin to occur. Miss Foley, a teacher, is terrified upon seeing her treasured little-girl identity eaten away by age in the maze of mirrors. The boys meet a boy who is revealed to be Cooger, having somehow returned to the age of 12, and through their accidental interference with the magical carousel that changes people's ages, they age him to 120.

The mirror maze and the carousel are the main instruments that the carnival uses to capture those lonely people who dream of gaining power by transforming themselves. The mirror maze shows them what they want to be and makes them fear old age and death. The carousel, by carrying them backward or forward, makes them the age they believe they wish to be. However, Dark, the show's proprietor, a version of the illustrated man from Bradbury's second story collection, always cheats, never giving people exactly what they believe they want but rather some extreme version of it. As a result, they tend to become his slaves, wanting another ride on his machine, and so they become part of his traveling freak show.

In Jim, Dark sees a potential partner, one who might help him carry on the show. Jim's desire is to become instantly older and more powerful. Bradbury does not explore this desire; rather, Jim seems to be a projection of the otherwise invisible dark side of Will. By the end of the first part, Will and Jim have gained enough knowledge of Dark's work to realize that he will catch and destroy them to use them if he can. In the second part, "Pursuits," the boys hide from him and try to discover a way to deal with him. By themselves, they find they cannot, though they are resourceful in their opposition. They enlist the help of Charles, Will's father.

Charles Holloway combines elements of both Jim and Will in his own past. He married late, after trying to make himself into his own ideal for thirty-nine years. He found eventually that life is not simple and fine, that one never becomes the ideal one dreams. Instead, as he tells Will, a person makes choices from one moment to the next, living into the future in a constant struggle against the temptations of nonbeing. There is no final arrival, only pursuit. Will's struggle to stay with Jim and protect him is parallel to Charles's struggle to come to terms with himself. Charles's main regret is that he took so long to begin his life, so he is susceptible to the carousel's temptation to roll back the years.

Charles is janitor at the Green Town library. There the most intense phase of the struggle begins. The second part ends when Dark makes his way into the library early Sunday evening, disables Charles, and captures Will and Jim. Charles almost gives in to death in this scene, to the power of the Dust Witch, one of Dark's accomplices, to stop one's heart. In the face of death, Charles realizes that human life is a bleak and meaningless joke. This nihilism leads him not to despair, however, but to laughter, for in the face of mortality, desire and temptation appear ridiculous. His laughter repels the witch and becomes the weapon by which he defeats Dark in the last part, "Departures."

Charles rescues Will and, together, they finally recover Jim from Dark's power, using the forces of laughter, kindness, and joy. With Dark's death, the freaks become free of their magic prison, represented by the tattoos that cover Dark's body. The carnival dissipates. Charles points out, however, that humanity is not free of temptation, for the desire for empty impossibilities is in them all, and there will be many other attempts to exploit this desire in their long lives.

Critical reaction to Bradbury's second traditional novel was mixed. Those who disliked it found it overwritten. There are many passages in the novel that remind one of Whitman's *Song of Myself* (1855), with sentences of many clauses celebrating and elaborating a scene or realization. As a result, the novel is not efficient in its development and, to some readers, seems inflated with unnecessary poetic prose. Others, however, respond positively to the fast pace of the action and to the marshaling of fantasy elements that produce an entertaining adventure/allegory.

SUMMARY

Throughout his career, Bradbury has exhibited both an enthusiasm for experience and an awareness of the weaknesses that repeatedly bring humanity to the brink of self-extinction; those elements are the hallmarks of his fiction. In his science fiction and in the fantasies based on his childhood, Bradbury has produced a memorable

and influential body of writing, notably in *The Martian Chronicles* and *Fahrenheit 451*. With moving and imaginative stories told in a lively, poetic style, he brought American science fiction and fantasy to the attention of a mass audience, helping to make possible a renaissance in these genres.

Terry Heller

DISCUSSION TOPICS

- Ray Bradbury seems always to have known what he wanted to do and how to get it done. Of the initiatives he has taken in his life, which do you think have contributed most fruitfully to his writing?
- Identify the resemblances between the Martians and American Indians in *The Martian Chronicles* and explain what they contribute to the total effect of the narrative.
- Montag is a grown man at the beginning of *Fahrenheit 451*, but what evidence do you see that he matures in the course of the novel?
- Some books probably intended for young readers turn out to be valuable reading for adults. Is *Dandelion Wine* such a book? Explain your response.
- Is Bradbury more convincing in his depiction of the dark side of life or in his hopefulness?
- Critics are inclined to discount the importance of popular writers in popular modes such as those Bradbury practices. What aspects of Bradbury's work entitle him to the status of serious writer?

BIBLIOGRAPHY

By the Author

SHORT FICTION:
Dark Carnival, 1947
The Martian Chronicles, 1950
The Illustrated Man, 1951
The Golden Apples of the Sun, 1953

The October Country, 1955
A Medicine for Melancholy, 1959
Twice Twenty-two, 1959
The Machineries of Joy, 1964
Autumn People, 1965
Vintage Bradbury, 1965
Tomorrow Midnight, 1966
I Sing the Body Electric!, 1969
Long After Midnight, 1976
"The Last Circus," and "The Electrocution," 1980
The Stories of Ray Bradbury, 1980
Dinosaur Tales, 1983
A Memory of Murder, 1984
The Toynbee Convector, 1988
Quicker than the Eye, 1996
Driving Blind, 1997
One More for the Road: A New Short Story Collection, 2002
Bradbury Stories: One Hundred of His Most Celebrated Tales, 2003
The Best of Ray Bradbury: The Graphic Novel, 2003
The Cat's Pajamas, 2004

LONG FICTION
Fahrenheit 451, 1953
Dandelion Wine, 1957
Something Wicked This Way Comes, 1962
Death Is a Lonely Business, 1985
A Graveyard for Lunatics: Another Tale of Two Cities, 1990
Green Shadows, White Whale, 1992
From the Dust Returned: A Family Remembrance, 2001
Let's All Kill Constance, 2003

DRAMA:
The Anthem Sprinters and Other Antics, pb. 1963
The World of Ray Bradbury: Three Fables of the Future, pr. 1964
The Day It Rained Forever, pb. 1966
The Pedestrian, pb. 1966
Dandelion Wine, pr. 1967 (adaptation of his novel)
Madrigals for the Space Age, pb. 1972
The Wonderful Ice Cream Suit, and Other Plays, pb. 1972
Pillar of Fire, and Other Plays for Today, Tomorrow, and Beyond Tomorrow, pb. 1975
That Ghost, That Bride of Time: Excerpts from a Play-in-Progress, pb. 1976
The Martian Chronicles, pr. 1977
Fahrenheit 451, pr. 1979 (musical)
A Device Out of Time, pb. 1986
On Stage: A Chrestomathy of His Plays, pb. 1991

SCREENPLAYS:
It Came from Outer Space, 1952 (with David Schwartz)
Moby Dick, 1956 (with John Huston)
Icarus Montgolfier Wright, 1961 (with George C. Johnson)
The Picasso Summer, 1969 (with Ed Weinberger)

POETRY:

Old Ahab's Friend, and Friend to Noah, Speaks His Piece: A Celebration, 1971
When Elephants Last in the Dooryard Bloomed: Celebrations for Almost Any Day in the Year, 1973
Where Robot Mice and Robot Men Run Round in Robot Towns: New Poems, Both Light and Dark, 1977
Twin Hieroglyphs That Swim the River Dust, 1978
The Bike Repairman, 1978
The Aqueduct, 1979
The Haunted Computer and the Android Pope, 1981
The Complete Poems of Ray Bradbury, 1982
Forever and the Earth, 1984
Death Has Lost Its Charm for Me, 1987
With Cat for Comforter, 1997 (with Loise Max)
Dogs Think That Every Day Is Christmas, 1997
I Live By the Invisible: New and Selected Poems, 2002

NONFICTION

Teacher's Guide to Science Fiction, 1968 (with Lewy Olfson)
Mars and the Mind of Man, 1973
"Zen and the Art of Writing" and "The Joy of Writing": Two Essays, 1973
The Mummies of Guanajuato, 1978
The Art of the Playboy, 1985
Zen in the Art of Writing: Essays on Creativity, 1989
Yestermorrow: Obvious Answers to Impossible Futures, 1991
Conversations with Ray Bradbury (Steven L. Aggelis, editor), 2004

CHILDREN'S LITERATURE:

Switch on the Night, 1955
R Is for Rocket, 1962
S Is for Space, 1966
The Halloween Tree, 1972
Fever Dream, 1987
Ahmed and the Oblivion Machines: A Fable, 1998

EDITED TEXTS:

Timeless Stories for Today and Tomorrow, 1952
The Circus of Dr. Lao, and Other Improbable Stories, 1956

About the Author

Bloom, Harold, ed. *Ray Bradbury*. New York: Chelsea House, 2001.
————. *Ray Bradbury's "Fahrenheit 451."* New York: Chelsea House, 2001.
Eller, Jonathan R., and William F. Touponce. *Ray Bradbury: The Life of Fiction*. Kent, Ohio: Kent State University Press, 2004.
Reid, Robin Ann. *Ray Bradbury: A Critical Companion*. Westport, Conn.: Greenwood Press, 2000.
Touponce, William F. *Naming the Unnameable: Ray Bradbury and the Fantastic After Freud*. Mercer Island, Wash.: Starmont House, 1997.
Weist, Jerry, and Donn Albright. *Bradbury, an Illustrated Life: A Journey to Far Metaphor*. New York: William Morrow, 2002.
Weller, Sam. *The Bradbury Chronicles: The Life of Ray Bradbury*. New York: William Morrow, 2005.

ANNE BRADSTREET

Born: Northampton, Northamptonshire, England
   c. 1612
Died: Andover, Massachusetts Bay Colony
   September 16, 1672

Blending Puritan religiosity, an awareness of the English literary tradition, and a talent for depicting domestic themes, Anne Bradstreet, one of the earliest Massachusetts Bay settlers, became America's first authentic poet.

BIOGRAPHY

Despite the prominence of both her father and her husband in the Massachusetts Bay Colony, facts about Anne Bradstreet are scarce, and her poems are the major source of biographical information. She was born Anne Dudley in Northampton, England, probably in 1612. From the age of seven, she lived in the household of the earl of Lincoln, whom her father served as a steward for more than a decade. As the child of a Puritan family, she became conscious of sinfulness early in life. Her physical health suffered. She regarded smallpox, which afflicted her at age sixteen, as a punishment for her "carnal" desires. In 1628, she was married to Simon Bradstreet. Two years later, the Bradstreet and Dudley families sailed to the New World on the *Arbella* along with John Winthrop and the original Massachusetts Bay colonists.

In the New World, the Bradstreets lived in several places before settling permanently in Merrimac (now Andover). Both her father and husband assumed leadership roles in the colony from the start. The former remained politically active into his seventies, serving four one-year terms as governor between 1634 and 1650 as well as thirteen terms as deputy governor. Her even more durable husband began as secretary of the colony, served thirty-three years as a commissioner of the New England Confederation, and in his seventies and eighties served as governor. He was also interested in frontier trading, and his frequent absences from home became the subject of two of his wife's best poems.

For some years after her marriage, Bradstreet continued to suffer from poor health and the added humiliation of not being able to bear Simon any children. It is not clear when she began writing poetry, but by the late 1640's she had written enough to justify, at least in the opinion of her admirers, a book. A family member or friend, probably her brother-in-law John Woodbridge, carried a manuscript of her poems to England. In 1650, the first book of poems by an American author, Bradstreet's *The Tenth Muse Lately Sprung Up in America*, appeared in England.

In the meantime, one of her concerns had been resolved, for she gave birth to eight children. From the evidence of her poems, she was a conscientious wife and mother. As Simon Bradstreet's wife, she was probably spared the worst household drudgery, but colonial life imposed severe hardships on a woman in any station. Nevertheless, she found time to compose long poems with such titles as "The Four Elements," "The Ages of Man," "The Humours," "The Four Seasons of the Year," and "The Four Monarchies." Today these poems seem derivative and amateurish, but "The Prologue," which is a defense of her resolution to pursue the male-dominated literary profession, remains an intriguing work.

Once it was in print, Bradstreet, conscious of the defects of her earlier work, revised it for a possible second edition. In "The Author to Her Book," she expresses chagrin over poems she characterizes as "ill-formed offspring"; she also composed additional poems of a quite different sort, including love poems to her husband and poems to and about her children. Her inclination to memorialize family events such as illnesses, deaths, and "deliverances" from these troubles sheds light on her life. Because she wrote a poem on the incident, for example, it is known that her house burned down on July 10, 1666. She also wrote religious meditations in both prose and verse. These more personal poems are much more concrete and vital than her earlier ones.

Bradstreet did not live to see the second edition of her book in print. She died on September 16, 1672, six years before the publication of the expanded edition. Another set of poems and prose meditations remained in manuscript until 1867. Bradstreet's legacy also includes her numerous descendants, among them such distinguished Americans as Wendell Phillips, the great abolitionist; Richard Henry Dana, Jr., author of *Two Years Before the Mast* (1840); the poet Oliver Wendell Holmes and his son, who served as a United States Supreme Court justice; and one of America's most important twentieth century poets, Edwin Arlington Robinson.

Though delicate in health, Bradstreet proved to be a woman of great interior strength and endurance. She not only ranks as America's first woman poet but also was America's first poet of indisputable literary quality.

ANALYSIS

Bradstreet benefited from an education unusually thorough for a woman of her time. Knowledgeable about history, theology, and science, she also demonstrates a familiarity with numerous earlier poets. She wrote an elegy on the famed soldier, diplomat, and poet Sir Philip Sidney that displays a keen interest in his sonnet sequence *Astrophel and Stella* (1591). She also appears to have been influenced by the English meditative poets of her own century. The poet she honors most highly, however, is the French religious poet Guillaume de Salluste (Seigneur du Bartas), whose epic *La Semaine* (1578; *The Divine Weeks*, 1608) was a favorite among Puritans.

In her early writing, Bradstreet favored quaternions, poems with subject groups of four. For centuries, the material world was believed to be composed of four elements: fire, air, earth, and water. Thus, human temperaments and physiological types were explained as various mixtures of these elements and were called "humours." Two of

Bradstreet's quaternions consist of successive speeches by the respective elements and humours in which they boast of their own importance. "The Ages of Man" follows a similar pattern, with Childhood, Youth, Middle Age, and Old Age speaking in turn. While rather stiff and uninspired, these poems show that Bradstreet had accumulated considerable astronomical, geographical, historical, theological, medical, and psychological information. "The Four Seasons of the Year," though occasionally betraying a love of nature, is similarly conventional and bookish.

Her longest poem, "The Four Monarchies," versifies in 3,432 lines a portion of ancient history for which her chief source was Sir Walter Raleigh's *History of the World* (1614). The last and shortest history is of the Roman monarchy, and it culminates in "An Apology" for being unable to carry it out to its projected length. The loss is not great, for "The Four Monarchies," which labors to show the vanity and futility of ancient pre-Christian ambition, is a tedious poem.

Those and a dozen other, shorter poems make up her *The Tenth Muse Lately Sprung Up in America.* Except for the introductory poem, "The Prologue," which provocatively asserts her commitment to poetry even as it seeks to disarm masculine criticism of her pioneering work, this collection was not responsible for establishing her reputation as one of the two most significant poets of the colonial era in America (Edward Taylor being the other). Readers must turn to the posthumously published poems to appreciate Bradstreet's poetry.

Motherhood became a paramount fact of her life and also one of her favorite metaphors. In "The Author to Her Book," her book is an ill-favored child whom she has labored to improve. She wittily bids her child not to fall into a "critic's hands" but to explain that her mother has had to turn her "rambling brat" out of the house because of poverty. This metaphor is useful in establishing the mock-modest tone that she employs when referring to her own work. Bradstreet is not being hypocritical; rather, she enjoys assuming the role of the hard-working amateur—a role made somewhat more difficult to sustain by the publication of her book. She reminds her critically inclined readers that few parents would care to be held completely responsible for their offspring.

Her own children are often her true subject as

well. Her family poems avoid sentimentality and brim with the honest sentiment of a woman who trusts in heaven but loves her husband and children beyond any other earthly thing. If her book becomes her child, her children in one poem become the birds of her nest. Inevitably the theme of death arises. "Before the Birth of One of Her Children," which is addressed to her husband, expresses the fear of the colonial housewife—for whom each pregnancy is the prelude to a possible death. Several other poems memorialize grandchildren who died in infancy or early childhood. The feeling in these poems is artistically restrained, and the attitude is one of resignation to God's mysterious will, yet there can be no doubt of the genuineness of her grief on each occasion.

Two poems occasioned by her husband's absence on business focus on her intense love for him. In one, she argues that her love exceeds that of the female deer, dove, and fish for their absent mates; when he returns, they will "browse," "roost," and "glide" together. In the other, "A Letter to Her Husband, Absent upon Public Employment," she uses the sun to describe her husband and her love for him.

Like most of the 1650 poems, "Contemplations" is conventional and rather general in its thought, but the voice is unmistakably Bradstreet's. It is a compact spiritual autobiography affirming that the hope of heaven is the only security worth striving for. Her fine prose work, "Meditations Divine and Moral," addressed to her son Simon and unpublished until 1867, demonstrates her good sense, poet's ear, and talent for grounding her religious outlook in close observations of the world around her.

Bradstreet was a poet of considerable talent who, lacking fruitful contact with other poets, nevertheless learned to write by studying the works of past poets. Discovering her true subject matter in religious and domestic themes, she also fulfilled the demanding role of a colonial housewife with a large family. American critics were somewhat tardy in recognizing her accomplishments, but it is safe to say that her best poems will be long remembered.

"THE PROLOGUE"

First published: 1650 (collected in *The Tenth Muse Lately Sprung Up in America*, 1650)
Type of work: Poem

A colonial woman begins her book of poems by defending it against captious criticism.

"The Prologue" is Bradstreet's apology for her book of poems. At first, it seems like an apology in the common sense of the word, for she refers to her "foolish, broken, blemished Muse" and begs elaborate pardon that her poems are not so fine as those of other poets, although she insists that she is doing the best she can. Upon closer inspection, "The Prologue" turns out to be an apology in the literary sense of a defense of her art. One of her favorite poets, Sir Philip Sidney, also referred to his own work condescendingly. This attitude has a special meaning when expressed by a woman writing in a New World Puritan outpost before 1650.

"The Prologue" is written in eight six-line iambic pentameter stanzas, using the rhyme scheme *ababcc*. Bradstreet begins by advising her reader that she has no ambition to write an elaborate, important poem such as an epic. She lauds the sixteenth century French poet du Bartas but notes that her work will be much simpler. She hopes it will not be judged too harshly, for her ability is severely limited.

In the second half of the poem, she modifies her defense. She acknowledges that men expect women to practice feminine arts such as needlework and refuse to recognize any value in a woman's poem. She intimates that the Greeks, in making the Muses feminine, had more regard for feminine creativity but concedes that this argument will not convince the men. She then concludes with two stanzas confessing the superiority of male poets but asking "some small acknowledgment" of women's efforts. After all, Bradstreet's "lowly lines" will simply make men's poetry look better by comparison.

Even read literally, as it often has been read, this poem displays clever strategy. How could any fair-minded person expect competent poetry from uneducated people who had no opportunities to travel or associate familiarly with other poets and who spent most of their lives bearing children and serving their needs and those of their husbands? Even when blessed with talent and sufficient leisure to compose, such writers offered no threat to the male poets, many of whom could take education, frequent association with their peers, and leisure for granted. By displaying humility at the beginning of her book, Bradstreet hoped to forestall, or at least minimize, the inevitable criticism of a woman poet.

It is difficult, however, to escape the conviction that irony lurks everywhere in this poem. In the first place, it is scarcely possible that Bradstreet considered her brain "weak or wounded" as she styles it in the poem; talented people are usually aware of their talent. If she cannot write "of wars, of captains, and of kings," she has the resources to write about her husband, children and grandchildren, domestic life (including the cruel experience of watching her home burn), and the spiritual struggle common to all Puritans.

The last four stanzas of the poem betray signs of an ironic counterattack upon her critics. Her fifth stanza almost undermines the effect toward which she is working by nearly boiling over with indignation at men's refusal to accept the woman poet. Such criticism is "carping"; it maintains that any feminine poetic success must be the result of either plagiarism or "chance." Why did men call poetry "Calliope's own child"? The answer that she attributes to the men—that the Greeks did nothing but "play the fools and lie"—mimics a weak-kneed response.

In her final stanza, she catches the true satiric tone. Addressing "ye highflown quills that soar the skies," she asks not for the "bays," or traditional laurel wreath honoring poetic achievement, but for a "thyme or parsley wreath" befitting the woman who is expected to reign chiefly in the kitchen. She might as well have asked for a bay leaf, the common kitchen spice, but such a request might have reminded her audience that the laurel leaf and the bay leaf are closely affiliated. In effect, Bradstreet has asked for a recognition less humble than it seems. Her final point—that her "unrefined ore" will make the male poets' "gold" appear to shine more brightly—taunts the egotism of the males, who are probably flying too high to notice.

"A Letter to Her Husband, Absent upon Public Employment"

First published: 1678 (collected in *Several Poems Compiled with Great Variety of Wit and Learning, Full of Delight*, 1678)
Type of work: Poem

In a verse letter to her absent husband, a woman affirms her love.

"A Letter to Her Husband, Absent upon Public Employment" is one of two Bradstreet poems on this subject. She must have been familiar with the classical epistle, or verse letter, which English poets had begun imitating in the sixteenth century. She addresses her husband by a series of metaphors, the main one being the sun. She likens herself to the earth in winter, lamenting "in black" the receding light and feeling "chilled" without him to warm her. She is home with only "those fruits which through thy heat I bore"—her children—as reminders. With her husband "southward gone," she finds the short winter days ironically long and tedious.

She continues to project her sun metaphor into the future. When he returns, the season will be summer figuratively and perhaps literally: "I wish my Sun may never set, but burn/ Within the Cancer of my glowing breast," a zodiacal allusion to early summer. She closes by reaffirming their married oneness: "Flesh of thy flesh, bone of thy bone,/ I here, thou there, yet both but one."

Though neither so intricate in form nor elaborate in imagery as John Donne's famous "A Valediction: Forbidding Mourning," published in 1633, this poem on the same theme shows Bradstreet's resourcefulness with imagery and able handling of her favorite pentameter couplets. While exhibiting great devotion to Simon, this poem succeeds because it also reflects devotion to the art of lyric verse.

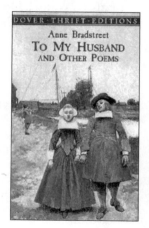

"In Reference to Her Children, 23 June 1659"

First published: 1678 (collected in *Several Poems Compiled with Great Variety of Wit and Learning, Full of Delight*, 1678)
Type of work: Poem

A mother bids a loving farewell in turn to each of her eight children.

One of Bradstreet's most charming poems, "In Reference to Her Children, 23 June 1659" distinguishes and describes each of the "eight birds" from her "nest." Several times she indicates precise dates for her poems or the events they describe; this one suggests a time of relative leisure after five of the eight have left home.

She maintains the bird metaphor throughout the poem's ninety-six lines, describing the various "flights" of five of her children and her concerns about those remaining in the nest. Four are "cocks," four "hens." The oldest having flown "to regions far," she longs for his return. The next two, both girls, have been married, while the second son is at "the academy," where he will learn to sing better than nightingales. Number five is "mongst the shrubs and bushes," which may mean that he has taken up farming. She hopes that the youngest three will not fall victim to birdcatchers, stone-throwers, or hawks.

Recalling the pains and cares of their early childhood, she notes that their growing up has not ended her constant concern for their welfare. Going on to remind the children that her own days are numbered, she tells them that she expects to be singing among the angels soon. The closing lines beg her brood to emulate in their own families the loving attention and moral instruction she has bestowed on them, thus keeping her alive in a way. She ends by bidding her offspring farewell and assuring them that she will be happy if all goes well with them.

Forty-eight tetrameter couplets might seem rather a long time to keep the bird metaphor going, but Bradstreet's light touch sustains the reader's interest. Because she evokes her children as individuals and conveys her tender feeling for each of them, this poem written on a particular day for a particular family expresses the universality of mother love.

Summary

Beginning with ambitious but uninspired poems on remote subjects, Bradstreet proceeded to discover her vocation as a poet of more personal matters. Of the poems in the first edition of her book, only "The Prologue" anticipates the more intimate kind of poem for which she is now best known. Her typical subjects became birth, illness, recovery, death, leave-takings, and her love for her husband, her children, and God. Her witty elaborations of basic metaphors—her book as her child, her children as birds, her husband as the sun—show Bradstreet's poetic imagination at its best.

Robert P. Ellis

Discussion Topics

- Show how Anne Bradstreet exemplifies the commonplace that ambitious writers have to learn to concentrate on subjects and themes best suited to their own knowledge and understanding.

- Bradstreet pays much attention to formal poetic devices. Are her meters, stanzas, and rhymes appropriate to her subject matter and varied enough to be pleasing?

- Bradstreet writes rather frequently about what she has produced: her children and her poems. Discuss the metaphors she uses to characterize both.

- Do you agree that Bradstreet's "The Prologue" is a heavily ironic poem, or did she really fear that her work would not pass muster with able readers? Explain your answer carefully.

- Bradstreet is adept at turning the hardships of life into poetry. Cite some examples. What techniques does she employ in this endeavor?

- How does Bradstreet demonstrate her awareness of European Renaissance poetry?

BIBLIOGRAPHY

By the Author

POETRY:

The Tenth Muse Lately Sprung Up in America: Or, Several Poems Compiled with Great Variety of Wit and Learning, Full of Delight, 1650; revised and enlarged 1678 (as *Several Poems Compiled with Great Variety of Wit and Learning, Full of Delight*)

MISCELLANEOUS:

The Complete Works of Anne Bradstreet, 1981 (Joseph R. McElrath and Allan P. Robb, editors)

About the Author

Cowell, Pattie, and Ann Stanford, eds. *Critical Essays on Anne Bradstreet.* Boston: G. K. Hall, 1983.

Dolle, Raymond F. *Anne Bradstreet: A Reference Guide.* Boston: G. K. Hall, 1990.

Hammond, Jeffrey. *Sinful Self, Saintly Self.* Athens: University of Georgia Press, 1993.

Harde, Roxanne. "'Then Soul and Body Shall Unite': Anne Bradstreet's Theology of Embodiment." In *From Anne Bradstreet to Abraham Lincoln: Puritanism in America,* edited by Michael Schuldiner. Lewiston, N.Y.: Edwin Mellen Press, 2004.

Martin, Wendy. *An American Triptych: Anne Bradstreet, Emily Dickinson, Adrienne Rich.* Chapel Hill: University of North Carolina Press, 1984.

Scheick, William J. *Authority and Female Authorship in Colonial America.* Lexington: University Press of Kentucky, 1998.

Stanford, Ann. *Anne Bradstreet: The Worldly Puritan.* New York: Burt Franklin, 1974.

White, Elizabeth Wade. *Anne Bradstreet: The Tenth Muse.* New York: Oxford University Press, 1971.

RICHARD BRAUTIGAN

Born: Tacoma, Washington
January 30, 1935
Died: Bolinas, California
September, 1984

Known for his gentle narrators and the unusual central characters of his novels, Brautigan is the principal transitional figure between the Beat writers and the youth culture of the 1960's.

Library of Congress

BIOGRAPHY

Richard Brautigan was born in Tacoma, Washington, on January 30, 1935, the son of Bernard Brautigan and Lula Mary Keho Brautigan. A series of stepfathers made Brautigan's early life rather chaotic and unstable. He began to write while attending high school, and the Beat movement drew him to the San Francisco Bay Area in the mid-1950's. There he met Philip Whalen, with whom he shared an apartment for a period, as well as Allen Ginsberg, Lawrence Ferlinghetti, and most of the other poets and fiction writers who congregated in the bookstores and coffeehouses. While Brautigan is primarily remembered as an offbeat novelist, he was first published as a poet; *The Return of the Rivers* appeared in 1957, the same year he married Virginia Dionne Adler. *The Galilee Hitch-Hiker* was published in 1958, *Lay the Marble Tea: Twenty-four Poems* in 1959, and *The Octopus Frontier* in 1960, the year his daughter Ianthe was born. During this period he worked at a succession of odd jobs while writing a considerable body of poetry.

During the four years Brautigan was married to Virginia Adler, he completed two of the three books of fiction upon which his literary reputation rests and began the third. Donald Allen was instrumental in bringing two of Brautigan's novels to the attention of an editor at Grove Press in New York, which published *A Confederate General from Big Sur* in 1964. When this work sold poorly, Grove had second thoughts about handling a second book. Allen

acted on Brautigan's behalf again by publishing *Trout Fishing in America* himself in 1967, and Brautigan's literary career quickly started to take shape. The "love generation" soon began to think it heard its own voice in the thoughtful, eccentric characters that peopled Brautigan's novels; Brautigan became a cult writer to a social and political movement with whom he shared only a few preoccupations.

Though he had never attended college, Brautigan became poet-in-residence at the California Institute of Technology in 1967. In 1969, the novelist Kurt Vonnegut helped Delacorte Press secure rights to *Trout Fishing in America* as well as Brautigan's new book, *In Watermelon Sugar*, which had been published by a smaller press a year before. With *The Abortion: An Historical Romance* (1971), Brautigan began to base more and more of his fictional works either on particular subgenres of the novel, such as the romance, or on specific earlier literary works, such as F. Scott Fitzgerald's short story "The Diamond as Big as the Ritz" (in *Tales of the Jazz Age*, 1922).

Brautigan's popularity grew, his book sales soared, and he began to wander more widely and more frequently than he had been able to before. In addition to his house in Bolinas, California, Brautigan acquired a strip of Montana ranch land near Livingston. The writer's fascination with this section of the United States influenced both *The Hawkline Monster: A Gothic Western* (1974) and *The Tokyo-Montana Express* (1980).

Brautigan married again, in Japan, and brought

his bride Akiko back to live with him in Montana. Like his first, this marriage was short-lived; the couple separated in 1981. Brautigan had earlier begun to drink heavily, and he grew despondent when the sales of his books declined steadily and critical reaction to his writing grew cool.

Experiments in fictional form and subgenre mark almost all the later and less important novels. *Willard and His Bowling Trophies* (1975) Brautigan subtitled *A Perverse Mystery*. *Sombrero Fallout* (1976) is subtitled *A Japanese Novel,* and *Dreaming of Babylon: A Private Eye Novel 1942* (1977) is an odd reworking of the 1940's private eye story. *So the Wind Won't Blow It All Away* (1982) seems to be based, at least in some ways, on Henry David Thoreau's *Walden* (1854). During this period, Brautigan grew more and more moody and reclusive, granting no interviews and delivering no public lectures on his works. Only with *The Tokyo-Montana Express,* his next to last book, did Brautigan again achieve anything resembling the brilliance, effervescence, and wit of his early works.

Self-absorbed, deeply depressed, troubled by debts, and abrasive even to those who cared for him, Brautigan went from bad to miserable. After the commercial failure of *So the Wind Won't Blow It All Away* (it sold fewer than fifteen thousand copies), no publisher was interested in a work that he offered them in 1983. In his house in Bolinas, sometime late in September of the following year, when even his closest friends did not know where he was, Brautigan put a borrowed Smith & Wesson .44 Magnum to his head and pulled the trigger. His body was not found until October 25, 1984.

ANALYSIS

The principal themes of Brautigan's fiction are concerned with different aspects of the same classical philosophical question: What constitutes the good life? For example, in *A Confederate General from Big Sur,* Brautigan explores the role of friendship in life—its obligations as well as its joys and tribulations. Lee Mellon, the book's central character, is an entertaining ne'er-do-well whose complex, disorganized life brings the first-person narrator, Jesse, as much trouble as it does pleasure—perhaps more. Lee is inventive and funny, but his behavior and morals are an increasing strain on Jesse's patience and sense of right and wrong. Lee's spontaneity and his direct contact with life cement the

friendship, but it is in almost constant danger of coming apart toward the close of the story.

Though the narrator feels "a sudden wave of vacancy go over me" when Lee treats another character harshly, Jesse remains loyal. One needs friends in this world, and sticks with them (the book implies) whether they are good or bad, right, or wrong. Such a youthful answer to one of life's tougher questions did not go unnoticed by those readers wearing bell-bottomed trousers or miniskirts.

Brautigan was concerned as well with the individual's need for a sense of community. In *A Confederate General from Big Sur,* community comes in the form of the little group that gathers around the bogus general Lee Mellon at his Big Sur encampment. Community nurtures the individual and helps both to create possibilities for each person and to establish the boundaries of his or her reality. *Trout Fishing in America* is concerned with this same question, though here the individual's "community" is national rather than local.

In Watermelon Sugar, set in a fantasy-embroidered commune, is especially concerned with how life is best lived in relation to other lives. The community of iDEATH represents for Brautigan one answer to the problem of how men and women may relate meaningfully to one another within a social unit. Freedom, respect, and gentleness are all-important qualities of the sort of social construct that fosters growth and trust, that makes life worth living. Just as important as community, however, in bringing meaning and purpose to life is a sound, deeply shared love between a man and a woman.

The narrator of *The Abortion* had drifted through a purposeless existence until he met and fell in love with Vida, a beautiful woman who brings him back in contact with life. Love gone sour and the consequences of this on the soul are the principal concerns of both *Willard and His Bowling Trophies* and *Sombrero Fallout*. Without love, Brautigan's books imply, life is a gray, pointless affair. Both his poetry and his prose point to healthy love and sexuality as a very important part of the good life.

Despite the strength and the consistency of themes in Brautigan's novels, this element is seldom, if ever, the emphasis in his fiction, and his readers probably did not buy his books for their ruminations on particular ideas. Instead, Brautigan was a scintillating prose stylist whose humor ran toward a zaniness that was seldom lame or strained. Lee Mellon, despite his flaws as a human being, is entertaining and fascinating because he is at the same time likable and humorously fantastic.

In *Trout Fishing in America*, the narrator goes to a strange sort of retail business establishment that sells trout streams by the foot (trees and birds are optional and at extra charge). Like Lee Mellon, the Cleveland Wrecking Yard is funny and sad at the same time; the reader is encouraged to laugh and ponder the odd ways of America—how it treats everything as commodity, even as Americans (both the reader and the author) try to imbue everything with meaning. Even in Brautigan's later books such as *The Hawkline Monster*, the humor of situation and character is frequently entertaining. A wry view of life animates Brautigan's early novels, and when that disappeared, so too did the joy that readers found in his books.

Besides being humorous, the writing is richly metaphoric. When he began writing fiction, Brautigan retained both the insights and the methods of poetry. The Cleveland Wrecking Yard shows Brautigan's use of figurative language as well as it shows his humor. This establishment represents the way America "does business," packaging myth with environment and selling both at a profit. As in all good metaphors, the point is both clear and striking.

Often, however, Brautigan's figurative language is harder to interpret. Every reader of *In Watermelon Sugar* has the impression that something besides a post-nuclear-war hippie commune is the topic under discussion, but even the critics have not been able to agree on what this extended figure of speech is intended to illuminate. Another type of figurative complexity is found in Brautigan's frequent analogies. The "Ice Age Cab Company" chapter of *The Tokyo-Montana Express* finds the narrator struggling to describe how a sunset on the mountains constantly changes as it is being watched.

To help readers understand his problem, he tells the story of a woman cab driver who seems preoccupied with an entirely different kind of change in the appearance of the mountains—that brought about by successive ice ages. At the end of her monologue, the narrator says, "When she started talking about the mountains, they looked one way and when she finished talking about them, they looked another way. I guess that's what I'm trying to say about this sunset." On the superficial level, one learns how long it takes her to tell her tale—in terms of the sunset. On another level, one is informed about the kinds of changes that take place in the mind as one views things from different perspectives. On the poetic level, one experiences an abrasion, one kind of change (a relatively rapid one, the sunset) grinding against a very different kind (the very slow change that glaciers bring about over eons). The result of such carefully wrought poetic language, though it often seems simple on the surface, is a discourse that is lean and spare and drenched in nuance.

A CONFEDERATE GENERAL FROM BIG SUR

First published: 1964
Type of work: Novel

A small band of bizarre nonconformists searches for Lee Mellon's connection with the past and, not finding it, survives with whatever comes to hand.

A Confederate General from Big Sur, Brautigan's first published novel, focuses the reader's attention on its characters. The narrator is Jesse, a young man whose gentle, strange personality has the capacity to delight the reader with metaphoric insights and uncommon attitudes toward love, friendship, and life in general. The central character of the novel, however, is Lee Mellon, a true eccentric. In the first part of the book, he tries to gather information about an ancestor, Augustus Mellon, who (at least as family history would have it) was a general in the Civil War. Jesse tries to help Lee in his quest and thus becomes enmeshed in Mellon's chaotic, rough-hewn life. At one point, Jesse calls his friend a "Confederate General in ruins," echoing Ralph Waldo Emerson's description of man as a god in ruins.

Lee Mellon is something of a narcissist and a bounder, but his character is compelling because he confronts life directly and leads the kind of wild, wide-open existence that invites readers to fantasize that they, too, could be more this way if they chose. Lee comes short of being truly offensive because he brings no lasting harm to anyone else.

Despite Jesse's and Lee's intensive search, they find no evidence that anyone by the name of Augustus Mellon was ever a Confederate general. Throughout the work Brautigan uses analogies

from the Civil War, and particularly writings about that mythic struggle, as an underlying conceit. As in Brautigan's later novels, an underlying literary work, a repeated allusion, acts as a source and inspiration, giving both information to the account and tone to the writing style. In fact, Brautigan identifies the principal source as Ezra J. Warner's *Generals in Gray* (1959).

After their failure to uncover any information about the hypothetical general, Lee and Jesse retreat to Mellon's ramshackle place on the coast at Big Sur and ponder the possibilities of life while they have affairs with local women, help control a psychotic millionaire driven from home by his greedy family, and generally share whatever adventures and misadventures come their way. Jesse, however, is troubled by the chaos and uncertainty of life at Big Sur with Lee Mellon in charge. He is further unsettled by Lee's increasing aggression toward others, especially the erratic millionaire Johnston Wade, who is also referred to as Roy Earle, the character portrayed by Humphrey Bogart in the film *High Sierra*. Despite all Lee Mellon's flaws, his rebelliousness, zaniness, and originality make him compelling and appealing.

This frankly experimental work is further complicated by Brautigan's providing not one but several endings for the book. In the first ending, the two friends and their girlfriends are high on marijuana and Jesse is unable to complete the sexual act initiated by the woman he is with. The second ending resembles a still photograph of the foursome on the beach. By the time readers reach the sixth ending, they learn that the book has more and more endings unraveling faster and faster—"186,000 endings per second," the speed of light.

While Brautigan's decision to provide multiple endings may adequately describe marijuana intoxication (through confusion and disorientation), it nevertheless forces readers to select their own version of how the tale ends and thus casts some of the burden of the meaning of the story on them. No matter which ending (or endings) readers select, the conclusion of the book is desolate. One is alone, though one may find oneself among friends, and the isolation is painful and lacking in hope. Intoxication, sex, or activity may numb the pain for a while, but eventually each individual must face whatever hollowness exists within his or her soul. The contrast between the pervasive humor and the desolation of the ending (that desolation is also found elsewhere in the book) gives the novel a tense, haunting quality. The contrast oddly blends the angst that is often found in the Beats and the joyous, carefree attitude that characterized the American youth movement of the 1960's.

TROUT FISHING IN AMERICA

First published: 1967
Type of work: Novel

Trout fishing becomes an extended metaphor for much that is either good or strange in the American experience: friendship, nature, commercialism, growing up, and love.

Trout Fishing in America is Brautigan's best-known and probably most important novel, but it is organized in a manner different from his other novels and from more conventional examples of the genre. For one thing, it has no easily recognizable plot structure. Rather, it weaves together (with apparent randomness) about forty episodes in the unnamed narrator's life and juxtaposes these with a few miscellaneous sections that illuminate the chapters in their vicinity. One thread of the story deals with the experiences of the narrator's boyhood. From these the reader gains a sense of his unusual personality—especially his separateness, vivid imagination, and highly individual way of viewing life.

Another thread consists of the narrator's trout fishing experiences, though these sometimes overlap with the boyhood episodes. Chapters set during the narrator's adolescence show him seeking comfort and meaning from nature, well outside organized American society. Yet another thread in this complexly textured novel deals with the narrator's life in beatnik San Francisco. By this point he has married and fathered a child. The reader will quickly notice that the chapters are not presented chronologically; instead, they occasionally form small thematic packets or sometimes appear to be arranged for the humorous relationships to one another.

The themes of *Trout Fishing in America* are at least as complex and various as the book's structure. Many values that can be observed in Brautigan's other books are upheld here. Certainly, friendship is important in life, the book implies, but so, too, are love, a direct contact with nature, freedom, individuality, and a good sense of humor.

Central to grasping the meaning of the novel is an understanding of Brautigan's many uses of the term "trout fishing in America." At its most fundamental level, the term refers to the actual act of fishing for trout—specifically, how this very act can rehabilitate a troubled mind. The term also represents nature itself in some sections and a state of mind that rises above the ordinary in others. Furthermore, the phrase is used as both a mythical character's name and a spirit of adventurousness in which freedom and rebellion combine to produce an idealized view of the possibilities of life. While this last use of the term tends to give the work a zestful quality in some places, the book is not fundamentally optimistic.

At the heart of *Trout Fishing in America* is a critique of contemporary American life and culture. Rampant commercialism, the packaging and selling of both the body and the myth of America, is shown in all its ugliness in the important "Cleveland Wrecking Yard" chapter as well as in several other parts of the novel. Nature and the environment have become secondary concerns in a country where an abundance of wildlife (including trout) and the purity of air and water have been taken for granted for centuries. Restrictions to personal liberty and the pressures on the individual to conform to American society's accepted roles are also criticized.

Such themes are not unique to this work; Brautigan's ideas are closely related to those of other artists of the Beat movement. Brautigan's extravagant humor masks the criticism implied by the work, however; the narrator never preaches, and if he does moralize, it is by means of a joke—often aimed at someone very much like himself. What is unique in the work is Brautigan's method of making both story and meaning.

Trout Fishing in America is probably best understood if it is viewed as a novel that owes much to poetry. While it was published after *A Confederate General from Big Sur,* it had been written previously, when all that Brautigan had published to that point were volumes of verse. The key phrase of the work, "trout fishing in America," acts much like an incantation or refrain in poetry—providing an echo of the main topic from beginning to end, while changing its meaning as the tale progresses and the reader sees more deeply into the theme. This refrain acts also as a unifying element in the work, as does the image of grass in Walt Whitman's *Leaves of Grass* (1855), itself a sprawling, seemingly disorganized work of poetry. Finally, the book is highly metaphorical, from its often repeated key phrase to the details of its description. *Trout Fishing in America* is a novel that only a modern poet could have written.

IN WATERMELON SUGAR

First published: 1968
Type of work: Novel

In a fantasy commune, the gentle, shy narrator tries to find peace and a sense of community while writing a book.

In Watermelon Sugar takes place in a world where life is lived simply and everything is made from watermelon sugar, a substance refined from both the watermelons grown on the commune and Brautigan's considerable imagination. The central character, another of Brautigan's gentle narrators, is the only writer in what seems to be the only settlement left on the planet. In fact, intellectual and artistic pursuits are allowed but not encouraged in the commune called iDEATH. Most of the residents live their lives on a more literal, physical plane: making stew for the gang, turning watermelons into building materials, and constructing transparent underwater tombs. Life at iDEATH moves at a leisurely, idyllic pace.

The novel consists of three books. In book 1, the reader is introduced to the gentle lives of most of the main characters. Pauline, whom the narrator describes as "his favorite," spends the night with him. When he was a child, a band of speaking, ironic tigers ate his mother and father—after sending him outside to play. Book 1 ends with the narrator wishing his former girlfriend Margaret would leave him alone.

Book 2 is both a dream and a flashback. In the narrator's dream, a band of misfits led by inBOIL, who seethes internally, rummages through the debris in the Forgotten Works, a place that seems to represent the remains of a demolished culture that placed its primary value in things instead of people. In its profusion of objects and its physical complexity, the Forgotten Works resembles a demolished twentieth century America. The residents of iDEATH seem to represent a postmodern settlement that has survived some great catastrophe by placing values where they rightfully belong: on simple living, friendship, and love. *In Watermelon Sugar,* more strongly than any other of Brautigan's books, espouses the ideals of the youth movement of the 1960's.

The drunken gang that follows inBOIL believes that they represent the real iDEATH. In an effort to prove this, they cut off their fingers and noses and consequently bleed to death. The residents of the commune watch this bloodletting with more relief than honor, finally collecting the dead and burning them in their cabins close to the Forgotten Works. At the end of book 2, after the carnage, the narrator realizes that all of his feelings for Margaret have turned sour.

The opening of book 3 shows the narrator awakening from his flashback dream. He joins his friends from the commune and appears to be little affected by it. Later, while gazing at the Statue of Mirrors, he has a vision of Margaret hanging herself. Margaret's body is found (she actually has hanged herself) and brought back to the commune for burial.

Margaret is buried on a Thursday; in the bizarre world of *In Watermelon Sugar* the sun shines black on Thursdays and no sounds can be heard. At the conclusion, all the members of the commune are waiting for the setting of the black sun so that the

social dancing, which customarily concludes a funeral, can begin. The narrator has finished his book, and the poetic wording of the ending reminds the reader of a similar incantation in the opening. One finds oneself reading the very book the narrator has been working on all along.

Upon publication of *In Watermelon Sugar,* many readers were tempted to see the work as a drug-induced fantasy. While the story may indeed by viewed as a many-colored distortion of the everyday world, it is doubtless a mistake to interpret it as a hymn to hallucinogens. Nothing in the content of the work suggests that drugs are either an issue here or a means to an end.

One of the main problems of interpreting this work accurately involves determining the meaning of the term "iDEATH." The death of "I" seems to represent the suppression of the ego, a feature of the Zen philosophy that was held in very high esteem by the Beats. In this system of thought, the ego is identified with selfishness and aggression. Surely inBOIL and his gang have misunderstood iDEATH. The ego is not to be done away with by self-torture or by punishing oneself. Those who value material objects above human values—kindness, love, and community—are on the wrong path. Instead, Brautigan's book recommends the simple life, as does Thoreau's *Walden.* Where Brautigan differs from Thoreau is in his view of society. Whereas *Walden* depicts a utopia for one, Brautigan suggests that life can be lived—indeed, is more meaningfully lived—in the company of others.

A key to attaining the death of the ego seems to consist of living in the present moment. Intellectual pursuits and even art apparently hinder this process. It is probably for this reason that the narrator's writing is considered something of an unnatural act in the commune. Because his scribbling harms no one, though, his foible is tolerated (if not encouraged). Important to this interpretation is the personality of the narrator; he is certainly more troubled than are the mainline iDEATH people with whom he associates. After the black sun sets and the writer concludes his work, he will be able to put aside whatever it was in his ego that made him want to write his book in the first place. In this way he moves toward greater and greater acceptance by those in the commune, and in the ending, with the completion of the book, the reader is, in fact, witnessing his final immersion into the community.

THE ABORTION: AN HISTORICAL ROMANCE

First published: 1971
Type of work: Novel

A reclusive librarian meets a beautiful woman who moves him farther and farther into the world by means of her having an abortion.

The Abortion: An Historical Romance was Brautigan's first book to which he gave a subtitle; by doing so he clearly indicated that the work was based on an already established subgenre. A writer of such originality, however, does not produce the sort of romance that most readers might expect. Instead, he infuses the form with his own themes and zany humor.

The unnamed narrator of *The Abortion*, though distinguished by eccentric attitudes and gentleness, is not as fully developed a character as the narrators of several other of Brautigan's books, most notably Jesse of *A Confederate General from Big Sur* and the unnamed narrator of *In Watermelon Sugar.* While he is admirable for his view of humanity, a self-imposed isolation and his chosen role in life reduce him in stature. Distant from most of society and remote in his feelings, he lives a life apart, both in the depths of his distinctly odd library (where he also lives) and in the labyrinth-like rooms of the Mexican abortion doctor later in the story.

Early in the story, the narrator describes his strange library: The books are all donated by the people who write them, society's sad losers and misfits, and Brautigan goes into considerable detail with titles (*Growing Flowers by Candlelight in Hotel Rooms, The Stereo and God*) and descriptions of the often unhappy or disturbed people who get to shelve their books themselves. Included in the catalog is a book called *Moose*, written by one Richard Brautigan, "who looked as if he would be more at home in another era."

In a flashback, the narrator relates how he met Vida, the extremely beautiful woman with whom he is living when the story opens. She, too, had brought her story, a tale of how her body does not really suit her, to be dutifully accepted and cataloged. Wherever she goes, even on the abortion trip to Mexico, her beauty brings chaos by the attention men pay to it. The stereotype of the mayhem-producing beautiful female can be traced in American literature from Katrina Van Tassel in Washington Irving's "The Legend of Sleepy Hollow" (1819) to Eula Varner in William Faulkner's *The Hamlet* (1940). Vida, as a character name, is derived from the Latin *vita*, meaning life.

This allegorical naming of a character is matched by the allegorical nature of the library itself. The narrator is the thirty-fifth or thirty-sixth librarian, which corresponds to the numbering of American presidents at the time the work was written—a split term for one president accounting for the confusion. In addition, the library is run by America Forever, Etc.

After they discover Vida's pregnancy, she and the narrator travel by plane to Mexico for the abortion, and this trip ironically represents the quest found in traditional romances. From beginning to end, Brautigan adheres closely enough to the traditional romance form so that readers familiar with it can recognize the various necessary items and feel its subjective intensity. At the same time, Brautigan's treatment of these essential forms is humorous, which casts an ironic light upon the entire novel.

Upon returning to San Francisco after the abortion, the narrator learns that he has lost his position at the library. While this forces him into the harsh realities of life outside his pleasantly numbing cocoon, where he had essentially retreated, Vida and his friend Foster welcome the change. He will become a hero in Berkeley, they assure him, and the final scene finds him outside among the students, contentedly collecting money for America Forever, Etc. Like the better-known *Trout Fishing in America*, this work deals with the problem of creating a meaningful life in the United States during the middle of the twentieth century.

The Abortion is the story of a man who has been strongly influenced by the literature he has read and obviously absorbed. The difficulties he encounters in the broader world are caused in part by his belief that life is—or ought to be—like literature. Literary forms, Brautigan suggests, provide a framework for thoughts and expectations. *The Abortion* shows how skewed a life based on these kinds of expectations can become.

Richard Brautigan

Summary

In his early novels, Richard Brautigan searches for the meaning of America. What he finds is a country debased by commercialism, shaken in its values, and haunted by loneliness. For the individual, love, humor, and the imagination can bring meaning to life.

Brautigan explored the American soul in the middle of the twentieth century; he believed gentleness and peace to be both means and end in this quest. His highly original, richly metaphoric books show him to be much more than a transitional literary figure. His finely crafted prose bears witness to his unique way of viewing the world.

Charles Hackenberry

Bibliography

By the Author

SHORT FICTION:
Revenge of the Lawn: Stories 1962-1970, 1971

LONG FICTION:
A Confederate General from Big Sur, 1964
Trout Fishing in America, 1967
In Watermelon Sugar, 1968
The Abortion: An Historical Romance, 1971
The Hawkline Monster: A Gothic Western, 1974
Willard and His Bowling Trophies: A Perverse Mystery, 1975
Sombrero Fallout: A Japanese Novel, 1976
Dreaming of Babylon: A Private Eye Novel 1942, 1977
The Tokyo-Montana Express, 1980
So the Wind Won't Blow It All Away, 1982
An Unfortunate Woman, 2000

POETRY:
The Return of the Rivers, 1957
The Galilee Hitch-Hiker, 1958
Lay the Marble Tea: Twenty-four Poems, 1959
The Octopus Frontier, 1960
All Watched over by Machines of Loving Grace, 1967
The Pill Versus the Springhill Mine Disaster, 1968
Please Plant This Book, 1968
Rommel Drives on Deep into Egypt, 1970
Loading Mercury with a Pitchfork, 1976
June 30th, June 30th, 1978

MISCELLANEOUS:
The Edna Webster Collection of Undiscovered Writings, 1995

Discussion Topics

- What is a "cult writer"? What factors played a major role in Richard Brautigan's becoming one?

- Cite instances of Brautigan's taking literary advantage of his wanderlust.

- Humor can be a saving grace for an individual and for literary works. Discuss this statement with brief reference to several of Brautigan's works or more extensively with respect to one.

- Brautigan's writing is notable for vivid sensory details. Examine some of them and explain how they function.

- For young people, friendships loom very important but often lead to disappointment. Discuss the ambivalence of friendships in Brautigan's fiction.

- What is the organizing principle of *Trout Fishing in America*? What does it have to do with poetry?

- Do Brautigan's poetic techniques work in a prose novel?

About the Author

Barber, John F. *Richard Brautigan: An Annotated Bibliography*. Jefferson, N.C.: McFarland, 1990.

Bradbury, Malcolm. *The Modern American Novel*. Oxford, England: Oxford University Press, 1983.

Brautigan, Ianthe. *You Can't Catch Death: A Daughter's Memoir*. New York: St. Martin's Press, 2001.

Chénetier, Marc. *Richard Brautigan*. New York: Methuen, 1983.

Foster, Edward Halsey. *Richard Brautigan*. Boston: Twayne, 1983.

Iftekharuddin, Farhat. "The New Aesthetics in Brautigan's *Revenge of the Lawn: Stories 1962-1970*." In *Creative and Critical Approaches to the Short Story*, edited by Noel Harold Kaylor. Lewiston, Ky.: Edwin Mellen Press, 1997.

Keeler, Greg. *Waltzing with the Captain: Remembering Richard Brautigan*. Boise, Idaho : Limberlost Press, 2004.

Mills, Joseph. *Reading Richard Brautigan's "Trout Fishing in America."* Boise, Idaho: Boise State University Press, 1998.

Seymore, James. "Author Richard Brautigan Apparently Takes His Own Life, But He Leaves a Rich Legacy." *People Weekly* 22 (November 12, 1984): 40-41.

Stull, William L. "Richard Brautigan's *Trout Fishing in America:* Notes of a Native Son." *American Literature* 56 (March, 1984): 69-80.

Wright, Lawrence. "The Life and Death of Richard Brautigan." *Rolling Stone* (April 11, 1985): 29.

HAROLD BRODKEY

Born: Alton, Illinois
October 25, 1930
Died: New York, New York
January 26, 1996

Concerned with examining his own life in close detail, Brodkey wrote largely about growing up as an adopted child near St. Louis and about his later life at Harvard University and in New York State.

© Jerry Bauer

BIOGRAPHY

Harold Roy Brodkey was born Aaron Roy Weintraub across the Mississippi River from and slightly to the northeast of St. Louis, Missouri, in Alton, Illinois, in 1930. His father, a junk man, was illiterate. Aaron's mother died when he was an infant, and his father, unable to care for the child, allowed Joseph and Doris Brodkey to adopt him. They changed his name to Harold and gave him their surname, a corruption of the family's original Russian name, Bezborodko.

In Brodkey's fiction, Joseph and Doris Brodkey become Leila and S. L. (perhaps to suggest St. Louis) Cohn. They figure prominently in early stories, in which Leila is portrayed as having adopted Aaron/Harold largely as a means of reclaiming her husband, from whom she was separated. Leila (variously Leah and Lila in Brodkey's stories) is shown as a woman too self-absorbed to offer much love to anyone else. There apparently was a daughter, somewhat older than Harold, who becomes Nonie in his stories.

One can speak only tentatively about the life of Brodkey; he kept the details of his personal life completely private except as they are revealed in his stories. For example, in an interview, *Esquire* journalist D. Keith Mano asked Brodkey if he had ever worked. Brodkey replied that he had but would provide no other details because he had not

yet written about that experience. So intensely personal are Brodkey's stories that he guarded assiduously the autobiographical details of which they are composed. His stories are generally thought to record with diary-like authenticity the actual events in his coming of age.

If one is to believe the information given in "Largely an Oral History of My Mother," Brodkey, in the persona of Alan Cohn, was discovered to have a remarkably high IQ—so high, in fact, that special training was recommended for him. The adoptive parents, by now having had their fill of Alan/Harold, used this opportunity to try unsuccessfully to return the boy to his birth father.

Brodkey apparently lived a childhood that was in many ways typically midwestern. He went to school, earned money as a baby-sitter, and belonged to the Boy Scouts. His family situation, however, was not typical. Having lost his real mother so early as to be unable to remember her, he tried to construct her in his imagination, using the small pieces of information that he was able to glean from people who knew her. Although she was not well-educated, his birth mother was bright, bookish, and fluent in five or six languages. Brodkey invented her and thus stirred his ability to create characters and situations by paying special attention to small details. This talent would later become the hallmark of his stories.

Having sustained the early loss of his real mother and, because of his adoption, his father, Brodkey would sustain similar losses in adolescence through the deaths of his adoptive parents.

Joseph Brodkey had a stroke when Harold was nine and was an invalid thereafter. He lived on for five years and required considerable attention. One year before her husband died, Doris Brodkey developed cancer. She lived a painful and increasingly isolated existence until her death, which occurred during Harold's undergraduate days at Harvard University. Never an easy or outgoing person, she became increasingly embittered as her health deteriorated.

A scholarship to Harvard and a small inheritance enabled Brodkey to live outside the Midwest for the first time, presumably beginning in 1948. Shortly after that, he spent part of a summer in Europe, which was his first trip outside the United States. The events of his life upon leaving college remain a mystery.

In 1957, Dial Press published his first collection of stories, *First Love and Other Sorrows*, which became an alternate selection of the Book-of-the-Month Club. This collection was received with considerable enthusiasm, and word was out that Brodkey was at work on a Proustian kind of novel, "Party of Animals," under contract to Farrar, Straus and Giroux. On June 4, 1976, *The New York Times* announced that Brodkey had delivered the more than two-thousand-page manuscript of this sprawling work to the publisher—sixteen years after the original contract was signed. Major sections of "Party of Animals" have been published in *The New Yorker, Esquire*, and *New American Review*. The three segments that make up *Women and Angels*, published in 1985, are from "Party of Animals," as are many of the stories in *Stories in an Almost Classical Mode*, published by Alfred A. Knopf in 1988. The latter, like Brodkey's first collection, was a Book-of-the-Month Club alternate selection.

Brodkey regularly published short stories and poems, particularly in *The New Yorker*. His output was small but well wrought. Typically, he took his stories through at least twenty revisions before he considered them finished. His attention to detail and the easy unfolding of his prose attracted a loyal following despite there having been only three collections in print for the first three decades of his productive life.

Brodkey was awarded both the Prix de Rome Magazine Award and the Brandeis Creative Arts Award in 1974. He received first prize in the O. Henry short fiction awards in 1975 and again in 1976. Brodkey was a fellow of the American Academy in Rome, the John Simon Guggenheim Memorial Foundation, and the National Endowment for the Arts. He taught writing and literature at Cornell University and at the City University of New York. Brodkey married Ellen Schwamm, a novelist, in 1980. He maintained a desk at *The New Yorker* and was an occasional lecturer on the college and university circuit.

Brodkey's life changed drastically in the early 1990's, when he was diagnosed as HIV positive. Full-blown AIDS followed and claimed his life in 1996. Brodkey had been quite closeted, but with the AIDS diagnosis, he became more forthright in discussing his homosexuality. He kept a journal that was published posthumously in 1996 as *This Wild Darkness: The Story of My Death*. He also published *Profane Friendship* (1994), in which he was more forthcoming in his presentation of homosexual relationships.

ANALYSIS

Brodkey wrote about the commonplace. His slow, sometimes agonizingly detailed unfolding of the commonplace distinguished him as a credible analyst of growing up Jewish and adopted in the Midwest. In the early stories, the cast of characters is identical: The story is told from the point of view of a boy, with an adoptive mother and father and an older sister given to tormenting him. Added to this ordinary American family configuration in some of the stories is a maid.

The first three stories of the nine that make up *First Love and Other Sorrows* are really the beginning of what might be called a *Bildungsroman*. They detail the childhood of the first-person narrator, who longs for love but is unable to attract it. The narrator was adopted by his foster parents in part because he was very attractive. In "The State of Grace," however, he is thirteen years old, is six feet tall, weighs 125 pounds, and has ears that stick out. He is self-conscious about being the gangly teenager new to adolescence.

A recurrent theme in Brodkey's work is that true selflessness does not exist. In his stories, as presumably in his early life, all Brodkey's characters have motives for what they do, and these motives are inextricably tied to self-interest. This attitude may seem cynical, but in Brodkey's work it appears more realistic than cynical. Sometimes he confuses reciprocity with selfishness. For example, in "Innocence," one of the later stories in *Stories in an Almost Classical Mode*, the protagonist is determined to give Orra Perkins her first orgasm, not so much to provide her with pleasure but rather to get a stronger hold on her and to increase the intensity of his own sexual pleasure with her. It is difficult in this story to know where the line is drawn between selfishness and selflessness.

Brodkey did not develop strong plots. His stories are essentially concerned with descriptive details about places and emotions. His prose style was shaped considerably by the style of *The New Yorker*. His style is unadorned, lean, and direct and is carefully calculated and assiduously polished to the point that it reads easily and is generally convincing. He succeeded best when he wrote about his midwestern childhood, perhaps because his uncomplicated style reflects the commonness of the situations in his life.

Verbal and typographical invention are an integral part of Brodkey's technique. He was always conscious of how sentences look on a page. He used punctuation in a unique and extremely calculated way. A typical example of his technique is found in a description of his adoptive mother in "Story in an Almost Classical Mode":

> What she did was get your attention; she would ask you questions in a slightly high-pitched pushy voice that almost made you laugh, but if you were drawn to listen to her, once you were attentive and showed you were, her voice would lose every attribute of sociability, it would become strained and naked of any attempt to please or be acceptable; it would be utterly appalling; and what she said would lodge in the center of your attention and be the truth you have to live with until you could persuade yourself she was crazy: that is, irresponsible and perhaps criminal in her way.

This complex sentence reveals Brodkey's fascination with semicolons and his typical use of the colon to emphasize that what follows is the most important part of the sentence. The colon simultaneously connects and separates. Brodkey sometimes combined his affection for semicolons with a fondness of parentheses, lodging a semicolon in the exact center of a parenthetical section of a sentence; he then placed the parenthetical section in the exact center of the sentence.

In *Women and Angels*, Brodkey explored his real mother in the story "Ceil" and his adoptive mother in "Lila." The philosophy that emerges from those stories, particularly the latter, is what one critic has dubbed the "tyranny of need." Brodkey viewed dependence as an essential ingredient of love. Close human relationships seem to be based on reciprocal weaknesses between two people rather than on the strengths of one or both of them.

Although Brodkey's parents, both real and adoptive, were Jews, it is difficult to classify his stories as notably Jewish. He was a Jewish boy growing up beside the Mississippi near the Missouri-Illinois border, but his life was shaped more by the convoluted emotions of the people who surrounded him for his first fifteen years or so than by the fact that he was Jewish. Formal religion did not play a significant role in his life. He had to handle larger, more personal discriminations as he grew up than anti-Semitism. His most developed statement of a religious philosophy occurs in "Angel," the last story in *Women and Angels*.

"FIRST LOVE AND OTHER SORROWS"

First published: 1957 (collected in *First Love and Other Sorrows*, 1957)
Type of work: Short story

The adolescent first-person narrator sees love around him and seeks it himself.

The title story of *First Love and Other Sorrows* takes place in the springtime when its narrator is sixteen years old and is dealing with a budding sexuality. He lives with his adoptive mother and his twenty-two-year-old sister, who seems as unhappy with her looks as the narrator is with his. She complains that her face is too round and that she does not look good in suits. The brother has peach fuzz and admits to shaving every three days; his mother and sister think he needs to shave more often. His adoptive father is dead.

The boy's mother warns him against playing too hard and about getting overheated in the springtime. This admonition seems to be a veiled warning that the heat of youthful sexuality can be as dangerous as the heat of April, which is the usual metaphor for youth. The boy certainly seems to feel that such is the case. The sister is dating Sonny Bruster, who, as the son of one of the town's leading bankers, is a good catch in the eyes of the mother. The romance between the two of them is not without problems; at one point, they stop seeing each other for several weeks. They get back together, however, and are engaged before the story ends.

The boy feels like an intruder in his mother's house. She makes it clear that she cooks only because he is there; were it only the two women, they would eat sandwiches. The family situation is not a hostile one, but little love is apparent. The mother, a controlling woman, is vitally concerned with having her daughter marry someone prosperous. She had known genteel living in a large house overlooking the Mississippi River, but the house was lost during a financial crisis, and she was reduced to living in more humble surroundings.

The boy's best friend is a schoolmate named Preston, who is shy, and—although the same age—more heavily bearded than the narrator. He is unimaginative and suspicious of imagination in others. The narrator is the aesthete, and Preston is the scientist who aspires to a career in physics.

Preston is the narrator's safe, dependable friend, with whom he enjoys athletics and double dating. Another boy in the school, however, is much more enticing. Joel Bush is so handsome that the other students can scarcely bear to look at him. He is described in ecstatic terms, but he is so perfect that people avoid him and admire him from a safe distance. Brodkey's effusive description of Joel may be read within a homosexual context, particularly when compared with his description of Orra Perkins in "Innocence."

One day, Joel reveals to the narrator that he had sex with an older woman the night before. He describes the event as masturbation with bells. Juxtaposed to this sexual revelation is a strenuous physical workout on the school's playing field, which serves as a sex substitute for many budding adolescents. The narrator spends an evening with Eleanor Cullen, who previously had had an uneventful date with Joel. Eleanor reveals that she does not regard herself as a basically happy person, which echoes the narrator's earlier statement that he is not popular because he is too gloomy.

The story ends with the narrator's sister en-

gaged to Sonny Bruster and wearing an heirloom engagement ring that she does not like. Her mother is in the kitchen writing letters to send to all of her relatives, telling them of the engagement. The boy and his sister come into the kitchen, and the mother offers to heat up some soup for them. Her eyes fill with tears of emotion, and the three embrace and kiss.

This story is typical of Brodkey's early work and gives a strong indication of the course his later work would follow. Nothing much happens in the story except that an adolescent boy makes tentative moves toward growing into manhood. He is uncertain and fearful of rejection and therefore cannot approach Joel. The closest he can get to him is to be friends with Eleanor. The story deals with situations and emotions but has little plot. The descriptions are accurate and evocative, filled with the carefully observed and presented sights, sounds, and textures that characterize most of Brodkey's writing.

"SENTIMENTAL EDUCATION"

First published: 1957 (collected in *First Love and Other Sorrows*, 1957)
Type of work: Short story

This third-person narrative is a delicate story of how two inexperienced college students discover love.

"Sentimental Education," one of the stories in *First Love and Other Sorrows*, was first published in *The New Yorker*. It is a tentative step in the direction of "Innocence," which was published sixteen years later. Set in Cambridge, Massachusetts, the story features the nineteen-year-old Elgin Smith, who is an undergraduate at Harvard University. The only other character to appear directly in the story is Caroline Hedges, a freshman at Radcliffe College.

The action takes place within a college year, during which time both Elgin and Caroline are forced to reassess their values. Their relationship grows, but the direction of their growth is not always toward each other. When the school year ends, they go their separate ways, although they do not break from each other decisively. They agree to meet again in the fall, but as friends rather than as lovers.

Elgin first sees Caroline on the steps of Widener Library and is instantly smitten. She does not know of his existence until two weeks later. Elgin drops his course in the Victorian novel and enrolls in a class on metaphysical poets because he knows that Caroline is also taking that course. He borrows a pencil from her during several class meetings and finally impresses her by his classroom contributions, though she is disturbed by his nasal, midwestern twang. When he invites her to have coffee with him, she declines but decides to say yes to his next invitation.

The relationship develops slowly, which gives Brodkey room to incorporate all the subtle detail that characterizes his stories. The detail in this story involves a careful analysis of the human emotions that are evoked by young love, particularly when both parties are unsure of themselves.

The relationship is platonic for some weeks, although both Elgin and Caroline want more. Both are too reserved to move toward expressing their feelings physically. Finally, however, after weeks of daily study sessions in Widener Library and of going out onto the Fenway, where Caroline tries to give Elgin elocution lessons, Elgin confesses his love to Caroline. Although Caroline does not immediately confess a reciprocal love, she does feel love for him, and they soon find their way into his bed.

The relationship initially surprises both of them. They have the feeling that such a drastic expression of love should offer something more than it has given them. Although they continue their affair, Caroline feels increasingly cheapened by it. She hates to admit to and surrender to her animal appetite, but she cannot deny that it exists. As time passes, the relationship changes; Elgin talks of marriage, but Caroline realizes how impractical that would be. She also thinks that she has lost her dignity by giving herself to Elgin and that he will not continue to love her because of that lost dignity.

During their last five weeks before the summer holiday, the two are chaste, although they see each other daily. They kiss, and touch, but they restrain their desires. On their last day together, they drink champagne. Caroline has to catch the night train to Baltimore and later go to Europe for the summer. Elgin is leaving too, presumably to return to the Midwest. They agree to see each other in the fall but only as friends. The story ends as Caroline walks back to her dormitory alone, at her own request. Walking away from Elgin, she feels a certain release, for she has shed the pressures of love and close daily association.

This story is different from any of the others in the collection. Unlike the first three, it is a third-person, author omniscient narrative. It is perhaps the most delicately presented of all the stories in *First Love and Other Sorrows*.

"INNOCENCE"

First published: 1973 (collected in *Stories in an Almost Classical Mode*, 1988)
Type of work: Short story

The first-person narrator struggles doggedly to give Orra Perkins her first orgasm.

Unlike many of Brodkey's short stories collected in *Stories in an Almost Classical Mode*, "Innocence" was not first published in *The New Yorker*. Instead, it appeared in *New American Review*, presumably because of *The New Yorker*'s reluctance to publish the common four-letter word that is used for copulation. "Innocence" is a story of young lust—as opposed to young love—in which the protagonist, a Harvard undergraduate, achieves what he feared was the unachievable: a sexual encounter with a very popular and beautiful Radcliffe undergraduate, Orra Perkins.

Orra is not inexperienced; she has been intimate with seven or eight men before she meets the narrator. She has never achieved an orgasm with them because, according to her, she is too sexual to have orgasms. She is not overly distressed by this omission and strenuously discourages the narrator from trying to give her the orgasm that he so much wants her to experience. His motive is twofold: He thinks that he will own Orra if he achieves his end, and he also thinks that his own sexual pleasure with her will be enhanced if she can respond more fully to his penetrations.

This story, generally considered to be among Brodkey's best, is some thirty pages long, of which two-thirds is devoted to presenting a highly detailed account of how Orra is brought to the pinnacle of passion. Before the story ends, Orra not only has her orgasm but, thinking back on it, also has another, multiple orgasm. Despite all the explicit physical detail the story contains, the result is neither prurient nor clinical. Rather it is realistic, direct, and detailed—so detailed, in fact, that the reader begins to long for Orra to achieve the orgasm.

This longing is part of Brodkey's technique. He does not seek to titillate his readers; rather, his aim is to walk them through the experience. As the two participants in the event strain through the seemingly endless encounter to achieve a climax, the reader is dragged along. Eventually, the reader is so worn down by the detailed narration of the event that he or she feels as physically spent as the perspiring participants when the moment of ecstasy finally arrives.

Brodkey's interest in beautiful people such as Orra reminds one of the fiction of F. Scott Fitzgerald. Brodkey's characters usually are well-to-do or quest after those who are. The original description of Orra is remarkably similar to that of Joel Bush in "First Love and Other Sorrows," leading one to speculate on whether Joel in that story was a first, unfulfilled homosexual love.

The title, "Innocence," may seem ironic, but it really is not. Despite having had some sexual experience, Orra is a neophyte in the bedroom. The narrator is little more experienced, although he knows his way around sufficiently to manipulate Orra's body to achieve the ultimate aim of giving her an orgasm.

True to the concerns in many of his other stories, Brodkey's theme involves dependency and achieving union through weakness—in this case, Orra's past inability to reach sexual fulfillment. The narrator's ability to bring her to the point of climax makes her dependent upon him in ways that she has never before been dependent upon anyone.

This story, virtually without plot, is an intricate depiction of both the physical and emotional details of a crucial event in the lives of two twenty-year-olds. The description engages all the senses, moving slowly through every second of the prolonged encounter and showing Brodkey as the recognized master of protraction.

"CEIL"

First published: 1983 (collected in *Women and Angels*, 1985)
Type of work: Short story

Through the recollections of others, Wiley Silenowicz attempts to know the mother he lost when he was two.

It is difficult to say definitively whether "Ceil," one of the three stories in *Women and Angels*, is a success. Some would question whether it is a story or merely a collection of fragments. "Lila" and "Largely an Oral History of My Mother," both depictions of Brodkey's adoptive mother, are more complete works.

Despite this caveat, "Ceil" is among Brodkey's most important works, for it reveals more than any other story the inner Brodkey, who yearns to establish a link with his past. Although the writing in "Ceil" is uneven, some of Brodkey's best images appear in the story, particularly when he writes about the great plains of the Midwest near Staunton, where his mother lived.

Ceil was the youngest of twenty or twenty-five children. Her father was a charismatic, highly intelligent rabbi, and her mother was remembered as long-suffering and remarkably fertile. Born in Russia near Odessa, Ceil was her father's favorite. He arranged a marriage for her, but she refused to go through with it. She was a bright, independent girl who, after her father had simultaneously forgiven her and put a curse upon her, set sail from Odessa for New Orleans.

Upon her arrival in New Orleans, Ceil goes directly to the beauty shop. Unhappy with the result, she is in another beauty salon within an hour, having it redone. Although appearances are important to her, success means more to her than anything else. She moves quickly from being a waitress to a housemaid to a successful businesswoman.

She is married to Max, a man much beneath her, who is originally from the Odessa area. Her success becomes legendary. Her self-satisfaction culminates with the birth of her son. Soon afterward, she falls ill and dies after a painful and lingering hospital confinement.

Brodkey strives in this story to capture a background of which he has only glimmerings. He sketches scenes of Russia by quoting passages from Anton Chekhov. He searches his own subconscious and resurrects a faint memory of having lived with his mother in a wooden house beside a single railway track; he recalls how its rooms shook as trains passed.

Part of "Ceil" is little more than fragmentary snatches, short single paragraphs set off from the rest of the story. Another part consists of italicized conversations with Lila or Ruthie, Wiley's adoptive mother and grandmother. What emerges is an incomplete portrait of a long-dead woman who necessarily remains sketchy in the eyes of her grown son. Part of Brodkey's creative genius is his ability to capture this quality so well.

THE RUNAWAY SOUL

First published: 1991
Type of work: Novel

This book chronicles Wiley Silenowicz's search for love and his inability to find it.

With the publication of *The Runaway Soul*, Brodkey published a book that many of his followers had been awaiting for thirty years. Weighing in at 835 pages, it was suggested that this book was the great "runaway novel." Most critics agreed that it made prodigious use of language and of grammatical structuring, which some of them referred to as "architecture." On the other hand, many critics considered the book flabby and contended that to make its greatest impact, it should have been much shorter. Certainly it would have benefited from a more drastic revision even than those that Brodkey, noted as a heavy reviser, accorded it.

Readers of Brodkey's short stories will find many familiar characters in *The Runaway Soul*, whose protagonist, Wiley Silenowicz, is Brodkey's alter ego. Wiley, like Brodkey, was brought up on the Illinois side of the Mississippi River just north of St. Louis. Like Brodkey, he is an adopted child and bears some of the baggage that goes with being adopted. Wiley is first introduced to readers at age fourteen

after Brodkey devotes only one page to his earlier life, much of which unfolds indirectly as the story evolves.

Wiley's stepfather, S. L. Silenowicz, a businessman, adores his adopted son. The stepmother, Lila, is somewhat less adoring. She has had to deal with many acute family problems. Her daughter, Nonie, ten years older than Wiley, may have been responsible for the deaths of two of her siblings.

Readers learn that Wiley was identified at age five as having a phenomenally high IQ. On learning of this, his birth father, an uneducated junk man, takes his son from his adoptive parents, which proves very traumatic for the boy, who feels more like an object than a human. When the birth father finds he cannot care for Wiley adequately, he returns the boy to the adoptive parents.

The basic story in *The Runaway Soul* is concerned with Wiley's need for love and his inability to find it. Whenever he is in relationships, be they with his adoptive parents, his stepsister, his various lovers, or his friends, the love he so fervently requires always has strings attached.

The chronology Brodkey imposes on this novel will bewilder some readers. It seemingly is random rather than sequential. Although authors frequently deal with chronology in heterodox ways, they usually can justify their doing so on solid artistic grounds. If such grounds lurk beneath the surface in *The Runaway Soul*, they elude most readers, as they did most critics.

SUMMARY

Critics have compared Harold Brodkey to such noteworthy American authors as Nathaniel Hawthorne, Ralph Waldo Emerson, Walt Whitman, F. Scott Fitzgerald, and Thomas Wolfe. In contrast to them, however, Brodkey was neither an eclectic nor a derivative writer. He brought to his writing a singular gift for detailed description of the commonplace and an occasional eerie penetration of the human psyche. A plodding perfectionist, Brodkey was clearly the son of the highly competent, intelligent, energetic, and hardworking woman he described in "Ceil."

R. Baird Shuman

BIBLIOGRAPHY

By the Author

SHORT FICTION:
First Love and Other Sorrows, 1957, 1986
Women and Angels, 1985
Stories in an Almost Classical Mode, 1988
The World Is the Home of Love and Death: Stories, 1997

LONG FICTION:
The Runaway Soul, 1991
Profane Friendship, 1994

NONFICTION:
Avedon: Photographs, 1947-1977, 1978 (with Richard Avedon)
This Wild Darkness: The Story of My Death, 1996
Sea Battles on Dry Land: Essays, 1999

MISCELLANEOUS:
My Venice, 1998

About the Author

Bawer, Bruce. "A Genius for Publicity." *The New Criterion* 7 (December, 1988): 58-69.
Bidney, Martin. "Song of Innocence and of Experience: Rewriting Blake in Brodkey's 'Piping Down the Valleys Wild.'" *Studies in Short Fiction* 31 (Spring, 1994): 237-246.
Braham, Jeanne. "The Power of Witness." *The Georgia Review* 52 (Spring, 1998): 168-180.
Brodkey, Harold. *This Wild Darkness: The Story of My Death*. New York: Henry Holt, 1996.
Dolan, J. D. "Twilight of an Idol." *Nation* 262 (March 25, 1995): 35-36.
Kermode, Frank. "I Am Only Equivocally Harold Brodkey." *The New York Times Book Review*, September 18, 1988, 3.
Mano, D. Keith. "Harold Brodkey: The First Rave." *Esquire* 87 (January, 1977): 14-15.
Weiseltier, Leon. "A Revelation." *The New Republic* 192 (May 20, 1985): 30-33.

DISCUSSION TOPICS

- Harold Brodkey's writing has been called "architectural." What do you think this term implies, and how apt is it in describing Brodkey's style?

- Discuss Brodkey's use of rounded and flat characters. Would you call him a creator of memorable characters?

- How does Brodkey use locale in his stories?

- Harold Bloom has said of Brodkey, "If he is ever able to solve his publishing problems, he'll be seen as one of the great writers of his day." Discuss this statement in the light of your reading of Brodkey.

- People have commented on Brodkey's "tyrannical use of punctuation." Discuss this statement in terms of your reading of his work.

GWENDOLYN BROOKS

Born: Topeka, Kansas
June 7, 1917
Died: Chicago, Illinois
December 3, 2000

Although she has published essays and a novel, Brooks is known primarily for her poetry, which realistically portrays African American life.

© Jill Krementz

BIOGRAPHY

Gwendolyn Elizabeth Brooks was born June 7, 1917, the first child of David and Keziah Wims Brooks. Her birthplace, Topeka, Kansas, was the home of her maternal grandparents, but at the age of five weeks, she and her mother returned to the Brooks's residence in Chicago, the city in which Brooks would live for most of her life. Her brother Raymond was born in 1918.

David Brooks, a janitor, made only modest wages. His children's lack of material luxury, however, was offset by a warm home atmosphere that nurtured culture and creativity. David loved to sing, tell stories, and recite poems, while his wife enjoyed singing, playing the piano, and directing plays for young actors.

As a child, Brooks was encouraged to read and to dream. By the time she was seven, she was expressing her thoughts in two-line verses. This precocity prompted her mother to predict that her daughter would one day become "the lady Paul Laurence Dunbar." Brooks continued to write, producing at least one poem per day, mostly about nature and romantic love. At thirteen, she published her first poem, "Eventide," in *American Childhood*. Three years later, she became a weekly contributor to the *Chicago Defender*'s column "Lights and Shadows." By the age of twenty, she had published poems in two anthologies.

Much of Brooks's inspiration came from James Weldon Johnson and Langston Hughes, two well-known African American poets to whom she had submitted several poems for criticism. Johnson concluded that she was indeed talented but needed to acquaint herself with more modern poets such as T. S. Eliot, Ezra Pound, and E. E. Cummings. Hughes also endorsed Brooks's ability and exhorted her to keep writing—especially about the things she knew.

After graduating from Wilson Junior College, Brooks worked briefly as a maid in a Chicago apartment building and as a secretary to one of its residents, a "spiritual adviser" who sold love potions. The building and its inhabitants would furnish the subject matter for her poem "In the Mecca," published in 1964.

Frustrated by the inability to find more fulfilling work, Brooks started a mimeographed newspaper that sold for five cents per copy. The paper, *News Review*, included stories about local events, discussions of cultural issues, brief biographies of successful African Americans, and cartoons drawn by her brother.

In 1939, Brooks married Henry Lowington Blakely II, another aspiring poet. They had two children, Henry in 1940 and Nora in 1951. Henry supported the family through a variety of jobs, while Gwendolyn wrote poems and reviewed books (both novels and collections of poetry) for *Negro Digest*, *The New York Times*, and *The New York Herald Tribune*.

Brooks's reputation as a poet began with the publication of individual poems in magazines such as *The Crisis, Cross-Section, Twice a Year, Common Ground,* and *Negro Story.* In 1945, however, she produced a volume of poems titled *A Street in Bronzeville,* published by Harper & Row. Four years later, she published *Annie Allen,* the work for which she won the 1950 Pulitzer Prize for poetry. She was the first black writer to win the award. Brooks also wrote poems for children (*Bronzeville Boys and Girls,* 1956, and *The Tiger Who Wore White Gloves,* 1974) as well as several essays, including "Poets Who Are Negroes" (1950) and "They Call It Bronzeville" (1951). In 1953, she published the novel *Maud Martha.*

Brooks succeeded Carl Sandburg as poet laureate of Illinois in 1968, and in 1985 she was appointed Consultant in Poetry to the Library of Congress. She was named to the American Academy and Institute of Arts and Letters and received many awards, including the American Academy of Arts and Letters Award, the Shelley Memorial Award, the Anisfield-Wolf Award, the Kuumba Liberation Award, two Guggenheim Fellowships, the Frost Medal from the Poetry Society of America, a National Book Award nomination for *In the Mecca* (1968), and the National Endowment for the Arts Lifetime Achievement Award in 1989.

Although she was reputed to be shy and introverted, she was eager to share her work and the art of writing poetry. She gave readings at many universities as well as in prisons and taverns. Moreover, she conducted a number of poetry workshops and organized writing contests in elementary and secondary schools, paying the prizes, which ranged from fifty to five hundred dollars, from her own pocket.

Despite her lack of an advanced degree, Brooks taught courses in literature and writing at Chicago's Columbia College, Northeastern Illinois State College, the University of Wisconsin at Madison, Elmhurst College, City College of New York, and Chicago State University, where she held the Gwendolyn Brooks Chair in Black Literature and Creative Writing. In 1969, however, health problems forced her to resign from teaching, and she devoted herself to the work she most loved: the production of poetry.

ANALYSIS

Critics have called Brooks's poetry "elegant and earthy." While she portrays black life in Chicago in realistic detail, she blends realism with lyricism, giving her poems beauty as well as truth. For Brooks, realism for its own sake is not enough; beauty is the essential ingredient that enables a poem to move its audience.

Brooks's style is characterized by its diversity. She employs a variety of poetic forms, including the sonnet, the ballad, the blues, free verse, and blank verse, sometimes in combination. Her language is also varied. In "We Real Cool" (from *The Bean Eaters*), she writes in black English; in some works, such as "The Anniad" (the second part of *Annie Allen*), she uses language reminiscent of the Renaissance and Middle Ages; in still others, she creates compound words such as "whimper-whine," "heart-cup," "wonder-starred," and "oak-eyed," producing the flavor of Anglo-Saxon poetry. In all of her works, she strives for one central image and gropes painstakingly for the exact words to convey her message. In an interview with writer Brian Lanker, she cautioned that if a line entered a poet's mind too spontaneously, it probably was not original; quite likely, the poet had read it in the work of someone else.

Although Brooks's poems depict black life, her themes (at least in the works written prior to the mid-1960's) are universal. The characters are black Chicagoans, but their problems and experiences are shared by people of all races and in all localities. An example of Brooks's universality is seen in "Gay Chaps at the Bar" from *A Street in Bronzeville.* In this poem, the black and white soldiers fighting in World War II are united in a cause. They have common fears, common disillusions, and common concerns about the future—if they survive. Even though the soldiers' caskets are designated for black or white bodies, a corpse sometimes ends up in the "wrong" box, but, the poet asks, "Who really gave two figs?"

During the 1960's, Brooks gradually became more interested in black identity, her African heritage, and the need for unity among African Americans in the struggle for equality. She had always advocated black solidarity but had also believed that achieving rapport with whites was the answer to racial inequality. Her poems of the 1940's and 1950's present African Americans simply as people; in "Gay Chaps at the Bar," for example, she notes the surprise of the white soldiers when the blacks look and behave like ordinary men. Another poem stressing the humanity of blacks is "I Love Those Little Booths at Benvenuti's" in *Annie Allen*. Benvenuti's was a restaurant in the black section of Chicago; white diners frequented the establishment, however, in the hope of seeing the black patrons clown or eat in a comical manner. In the poem, the whites are disappointed when the blacks' table manners and general decorum are as "normal" as their own.

Near the end of the 1960's, Brooks changed her mind about the effectiveness of racial integration. Undoubtedly, she was influenced by the Civil Rights movement, the death of Martin Luther King, Jr., and a growing unity among young blacks. In an interview with Ida Lewis, a writer for *Essence* magazine, she admitted her belief that blacks should work together for equal rights, independent of white aid, rather than hope for understanding and help from whites. Although Brooks never expressed hatred of whites (as did some of the students in her poetry workshops), she commented in her 1972 autobiography *Report from Part One* that it is rare for blacks and whites to establish true rapport.

Nevertheless, Brooks's later views of the racial situation did not change her from a poet into a prophet or a preacher. In *Report from Part One*, she counters critics who accuse her of sacrificing lyricism for political activism. She maintains that she still regards poetry as an art and still writes lyrically of the things she sees about her. In her maturity, however, she notices phenomena she overlooked in her youth. Two poems reflecting Brooks's growing awareness of racial conditions are "The Ballad of Rudolph Reed" and "Riders to the Blood-Red Wrath," both written in the early to mid-1960's. Rudolph Reed is a black man who purchases a home in a white neighborhood, only to be harassed and killed. "Riders to the Blood-Red Wrath" illustrates the pent-up anger of African Americans. Although he has learned to hold his tongue—as have most members of his race—the narrator of the poem implies that the era of black submission is coming to an end, for he concludes with the words, "We extend, begin."

Brooks's poetry reflects her attitude toward motherhood as well as racism. In her autobiography, she confides that she always wanted children. Not only did she desire offspring for their own sake, but she also wished to utilize the reproductive function of her body. Unlike some highly talented women, she did not view procreation and child-raising as impediments to art. For Brooks, motherhood represents wholeness in a woman's life. In "Sadie and Maud," a poem about two sisters from *A Street in Bronzeville*, Sadie, "one of the livingest chits," has two children out of wedlock, to the disgrace of her family. Maud, the respectable sister, attends college. It is Maud, however, whose life is empty and who ends up living alone "like a thin brown mouse." "The Empty Woman" echoes the theme of futility in a life without children. The "empty woman" takes great interest in her nieces and nephews, but her life is unfulfilling, as she has no children of her own. In "Children of the Poor" (from *Annie Allen*), Brooks begins by saying, "People without children can be hard." Brooks's poetry, then, presents the life she knows in stylistic beauty and also serves as the means of conveying her philosophies.

"KITCHENETTE BUILDING"

First published: 1945 (collected in *A Street in Bronzeville*, 1945)
Type of work: Poem

Brooks wonders whether dreams can germinate and survive amid the details of everyday life—especially in a small tenement apartment.

The efficiency apartment described in "Kitchenette Building," the first poem in *A Street in Bronzeville*, recalls the apartments in which Brooks and her husband lived prior to the early 1950's, when they purchased a house. Bronzeville, so named by the *Chicago Defender*, was a black ghetto consisting of forty square blocks on the South Side of the city. With its cross-section of people and lifestyles, Bronzeville provided Brooks with a wealth of subject material.

Written in an irregular rhyme scheme that moves toward pentameter, "Kitchenette Building" bears stylistic traces of the work of T. S. Eliot, Ezra Pound, and John Donne, while its message is reminiscent of that in Henry David Thoreau's *Walden, Or, Life in the Woods* (1854), which Brooks had read and admired. Discussing the need for simplicity,

Thoreau states that "our life is frittered away by detail." In a similar vein of thought, the narrator of the poem muses about whether dreams and aspirations can compete with the mundane details of life—onion fumes, fried potatoes, garbage rotting in the hall—especially in a cramped ghetto dwelling. She does not muse for long, however; another tenant has just vacated the communal bathroom, so she must scurry down the hall to use what is left of the hot water before someone else beats her to it. Practicality must supersede dreams.

The first line in "Kitchenette Building" suggests the wryness of Eliot: "We are things of dry hours and the involuntary plan/ Grayed in and gray." After this introduction, however, the poem moves into a lighter mood, as the narrator begins to wonder about dreams, which she describes as being violet and white. At age eleven, Brooks began writing her poems and reflections in notebooks; she noted that she associated colors with particular characteristics and images. These associations are found in some of her adult poetry. When the narrator says that she and her spouse are "gray," she means that they are gloomy, depressed with their surroundings. Violet, on the other hand, is a delicate shade of purple, which Brooks connects with art and beauty. In referring to the violet of dreams, she may also be thinking of the flower. Although its blossoms are fragile and short-lived, like many dreams, the violet is an independent, self-pollinating plant. Its independence suggests the individuality of dreams.

Brooks associates white with purity. In "Kitchenette Building," she may be wondering whether any dream can avoid becoming contaminated by the bustle and sordidness of a tenement apartment. In addition, "white" may refer to the white race, implying that only Caucasians have the time and opportunity to dream of the future.

Obviously, Brooks was able to dream and write in her small apartments, but her ability stemmed from her upbringing and innate talent. In the poem, she seems to be asking whether most people living in such places can nurture an aspiration amid the petty details of daily life.

"THE CHILDREN OF THE POOR"

First published: 1949 (collected in *Annie Allen*, 1949)
Type of work: Poem

A mother gives advice—her only gift—to the orphans of war.

"The Children of the Poor" is contained in the third part of *Annie Allen*. Partly autobiographical, *Annie Allen* consists of three sections: "Notes from the Childhood and Girlhood;" "The Anniad," a poem of forty-three stanzas, in which the central character, Annie, attains personhood; and "The Womanhood," in which Annie reaches maturity. In general, *Annie Allen* requires more concentrated reading than *A Street in Bronzeville*, as Brooks makes more obscure implications regarding human nature and uses more complex language marked by symbolism, figures of speech, twists of diction, and unusual combinations of words.

In "The Children of the Poor," Brooks looks at the ravages of World War II from a mother's standpoint. To her, the most vulnerable survivors were the children left fatherless, especially those whose widowed or abandoned mothers were economically impoverished. The poem consists of five sonnets in the Shakespearean and Petrarchan styles, each sonnet examining a different aspect of life from a maternal view.

In the first sonnet, Brooks describes the nature of motherhood by combining positive and negative images. For example, children's "softness" makes a "trap" and a "curse" for their mothers. Nevertheless, youngsters provide "sugar" for the "malocclusions" of the love that produced them. Motherhood is confining, yet fulfilling.

In the next sonnet, Annie declares the need to give her children something that will lend shape and meaning to their lives. Lacking material resources, she concludes that her gift will be a few lessons in coping with the world.

Sonnet 3 proceeds to examine the issue of religion. Having come from a Christian home, Annie retains a core of faith along with a degree of skepticism. Therefore, she advises her children to hold their faith in "jellied," or pliable rules; to "resemble graves," that they might bury doctrines that do not conform to their personal beliefs; and to become "metaphysical mules," stubbornly refusing to accept church teachings without first scrutinizing them. At the same time, she tells them that should their faith falter, she will be there to rebuild it, even if rebuilding involves reinterpreting Scripture or blinding the eyes of her young to disturbing doctrines.

In the following sonnet, Annie sets priorities: Although aesthetics are important, politics must come first. That is, if her children are to be productive, they must first attain a strong sense of self as well as a sense of the dignity of the black race.

In the final sonnet, Annie ponders whether her children will achieve justice for themselves and their race or succumb to "the universality of death." Ironically, Brooks presents dying in a positive light. By referring to death as completion and the grave as "familiar ground," she may be implying that for the poor, death is a release from the hardships of life and the only thing poor children really have to look forward to.

"THE LOVERS OF THE POOR"

First published: 1960 (collected in *The Bean Eaters*, 1960)
Type of work: Poem

Two women from the Betterment League visit a tenement apartment and are overwhelmed by what they see.

"The Lovers of the Poor" is one of thirty-five poems in *The Bean Eaters*, a collection that moves beyond the descriptive and autobiographical to show Brooks's growing social awareness. A satire on people with neither respect not genuine charity, the work was inspired by a visit Brooks received from two wealthy white women who wanted to see how the black winner of the Pulitzer Prize looked. In Brooks's words, they behaved "rather sniffingly." The women barge into Brooks's apartment, apparently without warning, and silently criticize, while their hostess copes with the usual business of the day. The women feel it their duty to step outside their affluent environment and help the less fortunate, but they are totally unprepared for the raw, teeming poverty that they encounter.

Brooks uses several devices to help the audience perceive the women's true attitude toward the poor. First, she employs sensual images that repel the visitors, such as the stenches of garbage, urine, and rotting food. The women are also put off by the myriad "Children, children, children—Heavens!" To the sheltered visitors, there is something repugnant in the prolific reproduction of the poor. Brooks reveals their genuine feelings regarding the poor through references to their "love so barbarously fair," their "loathe-love," and their intent to refresh with "milky chill."

Brooks's use of capitals, lowercase letters, and italics is also noteworthy. Words beginning with capitals imply a dry objectivity. Thus, the capitalization of "Ladies," to refer to the visitors, suggests a crushing, dehumanized force, without individual identity. (Brooks does not reveal until the end of the poem that there are two women.) Other capitalized words include "Slum" and "Possibilities." To the Ladies, the Slum is simply a geographic area, not a human community. Similarly, "Possibilities" is an abstract concept, having no connection to specific persons with potential.

Finally, the italicization of "heavy" in "*heavy* diapers" and "general" in "*general* oldness" accentuates the difference between the Ladies' experience and the present situation. The phrase "*heavy* diapers" suggests that the busy mother in the apartment is less meticulous in child care than the Ladies are or would be, and the "*general* oldness" of the building is not picturesque, like that of the Ladies' mansions, but signifies decrepitude.

In her youthful writings, Brooks associated pink with a mountain maiden, an image connoting innocence and remoteness from the world. Twice, she refers to the pinkness of the Ladies in their makeup and their "rose nails"—thus emphasizing their naïveté. She also mentions their "red satin hangings," associating red with the quiet anger they apparently feel, and "hangings" with slave punishment. Finally, she describes a rat as gray, the color of gloom. It is the rat that induces the Ladies to leave, feeling useless in this atmosphere of despair.

"WE REAL COOL"

First published: 1960 (collected in *The Bean Eaters*, 1960)
Type of work: Poem

Seven pool players at the Golden Shovel are immortalized in eight skinny lines totaling twenty-four words.

MAUD MARTHA

First published: 1953
Type of work: Novel

This short novel in shimmering language apparently derives in great part from Gwendolyn Brooks's own early life.

Gwendolyn Brooks said this in *Report from Part One*: "The WEs in 'We Real Cool' are tiny, wispy weakly argumentative 'Kilroy-is-here' announcements. The boys have no accented sense of themselves, yet they are aware of a semi-defined personal importance. Say the 'We' softly."

These young men should be compared to Jeff, Gene, Geronimo, and Bop in "The Blackstone Rangers," who were a gang of thirty seen by the "Disciplines" (the police) as "Sores in the city/ that do not want to heal." Yet despite the police officers' contempt for the adolescents on Blackstone Street and Helen Vendler's description of "We Real Cool" as a "judgmental monologue" that "barely conceals its adult reproach of their behavior," Brooks's insistence on a soft "We" suggests sympathy for lives at an impasse. The "basic uncertainty" of the "We" reveals no bold swagger but instead an awareness of the plight that circumstances have landed them in and represents a brave assertion that though their lives are short they are somebody too. The poem is an elegy for thousands of young black men whose growth has been stifled by prejudice and its resulting poverty and social confusion.

Placing the "We" at the end of the end-stopped lines results in a gaping hole at the end of the last line, a visual emphasis on the truth of how they "Die soon" and nothing follows. That is all for these truncated lives. The sound effects are conventional alliteration and rhyme. One critic has suggested that "Jazz June" includes a sexual image and that "Die" carries an old Renaissance metaphor for a sexual climax, but this interpretation may strike some readers as strained and out of place.

In the first of the novel's thirty-four brief chapters, the seven-year-old Maud Martha Brown yearns to be "cherished" in the way that she perceives her sister Helen, two years older, to be. The same motif of sibling envy pops up late in the novel when Maud Martha's mother, Belva, reveals that Helen wants to marry the family doctor, a man much older. This revelation (the girls' father is thinking of changing doctors) leads to Maud Martha's musing that "It's funny how some people are just charming, just pretty, and others, born of the same parents, are just not." The best answer that Belva can muster is "you make the best cocoa in the family."

These passages reveal something of the insecurity that Maud Martha feels, but her sensitivity to race and class issues troubles her much more. Her "first beau," Russell, is "decorated inside and out," but he is dismissed in favor of the "second beau," who longs to be an English country gentleman and envies the chaps who have mastered Vernon Parrington's classic work of intellectual history, *Main Currents in American Thought*. Maud Martha comes to an understanding, however, with Paul Phillips, who admits "I'm not handsome," and their generally contented marriage produces Paulette, who arrives in the world in comic confusion.

Some of Brooks's best chapters are stinging portraits of pretentiousness. When she goes to hear a popular black author speak, to his annoyance she tags along with him afterward toward the Jungly Hovel. His tone changes immediately when they meet up with a white couple, and Brooks's contemptuous portrait of this "rash representative from the ranks of the intellectual *nouveau riche.*" Equally cutting is the sketch of Mrs. Burns-Cooper, an elegant white lady who interviews Maud Martha as a potential house maid. Mrs. Burns-Cooper struggles to achieve the common touch as Maud Martha is peeling potatoes, but her tedious chatter about her imported lace, her sister-in-law's Stradivarius, and the charm of the Nile convinces Maud Martha never to return.

Maud Martha is a novel of acute observation of human behavior, and it is written in the bright language of a major poet.

SUMMARY

Writing from her own experience, Gwendolyn Brooks captures black life in both its poverty and its beauty. Her ability to portray beauty comes from her use of varied poetic forms and linguistic devices such as diverse rhyme schemes and diction from earlier eras. In her three best-known collections of poetry, *A Street in Bronzeville, Annie Allen,* and *The Bean Eaters,* she shows personal growth. In the first collection, she is objectively descriptive, in the second, reflectively autobiographical, and in the third, more consciously aware of widespread social and racial problems. Her poetry has touched many readers, regardless of their color.

Rebecca Stingley Hinton; updated by Frank Day

DISCUSSION TOPICS

- How does Gwendolyn Brooks present the poor in her works?

- What is Brooks's attitude toward the young men in "We Real Cool"?

- Children appear prominently in Brooks's poetry. How would you characterize her treatment of them?

- How does Brooks treat racial differences?

- What formal devices—such as rhyme, meter, figures of speech—can be discerned in Brooks's works, including *Maud Martha*?

- Discuss how Bronzeville becomes for Brooks a sort of microcosm, like William Faulkner's Yoknapatawpha and Thomas Hardy's Wessex.

- How does Mrs. Burns-Cooper offend the narrator in chapter 30 of *Maud Martha*?

- Chapter 25 of *Maud Martha* ends with the sentence "She kept on staring into Sonia Johnson's irises." Explain.

- Brooks is superb at catching people's personalities with a few striking phrases, as in chapter 23 of *Maud Martha*. Identify examples of this skill in both the poetry and the prose.

BIBLIOGRAPHY

By the Author

POETRY:
A Street in Bronzeville, 1945
Annie Allen, 1949
The Bean Eaters, 1960
Selected Poems, 1963
We Real Cool, 1966
The Wall, 1967
In the Mecca, 1968
Riot, 1969
Family Pictures, 1970
Aloneness, 1971
Black Steel: Joe Frazier and Muhammad Ali, 1971
Aurora, 1972
Beckonings, 1975
Primer for Blacks, 1980

To Disembark, 1981
Black Love, 1982
The Near-Johannesburg Boy, 1986
Blacks, 1987
Gottschalk and the Grand Tarantelle, 1988
Winnie, 1988
Children Coming Home, 1991
In Montgomery, 2003

LONG FICTION:
Maud Martha, 1953

NONFICTION:
The World of Gwendolyn Brooks, 1971
Report from Part One, 1972
Young Poet's Primer, 1980

CHILDREN'S LITERATURE:
Bronzeville Boys and Girls, 1956
The Tiger Who Wore White Gloves, 1974
Very Young Poets, 1983

EDITED TEXT:
Jump Bad: A New Chicago Anthology, 1971

About the Author

Brooks, Gwendolyn. *Report from Part One.* Detroit: Broadside Press, 1972.

Bryant, Jacqueline, ed. *Gwendolyn Brooks' "Maud Martha": A Critical Collection.* Chicago: Third World Press, 2002.

Kent, George E. *A Life of Gwendolyn Brooks.* Lexington: University Press of Kentucky, 1990.

Lanker, Brian. *I Dream a World: Portraits of Black Women Who Changed America.* New York: Stewart, Tabori & Chang, 1989.

Madhubuti, Haki R., ed. *Say That the River Turns: The Impact of Gwendolyn Brooks.* Chicago: Third World Press, 1987.

Melhem, D. H. *Gwendolyn Brooks: Poetry and the Heroic Voice.* Lexington: University Press of Kentucky, 1987.

Mootry, Maria K., and Gary Smith, eds. *A Life Distilled: Gwendolyn Brooks, Her Poetry and Fiction.* Urbana: University of Illinois Press, 1987.

Washington, Mary Helen. "Plain, Black, and Decently Wild: The Heroic Possibilities of Maud Martha." In *The Voyage In: Fictions of Female Development,* edited by Elizabeth Abel, Marianne Hirsch, and Elizabeth Langland. Hanover, N.H.: University Press of New England, 1983.

Wright, Stephen Caldwell, ed. *On Gwendolyn Brooks: Reliant Conversation.* Ann Arbor: University of Michigan Press, 1996.

PEARL S. BUCK

Born: Hillsboro, West Virginia
June 26, 1892
Died: Danby, Vermont
March 6, 1973

*Buck, in more than eighty books, delineated Asian culture in
forms that Westerners could embrace and understand.*

Edward Steichen/Courtesy, George Bush
Presidential Library and Museum

BIOGRAPHY

Pearl Comfort Sydenstricker was born to Absalom and Caroline Sydenstricker. The fourth of seven children, she was one of only three who lived to adulthood. Pearl was born when her Presbyterian parents were in the United States on temporary home leave from their missionary duties in China; when she was three months old they returned to Chinkiang, China. Her father's work there took him into the countryside for months at a time; her mother remained at home with the children, managing a dispensary for Chinese women.

Educated by her mother and a Chinese tutor, Pearl became proficient in both English and Chinese at an early age. She read the Bible, traditional Chinese tales, and the writings of Charles Dickens, whose character development techniques engaged her interest. Her mother encouraged her writing, convincing Pearl at age six to submit her letter titled "Our Real Home in Heaven" for publication. Beginning at age fifteen, Pearl attended boarding school in Shanghai for two years and worked at a shelter for slave girls and prostitutes. The Boxer Rebellion forced the family to flee to Shanghai until it was safe to return to Chinkiang.

In 1910, Pearl came to the United States to enroll in Randolph-Macon Women's College in Lynch-burg, Virginia. There she began seriously writing stories and poems, receiving two literary awards by her senior year. Graduating in 1914, she returned to China to nurse back to health her seriously ill mother.

Still in China in 1915, she met and then married (in 1917) a young agricultural economist, Dr. John Lossing Buck, a Cornell University graduate. They lived in a North China village, and Buck worked as a teacher and as her husband's interpreter. He worked in the fields among the peasant farmers, and Buck often accompanied him, absorbing details of place and character which she later used in such works as *The Good Earth* (1931).

In 1921, Buck's mother died, and her daughter Carol was born afflicted with phenylketonuria (PKU, which causes severe mental retardation in infants). At Carol's birth, doctors found a tumor in Buck's uterus. Its treatment required a hysterectomy for Buck, thus precluding her from having any more children. She and her husband tried to get medical treatment for Carol but eventually had her institutionalized at a New Jersey facility. They adopted another baby daughter, Janice, in 1925.

While in the United States seeking treatment for Carol, Buck attended Cornell, earning a master's degree in English. She taught and wrote newspaper articles and her first novel, *East Wind: West Wind* (1930). When she returned to China, her unhappy marriage worsened; she and her husband divorced in 1935.

In 1927, conflict among Nationalist and Communist forces and various warlords climaxed with foreigners being targeted and murdered in the Nanking Incident. Pearl and her family fled their home and hid out until American gunboats rescued them. They escaped to Japan for a year.

Buck moved to the United States in 1934, China having become too unsafe for Westerners. Her first novel and the stories and essays published in American magazines had established her reputation. Her second novel, *The Good Earth*, published in 1931 and a best seller through 1932, won the Pulitzer Prize and the Howells Medal and was made into a successful 1937 film. Along with *The Good Earth*, the biographies of Buck's parents, *The Exile* (1936) and *Fighting Angel* (1936), are credited by some for her receiving the Nobel Prize in Literature in 1938. She was the first American woman given the award, within ten years of her first book's publication.

Pearl's friendship with Richard Walsh, the John Day Company publisher of her first book, grew after she returned to the United States. When he divorced his first wife in 1935, he and Buck married. They bought a farmhouse, Green Hills Farm, in Pennsylvania. Pearl moved her daughter Carol to a Pennsylvania institution closer to where they lived. Over the years she and her new husband would adopt six more children.

Her literary output included novels, short-story collections, biographies, autobiographies, poetry, drama, children's stories, and translations from the Chinese. Some books were published under the pseudonym John Sedges. Buck also became involved in several organizations and causes. In 1949 she established Welcome House, the first international adoption agency for Asian and mixed-raced children. It has placed more than five thousand non-Caucasian children. She also established the Pearl S. Buck Foundation that sponsors children in Asian countries. She published essays in *Crisis* (the NAACP journal) and in *Opportunity* (the Urban League publication) in support of American civil rights issues. She was on the Howard University trustee board for twenty years and spoke widely on women's rights, civil rights, and her vision of China and other lands and cultures. On March 6, 1973, at age eighty, Pearl Buck died in Danby, Vermont. She is buried at her Green Hills Farm.

ANALYSIS

Most of Buck's novels deal with the confrontation of East and West. From her own life she knew how the Chinese people, rich and poor alike, lived, and she drew on her experiences to create the

events and the characters who lived those events. Because of her work with her first husband in the peasants' fields and the time she spent in Shanghai working at a women's shelter, she met real people whose lives and ways furnished the details that make her characters come alive.

Having missionary parents, she grew up steeped in the language and phraseology of the Bible. Though she read and appreciated other writings, she found the style of the Bible particularly fitting for many of her works. It was especially effective in *The Good Earth*. The rhythms and patterns of Chinese speech are captured through the biblical manner of expression. She uses a direct narrative approach, avoiding flashbacks and stream-of-consciousness techniques. Thus her stories move along in a strictly chronological mode from start to finish, simply, without confusion, and in language formal yet accessible.

In her 1938 Nobel lecture, she explains another strong influence on her writing. Reading Chinese novels, she says, was one of her early pleasures. The Chinese novel was not an art form conforming to arbitrary rules established by critics and scholars; it was a creation of the common people, who embraced oral storytelling and encouraged a simple narrative form when stories were finally put to paper. Because it evolved from an oral tradition, it was expressed in the language of the common people. Its primary purpose was to amuse its listeners (later readers), so it had not only to tell a clear, straightforward story, but also had to be expressed in words readily understood. It had to be fluid and uncomplicated in its printed form because it was often read aloud to a largely illiterate audience.

Polysyllabic words, convoluted sentences, philosophic meanderings, and lavish descriptive details had no place in such works. Descriptions were needed only to help the reader or listener visualize the scenery and characters. Actions and conversations alone would suffice to convey any philosophic concerns the writer wanted to mention. Most important, the story, though often dealing with myth and legend, must relate to familiar things, things that fill the lives of ordinary Chinese people: love, marriage, family, wars, pillagers, and heroic and villainous men and women.

Buck tried to achieve an unaffected naturalness. Though she deliberately varied her style from work to work to avoid sameness and predictability, certain characteristics recur in many of her novels because her readers can see themselves in her characters. Her heroines are often plain and ordinary-looking; her heroes are often less than brave. With many of her readers American or European, and therefore unfamiliar with the Chinese people she wrote about, she tried always to make her Asian characters and settings familiar in their ordinariness.

She wrote *East Wind: West Wind* with a focus on racial and gender issues, the plot dealing with the clash between Western and Chinese values and traditions. With the more epic *The Good Earth*, she describes a Chinese peasant family's struggles and triumphs, deprivations, and eventual prosperity. Buck's experiences as mother of a retarded child are suggested when Wang Lung and O-Lan's daughter suffers mental retardation. O-Lan's tumor recalls Buck's tumor. When *The Good Earth* was published, Americans were reading Erskine Caldwell's *Tobacco Road* (1932) and would soon be reading John Steinbeck's *The Grapes of Wrath* (1939). While those two books chronicled the American poor, Buck showed that poverty is a universal issue which everyone can understand, even when it occurs in far-off China.

Buck's other works highlight other aspects of Chinese society and history. She wrote two books about the lives of her missionary parents, conveying both their perceptions of Christianity as well as her own. The status of women is an important issue in Buck's work. Her female characters called attention to women's issues at a time when few others considered them worthy of discussion. Some of Buck's themes embrace the nature of love and the polarity of men and women, how marriage enforces or strains the spouses' concepts of fidelity, compatibility, and initial expectations about relationships.

Buck's novels have universal appeal because she is able to convey an understanding of humans in difficult yet ordinary circumstances, surviving hardships with a degree of grace and dignity, and living life with limited expectations. She tried, in most of her works, to promote understanding among peoples of different cultures.

THE GOOD EARTH

First published: 1931
Type of work: Novel

A Chinese peasant struggles with nature and family issues to gain prosperity, in the process losing many things dearest to him.

The Good Earth is Buck's masterpiece. Even though she wrote more than eighty books after its 1931 publication, it is her best-remembered work. Made up of thirty-four chapters dividing the story into two distinct parts, it tells of four generations of a Chinese family as it grows from poverty to prosperity. The narrative begins when young peasant farmer Wang Lung meets his bride, a slave girl named O-Lan, on the day of their arranged marriage. It ends when Wang Lung is an old man, a father and grandfather, placidly awaiting the end of his days.

The novel, a roman-fleuve, tells the saga of Wang Lung's family and its changes over the years. It is also an in-depth character study of Wang Lung, revealing the many sides of his personality. When first seen, he is a timid, humble young man on his wedding day with several admirable qualities: He is hard-working, unquestioningly doing the backbreaking work necessary to make his farm productive. He is respectful of his old father and to the gods he believes hold power over his farm's productivity. He may not love his wife, whom he meets for the first time on their wedding day, but he is as considerate of her as a good husband is expected to be and rarely has a harsh word for her. He even shows appreciation for her uncomplaining labor beside him in the fields, for her presenting him with three sons, and for her subservient kindness to his old father.

Though Wang Lung is illiterate, he is not a stupid man. He understands the value of his land and the importance of increasing his holdings whenever he can. Thus he shows shrewdness, saving money from his harvests and buying land until eventually he is one of the richest men in the region. When others around him sell their crops as soon as they are harvested, he understands the wisdom of holding back until demand is higher and prices are greater. By doing so, he manages to make a profit when others are only subsisting.

Still, when drought hits the region, even his thrifty ways do not prepare him for the famine that strikes everyone in the province. He must pack himself and his family off to a less stricken area in the south. There, in a city, his family begs while he, desiring to work instead of beg, pulls a ricksha. The southern city brings out another side of his character: When a frightened rich man whose home is being looted by rioting peasants thinks Wang Lung is a threat and offers him gold to spare his life, Wang Lung takes the money. He uses it to take his family back to his farm and to purchase additional acreage as well.

His resulting prosperity produces unpleasant qualities in Wang Lung. He spends less time actually working his farm; he hires workers to till his "good earth" and bring about the harvests. Bored and displeased with his plain-looking drudge of wife, he frequents a tea house, where he falls in lust with a young, pretty prostitute named Lotus. He takes her home as his concubine. He has no consideration for O-Lan's feelings about the arrangement; to him wives are for bearing sons, which O-Lan did, and concubines are for love. His sons, now old enough to understand how well-off the family is, urge their father to let them go to school and later to move the family into town so that they and their families can enjoy the lifestyle to which they are entitled.

Perhaps the most deplorable thing Wang Lung does in his fall from humility into arrogance and selfishness is to take two small pearls O-Lan saved from jewels she looted from a house in the southern city. She hoped one day to have the pearls made into earrings for herself. Wang Lung takes them from her to give to Lotus, effectively relegating O-Lan, mother of his sons, to the subservience she endured before marrying him.

Wang Lung shows cowardice and mean-spiritedness in at least one other situation. His father's indigent brother and family move in with Wang Lung once they realize that Wang Lung can support

them. They are disruptive and demanding, and Wang Lung wants them gone. When he tries to oust them, his uncle reveals his affiliation with a fierce robber band which terrorizes the countryside, though never assaulting the Wang household. Aware of the danger if he makes the uncle leave, Wang Lung, showing callous craftiness, concocts the idea of getting the uncle and his wife addicted to opium. He is happy to pay for the opium because keeping them in a drugged state guarantees his peace and quiet.

Wang Lung's educated sons show him how a man of means should dress and comport himself, so differently from how he dressed and acted when he was a struggling young farmer. Even he is surprised sometimes at how he has changed—and not for the better—over the years. Even so, he retains some virtues: he shows a tender devotion to his retarded daughter, his "poor fool." O-Lan had always cared for the girl, but after O-Lan dies, Wang Lung realizes no one else, not the sons surely, will care for the girl, so he is always sure she is fed and sheltered. One wonders if his devotion is altruistic or whether he simply finds an otherwise elusive peace in her undemanding company.

Wang Lung's sense of morality, though weakened over the years, does not die completely. When he takes a second concubine, this time the young slave girl Pear Blossom, even younger than any of his children, he is quickly disgusted with himself and regrets what he has done. He offers to give up the girl, but she chooses to stay with him, and their relationship assumes a father-daughter dynamic. The admirable quality Wang Lung retains throughout the story is his abiding regard for the land, for the "good earth," which he believes gives his family all that it is and has. He tries to persuade his sons to hold onto the land because of its spiritually nurturing value to the family.

A parallel can be seen between the rise of the Wang family and the decline of the House of Hwang. The rich Hwang family had owned the great house in the town near Wang Lung's farm. O-Lan, in her youth, had been one of the slaves there. As the Wang family grew in size, wealth, and prestige, the Hwang family declined. Its sons left the region, some going to live abroad. The family wealth was dissipated through luxurious living and apparently very little productive work. As Wang Lung acquired more land, the Hwangs sold off more of theirs. By the end of the novel, the sons of Wang Lung have also moved away from the land of their father. Being more town-bred than peasant-bred in their outlook, they see the farm only as a source of money once sold. Though they tell their father they will never sell the land, it is clear to the reader that they will repeat the mistakes that led to the decline of the House of Hwang. The good earth of Wang Lung's farm sustained him and his family and brought them prosperity. Divesting themselves of it promises to bring the family to grief.

SUMMARY

Buck's contribution to American letters is perhaps most obvious in *The Good Earth*. Her receiving the Pulitzer and Nobel Prizes for literature attests to the quality of her early work. Although some of her later works are considered propagandistic (*Dragon Seed* [1942], for example), inaccurate in their depiction of Chinese life, or simply not especially good writing, her best works about China have not been surpassed. She was one of the most widely read authors of her time. *The Good Earth* is the definitive story of Chinese peasant life before the Communist regime came to power. She said whereas her critics wanted China represented by its scholars and intellectuals, she wished to present a true view of the common people who were otherwise ignored.

In her lifetime, Buck produced more than one hundred writings. In them she tried to convey her

DISCUSSION TOPICS

- In chapter 18 of Pearl S. Buck's *The Good Earth*, when Wang Lung and O-Lan have a confrontation, O-Lan reveals a side of herself heretofore hidden. Characterize her as she was before and after that juncture.

- In chapter 16, Cuckoo describes the decline of the Hwang family. Discuss parallels with Wang Lung's family once he becomes prosperous.

- Which qualities of O-Lan and Lotus seem "typically" feminine or "typically" Chinese?

- Discuss qualities of Romanticism and of naturalism evident in *The Good Earth*.

- The Chinese government in the 1930's objected to much that was portrayed in *The Good Earth*. Discuss what you think was objectionable and why.

belief that people, no matter what their culture, were basically alike, with the same hopes, fears, expectations, and desires, and as a consequence, they should be able to coexist in peace and, ideally, harmony.

Jane L. Ball

BIBLIOGRAPHY

By the Author

LONG FICTION:
East Wind: West Wind, 1930
The Good Earth, 1931
Sons, 1932
The Mother, 1934
A House Divided, 1935
House of Earth, 1935
This Proud Heart, 1938
The Patriot, 1939
Other Gods: An American Legend, 1940
Dragon Seed, 1942
China Sky, 1942

The Promise, 1943
China Flight, 1945
Portrait of a Marriage, 1945
The Townsman, 1945 (as John Sedges)
Pavilion of Women, 1946
The Angry Wife, 1947 (as Sedges)
Peony, 1948
Kinfolk, 1949
The Long Love, 1949 (as Sedges)
God's Men, 1951
The Hidden Flower, 1952
Bright Procession, 1952 (as Sedges)
Come, My Beloved, 1953
Voices in the House, 1953 (as Sedges)
Imperial Woman, 1956
Letter from Peking, 1957
Command the Morning, 1959
Satan Never Sleeps, 1962
The Living Reed, 1963
Death in the Castle, 1965
The Time Is Noon, 1967
The New Year, 1968
The Three Daughters of Madame Liang, 1969
Mandala, 1970
The Goddess Abides, 1972
All Under Heaven, 1973
The Rainbow, 1974

SHORT FICTION:
The First Wife, and Other Stories, 1933
Today and Forever, 1941
Twenty-seven Stories, 1943
Far and Near, Stories of Japan, China, and America, 1947
American Triptych, 1958
Hearts Come Home, and Other Stories, 1962
The Good Deed, and Other Stories, 1969
Once Upon a Christmas, 1972
East and West, 1975
Secrets of the Heart, 1976
The Lovers, and Other Stories, 1977
The Woman Who Was Changed, and Other Stories, 1979

NONFICTION:
East and West and the Novel, 1932
The Exile, 1936
Fighting Angel: Portrait of a Soul, 1936
The Chinese Novel, 1939
Of Men and Women, 1941, expanded 1971
American Unity and Asia, 1942
What America Means to Me, 1943
China in Black and White, 1945

Pearl S. Buck

Talk About Russia: With Masha Scott, 1945
Tell the People: Talks with James Yen About the Mass Education Movement, 1945
How It Happens: Talk About the German People, 1914-1933, with Erna von Pustau, 1947
American Argument: With Eslanda Goods, 1949
The Child Who Never Grew, 1950
My Several Worlds: A Personal Record, 1954
Friend to Friend: A Candid Exchange Between Pearl Buck and Carlos F. Romulo, 1958
A Bridge for Passing, 1962
The Joy of Children, 1964
Children for Adoption, 1965
The Gifts They Bring: Our Debt to the Mentally Retarded, 1965
The People of Japan, 1966
To My Daughters with Love, 1967
China as I See It, 1970
The Kennedy Women: A Personal Appraisal, 1970
The Story Bible, 1971
Pearl S. Buck's America, 1971
China Past and Present, 1972

CHILDREN'S LITERATURE:
The Young Revolutionist, 1932
Stories for Little Children, 1940
The Chinese Children Next Door, 1942
The Water-Buffalo Children, 1943
The Dragon Fish, 1944
Yu Lan: Flying Boy of China, 1945
The Big Wave, 1948
One Bright Day, and Other Stories for Children, 1952
The Man Who Changed China: The Story of Sun Yat-Sen, 1953
The Beech Tree, 1954
Johnny Jack and His Beginnings, 1954
Fourteen Stories, 1961
The Little Fox in the Middle, 1966
The Chinese Story Teller, 1971

TRANSLATION:
All Men Are Brothers, 1933 (of Shih Nai-an's novel)

About the Author

Conn, Peter. *Pearl S. Buck: A Cultural Biography.* London: Cambridge University Press, 1996.
Doyle, Paul A. *Pearl Buck.* Boston: Twayne, 1980.
Harris, Theodore F. *Pearl S. Buck: A Biography.* 2 vols. London: Methuen, 1969-1971.
Spencer, Cornelia. *The Exile's Daughter: A Biography of Pearl S. Buck.* New York: Coward, McCann, 1944.
Stirling, Nora. *Pearl Buck: A Woman in Conflict.* Piscataway, N.J.: New Century, 1989.
Zinn, Lucille S. "The Works of Pearl S. Buck: A Bibliography." *Bulletin of Bibliography* 36 (October-December, 1979): 144-208.

CHARLES BUKOWSKI

Born: Andernach, Germany
August 16, 1920
Died: San Pedro, California
March 9, 1994

Recognized as one of the twentieth century's most influential and imitated writers, Bukowski, cult figure and "underground" poet, vividly documents the pain of the poor and dispossessed of urban Los Angeles.

Courtesy, Magnolia Pictures

BIOGRAPHY

Charles Bukowski was born in Andernach, Germany, on August 16, 1920, the only child of a German mother and an American soldier father. Because of social and economic difficulties, his parents brought him to the United States when he was three years old. They settled in Los Angeles, where he was raised and educated. His father spent most of his working life as a milkman until he lost that job during the Depression, a tragedy that turned an already difficult family life into an unbearable one. Bukowski's father was obsessed with pushing his son into attaining the American Dream to such an extent that young Charles left home after he graduated from high school in 1939. Their relationship was an extremely difficult one, and his father regularly beat him.

Though *Ham on Rye* (1982) purports to be a novel, it unquestionably documents the early life of Bukowski—his childhood, adolescence, and early manhood. The main character-narrator, Henry Chinaski, is certainly Bukowski himself as he records in vivid detail the poverty and oppression of the Depression years and the damage done to the poor and dispossessed during that bleak period.

Bukowski's two uncles both died young because of their excessive drinking, though his grandfather lived into old age in spite of an irresponsible life of drinking and womanizing. One of young Charles's earliest memories is the contrast between his family's disgust with his alcoholic grandfather and his own memory of him as a warm and generous presence. Bukowski identified with the outcasts early, the isolated and the alienated, and indeed became the writer whose major subject matter documented those empty, wasted lives.

His early family life is a litany of violent beatings from his father, who was unfaithful to his wife and beat her as well when she uncovered the marital infidelities. His grammar school days in the poorest sections of Los Angeles also consisted of endless battles with bigger and stronger boys who mercilessly taunted him because he was awkward, unattractive, and German. He spent much of his time alone, hiding out from the brutality of the daily routine of school.

While his teen years brought more self-assurance on the athletic field, they also brought violent bodily reactions in the form of acne and boils that became so inflamed that he had to be hospitalized. His face was permanently scarred, pitted and ravaged by the skin disease; in the shower room, his fellow athletes cruelly mocked his naked body covered with suppurating boils. During a time following surgery on his face and back, he first felt driven to create an alternate, imaginative world in which he could live outside the agony of reality. He realized that he could become a hero only in his imagination and that within that world nothing could hurt him. In short, he had found a refuge and power within himself that answered only to him,

This realization propelled him eventually into the life of a writer.

Several other key incidents reinforced his decision to become a writer. One took place in the fourth grade, when the teacher was asking all the students what their fathers did for a living; young Charles was struck by the fact that virtually everybody in the class lied, as most of their fathers had lost their jobs during the Depression; the teacher seemed to be accepting the lies at face value. The other incident occurred several years later when a sensitive teacher realized that young Charles's "eyewitness" account of Herbert Hoover's visit to Los Angeles was an elaborately constructed hoax and, instead of punishing him for lying, rewarded him for how accurately he presented his fiction.

Bukowski became a frequent visitor to the local library and would read a book a night. His early literary heroes were writers such as Sherwood Anderson, Theodore Dreiser, John Dos Passos, Aldous Huxley, and especially D. H. Lawrence and Ernest Hemingway. There is certainly little question which of these writers have influenced Bukowski's literary style. His work is frequently compared to that of Hemingway not only because of the journalistic prose and distinctly lean sentence style but also because of such shared obsessions as violence, alcohol, and sex.

Bukowski attended some classes at Los Angeles City College but learned little from his teachers there, preferring the company of the novels of Fyodor Dostoevski, Ivan Turgenev, Louis-Ferdinand Céline, and John Fante. He did, however, excel in college drinking contests and gained a reputation, which he retained for many years, for drinking everybody under the table. He left school without a degree and worked at many different menial jobs—as a stock boy, dishwasher, elevator operator, postman, slaughterhouse worker, and baker. His novel *Factotum* (1975) documents the variety of banal occupations he practiced during his post-high-school years. Except for some prolonged working periods in the postal service, he never stayed at one job for very long. He seems to have chosen a life of insecurity so that he could write without the distractions of duty and career. In fact, his work generally records the life of a rootless writer, a drifter whose only duty is to the poem or the story. In between the writing comes an endless round of drinking, barroom brawls, visits to the track, and short-lived liaisons with alcoholic women. These affairs take place in cheap hotels or boardinghouses that cater to such lost souls.

In 1955, however, Bukowski's excessive drinking landed him in the charity ward of one of the city hospitals, where he nearly died of a bleeding ulcer. After numerous blood transfusions, he left the hospital a shaken realist; he began compulsively writing and publishing poems in the many "little magazines" that were flourishing during the late 1950's and early 1960's. During the 1960's, in the literary ferment created by the Beat writers, Bukowski, who aligned himself with no literary or political group, became a prime example of the artist as maverick. Because he was completely isolated and owed allegiance to no one, he could write about anything he wished. He became the quintessential "underground" writer and, as a result, a major cult figure, having won the "outsider of the year" award in 1962 from the prestigious "little magazine," *The Outsider.*

He produced fourteen books during the 1960's, mostly poetry of uneven quality. Several volumes of poetry, however, such as *It Catches My Heart in Its Hands* (1963) and *The Days Run Away Like Wild Horses over the Hills* (1969), contained a number of highly moving poems that convinced the most anti-Bukowski critics that he could create poetry of deep feeling and substantial literary merit.

In 1970, John Martin of Black Sparrow Press convinced him to quit working at the post office after fourteen years to devote himself to writing full-time. Bukowski continued to produce prolifically during the 1970's, writing three highly acclaimed novels, *Post Office* (1971), *Factotum* (1975), and *Women* (1978), and many volumes of poetry and short stories. The 1980's brought forth two major novels which have met with generally high critical praise: *Ham on Rye* (1982) and *Hollywood* (1989). Bukowski gained further renown because of his screenplay for the motion picture *Barfly* (1987), starring Mickey Rourke and Faye Dunaway. Known for wasting nothing, Bukowski wrote a comic novel, *Hollywood*, which was essentially about the making of the film.

Bukowski continued to publish volumes of poetry, his first love, and many short stories even after becoming wealthy as a result of his royalties. He is still considered a major cult figure, especially in France and Germany, where his books were consistent best sellers. Though in the late 1980's his health took a downturn, he continued, as he put it, "playing with the poem." His last—and longest—volume of poetry published during his lifetime was *The Last Night of the Earth Poems* (1992). He died of leukemia in 1994.

ANALYSIS

Bukowski seldom commented on his own work, as most of his readers know that virtually all the novels, short stories, and poems are thinly veiled approximations of his actual life. Indeed, his highly acclaimed novel *Ham on Rye* (1982) is not only his autobiography but also an American portrait of the artist as a young man. Literary critics find his work difficult to interpret because it so closely resembles the actual day-to-day routine of an unapologetic, hard-drinking, womanizing gambler who loves playing the horses and brawling in barrooms. His work records the despairing lifestyles of the poor and infamous in Los Angeles in unrelenting detail. In *Hollywood*, his alter ego, Henry Chinaski, announces himself as "a historian of drink" who has no peer and wryly adds that he has outlived his drinking companions principally because he "never gets out of bed before noon."

The great French playwright and novelist Jean Genet called Bukowski "the best poet in America," words of high praise from an artist who rarely commented on another poet's work and is considered the archetypal "underground" writer of the twentieth century. Bukowski's themes are the same in most all of his poetry, novels, and short stories: violence, despair, poverty, hopelessness, alcoholism, suicide, madness, and how alcohol, sex, gambling, and, most important, writing can intermittently relieve the agony of these lives of dramatic desperation. He is among the United States' best-known existential writers and, many would claim, the most influential and imitated American poet. Bukowski owed allegiance to no one for the success of his work except the persistent integrity of the small presses that first published his work and especially Black Sparrow Press. The only literary assistance he ever received was from the books he read in his local public library.

Bukowski continued his work in spite of the psychological or physical traumas he was experiencing at any given moment; his fictive alter ego, Henry Chinaski, always finds time to jot down a few lines of a poem on the back of an envelope or a pa-per bag. What motivated Bukowski's commitment to the life of the imagination was his unflinching realization that without it, his life would be as meaningless and absurd as the rest of the trapped creatures he writes about. Wallace Stevens, one of the most important poets of the twentieth century, defined the imagination as the "violence within that protects us from the violence without." There is little doubt that Bukowski viewed its function in exactly the same terms, yet in an even more profoundly personal way. He survived on the mean streets of Los Angeles, after all, not (as did Stevens) in the comfortable safety of the office of vice president of one of the United States' largest insurance companies.

One of the more compelling poems from what is perhaps Bukowski's best-known collection of poetry, *The Days Run Away Like Wild Horses over the Hills*, concerns the plight of a poor man who discovers his beloved wife's infidelities and proceeds to castrate himself in her horrified presence, flushing his testicles down the toilet yet continuing to drink his wine while holding a bloody towel between his legs with a look of utter indifference on his face. The poem is called "Freedom." The ruling passions of the poor, the ugly, and the hopeless are, in Bukowski's view, much more significant to them than those of the wealthy are to them, simply because they are all that the poor have. In one of Bukowski's finest collections of poems, *It Catches My Heart in Its Hands*, he presents a world in which the young are "fenced in/ stabbed and shaven/ taught words/ propped up/ to die"—an existence in which "you and I ain't living well! or enough."

Critics often compare Bukowski to several of the so-called Beat writers (such as Jack Kerouac, William Burroughs, and Allen Ginsberg) but fail to mention that Bukowski's is a working-class background. He never had the opportunity to attend such prestigious universities as Columbia or Harvard, as did the other three writers. A number of his public school friends' fathers committed suicide during the Depression, while many others drank themselves into early graves. Though Kerouac emerged from a working-class New England background, he attended Columbia University on a football scholarship, while Allen Ginsberg and William Burroughs came out of college-educated families with traditions of reading and culture.

Though Bukowski is frequently compared to

Henry Miller in his graphic depiction of drinking and sexual freedom, one never feels that Bukowski is in any way romanticizing that lifestyle. Miller's characters could, if they chose, move on to an economically more rewarding life and, because of their intelligence, charm, or sexual prowess, find any number of amorous partners in countless cafés of the Latin Quarter of Paris during the 1930's.

What brings people together to form couples in most of Bukowski's works is that nobody else wants them; they are social outcasts who are desperate for sexual contact or for any kind of momentary intimacy that will temporarily assuage their empty despair. In the novel *Post Office*, the transient sexual liaisons with Betty, Mary-Lou, Joyce, and Fay do not last long, but they are vital in creating a meaningful life for Henry Chinaski (though he never thinks of his life in anything but temporary terms, because people are going mad or dying around him constantly). There is no aunt back East like the one to whom Sal Paradise, the fictive alter ego of Jack Kerouac in *On the Road* (1957), continually returns for solace, comfort, and forgiveness, Bukowski's heroes are denied the luxury of despair because there is literally no physical place to indulge in that kind of self-pity.

The desperate and unvarying patterns of lives that Bukowski presents in most of his novels, short stories, and poems can be summarized quite bluntly in an excerpt from his volume of poems titled *Dangling in the Tournefortia* (1981): "it was 11 A.M. and I was puking/ trying to get a can of ale down/ the whore in the bed next to me/ in her torn slip/ mumbling about her children in/ Atlanta." It is these stark imagistic scenes, repeated in book after book, that call to mind the literary advice from another stark poet, William Carlos Williams, and his rule for writers: "No ideas but in things." Bukowski's action immediately moves into image with no intervening philosophical speculations; his language records with unflinching accuracy scenes that tell all.

The critic John William Corrington captures the effect of Bukowski's direct language when he calls it "the spoken voice nailed to the paper." Not all of Bukowski's language, though, is so brutally naturalistic. He regularly offers a bittersweet comic side to the dreary life of cheap boardinghouses and the eternal quest for the rent check. In a poem titled "The Tragedy of the Leaves," he talks about the necessity for laughter in spite of depressing circumstances:

> what was needed now
> was a good comedian, ancient style, a jester
> with jokes upon absurd pain; pain is absurd
> because it exists, nothing more;
> . . . .
> and I walk into the dark hall
> where the landlady stood
> execrating and final,
> sending me to hell
> waving her fat sweaty arms
> and screaming
> screaming for rent
> because the world has failed us
> both.

There is also in these lines an empathetic quality of the poet as spokesman for all members of his tribe of down-and-outers, the losers in this world. The cadences are reminiscent of a bardic voice. One could certainly view Bukowski as the bard for his people in the poorer sections of Los Angeles where he originated. Bards have traditionally been viewed as the voices of their people but always of people in a very specific physical locale. Allen Ginsberg and William Blake project bardic voices and attempt to reconnect their readers to the truth of their own experiences. Bukowski's bardic voice, like that of William Carlos Williams, functions in a much more specific geographical place using the energies of the local, depleted though they may be, to generate utterance.

Though his message is consistently pessimistic, it is not the hopelessly bitter pessimism of his poetic idol, American poet Robinson Jeffers. Even in the midst of violence and death, Bukowski continues to offer hope. In lines reverberating with E. E. Cummings and William Carlos Williams, he declaims: "I want trumpets and crowing, . . . I want the whirl and tang of a simple living orange/ in a simple living tree." The great poet Robert Duncan once defined the word "responsibility" by breaking it down into its etymological units as "response-ability: that is, keeping the ability to respond." If one defines the word in those terms, Bukowski is arguably the most "responsible" poet that America has produced since Walt Whitman. He unquestionably kept and even celebrated his ability to respond vividly to his own life and the lives lived in his bardic realm with an affection, dedication, and faithfulness rarely encountered in contemporary American literature.

POST OFFICE

First published: 1971
Type of work: Novel

The normally jobless, transient Henry Chinaski attempts to live a normal life with a permanent job in the postal service.

Post Office is Bukowski's first novel; it became one of his best-selling works. He had published approximately twenty books of poems and short stories during the 1960's, with his hero, Henry Chinaski, as the major character in most of the stories. *Post Office* breaks no new literary ground but offers amplified versions of his typical narratives, now covering a fourteen-year period of employment in the postal service. The plot moves through various episodes of crises with his supervisors, coworkers, and lovers. *Post Office* presents a domesticated version of the picaresque hero. Chinaski certainly fits the major requirements of the typical picaresque hero, as he is a rogue who satirizes his authoritative supervisors in a series of loosely connected episodes. While his tone is consistently cynical, he usually projects a morally superior attitude.

The plot moves along on the intensity and energy of the particular crisis that involves Chinaski at any given moment. He initially seeks employment with the postal service because the monotonous work appears easy, and he seems exhausted with his transient living conditions; his betting at the race track has also drained his financial resources. The opening line, "It began as a mistake," sets the tone for the entire novel, which is divided into six major sections.

The first two sections present his beleaguered contacts with overly demanding customers and inflexible supervisors such as the thirty-year postal veteran Mr. Jonstone, known throughout the remainder of the novel as "The Stone." A bureaucratic bully of monstrous proportions, Jonstone spends most of his days doggedly carping at Chinaski and "writing him up" for the smallest infractions of postal rules. Chinaski, while suffering from The Stone's consistent pettiness, is clever enough to know exactly how far to go and when to utilize similar bureaucratic tactics to intimidate his supervisor into temporarily modifying his mean-spirited behavior. Chinaski's only solace during his apprenticeship is the warmth and sexual security that Betty offers him as they drink their way through most evenings.

As Chinaski's financial condition improves, he concentrates on playing the horses and begins to miss work. Betty, who has become jealous of his attentions to an attractive neighbor, gets a job and leaves Henry. His next amorous partner is a sexually indefatigable Texan, Joyce, who insists on marriage in Las Vegas and moving them to her small Texas hometown directly next door to her millionaire father. There, Chinaski works as a shipping clerk and eventually at the local post office. Joyce becomes bored with Chinaski's inability to keep her sexually satisfied and divorces him. He then returns to Los Angeles, moves back in with Betty, and goes back to the postal service. Betty soon succumbs to the effects of her alcoholic binges and dies in the city hospital.

Chinaski meets a number of interesting but irksome fellow workers in the sorting room, including David Janko, a novice writer who bludgeons him

night after night with the infinite details of both his sexual life and his novel in progress. He relates all these details in a strident vocal narrative that nearly pushes the regularly hungover Chinaski over the edge. The remaining three sections detail Chinaski's relationship with Fay, an aging hippie who bears his child and eventually moves into a commune in New Mexico. His highly successful performance at the track, letters of warning from his supervisors written in impeccable bureaucratic jargon, and his eventual resignation from the post office conclude the novel.

Adding a level of self-consciousness to this work, the concluding paragraph proposes that the seemingly pointless episodic nature of the narrative will be organized into a literary structure: "Maybe I'll write a novel, I thought. And then I did." The concluding paragraph of *Post Office*, though only three short sentences, qualifies this first novel as an embryonic version of a *Künstlerroman*, or a novel about the education and growth of the artist. A number of Bukowski short stories from the 1970's and 1980's such as "Scum Grief," "How to Get Published," and "Scream When You Burn," concern the specific day-to-day problems of the writer. He compares himself to his literary heroes and colleagues of the past and present, such as Dylan Thomas, Ginsberg, and Hemingway. In many stories and novels after *Post Office*, he frequently includes references to his creative work along with the typical drinking, gambling, and sexual scenarios that remain standard subject matter for virtually all his work.

HAM ON RYE

First published: 1982
Type of work: Novel

Bukowski's literary alter ego, Henry Chinaski, chronologically records his brutally poor childhood and adolescence in Los Angeles during the Depression.

Ham on Rye (1982) is not only a loosely constructed autobiographical novel of Bukowski's distressingly poor childhood during the Depression, but it also qualifies as the novelist's version of both a *Bildungsroman* and *Künstlerroman*. A *Bildungsroman* is a literary genre that usually deals with a young protagonist's growth, development, and education into the sometimes harsh realities of life—a fall from innocence into experience, from a condition of blissful ignorance into the potential agony of self-consciousness. D. H. Lawrence's *Sons and Lovers* (1913) is a classic example of this type of novel.

Ham on Rye can also be viewed as a *Künstlerroman*, or a novel that presents the growth and development of the young hero as an artist. James Joyce's *Portrait of the Artist as a Young Man* (1916) and Thomas Mann's *Tonio Kröger* (1903) are two of the better-known examples of this kind of apprenticeship novel. Even though Bukowski's second

novel, *Factotum*, recorded Henry Chinaski's failure to keep even the most menial of jobs, and *Women* documented a similar inability to maintain consistent relationships with his numerous lovers, *Ham on Rye* goes back to his earliest childhood memories, predating the chronic personal failures of Chinaski's middle years.

The structure of *Ham on Rye* resembles the episodic, loosely organized plot of his three earlier novels. It is divided into fifty-eight chapters, some as short as a page and a half. The title is a fairly obvious pun on Bukowski's legendary reputation as a "ham"—that is, a dramatic self-promoter—and his equally infamous reputation as a drinker of heroic proportions. His drink of choice is whiskey or rye. It is also quite obvious that the "wry" or comic attitude that Bukowski/Chinaski projects toward a life steeped in unrelenting pain and misunderstanding saves him from the madness and suicide that have swallowed up less resilient characters. His sense of humor and his ability to view himself ironically help him objectify his sufferings and enable him to accept his condition and work within it rather than hopelessly resigning himself to its despair. His comic imagination, then, transforms the merely grotesque into a vividly compelling work of literature.

While the time frame of the novel covers the young Chinaski from his birth in 1920 to the Japanese attack on Pearl Harbor in 1941, the major focus is on his relationship with his father and other authority figures during his elementary and secondary school years. It is unquestionably his father's sadistic cruelty toward him that becomes the novel's emotional and psychological core. Henry Chinaski somehow creates an interior life that generates an alternate kind of benign violence that enables him to regulate and utilize the destructive energies of his father for his own artistic growth rather than his self-destruction. Though he finds temporary solace in heavy bouts of drinking and mindless barroom brawling, he also discovers, in his local public library, fellow sufferers such as D. H. Lawrence, Ernest Hemingway, and, for humor, James Thurber. A sympathetic teacher encourages his precocious ability to create "beautiful lies"—that is, fictions that fulfill his imagination's yearning for some kind of satisfaction even though he seems buried in a life of poverty, violence, and hopelessness.

Again and again, Chinaski's wry or sardonic sense of humor saves him from the uncertainty and chaos of the Depression years:

> The problem was you had to keep choosing between one evil and another, and no matter what you chose, they sliced a little bit more off you until there was nothing left. At the age of 25 most people were finished. A whole god-damned nation of assholes driving automobiles, eating, having babies, doing everything in the worst way possible, like voting for the presidential candidate who reminded them most of themselves.

It is precisely Henry's resolution not to be "finished" by the time he is twenty-five that drives him to read and write himself out of the despair. It is in a scene in which he attends his high school prom as an onlooker because he has neither money for formal attire nor a date with whom to go, that Henry comes into his deepest realization of his isolation and alienation. He sees himself infinitely separated from the rich "laughing boys" and confesses his hatred of their beauty, their untroubled lives, and their unconscious participation in the joys of youth. He resolves at that moment that "someday I will be as happy as any of you, you will see."

Ironically, *Ham on Rye* dramatically documents that Bukowski not only survived but prevailed by transforming his brutally isolated childhood and adolescence into a critically acclaimed novel for the more privileged members of the class of 1939 to read and envy.

HOLLYWOOD

First published: 1989
Type of work: Novel

A novel about writing a screenplay and the chaos of trying to deal with Hollywood producers who are interested only in huge financial profits.

Hollywood is Bukowski's version of a subgenre of the novel called a roman à clef or a "novel with a key or secret meaning." The key will be immediately apparent to anyone who has seen the film *Barfly*, as the content of the novel *Hollywood* concerns the difficulties in writing and producing that film, for which Bukowski wrote the screenplay.

Though Bukowski has altered the proper names in the novel, many of them are easily recognizable if the reader uses some imagination. The film *Barfly* is called *The Dance of Jim Beam*, and certain well-known foreign directors appear from time to time with names such as Jon-Luc Modard and Wenner Zergog. The major difference between Bukowski's four previous novels and *Hollywood* is that most of the action takes place in Beverly Hills and Hollywood rather than the usual sordid neighborhoods of urban Los Angeles. Some of the sleazier film scenes, however, are actually shot in several of Bukowski's favorite gin mills, which have now become "sets" for the film. The French director Jon Pinchot, in his quest for authenticity, also decided to use the real inhabitants of these places, the barflies themselves, instead of Hollywood actors. Chinaski himself is regularly called in to demonstrate to the actor portraying him exactly how he conducted himself during his habitual barroom brawls.

The plot consists of the endless ups and downs of acquiring funds for producing the film. Bukowski also reveals that greed, and greed alone, constitutes the primary motivation for filmmaking and that producers and backers will do anything to increase profits. He finds that Hollywood has nothing to do with art, truth, or beauty in any form.

The comic aspects of *Hollywood* work on a number of complex levels because the content of the novel is also its form: It is a novel about writing a screenplay, but it is also a novel written by a barfly trying to write a screenplay about the life of a barfly. Not only is the barfly, Henry Chinaski, drinking to excess and trying to recover long enough to produce some acceptable scenes, but also one of Chinaski's major complaints is that everyone else involved in the direction, production, and promotion of the film is also debilitated by their alcoholic drinking. Indeed, when Chinaski is first asked what the screenplay is about, he states unequivocally: "A drunk. Lots of drunks." Later, he adds: "But the whole movie is *about* drinking." During an interview just before the preview of the finished film, he summarizes quite clearly his attitude toward drinking:

> "Isn't drinking a disease?"
> "Breathing is a disease."
> "Don't you find drunks obnoxious?"
> "Yes, most of them are. So are most teetotalers."

Finally, Henry honestly admits to himself as he watches his film, *The Dance of Jim Beam,* in his local theater: "I only wanted to show what strange and desperate lives some drunks live and I was the one drunk I knew best."

Although Henry Chinaski's financial situation has improved by the conclusion of the novel, he and his companion, Sarah, still enjoy going to films together, coming home to the five cats, and watching Johnny Carson on television. Sarah asks Henry what he intends to do now that the film is completed, and he responds that he will now write a novel about "writing the screenplay and making the movie." When asked what he might call the novel, he answers that it will be titled *Hollywood.*

SUMMARY

The literary quality of Bukowski's novels progressively improved, principally because each became more refined and sophisticated in terms of its form. The structure of *Post Office* consisted of a raw chronology of his years in the postal service, while *Ham on Rye* adhered to the pattern of a *Künstlerroman. Hollywood* has the advantage of being a full-fledged modernistic work because its form and content are virtually identical: It is a novel about writing a screenplay as it simultaneously records the difficulties that people encounter who drink too much. What saves Bukowski's work from becoming a dreary record of the hopeless lives of a group of helpless alcoholics is his refreshing sense of humor, his ability to see the irony of his own behavior, and his complete lack of self-pity. His work moved more clearly toward satire with each new novel, demonstrating his ability to see himself and his world in increasingly objective and compassionate terms.

Patrick Meanor

DISCUSSION TOPICS

- What circumstances of Charles Bukowski's life show him to be a real, and not just a would-be, outsider? How are these circumstances mirrored in his fiction?

- Is honesty the best policy for Bukowski's characters?

- Is Bukowski's usual protagonist, Henry Chinaski, more characteristically a victim or an instigator of the afflictions he suffers? Defend your choice by specific references to the novels.

- Cite instances that show Chinaski developing as an artist in *Ham on Rye.*

- Determine what is meant by the expression "bardic voice." Refer to passages in Bukowski's poetry that illustrate a bardic voice and comment on their effectiveness.

BIBLIOGRAPHY

By the Author

POETRY:
Flower, Fist, and Bestial Wail, 1960
Poems and Drawings, 1962
Longshot Poems for Broke Players, 1962
Run with the Hunted, 1962
It Catches My Heart in Its Hands, 1963
Crucifix in a Deathhand, 1965
Cold Dogs in the Courtyard, 1965
The Genius of the Crowd, 1966

The Curtains Are Waving, 1967
At Terror Street and Agony Way, 1968
Poems Written Before Jumping out of an Eighth Story Window, 1968
A Bukowski Sampler, 1969
The Days Run Away Like Wild Horses over the Hills, 1969
Fire Station, 1970
Mockingbird Wish Me Luck, 1972
Me and Your Sometimes Love Poems, 1973 (with Linda King)
While the Music Played, 1973
Burning in Water, Drowning in Flame, 1974
Africa, Paris, Greece, 1975
Scarlet, 1976
Maybe Tomorrow, 1977
Love Is a Dog from Hell, 1977
We'll Take Them, 1978
Legs, Hips and Behind, 1978
Play the Piano Drunk Like a Percussion Instrument Until the Fingers Begin to Bleed a Bit, 1979
Dangling in the Tournefortia, 1981
The Last Generation, 1982
War All the Time: Poems, 1981-1984, 1984
The Roominghouse Madrigals: Early Selected Poems, 1946-1966, 1988
The Last Night of the Earth Poems, 1992
Bone Palace Ballet: New Poems, 1997
What Matters Most Is How Well You Walk Through the Fire, 1999
Open All Night: New Poems, 2000
The Night Torn Mad with Footsteps, 2001
Sifting Through the Madness for the Word, the Lie, the Way: New Poems, 2003
The Flash of Lightning Behind the Mountain: New Poems, 2003
Slouching Toward Nirvana, 2005

LONG FICTION:
Post Office, 1971
Factotum, 1975
Women, 1978
Ham on Rye, 1982
You Get So Alone at Times That It Just Makes Sense, 1986
Hollywood, 1989
Pulp, 1994

SHORT FICTION:
Notes of a Dirty Old Man, 1969
Erections, Ejaculations, Exhibitions, and General Tales of Ordinary Madness, 1972
Life and Death in the Charity Ward, 1973
South of No North: Stories of the Buried Life, 1973
The Most Beautiful Woman in Town, and Other Stories, 1983
Bring Me Your Love, 1983
Hot Water Music, 1983
There's No Business, 1984
The Day It Snowed in L.A., 1986

Charles Bukowski

SCREENPLAY:
Barfly, 1987

NONFICTION:
Shakespeare Never Did This, 1979 (photographs by Michael Montfort)
The Bukowski/Purdy Letters: A Decade of Dialogue, 1964-1974, 1983
Screams from the Balcony: Selected Letters, 1960-1970, 1993
Reach for the Sun: Selected Letters, 1978-1994, 1999
Beerspit Night and Cursing: The Correspondence of Charles Bukowski and Sheri Martinelli, 1960-1967, 2001

MISCELLANEOUS:
You Kissed Lilly, 1978
Septuagenarian Stew: Stories and Poems, 1990
Run with the Hunted: A Charles Bukowski Reader, 1993
Betting on the Muse: Poems and Stories, 1996

About the Author

Baughan, Michael Gray. *Charles Bukowski*. Philadelphia: Chelsea House Publications, 2004.

Cain, Jimmie. "Bukowski's Imagist Roots." *West Georgia College Review* 19 (May, 1987): 10-17.

Cherkovski, Neeli. *Bukowski: A Life*. South Royalton, Vt.: Steerforth, 1997.

Harrison, Russell. *Against the American Dream: Essays on Charles Bukowski*. Santa Rosa, Calif.: Black Sparrow Press, 1994.

McDonough, Tom. "Down and (Far) Out." *American Film* 13 (November, 1987): 26-30.

Pleasants, Ben. *Visceral Bukowski: Inside the Sniper World of L.A. Writers*. Northville, Mich.: Sun Dog Press, 2004.

Sounes, Howard. *Charles Bukowski: Locked in the Arms of a Crazy Life*. New York: Grove, 1999.

_____, ed. *Bukowski in Pictures*. Edinburgh: Rebel, 2000.

Wakoski, Diane. "Charles Bukowski." In *Contemporary Poets*, edited by James Vinson and D. L. Kirkpatrick. 4th ed. New York: St. Martin's Press, 1985.

Weizmann, Daniel, ed. *Drinking with Bukowski: Recollections of the Poet Laureate of Skid Row*. New York: Thunder's Mouth Press, 2000.

CARLOS BULOSAN

Courtesy, APIHDC

Born: Binalonan, Pangasinan, Luzon, Philippines
November 2, 1911
Died: Seattle, Washington
September 11, 1956

Bulosan was the first Filipino writer to have a major impact on American literature, and his America Is in the Heart *has become an important model for the ethnobiographies that followed his work throughout the twentieth century.*

BIOGRAPHY

Carlos Bulosan emigrated to the United States from his native Philippines in 1930. Like countless other young men who had been driven to the United States by the promise of better jobs, Bulosan found instead the crushing defeats of the worst economic depression in U.S. history. The story of his struggles during the 1930's and early 1940's, chronicled in the autobiographical *America Is in the Heart* (1946), had a profound impact on ethnic writing after it was republished by the University of Washington Press in 1973.

It is difficult to piece together Bulosan's real life story, in part because his most important literary legacy is itself a creative mix of fact and fiction. Even the basic outline of his life is in some dispute: Scholars disagree about the date of his birth, the date and location of his death, and his age when he died. What is known is that he was born in the village of Mangusmana, near Binalonan (in Pangasinan province, on the island of Luzon) in the Philippines and was one of several children. Like many rural Filipino families at that time, his parents suffered economic hardship due in part to U.S. colonialism. He completed only three years of schooling and, drawn to the United States by the promises of wealth and education and the dream of becoming a writer, he followed two older brothers and purchased a steerage ticket to Seattle for seventy-

five dollars, arriving on July 22, 1930, while still a teenager. He would never return to the Philippines, and he would never become an American citizen. He worked at a series of low-paying jobs in an Alaskan fish cannery and as a fruit and vegetable picker in Washington and California. Conditions in the early 1930's were miserable for all migrant workers (as documented in John Steinbeck's 1939 novel *The Grapes of Wrath*) but particularly for Filipinos (then called "Pinoys") such as Bulosan, and he experienced racial discrimination and poverty. However, he slowly improved his English, befriended other immigrant laborers suffering similar conditions, and soon was writing for and editing union and immigrant papers such as *New Tide*. He also became involved in organizing workers and, with his Filipino friend Chris Mensalves, formed the union that would later become the United Cannery, Agricultural, Packing and Allied Workers of America (UCAPAWA).

Never a healthy man, Bulosan was diagnosed with tuberculosis in 1936, and he spent the next several years in Los Angeles General Hospital, undergoing surgeries and convalescence. He used his time productively, however; he later claimed that he read a book a day, many by the classic authors of American literature, including Edgar Allan Poe, Walt Whitman, Theodore Dreiser, and Ernest Hemingway. He never abandoned his early dream of becoming a writer and soon was publishing poetry and essays. By the early 1940's, he was gaining national recognition.

In 1942, he published his first book of poems,

Letter from America, and *The Voice of Bataan* was published the following year. Also in 1943, the *Saturday Evening Post* commissioned articles on the Four Freedoms, and Bulosan was paid one thousand dollars for "Freedom from Want," an essay that was illustrated in the magazine by the famous artist Norman Rockwell. Stories, poems, and essays by Bulosan began to appear during the early 1940's in magazines such as *Town and Country, Harper's Bazaar,* and *Poetry.* Bulosan's first collection of stories, *The Laughter of My Father,* was published in 1944 and was broadcast around the world to American troops fighting in World War II; it soon became a best seller.

In 1946, Harcourt Brace published *America Is in the Heart,* which also became popular, but Bulosan's career was already beginning to falter, in part because of two factors beyond his control. In 1944, he had published a short story, "The End of the War," in *The New Yorker,* and he was accused of plagiarism by another writer. The charges were never proven, but the claim and the publicity it aroused damaged Bulosan's career. Perhaps more important, the end of World War II saw the rise of anticommunist hysteria in the United States, peaking in the early 1950's with the witch hunts of the notorious House Committee on Un-American Activities and Senator Joseph McCarthy. Bulosan was investigated for his 1930's union activities and eventually—like many other important American writers—blacklisted. During this time, Bulosan was back in Seattle working as a labor editor but was in poor health. On September 11, 1956, he died of tuberculosis and is buried in Mount Pleasant Cemetery in the city's Queen Anne Hill neighborhood. He was originally buried in an unmarked pauper's grave, but, since 1982, his grave has been marked with a black granite headstone erected by admirers of the Filipino labor organizer and writer.

Bulosan wrote other books, including novels, but most of his later works were published posthumously by scholars who went through his papers and assembled individual titles. E. San Juan, Jr., has been responsible for many of these volumes, including *The Philippines Is in the Heart: A Collection of Short Stories* (1978), *On Becoming Filipino: Selected Writings of Carlos Bulosan* (1995), and *The Cry and the Dedication* (historical fiction, 1995), a novel set in the Philippines during and after World War II.

ANALYSIS

While debate about Bulosan's life continues to exist, the importance both of his career and particularly of *America Is in the Heart* is clear. In this fictional immigrant narrative, he combined fact and myth to create an ethnobiography of his people's experience in the United States in the early decades of the twentieth century. He fictionalized much of his own life in the story but was true to the oppression and discrimination that he and his fellow Filipino immigrants experienced during the 1930's. Unlike the authors of ethnic autobiographies that had been produced in earlier waves of immigration (such as the *Autobiography of Andrew Carnegie* or *The Americanization of Edward Bok*, both published in 1920), Bulosan stressed the class struggle which he saw played out in his own life and created a counterpoint to the standard American Dream portrayed in such works. The result is a powerful story which tells of his own life and that of his people from an anti-imperialist and working-class perspective.

Bulosan's other works have broadened his reputation, but *America Is in the Heart* remains the book by which he will be best remembered. Like other Asian American fiction (written by, for example, Amy Tan and Gish Jen), it explores a number of ethnic issues, including the theme of dual identity—the conflict between the protagonist's roots in an ethnic community and culture and the character's search for an individual identity. Furthermore, like a number of classic American works, from Mark Twain's *Adventures of Huckleberry Finn* (1884) to Jack Kerouac's *On the Road* (1957), *America Is in the Heart* is also the story of a journey of self-discovery. The narrator witnesses countless instances of violence and discrimination but by the end of the story comes to an understanding of himself and of the country he has chosen as his own. Like a number of works from the 1930's (not only that of Steinbeck's *Grapes of Wrath*, but also the novels of writers such as Jack Conroy and John Dos Passos), the book depicts life at its most miserable during the worst economic depression in American history.

Many ethnic American literary works have uncovered an American history that the dominant culture has arguably ignored, including slavery, the extermination of Native American tribes, and the expropriation of Mexican lands. Bulosan's work amplifies two important aspects of these ignored topics, first exposing what U.S. imperialism meant in the Philippines in the early years of the twentieth century and then what further injustices befell the victims of that imperialism who fled to the United States looking for its fabled riches. In the first part of *America Is in the Heart* and in numerous short stories and the later novel *The Cry and the Dedication*, Bulosan writes about his homeland and what has happened to it as a result of American intervention, beginning with the Spanish-American War in 1898. Moreover, in much of Bulosan's works, including the remaining four parts of *America Is in the Heart* and his short stories and essays, to say nothing of the trajectory of his own career, Bulosan documents how he and his fellow Filipinos have been systematically mistreated and brutalized in the American land of promise. Few ethnic writers can ignore their history, but Bulosan lived his and wrote about it almost obsessively.

AMERICA IS IN THE HEART

First published: 1946
Type of work: Autobiographical novel

Allos emigrates from his native Philippines in 1930 and spends a decade working as a migrant laborer up and down the West Coast before finding his calling as a labor organizer and writer.

Carey McWilliams, who wrote a classic study of migrant farm labor in California titled *Factories in the Field* (1939), also wrote the introduction to the University of Washington reprint of *America Is in the Heart*, the paperback which brought Bulosan's work back into national literary consciousness. McWilliams called the book "a social classic" that "reflects the collective life experience of thousands of Filipino immigrants who were attracted to this country by its legendary promises of a better life or who were recruited for employment here." The work must thus be read on multiple levels at the same time: as a greatly fictionalized memoir or life story but perhaps even more important, as a study of Filipino immigration—which in turn is also part novel, part autobiography.

The work is divided into four parts. In part 1, the narrator (named "Allos") describes his life in rural Luzon following World War I, when his brother Leon returns from service. His family is slowly disintegrating under multiple economic pressures, as absentee landlords are crippling the peasant farming economy, and eventually Allos is sent to the city to work. However, the perspective is not that of a young boy: Bulosan is clearly looking back as a writer in the United States. This adult narrator understands the exploitation of the peasants by landowners and the church and sees that radical social change is on the horizon. (The parallels to

AMERICA IS IN THE HEART

by Carlos Bulosan
Introduction by Carey McWilliams

the events on the West Coast—the labor organizing and strikes—in the 1930's of part 2 are clear.) Part 1 ends with Allos standing on the deck of the ship that will take him to the United States "and looking toward the disappearing Philippines" that he will never see again.

Part 2 focuses largely on the racial discrimination and violence that Filipinos and other minorities experienced in the United States. Allos arrives in Seattle with twenty cents, he says, and he is immediately exploited by a Filipino labor contractor who sells him to the fish canneries in Alaska. "It was the beginning of my life in America, the beginning of a long flight that carried me down the years, fighting desperately to find peace in some corner of life." His "pilgrimage, this search for a door into America," takes him instead through a world of gamblers and prostitutes, brutality and bestiality, and disorientation and oppression. He travels south in search of work and comes to realize "that in many ways it was a crime to be a Filipino in California. I came to know that the public streets were not free to my people. . . ." Bulosan relates a series of awful stories in this section, of hunger and pain, poverty and loneliness, racism and exploitation. Unlike the traditional American rags-to-riches story (compare Benjamin Franklin's *Autobiography* from 1793, and the story of how he arrived in Philadelphia with only pennies and within weeks had found friendship and success), Bulosan's story in this second part is an almost unremitting tale of violence and persecution. His "flight" here has taken him to a "crossroads" in his life journey, and he commits himself to broadcast his experience and organize his people.

Part 3 documents Bulosan's intellectual awakening. He becomes part of the labor movement, participates in a strike, and starts writing for *New Tide*. Just as he is beginning this activist role, however, he is diagnosed with tuberculosis and hospitalized. Yet, despite his illness, his "insatiable hunger for knowledge and human affection" begins to be satisfied. Several white women help him get books—he claims he reads a book a day, "including Sundays"—and encourage his literary ambitions. Throughout the work, Bulosan identifies with Robinson Crusoe and his castaway loneliness, but Bulosan's survival was possible only because of the various communities, both white and Filipino, that he found or forged in his new home.

In the short, concluding part 4, he continues to detail the writers who are influencing him—Younghill Kang, John Fante, Louis Adamic (all, like Bulosan, ethnic authors who wrote about their life journeys)—and to describe his organizing activities as his radical consciousness grows. He also begins to write in the same period that the Japanese bomb Pearl Harbor and World War II begins in the United States. Bulosan concludes his narrative with a song of praise to an America that the text itself seems to deny: "the American earth was like a huge heart unfolding warmly to receive me. . . . It came to me that no man . . . could destroy my faith in America again."

The contradictions within *America Is in the Heart* are everywhere. At the same time operating as both history and fiction, a work that praises America at the very moment that it is describing its multiple injustices, the book is a perfect metaphor for the paradox of America itself—its possibilities and cruelties. As a number of scholars have pointed out, the story fictionalizes much of Bulosan's life; on one hand, he came from a better-off family in the Philippines than Allos, and on the other, given his frail health, he could never have worked all the arduous jobs he describes Allos undertaking on the West Coast. The book is, however, true to his ethnic life story and is an accurate collective biography of the first wave of Filipino immigration to America, where exploitation and discrimination were the rule. Its theme thus places it in the mainstream tradition of American autobiography, from Benjamin Franklin through to Younghill Kang (*East Goes West: The Making of an Oriental Yankee*, 1937), as a story of someone who will, against almost insurmountable odds, overcome the obstacles thrown in his path. The two closest comparisons, however, are Depression-based autobiographies: Mike Gold's *Jews Without Money* (1930) and Richard Wright's *Black Boy* (1945). Like both these writers, Bulosan fictionalizes his experience and blurs the distinctions between fact and myth. Moreover, also like these authors, he tells a story of internal exile, of living in America and drawn to its dreams and yet feeling separated from real participation in American life.

SUMMARY

Carlos Bulosan's career has been unique in American literature. An ethnic writer who found fame before most others, he fell into obscurity, died young, and was rediscovered when the recovery of ethnic American literature accelerated in the last decades of the twentieth century. *America Is in the Heart* came to be considered a major work in the Asian American literary canon, but that is where agreement ends. Part myth, fiction, and history, *America Is in the Heart* puzzles critics, for it breaks the genre boundaries that scholars are usually intent on establishing. Still, the work remains Bulosan's most important legacy, a powerful retelling of one important chapter in Asian American history, what the critic Elaine Kim has called "a composite portrait of the Filipino American community, a social document from the point of view of a participant in that experience," and what E. San Juan, Jr., considers "a massive documentation of the varieties of racism, exploitation, alienation, and inhumanity suffered by Filipinos in the West Coast and Alaska in the decade beginning with the Depression and extending to the outbreak of World War II." Carlos Bulosan will hold his place in American literature as long as this country's rich multiethnic history is celebrated.

David Peck

BIBLIOGRAPHY

By the Author

LONG FICTION:
The Power of the People, 1986
The Cry and the Dedication, 1995 (E. San Juan, Jr., editor)
All the Conspirators, 1998

SHORT FICTION:
The Laughter of My Father, 1944
The Philippines Is in the Heart: A Collection of Stories, 1978
If You Want to Know What We Are: A Carlos Bulosan Reader, 1983 (E. San Juan, Jr., editor)
The Power of Money, and Other Stories, 1990
On Becoming Filipino: Selected Writings of Carlos Bulosan, 1995 (San Juan, Jr., editor)

POETRY:
Letter from America, 1942
The Voice of Bataan, 1943
Now You Are Still, and Other Poems, 1990

NONFICTION:
America Is in the Heart, 1946
Sound of Falling light: Letters in Exile, 1960

MISCELLANEOUS:
Bulosan: An Introduction with Selections, 1983 (compiled by E. San Juan, Jr.)

EDITED TEXT:
Chorus for America: Six Philippine Poets, 1942

DISCUSSION TOPICS

- How does the narrator of Carlos Bulosan's *America Is in the Heart* find his own identity?

- Which institutions (the church, the police, and so on) help his growth? Which ones hinder it?

- List all the incidents of violence, cruelty, and racial discrimination in the novel. What patterns do they reveal?

- Is this a story of assimilation into the American mainstream? How so?

- Where does Allos finally find community? Who helps him the most?

- Compare this work with other books about writers coming of age, such as James Joyce's *A Portrait of the Artist as a Young Man* (1916) or Sherwood Anderson's *Winesburg, Ohio* (1919). What do they have in common?

About the Author

Campomanes, Oscar V. "Filipinos in the United States and Their Literature of Exile." In *Reading the Literatures of Asian America*, edited by Shirley Geok-lin Lim and Amy Ling. Philadelphia: Temple University Press, 1992.

Evangelista, Susan. *Carlos Bulosan and His Poetry: A Biography and an Anthology*. Quezon City: Ateneo de Manila University Press, 1985.

Kim, Elaine. *Asian-American Literature: An Introduction to the Writings and Their Social Context*. Philadelphia: Temple University Press, 1982.

Libretti, Tim. "*America Is in the Heart* by Carlos Bulosan." In *A Resource Guide to Asian American Literature*, edited by Sau-long Cynthia Wong and Stephen H. Sumida. New York: Modern Language Association of America, 2001.

Morantte, P. C. *Remembering Carlos Bulosan: His Heart Affair with America*. Quezon City: New Day, 1984.

San Juan, E., Jr. *Bulosan: An Introduction with Selections*. Manila: National Book Store, 1983.

_____. *Carlos Bulosan and the Imagination of the Class Struggle*. Quezon City: University of the Philippines Press, 1972.

OCTAVIA E. BUTLER

Beth Gwinn

Born: Pasadena, California
June 22, 1947
Died: Seattle, Washington
February 25, 2006

Butler, as an African American feminist writer, brought a unique perspective to the science-fiction genre.

BIOGRAPHY

Octavia Butler's father died when she was an infant; she was raised by her widowed mother in California. A shy, quiet child, she was bullied by her classmates because she was dark-skinned and unusually tall. She began writing imaginative stories in a notebook, retreating into her own solitary world. She was a voracious reader; her mother, a domestic worker, brought home books that she had found in the trash. Young Octavia was disappointed to find no African American characters and only stereotyped portrayals of women characters in the science-fiction stories she favored. When she was ten years old, she began writing her stories on a portable typewriter, a gift from her mother.

Although Butler's early stories were routinely rejected by magazines, she persisted in her writing. A short story she wrote as a freshman at Pasadena City College won first prize in a school contest. She also attended California State University, Los Angeles, and the University of California, Los Angeles. For several years she did factory and office work, getting up early in the morning to write. She continued to get rejection slips. She credits the Open Door Program of the Screen Writers Guild of America and the Clarion, Pennsylvania, Science Fiction Writers' Workshop for giving her the critical feedback she needed. She sold her first story when she was twenty-three.

Butler attracted the attention of science-fiction fans with her Patternist series of five novels published between 1976 and 1980. She followed with her Xenogenesis trilogy, published between 1987 and 1989. Her short story "Bloodchild" (1985) won the prestigious Nebula and Hugo Awards. Her novel *Kindred* (1979), published as a mainstream work, explored American slavery. Her novels *Parable of the Sower* (1993) and *Parable of the Talents* (1998) were the first two books of a projected trilogy tracing the development of the philosophy of Earthseed.

In 1995, Butler won a MacArthur "genius" award of $295,000, which was paid over a five-year period. A longtime resident of Pasadena, California, she moved to Seattle in 1999 and published *Fledgling* (2005). A stroke ended her life in 2006 at the age of fifty-eight.

During her career, Butler published twelve novels and a collection of short stories and essays. She preferred writing novels, saying she needed the longer form to explore her ideas. While she discussed her work with audiences, she was uncomfortable reading her work aloud because she was dyslexic. She called herself an obsessive writer and believed that science fiction stimulates the imagination and creativity of both readers and writers.

ANALYSIS

Butler's work, although usually labeled as science fiction, is not easily categorized. Critics praised her straightforward, clear prose style and economy of description. She read widely and was especially fascinated by current issues in the biological sciences. Reviewers agree that Butler's attention to the psychological development of her characters distinguishes her work from that of others in the science-fiction genre.

Butler told several interviewers that she believed that the conflict between the gift of intelligence and the inborn tendency toward hierarchical behavior is the root of human problems. The central tensions in her artistic vision explore the divisions between rich and poor, male and female, people of different races, and humans and extraterrestrials. She is unsparing in her descriptions, whether the graphic savagery of a slave whipping or the depraved barbarity of drugged young hoodlums who mutilate and burn their victims. Butler's fiction is skillfully plotted, and although she was not a didactic writer, her work implies a severe criticism of the moral laxity of the contemporary United States.

Although Butler's African American heritage strongly influenced her writing, she saw racial issues in a wider context, beyond black-white confrontations and even between extraterrestrial and human species. Her positive characters often develop close friendships or sexual ties to those who are "different," in gender, race, sexual orientation, or social class.

Butler's science fiction novels include the Patternist series: *Patternmaster* (1976), *Mind of My Mind* (1977), *Survivor* (1978), *Wild Seed* (1980), and *Clay's Ark* (1984). These works, and the Xenogenesis trilogy of *Dawn* (1987), *Adulthood Rites* (1988), and *Imago* (1989), explore the complex power relationships between human beings and extraterrestrials and feature such science-fiction themes as genetic engineering and human/alien sexual encounters. *Kindred* (1979) projects a twentieth century African American woman into the past as a free black woman in the nineteenth century slaveholding South.

Parable of the Sower and *Parable of the Talents* were the first two novels of a projected trilogy left unfinished by her sudden death. Based on parables from the biblical New Testament, these novels portray a dystopic America of the twenty-first century in which social issues such as gang warfare, drug abuse, environmental destruction, racism, and religious fanaticism are carried to their extremes.

The publication of *Fledgling* ended seven years of writer's block for Butler. The novel tells the story of the Ina, an ancient, vampirelike race that takes humans as symbionts.

Butler's fiction resists classification. Whether writing science fiction or historical novels, such as *Kindred*, she consistently sought a philosophical basis to explore the imperfect world which her characters inhabit. Butler described her writing as a positive obsession and advised young writers to persist in the face of repeated rejection.

If civilization is to survive, Butler's work implies, it will be the strong, black feminists such as those who dominate her fiction who will assure society's salvation. However, her artistic vision offers scant hope that human beings can acknowledge the failures of history and build on this understanding unless they make a heroic effort to overcome their flawed nature.

KINDRED

First published: 1979
Type of work: Novel

A twentieth century black woman is transported to nineteenth century Maryland, where she must survive as a free person on a slaveholding plantation.

Kindred is a historical novel which explores slavery in the nineteenth century United States. The novel is classed as fantasy because of its use of time travel, which allows the protagonist to be transported by unspecific means between two centuries.

Dana, a twentieth century California writer who works at menial jobs assigned by a temporary employment agency, is married to Kevin, a white man. In her first time-travel experience Dana is unwittingly transported in time and space to a plantation in nineteenth century Maryland, arriving just in time to save the life of Rufus, the son of the plantation owner. She is sent back there five more times when Rufus's life is endangered. She returns to her own time and place when her life in the nineteenth century is threatened. During Dana's journeys into the past, Rufus grows from a young child to adulthood; however, elapsed time in Dana's twentieth century life ranges only from a few seconds to eight days.

Dana learns, through genealogical research, that Rufus is her ancestor, and unless she assures his survival to father the child who will be known as Hagar, Dana herself will never be born. The plot is driven by Dana's urgent need to protect the life of Rufus, a self-indulgent, accident-prone child and eventually an impulsively cruel adult. Dana also hopes to influence his character and to mitigate the evils of slavery. The carefully researched details of plantation life in the slaveholding South are graphically portrayed. As Dana notes, while being forced to watch the master whipping a slave, the sensory details of this brutality come alive in ways that cannot be felt by television and film viewers in later centuries.

Dana's predicament is complicated by the author's insight into the psychological conflict among, and within, her characters. As a twentieth century feminist, Dana is at first critical of the slaves' submission to their white master. For instance, Dana judges Sarah, the family cook, harshly as the stereotypical "Mammy" who appeases the master. However, Dana comes to understand that Sarah's submissive behavior assures the survival of her family, several of whom have already been sold down river to certain death from overwork.

On one journey into the past, Dana's white husband, Kevin, accompanies her. She must pretend to be his slave mistress in order to save her life; her attempts to act out this role are nearly her undoing. An unpleasant revelation is Kevin's obvious pleasure in his role as a nineteenth century adventurer, free to travel as he pleases, while Dana is confined to her quarters on the plantation.

Finally Dana must arrange for the young slave Alice to agree to a sexual liaison with Rufus, the event that will lead to the birth of Hagar, Dana's ancestor. This choice is abhorrent to Dana, a twentieth-century feminist. She acknowledges that she herself has become the hated "Mammy" figure, submitting to the master's wishes in order to assure her own survival.

At the conclusion, Alice, the slave mother of Rufus's children (including Hagar), hangs herself when Rufus tells her that he has sold her children. This is a cruel ruse, however, intended to demonstrate his power. He turns his attention to Dana, who bears an uncanny resemblance to Alice. During his attempted rape, Dana stabs Rufus to death. Having assured her own survival, Dana returns to the twentieth century but not unscathed. She bears the scars of two beatings and has lost part of her arm during her violent transport.

Kindred, written in the tradition of the slave narrative, is a study of power and its abuses. In the author's hierarchical world, unusual strength of character is required to overcome the hatred that leads to violence, whether the person is the victim or the oppressor. Some feminists have criticized the author's female characters who, like Dana, are "mothering" figures. However, a recurring motif in Butler's fiction is the agonizing trade-off that circumstances force upon strong women in their quests for survival.

"BLOODCHILD"

First published: 1984 (collected in *Bloodchild, and Other Stories*, 1995)
Type of work: Short story

Gan, a human boy, agrees to be impregnated by the female alien T'Gatoi in order to save his family.

"Bloodchild," which won both the Hugo and Nebula Awards, was first published in Isaac Asimov's *Science Fiction* magazine. Butler has said that she wanted to experiment with the idea of a man bearing children. The "children" in the story are worm-like creatures that will grow into adults resembling sea serpents with tentacles. The central event is the horrifying birth of the alien worms, which are torn from the body of the male host in a bloody operation.

Butler imagines an alien planet to which Terrans have escaped from the disasters of their native

Earth. The alien Tlics cannot bear their own young and must use the male Terrans as hosts. The Tlics use a form of narcotic to seduce the Terrans and develop familial bonds with their hosts, a strange love-hate relationship which foregrounds the conflict.

Gan is a young man whose mother, in exchange for the right to bear her own human children, has agreed to sacrifice her son as a host for the alien embryos. The female Tlic T'Gatoi has an honored place in the home, but the original friendship between the mother, Lien, and T'Gatoi has turned into hostility. Gan, torn between his horror at witnessing an alien birth and his desire to secure his family's well-being, agrees to be impregnated by T'Gatoi. This impregnation is grotesquely reminiscent of human sexuality but with the reversal of the male and female roles.

In this story Butler explores favorite themes: the reversal of gender roles and the inevitable power struggle between two species who must become interdependent if they are to survive. Butler called this a love story, but readers who find the explicit details repulsive might not agree.

PARABLE OF THE SOWER

First published: 1993
Type of work: Novel

Lauren Oya Olamina, a survivor living in devastated Southern California in 2024, journeys north to found the community of Acorn in the hope of fulfilling her prophetic vision of Earthseed.

In *Parable of the Sower*, Southern California in 2024 is a landscape of devastation caused by environmental disasters and governmental corruption. Evil flourishes because of power conflicts between the rich and the poor, who are sharply divided in a segregated society. Lauren Oya Olamina (an African tribal name) is the daughter of a Baptist preacher and educator. Her mother has died of a drug overdose. The family lives in the walled town of Robledo, near Los Angeles. Lauren is a "sharer," one who suffers from hyperempathy, the ability to feel the pain of others, a delusional condition which inhibits her ability to act in a crisis.

Environmental disasters have caused a scarcity of natural resources. There has been no rain for years; people will kill for water. Only the wealthy can afford to bathe and wash their clothing; the poor are identified by their filthiness. Police and firefighters are corrupt and must be paid for their services. Feral dogs rove the countryside, killing humans. Lauren, fifteen, admires her father but re-

jects his traditional Christianity. She has begun a notebook with a series of short poems which reflect her growing belief in her original philosophy, which she calls Earthseed. God, she believes, is Change, and there is no heaven to offer comfort. People must adapt and depend on one another and on their own natural abilities to live in an indifferent world.

Butler's description of life under these conditions is unsparing. Drug-addicted gangs of pyromaniacs kill for pleasure and burn their victims alive. Robledo is an armed camp, walled in against the outside world. Corporations exploit their indentured workers in a revived form of wage slavery. Women and children are frequent victims of rape. Lauren believes that her father's traditional religion is useless in this state of anarchy.

The mutilation and murder of Lauren's fourteen-year-old brother, Keith, by a crazed gang of drug addicts signals the community's coming destruction. Her father goes missing and is presumed dead. When arsonists set fire to the town, Lauren escapes with her emergency backpack, along with several surviving friends. Lauren, who is unusually tall, dresses as a man for her own protection and begins her journey north among the countless refugees walking on the California freeways.

Lauren's first-person narration is a detailed account of her hellish odyssey, with numerous deaths and narrow escapes. Finally the group that she has gathered, which has survived by killing in self-defense, arrives at a coastal California town. Here Lauren, eighteen, marries an older man, Taylor Bankole, who protects and loves her. Although Bankole is a physician without religious convictions, he supports Lauren's missionary commitment to Earthseed and the community she founds.

Lauren's journey chronicles her growing leadership qualities and is an incisive psychological profile of the challenges a prophetic leader faces in forging a community from a diverse collection of survivors. Both Lauren and the community grow successfully because they respect racial diversity and gender and age differences. They also tolerate discussion and dissent.

The narrative portrays keen psychological insight, perceptive character development, and a clear call for tolerance for human difference as the key to survival. The story concludes with a passage from the Gospel of Saint Luke, the parable of the sower whose seed falls on good ground and bears fruit. Earthseed, the ideal self-contained community with its humane principles of inclusion and hard work, offers some hope that it will bear fruit in a hostile world.

PARABLE OF THE TALENTS

First published: 1998
Type of work Novel

The story of Lauren Oya Olamina, begun in Parable of the Sower, *continues with her daughter Larkin's commentary on her mother's journals.*

Parable of the Talents introduces Larkin, commenting on the journals left by her mother, Lauren Olamina. Early in the twenty-first century, Olamina founded Acorn, a community of believers in Earthseed, a collection of philosophical statements based on the belief that God is Change. In the prologue Larkin reflects on her mother's death. She believes that Olamina was a misguided prophet who neglected her family in order to promulgate her beliefs. The novel is both an account of Olamina's life after the events of *Parable of the Sower* and the psychological journey of Larkin as she comes to terms with her own beliefs.

In *Parable of the Sower*, the United States in the early twenty-first century was a nation in chaos. The natural environment was devastated, and most people lived in poverty and degradation. Marauding gangs of drug addicts roamed Southern California, raping and burning and destroying the small, walled communities. Acorn, the working community founded by Olamina to live by the principles of Earthseed, was just barely surviving within its walls. The new president of the United States, Andrew Steele Jarret, imposed his fanatical religion, Christian America, on the nation.

Olamina's journals reveal an obsessive missionary zeal to spread the philosophy of Earthseed; its central belief is that God is Change and that hope lies only in the willingness of human beings to control their own destinies. Larkin learns that her father, Taylor Bankole, a physician, had urged the family to join a safer community, but her mother refused. Acorn is raided by Jarret's Crusaders, a fanatical sect of Christian America. Larkin's father, along with other members of the community, is killed. The remaining inhabitants are enslaved and forced to wear electronic collars which deliver excruciating pain at the flick of a switch.

The Crusaders run slave labor camps and force their slaves to watch public electronic lashings. They routinely rape women as a form of control. The Crusaders force their victims to memorize and recite Bible verses and punish homosexuality with death. The infant Larkin, along with the other children of Acorn, is taken away to be raised by a Christian family and renamed Asha Vere, after the character in a form of popular electronic entertainment called Dreamask.

Olamina's harrowing escape from her slavery and her journey with her growing band of followers northward into Oregon is the principal narrative strain. Larkin's parallel story reveals her connection with her uncle Marc (Marcus), Olamina's brother from whom she was estranged because of their conflict between his traditional Christianity and Earthseed.

The followers of Earthseed, under Olamina's leadership, become a wealthy sect after Jarret and his followers are defeated. The adult Larkin finally meets with her mother in a bittersweet reunion. Larkin learns that her uncle Marc, whom she reveres, has lied about her mother's death. Olamina is devastated by her brother's betrayal. Larkin believes that her mother had abandoned her, choosing instead to follow her beliefs, which Larkin regards as a fanatical cult. She calls herself Asha Vere, rejecting both her mother and her birth name.

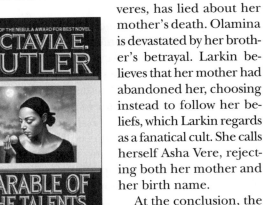

At the conclusion, the followers of Earthseed, despairing of reforming the United States, are transporting themselves through suspended animation to their destiny among the stars. Olamina dies at the age of eighty-one. Her ashes will travel into space to fertilize the fruits of the new colonies of Earthseed—her chosen immortality.

Although classified as science fiction, this portrait of a devastated America is recognizable as an extreme extension of the evils of the late twentieth century: useless warfare, fanatical religion, gang violence, environmental despoliation, and sharp divisions between social classes.

Butler said that the philosophy of Earthseed mirrored her own beliefs. She extended the motif of *Parable of the Sower*, offering the scant hope that human beings can succeed only through a new beginning in space. The story concludes with a passage from the Gospel of Saint Matthew in which the servant who increases the value of his money (talents) is rewarded by his master. If Olamina represents the faithful servant who has used her talents wisely, it is ironic that her eulogy is framed in the parable of the Christian Bible that she has rejected.

SUMMARY

Butler brought a unique perspective to the genre of science fiction, usually the domain of white male writers. As an African American woman, she was attentive to issues of gender, race, and social class. However, she did not view these narrowly as black/white or male/female relationships but extended these explorations to include differences in sexual orientation and even extraterrestrial/human relationships. A consistent motif in her work was her interest in family relationships, especially the painful experiences of her female characters who must choose between their own desires and the needs of loved ones.

Critics praised her attention to character development and her inquiry into the moral choices that confront humanity at the beginning of the twenty-first century. Butler dramatized the complex interaction among the past, present, and future, seeing the acceptance of difference and tolerance for others as a condition for the survival of the human race.

Marjorie J. Podolsky

DISCUSSION TOPICS

- The author called "Bloodchild" a love story. Do you agree or disagree?

- In *Kindred*, what lessons about the past does Dana learn that she will bring into her life in the twentieth century?

- Show how the female characters in Octavia E. Butler's fiction must make difficult choices between their own needs and desires and those whom they love.

- What possible solutions does the author suggest that might avoid the disastrous future she describes in her fiction?

- There are numerous references to African American history in Butler's fiction. Find examples and suggest reasons why she included them.

- Butler called herself a pessimist. Considering the conclusions of her novels, do you agree or disagree?

- Butler believed that the inborn human tendency for hierarchical behavior is the root of social problems. Cite examples of this behavior.

BIBLIOGRAPHY

By the Author

LONG FICTION:
Patternmaster, 1976
Mind of My Mind, 1977
Survivor, 1978
Kindred, 1979
Wild Seed, 1980
Clay's Ark, 1984
Dawn, 1987

Adulthood Rites, 1988
Imago, 1989
Parable of the Sower, 1993
Parable of the Talents, 1998
Fledgling, 2005

SHORT FICTION:
"Crossover," 1971
"Near of Kin," 1979
"Speech Sounds," 1983
"Bloodchild," 1984
"The Evening and the Morning and the Night," 1987

NONFICTION:
"Birth of a Writer," 1989 (later renamed "Positive Obsession")
"Furor Scribendi," 1993

MISCELLANEOUS:
Bloodchild, and Other Stories, 1995 (collected short stories and essays)

About the Author

Allison, Dorothy. "The Future of Female: Octavia Butler's Mother Lode." In *Reading Black, Reading Feminist,* edited by Henry Louis Gates, Jr. New York: Meridian, 1990.

Fry, Joan. "Interview with Octavia Butler." In *Poets and Writers Magazine* 25, no. 2 (March/April, 1997): 58-69.

Govan, Sandra Y. "Octavia Butler" in *Notable Black American Women.* Detroit: Gale, 1992.

Potts, Steven W. "We Keep Playing the Same Record: A Conversation with Octavia E. Butler." *Science Fiction Studies* 23 (November, 1996): 331-338.

Stevenson, Rosemary. "Octavia Butler" in *Black Women in America: An Historical Encyclopedia.* Brooklyn, N.Y.: Carlson, 1993.

Zaki, Hoda. "Utopia, Dystopia, and Ideology in the Science Fiction of Octavia Butler." *Science Fiction Studies* 17, no. 2 (1990): 239-251.

ROBERT OLEN BUTLER

Gray Little

Born: Granite City, Illinois
January 20, 1945

Butler's novels and stories, many of them about American and Vietnamese protagonists and their connections to the Vietnam War, give eloquent voice to a wide range of unusual, funny, and touching characters.

BIOGRAPHY

Robert Olen Butler was born in Granite City, Illinois, on January 20, 1945, the son of Robert Olen Butler, Sr., a theater professor at St. Louis University, and Lucille Hall Butler, an executive secretary. Granite City, a steel-mill town in the St. Louis area, attracted exiles from the Deep South and the Midwest, bringing to the area what Butler terms "a collision of cultures." In the summers of his college years, Butler worked in the steel mills and found himself as comfortable talking baseball with the other workers as he was talking aesthetics with his father and his father's academic colleagues.

Butler received a B.S. in Oral Interpretation from Northwestern University in 1967. On his twenty-first birthday, he decided to write the words rather than act them. To this end, he enrolled in the University of Iowa to pursue a master's degree in playwriting. Immediately after receiving his M.A. in 1969, Butler enlisted in the U.S. Army, leading to service in the Vietnam War, an experience that deeply affected his life and his writing. Trained as a counterintelligence special agent and a Vietnamese linguist, Butler gained "professional proficiency" in the language after a full year of study. The immersion course was taught by a Vietnamese exile who gave Butler a glimpse into the Vietnamese culture and the struggle of an exile. Butler

served his tour of duty in Saigon as administrative assistant to a U.S. Foreign Service officer who was adviser to the mayor of Saigon.

Butler's early experiences with a wide variety of people while growing up in Granite City and his Army service during the war are the two elements in his life that most strongly influenced his writing. In Vietnam, Butler came into contact with a wider variety of Vietnamese people than most Army personnel did. The quality of his contact with the Vietnamese and their culture was enhanced by his command of the language. His total immersion in Vietnam, its people, and its culture shaped the worldview that would become apparent in Butler's fiction.

Following his stint in the military, Butler worked as a substitute high school teacher for a year in his hometown. In 1975, he became editor in chief of the New York City-based *Energy User News*, an investigative newspaper he created. During this time, it occurred to him that he should be writing fiction, not plays. He enrolled in postgraduate work in advanced creative writing at the New School for Social Research in New York City, studying fiction writing with Anatole Broyard. Butler wrote short stories that were published in such magazines as *Redbook*, *Cosmopolitan*, *Fame*, and *Genre*. He eventually turned to the longer and more satisfying form of the novel.

During the daily train commute from his office in Manhattan to his home in Sea Cliff, New York, Butler wrote his first novel, *The Alleys of Eden* (1981), in longhand on a lapboard. Twenty publishing houses rejected the novel. One publishing house, Methuen, brought the book to the galley stage before canceling it. Publishers doubted the novel's marketability, believing that no one would want to read the story of an Army deserter and a Vietnamese prostitute. *The Alleys of Eden* was finally published to critical acclaim by Horizon Press.

In 1985, Butler assumed an assistant professorship at McNeese State University in Lake Charles, Louisiana, where he became the sole teacher of fiction writing in the university's master of fine arts in creative writing program. He settled in Lake Charles, a city with a community of Vietnamese exiles, with his second wife, Maureen, and his son from his first marriage, Joshua Robert. Butler married again, to writer Elizabeth Dewberry.

Butler has received many awards for his fiction, most notably the 1993 Pulitzer Prize in fiction for his 1992 collection of short stories, *A Good Scent from a Strange Mountain*. Additionally, he was a charter recipient, along with only three other fiction writers, of the Tu Do Chinh Kien Award given by the Vietnam Veterans of America for "outstanding contributions to American culture by a Vietnam veteran." Since 2000, Butler has been Eppes Professor of Creative Writing at Florida State University. In the fall of 2001, Butler wrote a short story, "This Is Earl Sandt," from first conception to final draft in seventeen real-time Internet Webcasts to demonstrate the creative process. The story appears in the collection *Had a Good Time* (2004), and the entire event is archived at www.fsu.edu/butler.

ANALYSIS

In a 1993 interview, Butler noted that his military service, his intimate encounter with the people of Vietnam, and his intense experience with the ravishing sensuality of that country turned him into a fiction writer. Butler said, "I had the impulse—that is the impulse of art which is a deep but inchoate conviction that the world makes sense under its surface disorder or chaos—I wanted to write to articulate that vision."

Butler's experience in Vietnam served as the basis for three of his major novels, *The Alleys of Eden*, *Sun Dogs* (1982), and *On Distant Ground* (1985). The major theme of this Vietnam War trilogy is the outsider abroad and at home, an alien in a country at war and an alien in his own country after the war. The three novels share characters, incidents, scenes, and symbols. In these novels, the protagonists are all soldiers who have served together as part of an American intelligence-interrogation unit stationed near Saigon.

In *The Alleys of Eden*, Clifford Wilkes is an Army deserter who escapes from Vietnam during the fall of Saigon with Lanh, his lover, a Vietnamese bargirl. Wilson Hand, Wilkes's fellow soldier and the protagonist of *Sun Dogs*, carries the war with him in his soul to the oil fields of Alaska, where he is on an investigative mission that uncovers industrial espionage. *On Distant Ground* is the story of the court martial of David Fleming, a fellow enlisted man of Wilkes and Hand, who becomes obsessed with the notion that he has a son in Vietnam, whom he returns to that country to find.

In this trilogy, which critic Philip D. Beidler has called "a master vision of Vietnam memory," Butler fashions archetypal scenes of war that personalize the Vietnam experience for the protagonists. In *The Alleys of Eden*, Clifford Wilkes is part of the American torture-interrogation squad (of which David Fleming is a member) that deals with a Viet Cong prisoner. The prisoner is stripped naked and lies near a stream. The American soldiers place a wet handkerchief over the prisoner's face to torture him during his interrogation. The prisoner suffers a heart attack and dies.

For Wilson Hand in *Sun Dogs*, the scene is his kidnapping by the Viet Cong during a visit to an American-supported orphanage. The novel records Hand's ensuing solitary confinement and eventual rescue by David Fleming in a mission where all of Hand's captors are slaughtered.

In *On Distant Ground*, the crucial scene occurs between David Fleming and a Viet Cong prisoner, Tuyen, who has scrawled, "Hygiene is Beautiful" on a prison-cell wall. Fleming sees the graffiti as his mental link to Tuyen, and he liberates his foe, which leads to Fleming's court martial and eventual return to Vietnam to find the son he believes is the product of an affair he had with a Vietnamese woman. In each case, these scenes are interspersed in the texts, creating the effect that they might be the memories of the reader, which Butler says is his aim.

In *Countrymen of Bones* (1983) and *Wabash* (1987), Butler chooses the burden of American history as his theme. *Countrymen of Bones* takes place at Alamogordo, New Mexico, and a nuclear test site in the nearby desert. The conflict of the novel is between Darrell Reeves, an archaeologist who wants to preserve a burial-ground excavation, and Lloyd Coulter, a scientist and disciple of J. Robert Oppenheimer, the American physicist who helped to design the atomic bomb. The burial ground represents a vanished culture unspoiled by American culture; the test site represents the overpowering, destructive force of American culture. The conflict between Reeves and Coulter is also played out in their shared pursuit of a woman who represents the salvation of love for Reeves and an object of obsession for Coulter.

Wabash, set in Wabash, Illinois, the fictional version of Butler's hometown of Granite City, is the story of Jeremy Cole and his wife, Deborah. Jeremy's story addresses the economic and political exploitation of workers and the attendant forces of revolution. Deborah's story concerns itself with domestic conflict, as she navigates the worlds of her relatives and her marriage in an attempt to reconcile the two. As in Butler's other novels, the possibilities of love in *Countrymen of Bones* and *Wabash* are redemptive forces that free the protagonists from the cultural dictates of society.

The Deuce (1989), Butler's sixth novel, is his first novel in which the point of view is that of a Vietnamese boy. It is written in the voice of a sixteen-year-old Amerasian boy, Tony Hatcher. Snatched from his bargirl mother in Saigon by his father, a former Army officer turned district attorney, Tony grows up as unhappy in affluence on the Jersey Shore as he was while a despised mixed-blood child in Saigon. Running away from home, Tony finds himself in New York City, where he must come to terms with his dual heritage and with America. In *The Deuce*, Butler addresses the theme of a collision of cultures by showing two cultures united in the mind and body of a single human being.

This theme is again addressed in all fifteen of the short stories that make up Butler's *A Good Scent from a Strange Mountain*. Each of the stories is told from the point of view of a Vietnamese expatriate living in the United States, an experience that gives resonance to the historical term "New World." Just as the soldiers in Butler's Vietnam trilogy are aliens in a strange land, so are the diverse narrators of these stories of love and betrayal, myth and tradi-

tion, wartime and peacetime. Butler shows that the experience of Vietnamese Americans is the human experience, with all of its pain and joy. Butler's second collection of short stories, *Tabloid Dreams* (1996), takes lurid tabloid-style titles ("Jealous Husband Returns in Form of Parrot") and then transforms and humanizes the absurd premises by delving into the consciousness of the characters involved.

In *They Whisper* (1994), Butler explores the erotic reminiscences of thirty-five-year-old Ira Holloway, whose first-person narration is interspersed with his attempts to "give word to whispers" by re-creating the voices of the women he has loved. *The Deep Green Sea* (1997), a love story with the Vietnam War in the background, creates a similar effect of multiple first-person narrations as Butler alternates between the points of view of Le Thi Tien, a Vietnamese woman, and Ben Cole, an American veteran. *Mr. Spaceman* (2000), a fantasy about the first alien visitor to publicly reveal himself to humans, seems in many ways distant from Butler's other generally realistic novels, but may also be seen as merely an extension of his trademark theme of the combination of multiple cultures and psyches within a single character. Desi, the empathetic alien who absorbs the thoughts of twelve very different humans, is simply the most literal version of Butler's many characters who need to understand alien cultures and ideas. *Fair Warning* (2002) was expanded from a short story commissioned for Francis Ford Coppola's *Zoetrope* magazine into a novel about a forty-year-old female auctioneer's search for love and authenticity.

Butler produced his third volume of short stories with *Had a Good Time* (2004), writing fifteen stories directly inspired by old American postcards from his personal collection. The postcards were all written in the early twentieth century, giving the collection an overall focus and unity, but Butler's imaginative development of the brief messages produces a typically varied range of distinctive first-person narratives. Butler's two decades as a teacher of creative writing are represented with a nonfiction guide for writers, *From Where You Dream* (2005), edited from a series of his classroom lectures.

Robert Olen Butler

THE ALLEYS OF EDEN

First published: 1981
Type of work: Novel

A U.S. Army deserter and a Vietnamese prostitute flee Saigon for the United States, where their relationship cannot withstand the clash of cultures.

Butler's first published novel, *The Alleys of Eden*, explores his often-repeated theme of the spiritual and cultural displacement of people by the Vietnam War. The book tells the story of U.S. Army Intelligence officer Clifford Wilkes and his girlfriend, Lanh, a Vietnamese bargirl.

When a prisoner he is interrogating dies of a sudden heart attack, Wilkes decides to desert; he feels that he can no longer believe in the United States, a country defined in his view by vanity and arrogance. He goes to live in an apartment on a Saigon alley with a bargirl named Lanh. She wonders why Wilkes loves her, as they are so different, both physically and culturally, from each other. Wilkes is as attracted to Lanh as he is to her country. For him, Vietnam has an integrity, a sense of self that he believes America no longer possesses. Lanh comes to understand this and tells Wilkes what he cannot articulate: that he can no longer go home because home is a place where a person feels innocent. She knows that Wilkes will no longer feel innocent in America. Butler writes, "The country he left was empty, the country he was in was doomed."

During the fall of Saigon, Wilkes and Lanh flee Vietnam for the United States and an Illinois town. In the United States, Wilkes is a fugitive, and Lanh, who speaks no English, is overwhelmed. Everything about the Midwest scares Lanh, even the size of the people. She points out that she "did not feel Vietnamese in Vietnam," but she feels Vietnamese in America, a stranger in a strange world.

As Lanh's sense of cultural displacement intensifies, her relationship with Wilkes unravels. Wilkes tries to save their relationship until he finds Lanh praying one day. He asks what she is praying for, and she answers that she does not know. As Lanh's personality diminishes, Wilkes comes to understand that the woman he loves is being tortured, just as they believed they would have been tortured if they

had remained in Saigon. The torture, however, is not physical; it is mental and is inflicted upon them both by the collision of cultures they find in America. Lanh goes to live with a Vietnamese family, where she at least has her language. Wilkes, who had expected to feel like a stranger in America, finds his growing retrospective alienation with Vietnam to be something he had not expected. Wilkes flees to Canada and leaves Lanh to live with the American representatives of her people, the Binh family.

In *The Alleys of Eden*, Butler writes about the American misadventure in Vietnam. The sexual collision between the American soldiers and Vietnamese prostitutes serves as a symbol of the war, just as the clash of cultures heightens the sense of a war fought on American soil. *The Alleys of Eden* provides a vision of what it is to be American and what it is to be Vietnamese.

"SNOW"

First published: 1992 (collected in *A Good Scent from a Strange Mountain*, 1992)
Type of work: Short story

A Vietnamese American woman makes a personal connection with a Jewish widower and comes to understand that despite culture or religion, people are fundamentally alike.

In "Snow," a short story from his 1992 Pulitzer Prize-winning short-story collection *A Good Scent from a Strange Mountain*, Butler weaves the tale of a Vietnamese refugee, Giàu, and a Jewish lawyer, Mr. Cohen. Butler's theme is once again the fracturing of community by the alienating sense of dislocation felt by outsiders.

On Christmas Eve, Giàu is working in the Plantation Hunan restaurant in Lake Charles, Louisiana. The product of a patriarchal society, she is a woman without a man, a position she finds uncomfortable. Everything about America makes her feel alien. In America, people are Christian; she is Buddhist. In America, people are always concerned about time; she had not seen a clock until she came to America (however, she likes the name of the "grandfather" clock, which conjures comforting images for her). She does not feel like those who live in the Vietnamese community in Lake Charles; she does not feel like a "real" American, like she supposes others do. Giàu compares herself to the building housing the restaurant, a former plantation home, noting that the life of a restaurant is not the life the house once knew.

Giàu remembers the first time she saw snow, while working in a St. Louis restaurant. The snow covered all that was familiar to her, frightening her. Just as she is frightened of snow, she is frightened to live her life without a man. When Mr. Cohen walks into the Plantation Hunan, she finds refuge in his face, as if it is a place to hide from the snow. She finds his voice reassuring, like a grandfather's voice. She asks why he is not celebrating Christmas. He explains that it is not the custom of Jews.

Mr. Cohen, a Polish man also displaced in America, is also afraid of snow, which reminds him of his father's death. His father's literal death is linked to the metaphorical death of his Polish and Jewish heritage through his displacement to America. Giàu understands this; it is how she, too, feels. When she saw the snow, she realized that her culture was lost to her. She adds, "I was dead, too."

"Snow" ends on an optimistic note when Mr. Cohen and Giàu agree to a New Year's Eve date. In the story's ending, Butler fuses images and metaphors, cultures and people. Giàu knows, just as her Vietnamese brothers and sisters know, that people should celebrate whatever holiday comes along. She sits in the restaurant, waiting for Mr. Cohen, listening to Grandfather, the clock, tell his story of time. She still has time to make her life whole, to recapture her culture. As two people displaced from their cultures, Giàu and Mr. Cohen can find wholeness and completion in each another as they together face the demands of their new world, the demands of America.

"CRICKETS"

First published: 1992 (collected in *A Good Scent from a Strange Mountain*, 1992)
Type of work: Short story

A Vietnamese father learns to accept the Americanization of his son when he attempts to teach his son a Vietnamese game, Crickets.

From the short-story collection *A Good Scent from a Strange Mountain*, "Crickets" is the story of a Vietnamese family displaced to Lake Charles, Louisiana, and the rift that develops between a father who would like to retain his Vietnamese heritage and a son who prefers all things American. Butler repeats his trope of the collision of cultures, this time as embodied in a second-generation Vietnamese American.

Thiệu is a chemical engineer in a Lake Charles refinery. His American coworkers insist upon calling him Ted; he believes that they call him Ted because they want to think of him as one of them. Thiệu knows that he will never truly be one of them; everything about him and them is so radically different, right down to size. He gives in to the name change because he believes that he has done enough fighting for one lifetime.

As part of the acculturation process, Thiệu has given his son an American name, Bill. The son speaks no Vietnamese and is embarrassed when his father tells him goodbye in Vietnamese. In an attempt to instill some of his heritage in his son, Thiệu decides to teach his son one of his own childhood games from Vietnam, Crickets. Thiệu has difficulty in keeping his son engaged as he explains the game and as they search for crickets.

Thiệu tells his son that there are two types of crickets, charcoal crickets and fire crickets. The charcoal crickets are large and strong but slow and easily confused. The fire crickets are small and brown, not as strong as the charcoal crickets but very smart and quick. The fights between the two types of crickets take place in a paper tunnel made for the game. The game Thiệu explains to his son cannot take place, however, because they can find no fire crickets. Bill loses all interest in the game when he sees that he has soiled his Reebok tennis shoes. Thiệu continues the search for fire crickets but finds none. He comes to believe that a fire cricket is a precious and admirable thing.

The game symbolizes the struggle between the Americans and Vietnamese in the Vietnam War. The charcoal crickets represent the Americans; the fire crickets represent the Vietnamese. Because he lives in America, Thiệu cannot find any fire crickets. Just as there are no fire crickets to fight the charcoal crickets, Thiệu decides not to fight his son's Americanization any longer. Thiệu understands that his son's concern over a pair of Reeboks, a symbol of America, is more important than the boy's lack of interest in the game, a symbol of the Vietnam of Thiệu's past, a Vietnam that does not exist for Bill. The next morning, when Bill leaves for school, Thiệu tells him goodbye in English rather than Vietnamese.

"A GOOD SCENT FROM A STRANGE MOUNTAIN"

First published: 1992 (collected in *A Good Scent from a Strange Mountain*, 1992)
Type of work: Short story

An old Vietnamese man converses with Ho Chi Minh's ghost and gradually realizes that his son-in-law and grandson are implicated in a recent political murder.

The title story in Butler's 1992 collection begins with Dao, a very old Vietnamese man who now lives in New Orleans with his family, recounting his most recent dream in which he is visited by the ghost of former Vietnamese leader Ho Chi Minh, whom he had known in London in 1917 and in Paris in 1918. Dao's three dreamed conversations with Ho Chi Minh alternate with his narration of scenes in which he becomes convinced that his extended family is keeping a secret from him. He suspects, however, that the mystery is connected with the recent murder of the publisher of a Vietnamese newspaper in New Orleans. Dao engages in dream conversations with Ho Chi Minh in which they debate the two divergent paths they chose: Dao became a Buddhist, and Ho Chi Minh led a political revolution and then a war. Dao finally comes to realize that his son-in-law and grandson were directly involved in the recent political murder.

Dao's story interlaces the past and his dreams with the present, a plot structure realistically motivated by the aging narrator's inability to separate reality and fantasy, past and present. At the level of technique, this intertwining of the three strands is reinforced with multiple patterns of imagery. The title of both the story and the book, the image of "a good scent from a strange mountain," illustrates Butler's method. The phrase itself is a translation of the four Chinese characters Bao Son Ky Huong,

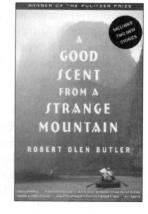

the saying of the Hoa Haos, the Buddhist sect to which Dao belongs. The story uses a variety of scents, particularly that of sugar (Ho Chi Minh had been a pastry cook) as vehicles for exploring and giving nuance to the story's main themes.

The three subplots of historical narrative, fantasy encounter, and contemporary violence intertwine to make the thematic point that the causes and effects of the Vietnam War extend deep into the past, involve spiritual as well as political issues, and, perhaps most significantly, that they persist today, not just in Vietnam but in the United States. Ho Chi Minh's decision to follow the Western materialist teachings of Karl Marx and Dao's decision to follow the Eastern spiritual teachings of Buddha represent a split within the national character that is simultaneously political and psychological, fragmenting both the nation and its individuals. Whether this political and psychic fragmentation can ever be brought together again is left ambiguous at the end.

"JEALOUS HUSBAND RETURNS IN FORM OF PARROT"

First published: 1996 (collected in *Tabloid Dreams*, 1996)
Type of work: Short story

A jealous man is reincarnated as a parrot in a pet store, then bought as a pet by his former wife.

As the title promises, the story revolves around a compulsively jealous husband, who is, as the story opens, sitting on a perch in a cage in a pet store in Houston, reincarnated somehow as a parrot. The reincarnation of the human narrator's consciousness into the animal body is established as the opening premise with the very title and is never explained. However, once Butler makes this stipulation, the story proceeds realistically. Rather than simply imagining a person in a parrot suit, Butler imagines the limitations of the parrot's brain and nervous system. When his former wife, who enters the store and is drawn to him, says, "Hello," he can say it back, but when she then says "Pretty bird," he can only repeat "Hello": "She said it again, 'Pretty bird,' and this brain that works like it does now could feel that tiny little voice of mine ready to shape itself around those sounds." Butler thus provides a foundation for both the recognizably human aspects of the tale and the animal point of view that defamiliarizes them for the reader. The initial encounter with his former wife exemplifies the method: "She knows that to pet a bird you don't smooth his feathers down, you ruffle them. But of course she did that in my human life as well."

She buys him and keeps him in a cage in his former den. The physical transformation of the narrator provides opportunity for comedy, while his more gradual psychological transformation provides the primary thematic elements. At first jealous and combative toward his wife's lovers (he waits for one "to draw close enough for me to take off the tip of his finger"), he comes to love his wife more than he had when alive, to regret his own failures in their relationship, and even to feel pity for her latest lover. He realizes that his consciousness had always been divided, that he had always had another creature inside who might have felt love while he had only felt jealousy and anger. Butler contrives, however, to leave it an open question as to how much of the narrator's emotional change is genu-

ine compassion brought about by his new perspective and how much of it is merely the effect of the supplanting of his human emotional responses by his increasingly parrotlike nature.

One day his wife left the door to his cage open, and he tried to fly to freedom only to fly headfirst into sliding glass doors. He resolves nevertheless to continue to throw himself against the glass. By the end of the tale, the avian elements predominate, but the human narrator's presence, once established, can not be forgotten, and his final desire for flight and freedom, even at the cost of his life, must be read both literally and metaphorically as a desire shared by the human and the bird. The story ends with the implication that his response to this new existence may have the same fatal result as his response to his former situation. As in Franz Kafka's *Die Verwandlung* (1915; *The Metamorphosis*, 1936), which provides one of the few close literary analogues to Butler's tale, the reader is led to consider whether the transformation is really as profound at all levels as one might initially suppose.

SUMMARY

In his novels and short stories, Butler depicts characters that are haunted by the past, ambivalent about the present, and in search of truce for the various wars—not just Vietnam—that they carry within them. Butler's ceaseless experimentation with techniques for representing unusual voices has led to his being lauded as "our pre-eminent practitioner of first-person narrative."

Tom Petitjean; updated by William Nelles

BIBLIOGRAPHY

By the Author

LONG FICTION:
The Alleys of Eden, 1981
Sun Dogs, 1982
Countrymen of Bones, 1983
On Distant Ground, 1985
Wabash, 1987
The Deuce, 1989
They Whisper, 1994
The Deep Green Sea, 1997
Mr. Spaceman, 2000
Fair Warning, 2002

Robert Olen Butler

SHORT FICTION:

A Good Scent from a Strange Mountain, 1992

Tabloid Dreams, 1996

Had a Good Time: Stories from American Postcards, 2004

NONFICTION:

From Where You Dream: The Process of Writing Fiction, 2005 (Janet Burroway, editor)

About the Author

Beidler, Philip D. *Re-Writing America: Vietnam Authors in Their Generation.* Athens: University of Georgia Press, 1991.

Broyard, Anatole. Review of *The Alleys of Eden,* by Robert Olen Butler. *The New York Times,* November 11, 1981, 29.

Lohafer, Susan. "Real-World Characters in Fictional Story Worlds: Robert Olen Butler's 'JFK Secretly Attends Jackie Auction.'" In *The Art of Brevity: Excursions in Short Fiction Theory and Analysis,* edited by Per Winther et al. Columbia: University of South Carolina Press, 2004.

Myers, Thomas. *Walking Point: American Narratives of Vietnam.* New York: Oxford University Press, 1988.

Packer, George. "From the Mekong to the Bayous." *The New York Times Book Review* 97 (June 7, 1992): 24.

Ryan, Maureen. "Robert Olen Butler's Vietnam Veterans: Strangers in an Alien Home." *The Midwest Quarterly* 38, no. 3 (1997): 274-294.

Sartisky, Michael. "A Pulitzer Profile: Louisiana's Robert Olen Butler." *Cultural Vistas: Louisiana Endowment for the Humanities* 4 (Fall, 1993): 10-21.

Womack, Kenneth. "Reading the Titanic: Contemporary Literary Representations of the Ship of Dreams." *Interdisciplinary Literary Studies* 5, no. 1 (2003): 34-44.

DISCUSSION TOPICS

- Robert Olen Butler often creates first-person narrators who are far different from him in terms of nationality, gender, age, and so on. What are some of the techniques he uses to make these different voices authentic and believable?

- The Vietnam War and its aftermath have affected many of Butler's protagonists. Critic Maureen Ryan argues that Butler's are among the most successful Vietnam books because he always subordinates the war story to larger, more complex themes: "in these books the challenges and lessons of the war only complement the main character's life experiences." Test Ryan's idea by applying it to one or more of Butler's protagonists.

- Many of Butler's works introduce mythic or supernatural elements into otherwise realistic narrative worlds. What are the effects of this combination of fact and fantasy?

- Go to the Web site www.fsu.edu/butler and see how Butler created one of his stories from beginning to end. How does this Web site contribute to your understanding of Butler's other works?

- How does Butler reveal the nature of his first-person narrators? Do they simply tell us what kind of people they are, or do we learn about them in other ways as well?

AP/Wide World Photos

JAMES M. CAIN

Born: Annapolis, Maryland
July 1, 1892
Died: Hyattsville, Maryland
October 27, 1977

Cain's best work exemplifies the definitive American mastery of the so-called hard-boiled style of writing, which gained prominence during the 1930's and won international favor for economy of expression.

BIOGRAPHY

James Mallahan Cain, son of James William and Rose Mallahan Cain, was born in Annapolis, Maryland, on July 1, 1892. He was the eldest of five children, including his three sisters—Rosalie, Virginia, and Genevieve—and his brother, Edward. His youthful aspirations, neither of which he completely surrendered during his entire life, were music and playwriting. He abandoned his plans to sing professionally but retained a critical appreciation of music that is evident in works such as *Serenade* (1937), *Career in C Major* (originally "Two Can Sing," 1938), and *Mildred Pierce* (1941). His exceptionally good ear for dialogue failed to ensure his success as a playwright. Between 1926 and 1955, his five attempts to write for the stage all resulted in failure of one kind or another; yet the effective dialogue and swiftly paced plots that did not function for him in drama became the core of his best-selling and most critically praised fiction.

In 1910, Cain graduated from Washington College (in Chesterton, Maryland), of which his father was president and to which, after unsuccessful forays into the world of professional singing, he returned as a teacher of English and mathematics from 1914 through 1917.

During the following decade, Cain worked as a newspaperman for *The Baltimore Sun*. After military service in France, where he worked on the newspaper of his World War I infantry company, he returned to *The Baltimore Sun* as a columnist and feature writer. He published articles in *The Atlantic Monthly*, *The Nation*, and, as a protégé of H. L. Mencken, *American Mercury*. Mencken recommended him to Walter Lippmann, who subsequently installed him as an editorialist for the *New York World*.

Cain's marriage to Mary Rebekah Clough in 1920 came to an end in 1927, at which time he married Elina Sjostad Tyszecka, who was to be his wife during the golden years of his career, 1927-1942. His first short story, "Pastorale," appeared in 1928. He published his first book in 1930, a collection of satirical dialogues titled *Our Government*. In 1931 he served briefly as managing editor of *The New Yorker* magazine and then moved to Hollywood. It was while he was earning his living as a scriptwriter that he produced the novels which, along with his first short story, guaranteed his inclusion in the canon of American literature. He achieved national fame in 1934 with his first novel, *The Postman Always Rings Twice*. This was followed by *Double Indemnity* (1936), *Serenade* (1937), *Mildred Pierce* (1941), and *Love's Lovely Counterfeit* (1942). His second marriage ended in divorce in 1942.

Cain remained in Hollywood for five more years, during the last three of which he was married to Aileen Pringle, a former actress. The marriage, troubled in large part by Cain's drinking problem, ended in divorce in 1947. This was the year in which the last of his best novels, *The Butterfly*, was published. It was also the year of his marriage to Florence Macbeth, the last of his four wives—with none of whom he had any children of his own.

As a writer, Cain had begun to aim at higher creativity, to which end he intensified not so much the profundities of style and thought as the niceties of research. *Past All Dishonor* (1946) was a heavily researched novel set in California amid the silver boom of the 1860's. Following his determination to devote himself to serious literary enterprise, he moved with Florence to Hyattsville, Maryland, in 1948. The best of his post-Hollywood fiction, *Galatea* (1953) and *Rainbow's End* (1975), merely echo his achievements of the 1930's and 1940's.

The major effort of his later period was *Mignon* (1962), his first published novel in the ten years that followed *Galatea*. Like *Past All Dishonor*, it is set in the 1860's, and it entailed painstaking research. The setting is the Red River Expedition to western Louisiana in the last year of the Civil War. Unlike *Past All Dishonor*, which, at the peak of Cain's fame, enjoyed mixed but generally enthusiastic reviews and a successful market, *Mignon* was a disappointment in both areas. Florence died in 1966; Cain himself, writing constantly to the last, died in Hyattsville on October 27, 1977, at the age of eighty-five. *Cloud Nine*, a novel published posthumously in 1984, adds nothing to his reputation.

ANALYSIS

The substance of Cain's fiction coincides with the undercurrents of Greek tragedy—violently satisfied ambitions, incest, hubris, adultery, murder, betrayal, and nemesis. Greek tragedy also comprises drama and music, the two modes of artistic expression to which Cain vainly aspired. Cain's work is best approached in this context of tragedy and auctorial frustration, even if one agrees with W. M. Frohock that the tragedy is "bogus" or "tabloid." (Frohock judges all Cain's work to be "trash" yet recognizes in it a readability to which many first-rate writers are drawn.) Like the major figures in his stories, Cain never got what he truly wanted; yet, in creating those figures, he wrote what he truly wanted to write and, although he did not become a dramatist and creator of high literature, he fathomed the currents of truth that may be the consciously or unconsciously sought goal of all art.

Cain's antiheroes mainly achieve, not their true desires, which may or may not remain unknown to them, but the surfaces of their dreams; the coalescence of the dreamer with the surface of the dream is the guarantee of disaster. Cain appears to have detected the fallacy of the American Dream, which rises brightly but upon unseen and unadmitted props of crime, violence, promiscuity, and sexual waywardness. The first sentence of *The Postman Always Rings Twice* encapsulates the quality and direction of Cain's fiction: "They threw me off the hay truck about noon." In addition to arresting the reader's interest with perfect verbal economy, the sentence connotes the alienation of the unsettled individual ("me") from the establishment ("they"), those who have harvested the fields of the American Dream at the temporarily shadowless (it is "about noon") surface of a society that has been wounded by the dream-destroying reality of the Depression of the early 1930's.

The story that follows is, at the literal level, the working out of Cain's fictional formula: A man and a woman seek sexual gratification and monetary profit from the murder of the woman's husband. At the emblematic level, it presents the American Dream as a sublimation of the quest for sex and cash.

The hard, lean, unembellished, and fast-paced narratives of Cain's characteristic works earned for his fiction the epithets "tough-guy" and "hard-boiled." He objected to these terms both because they placed him in a specific category, which placement as a critical device he abhorred, and because they were also associated with Ernest Hemingway, whose works Cain admired but whose influence upon himself he sternly denied in his preface to *The Butterfly*. In that preface, Cain, differentiating himself from Hemingway, says, "I . . . write of the wish that comes true, a terrifying concept."

The terror derives from the fact that it is chiefly the materialistic surface of the wish that comes true, not the true wish. There are precedents in Greek tragedy. The wish of Sophocles' Oedipus for material success, for example, comes true, but only by way of patricide and incest, the factors which ultimately defeat him; his true wish, unknown to himself until he is brought down by his wish come true, is for spiritual peace, which he learns, at last, is found in love. Cain's antiheroes fulfill their wishes for sex and money but, in doing so, must contend with the destructive forces loosed by the woman— the equivalent of "the first woman," as Cain says in the preface to *The Butterfly*, naming the Greek mythical Pandora.

The woman in *Serenade* murders a man's homosexual lover and restores to the man, through his heterosexual relationship with her, the fine singing voice which readers are given to understand his homosexuality had flattened. Then the basis of the man's successful new career asserts itself as the very destruction of that career. The man learns, after his singing voice reveals his identity and the law then finds and kills his fugitive woman, that his love for the woman was the real meaning of his life.

Love for a woman whom a man mistakenly assumes to be his daughter is the nexus of the tragedy in *The Butterfly*. Here the true love is incestuous, although to himself the man does not acknowledge it as such. His love increases in direct proportion to the strengthening of the unadmitted assumption that she is his daughter.

A virtual companionpiece to *The Butterfly* is *The Moth* (1948), in which a man's love for a twelve-year-old girl is as true as it is conventionally exceptionable. *The Moth* antedates Vladimir Nabokov's *Lolita* (1955) by seven years. Oddly, Nabokov's comic novel about a middle-aged man in love with a twelve-year-old girl ends unhappily, while Cain's novel is one of the few to which he gave a happy ending.

The happy ending is not Cain's specialty. His murder mysteries, *Sinful Woman* (1947) and *Jealous Woman* (1950), end happily and are both among Cain's least effective accomplishments. *Sinful Woman* is representative of another of Cain's infrequent devices, third-person narration. *Mildred Pierce* and *Love's Lovely Counterfeit* carry the device creditably, but the same cannot be said of either *Sinful Woman* or *The Magician's Wife* (1965). Departures from the techniques of *The Postman Always Rings Twice* were, except in the composition of *Mildred Pierce*, not felicitous for Cain. He is essentially a master of the short, brisk, unsentimental, first-person narrative tragedy of people pulled to destruction by the inevitable consequences of their fulfilled material wishes, which at first obscure and then either delay or preclude the experience of their true subjective wishes.

THE POSTMAN ALWAYS RINGS TWICE

First published: 1934
Type of work: Novel

Adulterous lovers who get away with murder cannot escape their fate.

The Postman Always Rings Twice was Cain's first novel and came to stand as his finest work of fiction. It is both classical Cain, with its hard-boiled, first-person narrative of a wrenching love triangle, wish fulfillment, and retribution, and classical in its tragic theme and episodic structure. A very attractive young woman, Cora, is unhappily married to Nick Papadakis, the proprietor of a restaurant. A drifter, Frank Chambers, falls in love with Cora, hires on as Nick's employee, and enjoys Cora's requital of his love. The adulterers successfully conspire to murder Nick, thereby gaining his restaurant business and their own life together. Much of their planning materializes through fortuitous as well as engineered accidents.

It is also an accident that finally destroys both of them, Cora as accident victim and Frank as the victim of circumstances. Having been acquitted of contriving the accident that was supposed to have taken the life of Nick Papadakis, a charge of which he was actually guilty, Frank is now ironically convicted of contriving the accident that killed Cora, despite his innocence. The structure, like that of Greek tragedy and classical literature in general, is symmetrical: Cora and Frank are denied free union by societal and economic restrictions, Cora and Frank achieve free union through their crime, Cora and Frank are destroyed precisely in the context of their achievement of free union. The symmetry is that of separation-union-separation.

Cain's special skill is in presenting a story with the immediacy and relevance of a news item. Stories, historical or otherwise, that did not speak to his own time defeated his interest. He insisted in a Hearst newspaper column for November 11, 1933, that he could not sustain his interest in certain regarded contemporary novels—among them Hemingway's *A Farewell to Arms* (1929), William Faulkner's *Sanctuary* (1931), and Nathanael West's *Miss Lonelyhearts* (1933)—because "they bear no relation . . . to the times in which I live." He believed that "the destiny, the national purpose of the deal" had to be there before a writer could have anything to say; the destiny of the American Dream antecedes *The Postman Always Rings Twice*.

The "they" who throw Frank Chambers off the hay truck also give him a cigarette. He is then given a job by Nick, a businessman whose financial security Frank would like to have, but without the attendant responsibilities; he would also like to possess Cora. Frank does not understand that Nick and Cora are extensions of the "they," reversing the process of gift giving—Nick tendering a job, Cora her body—and causing him to be thrown. The classical symmetry appears as thrown-gift-gifts-thrown.

Behind or beneath Frank's wish for money and sex is his true wish, unrecognized until too late, for love. The establishment, moreover, as the repository of superficial wishes, always defeats the individual whom it ostensibly accommodates. The last paragraph of the novel begins with "Here they come." (These are also the very last words of *Past All Dishonor*.) The "they" of the novel's beginning have, at the novel's ending, become Frank's executioners. Cain makes use of appropriate names in *The Postman Always Rings Twice*: "Nick" and "Cora" are both Greek names, and their characters embody the money and sex that Frank Chambers, whose name is not Greek, wishes to have. Frank's error is much the same as that of the Trojans who refused to share Laocoön's apprehension about Greeks bearing gifts.

DOUBLE INDEMNITY

First published: 1936
Type of work: Novel

A woman and her lover murder the woman's husband for insurance money, after which their mutual desire culminates in a death wish.

Double Indemnity was written by Cain in approximately two months; it appeared initially in *Liberty* magazine as an eight-part serial. It was, as Cain himself admitted, practically a rewriting of *The Postman Always Rings Twice*. In both novels, a man, obsessed with desire for a married woman and tempted by the prospect of easy money, contrives under the woman's encouragement a scheme to murder the husband and profit from the murder. In each novel the effect of the successful criminal enterprise is the self-destruction of the principals in tandem with their ultimate realization of their true love for each other.

Although neither title was Cain's inceptive selection—the original title of *The Postman Always Rings Twice* was *Bar-B-Que*, and *Double Indemnity* was suggested to Cain by James Geller—both include an ironic play on types of dualism. Fatal accidents happen twice, one staged and one actual, in the first novel. In the later novel, there are two double compensations for an accidental death that is actually a murder: The first is the double-indemnity insurance award, and the second is the self-execution decided upon by the two murderers who collected the insurance.

Despite the similarities, the novels remain distinct; each has its special characteristics, and each is a masterwork. The murderers in *Double Indemnity* are Phyllis Nirdlinger, a very attractive, unhappily married woman, and Walter Huff, an insurance agent who falls in love with Phyllis and whom she uses as the instrument of gaining her ends. Phyllis is more cunning and venomous than Cora Papadakis, and Walter is superior to Frank Chambers in both industry and intelligence. The intricacies of the legal profession inform the plot of the earlier novel, and the complexities of the insurance business inform the plot of *Double Indemnity*.

The love story in *The Postman Always Rings Twice* is fashioned against images of purgative swimming (off the seashore) and fertility (Cora is pregnant when the accident takes her life). In *Double Indemnity*, the love story is cast against images of sterility (hearth fire, the moon, Phyllis's thinking of herself "as Death") and culminates in the suicide pact of leaping from a ship into shark-filled waters.

Double Indemnity has other elements that are absent from Cain's first novel. There is a deep friendship between Huff and a father-figure named Keyes, who is head of the insurance company's claims department. There is a subplot involving Phyllis's stepdaughter Lola and Beniamino Sachetti, Lola's suitor. Huff's affection for the stepdaughter results in a double love triangle: Phyllis-Huff-Lola and Lola-Sachetti-Huff. These elements add depth to the story without even slightly curtailing its pace. Raymond Chandler, who wrote the screenplay for *Double Indemnity*, considered the novel, and Cain's work in general, to be "the offal of literature." The judgment, although seconded by not a few critics of Cain's fiction, is rash. In *Double Indemnity*, Cain manages not only to tell a gripping story in very few words but also to introduce a credible love story and a moving friendship into the lives of its concisely sketched characters. Furthermore, Cain's theme, materialistic and selfish dreams as leading eventually to an awakening into the reality of human affections, is far from negligible.

MILDRED PIERCE

First published: 1941
Type of work: Novel

A businesswoman sublimates an erotic need for her unconscionably selfish daughter.

Mildred Pierce is a domestic tragedy in which wife-husband and mother-daughter relationships are perversely confused. Mildred Pierce's husband, Herbert (or Bert), is not a good provider, and his need in a wife is for maternal solicitude. Mildred is a capable and intelligent woman who suffers an obsession with her daughter, Veda, which she thinks is mother love. Veda is a talented coloratura soprano whose obsession is herself. Bert deserts his family for a woman who is a mother figure. Mildred, thrown upon her own resources, becomes a successful entrepreneur in the restaurant business and finances her daughter's musical education, which leads to a bright career. When Veda, constantly betraying her mother, finally deserts her, Mildred is crushed, having lost her unconsciously desired love mate. Cain handles the incest motif more subtly, or perhaps more covertly, and decidedly more effectively here than he does in *The Butterfly*, published six years later. The novel concludes

with Mildred and Bert reunited.

The transformation of Mildred from a mother who would be wife to her daughter to a wife who resigns herself to mothering her husband is signaled in two keynote episodes. The first is the one in which Mildred learns that Veda is pregnant. Her immediate reaction is neither maternal protectiveness nor the murderous anger that Bert will feel toward the man responsible, but a fierce "jealousy . . . so overwhelming that Mildred actually was afraid she would vomit." This response is a betrayed lover's reaction, not a mother's. The distraught Mildred asks Veda "if she'd like to sleep with her, 'just for tonight.'" Veda declines, and Mildred spends a wakeful night "with the jealousy gnawing at her."

The second episode is the conclusion of the novel. Bert says to Mildred "to hell with" Veda, and Mildred, sensing his meaning, manages to swallow her sobs "and draw the knife across an umbilical cord." The indefinite article is functionally ambiguous, referring both to Veda, whose frustrated lover Mildred ceases to be, and to Bert, whose resigned mother she now becomes.

Mildred Pierce, as a long novel in third-person narration which is not a crime story or thriller, is not standard Cain; its pessimism, however, is standard Cain. Its emphasis upon vacuous materialism in the worlds of business and professional entertainment and its disclosure of affections transmuted by sublimation make it Cain's most pessimistic work. That it is, at the same time, not bitter or misanthropic in its effect is attributable to the author's sympathetic understanding of the forces and the emotions that move its characters; in this novel, Cain created his finest characterizations.

SUMMARY

Cain was an observer of the American character and a commentator on its dark vagaries. The height of his career coincided with the arrival of film noir, of which the film versions of *The Postman Always Rings Twice* (1946), *Double Indemnity* (1944), and *Mildred Pierce* (1945) are examples. What Ruth Prigozy, in her article on the film version of *Double Indemnity*, says about film noir is equally descriptive of the direction of Cain's fiction:

> The murder-detective story crime film was popular in the war years, for it enabled filmmakers to depict . . . the violent, nightmarish quality of the era, without explicitly criticizing America. In film noir, the optimism of the previous decade was rejected, perhaps unconsciously, in favor of an overtly skeptical view of human nature and society.

With his antiheroic characters and his theme of successfully but self-destructively pursuing the material side of personal gratification, Cain exposes the treacherous shoals of American aspirations.

Roy Arthur Swanson

BIBLIOGRAPHY

By the Author

SHORT FICTION:
"Pastorale," 1928
"The Taking of Monfaucon," 1929
"Come-Back," 1934
"Dead Man," 1936
"Hip, Hip, the Hippo," 1936
"The Birthday Party," 1936
"Brush Fire," 1936
"Coal Black," 1937
"Everything but the Truth," 1937
"The Girl in the Storm," 1940
"Payoff Girl," 1952
"Cigarette Girl," 1953
"Two O'Clock Blonde," 1953
"The Visitor," 1961
The Baby in the Icebox, and Other Short Fiction, 1981 (posthumous, Roy Hoopes, editor)
Career in C Major, and Other Fiction, 1986 (Hoopes, editor)

LONG FICTION:
The Postman Always Rings Twice, 1934
Double Indemnity, 1936
Serenade, 1937
The Embezzler, 1940
Mildred Pierce, 1941
Love's Lovely Counterfeit, 1942
Past All Dishonor, 1946
The Butterfly, 1947
Sinful Woman, 1947

DISCUSSION TOPICS

- Trace several examples of musical influences in either the subject matter or the techniques of James M. Cain's fiction.

- Several successful Hollywood films have been based on Cain's novels. What qualities do you see in his novels that might be expected to translate well to the screen?

- How well do the denouements of Cain's fiction exemplify his belief that a wish come true is a "terrifying experience"?

- Is Cain's work in general a denial of the validity of what is commonly thought of as the American Dream?

- In what ways is *Double Indemnity* superior to the thematically similar *The Postman Always Rings Twice*?

- Trace the stages in the development of the title character Mildred Pierce in Cain's novel of the same name.

The Moth, 1948
Jealous Woman, 1950
The Root of His Evil, 1951 (also pb. as *Shameless,* 1979)
Galatea, 1953
Mignon, 1963
The Magician's Wife, 1965
Rainbow's End, 1975
The Institute, 1976
Cloud Nine, 1984
The Enchanted Isle, 1985

DRAMA:
Crashing the Gates, pr. 1926
Trial by Jury, pb. 1928 (dialogue)
Theological Interlude, pb. 1928 (dialogue)
Will of the People, pb. 1929 (dialogue)
Citizenship, pb. 1929 (dialogue)
The Governor, pb. 1930
Don't Monkey with Uncle Same, pb. 1933 (dialogue)
The Postman Always Rings Twice, pr. 1936 (adaptation of his novel)
7-11, pr. 1938

SCREENPLAYS:
Algiers, 1938
Stand up and Fight, 1938
Gypsy Wildcat, 1944

NONFICTION:
Our Government, 1930
Sixty Years of Journalism, 1986 (Roy Hoopes, editor)

MISCELLANEOUS:
The James M. Cain Cookbook: Guide to Home Singing, Physical Fitness, and Animals (Especially Cats), 1988 (essays and stories; Roy Hoopes and Lynne Barrett, editors)

About the Author

Cain, James M. "An Interview with James M. Cain." Interview by John Carr. *The Armchair Detective* 16, no. 1 (1973): 4-21.
Fine, Richard. *James M. Cain and the American Authors' Authority.* Austin: University of Texas Press, 1992.
Forter, Gregory. "Double Cain." *Novel* 29 (Spring, 1996): 277-298.
Hoopes, Roy. *Cain.* New York: Holt, Rinehart and Winston, 1982.
_____. *Our Man in Washington.* New York: Forge, 2000.
Madden, David. *Cain's Craft.* Metuchen, N.J.: Scarecrow Press, 1985.
_____. *James M. Cain.* New York: Twayne, 1970.
Marling, William. *The American Roman Noir: Hammett, Cain, and Chandler.* Athens: University of Georgia Press, 1995.
Nyman, Jopi. *Hard-Boiled Fiction and Dark Romanticism.* New York: Peter Lang, 1998.
Skenazy, Paul. *James M. Cain.* New York: Continuum, 1989.

ERSKINE CALDWELL

Born: White Oak, Georgia
    December 17, 1903
Died: Paradise Valley, Arizona
    April 11, 1987

Enormously popular in the 1930's and 1940's, Caldwell brought to millions his bawdy, forcefully written, grimly comic stories of injustice and human irrationality, set chiefly in the American South.

Carl Van Vechten/Library of Congress

BIOGRAPHY

Erskine Caldwell was born in the community of White Oak, near Moreland, Georgia, on December 7, 1903, the only child of Ira Sylvester and his wife, Caroline Bell Caldwell. In following years, the little family moved often about the South, wherever Caldwell's father's duties as a minister and troubleshooter for his denomination took him, until they settled in Wrens, Georgia, in 1918. Caldwell's mother, like Ernest Hemingway's and Thomas Wolfe's, kept her son in shoulder-length curls; she refused to allow the boy to attend school until he entered the seventh grade.

In Wrens, the nearest thing to a hometown Caldwell had, the family lived an uneventful life. His father assumed a permanent pastorate, and both parents took jobs at the institute (or high school). Ira Sylvester, a man of great good will and unflagging philanthropy (though modest athletic ability), organized the school's first sports program and served for many years as its football, basketball, and baseball coach. Caroline Caldwell was a teacher of English. Known as Skinny, as much for his elongated frame as his first name, Erskine attended school under the watchful eyes of his parents and found his first job writing one summer for the *Jefferson Reporter.* In time he advanced to stringer status, serving as a correspondent for some city newspapers, mainly covering baseball games.

As son of a minister, Caldwell enjoyed a respectability in tiny Wrens very different from the reputation he was later to achieve after the shocking success in 1933 of the stage version of his *Tobacco Road* (1932). Misled by whopping lies that Caldwell told the gullible—as did many of his literary contemporaries—and by the subject matter of *Tobacco Road* (1932) and *God's Little Acre* (1933), books often read "behind the barn," Americans came to believe that Caldwell himself had emerged from the people he depicted. The tall, redheaded, freckle-faced youth who ran in the Wrens One-Mile Relay on New Year's Day, 1920, became in following decades the nemesis of the Watch and Ward Society, "America's No. 1 cracker-barrel pornographer" (*Time* magazine, 1957), and a suspected agent of the Kremlin.

In Wrens, Caldwell wrote newspaper copy and an occasional story and chauffeured a doctor on rural house calls, where he saw how blacks lived and discovered the living conditions of tenant farmers on the sandy roads that crisscrossed the countryside outside the town. In Wrens Caldwell developed the searing social conscience that boils below the apparent indifference of his fiction.

After finishing high school, Caldwell left for his father's alma mater, Erskine College, in South Carolina. He stayed there only a year and a half before transferring to the more challenging University of Virginia on an obscure scholarship for a descendant of a Confederate veteran. At Charlottesville,

Caldwell discovered the "little magazine," the trying ground for young writers, that he was soon to deluge with short stories from his own typewriter. There, too, he read Theodore Dreiser's powerful *Sister Carrie* (1900), some of the stories of the young Ernest Hemingway (just coming into prominence), and a book that affected his whole generation, Sherwood Anderson's *Winesburg, Ohio* (1919). He also studied writing formally.

At the end of his second year, Caldwell pushed north as far as Philadelphia, where he spent a summer term at the Wharton School of Finance before moving to Scranton, Pennsylvania, to unpack crates in the cellar of Kresge's—a discount store, the predecessor of Kmart. On the basis of limited football experience at Erskine College, he played right end for three games on a semiprofessional team, where he found himself completely outclassed. Experiences such as these, greatly exaggerated, eventually adorned his book jackets to serve as evidence of a life colorful enough to rival Jack London's.

The next spring Caldwell eloped with the first of his four wives and took a twenty-dollar-a-week job at the *Atlanta Journal*. In addition to reporting, he wrote book reviews which he sent to other papers and worked on short stories at night, determined now to be a writer himself. After a single year, he quit Atlanta for rural Maine to write only stories, and he sent them out until, in 1929, he got the first one published and then anthologized.

Soon F. Scott Fitzgerald, author of *The Great Gatsby* (1925), recommended that his own editor, Max Perkins of Scribner's, accept Caldwell's work. Not only did Perkins then print several of Caldwell's stories in *Scribner's Magazine*, but he also arranged for Caldwell to publish a collection, *American Earth* (1931). Further, he accepted Caldwell's new novel, *Tobacco Road*, which became a smash Broadway hit in Jack Kirkland's version. The notoriety the sexy play received guaranteed a huge audience for Caldwell's next novel; suddenly Caldwell's name was on everyone's lips, and the phrase "tobacco road," meaning a rundown white neighborhood, entered the American language.

As his marriage began to founder, Caldwell accepted offers from Hollywood and produced more short-story collections, another novel, and a book of reportage. These were less enthusiastically received. World War II gave brief impetus to his ca-

reer, as servicemen devoured his earlier, risque novels and Caldwell broadcast from Moscow while the Nazis poured into Russia. By then he had married Margaret Bourke-White, the photographer known for her combat photos in the pages of *Life* magazine. The end of the war marked the end of Caldwell's critical acclaim and, soon after, his popularity as well. Caldwell refused to acknowledge any decline, deliberately ignoring the judgment of those whom he felt were late to recognize him in the first place and whose opinions were not worth much anyway.

Although he wrote many more books, he had been so completely forgotten by the time of his death on April 11, 1987, that the obituaries of major American newspapers were obliged to explain in great detail who he was.

ANALYSIS

Caldwell is one of few American writers to achieve both enormous popular and critical success. Known to millions of his fellow Americans, many of whom actually read *Tobacco Road* or *God's Little Acre*, Caldwell's name mentioned on a radio program in the 1930's or 1940's would instantly evoke howls of snickering laughter, because his books suggested raw humor and sex. Ensign Pulver in Thomas Heggen's hit novel and play *Mister Roberts* (1946) was probably one of countless World War II sailors who had memorized the most scandalous passage in *God's Little Acre*, which he could recite "flawlessly."

If Caldwell meant "dirty books" to large numbers of Americans, he was something quite different to students of literature. Many considered him chiefly a protest or proletarian writer, one of those socially committed novelists of the Depression era who exposed injustices in American life, the plight of tenant farmers, or the outrageous conditions under which cotton mill workers or southern blacks lived. Left-leaning critics championed his work as properly Marxist, but they were often disappointed by what they considered irrelevant elements in his writing. What, they wondered, did all the slapstick and sex have to do with the class struggle? They wished he would simply concentrate on exposing the evils of capitalism. Even before World War II, the Soviet Union had put its stamp of approval on his work, and after the war the countries of Eastern Europe joined in so clamorously that

Caldwell became a figure of some suspicion during the Cold War years.

On the other hand, many compared him to William Faulkner, whose critical reputation was growing in the early 1930's but who could not command the sales that Caldwell could. Some said that Caldwell's southern gothic tales were as profoundly metaphorical as those of Faulkner. Faulkner himself joined the chorus of praise, calling Caldwell the best writer in America. Other critics insisted on comparing him to James Farrell, whose naturalistic novel *Young Lonigan* (1932), the first in his trilogy about Studs Lonigan, appeared the year of *Tobacco Road*. Like Farrell, Caldwell wrote about heredity and poor families whose unhappy destinies were largely determined by the world around them, an environment where people were strictly on their own.

Still others stressed Caldwell's humor. Not since Mark Twain, they said, had a southern writer made readers laugh so in showing humanity's hopeless irrationality. They pointed to stories such as "Mid-Summer Passion," in which Ben Hacket, fortified with fermented cider, pulls a pair of pink panties on Mrs. Fred Williams in a sort of panty raid in reverse, or to the shenanigans of "A Country Full of Swedes," which won for him a Yale Award for Fiction in the mid-1930's. Certainly readers found Jeeter Lester's attempt "to get on the good side of the Lord" with the help of the zany evangelist Sister Bessie Rice or Ty Ty Walden's gold-mining schemes—to mention only two of the obsessions of Caldwell's simple-minded characters—hilariously funny.

Like Twain's, too, was Caldwell's interest in American places in a period when regional distinctions were much stronger than they would become after generations of television and a mobile society worked their homogenizing effects. Caldwell wrote about the South, where he was born, and northern New England, where he spent the most productive decade of his life. In his later years he continued to travel about the United States and the world, showing interest in regional writers and expressing great pride in his editing in the 1940's *American Folkways*, a collection of studies of regional America by a host of writers. Although he left the South while still in his twenties, never to return except for temporary visits or Florida residencies, readers inevitably think of him still as a "Georgia boy."

Caldwell's writing, both his short stories and his novels, is uneven. It is not fair, however, to say that his muse abandoned him early in his career or that he sold out for big money after *God's Little Acre*, charges that were often leveled against him. Neither accusation is true. He wrote weaker stories, such as "Dorothy" (1931) and "Strawberry Season" (1930), as well as strong ones from the start. Two little-known novelettes that he published on small presses before *Tobacco Road*, *The Bastard* (1929) and *Poor Fool* (1930), most readers will find unrewarding. Indeed, Scribner's lost Caldwell as an author when the company decided not to accept his decidedly minor "Maine novel," the book he wrote after *Tobacco Road*, published years later as *A Lamp for Nightfall* (1952). Although Caldwell could command generous advances and profitable contracts in his heyday, he continued to write just as dutifully when there was little demand for his work.

Caldwell wrote a plain style of American English that F. Scott Fitzgerald perceptively recognized as resembling Hemingway's and told his stories, often about country folk, from an objective point of view—so objective, in fact, that many mistakenly thought he sympathized little with his characters. While the bulk of his writing is "realistic," providing recognizable details of everyday life, his use of grotesquerie, like that of such moderns as the Czech novelist Franz Kafka, is meant to show that the reaches of human experience cannot be captured by the photographic realism of the past, that something more is needed to depict, for example, the iniquity of the perverse preacher Semon Dye in *Journeyman* (1935) than merely faithful reproduction of externals.

Although he believed in the primacy of feeling and often seemed to view sex, as did the slightly older English novelist D. H. Lawrence, as bringing out the god in man, Caldwell's view of life is often as pessimistic as that of any naturalist. Jeeter Lester and his wife are killed in a fire in *Tobacco Road*. Will Thompson, the charismatic labor leader, is shot to death in *God's Little Acre*, as is Clem, the saintly black Christ figure in "Kneel to the Rising Sun" (1935). Semon Dye successfully bilks the town of Rocky Comfort in a revival meeting before moving on.

Thus an unresolved contradiction underlies much of Caldwell's work. He trusts that social justice will eventually bring better times to poor whites and blacks; he believes that the human spirit is indomitable, that there is a mystic force in the blood and soil, and that in listening to one's deepest instincts one listens to the voice of God. At the same time, he acknowledges that people are irrational and the world is a cruel place where the wicked often triumph over the good. Caldwell himself saw no such contradiction; rather, he called his work only a realistic balance between "the depiction of the violent and ugly, of poverty and class conflict" and "spasms of laughter, the horseplay of humor, and the enjoyment of living."

TOBACCO ROAD

First published: 1932
Type of work: Novel

Dirt-poor Georgia tenant farmers lose their family and their lives at planting season.

Tobacco Road, Caldwell's fourth novel (counting *The Bogus Ones*, discovered in 1978), remains the book for which he is best remembered. Narrated in an episodic fashion, it quickly reveals more of theme and meaning than would a more organically developed effort. In *Tobacco Road,* Jeeter Lester and his wife, Ada, live in a decaying cabin with his silent mother and two of their fifteen children, the harelipped Ellie May and her younger brother Dude. Like the tobacco road on which they live, once a means of delivering hogsheads of tobacco to the Savannah River, and like the fields around them, they are obsolete and worn out.

When Lov Bensey arrives to seek Jeeter's help in getting his child-wife, one of Jeeter's daughters, to speak to him and sleep with him, Jeeter regards the visit as an opportunity to steal turnips he suspects are in the sack Lov carries. Times in Georgia are so hard that "Captain" John has moved to Augusta, cutting off the credit that his tenant farmers like Jeeter need to eat and to acquire seed cotton and fertilizer for the tired soil. In no more than three brief chapters of *Tobacco Road*, Caldwell reveals the silent, loveless existence of his exploited country people and exposes the obsolete sharecropping system that controls their empty lives.

Lov is soon robbed of his turnips and seduced by Ellie May in a scene that is mostly suggested in the novel but was graphic enough to have titillated a decade of theatergoers. Seen from another perspective, Ellie May's seduction appears only the desperate act of a neglected teenager, starved for affection. Indeed, Caldwell later suggests that Ellie May is the proper mate for Lov, who married her sister mostly because she lacked Ellie May's disfigurement. In *Tobacco Road*, Caldwell comments obliquely and with great economy on a number of problems: human sexuality and love, agriculture in the South, hunger in America, the plight of the old, the place of labor in human life, and people's relation to God.

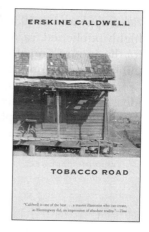

With the appearance of Sister Bessie Rice, Caldwell investigates this latter theme, though not to the extent that he does in *God's Little Acre*. Bessie, almost forty, decides that God has directed her to marry Dude and conduct a revival crusade. Like so many Protestants of fundamentalist background, Caldwell distrusts clergy, believing that a person's relationship with God must be direct, not attained through the office of fallible intermediaries—let alone via half-baked ignoramuses such as Bessie.

Although he is lazy, dishonest, mean-spirited, and lecherous, Jeeter often provides the reader with the author's viewpoint. Caldwell approves of Jeeter, who, despite his myriad faults, obeys his deepest instincts and trusts in God and the land. Strangely enough, the reader comes to feel the same way. Although there is little reason to believe that Jeeter will ever change his ways, in death he seems a sacrificial victim. Ultimately, one is ready—or almost ready—to believe Dude, who, in eulogizing his father, suddenly speaks about growing "a bale to an acre like Pa was always talking about doing."

GOD'S LITTLE ACRE

First published: 1933
Type of work: Novel

Shifting again the acre consecrated to God, Ty Ty Walden makes a last effort to find the gold he believes lies beneath his Georgia farm.

God's Little Acre, published on the heels of *Tobacco Road*, appeared in 1933 to favorable reviews and a highly publicized fracas with the New York Society for the Suppression of Vice that focused enormous public attention on the new novel. Here Caldwell brought in more concentrated form many of the ideas that had interested him in the earlier book. Again he sought to explain that "feeling," trust in oneself and in God—a state very similar to Ralph Waldo Emerson's self-reliance—is the natural goal of humankind.

In *God's Little Acre*, as in *Tobacco Road*, Caldwell treads an uneasy line between preaching that a divinity waits inside human beings to be freed and showing humans at their most irrational. In other words, he is never quite sure if he is a romantic who believes that humans are limitless or a naturalist who sees them as helpless victims of economic forces, their emotions, and their biology.

In depicting Will Thompson, the visionary leader, Caldwell resorts to an even more poetic style than he used in describing Jeeter's love for the soil, one that recalls Caldwell's early ambitions as a poet and his impressionistic prose poem *The Sacrilege of Alan Kent*, privately printed in 1936, though written in stages much earlier. When Will Thompson reluctantly appears at Ty Ty Walden's farm to help his father-in-law in his foolish search for gold, Caldwell's episodic story takes an aberrant turn. What at first seems to be only a rollicking story of rural eccentrics becomes an account of labor unrest, infidelity, and murder.

In *God's Little Acre*, as in *Tobacco Road*, a patriarchal figure embodying a host of contradictions becomes a sort of spokesman for Caldwell in the solemn stillness of the book's conclusion. Ty Ty Walden endorses the strength, joie de vivre, and sexual vitality of his daughter's husband and recognizes (unlike his jealous sons) Will's qualities of leadership. Though Will represents a threat to familial unity and to the virtues of his sister-in-law Griselda (his other sister-in-law, Darling Jill, has no virtue to worry about), Ty Ty must acknowledge the divinity he discerns within him. Will's raging libido becomes, in the course of the novel, a positive force, as it is from the love and admiration of three women that he acquires the strength to lead the mill workers in opening the mill, shut by selfish monied interests.

After Will, who has gradually been identified with Christ, has distributed his garments (by throwing his torn-up shirt out the window of the seized mill), he is killed by soldiers (out-of-state guards hired by the mill owners). In the aftermath of his death comes more tragedy, but readers are left with the belief, haltingly explained by Ty Ty, that Will's life has been a model for all and that conventional morality plays little role in the lives of heroes whose lives are at the service of the masses.

SUMMARY

Caldwell's two-fisted stories of baffled rural Americans struggling to survive in the merciless world around them won him the devotion of millions of readers who found his voice strong, his depictions honest, his prose style readable, and his courage admirable. He wrote forcefully about subjects other writers were afraid to confront, and he did so with a wild comic touch. If he emphasized sex, he did not neglect to expose the injustices everywhere in American life in the Depression years. Called a sensationalist by his detractors, he conveyed what Thoreau called "the stark twilight and unsatisfied thoughts which all men have."

James E. Devlin

BIBLIOGRAPHY

By the Author

SHORT FICTION:

American Earth, 1931
Mama's Little Girl, 1932
Message for Genevieve, 1933
We Are the Living: Brief Stories, 1933
Kneel to the Rising Sun, and Other Stories, 1935
Southways: Stories, 1938
Jackpot: The Short Stories of Erskine Caldwell, 1940
Georgia Boy, 1943
Stories by Erskine Caldwell: Twenty-four Representative Stories, 1944
Jackpot: Collected Short Stories, 1950
The Courting of Susie Brown, 1952
Complete Stories, 1953
Gulf Coast Stories, 1956
Certain Women, 1957
When You Think of Me, 1959
Men and Women: Twenty-two Stories, 1961
Stories of Life: North and South, 1983
The Black and White Stories of Erskine Caldwell, 1984

LONG FICTION:

The Bastard, 1929
Poor Fool, 1930
Tobacco Road, 1932
God's Little Acre, 1933
Journeyman, 1935
Trouble in July, 1940
All Night Long: A Novel of Guerrilla Warfare in Russia, 1942
Tragic Ground, 1944
A House in the Uplands, 1946
The Sure Hand of God, 1947
This Very Earth, 1948
Place Called Estherville, 1949
Episode in Palmetto, 1950
A Lamp for Nightfall, 1952
Love and Money, 1954
Gretta, 1955
Claudelle Inglish, 1958
Jenny by Nature, 1961
Close to Home, 1962
The Last Night of Summer, 1963
Miss Mamma Aimee, 1967
Summertime Island, 1968
The Weather Shelter, 1969
The Earnshaw Neighborhood, 1972
Annette, 1974

DISCUSSION TOPICS

- Identify the criticisms frequently made of Erskine Caldwell's work in the 1930's. Are any of them based on common obsessions of the time and might well be judged unfair from today's perspective?

- What character traits of Jeeter Lester in *Tobacco Road* help make him an acceptable protagonist despite his many serious faults?

- What themes in *Tobacco Road* and *God's Little Acre* most clearly mark them as Depression-era novels?

- What distinctively southern attitudes and values permeate Caldwell's fiction?

- Caldwell is reputed to possess a "comic vision." Is a comic vision more than merely seeing "the funny side of life"? Does it require happy endings? What do you think is the essence of a comic vision?

NONFICTION:
Tenant Farmer, 1935
Some American People, 1935
You Have Seen Their Faces, 1937 (with Margaret Bourke-White)
North of the Danube, 1939 (with Bourke-White)
Say! Is This the U.S.A.?, 1941 (with Bourke-White)
All-Out on the Road to Smolensk, 1942 (with Bourke-White; also known as *Moscow Under Fire: A Wartime Diary,* 1941)
Russia at War, 1942 (with Bourke-White)
The Humorous Side of Erskine Caldwell, 1951
Call It Experience: The Years of Learning How to Write, 1951
Around About America, 1964
In Search of Bisco, 1965
In the Shadow of the Steeple, 1967
Deep South: Memory and Observation, 1968
Writing in America, 1968
Afternoons in Mid-America, 1976
With All My Might, 1987
Conversations with Erskine Caldwell, 1988
Erskine Caldwell: Selected Letters, 1929-1955, 1999

CHILDREN'S LITERATURE:
Molly Cottontail, 1958
The Deer at Our House, 1966

MISCELLANEOUS:
The Caldwell Caravan: Novels and Stories, 1946

About the Author

Arnold, Edwin T. *Erskine Caldwell Reconsidered.* Jackson: University Press of Mississippi, 1990.
Cook, Sylvia Jenkins. *Erskine Caldwell and the Fiction of Poverty: The Flesh and the Spirit.* Baton Rouge: Louisiana State University Press, 1991.
Devlin, James E. *Erskine Caldwell.* Boston: Twayne, 1984.
Klevar, Harvey L. *Erskine Caldwell: A Biography.* Knoxville: University of Tennessee Press, 1993.
McDonald, Robert L., ed. *The Critical Response to Erskine Caldwell.* Westport, Conn.: Greenwood Press, 1997.
MacDonald, Scott, ed. *Critical Essays on Erskine Caldwell.* Boston: G. K. Hall, 1981.
Miller, Dan B. *Erskine Caldwell: The Journey from Tobacco Road, a Biography.* New York: Alfred A. Knopf, 1995.
Silver, Andrew. "Laughing over Lost Causes: Erskine Caldwell's Quarrel with Southern Humor." *The Mississippi Quarterly* 50 (Winter, 1996/1997): 51-68.
Stevens, C. J. *Storyteller: A Life of Erskine Caldwell.* Phillips, Maine: John Wade, 2000.

TRUMAN CAPOTE

Born: New Orleans, Louisiana
September 30, 1924
Died: Los Angeles, California
August 25, 1984

Capote's greatest accomplishment was his merging of the dramatic narrative techniques of fiction with the objective reportage of journalism in what he termed "the nonfiction novel."

Library of Congress

BIOGRAPHY

Truman Capote was born Truman Streckfus Persons, the only child of J. Archulus Persons and Lillie Mae Faulk Persons. During the first six years of his childhood, the boy frequently was handed off to the care of relatives by his carefree and irresponsible parents. Following his parents' permanent separation when Truman was six, he was left fully in the care of relatives in Monroeville, Alabama.

Being raised by a series of relatives, Capote had a lonely childhood existence; the experience forced him, as he said in many interviews as an adult, to create his own world, personality, and sense of identity. The search for that sense of selfhood was to be a frequent theme in his literary work, both fiction and nonfiction. One imaginative influence on the young Capote was his eccentric cousin Sook Faulk, who encouraged the boy's propensity for fantasy invention. He was later to recall Sook as the doting parent surrogate in his short story "A Christmas Memory."

Capote's childhood days can be seen in the novel *To Kill a Mockingbird* (1960), written by his childhood friend Harper Lee, in which the youthful Capote appears as the character Dill. Following his parents' divorce in 1931, Capote spent most of his time in Monroeville until his mother was remarried in 1932 to Joseph Capote. Following their marriage, the boy was to change his name legally to Capote and eventually move to New York to live with his mother and stepfather.

Capote attended private schools in Manhattan and ultimately graduated from the Franklin School, although his attendance had been, at best, irregular. The boy's time in an exciting metropolitan New York environment came at an impressionable age, and Capote, like one of his later heroines, Holly Golightly in *Breakfast at Tiffany's* (1958), loved the pace, sophistication, and glamour of New York.

Capote's childhood fascination with words continued in his teenage years as he served as a copyboy and file clerk at *The New Yorker* magazine. Although none of Capote's early work in fiction was published by *The New Yorker,* in 1945, the twenty-one-year-old writer published several short stories that gained for him almost instant literary attention: "Miriam," which appeared in *Mademoiselle* magazine; "A Tree of Night," in *Harper's Bazaar;* and "My Side of the Matter," in *Story* magazine. The appearance of these stories, and the subsequent publication in 1948 at age twenty-three of his first novel, *Other Voices, Other Rooms,* achieved for the young writer overnight international acclaim.

Capote often described the novel as a poetic version of his own lonely childhood—sensitive, abandoned, and isolated. The book was, he said, an emotional, or spiritual, autobiography, if not an actual literal one. The novel's romanticized treatment of a homosexual theme made it a sensation in the late 1940's, when only one other contemporary novel, Gore Vidal's *The City and the Pillar* (1948), had dealt with homosexuality. The controversy over Capote's book was further intensified by the now-famous picture of the youthful author on its back cover sprawled seductively on a chaise longue with his blond bangs hanging over his elfin face. Capote quickly added to his reputation as a master of prose style with his 1949 short-story collection *A Tree of Night, and Other Stories* and the 1951 novella *The Grass Harp.*

In the 1950's, Capote began to explore a variety of journalistic approaches to writing, including the travel recollection of *Local Color* (1950), an extended account of an American opera company's tour of the Soviet Union in *The Muses Are Heard* (1956), and his 1959 volume of commentary accompanying the photographs of Richard Avedon, *Observations*. In 1958, he produced his successful novella *Breakfast at Tiffany's*, which further enhanced his reputation as a fiction writer. An equally popular film version of the novella followed in 1961.

In the 1950's and 1960's, Capote applied his talents to other literary forms, adapting two of his works for the theater—his novella, *The Grass Harp*, and later his short work *House of Flowers*, which was made into a musical. He also wrote two screenplays for films, *Beat the Devil* (1953) and a film version of Henry James's gothic novella *The Turn of the Screw* (1898), released under the title *The Innocents* (1961). During the 1960's, Capote also published the first two parts of what was to be a trilogy of emotionally etched stories of his childhood in the South: *A Christmas Memory* appeared in 1966 (it had originally been printed in *Mademoiselle* in 1956), followed by *The Thanksgiving Visitor* in 1967. A year before his death, a third volume, *One Christmas* (1983), was published, dealing with the visit of a boy to see his father, separated from him by divorce.

Capote's major achievement in the 1960's, however, was to be the 1966 nonfiction book *In Cold Blood: A True Account of a Multiple Murder and Its Consequences*. This work, which describes the murder of the Clutter farm family in Kansas, required six years of research by the author. Many critics view *In Cold Blood* as Capote's finest work; the author maintained that he had created a new art form, the "nonfiction novel." This new form combined the detached observation of journalistic reportage with the dramatic story-telling techniques of fiction. Capote spent years in Kansas after the crime

was committed and, upon the capture of the two men charged with the killings, more time investigating the lives and motives of the killers right up to the time of their execution. The publication of *In Cold Blood*, first in installments in *The New Yorker* and later as a book, made Capote wealthy and gave him unparalleled celebrity as an author.

Following the success of *In Cold Blood*, Capote announced that the next literary project he would undertake was to be a *roman à clef* about New York and the international jet set with which he personally had become so familiar. Its title was to be *Answered Prayers*, and when completed, Capote predicted, the work would rival the achievement of French novelist Marcel Proust's monumental *À la recherche du temps perdu* (1913-1927; *Remembrance of Things Past*, 1922-1931), a claim Capote made repeatedly in television talk show appearances.

His personal life and physical well-being, however, became increasingly chaotic during the 1970's. He wrote in a personal reminiscence, an interview with himself in his 1980 volume, *Music for Chameleons*: "I'm an alcoholic. I'm a drug addict. I'm homosexual. I'm a genius." The complications from all those conditions simultaneously caused erratic behavior by the writer in his last decade and greatly diminished his writing volume, which had never been great because of his insistence on perfection of style.

In 1973, he had published a collection of short pieces, *The Dogs Bark: Public People and Private Places*. *Music for Chameleons* included not only more personal profiles but also a new short account of another true crime, "Handcarved Coffins," a kind of *In Cold Blood* in miniature. In 1983, the third of his childhood recollections appeared, a slender story in book form, *One Christmas*.

Only four portions of *Answered Prayers* ever appeared. These four parts ran in 1975 and 1976 in *Esquire* magazine, and their appearance created a personal disaster for the writer, as many of the thinly disguised portraits of his friends grievously offended their models. Many of the writer's wealthy friends simply cut all contact with Capote.

In his last years, Capote was subject to frequent bouts with and recuperations from his many substance dependencies. He died in 1984, shortly before his sixtieth birthday, while on a visit to Los Angeles. Following Capote's death, an extensive search was made for the missing portions of *An-*

swered *Prayers*, those segments the author so often said that he had completed. No portions of the work—other than those already published in magazine installments—were ever found. Some believe that Capote did write the complete book and destroyed the remaining sections. Others think the missing portions may exist somewhere, but the majority opinion holds that Capote never really wrote the rest of what he had promised would be his most revealing, most stylistically controlled work. The known segments were published after his death under the title *Answered Prayers: The Unfinished Novel* in 1986.

ANALYSIS

In the preface to the last collection of his work published in his lifetime, the 1980 volume *Music for Chameleons*, Capote discussed in detail his views about the ordeal of writing as a creative activity and his own lifetime commitment to that pursuit. Writing was an occupation with a great risk to it: One had to take chances or fail. Indeed, Capote compared writing to professional pool playing and to a professional card dealer's abilities. He also explained that he began writing as a child of eight and was, by his view, an accomplished writer at seventeen. Thus, when *Other Voices, Other Rooms* appeared in 1948, he viewed it as the end result of fourteen years of writing experience.

The substance of writing—and its accompanying pain of creation—Capote explained with a phrase he borrowed from Henry James; it was the "madness of art." All imaginative writing was, he explained, the artist employing his creative powers of observation, of description, of telling detail; it was that act that led Capote in his later writing to see the possibilities of journalism (which is factual, detailed observation of truth) as an art form that could be as powerful as fictional writing. So it was that he shifted from fiction to nonfiction in midcareer with works such as *The Muses Are Heard* and his most famous work, *In Cold Blood*.

For Capote, the writer is, by nature, an outsider, the observer seeing and hearing that which is about him but comprehending the witnessed events with an artistic sensitivity unknown to others. The outsider's perspective is—simply because it is detached from the observed society—more comprehensive. As he was an artist "outside," it was natural that Capote's works often dealt with the

conflict between vulnerable persons similarly outside their more conventional environment. This theme can be seen in a number of his works, such as *Other Voices, Other Rooms*, and even in the real-life killer of his masterwork, *In Cold Blood*. Often this theme is played out in his work through a confrontation of an unconventional outsider with the conforming, ordered world.

In *Other Voices, Other Rooms*, Cousin Randolph, the homosexual older relative, states the outsider's lament as he attempts to explain the search for love to the youthful Joel, explaining that all men are isolated from one another, that everyone, in the end, is alone:

> Any love is natural and beautiful that lies within a person's nature; only hypocrites would hold a man responsible for what he loves, emotional illiterates and those of righteous envy, who, in their agitated concern, mistake so frequently the arrow pointing to heaven for the one that leads to hell.

A similar idea occurs in *The Grass Harp* when Judge Cool, having joined a rebellious group hiding in a tree house, speaks of those who are pagans or spirits and defines them as accepters of life, because they are those who grant life's differences.

Some of the more flamboyant examples of the free, nonconforming spirit are seen in Capote's female characters, specifically Idabel, the tomboy twin of *Other Voices, Other Rooms*, who outwrestles young Joel in one scene and whose lack of femininity is an obvious counterpoint to Joel's boyhood homosexual longings. Another such unconventional personality is Holly Golightly of *Breakfast at Tiffany's*, who has run away from her background of poverty and also from a childhood marriage to seek glamor and to indulge her New York encounters with a series of wealthy men. Holly's defiance of convention is as meaningful as Joel's and Idabel's or, for that matter, the runaways in *The Grass Harp*, whose tree house retreat is Capote's symbol for all places of security for those who may be yearning for a place for their differences, their individual spirits, their ideal fantasies to be at home.

Capote frequently said in interviews that he saw in the real-life killers—particularly Perry Smith—of *In Cold Blood* the man he might have become had his own life taken a different turn. His realization was that the killers were the evil side of the same yearning for love, acceptance, even artistic achievement (especially with Smith) that he had known. That desire is seen in a key scene in Miami after the murders, as Perry realizes that all his hopes and ambitions are a dead end:

> Anyway, he couldn't see that he had "a lot to live for." Hot islands and buried gold, diving deep in fire-blue seas toward sunken treasure—such dreams were gone. Gone, too, was "Perry O'Parsons," the name invented for the singing sensation of stage and screen that he'd half-seriously hoped some day to be.

In Capote's musical, *House of Flowers*, one of the characters sings a song of yearning for escape from the everyday titled "I Never Has Seen Snow," and snow is a recurring image in many Capote works for the elusive dreams of life. One of the young boyfriends of the Clutter girl recalls becoming lost in a snowstorm in *In Cold Blood*. The cook, Missouri, hopes to run away north to see snow in *Other Voices, Other Rooms*. Judge Cool's distant wife had died in the snows of Switzerland in *The Grass Harp*. Ultimately, in a world that fails to understand or make room for the sensitive, artistic spirits, the "different," Capote returns frequently to the idea, stated by Judge Cool, that whatever passions compose them, private worlds are good—that is, unless turned to evil ends by the greater uncomprehending world.

OTHER VOICES, OTHER ROOMS

First published: 1948
Type of work: Novel

A young boy, seeking his lost father, moves into a strange household in Mississippi where he encounters bizarre relatives while trying to find love.

Other Voices, Other Rooms, Capote's first published long work, is a moody and atmospheric tale characterized both by its strange setting—a decaying mansion in rural Mississippi—and by the host of peculiar characters it presents to the reader.

The book details the encounters of thirteen-year-old Joel Knox Sansom, who travels to an old mansion, Skully's Landing, where he hopes to meet his long-lost father, Edward Sansom. In its emphasis on romantic and ghostly settings and its use of strange, eccentric characters, *Other Voices, Other Rooms* is typical of what has been termed the southern gothic school of fiction, a style of fiction marked by its use of the grotesque both in locale and in characterization.

This category can be seen in the works of other southern-born fiction writers such as William Faulkner (his short story "A Rose for Emily" and his 1931 novel *Sanctuary* both offer elements of southern gothic), Tennessee Williams (his 1958 play *Suddenly Last Summer* deals with incest, homosexuality, insanity, lobotomy, and cannibalism), Carson McCullers (her 1941 novel *Reflections in a Golden Eye* and her story "Ballad of the Sad Café" both have grotesque situations and characters), and Flannery O'Connor (her 1952 novel *Wise Blood* deals with religious obsession and madness). In *Other Voices, Other Rooms*, Capote uses this sense of the strange and the mysterious to convey the loneliness, isolation, and naïveté of Joel.

When Joel arrives at Skully's Landing, he meets a variety of unusual characters: an ancient black man, Jesus Fever; Jesus Fever's granddaughter, a twenty-one-year-old cook named Missouri (nicknamed "Zoo"); Joel's father, the bedridden invalid Edward Sansom (who communicates with the rest of the household by rolling red tennis balls down the stairs); his father's new wife, Miss Amy; and a much-talked-about cousin, Randolph. En route to the Landing, Joel also has met two young girls, the twins Florabel Thompkins and her tomboy twin sister, Idabel. (Many interpreters of Capote's work see Idabel as Capote's fictional version of his own childhood friend, Harper Lee.)

While the main plot of the book appears to be dealing with Joel's attempt to find and, later, to talk with his father, Capote really is presenting the plight of Joel as a lonely, sensitive youth who is, in fact, trying to come to terms with his own identity in an environment where he has no moorings. In one key scene, he tries to pray; he finds it almost impossible to ask God for someone to love him, yet that is really what the boy is seeking.

It is the search for love that defines the lives of many of the characters in *Other Voices, Other Rooms*: Cousin Randolph, Joel's homosexual older relative, still laments the loss of his great love, a boxer named Pepe Alvarez, and Miss Amy has married Joel's father—even though the man is an invalid—to have someone to care for and love. These aspirations to love are reflected in the desperation of other characters: At a carnival, Joel is pursued by the midget woman, Miss Wisteria, who, throughout her tragic life, has never found anyone her own size to love.

Similarly, the cook, Zoo, has suffered from her first experience with love; at age fourteen, she had married a man named Keg Brown who tried to kill her. Zoo seeks a place of beauty and purity, which, in her fantasy, she believes she will find in the North, where she hopes to go to see snow for the first time.

At the end of the novel, Joel, after recuperating from a severe illness during which he was cared for by Cousin Randolph, makes a decision about his life. He realizes that Randolph is, in many ways, a child like himself who has simply sought love in his life. Joel decides that he must abandon his childhood and accept his own sexual nature; at the end of the novel, the mature Joel ascends from the haunted garden at Skully's Landing to Randolph's room to embrace Randolph, leaving behind both his youth and his own sexual longing.

THE GRASS HARP

First published: 1951
Type of work: Novella

In a rigid, small-town, southern setting, an odd assortment of local people attempt to assert control over their lives by their defiance of convention.

The Grass Harp, Capote's sadly humorous tale about a curious collection of small-town southern eccentrics, continued the romantic and occasionally bizarre mood of his earlier *Other Voices, Other Rooms*, but his emphasis in this work more often is on the possibilities for humor in such strange behavior rather than on shock value. Capote captured the same tone of southern small-town hilarity that one also finds in many of the short stories of Eudora Welty.

Eleven-year-old Collin Fenwick, from whose point of view the work is told, is sent as a young boy by his grieving father to live with two unmarried cousins, Verena and Dolly Talbo. The father was distraught over the death of Collin's mother, so much so that he took off his clothes and ran naked into the yard the day of her death.

Collin is similar to Joel Knox Sansom of *Other Voices, Other Rooms* (and to the real-life youthful Capote) in that he is a lonely boy being raised by odd relatives. The Talbo household consists of Verena, the domineering force, who also has a head for business activities in the town; Dolly, the somewhat addled but good-hearted sister; a black woman, Catherine Creek, a companion to Dolly, who insists that she really is an Indian; and Collin, the boy who frequently spies on the household residents in different rooms through peepholes in the attic floor.

As a study of human loneliness, *The Grass Harp* echoes the themes of *Other Voices, Other Rooms:* the isolated, unloved, and unwanted child as well as the quiet desperation of many adults in small communities who suffer their own private terrors and despair. Dolly, Catherine, and Collin spend time regularly on picnics held in the hidden tree house of two lofty China trees outside the town. The tree house becomes a vehicle for their transport away from their real lives in the constricting town and into worlds of their imaginings. Verena, too—though not in their group—has suffered rejection; her intense friendship with another woman, Maudie Laurie Murphy, was lost when Maudie married a liquor salesman from St. Louis, left on a wedding trip (paid for by Verena), and never returned.

While *The Grass Harp* covers Collin's life from age eleven to age sixteen, the primary conflict of the work develops when sisters Dolly and Verena quarrel over a dropsy medicine formula known only by Dolly but which Verena hopes to develop commercially with a new man friend, Dr. Morris Ritz, a confidence man she met in Chicago. Dolly, viewing her formula as her own, decides to leave the house, taking both Collin and Catherine Creek with her. With no real destination or other home, the group moves into the tree shelter, while Verena arouses the town in a search for the runaways.

There are several comical encounters as a posse, including the local sheriff and a stuffy minister, attempts to get the group out of the tree. The group's rebellious independence is attractive to others, however, including a teenage loner, Riley Henderson, and the elderly Judge Charlie Cool, and both soon join the tree-dwellers in their defiance of the town's authority figures. At one point, the Judge summarizes the shared plight of the tree's inhabitants, telling them that there may not be a place in society for characters such as they are; he thinks there may be a place for them somewhere, however, and that the tree just might be the spot.

The search for that true, spiritual, home—for a place of real belonging—haunts each of the sympathetic characters in *The Grass Harp*. The Judge further defines for the group their role in life, as "spirits," or persons willing to grant differences in human behavior. He recalls, too, how he once almost had to imprison a man because that man defied custom and wanted to marry a black woman he loved. He reveals that his family views him as scandalous because he once maintained a long, friendly correspondence with a lonely thirteen-year-old girl in Alaska.

Capote sketches a variety of townspeople—some curious types, others mean and petty. There are the owners of the Katydid Bakery, Mr. and Mrs. C. C. County, and there is the traveling evangelist Sister Ida, the mother of fifteen children, one of whom is a star in her religious show and regularly lassoes souls for Christ. Ultimately, Sister Ida's troupe joins forces with the tree-house group in a battle with the town's conformist faction. A reconciliation becomes possible when Dolly realizes that she truly is needed by her sister, Verena. Verena, by this time, has been robbed of her cash and bonds by the smooth-talking Dr. Ritz, whom she had hoped to marry.

The last sections of the work deal with the maturing of Riley Henderson, his falling in love, and his eventual marriage to Maude Riordan. As Collin also matures, he plans to go away to law school and thus leave the town. Dolly, Verena, and Catherine Creek live together until a stroke kills Dolly, after which Catherine retires to live in seclusion in her own cabin. As Collin prepares to leave the town, he notes that the town remains—like the stories of the people in it—in memory. *The Grass Harp* reverberates with themes of alienation, loneliness, and the search for a secure and meaningful place in life, ideas Capote used in *Other Voices, Other Rooms* and was later to employ in *Breakfast at Tiffany's*.

BREAKFAST AT TIFFANY'S

First published: 1958
Type of work: Novella

A romantic, nonconformist runaway seeks glamour, self-identity, and freedom in Manhattan during World War II.

Breakfast at Tiffany's is a first-person narrative with a young male writer as its single point of view. The narrator relates what he observes of the life and experiences of Holly Golightly, a young Texas woman who has come to New York in the early 1940's seeking new life, excitement, and glamour, which she feels is in keeping with her freewheeling, sometimes irresponsible, approach to life.

Like *Other Voices, Other Rooms*, which preceded it, *Breakfast at Tiffany's* presents a free-spirited person trying to escape from the tawdry aspects of a past life by finding a lifestyle more compatible with her dreams and fantasies. Capote's story of Holly develops as a remembrance triggered in the writer-narrator's memory by an encounter with a Lexington Avenue bar proprietor, Bell, who had known Holly as a frequent and colorful patron of his bar.

Bell reports to the narrator that Holly in 1956 may have been seen in East Anglia, in Africa, where a Japanese photographer (who also had known Holly in New York) has encountered a wooden replica of Holly's face in a remote native village. The writer then recalls his first encounter with Holly when he had rented an apartment in the same building as she (and the photographer) during the early years of World War II.

The writer (whom Holly calls "Fred," after her brother, who is in the military service) grows more familiar with the irrepressible Holly after their first meeting. He finds that she views life essentially as a continuing party; some noisy parties occur in Holly's apartment. Holly first met the writer as she slid into his apartment from the fire escape one evening. He soon learns that Holly plays host to a wide assortment of mostly male friends, ranging from soldiers to Hollywood agents to an occasional gangster. Holly also is a regular visitor to Sing Sing Prison, where she is a paid messenger for a gangster named Sally Tomato. Holly is a vivacious blond who speaks in a kind of butchered French-English, which is her attempt at city sophistication.

Holly fascinates everyone who meets her: the young writer, her former agent, the bar owner, a rich playboy named Rusty Trawler, and a handsome Brazilian, Jose Ybarra-Jaegar, whom she hopes to marry. Holly is, in effect, a kind of free-spirited earth goddess, the kind of myth men tend to worship, a myth suggested by the wooden carving in the story's opening. The freedom to love as one desires is one of Holly's obsessions. She tells the narrator that she believes people should be allowed to marry as they like, either male or female. In another conversation, she expresses her open-minded attitude toward lesbians and even considers taking in a lesbian roommate. She further reveals that she is attracted to older men (such as Wendell Willkie) but that she could as easily be interested in, ideally, Greta Garbo.

The novella is a slowly unfolding character study of Holly through a series of episodic events: her parties; her free lifestyle; her taking in a model, Mag Wildwood, as a roommate; the visit of her older Texas husband, Doc; her aspirations to marry the rich Brazilian Ybarra-Jaegar; and her arrest and scandal because of her associations with Sally Tomato. Most important of all these casually related events is the sudden death of Holly's brother, Fred, killed in overseas combat. Faced with scandal and the end of her planned marriage, Holly, at the end of the story, leaves New York, abandoning her only commitment—the pet cat with no name—and heads to South America to seek further that glamorous place of safety for which she yearns.

The book's title is a symbol of that search; Holly likes the environment of Tiffany's jewelry store in New York, because nothing bad (she thinks) could happen to anyone there. A quiet, assured place of the security, wealth, and glamour—a place of calm belonging—that Holly so desperately seeks, she sees it as an alternative to the despair that grips her, the depression she calls the "mean reds." Although frivolous and exasperating to those who

know her, Holly Golightly (her name obviously suggests her attitude toward life) captivates all who meet her so that, in their minds, she takes on the substance of an elusive mythic dream, her appeal carved in their memories just as it was in the African wooden figure.

IN COLD BLOOD

First published: 1966
Type of work: Nonfiction novel

A Kansas farm family is mysteriously murdered by two ex-convicts who flee the scene but are eventually captured, tried, and executed.

In Cold Blood was created as a work of deliberate literary experiment. Having written extensive journalistic coverage in his account of an opera company's tour of the Soviet Union (*The Muses Are Heard*) and in various travel writing, Capote desired to combine the reportorial techniques of journalism—the gathering of detailed factual material by observation and interviewing—with the narrative and dramatic scene devices of fiction. The grisly, senseless murders of a Kansas farm family (Herbert W. Clutter, his wife, and two children) on November 15, 1959, in Holcomb, Kansas, provided the opportunity for the writer to try his experiment.

In Cold Blood is a documented record of those murders, but it is also a documentation of the backgrounds, motives, attitudes, and perspectives of hundreds of local townspeople as well as those of the two killers, ex-convicts Richard Eugene Hickock and Perry Smith, who are arrested eventually for the crime, tried, and executed. Shortly after the crime was committed, Capote went to Kansas to begin the massive accumulation of material that forms the substance of the book. At the outset, the murders were baffling because of the lack of any apparent motive for the slayings. There also were few clues.

Initially Capote envisioned his work as a short one in which he would explore the background of the murders and the reaction of the town to them. With the discovery, capture, and confession of the two killers, however, Capote's concept changed fo-

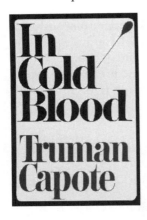

cus and became not only a study of the crime and its impact on the local community but also an investigation into the lives and motives of the two killers. While describing present action—the arrest, incarceration, trial, and conviction, then the appeals process. and finally the execution by hanging in Lansing, Kansas, in 1965—Capote also delves back into the murderers' past—their families, aspirations, and personal defeats. Writing the book took more than six years.

The organization of the material was ingeniously handled. Capote once said he had taken more than six thousand pages of notes. The book has four sections, all of which offer the reader shifts in time and place, rather like the cinematic technique of parallel editing, thus allowing the reader to experience simultaneous events with different persons in different locales. The four sections are titled "The Last to See Them Alive," "Persons Unknown," "Answer," and "The Corner." In the first section, Capote traces the members of the Clutter family through their activities on the last day of their lives, going through their routine in remarkable detail (even clothing is noted, as is music heard on the radio.)

While following the family, Capote also allows the readers to follow the ongoing progress of the two killers, Dick and Perry, as they move inexorably toward their victims in Kansas. The shifts between the killers' activities and those of their intended victims come to seem as fatalistic as Greek tragedy, and they add to the sense of tension and suspense (even though the reader is aware of the outcome of the impending meeting). Capote further heightens the reader's sense of dramatic anticipation by having section 1 end with the discovery of the bodies by local people. He carefully withholds the actual murder scenes until much later in the work; once the killers have been captured, the murder scenes are revealed in their confessions.

Part 2 catalogs the investigation of the crimes and the town's reaction to them. Against the ongoing investigation, the reader also follows the travels of Dick and Perry as they flee from Kansas—first to Mexico, later to Florida, and eventually back to Texas. As the authorities try to find leads to what seems a motiveless act, the reader sees the murderers as they fish, drink, and go to beaches. Capote also begins to introduce background information about the killers. A letter by Perry's father is included, as are a letter from Perry's sister written to him in prison and another convict's lengthy commentary on her letter. These revelations are juxtaposed against the frustration of investigator Alvin Dewey as he tries to find leads in the case.

Part 3, "Answer," brings the break in the case: A convict in prison reveals that Dick Hickock once told him of a plan to rob the Clutter household and leave no witnesses. As the net draws slowly about the killers after that revelation, the reader is given a sadly humorous episode in which a young boy and his ailing grandfather are given a ride by the murderers. The meeting of the open, honest, good-natured child with the killers is an example of how Capote has skillfully manipulated his material for maximum ironic effect. The killers join with the boy in a game to find empty soft-drink bottles in the barren Texas countryside.

Part 4 deals with events after Dick and Perry's arrest: their trial and conviction, the innumerable appeals in the courts as they seek to avoid execution, and, finally, their deaths by hanging in the Kansas State Penitentiary. Of particular interest in this section of the book is Capote's study of Dick and Perry's time on death row and his look at the lives of others who were death-row prisoners at the same time.

Capote's book does not end with the hanging of Dick and Perry; instead, there is a tranquil scene back in Holcomb, at the cemetery where the Clutter family is buried. Detective Alvin Dewey visits the graves and, while there, meets a young girlfriend of the Clutter girl. Their talk is routine—about school, college plans, marriages, hopes, aspirations, ambitions, the stuff of everyday life. These are exactly the details of routine life that have been denied the Clutter family and, indeed, their killers, by the tragic turns that fate works in people's lives. With the contrast between retribution and innocent hope, the book's final irony is eloquently achieved.

SUMMARY

Capote frequently depicted isolated, alienated personalities engaged in a desperate pursuit of love, seeking a place of security and belonging. That search is seen in the plights of characters as varied as Joel Sansom, Holly Golightly, and Judge Cool and the tree dwellers of *The Grass Harp*; it is found even in the real-life personalities of the killers in *In Cold Blood*.

The sense of personal desolation and anxiety is depicted with varying styles; Capote's early work has a romantically dense and suggestive metaphorical style, whereas later in his career he developed the stylized but factually based approach that he called the "nonfiction novel." All writing, Capote often said, like all art, has at its center a perfectly wrought core and shape. It is this distilled essence in his writing, coupled with his theme of the individually bruised soul seeking safety, that gives his works their almost unbearable tension.

Jere Real

BIBLIOGRAPHY

By the Author

LONG FICTION:
Other Voices, Other Rooms, 1948
The Grass Harp, 1951
A Christmas Memory, 1956 (serial)
The Thanksgiving Visitor, 1967 (serial)
Answered Prayers: The Unfinished Novel, 1986

SHORT FICTION:
A Tree of Night, and Other Stories, 1949
Breakfast at Tiffany's: A Short Novel and Three Stories, 1958
One Christmas, 1983
I Remember Grandpa: A Story, 1986
The Complete Collected Stories of Truman Capote, 2004

DRAMA:
The Grass Harp: A Play, pr., pb. 1952 (adaptation of his novel)
House of Flowers, pr. 1954 (with Harold Arlen)

SCREENPLAYS:
Beat the Devil, 1954 (with John Huston)
The Innocents, 1961

NONFICTION:
Local Color, 1950
The Muses Are Heard, 1956

DISCUSSION TOPICS

- How do the mysterious details of setting and the various eccentric characters contribute to the characterization of Joel in *Other Voices, Other Rooms*?

- Discuss the following assertion: Truman Capote's insistence on the originality of his "nonfiction novel," *In Cold Blood*, enhanced its popular success but misdirected criticism of the work.

- What did Capote ultimately learn and reveal about the motivation of the killers in *In Cold Blood*?

- Are there important mutually exclusive values in journalism and fiction? Has Capote been a bad influence on the recent journalists who have betrayed journalistic standards by incorporating fictitious material in their reports?

- Does Capote's literary output after *In Cold Blood* demonstrate that celebrity—and especially his practice of cultivating his own celebrity—damaged his integrity as an artist?

- What work of Capote's do you think best illustrates his conviction that "all writing has at its center a perfectly wrought core and shape"? Describe the core of that work.

Observations, 1959 (with Richard Avedon)
In Cold Blood, 1966
The Dogs Bark: Public People and Private Places, 1973

MISCELLANEOUS:
Selected Writings, 1963
Trilogy: An Experiment in Multimedia, 1969 (with Eleanor Perry and Frank Perry)
Music for Chameleons, 1980
A Capote Reader, 1987
Too Brief a Treat: The Letters of Truman Capote, 2004 (edited by Gerald Clarke)

About the Author

Bloom, Harold, ed. *Truman Capote.* Philadelphia: Chelsea House, 2003.

Brinnin, John Malcolm. *Truman Capote: Dear Heart, Old Buddy.* Rev. ed. New York: Delacorte Press, 1986.

Clarke, Gerald. *Capote: A Biography.* New York: Simon & Schuster, 1988.

Dunphy, Jack. *"Dear Genius": A Memoir of My Life with Truman Capote.* New York: McGraw-Hill, 1989.

Garson, Helen S. *Truman Capote: A Study of the Short Fiction.* New York: Twayne, 1992.

Plimpton, George. *Truman Capote: In Which Various Friends, Enemies, Acquaintances, and Detractors Recall His Turbulent Career.* New York: Doubleday, 1997.

Rudisill, Marie. *The Southern Haunting of Truman Capote.* Nashville, Tenn.: Cumberland House, 2000.

Windham, Donald. *Lost Friendships: A Memoir of Truman Capote, Tennessee Williams, and Others.* New York: William Morrow, 1987.

RAYMOND CARVER

Born: Clatskanie, Oregon
  May 25, 1938
Died: Port Angeles, Washington
  August 2, 1988

© Marion Ettlinger

In his relatively short career as a professional author, Carver established a critical reputation as one of the most powerful and innovative short-story writers of his generation.

BIOGRAPHY

Raymond Carver was born on May 25, 1938, in the small town of Clatskanie in northwestern Oregon. Before he started school, his family moved to Yakima, Washington, where his father worked as a logger. Carver went to elementary school and high school there and spent his leisure time fishing and hunting. He once said that growing up in the rugged and rural Pacific Northwest made him want to be a "writer from the West." He also once declared that the most important, although in many ways the most negative, influence on his early hopes to become a writer was the fact that he married and became a father before he was twenty. The pressures of supporting his young family made it almost impossible to find time to write.

Carver has said that he could not remember when he did not want to be a writer; he even took a correspondence course in writing when he was a teenager. He was never really interested in writing a novel but rather liked short stories—a form which he said best suited the circumstances of his life, for they could be finished in a few sittings. As a young man, his reading tastes were relatively unformed and undisciplined. He read Zane Grey Westerns, the science-fiction works of Edgar Rice Burroughs, and such men's magazines as *True, Argosy, Sports Afield,* and *Outdoor Life*—a masculine reading list which may partially account for the laconic, no-frills style of his short stories.

Carver moved his wife and two children to Northern California in 1958, where he registered as a student at Chico State College (now California State University, Chico). An important positive influence on his career while at Chico was his enrollment in a creative writing class taught by John Gardner, who was soon to make a name for himself as a writer. Carver was lavish in his praise for the help Gardner gave him, comparing him to the great maestros of the past who nurtured their apprentices. Because of Gardner, Carver began to think of writing as a high calling, something to be taken very seriously.

Carver transferred to California's northern coastal college, Humboldt State, where he studied under short-story writer Richard Day and received his B.A. in 1963. Soon after, he left for the University of Iowa Writers' Workshop with a small graduate grant of five hundred dollars. Unable to support his family and write, however, he went back to California before the end of the academic year. After returning, Carver held a number of minor jobs in Sacramento as a mill hand and a delivery boy, but perhaps his most fortunate job was a two-year stint as a night watchman at a hospital, where he was able to squeeze in some time writing. In 1967, Carver got a job as a textbook editor for Science Research Associates in Palo Alto, California. In 1968, the English Club at Sacramento State College, where he had taken a poetry-writing course, published twenty-six of his poems in a collection titled *Near Klamath.*

Although Carver was busy writing during the 1960's and was publishing his poetry and fiction in various small magazines, his big break did not come until 1970, when he was fired from his Science Research Associates job and when he received a National Endowment for the Arts Discovery Award for Poetry. With the money from the grant (plus his unemployment benefits and severance pay), he found the time to revise many of the stories that appeared in his first important book, *Will You Please Be Quiet, Please?* (1976). He was soon publishing in reputable journals and better-paying slick magazines such as *Esquire* and *Harper's Bazaar* and gaining recognition by having his stories chosen to appear in the O. Henry Award collections.

In 1971 and 1972, Carver had a lectureship at the University of California, Santa Cruz, and in the fall of 1972 he held a Wallace Stegner Creative Writing Fellowship at Stanford University. During the fall semester, 1973, he also had a visiting writer's appointment at the Iowa Writers' Workshop. By this time, however, he was plagued with the disease of alcoholism. He has said that he and his colleague, well-known writer John Cheever, were drinking so heavily during their tenures at Iowa that they never took the covers off their typewriters.

In 1977, when *Will You Please Be Quiet, Please?* was nominated for the National Book Award, Carver had to be hospitalized several times. He has said that June 2, 1977, was the date he stopped drinking for good. Carver's professional career began to blossom in the late 1970's and 1980's: He received a Guggenheim Fellowship in 1979, published a highly praised collection of stories titled *What We Talk About When We Talk About Love* in 1981, and another significant collection titled *Cathedral* in 1983.

Moreover, his personal life improved significantly. Following his divorce from his first wife in the late 1970's, Carver met and began living with writer Tess Gallagher. Also in 1983, he was awarded the Mildred and Harold Strauss Living Award, a five-year grant of $35,000 a year. His works have been translated into more than twenty languages. In 1987, after he had put together still another collection of both old and new stories, Carver, a heavy smoker, was diagnosed as having lung cancer. He underwent surgery in the fall, then radiation treatments. His disease had already progressed too far, however; he died in Port Angeles, Washington, on August 2, 1988. His final collection, *Where I'm Calling From,* was published that year.

ANALYSIS

Carver's first two collections of short stories shocked readers with their violence and puzzled them with their laconic, Chekhovian style. *Will You Please Be Quiet, Please?* contains twenty-two stories that provide stark images of lives lived in quiet desperation. In many of the stories in this collection, the characters are thrown out of their everyday routines and caught in situations in which they feel helpless and estranged.

Whereas the stories in Carver's first important collection are relatively drained of imagery and recall the style of Ernest Hemingway, the stories in his second major collection, *What We Talk About When We Talk About Love,* are even more radically sparing in their language; indeed, they are so minimal that they seem mere dehumanized patterns with no life in them at all. Whatever theme they may have is embodied in the bare outlines of sometimes shocking, sometimes trivial events and in the spare and reticent dialogue of the characters, who seem utterly unable to articulate the nature of their isolation. Characters often have no names or only first names and are so briefly described that they seem to have no physical presence at all.

The lyricism of Carver's style lies in a "will to style" in which reality is stripped of its physicality and exists only in the hard, bare outlines of the event. Carver's stories have more of the ambience of dream than of everyday reality. They are unconcerned with social issues, yet the stories are not parables in the usual sense. His characters give a feeling of emotional reality that reaches the level of myth, even as they refuse to give a feeling of physical or simple psychological reality. The most basic theme of Carver's stories is the tenuous union between men and women and the mysterious separations that always seem imminent.

The stories that appear in Carver's last two collections, however, *Cathedral* and *Where I'm Calling From,* perhaps because they were mainly written after Carver had been cured of alcoholism and had met Gallagher, are more optimistic and hopeful than the earlier stories; they also are more voluble and detailed, exhibiting an increasing willingness by Carver and his narrators to discuss, explain, and explore the emotions and situations that give rise to the stories.

Instead of separation, Carver's later stories move toward union or reunion. They are characterized by a mood of reconciliation and calm self-knowledge and acceptance. Although this shift in moral perspective moves Carver's fiction toward a more conventional short-story form, all of his stories are told in such a way that the universal human mystery of union and separation is exposed, even if it is not always explained. The simple, yet complex humanity revealed by Carver can neither be understood nor cured by the pop psychology of modern life; as in the great short stories of his predecessors, it can only be captured in the pure and painful events of human beings who mysteriously come together and come apart.

Carver was the most important figure in the renaissance of short fiction sparked in American literature in the 1980's. He belongs to a line of short-story writers that begins with Anton Chekhov and progresses through such masters of the form as Sherwood Anderson, Katherine Anne Porter, Ernest Hemingway, and Bernard Malamud. On the basis of a small output of stories, Carver will remain a significant figure in the history of modern American literature.

"NEIGHBORS"

First published: 1976 (collected in *Will You Please Be Quiet, Please?*, 1976)
Type of work: Short story

A young couple fantasize about taking the place of their vacationing neighbors.

"Neighbors" is one of the most puzzling and shocking stories in Carver's collection *Will You Please Be Quiet, Please?* It focuses on Bill and Arlene Miller, a young couple who feel that the lives of their neighbors Harriet and Jim Stone are somehow brighter and fuller than their own. The story begins when the Stones go on a trip and ask the Millers to look after their apartment and water the plants. When Bill begins routinely to perform this task, however, his visits to the apartment make him sexually aroused. Moreover, he begins to stay longer and longer in the apartment, taking trivial things such as cigarettes and a container of pills, and nibbling food from the refrigerator.

Bill's fascination with the apartment becomes

more bizarre when he secretly takes time off from work and slips in to spend the day alone there. He first tries on a pair of Bermuda shorts belonging to Jim Stone, then a brassiere and pair of panties belonging to Harriet. The story comes to a climax that evening when his wife goes over to the apartment and the reader discovers that she is similarly fascinated, telling her husband that she found some pictures in a drawer. Although the reader is not told what kind of pictures they are, one may assume they depict the secret life of the Stones. When the couple go back across the hall to their own apartment, they consider that maybe the Stones will not come back. When they discover that they have locked the key to the Stones' apartment inside, they feel desperate.

> "Don't worry," he said into her ear. "For God's sake, don't worry." They stayed there. They held each other. They leaned into the door as if against a wind, and braced themselves.

Typical of Carver's early work, the story offers no explanation for the fascination the apartment holds for the young couple; the closest Carver will come to an explanation is Arlene saying, "It's funny . . . to go in someone's place like that," to which her husband replies, "It *is* funny." This is not a story about a sexually perverted couple; rather, it is a story about the fascination of visiting the secret inner reality of someone else and the excitement of temporarily taking on his or her identity. To enter into the dark and secret world of the "neighbors" is to experience a voyeuristic thrill.

The dissatisfaction that everyone feels at times with being merely themselves and the universal inner desire to change places with someone else is delicately handled in the story. For example, Bill's fantasy of changing places with his neighbor is suggested by the simple act of his looking into the bathroom mirror, closing his eyes, and then looking again—as if by that blink, a transformation could take place. Moreover, the fact that Bill wants to make love to his

wife after visiting the apartment reflects the erotic thrill of peeking into the life of someone else and then, almost in an act of autoeroticism, fulfilling that fantasy with whomever is at hand. The desperation the couple feel at the end as they find themselves locked out of the apartment, bracing themselves "as if against a wind," points to the impossibility of truly entering into the lives of others, except to visit and, inevitably, to violate.

"Why Don't You Dance?"

First published: 1981 (collected in *What We Talk About When We Talk About Love*, 1981)
Type of work: Short story

A young couple inspects the furniture a man has set up on his front lawn, but more is at stake than a yard sale.

This first story in Carver's controversial collection *What We Talk About When We Talk About Love* is characteristic of the qualities of his short fiction at the high point of his career. The story begins with an unidentified man who has, for some unexplained reason, put all of his furniture out on his front lawn. What makes this event more than merely a yard sale is the fact that the man has arranged the furniture exactly as it was when it was in the house and has even plugged in the television and other appliances so that they work as they did inside. The only mention of the homeowner's wife is the fact that the bed has a nightstand and reading lamp on his side of the bed and a nightstand and reading lamp on "her" side of the bed; this is Carver's typical unstated way of suggesting that the man's marriage has collapsed and that his wife is no longer around.

The story begins its muted dramatic turn when a young couple furnishing their first apartment stop by and begin to inspect the furniture. As the young woman tries out the bed and the young man turns on the television, their dialogue is clipped and cryptic, reminiscent of the dialogue of characters in stories by Ernest Hemingway. When the homeowner returns from a trip to the store, the dialogue continues in its understated and laconic way as the couple makes offers for some of the furnishings,

and the homeowner indifferently accepts whatever they offer. The homeowner plays a record on the phonograph; the young man and the young woman, then the homeowner and the woman, dance. The story ends with a brief epilogue as, weeks later, the woman is telling a friend about the incident. The story ends: "She kept talking. She told everyone. There was more to it, and she was trying to get it talked out. After a time, she quit trying."

The story is an embodiment of the way that modern short fiction since Anton Chekhov has attempted to embody inner reality by means of the simple description of outer reality. By placing all his furniture on his front lawn, the man has externalized what had previously been hidden inside the house. When the young couple arrives, they embody the ritual process of replacement of the older man's lost relationship with the beginnings of their own, creating their own relationship on the remains of the man's.

The story is not a hopeful one, however, for the seemingly minor conflicts that the dialogue reveals between the two young people—his watching television and her wanting him to try the bed, her wanting to dance and his drinking—presage another doomed relationship, exactly like the one that has ended. Indeed, there is more to it, as the woman senses, but she cannot quite articulate the meaning of the event; she can only, as storytellers must, retell it over and over again, trying to get it "talked out" and intuitively understood.

"The Bath"

First published: 1981 (collected in *What We Talk About When We Talk About Love*, 1981; revised as "A Small, Good Thing," 1983)
Type of work: Short story

A husband and wife lose their young son in an automobile crash and are plagued by a mysterious telephone caller.

"The Bath," which originally appeared in *What We Talk About When We Talk About Love*, reappeared in the *Cathedral* collection, revised and renamed "A Small, Good Thing." The second version is also reprinted in Carver's final collection, *Where I'm Calling From.*

Both versions of the story focus on a couple whose son is hit by a car on his eighth birthday and who is hospitalized and in a coma. This horrifying event is made more upsetting by the fact that the couple receives annoying anonymous telephone calls from a baker from whom the wife had earlier ordered a custom-made birthday cake for the child. "The Bath" is a brief story, told in Carver's early, neutralized style, focusing less on the feelings of the couple than on the mysterious and perverse interruption of the persistent anonymous calls.

The revision, "A Small, Good Thing," is five times longer than "The Bath." It develops the emotional life of the couple in more sympathetic detail, suggesting that their prayers for their son bind them together in a genuine human communion that they have never felt before. The parents are given more of a sense of everyday human reality in the revision, and their situation is made more conventionally realistic. The father feels that his life has gone smoothly until this point, and the story thus suggests that neither he nor his wife have ever had their comfortable, middle-class lives threatened by such a terrifying disruption before. Much of the detail of the revision follows the parents as they anxiously wait for their son to come out of his comatose state. Whereas the mysterious voice on the phone throughout "The Bath" suggests some perverse interference in their lives, in "A Small, Good Thing" the voice suggests a more concerned presence who always asks them if they have forgotten about their son Scotty.

The most radical difference in the revision, however, can be seen in the conclusion. Whereas in the first version the child's death abruptly ends the story, in the second, the couple discover that it is the baker who has been calling and go visit him after the boy's death. He shares their sorrow; they share his loneliness. The story ends in reconciliation in the warm and comfortable bakery as the couple, in an almost Christian ritual of breaking bread together, eat the baker's bread and talk into the early morning, not wanting to leave—as if a retreat into the communal reality of the bakery marks the true nature of a healing unification.

Although the earlier version of the story seems to have been repudiated by Carver, the revisions that created the new story, "A Small, Good Thing,"

provide a striking example of how Carver's writing style and thematic concerns changed after his first two collections. Whereas "The Bath" is a story about a mysterious eruption into any life, "A Small, Good Thing" is a story that moves toward a more conventionally moral ending of acceptance. The image of the parents in the warm, sweet-smelling bakery, momentarily reconciled by their sense of communion with the baker, is a clear indication of Carver's moral shift from the skeptical to the affirmative, from the sense of the unspeakable mystery of human life to the sense of how simple and moral life is, after all.

"CATHEDRAL"

First published: 1983 (collected in *Cathedral*, 1983)
Type of work: Short story

A cynical man has his prejudices challenged by an encounter with a blind man.

The title story of Carver's third collection is typical of how his technique and thematic concerns changed after his personal life became more stable. The story contains much more exposition and discussion, more background and efforts at clarification, than the stories in Carver's first two cryptic collections. "Cathedral" is told by a first-person narrator, a young man who resents the visit of an old friend of his wife—a blind man for whom the wife once read.

Unlike Carver's earlier stories, which focus primarily on the immediate situation detached from its background, the first quarter of "Cathedral" recounts the narrator's knowledge of his wife's previous married life, her friendship with the blind man (especially the fact that they have sent audiotapes back and forth to each other), and even of the blind man's wife, Beulah, who has recently died. Although the relevance of all this information to the final, epiphanic revelation of the story is not made clear, it does reveal the cynicism of the narrator, who obviously resents his wife's relationship with the blind man. It also reveals him as an insensitive character who has prejudiced notions about a variety of subjects. For example, his only notion of blind people comes from films, and he asks if the blind man's wife was "a Negro" only because her name was Beulah.

The conversation among the narrator, his wife, and the blind man that makes up the center of the story is inconclusive, mainly devoted to the blind man's dispelling many of the prejudiced expectations the narrator has about the blind. The climax toward which the story moves—a confrontation between the narrator and the blind man—begins when the wife goes to sleep and the two men drink and smoke marijuana together. The encounter is triggered by a program on television about Christianity in the Middle Ages—which the narrator watches because there is nothing else on. When the program features a cathedral, the narrator asks the blind man if he knows what a cathedral is. The blind man says he has no real idea and asks the narrator to describe a cathedral to him. When the narrator fails, the blind man asks him if he is religious, to which the narrator says he does not believe in anything.

The blind man then asks the narrator to find some paper and a pen so that they can draw a cathedral together. The blind man puts his hand over the hand of the narrator and tells him to draw, with the blind man's hand following along with him. The blind man even asks the narrator to close his eyes as they continue drawing. When they finish, the blind man asks him to look at the drawing and tell him what he thinks; the narrator keeps his eyes closed. He knows that he is in his house, but he says that he does not feel like he is inside anything. His final statement is typical Carver inconclusiveness: "It's really something."

"Cathedral" is a much-admired Carver story, often finding its way into literature anthologies for college classes; however, it is less experimental and innovative, more explicit, and more conventionally optimistic and moral than his earlier stories. The narrator has obviously reached some sort of traditional epiphany at the end. Ironically, whereas he had been morally blind before, now he is able to see. The story is about his ultimate ability to identify with the blind man, about the two men blending together into one entity. The narrator's experience is a religious experience in the broadest sense; the fact that a cathedral brings the two men together makes that clear enough.

The story is much more "talky" than Carver's earlier stories, partially because it is a first-person narrative in which the personality of the narrator is the very thematic heart of the story itself, but also because Carver seems to believe he has an explanation for things that he did not try to account for previously. The tendency toward explanation moved his later work closer to the kind of moral fiction of which his first mentor, Gardner, would have approved.

"Errand"

First published: 1987 (collected in *Where I'm Calling From,* 1987)
Type of work: Short story

The death of Russian writer Anton Chekhov is imagined by Carver with a poignant Chekhovian touch.

"Errand" has special significance in the Carver canon, for it is the last story in his last collection, *Where I'm Calling From.* Because it was published not long before Carver's death, when he knew he had cancer, and because it deals with the death of one of Carver's most treasured progenitors, Chekhov, it takes on a particular poignancy as a kind of farewell tribute to the short-story writer's craft and art.

Much of the story seems less a unified narrative than a straightforward report of Chekhov's death in a hotel in the resort city of Badenweiler, Switzerland. The story recounts without comment Chekhov's last hours, as a doctor visits him in his room and as his wife, Olga Knipper, stands by helplessly. Knowing that it is hopeless and that it is only a matter of minutes, the doctor orders champagne and three glasses from the kitchen. A few minutes after taking a drink, Chekhov dies.

Up to this point, "Errand" is not really a story at all, for it does not have the implied "point" that is typical of the short story—especially since the innovations were introduced by Chekhov himself. What makes it a story is the appearance of the young waiter who brings the champagne. When the young man returns to the room the next morning to bring a vase of roses and to pick up the champagne bottle and glasses, Olga Knipper, who has spent the remainder of the night sitting alone with

Chekhov's body, urges him to go into the town and find a mortician, someone who takes great pains in his work and whose manner is appropriately reserved.

The young man listens as Olga tells him in great detail what to do. He should behave as if he is engaged on a great errand, moving down the sidewalk as if he were carrying in his arms a porcelain vase of roses that he has to deliver to an important man. He should raise the brass knocker on the mortician's door and let it fall three times; the mortician will be a modest, unassuming man with a faint smell of formaldehyde on his clothes. As the young man speaks to him, the mortician will take the vase of roses.

As Olga tells this "story" of the errand the young waiter must fulfill, it becomes so real that it seems to be actually happening—it becomes, in itself, an example of the storyteller's art. Meanwhile, the boy is thinking of something else: On the previous night, just after Chekhov died, the cork which the doctor had pushed back into the champagne bottle had popped out again; it now lies at the toe of the boy's shoe. He wants to bend over and pick it up, but he does not want to intrude by calling attention to himself. When Olga finishes the storylike description of the errand she wishes the boy to perform, he leans over—still holding the vase of roses—and without looking, reaches down and closes his hand around the cork.

It is this single, simple detail that makes "Errand" a story rather than a mere report and thus a fitting tribute to the short-story writing art of both Chekhov and Carver. The cork is not a symbol of anything; it is a concrete object in the world that one can almost tangibly feel as the boy closes his hand around it. It is the unique and concrete act of picking up the cork that humanizes the otherwise abstract report of Chekhov's death. It fulfills Chekhov's dictum that if a gun is described hanging on a wall early in a story, then it must be fired before the end. It also embodies the most important lesson that Carver learned from Chekhov—that human meaning is communicated by the simplest of gestures and the most trivial of objects.

DISCUSSION TOPICS

- What events in Raymond Carver's life crystalized his development as a short-story writer?

- Identify the "inexplicable separations" in two or three of Carver's short stories. What makes them inexplicable?

- The short-story form often allows readers to put themselves briefly into someone else's shoes. Find a few Carver stories that seem particularly effective in this respect. What techniques account for this success?

- Carver's *Cathedral* has been translated into more than twenty languages—a fact which suggests the existence of many readers in societies quite different from the United States. What themes, elements of his style, or other aspects of his stories seem best to account for the universality of his appeal?

- The stories in *Cathedral* are fairly evenly divided into first- and third-person narratives. What can you determine about the advantages and disadvantages of each of these modes of narration?

SUMMARY

After years of neglect, the short story enjoyed a true renaissance in the 1980's; Carver was arguably the most important figure in that revival. His understanding of the merits of the short-story form and his sensitivity to the situation of modern men and women caught in tenuous relationships and inexplicable separations has made him a spokesman for those who cannot articulate their own dilemmas. Although critics are divided over the relative merits of Carver's early, bleak, experimental stories and his later, more conventional and morally optimistic stories, there is little disagreement that he is a modern master of the "much-in-little" nature of the short-story form.

Charles E. May

BIBLIOGRAPHY

By the Author

SHORT FICTION:
Put Yourself in My Shoes, 1974
Will You Please Be Quiet, Please?, 1976
Furious Seasons, and Other Stories, 1977
What We Talk About When We Talk About Love, 1981
Cathedral, 1983
Where I'm Calling From, 1988
Elephant, and Other Stories, 1988
Short Cuts: Selected Stories, 1993

POETRY:
Near Klamath, 1968
Winter Insomnia, 1970
At Night the Salmon Move, 1976
Two Poems, 1982
If It Please You, 1984
This Water, 1985
Where Water Comes Together with Other Water, 1985
Ultramarine, 1986
A New Path to the Waterfall, 1989
All of Us: The Collected Poems, 1996

SCREENPLAY:
Dostoevsky, 1985

EDITED TEXT:
American Short Story Masterpieces, 1987 (with Tom Jenks)

MISCELLANEOUS:
Fires: Essays, Poems, Stories, 1983
No Heroics, Please: Uncollected Writings, 1991, revised and expanded as *Call If You Need Me: The Uncollected Fiction and Other Prose*, 2001

About the Author

Bethea, Arthur F. *Technique and Sensibility in the Fiction and Poetry of Raymond Carver.* New York: Routledge, 2001.

Campbell, Ewing. *Raymond Carver: A Study of the Short Fiction.* New York: Twayne, 1992.

Gallagher, Tess. *Soul Barnacles: Ten More Years with Ray.* Edited by Greg Simon. Ann Arbor: University of Michigan Press, 2000.

Halpert, Sam. *Raymond Carver: An Oral Biography.* Iowa City: University of Iowa Press, 1995.

Lainsbury, G. P. *The Carver Chronotope: Inside the Life-World of Raymond Carver's Fiction.* New York: Routledge, 2004.

Nesset, Kirk. *The Stories of Raymond Carver: A Critical Study.* Athens: Ohio University Press, 1995.

Powell, Jon. "The Stories of Raymond Carver: The Menace of Perpetual Uncertainty." *Studies in Short Fiction* 31 (Fall, 1994): 647-656.

Runyon, Randolph Paul. *Reading Raymond Carver.* Syracuse, N.Y.: Syracuse University Press, 1992.

Saltzman, Arthur M. *Understanding Raymond Carver.* Columbia: University of South Carolina Press, 1988.

Stull, William L., and Maureen P. Carroll, eds. *Remembering Ray: A Composite Biography of Raymond Carver.* Santa Barbara, Calif.: Capra Press, 1993.

WILLA CATHER

Born: Back Creek Valley, near Gore, Virginia
December 7, 1873
Died: New York, New York
April 24, 1947

Known primarily for her literary portraits of frontier life, Cather has achieved critical recognition as one of the leading American novelists of the twentieth century.

Edward Steichen/Courtesy, George Bush
Presidential Library and Museum

BIOGRAPHY

Willa Cather was born in Back Creek Valley, near Gore, Virginia, on December 7, 1873. Christened Wilella and called by the nickname "Willie" throughout her childhood, Cather later adopted the name Willa. The daughter of Charles Cather, a farmer, and his wife, Mary Virginia Boak Cather, she was the eldest of the couple's four children, who also included brothers Roscoe and Douglass and a second daughter, Jessica.

Although the Cather family had long been established in the small Virginia community where Willa was born, a general westward migration of family members, sparked by the railroad's opening of the Great Plains states to increasing numbers of settlers, was already under way at the time of Cather's birth. Cather's aunt, uncle, and grandparents had already left Back Creek for the Nebraska farming community of Red Cloud when Charles Cather decided to follow suit in 1883. Auctioning off the family farm, the Cathers left Virginia and traveled by train to Red Cloud. At the age of nine, Willa Cather arrived in the region that would provide the setting for most of her best-known works.

The tiny area where the Cathers and their relatives established homesteads had already come to be known as Catherton, but that did not increase Charles Cather's luck as a prairie farmer. After an unsuccessful first year, he sold his homestead and moved his family into Red Cloud, where he began a farm loan and insurance business. It was in Red Cloud that young Willa passed the next six years of her life, becoming an avid reader and diligent student whose sharp intellect and forceful personality left a lasting impression on friends and teachers alike.

In 1890, at the age of sixteen, Cather left Red Cloud for Lincoln and the University of Nebraska. After a year's preparatory study, she entered the school and quickly established herself as one of its brightest—and most individualistic—students. Severe and mannish in her dress, she was self-confident and sometimes aloof in her manner, and she was already beginning to establish herself as a writer. An editor and contributor to the campus's two literary magazines, she also had two articles published in the *Nebraska State Journal*, to which she began contributing a regular column during her junior year. That assignment soon changed to one as the paper's theater reviewer, a post she held until after her graduation. She earned a reputation as a tough and eloquent critic impatient with the third-rate fare often served up by touring companies from larger cities.

A year after her graduation, Cather moved to Pittsburgh, Pennsylvania, where she would remain for the following ten years. For much of that time she lived with the family of her close friend, Isabelle McClung, with whom she made her first trip abroad in 1902. During this period, Cather worked as an editor of *Home Monthly* magazine and taught high school. She continued the writing she had begun in Nebraska and published a book of poetry, *April Twilights,* in 1903 and a collection of short stories, *The Troll Garden,* in 1905. The following year, Cather moved to New York to work for *McClure's* magazine. Six years later she published her first novel, *Alexander's Bridge* (1912).

That same year, Cather made the first of many trips to the American Southwest, where her brother Douglass worked for the Sante Fe railroad. There, she visited the ruins of cliff-dwelling Indian structures and discovered the striking vistas and ancient culture that would play an important role in several of her later novels. Cather's next work, however, was *O Pioneers!* (1913), a story set among the landscapes and people of her Nebraska childhood. The book earned critical acclaim, as did her 1915 novel, *The Song of the Lark,* which examines the career of a singer.

Cather's next novel, *My Ántonia,* published in 1918, is recognized as one of her major works. Its story of an immigrant girl's life on the Nebraska plains draws its inspiration from many actual people and events Cather remembered from her youth. After publishing a collection of short stories titled *Youth and the Bright Medusa* (1920), Cather wrote *One of Ours* (1922), a novel set against the action of World War I, for which she was awarded the Pulitzer Prize in fiction.

Throughout the 1920's, Cather's popularity grew with critics and readers alike. She had achieved international recognition as one of America's finest writers, and her work continued to reflect the important influences on her life. *A Lost Lady* (1923) takes as its theme the end of the frontier days in the Midwest, while *The Professor's House* (1925) includes a long segment on the discovery of Southwestern Indian ruins. Now in a period of great productivity, Cather published *My Mortal Enemy* in 1926 and, in 1927, *Death Comes for the Archbishop,* which many critics regard as one of her finest works. Set in the Southwest, its story chronicles the life of a priest ministering to the Indian tribes.

In 1930, Cather was awarded the Howells medal for fiction by the Academy of the National Institute of Arts and Letters. During the decade that followed, she published three novels, *Shadows on the Rock* (1931), *Lucy Gayheart* (1935), and *Sapphira and the Slave Girl* (1940), a book of short stories titled *Obscure Destinies* (1932), and a collection of essays, *Not Under Forty* (1936). In 1944, she was awarded the gold medal of the National Institute of Arts and Letters. Despite the increasingly fragile state of her health, Cather continued to write until the time of her death from a cerebral hemorrhage on April 24, 1947. Two volumes of her later work— essays and short stories—received posthumous publication.

ANALYSIS

Cather is a rarity among writers: a woman who has managed to escape classification as a "woman writer." As a novelist, she is closely identified with a particular region but has nevertheless avoided the label "regional writer." It is the depth and universality of the themes that run through her work that have allowed Cather to transcend such limiting definitions of her voice as a writer, permitting its individuality to achieve full critical recognition.

Central to much of her work is Cather's fascination with the men and women who struggled to build lives for themselves and their families in the sometimes hostile environment of the American frontier. As the daughter of a farmer and, briefly, a homesteader, Cather was intimately acquainted with the conditions faced by the pioneers, many of them immigrants adjusting to new lives far from their native lands and the level of courage, endurance, patience, and strength that was demanded of them in their efforts to tame the frontier. In books such as *O Pioneers!* and *My Ántonia,* Cather creates vivid fictional portraits of the individuals who peopled the world of her Nebraska childhood. Her sensitivity to the problems faced by the immigrant homesteaders is especially acute, and her admiration for their ability to outlast the difficulties awaiting them in their new land is boundless.

In Cather's world, the pioneer experience draws on the depths of an individual's character. Cather's particular talent lies in her ability to translate this experience into universal terms, turning a pioneer woman's simple life into a glowing tribute to the human spirit. Cather sees in her characters—as she did in the figures surrounding her in her youth— people whose individual stories of courage and endurance form a heroic pattern that changed the face of a nation.

Cather also recognizes, certainly to some extent from personal experience, that a life tilling the soil can be restrictive and unfulfilling for anyone whose aspirations lie beyond the horizons of the

Midwest's farms and small towns. Claude Wheeler, the central character in *One of Ours*, is ill-suited to the life of a farmer and finds his escape in the battlefields of France. Jim Burden, the narrator of *My Ántonia*, is impatient to leave his small community for the larger world.

Cather also deals in her work with the passing of the frontier spirit as larger communities draw an influx of people to the region. There is a strong nostalgia for times past in many of her novels and an increasing dislike of modern society and modern ways that sometimes drew critical fire later in her career. In *A Lost Lady*, the charming Marian Forrester—a gracious, aristocratic presence in the small town of Sweet Water—gradually enters a decline that leads her to an affair with her husband's friend and an association with the town's unscrupulous lawyer. The book is sympathetic in its portrait of Marian, who represents the fading past, and harsh in its portrayal of Ivy Peters, the attorney whose ways represent a break with traditions such as honor and respect.

Hand in hand with Cather's reverence for the pioneer spirit is her admiration for individuality. One of the recurring themes in her work is that of the individual whose dreams and ambitions place him or her at odds with society. The choices a person makes, and the repercussions those choices have, is the theme of both *The Song of the Lark* and *The Professor's House*. In the former, a singer sacrifices everything for her career, leaving behind her midwestern home and family and relegating her social life to secondary status in order to pursue her dream. When she has achieved her goals, she is able to look back, clear-eyed, on the decisions she has made along the way and accept that they were necessary in obtaining her goal. For Cather, this was a highly personal subject, and the novel's story line has many similarities to her own life.

The Professor's House examines the life of a man who has not made such a decision and who reaches the beginning of old age only to come face to face with the unique individual spirit he suppressed years ago. Although outwardly successful, he feels less and less at home in the life he has gradually allowed to become his own. He at last releases his connection to his earlier self and resigns himself to living out what his life has become. His own choices are contrasted with his reminiscences concerning a former student, Tom Outland, whose ability to live in harmony with his own spirit reminds the professor of what he has lost.

Cather also had a strong feeling for the land itself, both the midwestern prairies and the more dramatic landscapes of the southwestern region she later came to love. The land is an intrinsic part of several of her best works, and it was frequently the inspiration for the poetry she wrote earlier in her career. It is in her descriptive passages that Cather's prose style is at its most eloquent, capturing with vivid imagery the colors, physical features, and shifting moods and impressions that a particular landscape evokes in its human inhabitants. In *O Pioneers!* and *My Ántonia*, the unique and subtle beauty of the prairie landscape is strongly felt throughout the stories, while *Death Comes for the Archbishop* and *The Professor's House* both offer striking portraits of the Southwest.

The latter two books also draw on Cather's fascination with Indian culture and the history of the land prior to the arrival of white settlers. Tom Outland's discovery of the cliff-dwelling Indian ruins in *The Professor's House* and his complete absorption in them over the following year of his life provide the book with its most compelling segments. *Death Comes for the Archbishop* is a historical novel that brings to life the missionary work of two priests whose lives span the dramatic changes in the southwestern frontier that took place in the latter half of the nineteenth century. The love they come to have for the land and its people reflects Cather's own feelings, even as the book gives voice to a unique period in American history.

MY ÁNTONIA

First published: 1918
Type of work: Novel

An immigrant pioneer woman's life is recalled by her childhood friend.

One of Cather's best-loved novels, *My Ántonia* is a moving tribute to the spirit of the pioneers whose strength and endurance made possible the settlement of the American frontier. In its portrait of its title character, the book gives an individual face to the myriad experiences facing the immigrants who composed a large portion of the Midwest's early homesteaders.

The story is told from the point of view of Jim Burden, a young boy from Virginia who has lost his parents and travels to Nebraska to live with his grandparents. On the same train as Jim is an immigrant family, the Shimer-

das, whose oldest daughter, Ántonia (pronounced in the Eastern European manner, with accents on the first and third syllables), will become the companion of Jim's childhood days. Through Jim's eyes, the reader sees the family's early struggles as they suffer cold and deprivation in a dugout house, lose the sensitive Mr. Shimerda to suicidal despair, and gradually begin to pull free of hardship through diligence and hard work.

Ántonia Shimerda is an intelligent girl who must forgo any thought of serious study in order to work for her family. First in the fields and later as a "hired girl" in Red Cloud, she is cheerful and uncomplaining, shouldering her share of the backbreaking work required to support a family farm. Ántonia's patient, gentle spirit stays with Jim long after he has left his small community, coming to represent for him the very best of what the pioneer experience can draw from the individual.

Ántonia is not, however, a simplistic character or a lifeless symbolic figure. Cather brings her fully to life, flawed and warmly human, and her story is both specific in its details and universal in its larger themes. A practical, sensible girl, she is nevertheless passionate in her love of the dances that provide all the hired girls with one of their few pleasures, and her trusting nature leads her into trouble—in the form of an illegitimate child—when she is unable to recognize dishonesty, so foreign to her own nature, in the man she loves.

My Ántonia draws its inspiration from Cather's own childhood memories, and Ántonia herself is modeled after a woman named Annie Sadilek, who worked as a maid for the Cathers' neighbors in Red Cloud. Like Ántonia, Annie's father had tragically committed suicide when faced with the hardships

and cultural deprivations of his new home, and Annie's strength and perseverance left a deep impression on Cather over the years. The book's narrator, Jim Burden, who leaves his small community first for college and then to become an attorney for the railroad, is essentially Cather herself, and Jim's growing understanding in the book's later passages of the importance of those early years parallels Cather's own.

My Ántonia is also filled with a wealth of memorable supporting characters: Jim's strong, loving grandparents, the family's colorful farmhands, Ántonia's friends, Lena Lingard, who becomes a successful dressmaker, Tiny Soderball, who makes her fortune in the Alaska gold rush, and Cuzak, the good-hearted immigrant who marries Ántonia and makes his life as a farmer although he longs for the city life he knew as a boy. The novel is peopled with a rich cast of characters culled from Cather's memory and transformed by her writer's imagination.

There is perhaps no other book that captures quite as well as this one does the look and feel of the prairie. An eye accustomed to more spectacular landscapes may miss the subtleties of the land's beauty, but Cather's deep feeling for the Midwest, with its rolling plains, wildflowers, and open sky, creates an almost palpable picture of her story's setting—one that is crucial to the reader's understanding of the characters and their lives. In the beauty of its language and the humanity of its characterizations, *My Ántonia* remains a major achievement among Cather's work.

A LOST LADY

First published: 1923
Type of work: Novel

An aristocratic woman's gradual decline mirrors the changes in the life of a small midwestern town.

A Lost Lady is Cather's elegiac portrait of the spirit of an earlier age. In her depiction of Marian Forrester, the much-admired figurehead of culture and society in the town of Sweet Water, Cather evokes a quality of life that began, for her, to vanish sometime around the beginning of the twentieth century. To Cather, much of what was wrong with twentieth century life was the absence of those qualities that Mrs. Forrester embodies: charm, warmth, and a certain graciousness of manner that has no place in the harsher climate of an industrialized society.

The novel traces the fortunes of the Forresters from their position in the book's opening chapters as wealthy and prominent citizens who divide their time between Sweet Water and the more sophisticated society of Denver, to their financial ruin and the decay of spirit that it precipitates. As in *My Ántonia*, the title character is seen through the eyes of a young man, Niel Herbert, although the voice here takes the form of a third-person narrator. From the time he is twelve and is nursed by Mrs. Forrester after a fall from a tree, Niel regards Marian as the standard against which all other women are measured. His devotion to her continues throughout his teenage years until the morning when he becomes aware that she is involved in an affair with a friend of her husband. For Niel, the shock is overwhelming. As Cather phrases it, "It was not a moral scruple she had outraged, but an aesthetic ideal."

The revelation of Mrs. Forrester's secret life coincides with the Forresters' financial ruin, brought on, in large part, by Captain Forrester's sense of honor. The captain had made his money in railroads and is serving on the board of directors of a bank when the bank's failure threatens to wipe out the savings of many investors for whom the captain's name has been an important draw. Determined not to let his investors down, Forrester liquidates his own fortune and pays it out to the investors. The strain brings on a stroke from which he never fully recovers.

The change in their fortunes quickly takes its toll on Marian Forrester. Ill-equipped to cope with a life uncushioned by her former wealth, she quickly declines to the point where Niel returns from school to Sweet Water to stay with the couple and see them through their difficulties. No longer able to travel, Marian soon feels the narrow constraints of small-town life and begins to drink. As time passes, she comes to rely more and more on Ivy Peters, an unscrupulous lawyer with a long-standing grudge against the Forresters, who takes advantage of Marian's helplessness.

It is clear that, for Cather, Marian Forrester represents a way of life that has been lost in the face of changes in modern society. Ivy Peters personifies those changes, emerging as an unsavory representative of an age in which money has replaced loyalty and honor as the standards by which a man is judged. The contrast between Captain Forrester and Peters is stark and not at all favorable to the latter, making the reversal in their fortunes—one beginning the novel in a position of wealth and authority and the other having seized the reins by its close—all the more painful. In an episode that saddens Niel greatly, Marian invites several of Ivy Peters's group of friends to dinner for an evening which seems to Niel a coarse mockery of the earlier days when an invitation to the Forresters was a much-sought-after prize.

Marian Forrester rallies, surprisingly, at the book's close, leaving Sweet Water and marrying again, to a husband who treasures her as Forrester had. Ultimately, however, she remains for Niel—and for Cather—a figure from a lost era and a reminder of the ways in which the world has changed.

THE PROFESSOR'S HOUSE

First published: 1925
Type of work: Novel

An older man reassesses the choices he has made in his life, comparing himself to a former, much-loved student.

In *The Professor's House*, Cather explores the thoughts and emotions of a man making the difficult transition from middle to old age and finding, as he looks back over his life, that he has lost sight of the person he once was. The first symptom of Professor Godfrey St. Peter's growing internal crisis is his reluctance to leave his attic study when he and his wife move to a new house. For St. Peter, the study—uncomfortable and inconvenient as it has always been—represents the constancy of his working life and the years devoted to his massive history of the Spanish explorers in North America. Unwilling to relinquish this tie to the past, the professor continues to rent his old house and visit it when he works.

As time passes, however, a growing sense of alienation from his family and even his work seems to overtake St. Peter. His two daughters have grown and have developed qualities with which he is impatient, and his relationship with his wife has become a matter of habit rather than interest. Questioning whether he has followed the right path in his life, he finds himself thinking that he has lost the boy he once was, opting instead for a set of social conventions. The spiritual malaise that has seized hold of him very nearly brings the professor to tragedy when he realizes that his life is in danger from a gas stove and he chooses to do nothing. Saved by the family's longtime sewing woman, St. Peter finds that he has somehow let go of those remnants of his boyhood self and is now able to resign himself to the years ahead of him.

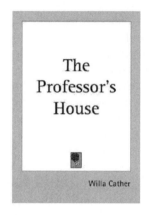

Many critics feel that *The Professor's House* is Cather's most revealing book in terms of her state of mind and her own conflicts regarding the artist's uneasy relationship with society. For Cather, it was essential that her work remain the top priority in her life, and she was prepared to make whatever sacrifices that decision might require. For the professor, social obligations in the form of a family have deflected him from the path he originally set out to follow.

Although they make up the greater portion of the book, Godfrey St. Peter's self-doubts and psychological quagmire are not the most memorable segments of *The Professor's House*. The remarkable section of the novel titled "Tom Outland's Story" comes alive in a way that the longer sections dealing with St. Peter never do. Indeed, Outland's presence—or memory—is the spark that enlivens even those sections of the book in which he does not play a prominent role.

An outstanding student and self-made scholar, Outland has already invented a lucrative engine when he is killed in World War I. The money from the invention leaves his fiancé, St. Peter's daughter Rosamond, a wealthy woman, yet it is a source of great strife within the family. A close friend as well as a student, Outland has come to represent for the professor a man who followed his natural inclinations wholeheartedly. At the time of his own turmoil, St. Peter is editing Outland's journal account of a year spent exploring and excavating Indian ruins. Outland is from Cather's beloved Southwest, and his discovery of a long-vacant village of cliff-dwelling Indians has a transforming effect on his life, one which illuminates his segment of the book and gives it a tone of energy entirely different from those devoted to the professor.

It is a difference that captures the contrast between the way in which the professor has lived and the total absorption that marks Outland's own approach. Recalling his young friend, St. Peter cannot help but find his own life pale and unfocused by comparison, and Cather illustrates this contrast with the marked shift in tone that characterizes Outland's segment—and, indeed, his every appearance—in the book. Whereas the novel as a whole needs the segment to balance and inform its story line, "Tom Outland's Story" could stand alone as a novella.

The Professor's House is interesting both for its insights into Cather herself and for its reflective quality, which marks its author's approaching later years. Yet it is Tom Outland that one remembers—a fact that eloquently bears out Cather's premise regarding the merits of each person's chosen path.

DEATH COMES FOR THE ARCHBISHOP

First published: 1927
Type of work: Novel

Two missionary priests, sent by Rome to bring order to the American Southwest, experience a growing love for the land and its people.

Death Comes for the Archbishop is the book that Cather believed to be her finest work. Like *The Professor's House*, it is a novel that explores the life of a man and draws on the American Southwest for its setting. Here the similarity ends, however, as the tone of the two books is quite different.

Unlike the earlier books, *Death Comes for the Archbishop* celebrates the life choices of its central characters, finding in the lives of Father Joseph Vaillant and Father Jean Marie Latour a simple dignity and extraordinary fulfillment.

Cather based her story on William Howlett's account of the life of Father Macheboeuf, vicar to Archbishop Lamy of New Mexico. Set in the mid-nineteenth century, the book follows the fortunes of Father Latour and his assistant and friend, Father Vaillant, as they organize the disjointed religious structure of the southwestern missions. The two face a formidable task, made more difficult by powerful priests long in control of the area who are loathe to abandon the corruption into which they have fallen. Working together diligently and with an unshakable faith, Father Latour and Father Vaillant eventually reclaim the region and bring its far-flung communities under the guidance of a single diocese.

The actual course its story takes, however, is less important than the novel's moving exploration of the human spirit as it is revealed in the two priests. Father Latour and Father Vaillant, both men of deep faith and dedication, willingly sacrifice much in the way of personal desires for the sake of the mission they have undertaken, and the book shines with the integrity and nobility of their efforts.

Cather was often asked how much of the story of the two priests was based on historical fact. Perhaps the most accurate answer would be that the skeletal outline of the book is drawn from reality, but everything else is what Cather referred to as a "work of the imagination." The book could be described as historical fiction, or perhaps fictionalized history, but whatever term one chooses to apply, it is clear that those elements that make *Death Comes for the Archbishop* remarkable are Cather's. Her extraordinary prose style is much in evidence, painting vivid literary portraits of the southwestern landscapes and bringing to life a chapter in frontier history.

Cather's love for the Southwest is evident throughout the book, and it reverberates in the love the two priests come to feel for the land and its people. Father Vaillant, in particular, is a man of the people—a dedicated priest who is happiest when he is able to minister to those cut off from the Church by distance or circumstance. Father Latour is a reflective man who sees his greatest dream accomplished in the building of a stone cathedral in Santa Fe, a building that combines the Romanesque architectural style of the Old World with the raw building resources of the New. In the novel's moving final image, it is at the altar of this cathedral that Father Latour is laid after his death.

Death Comes for the Archbishop is rich in unforgettable set pieces and unique secondary characters. Among the book's most memorable segments is the priests' encounter with a dangerous man who offers them shelter for the night, fully intending to murder them and steal their mules. They are warned by his Mexican wife, whom they later assist after she, too, has fled. This event leads to an encounter with frontiersman Kit Carson, in an effective blending of fiction and history that typifies the skill with which Cather brings the past to life.

Ultimately, *Death Comes for the Archbishop* is, like much of Cather's work, a tribute to the courage and perseverance of those who settled the American frontier. What Cather evokes so well in her depiction of Father Latour and Father Vaillant is the depth of purpose that led these men, and so many others like them, to leave behind the world they knew and undertake a mission that would transform their lives into an act of faith.

SUMMARY

In novels as varied as *My Ántonia* and *Death Comes for the Archbishop*, Cather created eloquently written portraits of individuals whose lives achieve a universality of experience and feeling within the confines of very specific, and often unremarkable, settings.

In Cather's best works, the courage and strength of the human spirit are brought vividly to life in stories that capture crucial moments in the history of the American frontier. In the midst of situations that test the limits of their endurance, Cather's characters are helping to shape the face of a changing nation as the threads of their quiet, individual stories are woven together in the fabric of history.

Janet Lorenz

BIBLIOGRAPHY

By the Author

LONG FICTION:
Alexander's Bridge, 1912
O Pioneers!, 1913
The Song of the Lark, 1915
My Ántonia, 1918
One of Ours, 1922
A Lost Lady, 1923
The Professor's House, 1925
My Mortal Enemy, 1926
Death Comes for the Archbishop, 1927
Shadows on the Rock, 1931
Lucy Gayheart, 1935
Sapphira and the Slave Girl, 1940

SHORT FICTION:
"Paul's Case," 1905
The Troll Garden, 1905
Youth and the Bright Medusa, 1920
Obscure Destinies, 1932
The Old Beauty and Others, 1948
Willa Cather's Collected Short Fiction: 1892-1912, 1965
Uncle Valentine, and Other Stories: Willa Cather's Collected Short Fiction, 1915-1929, 1973

POETRY:
April Twilights, 1903

NONFICTION:
Not Under Forty, 1936
Willa Cather on Writing, 1949
Willa Cather in Europe, 1956
The Kingdom of Art: Willa Cather's First Principles and Critical Statements, 1893-1896, 1966
The World and the Parish: Willa Cather's Articles and Reviews, 1893-1902, 1970 (2 volumes)

MISCELLANEOUS:
Writings from Willa Cather's Campus Years, 1950

About the Author

Bloom, Edward A., and Lillian D. Bloom. *Willa Cather's Gift of Sympathy.* Carbondale: Southern Illinois University Press, 1962.

Bloom, Harold, ed. *Modern Critical Views: Willa Cather.* New York: Chelsea House, 1985.

Gerber, Philip L. *Willa Cather.* Rev. ed. New York: Twayne, 1995.

Goldberg, Jonathan. *Willa Cather and Others.* Durham, N.C.: Duke University Press, 2001.

Nettels, Elsa. *Language and Gender in American Fiction: Howells, James, Wharton, and Cather.* Charlottesville: University Press of Virginia, 1997.

O'Connor, Margaret Anne, ed. *Willa Cather: The Contemporary Reviews.* New York: Cambridge University Press, 2001.

DISCUSSION TOPICS

- Willa Cather frequently gave her characters suggestive names. Consider several characters whose names suggest their traits or circumstances.

- Authors often combine some of the characteristics of two or more real person to fashion one fictional one. Consider Ántonia Shimerda as an instance of this practice.

- What is Cather's attitude toward social change as revealed in her novels? Nostalgic? Accepting? Resistant? Ambivalent? Does it vary from one work to another?

- Discuss Cather's work ethic as revealed in her life and in the characterization of the professor in *The Professor's House.*

- Describe some of the "unique secondary characters" in *Death Comes for the Archbishop.*

- Edward A. Bloom and Lillian D. Bloom published a book about Cather in 1962 titled *Willa Cather's Gift of Sympathy.* What evidence of her sympathy do you find in a novel of your choice?

Romines, Ann, ed. *Willa Cather's Southern Connections: New Essays on Cather and the South.* Charlottesville: University Press of Virginia, 2000.

Shaw, Patrick W. *Willa Cather and the Art of Conflict: Re-visioning Her Creative Imagination.* Troy, N.Y.: Whitston, 1992.

Skaggs, Merrill Maguire, ed. *Willa Cather's New York: New Essays on Cather in the City.* Madison, N.J.: Fairleigh Dickinson University Press, 2001.

Stout, Janis P. *Willa Cather: The Writer and Her World.* Charlottesville: University Press of Virginia, 2000.

————, ed. *Willa Cather and Material Culture: Real-World Writing, Writing the Real World.* Tuscaloosa: University of Alabama Press, 2005.

Wasserman, Loretta. *Willa Cather: A Study of the Short Fiction.* Boston: Twayne, 1991.

Woodress, James. *Willa Cather: A Literary Life.* Lincoln: University of Nebraska Press, 1990.

RAYMOND CHANDLER

Born: Chicago, Illinois
     July 23, 1888
Died: La Jolla, California
     March 26, 1959

Chandler helped to shape the American school of detective fiction in the 1930's, attempting to write detective novels that could be considered serious literature.

Library of Congress

BIOGRAPHY

Raymond Thornton Chandler was born in Chicago on July 23, 1888. He was the only child of Maurice Benjamin Chandler, a railroad worker, and Florence Dart Chandler (né Thornton), an Irishwoman who immigrated to Plattsmouth, Nebraska. Maurice was an alcoholic, and he and Florence were divorced when their son was seven years old. Raymond and his mother moved to London to live with his severe grandmother and his unmarried Aunt Ethel. His uncle, Ernest Thornton, an Irish solicitor, reluctantly supported this entire household. Chandler felt abandoned by his father and so developed a strong loyalty to his mother and a sense of justice that manifested itself later in his novels.

Chandler attended Dulwich College, a typical English public school. There he studied the Bible and the Greek and Roman classics, a course of study designed to teach a strict Victorian moral code emphasizing honor, public service, and self-denial. This code profoundly affected Chandler's personality, and it formed the basis for the character of Philip Marlowe, the hero of Chandler's best-known works.

In 1905, when he was seventeen, Chandler graduated from Dulwich near the head of his class. He wanted to go to a university to study law, but his uncle refused to pay his tuition, deciding instead that

Chandler should seek a career in the government. Chandler spent a year studying in France and Germany and became a British citizen to qualify for the civil service examination, which he passed easily. Yet, after six months in his job as an accountant for the navy, he quit to become a writer, much to the chagrin of his Uncle Ernest.

Chandler spent the next few years writing for newspapers and submitting articles and reviews to literary magazines but made very little money from his writing. In 1912, when he was twenty-three years old, he borrowed five hundred pounds from his uncle and sailed to the United States. Chandler went to St. Louis, then to Nebraska. He soon moved on to Los Angeles, however, to stay with a family he had met on his passage to America. Warren Lloyd, the father, was a Ph.D. in philosophy who became moderately wealthy from his dealings in the oil business. He found Chandler a job, and Chandler joined his social circle. There Chandler met Cissy Pascal, who was then married to one of Lloyd's friends.

Chandler's mother joined him in Los Angeles in 1916. In 1917, he went to Canada to join the army to fight in World War I. He was the only member of his unit to survive a German artillery barrage in France in June, 1918. By 1919, he was back in the United States. He felt rootless, and he wandered up to the Pacific Northwest, then to San Francisco, where he worked in a bank. He soon returned to Los Angeles, however, and began his affair with Pascal. She was divorced from her husband in 1920, but she and Chandler did not marry until 1924, after his mother died. At this time, Chandler

424

was thirty-five years old; Cissy was fifty-three, although she looked younger. Their marriage was often troubled, but they remained together for thirty years, until she died.

By this time, Chandler had taken a job with the Dabney Oil Syndicate, of which he eventually became vice president. During his years in the oil business, he developed a problem with alcoholism that eventually led to his dismissal. He was now forty-five years old. He gave up drinking and began to write for the pulp magazines, contributing his first story to *Black Mask* magazine in 1933. He supported his family this way for six years. Finally, in 1939, when he was fifty years old, his first novel, *The Big Sleep*, was published.

Although the book sold well, Chandler made only two thousand dollars on it. His second book, *Farewell, My Lovely*, published in 1940, received good critical reviews but sold sluggishly, as did his third novel, *The High Window* (1942). He achieved his best sales with his fourth book, *The Lady in the Lake*, published in 1943. Now he had established himself as a novelist, and he had attracted the attention of Hollywood.

In 1943, he went to Paramount Studios to work with Billy Wilder on the screenplay for the novel *Double Indemnity* (1936) by James M. Cain. Both this script and the script Chandler wrote for *The Blue Dahlia* in 1946 were nominated for Academy Awards. The years in Hollywood were profitable for Chandler, but they were also destructive. In the sociable studio atmosphere, he began to drink again, and he had several affairs. His screenwriting career ended in a series of bitter, petty quarrels.

Chandler escaped Hollywood in 1946, when he and Cissy moved to La Jolla, California. He gave up alcohol again and wrote two more novels: *The Little Sister*, published in 1949, and *The Long Goodbye*, published in 1953. Although he finally had fame and enough money to be comfortable, he could not be happy. He became ill with shingles and developed a skin allergy that caused the tips of his fingers to split open. It was so painful that he had to wear gloves to read and bandage his fingers to type. When this allergic rash spread over his chest, he required morphine to withstand the pain. Cissy's health also deteriorated, and she died of fibrosis of the lung in 1954.

Cissy's death drove Chandler to despair, and he began drinking again in earnest. He attempted sui-

cide early in 1955. During the last four years of his life, he divided his time between London and La Jolla. Under the influence of his literary agent, Helga Greene, he remained sober long enough to publish one last novel, *Playback*, in 1958.

In February, 1959, the Mystery Writers of America elected him president, and he flew to New York to accept his office. He caught a cold there and returned to La Jolla alone. He secluded himself and began drinking heavily. His cold developed into pneumonia, and he died at the Scripps Clinic in La Jolla on March 26, 1959.

ANALYSIS

In May, 1948, in an article in *Harper's* magazine titled "The Guilty Vicarage," W. H. Auden wrote, "Chandler is interested in writing, not detective stories, but serious studies of a criminal milieu, the Great Wrong Place, and his powerful but extremely depressing books should be read and judged, not as escape literature, but as works of art." This assessment pleased Chandler, for it confirmed that he had moved detective fiction toward the realm of literature.

Chandler's education in an English public school taught him high standards for writing. It also left him with a distinctly British writing style. In the five years he worked for *Black Mask* magazine, Chandler taught himself to write in the voice of the American vernacular. He both transmitted and invented colloquialisms. Chandler's hero, Philip Marlowe, the narrator of all seven of Chandler's novels, speaks in colorful slang that captures and holds the reader's interest. He is famous for his startling similes, such as the one at the beginning of *Farewell, My Lovely* in which he describes the thug Moose Malloy: "He looked about as inconspicuous as a tarantula on a slice of angel food."

Mystery stories often rely on dramatic irony—that is, the reader knows something that the detective does not know. Chandler sets himself a difficult problem when he makes Marlowe the narrator, because the reader cannot have any knowledge of events that occur outside the detective's perceptions. On the other hand, the reader becomes privy to Marlowe's thoughts and emotions, which lends Chandler's novels a greater depth than that found in most other mystery stories.

The name Marlowe may be a play on the name of Sir Thomas Malory, who wrote the Arthurian romance *Le Morte d'Arthur* in 1485. Indeed, Philip Marlowe behaves like a valiant knight fighting evil in the tradition of chivalry, and there are references to the world of knights in shining armor throughout Chandler's novels. In *The Big Sleep*, Marlowe approaches his client's house and notices a stained-glass window above the entrance that shows "a knight in dark armor rescuing a lady who was tied to a tree and didn't have any clothes on but some very long and convenient hair." Marlowe speculates that he might eventually have to go up and help him. Later in the novel, he looks down at his chessboard and comments, "The move with the knight was wrong. . . . Knights had no meaning in this game. It wasn't a game for knights." The title of the novel *Lady in the Lake*, in fact, refers to the woman who gave King Arthur the sword Excalibur. In *The High Window*, when Marlowe rescues a secretary held captive by her domineering boss, her attending physician calls him a "shop-soiled Galahad."

Philip Marlowe remains true to his knightly code of honor in a sinful world by avoiding its temptations: money and sex. He will never accept more than his standard fee, though he works overtime and often gets beaten up. He always refuses a bribe. He is working not out of a desire for money, but out of a sense of compassion for the weak victims of the world. He expresses contempt for the idle rich and for policemen who allow themselves to become corrupt.

He remains chaste through most of the novels as well. Beautiful, blond women often tempt him, but they usually turn out to be evil or crazy. When Carmen Sternwood shows up naked in his bed in *The Big Sleep*, he kicks her out of his apartment. Then, in a fit of revulsion, he savagely tears the sheets off his bed. When Marlowe meets a nice girl, such as Anne Riordan in *Farewell, My Lovely*, he describes her by saying, "Her nose was small and inquisitive, her upper lip a shade too long and her mouth more than a shade too wide." Her hair is brown, not blond, however, so Marlowe is not really attracted to her. "She looked as if she had slept well. . . . Nice teeth, rather large." He is trapped in that traditional male quandary: He respects the nice woman, the madonna, but he is sexually attracted to the whore.

Eventually Marlowe does sleep with a woman: Linda Loring in *The Long Goodbye*. Their encounter is a perfunctory one-night stand during which she begs him to marry her and he refuses. In *Playback*, Chandler's last and least respected novel, Marlowe actually marries, yet his sexual escapades seem gratuitous and sadistic. His "romantic" interlude with the character Berry Mayfield sounds almost like a rape:

> She started for the door, but I caught her by the wrist and spun her around. . . . I must have been leering a little because she suddenly curled her fingers and tried to claw me. . . . I got the other wrist and started to pull her closer. She tried to knee me in the groin, but she was already too close. Then she went limp and pulled her head back and closed her eyes.

Some critics have suggested that Marlowe remains chaste not because he is following a code of honor, but because he really prefers men to women. In *Farewell, My Lovely*, Marlowe meets a sailor, Red Norgaard, and describes him in a way that leaves no doubt that Marlowe finds him attractive:

> He had the eyes you never see, that you only read about. Violet eyes. Almost purple. Eyes like a girl, a lovely girl. His skin was as soft as silk. Lightly reddened, but it would never tan. . . . His hair was that shade of red that glints with gold.

Chandler defended his creation, Philip Marlowe, against accusations of homosexual tendencies. In fact, Marlowe's chastity can be understood as a manifestation of the moral code of an English public schoolboy.

THE BIG SLEEP

First published: 1939
Type of work: Novel

In a corrupt 1930's Hollywood, Philip Marlowe, a hard-boiled detective, solves the mystery of the disappearance of his client's son-in-law.

The Big Sleep was Chandler's first novel, and some critics say that it is his best, In it, Chandler's

knightly hero, Philip Marlowe, fights vice, particularly materialism and sex, and champions the virtues of loyalty and friendship.

Everything in this unseasonably wet October in Southern California is damp and unnaturally green, a color that Chandler associates with corrupt female sexuality. Marlowe meets his client, General Sternwood, an elderly invalid, in a steamy greenhouse filled with plants "with nasty meaty leaves and stalks like the newly washed fingers of dead men." Sternwood wants Marlowe to find out why he is being blackmailed for his daughter Carmen's gambling debts. Marlowe soon discovers that the blackmailer, Arthur Gwynn Geiger, is a pornographer who uses Carmen as a model. Carmen's boyfriend, Owen Taylor, kills Geiger, and then gets killed himself.

Joe Brody, a small-time racketeer, steals some nude photos of Carmen and tries to blackmail the Sternwoods. Carol Lundgren, Geiger's male lover, murders Brody in mistaken revenge for Geiger's death. The blackmail case is resolved. Yet, out of a sense of loyalty for General Sternwood, Marlowe continues work on the case, now to solve the disappearance of Sternwood's son-in-law, Rusty Regan, whom the old man loved.

Carmen has killed Rusty Regan, and her sister Vivian, Regan's wife, knows this. Vivian's loyalty to her father causes her to call on Eddie Mars, the most powerful mobster in Hollywood, to help her cover up her sister's crime. In return, Mars expects to be able to blackmail Vivian out of much of her father's fortune. Marlowe despises Mars because he values only money and power and will do anything to get it. Mars disguises the disappearance of Rusty Regan by holding his own wife, Mona, prisoner, then spreading the rumor that she ran off with Regan. In contrast, Mona is loyal to her husband and readily goes along with his plans because she loves him. Marlowe falls in love with her, as much for her moral beauty as her physical appearance.

Marlowe deduces that Carmen killed Regan; she is insane and will do anything to get sex.

Carmen had propositioned Regan, her sister's husband. When he refused her, she killed him. Out of the loyalty Marlowe feels for General Sternwood, he agrees to protect the general from the knowledge that his daughter killed his only friend. In return, Marlowe extracts a promise from Vivian to put Carmen in a mental hospital.

Marlowe has solved the crimes he was hired to investigate. Yet the two major criminals, Carmen and Eddie Mars, remain unpunished, so Marlowe is discouraged. All his effort and sacrifice did not make much progress against the evil and chaos in the world, General Sternwood, whom Marlowe worked so hard to protect, is old and nearly dead. Marlowe fell in love with Mona Mars, but in vain. Marlowe concludes by saying, "On the way downtown I stopped at a bar and had a couple of double Scotches. They didn't do me any good."

FAREWELL, MY LOVELY

First published: 1940
Type of work: Novel

Philip Marlowe helps a good-hearted thug find his old girlfriend among the demimonde of Los Angeles and Bay City (Santa Monica).

Farewell, My Lovely, Chandler's second novel, is filled with murder and corruption, yet it is essentially a love story. It begins on a warm day near the end of March in south central Los Angeles. Moose Malloy, a huge, dim-witted ex-convict, enters a bar called Florian's searching for Velma Valento, the girlfriend he left behind eight years before, when he entered prison. Marlowe happens to be there to see Malloy kill the manager of the bar and maim the bouncer. Malloy escapes, and Marlowe makes a report to the police.

Curiosity drives Marlowe to look for Velma. He follows the leads to the home of Jessie Florian, the alcoholic widow of the former bar owner. She acknowledges that Velma used to sing at the bar, and she gives Marlowe a photograph of the missing woman. Marlowe receives a call from Mr. Lindsay Marriott. Marriott hires the detective to accompany him to a remote canyon in Malibu, where he will deliver ransom for a stolen jade necklace.

When they arrive, Marriott is killed, and Marlowe is knocked unconscious.

When Marlowe comes to, he is met by Anne Riordan, a spunky, intelligent woman who happens by to check out the unusual lights in the canyon. She is the daughter of the former police chief of Bay City, and she decides to help Marlowe solve the case, although he balks at the idea. She discovers that the jade necklace belongs to Helen Grayle, the wife of a very rich man.

Marlowe discovers that Lindsay Marriott holds a mortgage on Jessie Florian's house; this is the indirect connection between Helen Grayle and Moose Malloy. Grayle invites Marlowe to her house. She is a beautiful blond, and Marlowe finds her very attractive. She is married, however, and so, according to Marlowe s chivalrous code of honor, she must remain unattainable as the Holy Grail. It is probably no accident that her name is homophonous with the elusive goal of the medieval knights. She throws herself into Marlowe's lap, and he succumbs to the temptation and kisses her. Just then, her husband walks in. Marlowe exits, embarrassed.

After he returns to his office, he is met by an American Indian named Second Planting. Planting drives Marlowe to the home of Jules Amthor, a phony psychic. There, Marlowe is beaten unconscious. He comes to, only to be beaten again by two Bay City police officers. When he reawakens, he realizes that he has been drugged by Dr. Sonderborg, a Bay City drug dealer. Marlowe escapes Sonderborg's clutches and flees to the home of Anne Riordan. She feeds him, dresses his wounds, and offers him her bed. His principles make him refuse and return to his apartment alone.

Lieutenant Randall of the Los Angeles Police Department warns Marlowe off the case. Marlowe continues anyway, by going to interview the corrupt chief of the Bay City Police, John Wax. Marlowe discovers that the town is being run by the racketeer Laird Brunette, who owns the Bay City Belvedere Club and two gambling ships anchored in international waters three miles offshore. Brunette is a friend of Helen Grayle.

That night, Marlowe hires attractive sailor Red Norgaard to take him out to one of the gambling ships so that he can talk to Laird Brunette. He gives the racketeer a message on his card for the missing Moose Malloy. Marlowe returns to his apartment at about 10 P.M. He telephones Helen Grayle and in-

vites her over for a drink. He falls asleep waiting for her, and, when he wakes, Moose Malloy is in his apartment.

When Grayle arrives, Malloy hides in Marlowe's dressing room. Marlowe accuses Grayle of killing Marriott, and Grayle pulls a gun on Marlowe. Malloy comes out of the closet because he recognizes Helen Grayle's voice as that of Velma Valento, his lost love. He suddenly realizes that she was the one who betrayed him to the police eight years previously. Grayle shoots Malloy five times in the stomach, then escapes and disappears. Malloy dies.

Anne Riordan congratulates Marlowe, but he still refuses to kiss her. Three months later, a detective finds Velma/Helen Grayle in Baltimore; she shoots him, and then herself, rather than be taken prisoner. Marlowe relates this story to Lt. Randall at the end of the novel. He ends on a note of regret: "I rode down to the Street floor and went out on the steps of the City Hall. It was a cool day and very clear. You could see a long way—but not as far as Velma had gone."

Velma is the "lovely" of the title to whom Marlowe is bidding farewell. He could never love the homey Anne Riordan as long as the dangerous, blond Velma obsessed him, as she did both Moose Malloy and Lindsay Marriott. Those two men loved her, and, in return, she murdered them.

THE HIGH WINDOW

First published: 1942
Type of work: Novel

A rich Pasadena widow hires Philip Marlowe to find a rare old coin.

Chandler's third book, *The High Window,* tells a story of personal tyranny and the misuse of money and power. The novel begins in front of an old, red-brick home in Pasadena, California. It is summer and much warmer there, in the San Gabriel Valley, than it is over the hill in Hollywood, where Philip Marlowe lives.

Marlowe is in Pasadena at the request of the wealthy widow Elizabeth Bright Murdock, a drunken, domineering matron. She wants Marlowe to find a valuable coin, the Brasher Doubloon, that has disappeared from her safe. She asserts that her flamboyant daughter-in-law, the former Linda Conquest, a nightclub singer, stole the coin. Linda's marriage to Elizabeth's son, Leslie Murdock, has been faltering, and Linda has moved out of the Pasadena house and gone into hiding.

Elizabeth Murdock has a secretary, Merle Davis, who intrigues Marlowe. She is blond and could be beautiful, but she wears no makeup. Merle is afraid of men because she suffered sexual harassment at the hands of Horace Bright, her former employer and Elizabeth's first husband. Marlowe feels attracted to Merle and protective of her. She gives him the names of Lois Magic, who was Linda's former roommate, and Louis Vannier, Lois's escort.

Leslie Murdock follows Marlowe to his office to find out why his mother hired a detective. His father was Horace Bright, who supposedly committed suicide when he lost all of his money in the stock market crash of 1929. Leslie is tied to his mother's purse strings, and he has rebelled by marrying a nightclub singer and running up twelve thousand dollars worth of gambling debts at Alex Morny's Idle Valley Club, a gambling house in the San Fernando Valley.

Marlowe discovers that Lois Magic, Linda's former roommate, has married Alex Morny. He confronts a man who has been tailing him, who turns out to be another detective, George Anson Phillips, who claims he has been hired to tail Leslie. Phillips asks for Marlowe's help on the case, but when Marlowe shows up at his apartment, he finds Phillips shot dead.

Marlowe goes downtown to interview a coin dealer, Elisha Morningstar, who, curiously, offers to sell him the Brasher Doubloon for a thousand dollars. When Marlowe returns to his office, however, he finds that the Brasher Doubloon has been delivered to him through the mail. He puts it in hock at a pawn shop for safekeeping. He telephones Elizabeth Murdock, who tells him that the doubloon has been returned to her. Returning to Morningstar's office, Marlowe finds him murdered.

The police are now suspicious of Marlowe, because he has discovered two dead men in as many days. After they interrogate him in his apartment, he receives a call inviting him out to the Idle Valley Club to talk to Alex Morny. He meets with Morny

and with Linda Conquest-Murdock, who explains that she hates her husband's mother because she mistreats Merle, her secretary.

Marlowe is summoned to his apartment, where he finds Merle, who is hysterical. She believes that she murdered Horace Bright in 1929 by giving him a fatal push out a window. Elizabeth has encouraged that idea in Merle and has let her believe that Elizabeth was protecting her by making the blackmail payments to Louis Vannier to keep that truth hidden. Now Merle has discovered Vannier dead in his house, and she believes that she killed him, too.

Marlowe calms Merle and goes to Vannier's place. There he discovers some photographs proving that Elizabeth pushed her husband out the window and that Leslie killed Vannier, who had previously killed Phillips and Morningstar. Leslie stole the doubloon from his mother to copy it with Vannier. They hired Phillips to sell the coin to Morningstar. Phillips got nervous and sent it to Marlowe. The other Brasher Doubloons were fakes. Marlowe returns the coin to Elizabeth, but he refuses to return her secretary. He personally drives Merle back to her family in Kansas, where she recovers from her big-city neuroses within a week. The "shop-soiled Galahad" had done his duty again.

THE LONG GOODBYE

First published: 1953
Type of work: Novel

A beautiful woman hires Philip Marlowe to protect her alcoholic husband, a successful author, from his self-destructive actions.

The theme of *The Long Goodbye*, the sixth of Chandler's seven novels, is again the corruption of American society, especially its rich. It is also about alienation and the need for love and friendship.

Marlowe befriends a charming drunk, Terry Lennox, in the parking lot of a swank Beverly Hills restaurant. Terry comes to him a few months later, and Marlowe drives him down across the U.S. border into Tijuana. It seems that Terry's wealthy wife, Sylvia, the daughter of Harlan Potter, a newspaper magnate, has been murdered, and the police suspect Terry. The police arrest Marlowe as an accessory when he pulls into the driveway of his Hollywood Hills home after the long trip back from the Mexican border town.

The police release Marlowe after they receive a written murder confession from Terry, as well as the news that he has died in Mexico. The police warn Marlowe off the case, as do several others, including Linda Loring. Linda, the disenchanted wife of a physician, is the sister of the murdered Sylvia. Later, she becomes Marlowe's lover for a single night.

Meanwhile, Eileen Wade, the beautiful wife of a successful writer, Roger Wade, hires Marlowe to rescue her husband from a disreputable clinic for wealthy alcoholics. After Marlowe does so, Eileen begs him to stay with her husband to keep him sober long enough to finish another novel. Marlowe remains for a while but then leaves, disgusted with Roger's drunken confessions of adultery with Syl-

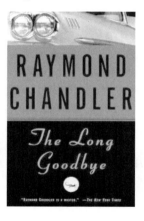

via Lennox and with Eileen's seductive behavior. Marlowe returns to the Wade house a week later to have lunch with Roger. Roger gets drunk and passes out, and Marlowe stays near the house to watch over him. When Eileen returns from shopping that afternoon, however, Roger is dead in the study, with a bullet through his head.

Lieutenant Bernie Ohls, Marlowe's old friend, investigates the death. He disagrees with the official finding, which ruled that Roger's death was a suicide. Instead, Ohls points out evidence to Marlowe that Eileen Wade sneaked into the house and shot her husband while Marlowe was outside and a noisy motorboat was passing by, covering the sound of the gun.

Marlowe and Howard Spencer, Roger's publisher, go to Eileen's house and confront Eileen with this evidence. Marlowe also reveals the fact that, in England during World War II, Eileen had been married to Terry Lennox, who used the name Paul Marston then. She thought that he had been killed by the Nazis. She learned that he was alive

only after she met him accidentally in Idle Valley (Chandler's name for the San Fernando Valley), after he had married Sylvia.

That night, Eileen commits suicide by swallowing an overdose of sleeping pills. She leaves a note confessing that she killed Sylvia Lennox because she felt that Sylvia had stolen both of her husbands. Eileen killed Roger because she was angry about his affair with Sylvia and she wanted to make it look like he was guilty of her murder.

Marlowe publishes her confession to clear Terry Lennox's name of guilt in Sylvia's death. He makes love to Linda Loring, who is divorcing her husband, yet he refuses to marry her and live on her father's money. Lennox, who supposedly died in Mexico, comes to Marlowe with a darkened complexion and a new name, Señor Maioranos ("Mr. Better Years"). He faked his suicide with the help of some gangsters to make his murder confession seem more plausible.

Marlowe despises Lennox for his lack of integrity. He returns the five-thousand-dollar bill that Lennox had sent him earlier in payment for helping him escape the country. When Lennox asks him why he refuses the payment, Marlowe tells him, "You had standards and you lived up to them, but they were personal. They had no relation to any kind of ethics or scruples. . . . you were just as happy with mugs or hoodlums as with honest men. . . . You're a moral defeatist."

When Lennox leaves Marlowe's office, Marlowe realizes that he has lost a friend. He feels as empty as he had when Linda Loring left him after their one night of passion, when he said, "To say goodbye is to die a little."

Summary

Chandler's hero, Philip Marlowe, is a perfectionist who hates the shallow values of American society. By the time of *The Long Goodbye*, set in 1951, the pockets of corruption that Chandler had depicted infecting Hollywood and Bay City in the 1930's had spread over all Los Angeles, like the smog that now blanketed the city. Marlowe has grown tired and cynical. Still, he battles on, even while questioning his own motives and integrity.

Throughout Chandler's seven novels, the character of Marlowe becomes increasingly complex. *The Long Goodbye*, Chandler's penultimate book, is concerned more with theme, characterization, and description than it is with the mechanics of a mystery novel. It represents the fulfillment of Chandler's desire to lift detective fiction to the realm of serious literature.

Pamela Canal

BIBLIOGRAPHY

By the Author

LONG FICTION:
The Big Sleep, 1939
Farewell, My Lovely, 1940
The High Window, 1942
The Lady in the Lake, 1943
The Little Sister, 1949
The Long Goodbye, 1953
Playback, 1958
The Raymond Chandler Omnibus: Four Famous Classics, 1967
The Second Chandler Omnibus, 1973
Poodle Springs, 1989 (incomplete manuscript finished by Robert B. Parker)
Later Novels and Other Writings, 1995

SHORT FICTION:
Five Murderers, 1944
Five Sinister Characters, 1945
Finger Man, and Other Stories, 1946
Red Wind, 1946
Spanish Blood, 1946
Trouble Is My Business, 1950
The Simple Art of Murder, 1950
Pick-up on Noon Street, 1952
Smart-Aleck Kill, 1953
Pearls Are a Nuisance, 1958
Killer in the Rain, 1964 (Philip Durham, editor)
The Smell of Fear, 1965
The Midnight Raymond Chandler, 1971
The Best of Raymond Chandler, 1977
Stories and Early Novels, 1995

NONFICTION:
The Blue Dahlia, 1946 (Matthew J. Bruccoli, editor)
Raymond Chandler Speaking, 1962 (Dorothy Gardiner and Katherine Sorely Walker, editors)
Chandler Before Marlowe: Raymond Chandler's Early Prose and Poetry, 1973 (Bruccoli, editor)
The Notebooks of Raymond Chandler and English Summer, 1976 (Frank MacShane, editor)
Raymond Chandler and James M. Fox: Letters, 1978
Selected Letters of Raymond Chandler, 1981 (MacShane, editor)
The Raymond Chandler Papers: Selected Letters and Non-fiction, 1909-1959, 2000 (Tom Hiney and MacShane, editors)

DISCUSSION TOPICS

- What is chastity? Is Philip Marlowe chaste?
- Does Raymond Chandler oversimplify his female characters? In general do they strike you as resembling women in the real world?
- How extensive is Chandler's influence on contemporary detective fiction?
- Is the character of Philip Marlowe "hard-boiled" primarily by nature or as a consequence of his experiences as a detective?
- Compare one of Chandler's novels with the film based on it. How faithful to the original story is the motion picture?
- How successful was Chandler's aim to achieve the level of serious literature in his novels?

431

About the Author

Bruccoli, Matthew J., and Richard Layman, eds. *Hardboiled Mystery Writers: Raymond Chandler, Dashiell Hammett, Ross Macdonald—A Literary Reference.* New York: Carroll & Graf, 2002.

Hiney, Tom. *Raymond Chandler: A Biography.* New York: Atlantic Monthly Press, 1997.

Lehman, David. "Hammett and Chandler." In *The Perfect Murder: A Study in Detection.* New York: Free Press, 1989.

MacShane, Frank. *The Life of Raymond Chandler.* New York: E. P. Dutton, 1976.

Marling, William. *Raymond Chandler.* Boston: Twayne, 1986.

Moss, Robert F., ed. *Raymond Chandler: A Literary Reference.* New York: Carroll & Graf, 2003.

Norrman, Ralf. *Wholeness Restored: Love of Symmetry as a Shaping Force in the Writings of Henry James, Kurt Vonnegut, Samuel Butler, and Raymond Chandler.* New York: Peter Lang, 1998.

Phillips, Gene D. *Creatures of Darkness: Raymond Chandler, Detective Fiction, and Film Noir.* Lexington: University Press of Kentucky, 2000.

Skinner, Robert E. *The Hard-Boiled Explicator: A Guide to the Study of Dashiell Hammett, Raymond Chandler, and Ross Macdonald.* Metuchen, N.J.: Scarecrow Press, 2002.

Van Dover, J. K., ed. *The Critical Response to Raymond Chandler.* Westport, Conn.: Greenwood Press, 1995.

Widdicombe, Toby. *A Reader's Guide to Raymond Chandler.* Westport, Conn.: Greenwood Press, 2001.

© Nancy Crampton

JOHN CHEEVER

Born: Quincy, Massachusetts
May 27, 1912
Died: Ossining, New York
June 18, 1982

Cheever is one of the very few postwar American writers to have achieved major status both as a novelist and as a writer of short stories.

BIOGRAPHY

John Cheever was born in Quincy, Massachusetts, on May 27, 1912. He was descended not, as he liked to claim, from Ezekiel Cheever, master of the Boston Latin school eulogized by Cotton Mather, but instead and more prosaically from Daniel Cheever, one of Ezekiel's cousins and the keeper of the prison at Cambridge.

Cheever grew up during what he called the twilight years of Athenian Boston culture. The accelerating pace of the decline that another Quincy man, Henry Adams, had noted a few years earlier in his *The Education of Henry Adams* (1907) manifested itself not only in the Boston area but in Cheever's personal life as well. As a result of the stock market crash of 1929, Cheever's father, Frederick, lost first his position as a shoe salesman (not a shoe manufacturer, as his son liked to claim), then his investments, and finally his self-esteem when his independent-minded wife, Mary, opened a gift shop in order to support the family.

As their parents grew gradually apart, Cheever and his brother, Fred, seven years senior, grew closer—unnaturally so, Cheever came to believe. Dismissed from Thayer Academy for smoking and poor grades, Cheever wrote a semi-autobiographical, quasi-Cubist story, "Expelled," which Malcolm Cowley selected from a pile of unsolicited manuscripts for publication in the October 1, 1930, issue

of *The New Republic*. After a walking tour of Germany, the brothers settled in Boston, where Fred supported them both while Cheever devoted himself to his writing. By 1934, "Jon" (or "Joey") as he then styled himself, decided to make a break.

He spent part of the summer at Yaddo, the writers' retreat in Saratoga Springs, New York, thus beginning what was to be one of the several long and immensely useful literary relationships. It was Cowley who helped him secure a foothold there, and it was again Cowley to whom Cheever turned upon his arrival in New York in July. Living in a squalid room on Hudson Street, Cheever, helped by Fred, supported himself by writing book reviews and synopses of novels for Metro-Goldwyn-Mayer. The money was meager, but friendships with E. E. Cummings, John Dos Passos, Sherwood Anderson, Walker Evans, James Agee, Gaston Lachaise, and Cowley (his mentor and surrogate father) were rich.

Cheever's story "Brooklyn Rooming House" appeared in the May 25, 1935, issue of *The New Yorker*, the magazine that would, over the next three decades, publish more that one hundred Cheever stories (only John O'Hara would publish more). His efforts to publish a novel at this time were hampered as much by conservative literary tastes as by Cheever's need for the quick money that the writing and the sale of stories could provide. He still could not support himself by fiction writing alone and so spent part of 1938 in Washington, D.C., on the staff of the Federal Writers' Project.

Back in New York the following year, he met Mary Winternitz, daughter of the dean of Yale

Medical School. The couple were married on March 22, 1941. Cheever enlisted in the Army the following year and was serving in the South when his first book appeared on March 8, 1943. Although this collection of thirty short stories (including one of his best, "The Brothers") netted its author only four hundred dollars, *The Way Some People Live* received a number of encouraging reviews and soon resulted in Cheever's transfer to a Signal Corps staff that included William Saroyan and Irwin Shaw and was stationed in Astoria, Queens. (Because nearly half of Cheever's infantry regiment died in World War II, the book and transfer may very well have saved his life.)

After the war, Cheever continued living in New York, writing stories and working on a novel. The Boston opening of *The Town House*, a play adapted from several Cheever stories and produced by George S. Kaufman, seemed promising, but the New York production soon folded, and whatever financial relief Cheever had hoped to realize came to nothing. In 1951, the Cheevers moved to suburban Scarborough, New York. Getting a grant from the Guggenheim Foundation to support his writing proved easier than getting his next book, *The Enormous Radio, and Other Stories* (1953), accepted. Rejected by Random House in 1952, it was published by Funk & Wagnalls the following year to less than enthusiastic notices.

Although Cheever would later claim that "something went terribly wrong" in the mid-1950's, in all outward respects his prospects seemed to be brightening: a $2400 advance from Harper & Brothers for a novel, the Benjamin Franklin Award for "The Five-Forty-Eight," an O. Henry Award for the "The Country Husband," election to the National Institute of Arts and Letters (Cheever was elevated to the American Academy of Arts and Letters in 1973), sale of the film rights to "The Housebreaker of Shady Hill," a year in Italy (at Cowley's suggestion), the birth of his second child, Ben (Susan, his first, was born in 1943; Frederick, his third, in 1957). His first novel (something of a psychological as well as financial necessity), *The Wapshot Chronicle* (1957) was a Book-of-the-Month Club selection and winner of the National Book Award.

The Housebreaker of Shady Hill, and Other Stories appeared in 1958; two years later he received a second Guggenheim and, with Philip Roth and James Baldwin, spoke at *Esquire* magazine's "Writing in

America" symposium. Despite misgivings and after a for-money-only stint in Hollywood writing a screenplay of D. H. Lawrence's *The Lost Girl* (1920), Cheever purchased a restored late eighteenth century house in Ossining, New York, some forty miles north of New York City. The house was expensive enough to fuel his anxieties over money but also provided exactly the right setting for the myth of the refined, well-to-do country squire, which Cheever, with the unwitting help of interviewers and writers of feature articles, would perpetuate over the next twenty years.

Soon after the publication of his strangely titled fourth collection, *Some People, Places, and Things That Will Not Appear in My Next Novel* (1961), Cheever suffered two emotional setbacks: the discovery of his brother Fred's alcoholism and his wife Mary's decision to work, teaching part-time at nearby Briarcliff College. Cheever, mindful of his mother's act of financial independence, was prepared to take the latter as something of a sexual attack and a further blow to an already shaky marriage. His marriage, however, would somehow manage to survive rebuffs, talk of divorce, and Cheever's infidelities for forty years.

Although his second novel, *The Wapshot Scandal* (1964), earned for its author a *Time* magazine cover story and a Howells Medal for the best novel of 1960-1964, financial worries led Cheever to break with *The New Yorker* and to sell the film rights to the two Wapshot books and to "The Swimmer." (The latter was made into a feature-length film starring Burt Lancaster in 1968. Cheever much preferred to sell the rights but have no film made; the two forms are, he maintained, entirely different.) He traveled with John Updike to Russia in 1964 as part of a cultural exchange, thus beginning his love affair with Eastern Europe. By the end of the decade he found a love more sexual than cross-cultural (though at times hardly less distant), beginning a long-term affair with the actress Hope Lange.

The writing of *The Wapshot Scandal* had depressed Cheever; writing *Bullet Park* (1969) exhilarated him, but when Benjamin DeMott's remarkably wrongheaded review appeared in *The New York Times Book Review*, Cheever became severely depressed. The early 1970's became for him a time of continued financial worries and sexual anxieties, much drinking, and little writing. The serenity which the poet Asa Bascomb achieves in the title story of *The World of Apples* (1973) collection eluded Cheever as he taught writing at Sing Sing Prison from 1971 until his first heart attack (brought on by his drinking) in 1972. He taught (when sober) in 1973 at the University of Iowa Writers' Workshop, where John Irving and Raymond Carver were also on the faculty. T. Coraghessan Boyle and Allan Gurganus were in his classes. His teaching stint at Boston University the next year ended prematurely with Cheever's complete physical collapse.

He entered a detoxification unit and afterward spent a month at Smithers Rehabilitation Clinic in New York. Free of his addictions to tranquilizers and alcohol, Cheever, now a regular at Alcoholics Anonymous, completed *Falconer* (1977), hailed as "Cheever's Triumph." *Falconer*'s success freed Cheever from the financial worries that had plagued him since his father's ruin and, like the novel's protagonist, from a number of other fears as well. As the awards and honors poured in—an honorary doctorate from Harvard University, a Pulitzer Prize, the National Book Critics Circle Award and American Book Award for *The Stories of John Cheever* (1978), the National Medal for Literature—Cheever became less reticent and more willing to be interviewed and to discuss his personal life, except his bisexuality.

The triumph was, unfortunately, short-lived. Cheever suffered two epileptic seizures in 1980 and was found to have cancer the following year. The illnesses were devastating to a man who had enjoyed physical activity his entire life. Despite the illnesses, he wrote an original screenplay, *The Shady Hill Kidnapping*, broadcast on the Public Broadcasting Service in January, 1982, and a novel, *Oh What a Paradise It Seems*, published in May of that year. Cheever died in his home on June 18, 1982. With the appearance of his daughter Susan's memoir, *Home Before Dark* (1984), his son Ben's selected *Letters of John Cheever* (1988), and Scott Donaldson's excellent *John Cheever: A Biography* (1988), the facts of Cheever's life have become nearly as accessible as his fiction. Excerpts from his journals appeared in *The New Yorker* in 1990.

ANALYSIS

"Fiction is not cryptoautobiography," Cheever warned with the insistence of a man either with a mission or with something to hide. Posthumously published biographical materials make it abundantly clear that Cheever's fiction follows Cheever's life rather closely but never deductively. "Fiction," he claimed, "is our most intimate and acute means of communication, at a profound level, about our deepest apprehensions and intuitions on the meaning of life and death"; it is "our only coherent and consistent, continuous, history of man's struggle to be illustrious." For Cheever, then, fiction was much more a spiritual than a biographical or psychoanalytical exercise, closer to hymn and prayer than to either confession or disclosure.

His essentially affirmative vision and lyrical style are not merely and superficially willed; rather, they are earned. His description of fiction as "the bringing together of disparate elements" places as great an emphasis on the apparent randomness of contemporary experience as it does on the elusive wholeness of being for which his characters yearn. "The most useful image I have today," Cheever noted in 1959, "is of a man in a quagmire, looking into a tear in the sky." One year later, Cheever would flatly assert that life in the United States in 1960 "is hell."

This apprehensiveness is every bit as much cultural as personal and could, Cheever felt, be attributed to a "loss of serenity in our lives," to a "loss of tradition," that forced him as well as his characters and readers into ceaseless acts of moral (and, for Cheever, aesthetic) improvisation. The decorous surface of his prose stands in marked contrast to the nonlinear development of his plots and his characters' lives. At its worst, this decorum (evident as well in the veneer of respectability of Cheever's suburban stories, the mask of a venereal itch that is itself a mask for or symbol of something deeper still) seems little more than a form of what in *Bullet Park* Cheever, perhaps not so tongue-in-cheek, calls "spiritual cheerleading."

This spiritual cheerleading may seem especially odd to find in the fiction of a writer whose early work was strongly influenced by that of Ernest Hemingway. Hemingway distrusted the very words—honor, love, courage, valor, and so forth—on which Cheever's lyrical vision came more and more to rely. Cheever's fiction convinces the reader on the basis not of what it denies but instead of what it affirms by virtue of its emotional effect and cumulative power. It evokes a nearly liturgical dimension that leads the reader to believe, as Cheever did, that the purpose of both writing and living is to enlarge humankind rather than to diminish it.

Because his vision is earned rather than willed, the fiction operates not at the extreme of faith but between the poles which Cheever variously described: expansion and constriction (or confinement), "grossness and aspiration," a world which "lies spread out around us like a bewildering and stupendous dream" versus a world grown suddenly incoherent, inhospitable, even "preposterous." In Cheever's stories and novels, opposites meet but do not necessarily merge as the narrative teeters precariously between the prosaic and the poetic, the practical and the visionary. Even Cheever's distinctive narrative voice proves hard to pin down, managing to be at once compassionate yet detached, celebratory yet satirical.

Cheever's characters often find themselves similarly (ambivalently, even ambiguously) situated—not so much placed as displaced, or what Cheever's friend Ralph Ellison would call dispossessed. They suffer, often seriocomically, from loneliness and from a loss of self-esteem; often (but by no means always) they live well (if precariously) financially, but they are generally bereft emotionally and spiritually impoverished. The discontinuity of their lives often drives them to an earlier time, to tradition, and to memory, but their nostalgic desire to recover what they have lost—a sense of purpose and security—is often one-sided and therefore mistaken in that they fail to realize that nostalgia is as much "a force of expectation" as it is a longing to recover the past.

At their most successful, the search for spiritual wholeness leads them "to build a bridge" in an effort to connect the discontinuous facts of their lives, including the unruliness of their sexual desires. Asked by John Hersey to explain the "blurted quality" of his prose, Cheever responded by attributing it to "some ungainliness in my spiritual person that I cannot master," least of all by psychoanalysis, which Cheever, like many of his characters, had tried and which, he believed, places too much emphasis on motivation and not enough on aspiration.

The critical response to Cheever's work has been uneven and unsure, less because of any difficulty in the fiction than from attempts on the part of reviewers and critics to apply the right kind of rigid formulas that Cheever's work both invites and

resists. For example, closely associated with *The New Yorker* magazine, Cheever was soon classified and accordingly dismissed as a *"New Yorker* writer." Reading him as a realist, critics paid scant attention to the strong element of fabulism in his fiction. Judged a writer of short stories, he had his novels discussed as proof of his failure to make the leap to the "more demanding" form of the novel. Seen as a comic writer, he was judged a literary lightweight, a naïve optimist, an apologist for the suburbs, or alternately a satirist of those same suburbs.

In fact, Cheever's settings kept changing—city, country, St. Botolphs, suburbs, Italy, prison—but his characters' predicaments remained essentially the same. At a time of considerable literary experimentation, Cheever found himself either praised or damned as a conservative in terms of both values and style—this despite the fact that his achievement derives in large measure from his having so successfully managed either to transcend or to undermine the very formulas used to pigeonhole his work.

Cheever not only gave new life to the short story and, thanks to the immense success of his retrospective *The Stories of John Cheever* (1978), opened up the market for other short-fiction writers, he also broke down the line separating story from novel, realism from fabulism, convention from innovation (or what he liked to call "improvisation") so unobtrusively that his efforts largely went unnoticed as he went about his chosen task of communicating modern people's deepest apprehensions and aspirations.

THE WAPSHOT CHRONICLE

First published: 1957
Type of work: Novel

In this family chronicle, the youngest generation of Wapshots encounters the waywardness of love and of contemporary life.

The Wapshot Chronicle, Cheever's first novel, begins with a Fourth of July celebration in St. Botolphs, "an old river town," a world of the imagination modeled loosely on Cheever's birthplace, Quincy, Massachusetts. Mishap—a firecracker exploding underneath the horse pulling a wagonload of the town's most upright women—is turned to narrative advantage; it is the excuse the novel needs to take the reader on a tour of the area. The pace changes and the continuity dissolves as the novel moves through three progressively shorter parts of seventeen, then ten, and finally five chapters, to end back in St. Botolphs on yet another Fourth of July a few years later.

Against the discontinuity of the intervening narrative, the novel's frame takes on a special but nevertheless ambiguous significance. It adds an element of ceremony but also of arbitrariness that corresponds to the relation between St. Botolphs and the world outside its borders, where much of the novel takes place. The relation between these worlds and between tradition and independence (itself an American tradition), between a past which both sustains and confines and a present which frees but also dismays and displaces forms the thematic center of a novel that is about the need to bridge the two worlds and all they represent.

Descended (in a double sense) from a long line of New England sea captains, the mythically named Leander Wapshot stands at the novel's moral center. Lusty, sometimes drunk, but always ceremonious, he is Cheever's diminished hero, captain of the *Topaze*, a barely seaworthy tourist ferry owned by his eccentric, sexless sister, Honora. When Leander loses his boat, he loses his usefulness and therefore his self-esteem and thus becomes the tragicomic epitome of humankind's "inestimable loneliness." His civic-minded wife, Sarah, like his sister, plays her part in Leander's temporary fall from grace when she turns the *Topaze* into a floating gift shop. His sons, Moses and the younger, "ministerial" Coverly, fare no better in their relationships with women in the world beyond St. Botolphs.

Once the brothers leave St. Botolphs (Honora, who controls the family inheritance, demands that Moses leave; Coverly departs because he cannot live at home without his brother), their lives become nomadic and the novel's plot ever more wayward, serving up several divergent yet oddly parallel and at times intersecting stories rife with chance meetings—a sign on one hand of life's versatility and romantic possibilities and on the other of its inexplicable randomness.

Moses goes to Washington, gets a government job that is so secret that the narrator cannot discuss it, has an affair with a married woman named Beatrice, gets fired, leaves Washington, goes fishing, comes to the aid of a wealthy man whose gratitude includes hiring Moses, and falls in love with and marries Melissa, the ward of a distant cousin, Justina Wapshot Molesworth Scaddon. Justina is the widow of a five-and-ten-cent store king, caricature of the American nouveau riche, and the novel's comic version of Charles Dickens's Miss Havisham.

Meanwhile, Coverly has gone to New York, where he does not get a job in the carpet business owned by the husband of yet another wealthy cousin (Coverly fails the days-long psychological testing), works in a department store, goes to night school to become a computer "taper," and falls in love with and marries his Georgia-born "sandwich shop Venus," Betsey Macaffery, like Melissa an orphan. (Absent parents, especially fathers, figure prominently in Cheever's fiction.) Moses's and Coverly's marriages are as full of interruptions as Cheever's narrative. Melissa soon turns aggressively asexual as the couple lives under the vast but confining roof of Justina's Clear Haven mansion.

Coverly's marriage begins to deteriorate when Betsey's efforts to make friends at the planned community of Remsen Park (where Coverly's work has taken them) all fail. Stylistically and narratively, *The Wapshot Chronicle* is as fractious as the brothers' marriages: Straightforward narrative sections alternate with Wapshot journals, lists, letters, phony biographies, Catch-22 logic, and frequent addresses to the reader, including such announcements as "now we come to the unsavory or homosexual part of our tale and any disinterested reader is encouraged to skip."

The ending of *The Wapshot Chronicle* proves no less curious than the chapters which precede it. Both couples reunite, and both Moses and Coverly father sons and so fulfill the terms Honora set for establishing trusts in their names, part of which the brothers will use to buy Leander a new boat. Before the boat can be bought, however, or the boys (now men) even return, Leander drowns, but his death becomes the occasion of Cheever's (and the town's) celebration of all that Leander represents. At the very end of this novel in which tragedy is undercut by humor and the absurd heightened by pa-

John Cheever

thos, Leander finally gets what neither Sarah nor Honora ever let him have in life—the last word—when quite by accident Coverly finds Leander's handwritten "Advice to my sons," which mixes practical advice with liturgical intensity, ending with the words "Trust in the Lord."

THE WAPSHOT SCANDAL

First published: 1964
Type of work: Novel

The comic waywardness of The Wapshot Chronicle *gives way to the confusions and discontinuities of the contemporary world.*

Similarities between *The Wapshot Scandal* and the work to which it serves as sequel, *The Wapshot Chronicle,* are readily apparent: the similar cast of characters (though Leander and Sarah are both dead), the use of a framing device (two Christmases at St. Botolphs), and the interweaving of multiple narratives. Honora, still eccentric but now more sympathetic, tries to escape persecution for nonpayment of taxes by traveling to Italy. There she finds herself homesick rather than free and, in the company of an equally lonely Internal Revenue Service agent, returns to St. Botolphs, where she must forfeit the family fortune and soon drinks herself to death (a death that Cheever somehow seems to make funny).

Cheever depicts the lives of Coverly and Betsey in a missile-site housing complex named Talifer and of Moses and Melissa in affluent Proxmire Manor. The differences between the two books, however, are of greater importance than the similarities. In *The Wapshot Scandal,* the narrative is more discontinuous (so much so that Cheever once described it as "an extraordinarily complex book built upon non sequiturs"). The temporal vagaries of *The Wapshot Chronicle* here seem more pronounced, resulting in a more mythified realism, a fictive world that is simultaneously now and never. (In this sense it resembles the strangely familiar setting of Shirley Jackson's "The Lottery," which significantly first appeared in *The New Yorker* in the 1940's.)

The narrator's relation to his story has also grown more problematic: It is at once more intimate and more detached. He claims to have personal knowledge of the Wapshots, who, he says, always made him feel like an outsider. Most important, *The Wapshot Scandal* is a darker and at times blackly humorous novel haunted by death, as the now-vacant Wapshot house is said to be haunted by the ghost of Leander, described here as a man who always looked like a boy but who in his last years "looked like a boy who had seen the Gorgon." Coverly cannot understand why his father would want to come back, least of all to a decidedly fallen world which seems to promise nothing ahead and offer nothing to which to return.

The modern world has almost entirely displaced the "old river town" of the earlier novel. The potency of this new world is almost entirely destructive, as figured most clearly in Dr. Lemuel Cameron, né Bracciani, director of the Talifer missile site and believer in the inevitability of nuclear war, who is more than willing to dispose of all who do not measure up to his intellectual and physiological standards, including his own son.

With Leander's death, the moral center of the Wapshot books shifts to Coverly, whose efforts to build a bridge between past and present and to adapt to the rootlessly and ruthlessly modern world without succumbing to it are fraught with difficulties. As his world grows increasingly resistant to his sense of what it should be, and as Betsey, still frustrated in her efforts to make friends with her neighbors, grows ever more distant, Coverly searches for some way to prove himself useful, even illustrious. A computer "taper" misassigned to a public relations department as the result of a computer error, Coverly does succeed in building a bridge of sorts when he runs a computer analysis of John Keats's poetry. He discovers that in their order of frequency the most commonly used words yield their own poetry—proof, Coverly believes, "that some numerical harmony underlay the composition of the universe."

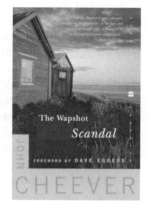

Moses is neither so fortunate nor so optimistic. Having given up his study

438

of banking for a job in "a shady brokerage house," he finds himself morally as well as financially in debt, soon to become both a cynic and a drunk. Moses, however, appears very little, Melissa very much, in this novel. The reader detects a corresponding shift from Betsey's loneliness to Melissa's boredom and disappointment. The bland assurances and apparent security of middle-class life in well-to-do Proxmire Manor come up against Melissa's all-consuming fear of death, which in turn releases her "unruly lusts" and "ruthless greed for pleasure."

Her problem is not so much sexual as it is spiritual, but when her minister advises her to see a psychiatrist, Melissa takes matters into her own hands and begins an affair with a nineteen-year-old grocery boy, Emile Cranmer. Each sees the other as divine, which is to say as representing the life neither has but for which both yearn. The yearning of Melissa, Emile, and indeed of the novel's characters is real enough, even if it generally manifests itself in bizarre, ultimately unfulfilling ways—in supermarket purchases or the golden egg which, thanks to Emile, Melissa finds and so wins a trip to Rome.

Rome, however, will not satisfy Melissa, any more than it does Honora. Nor will Emile, who, thanks to one of Cheever's numerous and entirely self-conscious plot contrivances, ends up in Italy on the block at a sex auction, where Melissa buys him. Last seen at the Supramarketto Americano in Rome, Melissa appears still dissatisfied, still yearning, still buying, still absurd.

At novel's end, Coverly, evicted from his house, returns to St. Botolphs, where, after Honora's death and in the company of a nagging Betsey and a randy, drunken Moses, he honors Honora's request to preside over a Christmas dinner for guests from the Hutchins Institute for the Blind. The sense of ceremony is played against the novel's second ending, however, in which the narrator claims that he will "never come back" to St. Botolphs and that even if he did there would be "nothing" to return to, "nothing at all." His words recall Prospero's speech at the end of William Shakespeare's *The Tempest* (1611) as spoken by Coverly over Leander's grave in accord with his father's request at the end of *The Wapshot Chronicle*.

Here, however, those words do not so much comfort as disconcert, and in this sense seem strangely linked to the "large, ugly, loaf-shaped and colorless escarpment of granite" around which a housing development has been built that Emile sees earlier in the novel and which Cheever ambivalently describes as "triumphantly obdurate and perverse," "useless," and "invincible," a fit emblem of both the Caliban to which Melissa succumbs and the Ariel to which Coverly aspires.

FALCONER

First published: 1977
Type of work: Novel

A man's attraction to the natural world and to spiritual light leads him out of the prison of self.

Hailed as "Cheever's Triumph," *Falconer* seemed to surprise many of its reviewers. They were surprised that a writer of short stories could, after three missteps, finally write a "real" novel, especially after the "broken-backed" performance of *Bullet Park* eight years before. They were also surprised that this "Chekhov of the exurbs," as one reviewer of *The World of Apples* (1973) put it, would set his latest fiction in a prison and, more shockingly, write so explicitly about fratricide and homosexuality.

Their surprise points all too well not to any change in Cheever's writing but instead to the shortcomings on the part of Cheever's critics and reviewers. The prison setting, as Cheever would point out, functions much as St. Botolphs and fictional suburbs such as Proxmire Manor, Shady Hill, and Bullet Park (as well as Italy and Sutton Place apartment buildings) do as metaphors of the confinement that figures in virtually all of his fiction.

Falconer is not a prison novel in any narrow sense, nor is it about Sing Sing, where Cheever taught in 1971 and 1972. Although it draws on information supplied by his inmates/students, *Falconer* represents what Cheever called "the sum of my experience." Just as important, *Falconer* is not any more "novelistic" than *Bullet Park* or the Wapshot books, though it is certainly more narrowly and more intensively focused.

Rather, all four employ the same parallel structure, which Cheever also uses in his short stories.

Finally, the homosexual theme in *Falconer* represents more a culmination than a new direction in his work; what is different about Cheever's handling of homosexuality in *Falconer* is his forgoing the comedy which previously allowed him to defuse the subject's personal and thematic explosiveness. Begun during Cheever's darkest period (not later than 1974), it was completed in a single year-long stretch following his release from Smithers Rehabilitation Clinic and from his addictions to drugs and alcohol.

Falconer differs most from the earlier works in its intensity. Never before, for example, had the close, often strained, occasionally hostile relations between brothers actually ended in death. ("I killed you off in *Falconer*," Cheever could jokingly say to Fred a few weeks before the latter's death on May 30, 1976.) Never before had the contrast between light and dark, spirit and flesh, "the invincible potency of Nature" and one's deadened sensibility to that potency, been so starkly portrayed. Never before was Cheever quite so clear or quite so determined about the need for spiritual redemption apart from all psychoanalytical explanations and excuses. Neither psychological nor sociological in its import, *Falconer* is an essentially religious work in which the criminals are "miscreants," the crime is "fratricide," and the meaning is "the mystery of imprisonment."

Falconer Prison is a world apart from affluent Indian Hill, Connecticut, and forty-eight-year-old Ezekiel Farragut's life there as husband, father, and professor. It is also the epitome of a life that has made addiction to heroin, to methadone, and ultimately to all forms of self-love and self-indulgence its center. Sentenced for up to ten years, Farragut must do more than serve his time; he must learn "to leach self-pity out of his emotional spectrum." It is a task made difficult not only by Farragut's self-pitying nature but also by the number of targets he blames for his condition: his narcissistic wife, Marcia; the father who wanted his fetus aborted; the mother who would spare him none of her time; the brother who (Farragut believes) tried to kill him. Yet none of them serves as adequate answer to the question that soon becomes the novel's refrain, "Farragut, Farragut, why is you an addict?"

The men Farragut meets in *Falconer* are all grotesques—the sadistic deputy warden, Chisholm; the immensely fat guard, Tiny; the Prussian-looking Marshack; and the "freaks" of F-Block: Chicken Number Two, Bumpo, the Cuckold (with his stores of food with which to bribe the others into listening to his stories), Tennis—each in his own way a distorted mirror image of what Farragut has or will become. Farragut's homosexual love for the youthful-looking Jody serves as the novel's turning point. Unlike all the other prisoners, Jody is willing to speak truthfully about himself, to blame himself for who, what, and where he is, and to admit that he has no future. (Jody's escape from prison is not so much unbelievable as miraculous, proof that *Falconer* is more religious than realistic, closer to romance than to realism.)

Farragut's love for Jody (as well as his doubts about that love) leads him out of the prison of self and eventually out of Falconer Prison as well. He takes his second step beyond self when he begins to build a contraband radio (another kind of bridge) to bring news of the riot at Amana Prison (modeled on the Attica riot of September, 1971) to Falconer's inmates and so, Farragut optimistically and mistakenly believes, to cause them to band together with their "brothers" at "the Wall." The idea is overly ambitious, bearing about as much relation to the reality of prison life, with each man in his own cell of self, as do Farragut's sexual fantasies. The torpor of the men, like the unchanging summer weather, proves as indomitable as it does perverse.

The riot is broken; the men stay as they were—torpid, selfish, and lonely—except for a change in the color of their clothing, from gray to a "noncommittal green." The change in Farragut is far more dramatic. Free of his addiction (though through no effort on his part), he attends to the dying Chicken Number Two and finally recalls the events leading up to his brother Eben's death. As the reader comes to understand, in killing Eben Farragut he was trying to kill a part of himself. Self-pity has become self-awareness.

It becomes, too, a selflessness that paradoxically—or miraculously—restores Farragut to himself, to the need to take his rightful place in the world. Employing courage and cunning, he undergoes a metaphorical death and rebirth. He puts himself in Chicken Number Two's body bag and coffin, is carried out of the prison, and makes his escape, having lost his fear of falling "and all his other fears as well." The ending is (again) unrealistic but nevertheless entirely convincing, a quiet but liturgically intense affirmation of faith: "Rejoice, he thought, rejoice."

"THE ENORMOUS RADIO"

First published: 1947 (collected in *The Enormous Radio, and Other Stories*, 1953)
Type of work: Short story

The Westcotts discover that evil lies within the heart, not out in the world.

What distinguishes "The Enormous Radio" from the Hemingway-like stories of Cheever's first collection, *The Way Some People Live,* is the unsettling mixture of realism and fantasy that characterizes the best of his later work. "The Enormous Radio" concerns the Westcotts, who live in a Sutton Place (New York) apartment building and who resemble other young (mid-thirties), college-educated, upwardly mobile couples of the immediately postwar period in all respects but one—their special fondness for classical music.

When their old radio breaks down, Jim buys Irene a new, rather expensive one as a present. Larger and more powerful than its predecessor, the new radio becomes a disturbing presence in the Westcotts' (especially in Irene's) life. She does not like its ugly gumwood cabinet, confounding complexities, violent forces, "malevolent green light," and "mistaken sensitivity to discord."

This "aggressive intruder" invades and disrupts not only Irene's world but also that of her neighbors. Irene is appalled, yet fascinated, by what she hears—evidence of her neighbors' financial, social, and sexual anxieties—but also worried that her neighbors may be able to hear what she and Jim say in the privacy of their own apartment. Irene becomes apprehensive, and this, in turn, leads Jim to express his own long-suppressed financial worries and finally to broadcast his wife's secret sins: taking her mother's jewels before the will was probated, cheating her sister, making another woman's life miserable, and going to an abortionist.

Like Nathaniel Hawthorne's Young Goodman Brown, Irene has entered the dark forest of moral ambiguity and emerged a different person— emerged, that is, as she truly is rather than as she

would like to appear. The breakdown of the old radio prepared the way for the breakdown of the Westcotts' moral facade and for their and the reader's discovery that the "heart of darkness" lies not without, as Irene wished to believe, but within. The ultimate truth may very well lie somewhere between the Westcotts' fondness for harmony and the radio's "mistaken sensitivity to discord."

"GOODBYE, MY BROTHER"

First published: 1951 (collected in *The Stories of John Cheever,* 1978)
Type of work: Short story

The conflict between two brothers centers on their different visions of the world and reflects the conflict raging within the narrator.

The theme of "Goodbye, My Brother," a story based on Cheever's relationship with his older brother, Fred, is one that preoccupied Cheever over the course of his entire career, from the early story "The Brothers" (1937) to the late novel *Falconer.* The story takes place on Laud's Head, on the New England coast, where the geographically distant but "close in spirit" Pommeroy clan (a widowed mother, one recently divorced daughter, and three brothers with wives and children) gathers at the family's summer house, built in the 1920's. The unnamed narrator, one of the brothers, is thirty-eight, a schoolteacher resigned to a future without much promise who, like the rest of his family (other than the youngest brother), believes that while the Pommeroys may not be distinguished, they are unique.

The late arrival of Lawrence, the youngest child and a lawyer, is the return of the prodigal son, only in reverse. Known variously as Tifty (from the sound his slippers made when he was a child), Croaker, and Little Jesus, he has no enthusiasm— indeed, much contempt—for the activities in which the rest of the family take so much pleasure: drinking, talking, dancing, playing games, and above all, swimming, which during Lawrence's visit they seem to do more as a way to cleanse themselves of his doleful presence than as a form of physical exercise.

"He could make a grievance out of everything," the narrator complains about a brother who sees moral as well as physical decay everywhere. Lawrence is not only gloomy, however; he is also at least partly correct in his unwanted judgments: There is indeed a crack in the sea wall, the summer house was built to appear old even though it was not, the family members do delude themselves in various ways, as even the narrator seems to realize if not quite admit.

It is as much Lawrence's willingness to articulate—or croak—these cracks in the Pommeroy dream as it is his failure to entertain that lyrical vision and sense of ceremony and decorum with which the other Pommeroys are so preoccupied that causes the narrator to strike him on the head. The ever-complaining and ever-departing, ever-disappointed Lawrence deludes himself in thinking that he has important things to do—things which his frivolous and now murderous family have kept him from doing.

Lawrence, too, appears to be marked for failure, branded like Cain by the Cain-like brother who has just tried to kill him.

The ending of the story compounds the ambiguity, for the richness of lyrical phrase and mythic allusion creates a sense of affirmation and illusion. The doubleness is crucial to Cheever's effect and to the reader's perception that the external conflict between the two brothers and their very different visions reflects the internal conflict raging within the narrator and, one suspects, within the author as well.

"The Country Husband"

First published: 1954 (collected in *The Housebreaker of Shady Hill, and Other Stories,* 1958)
Type of work: Short story

The comic hero takes a rather absurd route in an effort to reclaim his self-esteem and rightful place in the world.

"The Country Husband" typifies Cheever's use of humor to underscore the absurd ways in which people, like the hero Francis Weed, attempt to overcome a sense of having suddenly become displaced, socially or sexually. An emergency airplane landing in a field while returning from a business trip precipitates Weed's crisis; he will soon run the risk of becoming as unwanted as his namesake in his suburban Garden of Eden, Shady Hill. Once returned, he can find no audience for his tale of near-extinction: His children turn the house into a battlefield, and his wife, Julia, prepares, serves, and eats the family dinner while pretending to ignore the chaos.

Escaping into his back yard, Weed finds not the peace and understanding he craves but instead the proof of Shady Hill's essential triviality: old Mr. Nixon defending his bird feeder from the squirrels, while another neighbor, Donald Goslin, plays (as he does every night) the "Moonlight Sonata" in "an outpouring of tearful petulance, lonesomeness, and self-pity—of everything it was [Ludwig van] Beethoven's greatness not to know."

Curiously, Weed's awareness of the self-pity of others does not prevent him from succumbing to it himself as he falls madly in love with the teenage baby-sitter whose very name—Anne Murchison—adds to the story's comic absurdity, as it effectively undermines Weed's exalted image of her and his mistaken belief in her power to restore him to his rightful place in the world. As Weed's romantic fantasy grows ever more adolescent, his wife grows more perturbed and more absurd. His cutting remark to one of the community's most important women costs Julia a party invitation, thus putting her closer to that "most natural dread of chaos and loneliness," against which her only weapon is a hyperactive social schedule.

Julia (ignorant of Weed's love for Anne) claims that he has been subconsciously expressing his hatred for her by leaving his dirty underwear around the house. Weed does eventually regain his place, if not his self-esteem. On the advice of a psychiatrist, he takes up woodworking and in this way channels his desires into a harmless pursuit, not unlike Donald Goslin's piano playing. The ending—"Then it is dark; it is a night where kings in golden suits ride elephants over the mountains"—is clearly lyrical but perhaps duplicitously so, evoking both transcendental affirmation and ironic doubt.

"THE DEATH OF JUSTINA"

First published: 1960 (collected in *The Stories of John Cheever*, 1978)
Type of work: Short story

Adversity becomes absurdity as Moses discovers the fear of death upon which "the good life" is founded.

In "The Death of Justina" it is not merely a brush with death (as in "The Country Husband") but death itself that serves as catalyst not only for a change in the narrator-protagonist's life but for Cheever's comic genius as well. "So help me God it gets more and more preposterous, it corresponds less and less to what I remember and what I expect as if the force of life were centrifugal and threw one further and further away from one's purest memories and ambitions"; the speaker is a version of the figure Cheever imagined in 1959—the man in a quagmire looking up at a tear in the sky—but one whose predicament has somehow become funnier as well as more dire.

If, as the narrator would like to believe, fiction is art, and if art is the triumph over chaos brought about by the exercise of choice, then how is the writer or authorial narrator to continue to effect that triumph in a world in which change occurs too rapidly and in which the basis for making aesthetic as well as moral choices appears to have disappeared? How is one to build Coverly Wapshot's bridge between "memories and ambitions"?

Aside from the setting (Proxmire Manor) and names (Moses and Justina), "The Death of Justina" exists independently of *The Wapshot Scandal* in all but two important respects, structure and theme, and specifically in Moses's wanting to know how, in the world's most prosperous land, there can be so many disappointed people. "The Death of Justina" provides a possible answer. When his wife's cousin dies in his home, Moses suddenly learns that his neighborhood and the suburban good life it represents are not zoned for death. As the mayor explains, "The importance of zoning just can't be overestimated," and Moses will simply have to wait a few days or weeks until an exemption can be issued and the body can be legally disposed of. When Moses threatens to bury the corpse in his back yard, the mayor—acting illegally—relents.

Matters do not end there, however, for that night Moses has a dream in which a thousand grotesquely garbed shoppers, desexed and penitential, wander around a brilliantly lit supermarket, its windows darkened, the contents of all packages unknown. At the checkout counter, large men tear open the packages, express their disgust, and then push the humiliated shoppers out the door into a sea of tormented souls.

This blackly humorous updating of Dante's *Inferno* (c. 1320) manages to create a certain sympathy for those it satirizes and for modern humans' mistaken efforts to realize their deepest longings. Burying Justina in a cemetery which, like a dump, lies on the town's outskirts leads Moses to ask, "How can a people 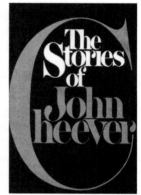 who do not mean to understand death hope to understand love, and who will sound the alarm?" Apparently, Moses will. Told by his boss to rewrite a commercial for a product called Elixircol, he first composes a parody, "Only Elixircol can save you." Then, when threatened with a kind of death—being fired—he copies out the Twenty-third Psalm. In the nightmare world of the supermarket of the soul, the words that Moses chooses, "the Lord is my shepherd, I shall not want," sound both sane and strangely convincing.

"THE SWIMMER"

First published: 1964 (collected in *The Stories of John Cheever*, 1978)
Type of work: Short story

An afternoon swim becomes a psychologically powerful fable of the Fall and of human expulsion from a modern Garden of Eden.

The comic absurdity and artful randomness of "The Death of Justina" differ sharply from the dark ambiguity and the tight, almost inexorable structure of "The Swimmer," another Cheever story concerning modern people's efforts to guard themselves from every painful memory and every proof of their own mortality. "The Swimmer" begins on a summer day around the Westerhazys' pool when the youthful Neddy Merrill decides to "enlarge and celebrate" the day's beauty and his own good fortune—including his wife and "four beautiful daughters"—by swimming home to Bullet Park, eight miles (sixteen pools) away. Thinking of himself as a legendary figure, a pilgrim, an explorer, "a man with a destiny," Neddy seems childlike, even comically childish, yet nevertheless preferable to the others who sit around the pool complaining of having drunk too much the night before.

The first half of the story moves along rapidly from their chronic plaint to Neddy's chosen plan and the swimming of nine pools in one hour. Neddy's odyssey is not without some difficulties—a thorny hedge, gravel that cuts the feet, drinks proffered and politely drunk, a brief storm, a sudden coolness in the air, a drained pool, and an overgrown yard. There is also a small plane "circling around and around and around in the sky with something like the glee of a child in a swing," which, twice noticed, delights Neddy but also distracts him and perhaps serves to remind the reader of not only the joy but also the futility of Neddy's act, the inexorable closure of his destiny.

In the story's first half, the disappointments and impediments are generally minor and cause neither Neddy nor the reader much inconvenience or delay. In the second half, however, the obstacles increase, and the pace of both the swim and the reading slackens. It takes a page, for example, to cross the divided highway where Neddy suddenly seems vulnerable, even pitiful, unable to turn back and unsure when this bit of afternoon play turned serious. As the pace slackens, the evidence mounts that Neddy's ability to repress all unpleasantness has "damaged his sense of truth" until inevitably, yet inexplicably, Neddy finally reaches the empty house that was once his home.

For the reader, Neddy's defeat is doubly troubling. Like Neddy, the reader must confront the emptiness at journey's end and all that this ironic reversal of Odysseus's homecoming suggests about Neddy and more generally about the precariousness of American upper-middle-class life. The reader must also face the fact that a story that began as more or less conventional, certainly comic, realism has transmogrified into a dark fantasy in which it is not only the day that has gone by but the seasons, indeed the years of a man's life, leaving him, like the narrator at the end of *The Wapshot Scandal*, with "nothing, nothing at all." While the specific cause of Neddy's downfall may be financial (as well as psychological), the power of this story (like Washington Irving's "Rip Van Winkle," which it resembles in certain ways) derives from some much deeper, less specific source whose tenor, as Edgar Allan Poe said of his own gothic tales, is "not of Germany"—or of the suburbs—but "of the soul."

SUMMARY

Cheever is one of the very few writers who have attained major status in both the novel and the short story, a form to which the retrospective collection *The Stories of John Cheever* (1978) brought renewed interest and a much greater measure of respect. Equally important, however, are the ways in which Cheever managed to combine so subtly and so successfully traditional storytelling with narrative innovation and conventional realism with lyrical fabulism, and to invest his middle-class characters and suburban settings with mythic resonance.

Robert A. Morace

BIBLIOGRAPHY

By the Author

SHORT FICTION:
The Way Some People Live, 1943
The Enormous Radio, and Other Stories, 1953
The Housebreaker of Shady Hill, and Other Stories, 1958

Some People, Places, and Things That Will Not Appear in My Next Novel, 1961
The Brigadier and the Golf Widow, 1964
The World of Apples, 1973
The Stories of John Cheever, 1978
Thirteen Uncollected Stories, 1994

LONG FICTION:
The Wapshot Chronicle, 1957
The Wapshot Scandal, 1964
Bullet Park, 1969
Falconer, 1977
Oh, What a Paradise It Seems, 1982

TELEPLAY:
The Shady Hill Kidnapping, 1982

NONFICTION:
The Letters of John Cheever, 1988 (Benjamin Cheever, editor)
The Journals of John Cheever, 1991
Glad Tidings, a Friendship in Letters: The Correspondence of John Cheever and John D. Weaver, 1945-1982, 1993

About the Author

Bloom, Harold, ed. *John Cheever.* Philadelphia: Chelsea House, 2004.

Bosha, Francis J., ed. *The Critical Response to John Cheever.* Westport, Conn.: Greenwood Press, 1994.

Byrne, Michael D. *Dragons and Martinis: The Skewed Realism of John Cheever.* Edited by Dale Salwak and Paul David Seldis. San Bernardino, Calif.: Borgo Press, 1993.

Cheever, Susan. *Home Before Dark.* Boston: Houghton Mifflin, 1984.

Coale, Samuel. *John Cheever.* New York: Frederick Ungar, 1977.

Collins, Robert G., ed. *Critical Essays on John Cheever.* Boston: G. K. Hall, 1982.

Donaldson, Scott. *John Cheever: A Biography.* New York: Random House, 1988.

_____, ed. *Conversations with John Cheever.* Jackson: University Press of Mississippi, 1987.

Meanor, Patrick. *John Cheever Revisited.* New York: Twayne, 1995.

O'Hara, James E. *John Cheever: A Study of the Short Fiction.* Boston: Twayne, 1989.

Waldeland, Lynne. *John Cheever.* Boston: Twayne, 1979.

DISCUSSION TOPICS

- John Cheever's accounts of his life and circumstances are sometimes at odds with the facts. Is prevarication a habit of the major characters in his stories?

- Cheever lamented the loss of such values as "serenity" and "tradition" in modern life. Are these losses important themes in his fiction?

- Examine the structure of *The Wapshot Chronicle* with particular attention to its framing Fourth of July settings.

- Decorum involves such qualities as propriety and good taste. Is the "decorous surface" of Cheever's prose a deception or does it reflect values affirmed in his stories?

- Cheever called *Falconer* "the sum of my experiences." Is this one of his misleading statements or does it seem to ring true?

- Judging from the evidence presented here, do you think that critics generally have understood Cheever's work properly?

CHARLES WADDELL CHESNUTT

Born: Cleveland, Ohio
June 20, 1858
Died: Cleveland, Ohio
November 15, 1932

The first African American novelist and short-story writer to produce a substantial body of fiction of widely recognized merit, Chesnutt was an important spokesman on race relations at the turn of the twentieth century.

Cleveland Public Library

BIOGRAPHY

Charles Waddell Chesnutt was born in Cleveland, Ohio, on June 20, 1858, the first child of Andrew Jackson and Ann Maria Sampson Chesnutt. Charles' parents had met as members of a northbound wagon train of free people of color leaving Fayetteville, North Carolina, where legal and social restrictions imposed on free blacks had become intolerable. Andrew served with the Union forces as a teamster in the Civil War, after which the family moved back to Fayetteville, where Andrew opened a grocery store with the aid of his father, Waddell Cade, a white man and former slaveholder.

Ann Maria died in 1871, the store failed soon after, and Charles was forced to drop out of the Howard School (which has since evolved into Fayetteville State University) to help support the family. Recognizing Charles's exceptional ability, his principal immediately hired him as a student-teacher at age fourteen. Chesnutt became the principal of the Howard School at age eighteen, then returned to the newly established State Colored Normal School in Fayetteville, a teacher-training institution for African American students, as a teacher and assistant to the principal.

Chesnutt married Susan Perry, a fellow teacher, in 1878 and became principal of the Normal School in 1880, at the age of twenty-two. Discour-

aged by the unjust treatment of blacks in the South, by 1883 he had trained himself in stenography well enough to resign from his position and find work in the North. He eventually settled in Cleveland, where he worked as a legal stenographer and studied law, passing the Ohio bar examination in 1887 with the highest scores in his class. Chesnutt capitalized on his stenographic and legal training to set up a court-reporting business, which quickly became profitable.

That same year, he published his first important story, "The Goophered Grapevine," in the August, 1887, issue of *The Atlantic Monthly*, and his career as a writer was launched. Chesnutt published more stories in 1888 and 1889 and gathered together three of them, along with four new stories, for his first book, *The Conjure Woman* (1899). The book was favorably reviewed and sold well, perhaps in part because of the interest generated by the public disclosure of Chesnutt's racial identity. He had never attempted to conceal his race, although he was often mistaken for a white man and could easily have "passed" as white. However, he refused to allow himself to be promoted as an African American writer, preferring to have his work judged on purely literary criteria.

His publishers decided to bring out a second volume of short stories before the end of the year, and *The Wife of His Youth, and Other Stories of the Color Line* (1899) was released in time for the Christmas market. Two months after signing the contract for the book, Chesnutt closed his court-reporting business to devote himself full-time to his writing. Unlike Chesnutt's more fanciful earlier stories, the tales in the second volume are generally serious in tone and contemporary in setting, focusing on the themes of miscegenation and the plight of people of mixed race in the United States. Perhaps because of the shift to weightier themes, the book was less successful with the public and the critics than *The Conjure Woman* had been. His two collections had made him enough of a reputation that another publisher commissioned him to write a biography of Frederick Douglass for high school students, and the book appeared in 1900.

Chesnutt next published two novels, *The House Behind the Cedars* (1900), the tragic story of a mixed-race heroine who attempted to pass for white, and *The Marrow of Tradition* (1901); these books are now generally agreed to be his major literary achievement. Neither book sold well enough to enable him to support his family, however, and in 1902 Chesnutt reopened his court-reporting business. He continued to write, producing short stories and essays on racial problems as well as a third novel, *The Colonel's Dream* (1905). Chesnutt made the protagonist of this novel a white man, perhaps in hopes that his predominantly white audience would be more likely to identify with the character, but the book's pessimistic social analysis failed to attract favorable criticism or a wide readership.

Chesnutt published little more fiction after this, although he worked actively for racial equality in local and national organizations and served on the General Committee of the National Association for the Advancement of Colored People (NAACP). In the 1920's, Chesnutt's work attracted belated interest from a new generation of readers, and *The House Behind the Cedars* and *The Conjure Woman* were brought back into print. In 1928, he was recognized by the NAACP with its Spingarn Medal for his literary and civic achievements.

ANALYSIS

As Chesnutt predicted in a journal entry on May 29, 1880, several years before he actually published any substantial work, "The object of my writings would be not so much the elevation of the colored people as the elevation of the whites." He knew that militant preaching to white Americans would be received with indifference or hostility, and he concluded that it would be necessary to entertain his white audience before he could have any hope of

leading them out of their prejudices: "The Negro's part is to prepare himself for recognition and equality, and it is the province of literature to open the way for him to get it—to accustom the public mind to the idea; and while amusing them, to lead people out, imperceptibly, unconsciously, step by step, to the desired state of feeling." The combining of these dual purposes, entertainment and moral education, constitutes the controlling strategy behind most of Chesnutt's fiction.

The stories collected in his first book, *The Conjure Woman*, appealed immediately to their predominantly white Northern audience as examples of two familiar popular genres, "local color" and "plantation" fiction. Local color stories presented readers with detailed depictions of unfamiliar customs and places, often reproducing the distinctive dialect of a given region and social class. Plantation novels typically described the antebellum South as an idyllic and peaceful setting for the supposedly harmonious relations between benevolent masters and loyal slaves. Both genres were appealing sentimental fantasies for both Northerners and Southerners in a period of rapid and often threatening social and economic change during which the failure of Reconstruction policies and the reinstatement of an increasingly harsh racism in the South became apparent.

In *The Conjure Woman* stories, an elderly former slave, Uncle Julius, recounts the beliefs and practices of plantation slaves in the antebellum South. Uncle Julius's stories, delivered in his distinctive dialect, were cleverly designed at one level for the diversion of Chesnutt's target audience of middle-class white readers familiar with the Uncle Remus dialect stories of Joel Chandler Harris. As Chesnutt must have anticipated, most readers identified the first-person narrator, John, who becomes Julius's employer, with the voice of the author. Such readers assumed that Chesnutt was white and viewed the tales, as John does, as light local color comedy, usually reflecting an attempt by Julius to gain money or privileges. More careful readers, however, could see that the tales Uncle Julius tells within this outer frame often constitute serious indictments of slavery and of the white characters' greed and abuse of power.

These two levels of interpretation, which correspond to Chesnutt's dual purposes of entertainment and moral education, are exemplified in the second tale in the book, "Po' Sandy." The tale is often regarded as the strongest of the conjure stories by modern critics who value Chesnutt's literary artistry and social criticism more than his contemporary audience did. Chesnutt appears to have fully realized the possibilities opened up by his creation of a fictional white audience for Julius's tales, and the frame includes the reaction of John's wife, Annie, whose compassion and understanding are much greater than her husband's. While John sees the story superficially, as a tall tale designed to trick him into letting Julius assume possession of an old building, Annie sees the serious indictment of the slave system that underlies the tale, which is for her more about the destruction of a slave family than about a conjuring feat.

John remarks at one point that "Some of these stories are quaintly humorous . . . while others, poured freely into the sympathetic ear of a Northern-bred woman, disclose many a tragic incident of the darker side of slavery." As critics have noted, John's inability to sympathize with this tragic level unfortunately mirrors that of the complacent mainstream white audience Chesnutt addresses, while Annie's response dramatizes that of the ideal reader that he hoped to educate into being through his writings.

While a white audience could easily have missed much of the implicit social commentary of the stories in *The Conjure Woman*, most of the stories in Chesnutt's second book, *The Wife of His Youth, and Other Stories of the Color Line*, are bold examinations of then-taboo subjects such as miscegenation and racial violence. The shift in approach does not really represent a new direction in Chesnutt's ideas—many of the stories in the more pessimistic and realistic second book were written before the more optimistic first book was assembled—but rather indicates the extent to which he conceived of each book as having its own thematic unity. The sequence of his books nevertheless suggests an ever-increasing distance between Chesnutt, who insisted on taking a hard, realistic look at racial problems, and the popular audience, which was reluctant to read anything that was not presented with a sugar coating.

The themes of the second book of short stories are further explored in *The House Behind the Cedars*, which documents at greater length the social circumstances that provoke a woman of mixed race to pass for white and the tragic consequences that follow. Chesnutt again hoped to educate his audience about a set of unfamiliar social and psychological conditions, with the hope of producing tolerance and reform. He further broadens his scope in *The Marrow of Tradition*, which introduces a much larger cast of characters from a broader spectrum of society. The novel is now recognized as an important example of early social realism in its effort to paint a comprehensive picture of the South at the turn of the twentieth century.

The Colonel's Dream continues Chesnutt's emphasis on socioeconomic analysis, depicting the unsuccessful efforts of an idealistic white businessman to reform the social injustices in the South. As Chesnutt had written to his publisher after the limited success of *The Marrow of Tradition*, "I am beginning to suspect that the public as a rule does not care for books in which the principal characters are colored people, or written with a striking sympathy with that race as contrasted with the white race." His use of a white protagonist failed to make this sympathy more palatable to the public, and reviewers were more prone to attack the book for its pessimism than to praise it for its honesty.

THE CONJURE WOMAN

First published: 1899
Type of work: Short stories

The shrewd former slave Uncle Julius entertains, manipulates, and sometimes tries to educate his young Northern employers with humorous tales of conjuring in the antebellum South.

With the stories collected in *The Conjure Woman*, Chesnutt discovered a way to introduce into apparently humorous tall tales depictions of black characters who avoided the negative stereotypes then current in fiction and to include, beneath the comic surface, a level of social criticism. John, a young white man from the North, goes to North Carolina after the Civil War to find a suitable climate to help his wife Annie's poor health and to buy a plantation for growing grapes. He and his wife meet Uncle Julius, an elderly former slave, who tells them anecdotes that revolve around instances of conjuring, or magic.

In "The Goophered Grapevine," Chesnutt's first major publication and still his most frequently anthologized story, Julius tells in minutely rendered dialect the tale of the slave Henry, whose health and appearance are magically linked with those of the bewitched, or "goophered," grapes that he has eaten from the plantation that John has come South to purchase. Henry's master takes advantage of the enchantment by selling him to a new owner every spring, when he is young and healthy, and buying him back every fall, when he becomes old. At one level, the tale is an attempt by Julius, who makes money selling the grapes, to dissuade John from buying the bewitched plantation. At a deeper level, however, the story can be read as social criticism of the owners' treatment of Henry, who withers away and dies.

Chesnutt again capitalizes on the device of having a dual audience discover dual meanings in "Sis' Becky's Pickaninny," in which a slaveowner first sells a baby's father and then trades the baby's mother for a horse, leaving the child alone in the world. A conjuring trick results in a relatively happy ending, to which John reacts by saying, "That is a very ingenious fairy tale, Julius." Annie, however, correctly sees the devastating critique of the inhumanity of slavery that underlies the fairy-tale elements. Implicit social commentary is also evident in "Mars Jeems's Nightmare," in which a slaveowner is temporarily transformed into a slave; his subsequent treatment at the hands of his own brutal overseer changes his view of slavery permanently. While the other tales in the book feature more comedy than tragedy, their depiction of sympathetic black characters in the context of their own folk culture allowed an ethnocentric white audience to learn something about the black experience in the South.

THE WIFE OF HIS YOUTH, AND OTHER STORIES OF THE COLOR LINE

First published: 1899
Type of work: Short stories

In these pioneering stories, Chesnutt explores a range of contemporary racial issues, including miscegenation and caste and color prejudice between and within ethnic groups.

Chesnutt summarized the theme of his second book of short stories in a letter to his publisher written a few months before it came out:

> I should like to hope that the stories, while written to depict life as it is, in certain aspects that no one has ever before attempted to adequately describe, may throw a light upon the great problem on which the stories are strung; for the backbone of this volume is not a character, like Uncle Julius in *The Conjure Woman*, but a subject, as indicated in the title—*The Color Line.*

Chesnutt's more direct approach to these highly charged racial issues presented a challenge that the conservative reading public often proved unwilling to meet. Particularly shocking to contemporary critics were such stories as "The Sheriff's Children," in which a young man of mixed race, Tom, is arrested as a murder suspect in a small town in North Carolina about ten years after the Civil War. A lynch mob attempts to break into the prison to hang him without a trial but is driven away by Sheriff Campbell. Tom then gains possession of the sheriff's gun and reveals that he is the son of Campbell and a slave woman whom Campbell had sold. Just as he is about to shoot the sheriff, Tom is shot and wounded by Campbell's daughter and disarmed. Campbell spends the night contemplating his past and decides to atone for his moral crime of neglect against his son, whom he now believes to be inno-

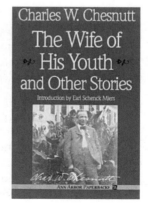

cent of the murder. When he returns to the jail the next morning, however, his son has torn off the bandage on his wound and bled to death in an apparent suicide.

Chesnutt focuses on the internal point of view of the relatively sympathetic white sheriff in the last third of the narrative, providing white readers with a moral role model within the story. Campbell's miscegenation and the lynch-mob scene, however, are more direct attacks on white society's treatment of African Americans than anything in the earlier book. Even in a story of superficially successful "passing" and miscegenation such as "Her Virginia Mammy," in which a young, mixed-race woman is kept ignorant of her black ancestry so that she may marry a rich white man, the emphasis is on the emotional cost to the black mother, who must never acknowledge their relationship, rather than on the daughter's happy future.

Particularly interesting are a series of tales that analyze the hitherto seldom-explored subject of racial prejudice within the black community. "The Wife of His Youth" presents the positive example of a prominent and wealthy leader of the "Blue Vein Society" ("no one was eligible for membership who was not white enough to show blue veins"), who publicly acknowledges his long-lost wife, an illiterate former slave with very dark skin. "A Matter of Principle" complements "The Wife of His Youth" with the humorous negative example of a light-skinned man whose bias against darker blacks costs his daughter a chance at a successful marriage.

THE MARROW OF TRADITION

First published: 1901
Type of work: Novel

Dr. Miller, a black physician, is called upon to help the dying son of the white Major Carteret, whose racist editorials had incited the riot in which Miller's son was killed.

The main plot of *The Marrow of Tradition* is based on newspaper and eyewitness accounts of the lynchings that occurred during the election riots in Wilmington, North Carolina, in 1898. Chesnutt added a number of subplots that enabled him to explore a wider range of social issues more thoroughly than the short-story form had permitted. Dr. Miller, a talented black surgeon, and Major Carteret, an aristocratic white supremacist, are somewhat melodramatically brought together when Carteret, having indirectly caused the death of Miller's child with inflammatory race-baiting editorials that incited riots, calls upon Miller at the end of the book to save the life of his own child. The connection between the two men is ironically underscored by the fact that they are married to half-sisters, one white and one of mixed race. This parallelism of characters from opposite sides of the color line is echoed within the black community by the paralleling of the middle-class, moderate Miller with Josh Green, a militant black laborer.

Miller seems to represent an effort on Chesnutt's part to find a middle ground that will avoid the extremism of either Green or Carteret. Miller refuses to lead the black community in what he correctly perceives as a hopeless attempt at armed defense against the white lynch mob; at the end of the book, he agrees to help Carteret's child. Dr. Evans, a youthful white physician who lacks Miller's expertise and is himself powerless to help the child, ends the book with a cautious optimism about the Carteret child's condition that the reader is invited to apply as a prognosis for America's condition with respect to the problems of race relations: "Come on up, Dr. Miller. . . . There's time enough, but none to spare."

Despite his evident intent to promote the moderate line, Chesnutt's involuntary admiration for Green's courage is unmistakable, and Green's heroic insistence that "I'd ruther be a dead nigger any day than a live dog" is never convincingly discredited. Even the moderate Miller is acutely aware that Green exemplifies not savagery but love of liberty. While Miller's wife urges him to help the child, she emphatically refuses to accept her white half-sister's long-overdue offer to recognize their relationship and to offer financial restitution. Chesnutt's realistic depiction of the brutalities that kept black citizens in their social places, and his implication that black pride and resistance were appropriate positions, could hardly fail to strike genteel white readers and critics as bitter and excessive. Chesnutt himself considered the novel his best, and later critics have generally found the novel a milestone in the movement of the African American novel toward social realism.

SUMMARY

Chesnutt failed to achieve his ambitious project of reforming the social consciousness of his white audience, but he nevertheless succeeded in earning national fame and the respect of the literary establishment. As Chesnutt himself said of his literary career, "My books were written, from one point of view, a generation too soon. . . . I was writing against the trend of public opinion on the race question at that particular time." Later generations of readers have proven more receptive to his insightful analyses of racial injustice. While his success in balancing the demands of entertainment and moral purpose has made the folklore tales of *The Conjure Woman* his more widely read work, critics have more recently come to appreciate the artistry and power of his later, more realistic short stories and novels.

William Nelles

DISCUSSION TOPICS

- Charles Waddell Chesnutt did not suffer the experience of slavery, but as a young man he experienced the bitter failure of Reconstruction. How does this fact color his stories?

- Chesnutt said that he wanted to "elevate" not black Americans but white ones. What does he mean? Identify a story which seems to reflect this ambition particularly well and explain why you think so.

- What reasons can you discover for Chesnutt's decision to call the novel *The Marrow of Tradition* his best? What does tradition have to do with the novel? Consult dictionary definitions of "marrow" that seem applicable to this work.

- One of Chesnutt's best-known stories, "The Sheriff's Children," shocked many readers. If you were to choose one of his stories in an anthology, would you consider this story an essential one? A representative one?

- Do the subtleties in Chesnutt's *The Conjure Woman* stories cause him to fail in his aim of educating his readers?

BIBLIOGRAPHY

By the Author

SHORT FICTION:
The Conjure Woman, 1899
The Wife of His Youth, and Other Stories of the Color Line, 1899

LONG FICTION:
Mandy Oxendine, wr. 1897, pb. 1997
The House Behind the Cedars, 1900
The Marrow of Tradition, 1901
The Colonel's Dream, 1905
Paul Marchand, F.M.C., wr. 1921, pb. 1998
The Quarry, wr. 1928, pb. 1999

NONFICTION:
The Life of Frederick Douglass, 1899
The Journals of Charles W. Chesnutt, 1993
To Be an Author: The Letters of Charles W. Chesnutt, 1889-1905, 1997
Charles W. Chesnutt: Essays and Speeches, 1999

Charles Waddell Chesnutt

Selected Writings, 2001 (SallyAnn H. Ferguson, editor)
An Exemplary Citizen: Letters of Charles W. Chesnutt, 1906-1932, 2002 (Jesse S. Crisler, Robert C. Leitz III, and Joseph R. McElrath, Jr., editors)

About the Author

Duncan, Charles. *The Absent Man: The Narrative Craft of Charles W. Chesnutt.* Athens: Ohio University Press, 1998.

Kulii, Elon A. "Poetic License and Chesnutt's Use of Folklore." *CLA Journal* 38 (December, 1994): 247-253.

Lehman, Cynthia L. "The Social and Political View of Charles Chesnutt: Reflections on His Major Writings." *Journal of Black Studies* 26 (January, 1996).

McElrath, Joseph R., Jr., ed. *Critical Essays on Charles W. Chesnutt.* New York: G. K. Hall, 1999.

McFatter, Susan. "From Revenge to Resolution: The (R)evolution of Female Characters in Chesnutt's Fiction." *CLA Journal* 42 (December, 1998): 194-211.

McWilliams, Dean. *Charles W. Chesnutt and the Fictions of Race.* Athens: University of Georgia Press, 2002.

Pickens, Ernestine Williams. *Charles W. Chesnutt and the Progressive Movement.* New York: Pace University Press, 1994.

Render, Sylvia Lyons. *Charles W. Chesnutt.* Boston: Twayne, 1980.

Wilson, Matthew. *Whiteness in the Novels of Charles W. Chesnutt.* Jackson: University Press of Mississippi, 2004.

Wonham, Henry B. *Charles W. Chesnutt: A Study of the Short Fiction.* New York: Twayne, 1998.

FRANK CHIN

Corky Lee

Born: Berkeley, California
February 25, 1940

Chin's acclaimed dramas and novels present the difficulties that Chinese Americans face in negotiating the majority culture, while his essays angrily denounce racial discrimination.

BIOGRAPHY

Frank Chew Chin, Jr., was born on February 25, 1940, in Berkeley, California, to a family prominent in the Chinese American community. His great grandmother owned a famous brothel, and his father was the president of the Chinese Six Companies, a combined business group and benevolent association. At the time, Chin's birth was exceptional; because of discriminatory laws, few Chinese women were allowed into the United States until the late 1940's.

At first, Chin's parents could not take care of him—his mother was only fifteen when he was born—and he was put in a foundling home. The home placed him with an impoverished white couple, with whom he stayed until his parents reclaimed him at the age of six. Even from that point, though, Chin's childhood was not to be an easy one; his father was strict and beat the boy to discipline him. These early years had obvious effects on his writing, both in his portraits of tortured, poisoned relations between fathers and sons and in his depictions of Chinese American boys who feel they have lost contact with their Asian roots.

Chin attended the University of California at Berkeley from 1958 to 1961 and then the Writers' Workshop at the University of Iowa from 1961 to 1963. From 1962 to 1965, he worked as clerk for the Western Pacific railroad. In 1965, Chin enrolled in the University of California, Santa Barbara, and graduated with a B.A. in English in 1966. In this year, he worked as a brakeman for the Southern Pacific railroad. He was the first Asian American to hold this latter position for the company. This was another important shaping experience for Chin, and his work makes repeated reference to railroad lines, both in connection to his own job and in discussions of the large part Chinese laborers played in building the Western railroads.

Through the late 1960's, the author taught in colleges and wrote for a broadcasting company. Also in this period, he founded the Asian American Theater Workshop in San Francisco. His first play, *The Chickencoop Chinaman* (pr. 1972, pb. 1981) was staged in New York City in the early 1970's. This was another Chin first, as the play was the first drama by an Asian American to be performed on Broadway. The work was acclaimed by the critics, yet the event was also a traumatic one for the fledgling dramatist. He wanted his mother to come from California to attend the opening night, but Chin's father would not permit her to leave, because he wanted her to attend a business party. On the way to the dinner, their car crashed, and Chin's mother was killed.

Although the playwright's father accepted his son as a man, he never accepted him as a writer. Chin once commented that his father "never respected my writing. He died believing I never worked a day in my life."

Chin's next play, *The Year of the Dragon* (pr. 1974, pb. 1981), was also a critical success. He also coedited the anthology *Aiiieeeee!* (1974), the first lit-

453

erary collection to focus on Asian American writers. Chin, however, did not immediately follow up these successes, partially because of his own absorption in teaching and running his theater and also because of a change in the literary climate. His militant writing, which castigated the mass media for stereotyping Asians, fell out of popularity with the public and lost acceptance from producers as the United States became increasingly conservative in the late 1970's.

Until the late 1980's, Chin devoted himself to teaching. In this period, he engaged in a drawn-out war of words with the Asian American novelist Maxine Hong Kingston. Their quarrel began when she asked him to write an endorsement for her first novel, *The Woman Warrior* (1976). Although he found merit in the novel, he could not sympathize with the general direction of her book, which seemed to him more aimed at endearing Kingston to white audiences than at recapturing or revivifying Chinese immigrant history. As Kingston's other novels appeared, Chin continued criticizing, especially scorning what he saw as her doctoring of Chinese mythology to fit Western misconceptions.

In the late 1980's, Chin returned to print with a book of short stories, *The Chinaman Pacific and Frisco R.R. Co.* (1988), and a novel, *Donald Duk* (1991), which worked to correct misinterpretations of the Chinese past. The novel presented a gallery of authentic Chinese heroes, while the earlier book went so far as to poke fun at Kingston in a short section that parodied her style and message.

With successful Chinese American author Amy Tan, Chin added another writer to his sworn enemies. In his introduction to his revised anthology, *The Big Aiiieeeee* (1991), he openly attacked Kingston, Tan, and David Henry Hwang as impostors who had faked Chinese mythology to curry favors with whites. His strong condemnation of Kingston and Tan took a misogynist tone for many critics and contributed to a bitter feud in the field of Asian American literature and literary criticism. Nevertheless, for 1992, the Lannan Foundation awarded Chin forty thousand dollars for its Fiction Fellowship in recognition of his talent.

Chin's next novel, *Gunga Din Highway* (1994), continued to explore questions of Chinese American identity, racism, stereotypes, and popular culture. Written with an angry attitude against assimilation, Chin's narrative begins like an early Thomas

Pynchon novel that irreverently mixes popular culture, surreal comedy, and philosophy and ends with the funeral of the protagonist's difficult father.

Chin's aggressive stance against his opponents, both Asian and white, turned passages of his collection of essays, *Bulletproof Buddhists, and Other Essays* (1998), into what some critics viewed as rather polemical. He certainly was an angry writer by the late 1990's, comparable to his friend the African American writer Ishmael Reed.

Increasingly feeling marginalized and persecuted, Chin published "Feminists Censor Frank Chin, Again" in the online journal *Ishmael Reed's Konch Magazine* in 1999. He described how the president of the Western Literature Association was forced to drop Chin as recipient of that organization's Distinguished Achievement Award for the coming year 2000 under the pressure of its executive council.

Suffering a stroke in 1999, Chin recovered and turned his eye on the story of the Japanese American internees during World War II who refused to pledge allegiance to an American government that imprisoned them and their families. In editing *Born in the USA: A Story of Japanese America, 1889-1947* (2002), he went as far as claiming that the president of the Japanese American Citizens League proposed interning Japanese Americans in the continental United States in camps for their own protection. The book caused a fierce historical debate.

In April, 2004, Chin donated his collected papers—filling forty-five cardboard boxes—to the Special Collections Department of the Donald Davidson Library of the University of California, Santa Barbara, his alma mater. Also at the university, Chin's longtime friend Curtis Choy directed a video documentary, *What's Wrong with Frank Chin* (2005), featuring Chin himself. In 2005, the documentary was shown widely at film festivals throughout America and brought Frank Chin fresh recognition.

ANALYSIS

Chin is centrally concerned with the psychological effects of assimilation on Chinese Americans who were born into the United States after World War II. He argues that the adaptation of Chinese Americans to their home was distorted by critical problems that Chinese immigrants have had since the nineteenth century in being accepted as equal to the children of European immigrants. Chin shows how real Chinese contributions to American life, such as the building of the railroads, have been downplayed or purposefully forgotten and how, in the place of real history, Chinese Americans have been saddled with degrading stereotypes.

This stereotyping plays into a second major problem Chinese Americans face, which involves their economic place. Either they do the real work of society—as laborers, cooks, and so on—and their activity is ignored, or they get high-profile jobs peddling the very stereotypes that disempower them. A character who holds this last type of job is Fred Eng in *The Year of the Dragon*. He gives tours of Chinatown and finds that, to make his business lucrative, he must repeat to his clients the same distortions they have heard about Asians from the media.

Chin is not a literary preacher who uses his work as a soapbox from which to make judgments; he is concerned with tracing the human effects of stereotyping and subordination. His views on the fate of Chinese Americans serve as a background to his portrayal of individuals and their families who are damaged by the roles that they are forced to play in white America's reality and dreams.

A special quality of Chin's work is that he stresses the disastrous effects of prejudice more on the relations between family members than on individual psyches. Above everything, Chin focuses on the relations of fathers and sons. (Although Chin can portray vivid female characters, these are decidedly secondary to his interests.) This is why, of all the popular caricatures of the Chinese, the one to which Chin reverts over and over is that of the fictional detective Charlie Chan, because central to this representation was the display of Charlie's relationship with his servile sons and the fact that the detective himself was played by a white actor. In *Gunga Din Highway*, the whole first section of the novel is devoted to this topic as the (fictional) last white actor to play Charlie Chan is sought out by his last film son, a Chinese American with hopes to be the first Asian to portray Chan.

Chin's discussion of stereotyping is a complex one. It is not so much that Charlie Chan films, for example, promoted the picture of Chinese sons as passive buffoons. Though this was bad enough, the real problem was that American-born Chinese sons, with no other available images of Chinese boys, began to believe in the stereotype. Thus, the protagonist of *Donald Duk*, who is sent to an American school where such stereotypes are promulgated, begins to hate other Chinese boys, who he thinks are physically weak and passive. The hero of *The Chickencoop Chinaman* is driven to despair by the parade of stereotypes in the media until he invents a Chinese role model, the Lone Ranger, a cowboy hero who never removes his mask— because, as the Chinese boy believes, he is concealing his Oriental eyes.

This second example suggests that Chinese sons do not simply submit to the endless negative images but may revolt against them, often putting them at odds with their uncomprehending fathers. Immigrant fathers, such as Pa in *The Year of the Dragon*, cannot sympathize with the feelings of the sons; the fathers are too steeped in original Chinese tradition to be really affected by American culture, and they are too impressed with the material success available in the United States to care about their images.

A division between the generations occurs because each requires a different degree of integration into their new society. The fathers are satisfied with economic acceptance, while the sons, who are necessarily more familiar with American ways, yearn for an unobtainable cultural acceptance. These disparate goals make for strife and misunderstandings in the family unit.

There is a clear change in Chin's attitude over the years. His earliest writings, his theater works, are unrelentingly bleak, showing protagonists who are painted into a corner by their own inabilities to either ignore or escape debilitating social strictures. In his later fiction, Chin does sketch avenues of psychic survival, ones that involve an honest appraisal of the Chinese place in America, a continued respect for the Chinese customs that can be salvaged in the new environment, and the choice of a career that can mediate between American and Chinese society. By the end of *Donald Duk*, for example, the twelve-year-old protagonist has grasped these essentials. He has learned of the Chinese contribution to building the transcontinental railroad, has come to appreciate the significance of the traditional Chinese New Year, and has seen the viability of his father's choice of occupation. His father is a chef who is popular with Americans but who also makes time to be involved in sustaining his own ethnic community—as when he closes his restaurant except to his friends so that he can create dishes only the Chinese palate can properly savor.

Chin's style is protean. His writing becomes especially lyrical and surreal when describing media fantasy worlds, as when the Lone Ranger or Charlie Chan appears, but can be matter-of-fact and prosy when describing the everyday lives of immigrants. Nevertheless, his virtuoso handling of varied styles is subordinate to his continued focus on the perils facing the Chinese American boy who strains to adapt to an American system that has little regard for his people's history and less for his present need for self-validation.

THE CHICKENCOOP CHINAMAN

First produced: 1972 (first published, 1981)
Type of work: Play

A Chinese American filmmaker comes to Detroit, ostensibly in search of material but really looking for his own identity.

The Chickencoop Chinaman established Chin's success and became the first play by an Asian American to be produced on Broadway. Yet the work is not one that would seem to recommend itself to the average theatergoer, given the play's dark theme, its depiction of the irreparable loss of a father, and its irresolute climax.

Ironically, of all Chin's works, this piece, which established his credentials as a Chinese American writer, is the one least concerned with the Chinese American experience. Rather, the play portrays the extravagant heterogeneity of the United States. Each character's life is an unstable ethnic mélange. The protagonist, Tam Lum, a Chinese American, was raised in a black area of Los Angeles. Now, as a young man, he devotes his energy to making a film about his idol, an African American prizefighter.

The play does not celebrate this diversity. Instead, it counts the cost in unhappiness for those who have no clear-cut allegiances: These charac-

ters, who have lost their natal culture, have not been able to attach themselves to any other tradition. Tam is making a film to prove himself, but at bottom, he is not sure what he is proving or to whom he has to prove something.

If *The Chickencoop Chinaman* were a conventional play, its plot development would probably concern how the characters recontacted their base cultures and relocated their fathers. In Chin's alternative dramaturgy, however, the plot does not conclude the characters' searches but rather cuts the few ties they have left. In the most disheartening and poignant confrontation of the play, for example, Tam goes for an interview with Charley Popcorn, the purported estranged father of his film's subject. Tam has gotten substitute satisfaction from hearing touching stories of father-and-son affection from his boxer subject. Now, though, he discovers that these stories were not reminiscences but fairy tales, as Popcorn was the fighter's manager but had no blood ties to him. In another blow to Tam, in a fantasy sequence he meets the Lone Ranger, whom he adored as a boy, thinking that the cowboy's mask concealed the fact that he was Asian. The Lone Ranger turns out to be white, and a racist to boot.

The play ends up in the air. The status of Tam's film project is in doubt, and no one has gained any clarity on their parentage or roots. Thus, Chin's play ends by underlining the point made at the beginning: Second-generation Americans are faced with a severe identity crisis seemingly out of all proportion to their ability to handle it.

"THE SONS OF CHAN"

First published: 1988 (collected in *The Chinaman Pacific and Frisco R.R. Co.*, 1988)
Type of work: Short story

The protagonist comes to Las Vegas on a dual mission: to interview a famous stripper and to kill Charlie Chan.

"The Sons of Chan" is the last story in Chin's short-story collection *The Chinaman Pacific and Frisco R.R. Co.* Chin's stories are the most stylistically idiosyncratic of his writings. Their prose is dense, allusive, and layered. In keeping with this individualism in style is the way that, in many of the stories, the protagonist concocts a subjective mythology. In the earlier *The Chickencoop Chinaman*, the hapless hero had tried to remold American pop iconography to his own ends; in the later *Donald Duk*, the hero locates a sustaining mythology by discovering forgotten pages from the Chinese past. In "The Sons of Chan," however, the hero dreams up his own personalized fantasy world, which is centered on the existence of a secret brotherhood; the imaginary actions are intercut with the more realistic events of the story's plot.

This brotherhood, The Sons of Chan, is made up of symbolic male children of Charlie Chan, that is, of Chinese American men who were crippled by media depictions of Asian sons. The vow of this order is to kill the actor who originally played Charlie Chan.

In the story, the symbolic attempt to break with the male stereotypes acquired in childhood intersects with the narrator's attempt to face down, in the real world, an example of the female type who has been put forward as the only worthy object of desire by American popular culture. This culture never portrays desirable Asian women but instead presents a pantheon of blond, curvaceous love goddesses whose seductiveness has distorted the narrator's own romantic life. He has had affairs with and been married to only white women, never finding himself capable of loving a fellow Chinese. In coming to Las Vegas to interview a has-been stripper for a magazine, he is also coming to grips with his own warped sexuality.

Because a major facet of the hero's problems is that he cannot disengage his mind from these oppressive stereotypes, it is unlikely that his encounters with these archetypes will be productive. In fact, the meetings are abortive. In fantasy, he meets Chan, but he lets slip the opportunity to assassinate him; the hero cannot even arrange a meeting with the stripper.

The real moment of learning for the narrator occurs outside his fantasies. He runs into an older Chinese American woman who is on a picket line, and he feels drawn to her. Half charmed and half disgusted with her pidgin English and aging flesh, he sympathizes with her and ends up sleeping with her. Though his misgivings about himself are hardly laid to rest by this one-night stand, the episode does show him breaking with his evasive circling around media creations. He broaches the more fragile but potentially fuller relationship to someone he is meeting as a person, not as a reflection of programmed stereotypes.

DONALD DUK

First published: 1991
Type of work: Novel

A Chinese American boy overcomes his resistance to Asian things as he locates the usable parts of his heritage.

Donald Duk presents characters in positions similar to the ones they occupy in Chin's earlier works, but the novel reverses the characteristics of those that hold the positions. Specifically, his short stories and plays show a young Chinese American man who is constructing a viable tradition to put in place of the soul-destroying one given him by America; this construction is interfered with by a father figure, who may be a media image, such as Charlie Chan, who perpetuates the hurtful culture. In *Donald Duk*, however, it is the father who has located the viable, laudable tradition and the son who fights against it.

This change in who plays what role can be seen as accounting for the changed tone and even changed writing style of the novel. Chin's earlier works, which showed protagonists battling tenaciously but mostly unsuccessfully for an acceptable heritage while being dragged down by their American cultural baggage, moved spasmodically and ended inconclusively. *Donald Duk*, in which a workable Chinese American identity has already been established by the father and his peers, has a more linear, progressive plot, with the leading character following a clear trajectory.

The hero of the book, Donald, has been turned against Chinese traditions by the influence of the nearly all-white special school that he attends. He is so indifferent to his ethnic culture that he wantonly destroys one of the model planes his father has made for a Chinese New Year celebration. His father learns of his deed and tries to awaken Donald to the subtleties and enhancing aspects of their shared culture. Meanwhile, the father's teaching is supplemented by Donald's dreams, which put him back in the days of the building of the cross-country railroad. In his dreams, Donald finds out something about the Chinese people's real contribution to the United States. By the end of the novel, Donald embraces his background, to the point of correcting his history teacher, who is ignorant of Asian American history.

As the novel presents a more definitive series of events than is seen in Chin's other fiction, so, too, is Chin's writing style less flashy and fragmentary, more workmanlike and plainer. This is not to say that one of these styles is preferable, either the earlier artsy one or the later simpler one; each is appropriate to its message and context. In *Donald Duk*, the point is that, through intelligent participation in and ongoing creation of a tradition, one can make a life that honors both individuality and one's ethnic group. The presentation of this message calls for a measured tone that is correspondent not with struggle but with struggle achieved.

GUNGA DIN HIGHWAY

First published: 1994
Type of work: Novel

A middle-aged Chinese American actor reviews his career, while his rebellious son experiences five decades of a turbulent life before his father's Hollywood funeral.

Gunga Din Highway is a passionately argued novel about Chinese American identity. It opens with Longman Kwan, a Chinese American actor who is given bit parts in Hollywood movies that stereotype Asians, generally dying for whites or as their enemy. Now, Longman reunites with the (fictional) last white actor who played the Chinese detective Charlie Chan opposite Longman's role as Chan's fourth son.

As throughout his oeuvre, Chin deftly mixes the real with the imaginary. Charlie Chan was indeed played by three different whites and never an Asian actor. His subordinate sons were played by Chinese Americans such as Keye Luke, whose real filmography looks much like Longman Kwan's imaginary one.

Soon the novel turns to Longman's third, rebellious son. Named Ulysses Kwan after James Joyce's modernist novel once banned in America for its erotic content, Ulysses's life is inspired by Chin's own. As a boy, Ulysses rebels against Chinese and whites alike and associates with African Americans. He torments his Chinese language teachers and forms a lifelong brotherhood with two friends, Diego Chang and Benjamin Han. Playing on Chin's concern with father-son relationships, Benjamin changes his last name to Mo, that of his father who was killed by his mother's lover, who then became his despised stepfather.

As a young man, Ulysses lives a bohemian lifestyle vindicated by the cultural upheaval of late 1950's and 1960's America when California became a haven of counterculture. Working as brakeman for a railroad company, Ulysses eventually moves up to Seattle. There, he and his father meet again at a Woodstock-like rock festival. Yet his father does not recognize the pony-tailed rock musician as his son, and on stage, the old man satirizes his own role as Charlie Chan's fourth son.

Benjamin bears traits of the author as well. Like Chin, Benjamin studies creative writing in Santa Barbara and becomes famous with a radical play. Benjamin's wife, writer Pandora Toy, is a thinly disguised caricature of Chin's female Asian adversaries. On the opening night of Benjamin's play, Pandora attempts suicide out of professional jealousy, and her *Conquering Woman* is an obvious allusion to Maxine Hong Kingston's *The Woman Warrior* (1976). Pandora fakes Chinese mythology just as Chin accused Kingston and Tan of doing.

The novel reaches a climax with Longman Kwan's funeral, organized by his first Chinese-born son who has become a millionaire in America. When the arrival of a white actor to play Charlie Chan in the remake adds to the insult of a Catholic funeral for Buddhist Kwan, Ulysses takes charge and delivers the eulogy. Now the meaning of the novel's title is revealed, as Ulysses quotes from the end of Rudyard Kipling's poem "Gunga Din" (1892). Ostensibly, the poem praises an Indian water carrier who sacrifices himself for a British soldier. In Ulysses's interpretation, the poem reveals what is wrong about Asian Americans sacrificing themselves for whites. He and his friends will not travel along his father's Gunga Din highway but will choose another road.

SUMMARY

Chinese immigrants to the United States would not have made the perilous voyage if they had not had high hopes. They were often disappointed. In Chin's opinion, however, it is not the immigrants but their children who were to feel the bitterest discouragement. His writings mull this theme, exposing how Chinese Americans are hit by both demeaning stereotypes and, often, occupational and social discrimination. Even at his most hopeful, Chin does not believe that the children can create an amalgam of American and Chinese ways. They must, instead, create a new Chinese culture, adapted to but not beholden to the largely antagonistic one of their new home.

James Feast; updated by R. C. Lutz

DISCUSSION TOPICS

- What are some of the reasons that so many of Frank Chin's characters hate the figure of Charlie Chan?

- Discuss Chin's portrayal of a son's conflict with his father in one of his plays, short stories, or novels.

- In what ways do racial issues affect the lives of Chin's protagonists?

- What is it that Chin has against fellow Chinese American writers Maxine Hong Kingston and Amy Tan?

- According to Chin's works, what makes life especially hard for second-generation Chinese Americans?

- Initially, many of Chin's young characters rebel against all things Chinese in their lives. Why do you feel they do this, and does their attitude change sometimes?

- What are some examples of Chin's dark humor in his texts, and what effect does this humor have on you as the reader?

- What part do American television series and films play in the lives of many of Chin's characters?

BIBLIOGRAPHY

By the Author

DRAMA:
The Chickencoop Chinaman, pr. 1972, pb. 1981
The Year of the Dragon, pr. 1974, pb. 1981

LONG FICTION:
Donald Duk, 1991
Gunga Din Highway, 1994

SHORT FICTION:
The Chinaman Pacific and Frisco R.R. Co., 1988

TELEPLAYS:
S.R.T., Act Two, 1966
The Bel Canto Carols, 1966

Frank Chin

A Man and His Music, 1967
Ed Sierer's New Zealand, 1967
Searfair Preview, 1967
The Year of the Ram, 1967
And Still Champion . . . , 1967
The Report, 1967
Mary, 1969
Rainlight Rainvision, 1969
Chinaman's Chance, 1971

NONFICTION:
Bulletproof Buddhists, and Other Essays, 1998

EDITED TEXTS:
Aiiieeeee! An Anthology of Asian-American Writers, 1974 (with others)
The Big Aiiieeeee!, 1991
Born in the USA: A Story of Japanese America, 1889-1947, 2002

About the Author

Abe, Frank. "Born in the USA: A Story of Japanese America, 1889-1947." *Amerasian Journal* 30, no. 2 (Summer, 2004): 107-113.

Cheung, King-Kok. "*The Woman Warrior* Versus *The Chinaman Pacific*: Must a Chinese American Critic Choose Between Feminism and Heroism?" In *The Woman Warrior: A Casebook,* edited by Sau-ling Cynthia Wong. New York: Oxford University Press, 1999.

Lee, Rachel. *The Americas of Asian American Literature: Gendered Fictions of Nation and Transnation.* Princeton, N.J.: Princeton University Press, 1999.

Leonard, Suzanne. "Dreaming as Cultural Work in *Donald Duk* and *Dreaming in Cuban.*" *MELUS* 29, no. 2 (Summer, 2004): 181-205.

Li, David Leiwi. "The Formation of Frank Chin and the Formations of Chinese American Literature." In *Asian Americans: Comparative and Global Perspectives,* edited by Shirley Hune, Hyung-chan Kim, Stephen Fugita, and Amy Lin. Pullman: Washington State University Press, 1991.

Nguyen, Viet Thanh. *Race and Resistance: Literature and Politics in Asian America.* New York: Oxford University Press, 2002.

_____. "The Remasculinization of Chinese America: Race, Violence, and the Novel." *American Literary History* 12, nos.1/2 (Spring/Summer, 2000): 130-157.

Richardson, Susan B. "The Lessons of *Donald Duk.*" *MELUS* 24, no.4 (Winter 1999): 57-78.

Wong, Sau-Ling Cynthia. "Autobiography as Guided Chinatown Tour? Maxine Hong Kingston's *The Woman Warrior* and the Chinese American Autobiography Controversy." In *The Woman Warrior: A Casebook,* edited by Sau-ling Cynthia Wong. New York: Oxford University Press, 1999.

Wong, Sau-ling Cynthia. *Reading Asian American Literature: From Necessity to Extravagance.* Princeton, N.J.: Princeton University Press, 1998.

KATE CHOPIN

Missouri Historical Society

Born: St. Louis, Missouri
February 8, 1851
Died: St. Louis, Missouri
August 22, 1904

Renowned for her literary naturalism and feminism, Chopin's fiction forthrightly challenged traditional roles for women and addressed other controversial themes, such as interracial relationships and human sexuality.

BIOGRAPHY

Kate O'Flaherty Chopin was born into a wealthy Catholic family in St. Louis, Missouri, on February 8, 1851. Her mother, Eliza Fans, was from an aristocratic French-Creole family, and her father, Thomas O'Flaherty, was an Irish immigrant who became a prominent merchant in St. Louis. After her father died in 1855, Kate was raised at home, among three generations of strong-willed and self-sufficient female relatives who undoubtedly influenced her attitudes about women.

On June 9, 1870, two years after graduating from a St. Louis convent school, Kate married Oscar Chopin, a French-Creole. After the marriage, she moved with her husband to New Orleans, where Oscar had a cotton-brokering business. In the first years of her marriage, Chopin's life revolved around the social obligations she bore as the wife of a notable New Orleans businessman and the raising of children. In 1879, however, Chopin found herself once again relocating, because of the failure of her husband's business. This time the family, which now included six children, settled in Cloutierville, in central Louisiana, where the Chopins managed a plantation store and a small farm belonging to Oscar's family. These were difficult years. The region, however, would provide the locale for many of Chopin's best short stories and novels.

On December 10, 1882, Oscar died unexpectedly from a fever. Chopin and her six children were left with surprisingly little financial security. At the time, the only choice seemed to be to remain on the plantation and assume its management. Within a few years, Chopin had regained her financial standing, and in 1884 she returned to her mother's home in St. Louis. As she had in New Orleans, she attempted to follow the life expected of a socially prominent widow, but in 1889 she turned to the writing career that would sustain her for the remainder of her life. Chopin became a prolific author of poems, short stories, novels, literary criticism, and drama. Within her first decade as an author, she had written three novels (one, destroyed by the author, was never published), twenty poems, several essays of literary criticism, and almost one hundred short stories.

While publishing short stories in local magazines, Chopin wrote her first novel, *At Fault* (1890). Using the southern plantation locale that she knew so well, this novel was conventional in style and, unlike her later works, sentimental rather than realistic, although it did address divorce and alcoholism, two controversial issues for the time. In spite of these topics, the novel received virtually no critical response.

Chopin continued to publish her short stories, and two volumes of her collected works appeared within a few years: *Bayou Folk* (1894) and *A Night in Acadie* (1897). A third collection, tentatively titled "A Vocation and a Voice," was never published in book form. Several of the published stories address the theme of women's lack of personal fulfillment under society's restrictive rules, and they present

461

women characters who, like the author, were beginning to challenge such traditions. Chopin soon gained a reputation as a gifted author of short stories, but it was with the publication in 1899 of her masterpiece, *The Awakening*, that she reached the culmination of her theme of women's oppressed lives.

Because this novel dealt openly with female sexuality and adultery, however, and because it presented a woman who refused, at all costs, to adhere to social restrictions, it received widespread condemnation from critics. The response of outrage was so pervasive that Chopin was socially ostracized in her own hometown. The novel was pulled from circulation, and it quickly went out of print until 1969 when Per Seyersted issued, in two volumes, *The Complete Works of Kate Chopin*. On August 22, 1904, five years after controversy arose from the publication of *The Awakening*, Chopin died.

ANALYSIS

In the late nineteenth century, when Chopin came of age as a writer, the prevailing attitude was that a woman's proper sphere was in the home and that her purpose in life should be to nurture and encourage her husband and her children. She was to be, as Chopin termed it in *The Awakening*, "a mother woman." Such definitions reveal the dependent, relational nature of woman's status in nineteenth century America: With no individual identity, a woman was notable only in relation to another—a father, a husband, or a child. Such restrictions were not only socially condoned but also legally enforced, as women, in spite of suffrage movements, did not have the right to the vote and thus were allowed no effective voice in political or civic matters. Against this background of oppression, Chopin chose to air these issues in her fiction and to challenge the validity of such assumptions about "true womanhood."

Chopin understood that if a woman was always seen in the context of another, relationships became the central issue of her life and, consequently, of her identity. Thus Chopin's fiction consistently explores interactions between men and women in their daily lives. Many authors of this period were exploring similar issues. In *McTeague* (1899), for example, Frank Norris studied the consequences for a marriage when the possibility of great wealth is interjected between the wife and husband.

Chopin's fiction, like Norris's, is often described as realistic or naturalistic; however, she was interested not in the exceptional situation but in the consequences of everyday interactions between spouses. Further, she extended her analysis of relationships to include the exchanges, intimate as well as public, between men and women who were not married and, perhaps most radically, to the interactions among women that enforced or negated women's traditional role in society.

Chopin explored these themes of social conflict throughout her writing career, beginning with her earliest published short stories, such as "A Point at Issue" and "Wiser than a God." Both stories, published in 1889, concern a woman's sense of stifled existence in a marriage; the women were required to subordinate their lives to those of their husbands. In the latter story, the protagonist decides to risk the insecurity of pursuing a career in music rather than opt for the social and financial security of marriage. She achieves success both in her artistry and in her personal life when she becomes a renowned pianist and develops a love relationship with her music instructor. As Chopin continued to explore the complexities of relationships between the sexes, however, she moved away from such romantic reconciliations and began to depict the incongruity for women of attaining public and private happiness in a culture that did not condone a woman's sense of individuality.

It would be erroneous to suggest that Chopin's themes related only to gender; she was equally concerned with racial relationships in the United States at the end of the nineteenth century. In her regional fiction, she realistically portrayed the diversity of American peoples and integrated Creole and Cajun lives and dialects into her literature. Many of her short stories were set in the Louisiana bayou country in which she had lived for so many years; the stories' realistic details and vivid descriptive passages suggest the keenness of her observations of the people and customs of that region.

These stories also acknowledge the class structures within groups as well as within American society as a whole: She depicts enslaved blacks and upper-class whites, impoverished Acadians and aristocratic Creoles. As Chopin's stories spread far beyond the local periodicals in which she first published to magazines with national circulations, her readers were allowed to explore vicariously a seemingly alien region but at the same time were exposed to the universal human dilemmas that her characters confronted.

As Chopin recognized, the maltreatment of minority peoples and the disparate economic and legal status of many Americans, and all women, were political issues. Although women did not have the power to enact legislation or elect their representatives, they were not spared the consequences of political machinations. Chopin recognized that one way in which women could comment politically, however, was through art. Thus, many of her women characters seek careers in the arts—especially in music and painting—and, certainly, her own career as an artist stood as testament to women's ability to combine intellectual and artistic activism.

In one of Chopin's most frequently anthologized short stories, "Désirée's Baby," she brings together many of her themes: miscegenation, women's restricted lives, the injustice of social codes. Désirée is happy in her married life; after the birth of her child, however, her husband suspects that she has hidden from him that fact that she has some "black blood" in her. The tragic consequences of miscegenation are rendered through Désirée's decision to drown herself and her child, an act that symbolizes the limited options for women who found themselves without male support (emotional as well as financial) and with no means to establish their own independence. As with many of Chopin's best short stories, this work's central, provocative concept would be brought to its culmination in the tragic conclusion to *The Awakening*.

Because of the controversial nature of Chopin's themes, especially as they culminated in the publication of *The Awakening*, her work was largely ignored for many years. She was relegated to the status of a "local color" short-story writer, and she received limited critical consideration at best. However, when Per Seyersted published the two-volume *Complete Works of Kate Chopin* in 1969, a new era in Chopin scholarship began. Her works have been analyzed in terms of the influence of American and French writers, including Nathaniel Hawthorne, Walt Whitman, and Guy de Maupassant.

Chopin's ability to work within numerous genres (essay, poetry, short story, and novel) and numerous literary modes (romanticism, realism, and naturalism) attest her original and influential art-

istry. With the advent in the 1970's of feminist critical interest in Chopin's writings, her work began to receive deserved attention for its feminist ideals and cultural critiques of patriarchal American society. She is recognized as a major literary artist whose psychological and sociopolitical insights have helped to reshape an understanding of her writings—and of the society within which they were created.

THE AWAKENING

First published: 1899
Type of work: Novel

In the repressive world of the nineteenth century United States, a woman awakens to a sense of herself but can find no socially acceptable means of self-fulfillment.

The Awakening begins with a seemingly insignificant event: Léonce Pontellier is disturbed while trying to read the newspaper. As Chopin reveals, however, this incident reflects the patriarchal structure of most late nineteenth century American marriages in which the entire family's activities are inordinately structured around the husband's wishes and moods, no matter how trivial.

The summer resort of Grand Isle is a setting that allows Léonce's wife, Edna, to confront her dissatisfactions with her marriage. Further, she can explore first her awakened sexuality through the attentions of Robert LeBrun and then the subsequent desires for an alternative lifestyle that this awakening creates. While they are at Grand Isle, Léonce has no objections to Robert's flirtations; indeed, he seems indifferent to the developing intimacy between Edna and Robert. When the family returns to New Orleans, Léonce assumes that Edna will return to the duties of a supportive wife.

Edna has awakened, however tentatively, to the excitement of personal liberty, and she discovers within herself a growing desire to control her own life. She has within her social circle two role models for women's lives: the beautiful Madame Ratignolle, "a faultless Madonna," who dedicates her life to her husband and children and who is, therefore, honored by everyone in the community; and

Mademoiselle Reisz, a single woman who has dedicated her life to her music but who, therefore, is distinctly a social outcast and whose life seems stale and isolated. Not surprisingly, neither choice appeals to Edna's growing excitement about the prospect of personal freedom.

Each woman counsels Edna on the decisions she is about to make: Madame Ratignolle asserts that Edna must place her children's needs before her own. Mademoiselle Reisz, though cautiously encouraging Edna, also notes that an artist must possess a courageous soul; she adds, "The bird that would soar above the level plain of tradition and prejudice must have strong wings." Each woman's advice represents societal truths. If Edna chooses to remain a traditional woman, the needs of her children and her husband must come before her own. If she seeks new avenues of self-fulfillment, however, she must recognize that she will be confronting tempest-like winds of controversy that will lead to social banishment.

At first, Edna believes that she can reject traditional wisdom and weather the brunt of conventional reactions. In spite of warnings, she becomes involved with the infamous Alcée Arobin, and she eventually moves into a home of her own. Yet, as the designation for her new residence—the pigeon house—suggests, Edna has not escaped the trappings of her marriage; she has only exchanged them for an illusion of freedom. Although she begins to paint and finds some success in selling her creations, Edna discovers that independence and art alone cannot fulfill her. Her sexuality has been awakened, and she does not want to confine herself to the sterility of an existence like Mademoiselle Reisz's.

If Edna's awareness of options for women has changed, society's perspective has not. Edna finds herself unable to escape the numerous demands and desires of her old and new lives: Though she is able to leave her husband, she cannot escape her maternal status, and her new independence is quickly separating her from old friends without affording her new support systems. She is unable to attain success as an artist and at the same time satisfy the sensual self that she has discovered. In the face of these irreconcilable realities, Edna returns to Grand Isle.

The conclusion of *The Awakening* has created interpretive controversies since its first publication and remains a point of debate among scholars. Some critics see Edna's final swim out into the ocean as one more instance of her capricious behavior; they believe that her death is an accident. Most critics, however, recognize Edna's act as a conscious recognition of the inescapable limitations of her life that continue to stifle her creative and sensual endeavors. That Chopin intended the ending to be ambiguous is indicated in the shifting allusions that surround Edna's final act: a broken-winged bird falls to the water, suggesting that Edna has been unable to withstand the social prejudices about which Mademoiselle Reisz had warned her.

As Edna contemplates her movement into the water, however, she removes all of her clothing, freeing herself of the symbols of society and suggesting that it is her awakened self that is preserved in this final act. By forcing the reader to consider these shifting perspectives, Chopin also forces the reader to confront the causes behind Edna's inability to find personal fulfillment; the oppressive nature of nineteenth century America is symbolized in the waves that wash over Edna as she enters the water. It is only by swimming far beyond the boundaries of the shore that she finally escapes and finds freedom. The tragedy is that this is the only kind of freedom a woman such as Edna could find in her society.

"THE STORY OF AN HOUR"

First published: 1894 (collected in *The Complete Works of Kate Chopin*, 1969)
Type of work: Short story

A woman with heart trouble dies—not when she hears of her husband's death but when she discovers that he is still alive.

In "The Story of an Hour," the fact that Mrs. Mallard is "afflicted with a heart trouble" becomes an ironic reality, for Mrs. Mallard's "heart trouble" in the beginning of the story is that she feels emotionally thwarted in her marriage. When her husband is believed to have been killed in a train accident, her friends notify her cautiously, assuming she will be devastated. The news, however, brings her tears of release rather than of grief. She is enlivened by her new situation and symbolically insists that all the doors of the house be opened. When Brently Mallard suddenly returns home, however, Mrs. Mallard's death is both literal and symbolic—in one hour, her freedom has been won and lost. For Chopin, Mrs. Mallard represents the numerous women who silently bear the feelings of being trapped in unhappy marriages but whose escapes could be ephemeral at best.

"THE STORM"

First published: 1969 (collected in *The Complete Works of Kate Chopin*, 1969)
Type of work: Short story

A married woman spontaneously commits adultery, then reacts not with shame but with joy at her sexual awakening and continued love for her husband.

Written only six months after the publication of *The Awakening*, "The Storm" continues Chopin's confrontation with the theme of women's sexuality and the complexities of the married state. In this five-part short story, the narrative structure allows Chopin to present varying perspectives on a single situation as a means of suggesting that "reality" is, at best, relative. The situation is simple enough: Calixta's husband, Bobinôt, and son, Bibi, are in town when a storm hits. Alone at home, Calixta is about to shut the windows and doors against the rain when her former lover, Alcée Laballière, rides into the yard seeking shelter. While the storm rages, Calixta and Alcée renew their passionate feelings for each other; their desire finally leads them into having sex. When the storm abates, Alcée departs, and Calixta welcomes her family back home. The story concludes, "So the storm passed and every one was happy."

Like all of Chopin's best fiction, "The Storm" does not offer pat moral truisms; indeed, the shocking element of this story's conclusion is that the retribution one might expect for the act of adultery never comes. In section 2, the crucial love scene is played out against ironic allusions to Christian symbolism: the Assumption, an immaculate dove, a lily, and the passion. Chopin offers a moral tale in which a woman's sexual experience is not condemned but celebrated and in which she uses that experience not to abandon her family but to accept them with a renewed sense of commitment. Unlike *The Awakening*, "The Storm" allows a woman to gain personal fulfillment and to remain happily married. As in most naturalistic fiction, morality—like reality—is relative.

SUMMARY

Chopin revealed through her artistry the realities of many women's stifled lives and the oppression of often-overlooked minority groups such as the Creoles and Cajuns. Chopin also depicted the beauty of these people's lifestyle in the Louisiana bayou region and the power of individuals to shape their own lives. Through lyrical depictions of natural settings, Chopin compared the powers of nature to the potential for human self-empowerment.

Sharon M. Harris

BIBLIOGRAPHY

By the Author

SHORT FICTION:
Bayou Folk, 1894
A Night in Acadie, 1897

LONG FICTION:
At Fault, 1890
The Awakening, 1899

NONFICTION:
Kate Chopin's Private Papers, 1998

MISCELLANEOUS:
The Complete Works of Kate Chopin, 1969 (2 volumes; Per Seyersted, editor)

About the Author

Beer, Janet. *Kate Chopin, Edith Wharton, and Charlotte Perkins Gilman: Studies in Short Fiction*. New York: St. Martin's Press, 1997.

Beer, Janet, and Elizabeth Nolan, eds. *Kate Chopin's "The Awakening": A Sourcebook*. New York: Routledge, 2004.

Bonner, Thomas, Jr. *The Kate Chopin Companion*. New York: Greenwood Press, 1988.

Boren, Lynda S., and Sara de Saussure Davis, eds. *Kate Chopin Reconsidered: Beyond the Bayou*. Baton Rouge: Louisiana State University Press, 1992.

Koloski, Bernard. *Kate Chopin: A Study of the Short Fiction*. New York: Twayne, 1996.

Petry, Alice Hall, ed. *Critical Essays on Kate Chopin*. New York: G. K. Hall, 1996.

Skaggs, Peggy. *Kate Chopin*. Boston: Twayne, 1985.

Stein, Allen F. *Women and Autonomy in Kate Chopin's Short Fiction*. New York: Peter Lang, 2005.

Taylor, Helen. *Gender, Race, and Religion in the Writings of Grace King, Ruth McEnery Stuart, and Kate Chopin*. Baton Rouge: Louisiana State University Press, 1989.

Toth, Emily. *Kate Chopin*. New York: William Morrow, 1990.

_____. *Unveiling Kate Chopin*. Jackson: University Press of Mississippi, 1999.

DISCUSSION TOPICS

- In what respects does Kate Chopin's fiction typify literary naturalism?

- Chopin's short stories have often been classified as local color fiction. Choose several stories from *Bayou Folk* and cite settings and characters that exemplify local color.

- Examine the sensory detail in one Chopin short story or one chapter from a novel and explain how it enhances the effect of the whole.

- What were Edna Pontellier's marital expectations beforehand, and how did they change in the course of *The Awakening*?

- With careful attention to the details in the final chapter of *The Awakening*, determine whether Edna's suicide should be interpreted as an act of despair or liberation—or should it be regarded in yet another light?